Men of the Inland Rivers

Interviews from the Age of Steamboats, Packets and Towboats

John Knoepfle

Burning Daylight

Colorado

Peggy Knoepfle, Consulting Editor, (Peggy retired after editing "Illinois Issues Magazine" for 17 years, she was the editor of a book the magazine published titled: *After Alinsky: Community Organizing in Illinois*, which had an article written by Barack Obama before he entered politics and became president).

Bonnie Amesquita, Assistant Editor
Megan Ryan, Cover Design, megantreverwebdesign.com
Becky Shadlich, Assistant Editor
Thanks to Paperwork for original word file setup.
Thanks to Jeremy Schmidt for Technical Assistance.
Photos provided by The Dave Thomson Collection at steamboats.com
Riverview photo from Joseph Sohm via Shutterstock.
Thanks to Tom Wood, University of Illinois, Springfield Library.
The font of the text is 11 point Times New Roman.

Library of Congress Control Number 2020935512

Knoepfle, John 1923-2019
Men of the Inland Rivers, by John Knoepfle
ISBN 978-0-9897242-9-6

Printed in the United States of America

First edition.

For Collum Davis

Contents

Introduction

In the early nineteen fifties, I was a producer director for WCET, Cincinnati's educational TV station. In the Queen City, if you drove along the bluffs you could see the Ohio River below and also see the river commerce, and as it happened the last of the steam-driven packets and tows. Stern and sidewheel river boats were called packets because for years they carried the mail. I suggested that the station might do a series of programs involving those that were engaged in that river commerce. Given the go ahead for my suggestion, I contacted a friend who worked on the landing. From there I was able to contact interview and record on my big box recorder some 70 men who worked on the river.

Fortunately, when I began teaching at Sangamon State University (now the University of Illinois at Springfield), Professor Cullom Davis was able to transcribe, store, and protect my fragile recordings. I should add that these included the recollections of men from the Allegheny, Tennessee and Kanawha rivers among others as well as the Ohio. The interviews featured captains, pilots, boat owners, show boaters, night watchmen, mates, roustabouts, lock masters, packet cooks, among others.

John Knoepfle, 2019

John Knoepfle read this paper, which was based on oral history, in the late 1950s at an MLA Conference. The room was packed full of people wanting to listen to him. He was astonished and encouraged by the response. It was published in "Midcontinent American Studies Journal," 4:1 Spring 1963, and is reprinted here as it first appeared. The tapes are archived in the University of Illinois, Springfield Library.

Some Notes on the Men of the Inland Rivers

The remarks which follow are based on material contained in a collection of tape recordings of the recollections of inland rivermen which is now deposited in the Division of Inland Rivers of the Public Library of Cincinnati and Hamilton County, Ohio. The subjects of the interviews were men whose work associated them with the last days of steam packetboats and tows on the Ohio, Mississippi and Missouri Rivers. Occupations varied widely among the seventy men interviewed by the present writer. They included deck-hands, lograftsmen, captains, pilots, civil engineers, mates, roustabouts, steam engineers, cooks, commercial fishermen, musicians and others. The form which the interviews took was a simple one: the men were asked to establish their occupations and backgrounds; and were encouraged to dwell at length on the phases of river activity which most interested them. As a result, although the tapes are often discursive, they contain a large quantity of information and also reflect individually the attitude toward the river of each of the speakers.

Generalizing from some of the recorded experiences, one can say that the old rivermen constituted a rather special society. Many of the survivors of the age of steam are the sons, grandsons and even great grandsons of rivermen. Their competitive instinct, though strong, was modified by an intricate network of blood relationship and acquaintance that crossed whole generations in time and spread out over the midcontinent with its three great rivers. If there was a tradition for a tough, cash on the barrelhead kind of business, there was an equally strong willingness to trust a man in a transaction. The value of a man's word was high, and deals were made with handshakes that involved the change in ownership of valuable packetboats. A captain could take possession of a boat by verbal agreement and pay it off with the profits from the next summer's run. He signed no paper that said he had to. This casual method of exchange makes documents relating to boat ownership somewhat untrustworthy. An owner's name on a steamboat list means merely that he was the owner of the vessel on the morning the information was gathered.

This willingness to do business on trust, it seems to me, is ancillary to the general attitude of independence of these rivermen. A captain hired his own crew, regardless of the boat owner's desires. After the dams were constructed on the upper Ohio, it became customary to pick up new hands at the locks. The captain's right to hire was a jealously guarded one, and even the United States

vi

Coast Guard had to acknowledge it. But the right expired with the demise of locally owned passenger carrying packets along the river. As for the company-owned towboats; the right was compromised during the depression years when the big steel and coal corporations began to furnish crews from records in the personnel offices. The action was benevolent, done to protect the hands and secure steadier employment for them in those hard days, but it left the captains with less status than they had formerly.

The decline in the power of the word is something for the social historian to puzzle. Those steamboatmen would have been hard put to understand the present frenzy for a man's signature, the ballpoint diabolism of our age. It may be that something more than the national fortune was broken in 1929. In any case, I think it is probably the most significant change that has taken place in American life since the first steamboats, those fire canoes, as the Indians termed them, plied the western rivers.

If these ideals of integrity and independence had been matched by an equal value placed on the dignity of labor, the men of the valleys might have presented the world with an enviable picture of democracy in action, but as the facts stand, the picture is not a pleasant one. For the roustabout, who was also a man captivated by the river, life consisted of hard, stiff and often demeaning work. He was expected to be able to carry his own weight. On a short-haul boat he labored in proportion to the demand: six hours loading apples on the north bank of the river, then six more on the south. His work was entirely done by hand, back and shoulder. There were no carts or trucks to ease his burden. He slept under the boilers on cold nights. And his surname, like his position, was without respect. He was like Friday in *Robinson Crusoe* in this regard. His name was given to him. He was called Wing, or Devil, or One-eyed or The Old Original Hog-head. And sometimes he became so used to his nickname that he forgot his real name, so that his Christian name was only established with difficulty when Social Security regulations required his proper identification. His badge of office was as common as he was. A spoon. That spoon was the one article a mate looked for when he had to take on a strange hand. It meant that the new man was not a drifter, but an experienced worker who knew that packet cooks did not supply eating utensils when grub was ladled out on trays for the roustabouts. Finally, he was an uneducated man who could not read or write. Because of this, of all rivermen, the picture of the typical rouster is the most distorted: he is remembered as a happy-go-lucky, smiling man, strangely savage at times, who lost his money gambling whenever the boats were underway. But there is another side to the profile. This shows the face of physical exhaustion. If a man fell dead in line, the coroner called it a heart attack, but for the rousters, the man just worked himself out.

In fairness, however, the position of river roustabout should be considered in terms of the general state of unskilled labor in this country before the First World War. When Italian work-gangs were employed in dam construction, as one salvage man stated it, the work-boss got down in the coffer dams with a pick handle to make them go. A dollar a day for a man, fifty cents for a boy, for work from dawn until sundown, were not unusual wages in the early 1900's. Perhaps, too, in the case of roustabouts, it was the position itself, rather than the man, that was demeaned. Negroes were used for the job in the last days of the packets; before the Negroes, German immigrants did the work, and before Germans, Irish immigrants. At the very end, when Negroes could not be made to work during the hot dogdays of summer, there was speculation that Italians might serve well as roustabouts because they had more tractable dispositions.

Perhaps more than the roustabout, the figure of the mate is left with a distorted image. He is remembered as a particularly tough individual who possessed an unlimited capacity for swearing, but at his best he was a man of character and capability on the river. He was a commander of men. He had to know how to stir the roustabouts up to get the most work out of them. He was always working against the clock, getting the boat in and out of the landings as quick as possible. If he was an experienced man, he had a refined sense of touch. He could tell merely by walking across a dark deck at night whether there were any strains in the boat due to improper loading. It was his job to see that the freight was so distributed that the packet would neither be stern nor bow down in the water. A bad job of loading caused leaks to spring in the wooden hulls of the boats and if the stern or sidewheels were too deep or shallow, they would not function at their full capacity, and steam and power would be lost as well as time. He needed to know a thousand practical tricks for meeting sudden and bizarre emergencies when underway. On the Cumberland River, for example, where boats were fragile constructions that drew fifteen inches of water, shipping a stud horse was a hazardous venture. If anywhere along the river the stallion scented the mountain mares, he would begin to stamp in his pen, an action powerful enough to break the wooden deck and sink the boat. But the mate knew how to handle the situation: he sent a roustabout down to chew on the stallion's ears and so pacify him. He had to be a man of some physical courage. If the roustabouts hid in the excelsior pile beneath the main deck (stored there for plugging leaks in the hull), it was the mate's responsibility to crawl in there and force the men out, sometimes at the risk of a knife slash or a bullet wound.

The mate's life was turbulent and demanding, the river a close-knit and long-remembering community. This may account for some of the brutality of the river, for certain mates did have a reputation for cruelty. If a mate had a history of savageness, he had to cope with a real or imagined fear of retribution. Someone would catch up to him some night and get him. Some mates carried sticks, and at least one, a cane reinforced with lead. Others condemned the practice. One such mate, a small man with a powerful voice and six knife slashes to show for his trade, speaking of the life of the roustabouts, accounted for much of the struggle and pain of the river in a single sentence: "It was the worst kind of inhumanity, but we were country boys, and we just didn't know any better."

The clerk was also a man who lead a life of hard work on the boats. He was always at odds with the mate. He told the roustabout where each load was going to be shipped, and the rouster relayed this information to the mate who then decided where to store the load on the boat. "Care" was the watch-word of the clerk, "speed" of the mate; it was a twain that seldom met. Some idea of the clerk's responsibility can be formed from an illustration of his work on a single trip during a good freight season on the upper river. In this example, so much had to be done in so short a time that two clerks were used. They had to get off as many as four hundred shipments on a run from Pittsburgh to Wheeling, a ninety mile journey with perhaps seven or eight landings where freight was picked up or put off. During this time they had to rate the freight bills, enter these in the freight book, make out the bills and write up calculations in the discharge book, meanwhile checking the freight out at various landings. The boat left Pittsburgh at two in the afternoon and arrived at Wheeling the next morning. Obviously, this work kept them busy.

Whatever other rewards there were for working on the river, for most men the wages were low. The clerk could make four dollars a day on a run such as the one just described, but more than likely it was less than this, and on the last boats that ran freight and passenger service the wage dropped as low as sixty cents a day for a twenty-four hour day. This was in the middle thirties, after the building of good roads liberated the back counties from dependence on the river for supplies and trucks could move quickly among big towns, making storedoor to storedoor deliveries. There were other reasons, too, for the decline of the packets. With unionization of the unskilled worker, it became increasingly difficult to get crews to work the boats. Government regulations following on the Moro Castle disaster in inland waters required the mounting of expensive fire prevention equipment on the packets which the owners could not afford to have installed. The despoliation of hardwood timberlands made it almost impossible to get good oak for the repair of hulls and wheels and checked what impulse there was to build new boats. Insurance rates were high and adjustments for damaged or destroyed boats made replacement financially impossible. Finally, the cost of coal to run the boats became a prohibitive factor when measured against the diminishing returns of the trade. These things, added together, broke the enthusiasm of even the most spirited and resourceful of the rivermen. The price was too high, and the age of steam was allowed to run itself out.

Question: I have come to the home of Mr. Yeatman Anderson who worked on the dam at New Richmond during the period of its construction. Mr. Anderson, maybe you can begin by giving us a little resume of your work on that dam.

Answer: My work on the dam actually occurred in the second year of my association with the engineers on the river, which occurred in the summertime between the school years at the University of Cincinnati. I was employed by the U. S. Engineers as a deputy inspector, and as such did all the little dirty jobs that happened on a big construction project of this kind. However, it was exceedingly fascinating and interesting to watch the dam grow as additional piles, additional concrete, additional forms were erected and taken care of. Many, many engineering problems, but that has very little to do with the actual construction of the dam or had very little to do with the history of the river excepting as dam 35 at New Richmond became a part of the channelization program for the entire river. I don't believe that there are many of the fellows that worked on that project that are still alive. Most of the other people there were considerably older than I. At least I've lost complete track of them.

When I joined the group they had just erected the cofferdam for the lock chamber, which of course is on the Kentucky side of the river and were just starting construction. Perhaps many people don't know that at least this dam and I believe most of the others were actually built on piles and that we drove piles day-and-night, twenty-four hours a day for seemingly months on end in order to provide a firm foundation for the super structure, namely the part that people see as today they ride up and down the river. All of us lived over at New Richmond, and our only method of getting across the river was a little outboard motor driven rowboat, which like all outboard motors often refused to work at the most inopportune moments and on several occasions we got caught in the current and we drifted far down stream and finally had to get out and walk back to our homes. I don't mean to walk in the river, but we had to get over to the shore and just leave the boat and send a steamer down after it. I don't know whether you are interested in the engineering stages of this thing and how it grew and all the parts of the dam? I could probably identify them from the photographs I have here but again that would be probably of secondary interest.

Q: I know this, that at least Evan Bone mentioned that each of those dams was a kind of unprecedented experience and a lot of it was pretty much trial and error. Because what was good for a dam upriver wouldn't be good for a dam downriver.

A: Well that's very true, of course that is true of any building project. Even within the confines of a given city you will find entirely different soil structures.

For example, very few people know that the downtown portion of the city of Cleveland is built on quicksand.

Q: It is?

A: But still they have the big buildings and one of the first projects of that sort for a building was what was originally called the Rockefeller Building in Cleveland where it was actually built on quicksand. But there again strangely enough that is related to not the Ohio River Valley but the Mississippi River Valley because the Eads Bridge at St. Louis is also built on quicksand, that is the foundations are on quicksand, and Mr. Eads was the man that discovered or decided that if he could confine the quicksand so that it couldn't run away from him, by building a cofferdam around it, and then put his foundation on the confined quicksand, why he could get a perfectly firm foundation and the fact that the bridge is still standing is certainly an indication that he knew what he was doing. So even going as far away as Cleveland, which you would certainly not definitely associate in your mind with a river, there is at least the precedent, that move to Cleveland. So that it's kind of hard to get away from this old thing you call the Ohio.

Q: Were there any particular problems associated with that dam that you know of?

A: Not that I know of, you see there had been a number of other dams completed, and while as you said there a minute ago, there is always problems, special problems, but they're not generally major. Past experience makes you anticipate the trouble you are going to get in. And while you may not solve the problem a hundred percent, and there is a certain amount of trial and error involved, nevertheless it's not anything that you complain about or worry about. You just take it in your stride. And as far as my one summer's association at that dam, I can recall nothing of any importance that occurred. My recollection is that at the time it was built, and this I can be quite wrong in, that the 600 foot lock chamber was the largest lock chamber that had been built on the river up to that time. Now as I say I could be very wrong in making that statement and I would hate to be quoted without having it checked out.

Q: Maybe you could go into some particulars about your own job? You said it involved a lot of the nasty little things, well could you explain that?

A: As a deputy inspector I was paid a tremendous salary of 60 dollars a month. I had to inspect the driving of piles, I had to count the number of bags of cement that went into every batch that was made to see that the mixture was correct. We did a little bit of surveying, we used to play around a little bit with explosives, not great quantities, nothing spectacular at all, but we ran into rock that had to be blasted out and had to see that it was properly cleared out and that we didn't have any loose rock underneath or shattered rock underneath. Everything that was loose or that could give way was taken care of. I think the most interesting part of building that dam occurred after I left when they got to installing the machinery and the gates and that sort of thing, but after all, the main portion of the dam was just big blocks of concrete and there is nothing very fascinating about pouring concrete.

Q: They already had its coffers when you got there?

A: Yes, the main cofferdam for the lock chambers. They built the lock chambers first and got it established so the traffic could continue, before they started the dam across the river, which would block off the main channel. In other words, they had to complete the lock chamber itself, tear down that cofferdam, then build a new cofferdam across the main channel.

Q: I see, well you were there in the summer I suppose?

A: That's right.

Q: Do you remember in that summer if the low water cut out the navigation?

A: That's another story. Not insofar as New Richmond was concerned, but the previous year I had also worked for the engineers and in an entirely different area of the river, entirely different part, and at that time they sent me down to do two jobs. One after the other. One was down at Golconda just below Golconda, Illinois, where we were building some, what were then known as loose stone dikes, actually in present parlance they would be called jetties, simply to try to divert the river into a definite channel on the Kentucky side rather than on the Illinois side. These jetties simply consisted of rock laid in a definite pattern so that the current in sweeping down on it would carry the sand and drop it out and the water would tend to go the other way. It happens that there was a big bend in the river at that point, so we were able to divert the water in the direction we wanted it by carefully planning the layout of these dikes. As part of that particular experience there was one man who was the contractor who was quite a well-known character on the river; unfortunately his name escapes me at the moment.

I took a trip on the *Delta Queen* last summer and got acquainted with the officers on that ship who are all of them old-timers and mentioned this man and they all remembered him and could call him by name. The man must have been in his 60s I guess when I was down there in the summer of 1913 and he was known for his very violent temper and very masterful way with dealing with people. And he had only the little finger left on his right hand and the story of how this accident occurred is what I am leading up to. Like all river contractors building structures on the river, he knew all about driving piles. The work wasn't going the way he wanted to so he went out to personally supervise it, and in doing so he put his hand out on top of the pile, which had a steel plate fastened to it, and then hollered at the engineer to drop the hammer. The engineer refused and refused because of his hand and tried to tell him to get his hand out of the way. This contractor being the adamant soul that he was, unmistakably said, "Drop the hammer you so and so." He dropped the hammer and cut his hand off, everything except his little finger.

Q: Is that so?

A: They were peculiar characters in those days.

John Knoepfle

Q: I understand upriver the labor crews often were made up of teams of Italians under a foreman. Do you remember anything about that?

A: No, I don't recall anything of that sort at all. Because all of the deckhands that we had were mostly people from the southern hills. Many of them came from around the Kanawha and in fact the Kanawha people were preferred. They were a rough and tough lot, but they were good workers and given their heads more or less on a job, once they understood what had to be done, why they did a very, very excellent job and it's my recollection that a man from the Kanawha was always given preference up in this area of the country anyhow.

Q: Up around New Richmond and in there?

A: You were speaking a while ago about whether or not the low water bothered us at New Richmond. Well I don't recall that it did, particularly at the dam site, and that may have been because the dam at, oh what is the one that is downstream?

Q: 37.

A: 37 I think 37 had been completed before the New Richmond Dam was started, which was 35. The Coney Island Dam 36 had not been started. That may have accounted for the fact that we had no difficulty since there was some pool, not a great deal, then of course those riverboats drew very, oh, only three or four feet.

Q: What month did you get out there on the dam proper?

A: Oh, it was probably around the 1st of June and I worked until school started again late in September or early October.

Q: I asked that because I know a lot of the commerce on the river in those days was made up of, there was a lot of logging coming out of West Virginia. Coal boats were coming down from the Kanawha and Pittsburgh.

A: As I say I don't recall that we had any difficulty with low water at the dam itself, but we did have great deal of difficulty the previous year after I had finished my stint on building those jetties, or as we called them, loose stone dikes. I was transferred to Henderson, Kentucky and put in charge of a dredge crew on the Henderson Island Pass. Our job was to try to cut a path through the bar, the Henderson Island bar, rather, had to keep a path open there for traffic and the water was so absolutely low, and the sand so soft, that the dipper off the dredge would just build up a roll in front of it so we couldn't even get our barges in to haul the sand away. We were just picking up sand on this side and leaving it over here, and picking up the same sand tomorrow. Part of our job on that assignment was to keep traffic moving on the river and towboat after towboat, mostly packet boats, not the big tows, but mostly packets would get stuck out there and we had a shallow draft and we'd go out there and try to pull them over. I've seen them break three and four inch lines without any difficulty at all trying to pull them over.

Q: Do you remember off-hand the name of the steamer?

A: Yes, here's a picture of it. Here is the crew. That's the dredge.

Q: That's the *Hoosier*?

A: That's the dredge, yes. Here are the barges, and that was a packet, this is the bridge at Henderson.

Q: Now let's get back if you will.

A: The towboat that I had under my jurisdiction was the *R. J. Armstrong* and again in making the trip on the *Delta Queen* last summer I inquired from the officers of that boat if they remembered the *Armstrong* and they said, "Yes, if you'll watch as we go upstream from Evansville you will see what's left of it being used there as a small boat harbor." And sure enough there was enough of it left so I could recognize it with the picture you have in your hand there. I gave you a picture of it, didn't I?

Q: Yes sir, I have it. It was an old beauty.

A: There is a picture of their engine room where they painted it any color just so it was red. Red and yellow are the two colors they used in there. That was the engineer and his younger brother who was the fireman.

Q: You don't know their names do you?

A: I don't remember their names at all anymore, I don't remember the captain's name even. However, again this is the captain of the boat, this fellow here, and there again the old-timers down on the *Delta Queen* called him by name but I didn't make a note of it at the time.

Q: So you broke those big lines trying to haul those packets over?

A: It's surprising the amount of strength or force that can be exerted by a stern wheel stream coupled with the capstan, a steam driven capstan on the front deck there. You can see it right there. One of the most interesting things to me is the part of all of this, the story of low water and so on in the river, was the fact that this *Armstrong* when I took over had just been reconditioned and they had not completed all the insulation on the steam-pipes and that sort of thing in the engine room and the boiler room. So one day this shantyboat appeared on the scene and they pulled in and tied up there at Henderson Island, and the old man in the rowboat came out to the boat and was greeted like a long lost friend and it turned out that he was an expert insulator. Probably the dirtiest human being I ever saw.

Living on the water you would think at least he would wash his hands, but I bet his hands hadn't been washed, hadn't even been wet except for pulling catfish out of the river, in years. The top of his head, he was bald, was just as black as this table. I never saw anything like it, it wasn't tan, it was just plain dirt. But he did a beautiful job, so I inquired about that, and the story was at that time many of the shantyboat people were marvelous artisans and had definite trades and could really do a beautiful job of work when they felt like working and this family, a man and his wife, and remember one possibly two children and a dog. You can see the little boy in the picture here, no, there's two little boys. Actually they were so well known the towboat captains would haul them upstream and then they would coast down the river, or drift down.

John Knoepfle

Q: It must have been an arduous summer you put in down there on all that shoal water?

A: Well it didn't bother me any, the other fellows had to do the work. I just went along almost for the ride, I was there to see what they were doing and to tell them what to do but beyond that they operated almost by themselves. It was a fascinating experience I thoroughly enjoyed, and met a lot of very interesting people in that way that I never would have met in any other way. I'm sitting here trying to remember, I remember one night a showboat got stuck on the bar. We went out, we tried to pull it over, in so doing got stuck ourselves, had to spend the night out there. It was really quite an interesting time to get to know the showboat people and we did, we had dinner together and they entertained us on the boat. We had a very, very enjoyable evening. The next day by proper manipulation with our wheel we were able to dig ourselves out and we did get them loose and they went on downstream.

Q: I wonder who they were?

A: I wouldn't know. I thought I had a picture of them, but I don't seem to have anymore. Thought I had taken a picture. Here is a typical old, the *Lowry*, the typical old packetboat and if I am not mistaken this is a boat that I made a trip on to Cincinnati and that was a fascinating experience because the packetboats in those days were literally the packetboats, the freight people, and they would put in where anybody would wave a handkerchief at them and take on two hogs or five sacks of wheat or something of that kind. Another interesting custom that I ran into on that boat was, and I've told a lot of people and they've never heard of it before was how the stevedores or the deckhands were paid for handling wheat and other freight on and off. The one time I have in mind particularly, we were loading on a lot of grain in sacks and when the gangplank went down the purser went out about halfway on the gangway and the deckhands went ashore and would grab or pick up a 100 pound sack of wheat on their back and as they walked up the gangplank the purser would hand them a penny and that was their pay for bringing that sack of grain on.

Q: A penny a sack?

A: A penny a sack transporting it from the shore over on to the boat and the same thing was done when they took the grain off. They were part of the ship's crew, but apparently I don't know that this was true, but apparently if they were paid anything it was very, very little. They slept on deck, or in the boiler room on the floor. There was no accommodations at all.

Q: What part of the country was this where you picked up the wheat?

A: I don't know exactly, it was somewhere downstream from here, somewhere between here and Paducah, I'm sure of that, but just where I don't remember.

Q: I am always curious when somebody tells about those men whether they remember a scrap of song they might have sung?

A: No, I don't in that connection. Later on in life I lived down south for about 14 years and I lived in the deep south and was in both the building business and several other businesses down there and the singing roustabout was always paid a premium because he led the group and they always worked in rhythm. While I don't recall it in connection with the wheat incident at all, I am certain there must have been a leader of the group who did sing because as I think back now, it seems that they didn't actually run, but they sort of jogged up the gangway there. Incidentally this penny a sack deal was open to anybody that wanted to do it, and on that particular occasion several of the passengers went out and got a sack and came in and picked up their pennies and of course gave it to one of the roustabouts afterward. The one thing that they did do in addition was to entertain the passengers and in the evening down on the fore deck they would sing, and dance and the passengers would toss them coins and that sort of thing. A trip on that sort of a boat was really a very, very interesting experience to a landlubber like me. Another thing that was so characteristic was that no packetboat ever came in shore or left shore without music. Even if it was just nothing but one single person playing the mandolin. He played you in and played you out and he was always there. Don't know whether you had ever run into that before.

Q: That was a delightful custom I think.

A: Yes, the music wasn't very much but nevertheless they were fulfilling a tradition.

Q: Wonder now if we can go back to New Richmond. Can you tell me about some of the other men who were working with you, if you remember them?

A: As I say the only name that I remember at New Richmond, incidentally that's a picture of the Evansville. Hey Bud! This is my son Guy. Son this is John Knoepfle.

Q: A pleasure to meet you. We are making your father immortal.

Guy: Oh, good, good.

A: The only name that I remember was this man Prell. P-R-E-L-L. He was a resident engineer up on the New Richmond dam. Unfortunately, I don't remember any of the other people. Prell himself was a man at that time in his 40s and had been with the engineers for a good many years and was very highly thought of and he was quite a driver, but in a very decent sort of a way. Actually I roomed in his home while I was there. I understand, I think back now, I remember hearing after having completed that dam he went on and they put him on another one. What one I don't know. Where is that engineering group? Let's see if I can remember any other names out of this bunch at all. I'm quite sure that this man here became one of the senior engineers stationed here.

Q: This is the man on the right end as you look at the picture.

A: Yes, this fellow with his hat in his hand here. And this man I have seen once or twice; I think he is a Cincinnati man.

Q: He's the second from the left with the watch fob?

A: Yes. The other fellows, I can't put a name to any of them at all. So I can't help you on personnel. Incidentally, again thinking of the low water, did you ever hear of them walking a boat over a bar?

Q: Well I've never had anyone describe it.

A: That's a very interesting thing and perhaps I can find it, well, here's a picture of Prell here, not a very good one.

Q: You were all happy in the group?

A: Oh well we had to be. Let me see where the close-up of the *Hoosier* is, maybe I can show you. Yes, you see these spiles as they were called standing up here in the air, well they were hooked up in such a way that they could be raised and lowered and also they were pivoted. Now they served two purposes: when the dredge was actually digging they were dropped down, or spuds they were called, not spiles but spuds, and they dropped down into the bottom to give stability to the boat while the dipper was working, but on the other hand, when they got stuck on a bar they would drive this one down, they could not only drop it but they could actually drive it into the ground, the one on the stern, pick up the two in the bow, swing them forward maybe four or five feet and drive them into the bed, and then force this back one to swing out from it a little bit and force this back one to push. The result was that the front end of the boat would rise up and go over. Actually they could put enough force on here to raise the bow of the boat virtually out of the water, and just by its own weight it would fall forward. I saw some boats down there, instead of having this single one on the stern had a pair near the back of the stern and it was sort of like the old poling idea that they used to use on some of the shantyboats.

Q: I bet those were Missouri boats they had those on, they used to run into that shoal problem all the time?

A: Yes, well, I saw it on the Ohio and a good many of the government boats were equipped at that time, they had snag pullers and stump pullers and what not, and they were all shallow water boats and they were set up that way and they could actually walk themselves over a bar. It was a long slow tedious job, but nevertheless they could do it. Those are things that, well I wish that I would have had a movie camera at the time. This old gal used to sit out here on the side deck peeling potatoes and chewing snuff. Sometimes we wondered whether we got snuff or whether we got potatoes.

Q: She must have been a mountain woman?

A: She was typical.

Q: I see you got her with a spittoon in front of her.

A: Oh yes, she carried that with her wherever she went.

Q: She was a cook on the dredge?

A: She cooked for all of us. Well I don't know whether I am saying anything that has any meaning to you or not or any interest but . . . .

Q: There are all kinds of little details that are interesting.

A: I haven't given any great thought to this whole picture for a long, long time. But there is Henderson, Kentucky, in the background, which was Henderson Island, now the river goes around the other side of the island more than it did when I was down, so they don't have that trouble. They have cut a new channel through. Here is another view of the dam down at Evansville. We went down there one day on a special trip.

Q: It was a big dam too, wasn't it?

A: Yes, the farther downriver you went the bigger they became. That's when I grew my mustache for the first time, trying to look older. I was about nineteen at that time. Don't remember whether I took that picture for the boat or for the bridge because I am a civil engineer by education and was interested in bridges of that sort at that time. I took this bunch of photographs with me on that *Delta Queen* and showed them to all these fellows and gee, even if they couldn't recognize a boat they were willing to bet money it was such and such a boat. I said you can't prove it by me. They got to arguing amongst themselves on the details they could see as poor a picture as that, which is indicative of how they learned their boats and how well they knew them.

Q: Looks like, I see, a Missouri boat, has a domed pilot house.

A: It could very well be.

Q: They didn't like domed pilot houses on the Ohio. They thought it was bad luck.

A: Was that so? I had never heard that. I do know one thing, this boat is going upstream because I remember the lay of the land. This picture was taken from the old wharfboat at Henderson, on the outer side of it. This railroad bridge had just recently been completed and it lay downstream from the wharfboat.

Q: Well you worked on the dams on the river here, maybe two or three summers while you were still in school?

A: Yes, two summers. I wasn't actually a co-op. I went out and got these jobs myself, but it is essentially the same thing.

Q: Then you went in the service when the war came out?

A: Not until 1918, by that time I had drifted far away from Cincinnati and had come back again. Not here, I went in the Army from Cleveland.

Q: Are you professionally a civil engineer?

A: Let's just say I'm an engineer. Because it doesn't take but a very few years to break away from the thing you studied, at least in my life, so I've been a salesman all my life, selling technical equipment or building equipment, but I can't say that I ever was an engineer as such professionally.

Q: Well there are lot of interesting things, Mr. Anderson.

A: Sure, sure I'm just talking at random here and we are jumping around, whether there is anything of interest there, I don't know, but what there is you are more than welcome to it and I am very glad to do it. One thing that I just thought of in connection with this, I don't know what you are going to get out of this thing.

John Knoepfle

Q: Well let's see. Come again on that jazz thing.

A: Well that happened on the 4th of July while I was down working on the loose stone jetties. We'd all gone up to Golconda, at least I always went up to Golconda and stayed at the hotel over the weekend, and they were giving a public dance. I suppose we would call it a subscription dance now, at some park, maybe five or ten miles front Golconda, so we all went over to this dance. They had a negro band supplying music and that was the first occasion that I had ever heard what we now call jazz. Typical jazz rhythm or at least, again I must say this was what we call jazz today may not be what I am referring to because there has been so much change in the rhythmic setup over the years, but nevertheless the clarinet player particularly did things with a clarinet that I had never seen done before. He could almost make it sound like a slide trombone by eliding the sounds; it didn't have the tone quality of a trombone but I'm trying to express or describe the way, in which he treated this instrument of his. It certainly was rousing music and it had that whole in good humor almost as soon as they played their first tune. They played all day long, and late that evening, why, we drove back.

Q: Wasn't what they call gutbucket, was it?

A: I never heard of that expression. It might have been. Another one of the interesting things, actually during the week while I was down there, we stayed at a little town called Bay Village and I roomed with the wealthiest woman in town. Her wealth consisted of the house that she lived in and a little plot of ground and some four or five hundred bushels of corn in the crib. She was quite typical of that area in that she cooked once a week over an open fire when she did her washing and she would cook enough to last us all week. That is in the way of vegetables and that sort of thing. She did fry eggs. I never will forget the first morning when I woke up in her house.

I was wakened by a rooster perched on the foot of my bed welcoming the dawn, which was not a very happy situation but nevertheless there it was. Every evening we would wait for the upriver packet and gather on the little porch of one of the two stores. The one that overlooked the river and we had only one subject of conversation and that was the size of the village. There were two schools of thought: one said that the town consisted of two stores and three houses; and the other group said that it consisted of two stores and five houses. The latter group insisted that by some right that nobody could discover the town limits were a mile square and these two houses were just about out from the center of town and as soon as the boat would come in and discharge whatever it had to discharge at this little wayside stop, why we would all go to bed, probably about eight o'clock and the roosters would wake us the next morning.

Again, that has nothing to do with the history of the river, but it was a rather interesting recollection that comes back to me. Oh yes, and the payoff on that was at the end of the first week that I stayed there I asked her how much I owed her and, I have forgotten the exact amount, but in addition to providing me with a room, the bed, my breakfast and my supper; she also had done some washing for me. I expressed surprise at the smallness of the bill. She explained it, "Well I charge 15 cents a night per room and five cents a meal and you only have breakfast with me, no, you have two meals a day so that's 25 cents a day." I says, "What about the washing?" She says, "I just threw that in cause you are living with me." Which has interest only in the difference and tremendous contrast between the cost of things then and the cost of things today.

I think some of my interesting recollections while associated with the river are not of the river themselves, but of going in over the weekends to this little hotel in Golconda. Well naturally at this woman's house where I spent all week there was no chance to take a bath so late Friday afternoon I would row out or have somebody row out and catch the up packet and we'd simply throw a line to the packet and one of the deckhands would catch it and I would clamber aboard and ride up to it, and then the rowboat would go back in to Bay Village again. But as I walked up to the street to the hotel, they had negro porter he would see me coming and just as I would walk in the door I would say, I've forgotten his name, but I would call him by name.

And he says, "Yes, Mr. Anderson, which room are you going to have tonight?" I said, "I don't know." Well he says, "I'll have your bath ready for you by the time you get upstairs." Well that was somewhat of an exaggeration but within a half hour he came up with a tin washtub and put it down in the middle of the room, and then two buckets of reasonably warm water and that was my bath, which I paid the tremendous sum of 25 cents for, in addition to the cost of my room for 50 cents a night. The hotel was operated by a man named Chin, and I think he had been a shoe salesman and retired and bought this little hotel and he used to go to bed every night about eight o'clock or eight-thirty and would leave a note on the desk: "I've gone to bed. If you want a room, go upstairs and try the doors until you find one that's unlocked, and I'll see you in the morning."

Q: Where was this?

A: At Golconda. It was just a typical little country town, unpaved streets and all that sort of things, dinky little old town. The other thing, at this Bay Village, the principal store was also the telephone exchange. Strangely enough they had telephones there, but the telephone exchange consisted of three switches and a wire connected to the trunk line coming in, the one trunk line; when anybody wanted to use the telephone they turned the crank and the bell rang, he would go over and answer it. He would pick up this piece or wire, connect it to the proper switch to get the proper combination that he wanted. I don't know you have kind of pumped me dry. I think I've wandered far away from the things that you really want probably.

Q: Well it's all right, there's a lot of fine material here, and I thank you for taking the trouble.

A: I was glad to do it.

John Knoepfle

James Ault, August 1, 1956

Question: I'm at the home of Mr. James Ault, on Dale Road in Norwood. Mr. Ault was a musician on a number of steamers in the 1920s.

Answer: The first time, I was in the music business a number of years before I ever worked any of the boats. I think the first time I ever worked on any steamer, though, was up as far as 1928. The *Island Queen,* and that was just a matter of up and down the river to the Island. That was going nowhere. In 1929 I did some work on the Greene Line; that was when they were running the *Chris Greene* and the *Tom Greene.* We were from Cincinnati to Charleston. They carried freight on the lower deck and the season was strictly a passenger business too, along with the freight. For entertainment they frequently had a few fellows that played music on the boat, and I made numerous trips on both of the boats at different times. Usually about a four or five piece orchestra, and what we did working out of Cincinnati here on those trips just about played the same on the boats, same type of music as we played for dances around here. Why that was to some extent was the people that usually took those trips in the summer were, oh, quite a few school teachers. Seemed to draw them for Indiana, Michigan, upper Ohio. They'd read literature at the travel agencies and they'd think, "Well, I would like to take a river trip."

Well they liked a lot of the older type of music, the older tunes, but once in a while there would be some young people on the boat and they would want to let their hair down so speak so we would play a little jazz, mix it in. But on this particular trip we just more or less played the average pop music of the days at that time. In 1929, February of 1929, I had a trip to New Orleans on the, back in those days it was called the *Cincinnati,* and the crew was made up of people from all along the river here that were from different lines, in other words, it was just a get together to make the trip. People from the Greene Line and people from the old L and C Line, some of the people from the Coney Island company. Pilots and such, some of the other help on the boat. That again was the case, playing the music on that trip to New Orleans and back was a case pretty much like the *Greene* boat; it was wealthy people who could afford the trip taking a winter vacation so to speak. So we played pretty much what we call now society music, in other words tunes from musical comedies and things of that type. We didn't play too much wild music or anything like that. In other words, in the music business you have to tailor your style of playing, if you can tailor it, to fit the occasion. Depending on where, who you are working for, and what they want. I know from what my experience through, speaking of the *Island Queen,* they used to make trips in the spring and fall after the season would close here. They would normally, originally they'd go all the way down to New Orleans. They'd make stops on the way down. Maybe Louisville for a couple of days, two or three days; at smaller towns, just one night, sometimes they would pick up three towns in one night. Evansville was good for two or three nights. Get on down to Memphis, stay there maybe a week, get down to New Orleans finally, stay a month or two.

This was back in the 1920s, and usually when any of the bands that would be playing at that time, when they would get down to New Orleans we would still play practically the same style they played up here. In other words they wouldn't change, that was the way the band played. Of course the regular New Orleans bands would play the style that they were accustomed to playing. A lot of times the people would, there were excursion boats working out of New Orleans, in fact the *Capitol* was down there. There was a colored band on the boat, either a ten or twelve piece band, and they played typical of how the bands played, the large colored bands. But a lot of times people would, instead of taking that excursion around the harbor of New Orleans, would come over and take the *Island Queen* excursion, which was a different boat to ride on, a different band to listen to, and like I say, it was a little different style than what they were accustomed to listen to. Even on the way down, like in Memphis the bands played pretty much in Memphis like they played up here. In other words, with people hearing tunes on records and radio, I mean maybe they didn't get some of the latest tunes quite as fast as they did, but in other words, the same type tunes predominated. We didn't go in for a lot of gutbucket or New Orleans jazz or anything like that. Not that we didn't want to play that style, but like I say, we were trying to fit the occasion where we were working. There was a case, speaking about boats along the river, the steamer *Avalon* now, I can't remember what the old name was, but that boat used to work out of Louisville. See a lot of times these boats changed names maybe three or four times.

Q: I think it was the *Idlewild* or something?

A: Yes, that could have been. There was a band out of Louisville, they used to come, it was an excursion boat, they would go up the river out of Louisville about ten mile, I forget where they went now. But I rode that boat several times just to, because they were doing afternoon trips, and we were only doing evening trips, just to hear the band and meet the fellows. And there again was a case of the band on the boat. I can't remember the fellows' names any more. But it was an eight piece band, and there again, they played about the same style that they would be doing for dances if they were playing in Louisville. The only time that I would hear any, oh, so called riverboat jazz would be like a lot of times some of the boats that were working out of St. Louis, the Streckfus Lines, when we'd run into one of those boats, like maybe playing the same town, like Memphis we'll say, and they were running an excursion, and we were running an excursion. A lot of times they would run an afternoon and we weren't, why we would go and hear the band. A lot of times they would have pretty much of a jazz band on those boats, but more of the style that was known as riverboat jazz. I used to go over, and catch bands like at different spots like that, when I got a chance to. Most of the boats that worked the Ohio was more

John Knoepfle

or less bands that, typical ballroom bands, because there were a lot of ballrooms back in those days and it was strictly ballroom bands; and a lot of times when the ballroom season wouldn't be going so great, they'd be doing work on the boats on the river.

Some of the boats that didn't go in for big bands like the old *Queen City* that ran from here to Pittsburgh for a while, they would have only maybe three pieces. It was stylish, something to keep the people happy or have them sing along with the band. Usually in a three piece group we used to be drums, piano and some horns, saxophone or something like that. Four pieces well could be drums, piano and then two of almost anything. Like a sax and trumpet. The Greene Line like I spoke of before was usually a four or five piece band. I can remember one time, though, when things were a little slow we took some extra fellows along just for the trip. We had an eight or nine piece band at that particular time. That got to be a pretty good deal. That's when I noticed about bands that I had occasion to run into and work with along the river was, like I say, you played more or less the same style that you played at dances.

In fact, I more or less, was for the older crowd because people making those trips as a rule were older people and they didn't want a lot of loud jazz. When we were working these tramp trips down the river on the *Queen* and such that was more or less younger people. I mean the typical crowd that you get along on an excursion. We were playing more jazz on those occasions than we would working on these pleasure cruises. Because we were working then for people that wanted to let their hair down and cut a rug, so we would play that style for them, although mixed in with the pop tunes of the day too. I got away from working on some boats for a while, and went back, I think it was in 1933, worked of course on the *Island Queen* some more that spring and that fall. That time they didn't go all the way to New Orleans. They were only going as far as Memphis. It was too competitive down around New Orleans, so they just went as far as Memphis. We usually took, oh, four or five weeks to get down, leisurely. I mean like I say stop in different places on the way down. Then we would end up staying at Memphis anywhere from five to ten days. Then we would do the same thing coming back up. We were gone for maybe seven or eight weeks in the fall and that was again playing for a younger crowd. We would mix up the style of music we played. We'd play a lot of jazz and a lot of pop music, mixed up. Because if they heard tunes that the radio programs and played records that they wanted to hear they'd ask for it and we would play it for them. Where a lot of those colored bands that I used to hear on some of the Mississippi boats, they played things that strictly were more their style and not to many so-called pop tunes. There were some good bands that I ran into at different times. I couldn't tell you off-hand the names of some of those bands anymore, but I know there were some good men in some of those bands that gradually came on up and got into better bands and became top flight men in their field on their respective instruments.

Q: I know that Satchmo came up on the boats.

A: Yes, that was before my time on the boat, they say according to history. I've met him and talked to him a good many years ago. I haven't ran into him recently. I hear his records and everything now, though, and see him on shows. That was along about 1925 or 1926. 1925 I would say he came up. Of course he would work on excursion boats, in New Orleans proper. He never made any of the trips coming up on the boats, but he would do excursion boat trips around the harbor of New Orleans because that's been going on for a long time down there. What did I say the name of one old boat was? The *Capitol*, yes. There were other boats besides that. Speaking of trumpet, this don't pertain to river especially, although he probably had some of it in his early days, he was from Davenport, Iowa, was Beiderbecke. He was around here in 1924 and a little bit of 1925; he worked a couple of spots around Cincinnati, but he didn't do any work on the river around here. I do think he did on the Mississippi in his early days before he came over this way, when he was working around Indiana and this part of Ohio. He worked around here about a year or year and a half in different spots before he went up to Detroit and joined the Goldkette Band. Of course from the Goldkette Band he joined the Whiteman Band and that's about as much as I can remember of him. Still have some of those old records of his.

Q: They are probably collectors' items now?

A: Some of them maybe. I used to have a lot more records than I have now. But I used to lend them out to people foolishly, that didn't take care of them. You didn't think of them as collector's items then. I just don't lend them out anymore. I haven't played a lot of them for a long time, but every once in a while I get a notion and I'll spin a few. Takes me back.

Q: I know there was a man named Sy Rhinehart in Louisville, did you know anything about him? He used to work on the Louisville excursion boats.

A: I only recall that I heard the name. I don't remember if I met him or not; if I did it was quite a while back. The name strikes some response.

Q: He composed some music I understand.

A: Sy Rhinehart. A lot of times I didn't get a chance to meet those people; they were working at the same time that I was. Unless they were doing an afternoon excursion and I wasn't, and I happened to be there. A lot of times we would be doing an afternoon excursion, and then we would have people come over to visit us. That's the way you would get to meet people from the different boats.

Q: What kind of a schedule would a musician have on one of those boats?

A: Well, which type boat, you mean the tramp trips on the *Island Queen*, a regular dance schedule, or the excursion boats?

Q: Well, both ways.

A: On boats like the *Island Queen*, that was running these dances, it was more or less on a schedule similar to a regular dance; it would be like eight to twelve, four hours, eight-thirty to twelve-thirty or nine to one. A lot of times we were running, picking up one small town, then another small town, then another

John Knoepfle

small town, it was worked out in such a way we'd start at eight, pick up the first town, half hour later pick up the next town, half hour later pick up the next town, and paddle around a bit and finally along about twelve drop the first town off, a half hour later drop the next town off. In other words they each got in approximately four hours. That was the usual times for those things. Eight to twelve, eight-thirty to twelve-thirty or nine to one. Now that held true on most of the excursion boats. Of course the dance boat, there was an afternoon sightseeing trip; the band usually had to do some playing. That was usually one of those two to five things probably, one to five or two to five. But you didn't play all that time, you would play a little bit to break the monotony, but it wasn't so much, those afternoon things, wasn't so much to listen to the music; it was more sightseeing, but you had to go along and break the routine a little bit, break the monotony. On the boats though that, the passenger boats, that were taking people on these trips to Charleston, to Huntington, Point Pleasant and such places as that, and even like the *Delta Queen* does now on down the Kentucky Lake, music is just an incidental thing like they may have some music on the boat. That evening, after the evening meal if the people are in a mood. They'll play maybe two or three hours. No set time, just when everybody is in the mood. Sometimes they will get customers that feel like dancing and other times they'll just want to sit around and listen; other times they'll want to sing, and you play old tunes that they'll sing along with you. But there was no set hour or anything of that type and usually it broke up, if you started about eight-thirty you may work not steady but to ten-thirty, sometimes eleven; sometimes you didn't start until nine, you would work until about eleven. Three hours would be a long time for something like that.

Q: Well 1929 must have been hard years for musicians; can you tell me what kind of wages musicians were making then?

A: A lot depended on where you were working out of. I couldn't say what the bands on the boats along the Mississippi were making. If they were on tour and hitting a lot of places, then more or less it was a wage, a combination of a wage that fit most locals, so to speak. In other words, what I mean by that, is if a group worked out of St. Louis on excursions and strictly were always in that jurisdiction, they had to get St. Louis scale, whatever it was in those days. If they worked out of New Orleans and New Orleans only, that prevailed. Now the way it used to work for us on the *Island Queen*, although we were out of this jurisdiction as soon as we left Cincinnati, it was usually Cincinnati bands on the *Island Queen* and the Cincinnati local made a rate, which wasn't as high as if we worked in town here and yet it was high enough that it would satisfy all the various locals whose jurisdiction would be in Louisville, Evansville and such places, Paducah. I would say roughly back in those days that that particular trip on the *Island Queen*, that thing only paid $20 or $25 a week, room and board. That was back around that time, and even during the depression, 1931-1932-1933, I don't think the price came up even there, I don't think the price came up beyond that $25, $30 a week until along about 1934 or 1935. I think it came up to around $45, $55, I think, finally well, like the *Queen* on their trip when they had the explosion up in Pittsburgh. Back in the 1940s wages were up and in pretty good shape, I mean a fellow, a sideman, not a leader, a sideman, could make himself usually 75 bucks a week, room and board at that time.

Getting back to the passenger boats though, that was more or less a flat rate, like when we used to make Mardi Gras trips, there would be a flat rate guaranteed for you for the trip. I figured an 18 day trip, 18 days to get there and back plus three or four days you could stay in New Orleans, and ordinarily you may make $50, room and board. You ate with passengers and had a good room. On those passenger boats the meals were good and you had a good room and on boats like the *Queen,* which wasn't really equipped for passenger service, you had to move right in more or less with the crew and eat when they ate and eat the food they ate, and it wasn't luxurious by any means, but these other boats, the Greene Line, the food was wonderful, the best they could obtain and the rooms were always nice, and it was just much better traveling conditions. The summer season on the Greene Line, small bands they used to use, there used to be either $15 or $20, room and board. Of course that was back in the 1920s, the late, late 1920s, and the depression, early 1930s. The bands who worked on the excursions, though, they'd be making anywhere, it seemed like the colored bands never seemed to make as much money as some of the other bands that worked out of here. Like along the Mississippi they would get them for cheap wages. In other words maybe $15 or $20 a week and their room and board. Of course that was a big item because they didn't have to worry about their food, didn't have to worry about a place to sleep. The money was just spending money to them. So wages, you didn't, up until it got into the 1940s, you didn't make much money on those type trips.

Q: Life is a little better now?

A: Oh yes, and of course wages did finally come along, and then too, the various locals, instead of trying to give breaks to them like they did create, back in the 1920s and 1930s, to create some work when there was a lot of other jobs to choose from, competition, the boats, the companies had to start paying more money because the people would go somewhere else and work. Plus the locals of the various cities would demand better pay. So it finally started coming up paying a little better than it did before.

Q: We never established what you played on the boats?

A: Back in those days, well when I first played on the boats, my first professional instrument I played, was banjo. Back when banjo was popular the first time. I guess it was along about 1929, 1928 or 1929 when banjo was starting to die out at that time and guitar was coming in. I thought, "Well, should I switch over or stay with it, stay with guitar?" I switched over to saxophone. In fact some of those trips I was telling you about like on the Greene Line I was playing sax then. The trips to New Orleans I was playing sax and on the *Queen* playing sax. Well then later on I still played sax, I have one left. I used to have a set of them. I switched over to trumpet and that's what I play even now, but I guess I've been playing trumpet, since about 1935-1936.

Q: Were there any particular combinations of bands that you remember names?

A: You mean that I was with?

Q: Yes, that you were with.

A: A band that use to be popular around here and also do some of those trips too, working the Coney Island season, plus these tramp trips, these trips up and down as far as New Orleans, sometimes up as far as Pittsburgh, Art Hicks, I worked with Art. He had a popular band around here and also was well-known up and down the Ohio and Mississippi, sometimes he would get to. Art Hicks, he had a pretty nice band. There was . . . trying to think of that other band that I, well, Billy Shaw used to have a band and we did similar, about the same type work Hicks was doing only a year or two later. Billy Shaw, he had the band, a fairly popular one around these parts. Wasn't too well known down the river because like I say we would only get there, every once or twice a year. I think Shaw, I worked with him, think we did about two seasons of those type trips that he had. Oh, I think up in 1940 I think it was, 1940 or 1941, I made a trip too, a tramp trip, I was on the *Queen* again, the *Island Queen*. We went as far as Memphis that time, stayed there about eight days. That band was led by Herman Kershner. That was back in the days when he had bands; now he has a spot downtown just doing piano work by himself. He has the Piano Lounge downtown in the Keith's Theatre building on the first floor on Walnut Street. But he used to run bands and I worked, I played trumpet in his band, some sax, and I used to score for the band, arrange for the band. That's what I've been doing for a good many years, arranging.

Q: You are with WLW-Radio, Cincinnati, now aren't you?

A: I was with them up until last October, was with them, lacked about a month being 21 years. Just when I thought the job was going to be steady. No, I'm not doing that type work now because the field is limited around here as to writing for bands, so I just more or less gradually edged out of the business.

Q: Cincinnati has left a lot of good things go.

A: There are some good potential musicians here in town right now. There is one trombone player I know, he is doing some selling. He, for my money, is one of the top ten in the country. He could go out with various current name bands like Jerry Anthony. But what it would cost him to make those trips plus trying to keep his home up here with his family, you just don't make it. If he made two hundred bucks a week, he still couldn't come out. So he is sitting making far less and picking up what scraps of jobs he can. Another trombone player, in fact he used to be on one of those old Bix Beiderbecke records, he is working over at Beverly Hills, and Bill Rank, he is one of the good top men in the country. There are some good trumpet players around town, some good sax men, a lot of good talent here in town. But rather than go out and beat their brains out on the road now, they are just sitting here and doing something else.

Q: Wonder if this fellow Rank is in Mississippi now?

A: No, I tell you his connection, how he happened to make records with Beiderbecke. Rank was playing trombone with Whiteman and when Beiderbecke joined Whiteman, all the time he was with Whiteman, I should say, even when he was making records even under his own name, he was usually using men out of the Whiteman band at that time. But when he made records in Chicago before he went with Whiteman, then it was fellows from around here or fellows from over around Indiana U. or fellows from Chicago. The men on some of those records used to vary a little bit although the name was always the same. But it got so there when he was making records in New York and the time he was with Whiteman, most all the time it was Rank on trombone, Bill Rank. Usually Trumbauer on saxophone and usually the pianist out of the Whiteman band, and bass. George Wettling, the drummer used to always be on those records. So there was a time about like then. Rank plays very good to this day. Plays real good.

Q: I would like to ask you some offbeat questions. I know as a musician you would have had a sharper ear for any of the singing the roustabout did. I know they sang a lot at their work.

A: Even on the boats working the Ohio River there would be, seems like there would be like a gang of them three or four assigned to one job. Seems like they'd, by this pattern, this rhythm shall we say of whatever they would sing, they would seem to get the work done quicker and better. Like do the work along and in time with the music they were singing. A lot of times they'd would make up something pertaining to the work they were doing. They'd sing, "This old job is sure hard, but it's got to be done." You know they would put it to some little melody of their own or compose it as they went along. A lot of those things that they used to do were just spur of the moment things. The ideas came to them, that's it. Usually the one fellow would set the pattern and the other two or three would join in and add to it.

Q: You don't remember any of the lines or anything offhand, do you?

A: No, I wouldn't, offhand, no.

Q: I am kind of interested in how they got those boats loaded.

A: In what way how they got them loaded?

Q: What kind of freight was carried on and off and how, where?

A: Well, I guess that would depend on the locality; I've seen along the Mississippi loads and loads of bales of cotton, which was a big commodity and was something they handled plenty of. On the Ohio here the boats that would haul freight, it was almost anything. Freight, period! In other words there would be hardware, stoves, furniture.

Q: Where did they get the stoves from, up around Ironton?

John Knoepfle

A: There was quite a few stove manufacturers here in Cincinnati and they would ship out of here, maybe on the way up the river, if we had maybe two hundred stoves, we'd drop some off at Portsmouth to the wholesaler up there, drop some off at Huntington, and take some over the Charleston. They were usually, if not manufactured here, at least manufactured somewhere in Indiana close by and hauled here by truck and then carried the rest of the way by boat because it was cheaper transportation. I remember the Greene Line used to have them, on the old *Chris* and *Tom Greene*, they used to have the contract to haul all the new Fords and Chevys to the up the river towns. So we would stop dropping them off anywhere, usually they could get, I don't remember the actual count, maybe as high as twenty cars. They'd find places for them on that bottom deck and they would drop them off at Portsmouth. They drop some off at Ironton, and some at Huntington. There for about three or four years they were making a big deal on hauling those. They weren't being driven up to those places. They were hauled up on the boat.

Q: Guess the roads were too bad at that time, maybe?

A: That could be.

Q: They just drove them off the boats onto the wharfboats up there.

A: That's right. Then whoever the dealer was that they were assigned to, he would come down and have people drive them on up from there. But I don't know where the Fords came from here; the Chevys were assembled here even then. The Fords must have been assembled somewhere close by. Because we used to haul Fords and Chevys. otherwise the freight consisted of, oh I said hardware, and such as that. A lot of those up the river towns used to get their wholesale groceries from these big wholesale grocery houses in Cincinnati. We used to carry a lot of crates and cartons of wholesale groceries, cereals, canned goods and things of that type. Of course there was a lot of times, at some of these small landings where the boat wouldn't ordinarily ever make a stop unless it was a scheduled thing, the farmer maybe had called in and made arrangements for the boat to stop there at the landing and pull up to this landing on the Ohio and put on some cows or some pigs or something and bring it on down to the market here. In other words they were going to the stockyards here in Cincinnati and a lot of times those farmers used to haul their cattle in, coming into Cincinnati. That would be like on the trip coming back down.

Q: I've been told that the rousters used what they called a chain bar. Two long handles joined by chain and they would haul things in those chain bars. Did you ever see them do that?

A: No, I don't recall that. Usually, I won't say it wasn't done, but usually it was just strictly brawn in loading or unloading. I mean if it was a big item two or three men handled it, if it was a small item, maybe weighing 50 to 75 pounds, they would get it up on their shoulders and haul it away, strictly picking it up and toting it so to speak. That's a term they used to use, tote.

Q: That's right. These terms crop into the speech.

A: Is there a word like that in the tune "Old Man River?" Tote that barge. Tote that bail. I don't remember the words, but the word tote is in there. But that's characteristic. I've heard that expression used a lot of times.

Q: Do you have any particular recollections that stand out in your mind about that upper river?

A: The upper Ohio?

Q: Yes.

A: I went up numerous times as far as Point Pleasant. And of course up the Kanawha there, but beyond there, I've gone up to Marietta several times, Wheeling, but I don't remember much about that because I didn't make many trips up that far, maybe one or two.

Q: I forget you'd probably be playing when you were going up through there too, wouldn't you?

A: A lot of times when we were going from one city to another during the daytime with nothing to do when we would be getting there, I would get myself a nice shady spot and watch the scenery. The upper Ohio had some nice scenic spots. I would say the upper Ohio is much more scenic than the lower part of the Ohio, I think.

Q: I have heard that. I have been through the upper myself.

A: Of course speaking of scenic the Mississippi surely has nothing to offer you. The lower stretch of the Mississippi is just from nowhere.

Q: The old wide water?

A: Once in a while you can see across, the top of the levee you can see tops of some houses of the small towns that you passed. Of course a lot of the, Natchez and such as that is built upon a bluff, so is Memphis. Away from the river and up so the water can't get to it. Strictly nothing scenic about the lower Mississippi. I've never been up the upper Mississippi. They say that is very nice. But the upper Ohio in fact I think is very beautiful. Never get tired of looking at it.

Q: I have never made it by water, but I would like to someday. I drove up through there last year.

A: It's just like other scenic spots down through the Smokies, I've been there several times. Still don't know if I would make a special trip or not but if I were close would probably drop myself around and go through it again. It's some-thing you like to see over and over again. Speaking about over and over again. A lot of these people, I would say a lot of old school teachers, used to make these summer trips on these boats. Lot of times they would be back the next year. Some of them would make it three or four times. If they made a trip one time up the river, the next year they would make it down on one of the other boats. Like Cincinnati to Louisville. A lot of those people enjoyed it. It was quiet and restful. I'm speaking of the passengers. Quiet and restful and if you wanted to get a good rest that was sure one way to do it. I know us musicians

John Knoepfle

on those type trips, all we had to do outside of the playing at night, was lay around, eat, get fat and lazy.

Q: One of the captains told me they would all get fat standing up in the pilothouse and the die of heart attacks trying to climb the riverbanks.

A: (chuckles) They could do something like that.

Q: Well, fine, I think you have given me a nice interview, Mr. Ault. And you'll be down there with the others.

A: Like I say, I didn't have too much actual boat experience on the Mississippi, that's a different thing, working steady over there, I mean they may have played different sounding music than we did. But my only contact was like I say was going down there occasionally and playing a few nights at some of those towns. We played the same like I say there that we did up here.

Q: And draw good crowds?

A: Yes, we did good business. That was usually all thought out time. They knew ahead of time how those things worked. Those tramp trips on the *Queen*. They were usually sponsored, each night would be sponsored by the American Legion or a group of sponsors, something. The fireman or police groups in these different cities and towns were real great at sponsoring those; sometimes the police and the firemen would go together. Sometimes it would be like an American Legion group, sometimes Veterans of Foreign Wars, sometimes a civic group of some sort. But each night, it wasn't a haphazard thing, those people were selling tickets, like I'm speaking now about the *Queen* and excursion boats. Those people would be out weeks ahead of time selling tickets, because over the guarantee in the amount that the boat cost them, in other words they had to guarantee the company a certain amount, and over that they made some money and the boat made still some extra money over that, but they had to get out and sell enough tickets to make something for themselves. In other words they were trying to build up their funds, the police or firemen thing, were trying to build up their retirement, or something like that.

Q: You just reminded me about something because we did that out of high school. I had my first date on the *Queen,* and it was one of the most miserable nights I ever spent in my life. (chuckles)

A: Speaking of the *Queen* a lot of fraternities and sororities would sponsor a lot of those, I remember that too. A lot of times it would be some big business. Some big company that would sponsor something.

Q: Well, guess the *Avalon* follows pretty much that pattern even now.

A: Yes, of course, the fellow that is running that business, running the *Avalon*, he was publicity man for years with the Coney Island people. He always made the advance trips up and down the river and set these dates, found out who was going to sponsor that particular dance. He did that for years and years. Incidentally he was an old time musician himself. He had a band around town back in the 1920s. I am trying to think of his name.

Q: His name was Meyer, I believe?

A: Yes, Meyer, I'm trying to think of nickname he had. Well, maybe, Woody Meyer? Woody? He had a band back in the 1920s around here. It wasn't a top flight band, but he did work, and he got in this publicity business, and he seemed to take to that. Like I say for 15 maybe 20 years he was going up there for the *Queen*. So he is probably following up the same, has been, since he's taken over the *Avalon* a number of years ago, probably following the same procedure as he used to do for the *Queen*. In other words contacting the same people. Only he covers more territory. He'll probably go the upper Mississippi and he may go into the Cumberland River, the Tennessee River, I don't know.

Q: They'll go anywhere on the Avalon.

A: The only requirement on those boats, that you will naturally if you have a business there. you always get men who have license that can take you on those rivers; because if your regular men can't do it, you hire people wherever you are going that have license to cover that.

Q: They are getting rarer and rarer, and older and older.

A: Yes, most people they are breaking in now, some of the old-timers are going in, working the towboats.

Q: They don't bother with a license?

A: Pilots still have to have licenses. They can't get up in that house unless they do.

Q: That's an odd thing, they don't need the kind of license a man would have needed if he was steam pilot.

A: Probably not but you still have to know your river.

Q: Oh, there is no question about that.

A: Which is only one of many of the requirements. I can remember back, oh, a lot of times we would hit some of these trips in the spring when the water would be high, the river would be high, and they'd have to know conditions, in other words, how high the water was, how high bridges were, that they could calculate, because a lot times they would take the top of, maybe the pilothouse off, the trimmings, the ornaments, lower the stacks back to get under a certain bridge, and they'd have it all worked out because they knew the height of the bridge, that was part of their business, they would know how high the water was by the government reports, so they figured how much they would have to lower those stacks. Some of them were made to bend back and they would take some of the ornaments off the top of the pilothouse. I would stand up on the top deck sometimes it would be like we were missing by about one or two feet. But they knew they could do it.

Q: I remember once the *Queen* went under the bridges here like that with the stacks back. It was quite a thrilling thing to be up there and watch that.

A: There was one time once this was down the river, we were down, oh, at least around Paducah, I can't remember if we were going there or coming from there, but we had to get to this next town and the river was coming up. So they figured they could beat the rise, and get under this certain bridge they had to get under before they were going to be held there and not going to be able to get under. So they figured, well we think we can do it if we get there quick enough. That was a case of missing it just by about a foot, but they can do a lot of calculations you know. Course they figured when they came back up a few weeks later the water condition would change. I don't remember anytime that we were ever completely stopped. But they got awfully close sometimes.

Q: Well fine, and I thank you for having taking the time out for this.

Question: We are talking to W. C. Beatty known here as Captain. He has spent many years on the river and knows a great deal about the Big Sandy country.
Answer: You want to know something about the batwing boats?
Q: Let's start with the logging.
A: The first logging that I did or had any part of was in 1906 and at that time we handled quite a bit of logs and timber for a company by the name of Whistler and Searcy Lumber Company. Searcy was a man that lived in Ironton, and he was a very wealthy man at one time. He was also associated with this Mr. Whistler who was from Hillsboro, Ohio. Mr. Whistler, if I'm not mistaken, had some kind of a mill, maybe a flour mill or something at Hillsboro, but he wasn't too active in the business, and these particular people bought timber out of Big Sandy River, and they bought timber out of Little Kanawha River, lots and lots of timber out of Little Kanawha River. They bought from M. R. Lowders. Branded his logs M. R. L. Company. And they bought from Pierces and there were two Pierce brothers, one of them was a doctor and his name was Charlie. That was C. S. Pierce, was the brand: C. S. P.; then the other one was Henry Pierce and they branded, well they had the two brands H. S. P. and C. S. P., which belonged to Pierce brothers and then they had an H made with one leg of the H made part of the P.

A good deal of their timber came out of, well it all came down the Little Kanawha River, but there was quite a bit of it that came out of Hughes River, which is quite a distance up in the Little Kanawha. That was floated out in what they called lockages because there was locks and dams in there at that time. But they were very little locks and they couldn't make very big rafts out of them, they weren't like a Big Sandy raft. A Big Sandy raft was much bigger than these little lockages and when they rafted these logs together the majority of the timber that came out of there was rafted with what they called a withe and two pins. They laid a tie across the logs; they bored a hole on each side of the tie pole. They would take a hickory withe and stick down in this hole, and then drive two wedges in so it wouldn't come off, like a yoke over it and that's the way that they rafted their logs. Of course then in later years, why, chain dogs, there was chain dogs at that time, but they didn't use them up there. They cost too much money.
Q: Was the withe across the logs?
A: No, across the tie pole. Like you would take, a chain dog was two dog wedges made out of three-eighths by inch and a quarter, maybe inch and a half iron with a hole in each end of it with a chain across the two of them, and you would stretch them across the pole, drive one on each side of the pole, and that held the logs. Then they would bring these logs out and they would hold them there. We would always have to go up there and measure them. I worked for

John Knoepfle

this Whistler and Searcy people, and we would go to Parkersburg, we'd measure this timber all up, and there was a couple of, well several little boats that brought timber out of there.

There was people by the name of Verian, Homer Verian and his brother. I don't recall his name. But they had a little boat, *Carrie V* was the name of the boat, and then after that they had another boat called the *Valley Belle*. The *Valley Belle,* the last that was ever heard of her she belonged to the Bryant Showboat people. They bought her and ran her towing the showboat back and forth. There was an old gentleman by the name of Sam Spencer that used to be captain on the *Carrie V.* He had great long chin whiskers come down to this belt. And there was a fellow was mate on there by the name of John Ruth, he was a Parkersburg man.

Q: Spencer's beard wasn't red was it?

A: No, it was white, white as the driven snow. The only redheaded and red-bearded man, well he didn't have a long beard, was a fellow by the name of Captain Doss Davis. But he never towed any timber that I ever knew of. Then they would keep this timber there and fleet it up in fleets and these boats would get it and they would bring it to Ironton or wherever it may go, in fact some of it was sold and went as far as Louisville. Went to what they called Point Lumber Company at Louisville, Kentucky. They would get behind this or in front of it and back it all way down. They didn't try to shove it or tow it.

They backed it and at night when they would get ready to tie up they would turn loose from that end, go around and get on the upper end of it and what we called rough lock it. They would back it in against the bank and make it drag. It would just keep dragging and dragging and of course they would run a line to help it and eventually it would stop and maybe you'd drag off a dozen logs. Well you had to go back up there with cant hooks, roll them in the river, bring them down, the next morning when you got ready to leave way they'd swing them around and put them back in the place where they belonged.

Q: I supposed if you tried to tuck them in without dragging them and that line broke . . .

A: Well it would just keep on going, and then it took a pretty good line to hold them, and you couldn't handle too big of a line because you had to handle it all by hand, and we would go out and tie it around a tree, and put it under a tie pole, put a toggle in it and check them in that way. Stopped many, many times.

Q: How big were some of those fleets, do you know?

A: I have seen them when they had, oh they would be 200 feet wide, 500 to 600 feet long.

Q: Would that be all hardwood?

A: No, all kinds. There would be oak, and maple, and birch, and sycamore, and buckeye, and gum, and elm, and ash, and hickory, and pine, and poplar.

Q: How did they ever get by them on the river, those packets?

A: They give them plenty of room. They kept out of their road, and if they were in a close place in the bend, why the packet would run in a notch in a bank someplace or someplace where there was good water and let them go by. They never bothered each other. Well it was no use because they would just get into trouble if they did. Of course at that time there was a lot of big coal boats that belonged to the river Combine. They run their coal boats, maybe you would pass a half dozen of them in the run of a day. Of course they had no choice, they just had to take what was coming to them because you couldn't get out of the road of them, they would, if they could hold them up on a point or something or keep them out of the bends. Ordinarily if they backed them slow and they kept them pointed, why they would go the way they were pointed. We hand run lots of them without any boat, with what they call a gouger oar on the end of it. I floated a lot of timber from the mouth of the Big Sandy and from the mouth of Twelve-pole to Cincinnati and tied them up right here, right here at this, right where we are sitting here. The old log way is down the hill, down there, when they had the sawmills here, for C. Crane and Company.

Q: Can you amplify that gouge oar navigation a little bit?

A: A gouger oar, ordinarily they were about, oh maybe, 12 to 14 feet long, that is the blade was. Had a tapered blade, it run from a half inch thick on one end to possibly two, two and a quarter thick on the other end, and would be any place from eight, maybe to ten, twelve inches wide. It had a long pole on it. The pole wasn't straight with it. It was put on in a, well, what you would call a little bit out of line, so that when it was hung, you bore a hole in the end of a log, put a pin in there; it had a hole in this oar, the hole in the bottom part of the oar was just a little bit bigger than the pin. Then about two inches up in that, what would be the handle or the pole on that oar, that would be cut out bigger so when you raised it, it would give you a chance that it wouldn't bend the pin every time, but the oar would work back and forth in that, see it had some like the bottom of it had, was down in and had a hole in the bottom.

When you made this bigger up here so when you raised this oar that pin stayed, and it gave you room to rock it. Then there was a hole bored in another pole that was put on the top of this pin, that you could put that on that oar, and that kept it from falling over sideways. See you had control of it end ways, but over sideways when you went to pull on it, a walk, and you walked across the logs. You would go to one side of the raft with that oar, stick it in the water and walk from across to the other side, well that made the raft follow you. Which way you was walking that raft, would make that raft follow you over there. Maybe you might have to hit it a hundred licks before you got it to where you wanted. If you was in a close place, a lot of times you would go to hit the bank and if you went to hit the bank and you did get out and they was going to hit something, you lifted that thing up off the top of your oar, and lifted your oar up out of the hole and pulled it back on the raft so it wouldn't tear your oar up, because without the oar you were done.

John Knoepfle

Q: How many men came down on those rafts?

A: Two to the raft. Unless you had more than two rafts, if you had more than two rafts, why, then a lot of times they would give you three men. That was two on the lower end with a gouger oar, one fellow on the upper end. The fellow on the upper end was always the captain. He did the running; he told you when to move. All he did, he didn't have anything to do, the fellows on the lower end was the guys that did the lifting. They would lift it out and that was a long time before the locks and dams came in. When they were building dam 19 at Little Hocking right below the mouth of Little Hocking, right no not dam 19, dam 22 at Ravenswood, and they were building that and we came through there close with some timber at that time and tore it up down there on those big rocks down there below Ravenswood, lot of rocks on the West Virginia side there.

Q: A big ledge of rock in there.

A: There is a big, well the Sandy Creek's in there and then that's all rocky shore down in there. That was about the last of the logging that came out of the Little Kanawha River. Then after that we took lots of them out of Big Sandy, and lot of them out of Twelve-pole, and lot of them out of Guyan. At one time there was 60,000 logs in a jam in the Guyan River. And a C & O Railroad engine went there, and a fellow by the name of Shorty Weaver was the engineer on it, and they tore that, them logs was causing that bridge, and that engine fell in the river there, like to never got her out.

Q: The logs broke up the bridge?

A: Yes, it jammed on the bridge, tore a pier out from under it. Yes, tore the pier out from under it, and a lot of times they would have those logs jammed, you couldn't get them loose and you used to have to dynamite them, if they got so bad that you couldn't, and looked like they weren't going to move their self. They would leave them. What they liked to do, they liked to leave them as long as they could possible leave them, leave jammed if they wanted to, with the hopes they would break, cause if they were broke they were sure then that they would all go at one time. And of course then if it didn't look like they were going to break, why they got in there and dynamited them.

Q: Guess the water backed up under them?

A: Oh it just backed up, backed up and got everything behind, you know, and then they had fellows, what they called "follow up" men, maybe they would be seven, eight, ten men. One log would catch on the bank and be a straggler, you know, and they would come up and roll him in and let him go on by himself. Of course that was up in the creeks up in there. That wasn't done in main Sandy. In main Sandy River, why you turned them loose they would catch them in there and make you pay for them. They would tie them up on you, of course in these creeks they wouldn't.

Q: They were all made in little rafts on the Big Sandy?

A: Yes, after they got down out of the forks, you know, down below the forks. You see main Sandy River is only 26 miles long. It goes to Louisa, that's right, it goes from Catlettsburg to Louisa and it's 26 miles. Then on the left fork as you go up the river it's Tug Fork, and the right side is Levisa. If you go to Pikeville and Prestonsburg and Beaver and all up in there and over on the other fork why you go to Williamson and Matewan up through that country. Blackberry, Chattaroy, and I was trying to think the first gasoline boat that ever I saw on the Kanawha River belonged to a fellow by the name of Jim Kennedy. He owned the first boat; he did quite a bit of fleeting of timber there in the mouth. What they call fleeting it, was take the rafts, build them up into fleets, see, so they could come on out in the river and deliver them to the mills. Course sometimes, why those mills over around Ironton and over in there, why a lot of times you would go over in there and only bring one raft over.

We would go up there on a streetcar and get on that raft and take about, oh it took you about five hours to float over there, ten miles; went over there in four and a half or five hours, unless you had pretty good water, and if you had pretty good water you could go over. Along with these logs there were millions of cross ties came out there. The majority of the cross ties that came out of there went to Ironton, took out over the elevator there, belonged to an old fellow by the name of C. C. Clark. He rafted his ties up in there and brought them there, and sold them to the various railroads. This fellow Kennedy that did this fleeting up there, he had that little boat, and then the next boat was built by some people down at Hanging Rock by the name of Icher. Old man Icher, and his boy's name was Wes; they had one of best boats, a boat called the *Comet*. They had her around there for a long, long time. And then there was a steamboat there that belonged to Carl Mace, and Ellis Mace his brother, called the *Sea Lion*. The *Sea Lion* afterwards left there and went around on Kentucky River to do something, and I think she burned up around there. They never did get her back out of there.

Q: For some reason I thought Cole Crane owned the *Sea Lion*.

A: No, no, Crane owned the *Crown Hill*, the *J. O. Cole,* and they owned, a little boat called the *Katrinka* and they owned a diesel boat called the *Goldie*. I came here to Cincinnati, and bought the *Goldie* in 1917, took her to Ironton and wintered her through the 1917 and 1918 ice and built a hull for her and she, a boat called the *Colonel,* and she belonged to the Ironton Lumber Company. I sold her to the Ironton Lumber Company.

Q: Now I think a man you may know from my information, he left Ironton before the 1913 flood and his name was Tom Wagner.

A: Yes.

Q: And he remembered a mill burning up there. It burned for days and they had left the insurance drop an hour before the fire started?

A: Yes, Newman and Spanner.

Q: Spanner? How do you spell the Spanner?

A: S-P-A-N-N-E-R, Spanner. They not only burned once but they burned a lot of times; then there was a mill next to them that belonged to an old fellow by the name of Pat Hart. He burned out at that time; the Fearon Lumber and Veneer Company burned up; the Whistler and Searcy Mill burned up. They tore the Fearon Lumber Company Mill down; they tore the Nile Lumber Company Mill down; they tore the Dockins Lumber Company Mill down. If I'm not mistaken the Yellow Poplar Lumber Company burned up at Coal Grove.

Q: All of that is a past age now, no more timber coming out and no mills running?

A: There is not a mill, the last mill that I knew of was a little sawmill belonged to Ulysses Parsley, and that was right on the bank above the mouth of the Big Sandy River. Ulysses Parsley and I understand that Lys got out of the lumber business, he had become a very wealthy man, and somebody told me that he went to Florida and that is the last I ever heard of him.

Q: When was the last of the timber brought out that was considerable?

A: The last considerable timber, I would say about around 1916, 1917, 1918, along in there. See there wasn't too much of it after that. There was some but not too much.

Q: I have one question about this Newman and Spanner. Wagner mentioned that fire killed Old Tee. Do you remember who Old Tee might have been?

A: It don't register right now. Talking about those little bat wing boats. Those things ran up in there a long time before my time, it was before the C & O Railroad went up Big Sandy. And they used those little boats to haul supplies up there because that was the only way that they had of getting them up there. About the time that they were finishing up the railroads, why these fellows that owned these boats, you know, saw the handwriting on the wall and they begin to want to dispose of them. So there was an old Jewish fellow there by the name of Fish Goldman and old Fish bought one of these boats. Yes, and you know Big Sandy is nothing but a big creek. It will rain, it will raise and fall and be done in 24 to 36 hours. The raise, the fall, and everything is done. So when they had water they had to go. So they had a big crowd on the boat, they was carrying a lot of passengers on there. This boat, I don't remember what the name of the boat was, this particular boat, but anyhow he bought this boat and they made a bank landing and the river was falling and they hit the bank a little bit too hard. The river kept falling and they kept carrying the freight off or on whatever they were doing, and the boat began to list pretty bad. Old Fish, he thought he would satisfy everybody that was on the boat and he went up to the top of the step and he said, "Ladies, don't be a bit alarmed, the boat is fully insured." So that cleared that up all right. Let's see, the *Thealka* and the *Guyandotte*, the *Sandy Valley*, now there was another one I can't think of that belonged to a . . .

Q: There was an old boat there in 1903 called the *Stafford*.

A: *Stafford*, before my time around there, see. I guess when I first went to going around the mouth of the Sandy, I was about seventeen. Let's see seventeen, would make 1903.

Q: You must remember some of the characteristics of those men that pulled the logs out? Can you talk about them?

A: That took them out of the river?

Q: I understand it was kind of rough country up there?

A: The last good timber that was taken out, I helped take it out, it was on Durbin Creek. It's about nine miles to the mouth of Durbin where we took them out down below the mouth of Durbin Creek, and then the next lot was on Bear Creek and Bear Creek comes in at Buchanan and Buchanan is right across the river from Prichard. Prichard is on the N & W and the C & O is Buchanan and Bear Creek goes back up in there. The Iron Lumber Company owned that timber and they went up in there and cut it and they throwed it over a rock cliff that was there, just liked they would go up there and they never cleaned the timber below it. There was a lot standing trees in there, and they never cut a one of them, they just dumped them logs in and made the awfulest log jam that you ever saw in your life there. It was costing them more than the logs were worth to get them out of there, and a fellow and I went up there and took some, rolled up enough poplar logs in the river to make a float out of and took a hoisting engine and went in there and pulled the end out and we floated them out of there. That was, let me see in 1910 or 1911 in there, that was the last that came out of that part of the country.

Q: Those trees were all sawed and axed I suppose?

A: They were chopped down and sawed and there was some mighty fine timber in there. It was one of the finest, and it belonged to some old people that never would let loose of it and of course they died and of course they settled up the estate, and that's how they come to get it. There was part of it come out of Bear Creek and part of it come out of, down at the other place, and we had to haul it across the C & O Railroad tracks to get to the river there at the mouth of Durbin. We hauled it in there and rolled over the bank and rafted it and brought it out.

Q: I understand those Big Sandy raftsmen wouldn't go into the Ohio?

A: No, all you had to do, and it was done a lot of times, those fellows had little boats, I had two different boats in there, you know, I had a boat called the *Eureka* at one time. Put her in there in 1907 or in 1908, right after that, during that panic. In fact I built her in 1907 and 1908, wanted to call her *Panic* and even had the letters cut out to call her *Panic*, and when I turned it into the Custom House they said, "Oh, oh, no, not that. This government has got enough trouble without stirring up anymore of it." So that was the answer on that. Then I put the *V. F. Searcy* in there after the 1913 flood or 1914. The boys would go up in around England Hill and up in there and they would see them folks coming out, and the Sandy would be running out, they'd holler, "Hey, buddy, you better get off of there," said, "You're going out in the big Ohio," those fellows they would just loaf overboard and swim ashore. They wouldn't go out in the Ohio at all. They'd ride out of the Big Sandy, and them things changing ends and everything else, coming out of there you know.

John Knoepfle

Q: I can't even visualize anybody on a raft going down the Big Sandy.

A: Oh yes, there were two men on there, one on each end of it. They had one of those gouger oars, and that was the only way you keep from hitting the bank. Those fellows agreed to deliver those for so much money. If they didn't deliver them, that was it. If they tore up and was lost, why that was just it.

Q: I guess that amount of money varied?

A: It depended on how far, now we used to go up there, when I first put them boats in up there, I worked them boats for a dollar and a half an hour, me and another man and I supported the man and myself and we got a dollar and a half an hour catch as catch can. Some days we would get an hour or two and some days we didn't. And other days we would work around the clock.

Q: That was for catching logs . . .

A: That was taking care of the rafts with the boat, see. When they would come out, for instance if there was a lot of current, and they were getting afraid that they were going out in the river, why we would go up and catch them and land them, you know shove them in because they had certain places that they were going to go. Maybe they were going to go to Wright and Kitchen. Now Wright and Kitchen would have a place along there where they tied their stuff up or Dansam and Kitchen would have a place to tie theirs up. Ironton Lumber Company had a place for theirs. Yellow Poplar and Coal Grove had a place for theirs and so on all the way down the line. What we would we'd try to, fellow would say, "Well, I've got six rafts a coming. When you come to the raft ask them who they are, who they are working for. If they are working for me, tie them up. Don't mince any words with them just tell them you have orders to tie them up." Then he would tell us which fleet to put it in. Ordinarily it tickled them guys to death, you know, because they didn't have to tie it up and they wasn't afraid of going on out on the river. I've seen it get blocked off up in there, and none of us could get in and none of us could get out. Then they had to go and get the United States Commissioner and make them move. Cause they would block her off, they get a jam. The biggest jam that you ever saw.

Q: Must have been fabulous days, guess some of those men got pretty agile on the logs?

A: Well when you were working you always wore caulk in your shoes you know, big spikes, why you walk in here on this linoleum you would pick it all up you know. Them things were sharp as razors and if you would walk on this it would just get ahold of you and pick out big chunks of it, you know. When you went home, you always had to take your shoes off at the door to keep from ruining the floor, because on the boats that we lived on or stayed on, why they were bare floors, you know.

Q: Now I understand there were three mills in this area here?

A: There were three double mills here. That was equal to six mills here. I think they called this was the Lower Mill, and then the New York Mill and another one. I know they had three mills, it was in three buildings, but they had double, a left hand mill and a right hand mill in the same building.

Q: Were those all Cole Cranes?

A: They all belonged to C. Crane and Company and there was a big planing mill right in here. I'll tell you where there is a picture of that up at Mrs. Daley's Saloon — up on Third Street here I believe — those mills and those logs and one thing or another.

Q: I will have to go up and look at that. Well then there was another mill that the Marine Way had.

A: Up at the Marine Way. Now I don't know whether the Marine Way sawed any timber or whether they got it from Crane. I think that possibly they got that from Crane.

Q: Maybe they had a mill of their own earlier.

A: Well if they did I didn't know about it. Now at one time somebody told me, in fact, I don't know whether it ever ran, I saw some of the machinery out of it setting on the bank down above Mill creek; that's before there was any flood wall. Somebody started or did have a mill in there. But that was before my time around Cincinnati. I was coming in and out of here on, that was back in 1925 and 1926 and 1927. I come here in 1929, and of course I was in and out of here all the time.

Q: I want to ask if you can give me approximate dates of the beginning and ending of the Crane Company here?

A: I could not. I could tell where you could find that out. You could find that out at possibly the 5th Third Bank because the Edwards used to be owners. Somewhere or other the Edwards and the Cranes, in fact I believe Charlie Crane is still living right here in Cincinnati, and the last I knew of him he was a watch-man for the night telegraph affair that goes around here in the buildings where they have burglar alarms for the burglar alarm people. And Charlie did live, I was going to say up on Walnut Hills here and I still think that that's right, on Walnut Hills. Look in the telephone book and see if there is a Charlie Crane in there. Spelled his name C-R-A-N-E. There was a fellow just died since the *Island Queen* blowed up and that was D. Butler.

Q: He was a famous pilot.

A: Yes, D. Butler was a pilot and he took care of their boats down here for years, C. Crane. Somebody around that could tell you that, I don't know, I'm not too familiar when they started. But I do know that they were a long, long way back. Gee whiz. You see it was the old Cole and Crane Company and then it became C. Crane and Company.

Q: I'll be able to check that. I notice you have a lot of pictures of towboats in this streetcar here and many of them are Combine boats.

A: They are very near all Combine boats.

Q: Wonder if you could tell me something about that Combine? We were just beginning to talk about the river Combine.

John Knoepfle

A: The river Combine?

Q: Yes.

A: I knew the river Combine when I was a little boy. As a kid I lived at Ironton and I rowed out in a john boat or a yawl and row out to them, and always took them a newspaper. See those fellows going by on a boat, they never had a newspaper or anything, and I would walk a mile and a half down from where I lived down to where they sold papers. I would go down and get a paper and come up and watch for them boats and when one would come up I would go out and they'd give me some scrap iron they had on the boat or they'd give me some old junk rope that they had on there where they had broke up a line or something. I would take it down to the junkyard and get me a few nickels out of it and one thing or another. They'd always pay you a quarter though for your paper. Always got a quarter for the *Cincinnati Enquirer*.

Q: So when did that Combine come into existence, do you know that?

A: No, there's a history on that but I don't know. I would be afraid to hazard a guess.

Q: I surmise that it broke up about 1915.

A: Well there were some of them in the 1917-1918 ice because that was where the *Sam Brown* got, see that fourth or fifth and the sixth picture there. The *Sam Brown* when she was up on the lock wall at dam 33 during the 1917-1918 ice. That ice was in March, so they were still some of them running then. Then they quit after that.

Q: I see. Well I guess their big problem was keeping the boats afloat?

A: Oh yes, they had a lot of old wooden stuff and well the only steel boat that I remember, the first one I remember, was a boat called the *Cruiser* and she belonged to them. I don't know whether the, it runs in my mind that the *Monitor* had a steel hull. I'm not too positive of that, but I do know that the *Cruiser* had a steel hull. I knew a lot of those old pilots and captains on there, there was some of the Goulds and old Frank Gould, and then after he had a boy that became a pilot and Joe "Old Man Doggy" Dippold, and Doggy Cross. Well Doggy Cross, I never knew him to be on any towboats, but he was a packetboat pilot and a very good one too. There were some of the Davises that were towboat pilots.

Q: Getting back to this leakage. Captain John, yesterday described some of those hand pumps they used, and we weren't able to get that down. Could describe that?

A: Springpole pumps. That's what they called springpoles. They would take a long hickory or a green white oak, when I say green I mean it was new, not painted green or anything. The pump was made square it was six inches square on the inside, made out of lumber and would go plumb to the bottom of the barge and it had two flat valves in the bottom of it made out of leather and had a little block nailed on them that helped them get down and the sucker was made out of leather and it was made so that when it would go in it was so formed it was square, it wasn't round, now if it was a tin pump, it would be round, but in this wooden pump it was a square affair. It had, it was on a pole, was all and had four snaps on it to hold it on and they would take that pump and put it in a barge. It had a pitcher spout on it just like a pitcher that would pour over the outside of a barge with a big spout, the spout on it was approximately eight or nine inches, and they put that in there and would take the little end of this pole, possibly be 16 feet long, maybe 17 or 18 long, and they would take a chain dog or a chain and staple that end of it down so it would be perfectly solid right on the gunwhale of the barge. Then they would take that and about three or four feet from where it was fastened down they would put a block in under it and block it up and make the little end of it stand up in the air head high, very near to the top of your head about six feet high. Then they would reach up and get that and pull it down and they would stick the handle on this pump through that. Then the guy when he shoved that pump down, the trouble was to pull it up, when you pulled it up you were pulling water, but it would go down easy when you shoved it down, but spring in that pole, by wanting to go up that high, that helps you pull it up. When they put you out there and you've got six hours of that boy, nobody had to rock you to sleep when you went to bed. Golly, whew, I'm telling you boy, that was something. Lot of times you had a bad leaker . . .

Q: They had pump boxes in each corner of those barges?

A: Pump boxes in the corner of the barges so they could put them down in there and then they kept them pretty clean so there was no coal got down in because if a little lump of coal got in under those valves they wouldn't pump. They had to keep them pretty clean. Of course the coal was dumped right on the bottom, there was no decks in those barges at all. It was dumped right down on the bottom. A coal barge was 26 feet wide and a 135 feet long and eight feet deep. A lot of them were only eight and some of them were nine. Then they built what they called a coalboat. That was a crackerbox and a crackerbox had about a 10 by 12 bottom gunwhale. There was very little caulking in them. When they put the bottom on them, they put it on, and they planked both ways from the end and put a key board in there and they drove that board in and that wedged it. Then of course if they had any leaks then they would nail a little batten or something over them. But that lumber was dry, they spiked it very thoroughly on there, and the sides then in this 10 by 12 gunwhale that went from one end to the other, they mortised and put some uprights in there and set them in an inch and half from the outside edge, and then they would side that up with that hemlock. They would take those barges and go all the way to New Orleans with them. They shipped a lot of coal. If they got them down there, if they didn't get them back they wasn't out too much money. But if there was any chance to get them back, they would get them back. They were so flimsy and thin that you wouldn't dare put a timberhead on them to try to stop them with, you would just pull the whole side off. So when they were loading them they would have a big log possibly 18 maybe 18 inches 2 feet in diameter, and they'd put that

John Knoepfle

right in the center of it, and then they would nail a lot of props and stuff to it and pour the coal in around it. They did that to keep that from pulling up, and instead of fastening it on one of them when they went to stop it they maybe would take a turn around this one and go to another one and turn around that one so that made them all pull, didn't put all the strain on any one of them.

Q: You sunk a lot them?

A: Oh, I've seen as many as 16 of them in one wreck, 16 of them laying down, that's all. The *Ironsides* hit the cofferdam at Ironton when they were starting to build that B & O bridge, which they never did finish. She hit there one morning and lost six and later on old man Gould came down there on the *Boaz* and the fog caught him and over what they call the Head of the Willows, that's right at the lower end of where American Rolling Mill is today, there below Ashland, he sunk 16 in there, they all sat down right in there.

Q: Hit the bottom I guess?

A: Hit the bottom, just hit the bottom. There was just bad bottom in there and they dug the coal out of them, much as coal they could get and tore the old wrecks up, and I don't think they salvaged a barge out of the whole thing, it was just all old rotten stuff.

Q: I understand they dynamited a lot of those barges, the government.

A: If the government come to them, see they had a snag boat here that they ran, that was the old *E. A. Woodruff*, she was built over there in the Licking River. They had her and when they could get her to these wrecks, she would go in there and tear them up. She had what they called a polly hook. She had a big hook on the end of an A frame and they just let that down in the water and she was a big sidewheel boat and they just backed out, and that wood you know, it would tear it right up. They cleaned up a lot of them that way and if there was someplace where you couldn't get the *Woodruff* to it and the river was low and these things came out and they found them, why then they would get somebody to dynamite them. I dynamited a lot of that stuff for the U. S. Engineers. There was a boat that sunk at Ironton called the *Bob Ballard*, and she was a transfer boat there. Where they transferred cars across the river. She went to back out in there and hit a rock and sunk. She sunk in the fall and they didn't get her up and the ice cut her all to pieces and it left her a wreck there. The hull was full of sand and mud and stuff. The river got down low and they couldn't get the *Woodruff* to her to tear out and I eventually shot her out of there. Just put down dynamite enough at different times until we got it all cleaned up.

Q: You don't know about what year that *Boaz* sunk?

A: All this coal. Well it was before I was married. It was back around 1907 or 1908, along in there someplace.

Q: I've talked to a lot of men on this and I'm getting a kind of picture coming all the way down.

A: I might be wrong on some of my dates on some of that stuff. Because it's only from memory, and I had no occasion to remember it. Something that you have occasion to remember why it's different. But I do know about 1913 and 1907 and 1908.

Q: That piloting in a fog must have been fierce with those barges?

A: Boy, listen, when it looked like fog they began to hunt a place to get in. You couldn't always find a place to get in. You had places that you tied, you know. You knew where the good holes were and, if you could get in them okay, and if you didn't, that was something. There wasn't a thing in the world you could do, because if you went to backing them, you're dead, you're just liable to back them in the bank and if one of them struck the corner of the bank why the whole corner would fly out of it and you lost one right there. Maybe you would sink one or two more before you could get off that or you might back in over a top of a pile of rock or something like that you can't see. It's good policy — when it looks like fog — is to tie up first.

Q: Norval Horton told me I think that below Manchester there are some rocks and the fog hit them and they lost three or four barges trying to get in.

A: Who was that?

Q: Norval Horton, he was an engineer. He's a stationary engineer now at Kahn's. He was on some of the big Combine.

A: Some of the Combine boats? He must be a pretty old man. He's in his sixties, he would have to be. He would have to be 21 years old before he could get a license. That is if he was an engineer, of course if he was an oiler or something like that why he might have been serving his apprenticeship on there.

Q: He told me a strange thing that I would like to get some man to verify. He said if the water rushed into those barges, boosted the air out, coal would pop.

A: Oh, it looked like a cloud. You couldn't see anything it looked like they blowed up.

Q: Is that so?

A: Yes sir, the damnest mess of coal that ever you have seen to see one of them with that fine coal and see that dust go up in the air, it's got to go someplace. Boy it will really drive it out of there.

Q: Shot lumps of coal out. I guess it's kind of dangerous to be a deckhand then.

A: The best thing is jump overboard and get away from it and go to swimming. If you didn't it would choke you to death.

Q: That's kind of a magnificent era in the history of the valley running all that coal down there.

A: They used to bring that coal out of Pittsburgh as you can see there that Pittsburgh Landing there was just room for the boats to go up through there waiting on water. Now they are towing coal from Huntington to Pittsburgh.

Q: I heard that.

A: A lot of them high barges, line barges, they call us and say don't put the lids on, pile them up on the end. They are going to pick up a load of coal. They can't load them with the lids on. We handle them, the lids, to pile them up here.

John Knoepfle

Q: Yes, there's a very significant change in the traffic pattern. Now I talked to a man who said that a lot of these big tows were laid up because the Consolidated Coal and Coke Company, let's see how he put that, they had a deal where they could ship coal to the lakes and bring ore back and make it both ways and they didn't need the tows to ship out of Pittsburgh anymore and that's how they happened to lay up. I wonder whether that was accurate. It's very hard to trace the particulars of that Combine.

A: Yes, there were a lot of things in there. The rest of the steamboat people didn't like them too much. They were too high and mighty, as the fellow said. They were just too big, the fellow says, for anybody to get along with.

Q: I heard they could pay such fabulous wages they just kind of broke up steamboating for smaller men.

A: They did. They just paid enough wages for them fellows that they had all the best, and the thing of it they hired them by the year, and they could have been out a helping somebody else, they didn't allow them to. They just paid them the year round. Oh there are some of those old fellows, they know, they were all good steamboat men. There was a fellow that used to be here was captain on that boat right there, on the *F. M. Wallace*. Captain Bill Brookhart and he was what they called a bridge pilot. The boats would come in up around Coney Island and they would tie off up in there because they wouldn't let those pilots run the bridges because they didn't know where the sets were in the water. Then they had a horse and buggy didn't do nothing, but when Bill Brookhart got through down the Mill Creek, they set him out on the bank; there was a horse and buggy there, and he went up and got another one and brought it down and that was Bill Brookhart's job. I knew him for, in fact in years after that, after the Combine broke up, I worked on a boat called the *Castalia*, he was on there for a while and he was on the *Val P. Collins*, the *Castalia*, the *Reba Reeves*, and I don't know whether he was ever on the *Marlen Riggs* or not. I had old big Jim Woodward, Scrip Woodward, on the *Marlen Riggs* when we had her chartered, and Old Jim was one of the old Combine guys. One of the best. His feet were about 14 inches long, had the awfulest feet on him, he would get up in the pilot house on that little *Marlen Riggs* and step in the wheel, you know. They used to call that, walk the wheel. She didn't have no steering gear on it, had to steer it by hand. Boy, when he would pull on that wheel, step them big feet in there, pretty near shake the pilot house off of it. Never will forget one time, he handled a boat up at Pittsburgh. I can't think of the name of it. There had been low water and the boats hadn't run for six or seven months and he stayed on the boat and they kept the mate on the boat. He and the mate, and they kept the cook, and Old Jim would go uptown every day and get all barreled up and come down long in the afternoon in time to eat supper and go to bed, there was no place to go. Old Jim had been up town and he came down this afternoon and the cook went out on the bank and she said see the boat had been laid up two or three months not doing a thing, she said, "Oh Captain, I saved the boat, I saved the boat." So Old Jim looked at her, and he says, "How'd you save the boat?" She said, "It was all a fire back in the kitchen. I carried water in a bucket out of the river." He said, "Get your clothes and get off of here, who hired you to put out fires, anyhow." He wanted to get the insurance on that boat, and it could have burned up if she hadn't of put the fire out.

Q: They used to bring boats down here with bowboats on the tow, didn't they?

A: They never ran very many bowboats, the boat was always on the bow of them, dragging them, but there wasn't anything along the stern.

Q: Oh was that so?

A: Oh no, that was what I say they backed them, they backed them all the way that was the boat that was on the bow of it. See the bow was always down the river when it was coming down.

Q: This is the coalboats I'm talking about.

A: Oh, on coalboats, oh, they used to steer them through the bridges here a lot of times. John does that yet. Every now and then some boat will come in here that has got more than he can handle and he's a little bit afraid and John will lay right across the head of his tow and move it back and forth for him when he gets to where he wants to go, why get out the road and let him go on.

Q: You don't remember whether they had any special signals for those boats?

A: Well there would be one to come ahead, and two to stop, and three to back or whatever they might arrange between themselves, and of course the main towboat on there would blow all passing signals. Because you were only helping that boat out and you had nothing whatever to do with the tow any more than to help him do what he wanted done. Any signal he would give you would be one to come ahead and maybe two to come ahead whichever way you would make up the signals on it. And that would only be toots to the whistle because there was a whistle and a pass he would say now don't confuse this short toot of the whistle with the long whistle I'm going to blow for this man for a pass maybe if he is going to pass one or if he is going to pass two. You always say you are passing a boat on one whistle or two whistles; you don't say, I'm going to the right . . . on the left . . . passing . . . whistles.

Q: I guess it was rough here when the water was about 30 or 35 feet?

A: 36 is the rough water on the bridges down there. That's what caused the whatcha-call-it to get in trouble that morning that she was tied up. She was laying right over there.

Q: *McBride*?

A: *McBride*, and my watchman I had here was pretty good steamboat team, in fact he and I steamboated together for years. He watched him when he backed out and he called me over home said, "Looks to me like the *McBride's* in trouble." See, she'd been tied up on account of fog. Been a little fog, too foggy to go through the bridges; ordinarily been out running, she possibly would have run. But it was too foggy to go through the bridges. And he called me, said, "If you don't get out of where he's at," said, "he's going to hit that pier." I said,

"Well, call me back." And it wasn't but a little bit he called me back. He said, "Well, she did." That was it. She disintegrated right there.

Q: Captain John told us quite a bit about that.

A: See, John took the derrick boat and went over there to do some work for the Ohio River Company. See, we had that derrick boat here that belonged to the Cincinnati Sheet Metal and myself at that time, it was before John bought it.

Q: Well this is a rich document and I want to thank you for taking the time out.

A: If there is anything in there that doesn't jibe with those fellows, with some of those others if you'll contact me on it. I have quite a lot of scrapbooks, but they don't date back too far. They only go back to about 1930. I think that's about as far as they go back 1929 or 1930. They couldn't go much farther than 1929 because I didn't start to keep them until after I came to Cincinnati. Now like the other day there was a piece in the "Waterways Journal" about the *Belfont*. Well the fellow that wrote it is all wet. I come out as captain on her. I went to the boatyard and got her and brought her out, and another fellow, but he never even worked on her and they got a lot of information from him, and it's all wrong.

Q: Well that's one of the big hazards.

A: See, I know that thing as well as I know anything, and it's like that piece that was in this magazine the other day, this what do you call it? The one that's got the piece in it about John, with John's picture in it, the new one that's out. I've never saw one of them until I saw that one with his picture in it.

Q: A new river magazine?

A: Yes, it's some fellow, it's changed hands here lately, I don't know what it is, but anyhow it's got a story in it that John gave the man. I know that John didn't give it to him that way because there is part of it is wrong. Some of it is wrong, I could correct but if John did it he's mixed up, because, it's not too bad. But it's something that I knew different, but it don't mean anything. My dad, you know, he used to steamboat before I was born. And he went every year in the fall of the year. He and a fellow by the name of Bill Nolte was buddies and they were both carpenters, they'd bug these towboat men. They'd get in the yawl and get somebody to get them out and they'd ask them how they was fixed for help. All they wanted, they would work their way for nothing all the way to New Orleans to get down in that country. They went down in that country down in there and they built cisterns. Wooden cisterns, see you couldn't dig a cistern in that country because it's all swamp and the mosquitos were bad, and they had to be very careful about their drinking water. They had a system of building them, they would get somebody to make them hoops, make the hoops for it and they would make these cisterns round, they'd take a board and stand it up on its edge and take a ballpeen hammer. That's a hammer with a round end on, a ballpeen, and they would take that board and beat a groove in it from one end to the other and turn it over and beat a groove in the other side of it. They would take a plane and plane that wood off that they didn't pound down to what had pounded down as far as they needed, and you'd take that and put them together and when you threw a bucket of water on them, why you can see what is going to happen. The tightest thing that you have ever seen that never would leak from sitting out in the weather. They made cisterns that way, and then they built schoolhouses. There was no schoolhouses in that country, and they would do carpenter work building schoolhouses down in there. Work till spring, back up in this country they would come. That is before I was born and then after that he went to work for an old man by the name of John J. Shipman and he built this dike at Coney Island, he built the dike at the Bonanza Bar at Portsmouth and he started the dike at . . . .

Q: This is the 15th day of August 1957. And I am talking again with Captain W. C. Beatty. Where are we this morning, Captain?
A: In the machine shop at Rookwood River Rail Terminal.
Q: All right, fine. Now let's see how we . . . well, I think we agreed to talk about the iron works up around Ironton.
A: Oh, yes. At Ironton, Ohio. Well, that particular part of the country up there was noted for its oh, in years gone by, for its charcoal iron. It was made on little blast furnaces out back of Ironton. There was one called Etna, and one called Vesuvius, one called Pine Grove, a small one at Hanging Rock that I don't remember the name of, and this Hecla furnace was later on changed to charcoal that they melted the ore with, and they made a coke furnace out of her. And she didn't, she made some special iron. There was a fella by the name of Jim Bird who was a foreman.
Q: B-I-R-D?
A: B-I-R-D, that come there, bought it and put it in blast, and they hauled their coke on the same kind of wagon that they hauled their charcoal on, which was a great big bed. There wasn't very much weight in it, and they hauled it all with oxen. All with oxen they depended each one of these little furnaces, of course, they had no wells or anything. They always made dams across some hollow someplace to have water for the furnace and so forth. And they had little, very small machinery that they blowed these little furnaces with. But this Hecla furnace was a pretty good sized furnace. She had blowing tubs. That's what they called the end of the steam engine that made the air, called a blowing tub. They were all vertical engines, I don't know why, but they were all vertical engines. Engine was down in a pit and the tub was up high. And then in Ironton proper, well, starting at the lower end of, starting in down at Hanging Rock, they was a furnace there. That made about oh, I guess, 250 ton of iron a day. And they later made her bigger and I think she got up to where she could make about 350. Then they had, the next one up was called Union Iron and Steel, and she was about the same size. And they got ready to make her into a bigger furnace, but they never did put the machinery in. They quit for some reason or other. Then the next one belonged to the Belfont Ironworks Company and they

John Knoepfle

also owned a part of a rolling mill, a steel plant over at Ashland, Kentucky. And they eventually merged with the Kelly Nail and Iron Company. They all made nails and wire and so forth out of their materials. This Belfont furnace they made her from all this iron that was made at any of these furnaces that I've mentioned was always poured out in a sand bed or they tapped it out of the furnace, and it run out in a sand bed, they called it sand iron. That's the reason why the iron, the pig iron, always sold for 2,240 pounds per ton. They allowed 240 pounds for sand and dirt and stuff that might be in the iron and it still goes today that all pig iron is sold 2,240 pounds, a long ton.

Q: I see.

A: Then they changed this Belfont over and they put in what they called a pig machine. They run this iron out in a big ladle, and then they had chills or molds on a strand of steel, like a conveyor, and instead of being a belt conveyor, it was made out of multiple molds that were hinged together and they would run round and round and they would, they poured, they put this iron, it was this furnace made about 250 tons at a cast, and they made their casts four times a day. They cast every six hours. And they would pour this, hold this ladle up over this chain as it went by and they filled each one of these little molds full and if they happened to run one over, why you'd just run over and run into the next one. They were overlapped so that they didn't have a mess out of the thing. And they ran her for a long time after that. Then when these two furnaces merged with the mills, the Kelly Nail and Iron Company, they merged with, they had a little furnace called Sarah. Sarah furnace and the, in fact the stack was named, Sarah furnace. Every blast furnace in that part of the country the stack had a name. And it was very near always the stack is what they melted the iron in, they called that the stack. And very near every one of those furnaces had a woman's name. Another one I'll mention to you had belonged to, Marting Iron and Steel eventually bought her and . . .

Q: How do you spell that?

A: M-A-R-T-I-N-G. Marting Iron and Steel. They eventually bought her and put her in blast, but she set idle for oh, for a number of years. She was idle for far back as I can remember, and then in about oh, in the early 1900s sometime they put her in blast. She had, one of the stacks on her she had, she was a double furnace. One of them was called Blanche and the other was called Alice after Blanche McGovny and Alice McGovny whose people were very wealthy, and they'd been in the iron business. Then the, this Belfont furnace, they kept her in blast oh, for after they changed her over, she probably ran 10, 12 year. And there's a funny thing about her, they had a foundry man there by the name of Earl Steinbacher. He was the foundry man — that's the fellow who blows the furnace you — know the boss, the superintendent. And by some hook or crook, I don't know, they let Earl go and he went, left there, and he went to Portsmouth to a blast furnace that they built down there that belonged to Whittaker Glessner. That's a forerunner of Wheeling Steel. And Earl went to that furnace and he broke a world's record on making iron on that furnace. Boy, I don't know how he did it, but anyhow he was, the last I knowed of him, he was still blowing that furnace. I presume he's dead today, I don't know. He was a much older man than I was at that time. And anyhow, the fellow that come in and took his place at the Belfont furnace came from Gary, Indiana. His name was George, well anyhow I can't think of his last name, but he took the same furnace over that Earl had been on and broke a world record for that size furnace.

Captain W. C. [John] Beatty, Part II

Q: Is that so?

A: On the same furnace, never did anything to her or anything of the kind, just the way they blowed her, the way they burdened them. When they put anything in a furnace, they called it burden, they put a burden on it, see. So much burden in there, and then they got so much back out of whatever the burden was. Coke, lime, two or three kinds of ore, and all that kind of stuff to make this iron. Then this Sarah furnace was a little bit of a furnace and I guess she made possibly 300 ton a day, something like that. And they ran her iron out on sand and sand iron and then they took this iron and sent it to Ashland, Kentucky, used to cross the river there on a car ferry, loaded these cars, take it down, take it over and work it into steel. Make the steel, and then they would bring the steel back over too, they had a rod mill and made rods, wire nails out of them. They had sheet steel or plate steel that they made cut nails, had as many as a hundred thousand keg nails at one time piled up in a building that during hard times and this the man that owned this furnace was named Oscar Ritchie who was a very wealthy man. And always when times was hard and you wouldn't get a job no place, that fellow always hired a few men. He could always hire a few men and hire them very cheap. I remember a lot of men worked for 90 cents a day, and that was many days, many days. Ten hours for 90 cents. And he made nails, then when times got good, why he was out of the labor market and he had nails to sell, had money enough to carry on his business.

Q: Now all those kegs were loaded by hand on the packets?

A: Every one, every one. They hauled those nails, well, in fact, they hauled pig iron from these little blast furnaces in and stacked them on the riverbank, just stacked them on the bank. If the river raised over them, it didn't make no difference. And they would stack it there and boats would come in there. They would load that iron. They would take it to Wheeling; they would take it to Cincinnati or wherever the market may be. They moved it all over the country to foundries here and there and every place, they had to have their iron. And that's the way it was all done by hand

Q: Must have been a hard life on a rouster up here.

John Knoepfle

A: Oh, oh. Fifty cents a day and board to sleep under the boilers on the boat. Eating out of a tin pan what was left on the table. Yes, boy, it was a rough time. And they built — and this Big Etna Furnace — they put her in blast. She was the first furnace that had a skip hoist on her. They eventually had skip hoists on all of them but Sarah furnace.

Q: Now what is a skip hoist?

A: Well a skip hoist, originally they had elevators just like in a building. They run the buggies, the buggies of this stuff on the wagon, whatever they may have it on. They called it buggies. They run these buggies on, they took them up and dumped in the top of the furnace. And in the top of a furnace to keep the heat from coming out, they had what they called a bell in there. A furnace was built like a funnel upside down. It was little at the top and big at the bottom like a churn. They hung a bell inside there. The bell in the furnace had to be put in when the furnace was down. They put the bell in first because after the furnace was built, you couldn't put it in. There was no place to put it in; it was bigger than the hole was. And they had that hung on a gallows spring at the top and they would go in there and when you'd go up there, there was a walkway all around this furnace. They'd go in there and pull one of those buggies off, shove it over, and you dumped it in, you dumped it on the bell. When they got dumped all the way around what they had, all the stuff they wanted dumped in there, they had a steam cylinder on that and they'd go over and let the steam run on it or over, take it off, and then it would all fall and fall down in the furnace, and they put the steam back off and the bell would go back up and shut her off. And that kept the heat in.

Q: Oh, I see.

A: Stoked her from the top.

Q: A kind of valve.

A: A valve was what it was.

Q: It didn't ring.

A: No, it didn't ring. And we'd, I expect some of those bells weighed maybe 7, 8, 10 ton. They were pretty heavy because some of those furnaces were 20 feet across the top. And that bell had to be that big, you know. Of course, the majority of them were smaller than that. And they cast those bells right there on the place. They was so big you couldn't ship them, you know. You'd take and build up a mound of sand and work it up and put something in between it, you know, like a core in there to take the place of the iron and then put the cover all the way around on top of that and pour their own iron right into it, make those bells. Have to do that in a pit. They dig a ditch and let that hot iron run through that ditch going over to get into that mold. Then this skip hoist was an incline with buckets on it and they filled these buckets and they were full from the bottom. When they got up to the top, they had a set of big wheels on the back of them. And on the front they had two wheels on them. That is they had a wheel on each side but it was a double wheel and when they would get up to the top, just as they'd go to, when they'd get up where you'd go straight like you were going to go up and go straight over to the stack, or over to where you dumped the bell, there was a set of covered wheels that come off and was stuck out. The track was built out and maybe they would catch on there and it would cause this buggy to up dump itself. Wasn't anybody there at all, just when it come their way, it was up dumped. It was standing right on its end when you got ready to let it back down. It went back down, went on its own track on there and that saved anybody working on top of the furnace, have a lot of men pass out from gas, carbon monoxide and stuff like that. Put the material up and dump it. That's what a skip hoist was.

Well, that was so much for Big Etna and she made about 500 tons of iron a day, 500 to 550. Then they built another furnace they called — I had it right on the point of my tongue — oh, it was called the New furnace, but it had another name and it was a real up-to-date furnace. Instead of having your old style blowing engines in it, why it had new blowers, rotary blowers, had a skip hoist, and everything was strictly up-to-date. And she made around 700 ton of iron a day. It was called New furnace. That's what it was. It belonged also to Marting Iron and Steel.

Q: Marting?

A: Yes.

Q: Well, all that tremendous iron out here, it's all gone now.

A: Every bit of it. And then there was another furnace that was out in the country called Large furnace and I eventually tore that furnace down. And made scrap iron out of it. And she belonged to the Marting Iron and Steel Company and they sold her, and she had what they called, instead of pouring and making sand iron out of her, they paired this iron in chills. They had big chills and there were enough of them laid on the floor to hold a whole cast that come out of the furnace and they would tap it in there, and they didn't have to make up the pig beds like they do, you know, on the sand. See, when they make sand iron, they had to mold them sand beds, so that would go in there. They had to have that sand at the right consistency so it wouldn't fall apart, and it couldn't be too wet because that hot iron running off would blow up and fly all over creation. And that was Large furnace; the place called Large furnace was right on the railroad and of course, she could, she got coke and ore and stuff on the, well just the same as anybody else did. The ore and the coke came from various coke ovens. But to my knowing, there never was any coke ovens in Ironton until the Cement Solvey Company come in there. And Cement Solvey, they did by-product coke and things like that.

Q: Now what year was that that they come in? Do you remember that?

A: Who? The Cement or the Coke company? Oh, that would be possibly . . . Oh, I'd be afraid to hazard a guess on that.

Q: That's no problem, we can find that out.

John Knoepfle

A: They, I was going to say something else. I was going to say something. I forgot what it was.

Q: Shouldn't have interrupted you, I think.

A: Oh. Another good industry, did you want that on there?

Q: Sure.

A: Tow industries that used to be there was the soap factories. They had two enormous big soap factories here. Weihle Soap Company and . . .

Q: How do you spell that?

A: W-E-I-H-L-E, Weihle. Weihle Soap Company and they shipped all their products or the majority of their products by boat. They had a landing of their own. They were way out in the east end of Ironton. And that's right where the Cement Solvey plant is at. Of course, Cement Solvey gets an enormous lot of their coal in by water. They get a lot in by rail. They ship a lot of coke by water. And the other soap company was? Well, anyhow, there were two big soap companies there. My sister and I were talking this morning at the Richter Stables about milk. And I mentioned something about some people that we knew when we lived in Ironton. She was born in Ironton, too. She keeps house for me now. And these people's names was Ensinger. And they had these black and white Holstein cattle. The Board of Health eventually broke that old man for watering his milk. He was supposed to be watering his milk and he told them he never put water in his milk. They even took the milk direct from the cows and it wouldn't pass the test. They gave an immense amount of milk, but it was no good and they eventually just fined him, fined him, fined him, till he took it right straight from the cow and they tested it and it was not any better.

Q: I'll be darned. How did you spell his name?

A: E-N-S-I-N-G-E-R. Christopher Ensinger.

Q: Did you know a family named Hafely?

A: Oh, yes.

Q: Captain Hafely, the shanty beater?

A: Yes, knowed him very well. Old Bill Hafely?

Q: Now this is where, see this dovetails with Tom Wagner because he used to be on that boat.

A: I've been on it many, many times. The only boat ever I seen in my life, with the exception of one, that had a piano on it.

Q: It had?

A: Had a piano on it. Oh, God, that goes back to 1902, 1903, way back in there.

Q: He said those girls used to leap out the window into the river.

A: Yes, there was Bill, young Bill and the old man. Two or three girls, they was beautiful girls, all of them. He was a fisherman, made his living fishing. They had a two-story boat. It was the first two-story boat ever I seen. It had a top cabin on it, and it laid right at where the Ironton Waterworks is, right between the waterworks and the public landing. Old man Bill Hafely. Little old, thin, skinny old fella. I bet he wouldn't weigh 90 pounds.

Q: He must have been . . .

A: Made his own nets, knit his own nets. Tarred them and fished them.

Q: He must have been a fine man.

A: Oh, he was, he was, they raised a wonderful family, too.

Q: That's what I heard.

A: Fine, fine old fellow. I can see him yet peddling the fish he got with his nets. He'd come up, he had them strung on a pole around his neck like they used to carry milk buckets.

Q: Did they ever string fish on wagons to sell? Do you ever remember anything like that?

A: Well, somebody sold fish, but I don't think it was Hafely. If he did, I don't remember him. I can see him, there were another one used to carry them up the hill. There was another old fellow there was about like him, the name was Eli Pyles. P-Y-L-E-S, Pyles. And he was a fisherman. Old Eli would — he made his own nets to fish and lived on a shanty boat. He did his fishing and the thing of it was when he come over to the boat, he had to roll over the bank to get on the damn boat, he was about half drunk half the time. But old man Hafely, I never, old man Hafely was a pretty good citizen, had a very good reputation.

Q: That's what Tom Wagner said about him.

A: Well, this Tom Wagner, I've heard, I've just, there's two or three sets of Wagners and there's a Tom I believe he must be the bunch from West Ironton.

Q: Maybe, he worked in the theater there as a stagehand, too.

A: Yes, he's from the Wagners from the lower end of town, yes.

Q: Well, that brings me around to the Bay brothers.

A: Oh yes, Bill Bay and George Bay. Yes, they were characters. They were in partners together and used to fight like cats and dogs and they oh, they had a number of boats. I can name quite a few of them. They had a boat, the first one I can remember was a *Volunteer* and she was a screw wheel boat, first screw wheel boat ever I heard of. The next screw wheel boat ever I heard of was *Lucy Coles*, and then there was another one called the *Gaylord* and she turned over in a storm up at Ashland and they never even looked for her. She just turned over and that was the end of her, never even found her, pretty deep water. But getting back to Bays. Then they had the *Minnie Bay* and they had the *Lizzie Bay*, the *Chevalier*, the *Urania*, the *Volunteer*, and the *Greyhound*, did I name *Greyhound*?

Q: Yes. Well, no, but you did now.

A: Now wait a minute. Then they had a low water boat. They had a low water boat called the . . .

Q: They had the *Louise*?

A: They had a boat called the *Louise*, too. But this low water boat was the *Bay Queen*, a low boat called the *Bay* . . .

Q: *Bay Queen.*

A: Yes. She'd run on the dew, that boat would.

Q: Was that a sandy gyper?

A: No, she was a little sternwheel boat, She had very small machinery on her. She was wide, didn't draw much water, and she ran when their other boats was laid up. And I think that *Greyhound* was the biggest money maker ever they owned. She was pretty fast. She eventually sunk in the 1917-18 ice over to Ashland right on the outside of the center bank there. She went to pieces there, the ice cut her up.

Q: Were you up in that territory then during the ice or down here?

A: Oh, I was up there. I bought a boat right here off of C. Crane in 1917 and took it to Ironton and wintered it over and built a new boat for her while the river was froze over. I worked every day on the levee there when snow was 18, 20 inches deep all winter. If you dropped anything on that levee, it went right on in the river. It was that slick there, just nothing but a glare of ice all the time. I worked there every day. I built that boat very near all by myself. Only time I'd have any help was when I had something I just couldn't do by myself and then I hired a man to help me.

Q: What boat was that, Captain?

A: A boat called the *Colonel*. By the way, it was first boat that the Ashland Oil Company owned.

Q: Is that so?

A: First boat they ever . . .

Q: Which was the boat you bought from Cole.

A: From Cole and Crane? That's the one, the *Goldie*, *Goldie*. And I built that I took her, and she had a 32 horsepower Fairbanks and Morse engine on her. And I took her there and wintered her all winter and she was the only boat that was saved in that part of the country during the ice and she was a rotten old wreck, but I saved her.

Q: Could you describe that ice?

A: Ho, that was something. Well, I'll never forget it, I had a contract to build this boat and I was working I got a fellow that had some machinery. He had a band saw, a planer and I got him to let me work in his shop. He agreed to let me use his machinery for $10 to build that boat and to do all the work that I wanted on his machines. His name was Willis. Did carriage work, wagon and carriage work. They made carriages and wagons and stuff like that. And then he had an old fellow that did his blacksmith work and he did the blacksmith work on it like making the rudder pedals, and anything that was in the black-smith line. I think it was either on my birthday or the day before my birthday, it turned down and went cold. That was the 11th day of December. And the river started to freeze up and it snowed, and we never saw the ground until March. Never saw the ground clear until in March. And the river was froze up from December until way in the latter part of March before it broke up. Of course when it broke up, it cleaned everything. You name a boat and I'll tell you where she went to.

Q: Yes.

A: The *Portsmouth* ferryboat, it shoved her out on top of the bank and when the river fell, she was forty feet up above the ground sitting on ice. That much ice under her, it just piled up and left her setting there. And they eventually took hose and washed and washed and washed and washed that ice, cut it, cut it, if she started to lean this way, they'd cut it out here. And they just eventually rocked her till they let her down. Let her down pretty close and they got a raise in the river and eventually floated her off. And that was the boat — the boat belonged to the C & O Railroad — called the *City of Portsmouth*.

Q: Must have gone out . . .

A: *Ashland* ferryboat went out, the *Huntington* ferryboat went out, the *W.K. Peter* sunk, all of this stuff that they had here at the public landing, you know, at that time, that's before ever started to come to Cincinnati. I'd been to Cincinnati, but I mean I never run in and out of here any.

Q: It must have gone out with an incredible roar.

A: You could hear it for a long ways. And then the worst trouble, it broke up and it went down to a place called Ferguson's Bar which is about five and a half miles below Ironton and lodged. It quit. It broke up that far down. I'll venture to say that the river raised forty feet in less than forty minutes.

Q: Is that so?

A: And when that let loose, it just took and went on with it, that was all. If you was in close to bank, you were beached up, that was all, you just set right down there. If you were out in the river, you went away. At that time, that's the time that the dry dock went out of Kanawha River, Big Kanawha River, belonged to Bill Smith, and had a little boat in it called the *W. S. Smith*. And that boat was in the dry dock and the dry dock and all got loose, and that boat went all the way down the Ohio River to above Evansville. And when they found her she was a half a mile up in the Green River, swirled and went up in Green River.

Q: Is that so?

A: Swirled and went up in Green River. Never hurt her, they towed her back to the dock and finished repairing her and she eventually was sold to the Wheeling Steel Company at Portsmouth.

Q: Well, can you tell me anymore about those fabulous Bay brothers?

A: Oh, yes. I'll tell you a story about, one time they had a fellow — I guess it doesn't make any difference to name names they're all dead whether you want them or not — but anyhow, I'll tell you they had a pilot on there, and he was quite a guy, had been with them a long, long time. They were going up the river on one of the boats and old Captain George had got on the boat, old George don't think he was over five feet tall and he might weigh 90 pounds, I doubt it, whether or not, but they were going along in about that, what they called Green Bottom up in that country, beautiful country. It is yet, and old George was up standing out on the forecastle of this boat, on the roof, and he hollered back it at this captain, and he said, "Who owns that farm over there?" He said, "They

John Knoepfle

got their fences all painted white. Everything's painted white. That's the prettiest place ever I seen." He said, "Why, Captain, that belongs to the clerk on this boat." And they never paid him but $.50 a day. That's all they paid him. I can see him yet, he was crippled in one arm and holding his hat in his hand and would go up, you know, and collect the money, you know, and always had his hat off, you know, when he talked, particularly if there were any ladies on the boat. The old man never said anything, so they got up a little bit further, and on the other side of the river, he said, "Gee," he said, "There's another beautiful place over there." He said, "Who owns that?" This pilot said, "Same fellow that owns the one on this side." He said, "He stole them off of us! He stole them off of us! He never made enough money to buy them places."

Q: I'll be darned. Well, they ran a lot of competition who was the pilot incidentally? Do you remember his name?

A: Yes. Tom Roush.

Q: Tom Roush.

A: Yes, he's dead. That Tom Roush ran on the boats and Pete Lallance, the fellow that got killed, got drowned on the *McBride* when she hit the bridge over there. Pete was on watch that morning. He's the guy that had the big diamond ring.

Q: He the mate?

A: He was the captain.

Q: Oh.

A: Lallance.

Q: Oh. How do you spell that?

A: L-A-L-L-A-N-C-E. Lallance.

Q: Oh, yes, must have been a Welshman with that double L.

A: But he sure as hell overshot his hand that morning

Q: Pete was a red-headed guy, very freckle faced, awful swell guy, good pilot. Well, tell me, the Bays ran a lot of competition with the Laidley Line, I understand.

A: Well, they did in a way. They used to fight them all the time. Old Captain Bill, he was a tough old scrapper. He eventually killed a fellow. Something happened, I don't know what it was, whether it was, I think they were throwing rocks at the boat, the boat went, they did it two or three times, he couldn't break it up. He sent them word, it was down by Portsmouth. He sent them word the next time that boat went into the landing and somebody throwed a rock he was gonna kill somebody. And by God, he did. They didn't do nothing with him, but they tried to. They did everything in the world, and he was justified in doing it, because the same thing has happened to us, not only to me, to my son, to the pilots, everybody else going up Licking River.

Them guys over there shoot you with an air gun. Yes, sir, you'd be right out on the head of a tow, we've been to the police over there many times over them. You'd be standing out there and wham, somebody'd take you. While they don't bust the skin on there, they don't go in very deep, but it's not very pleasant. When I ran on the *Belfont* over there, going in and out of there — I was in there three times every week, made three round trips to Licking River every week on a boat called the *Belfont* — and they got to shooting over there and I said, "Well, I'm going to break it up." I told the police about it and they said, "How you going to break it up?" I said, "I'm going to kill somebody if they don't quit it." So I got a shotgun and put it on the boat and the next time it happened, the next trip we come in down there and it happened, I shot up in the willows and I bet there was twenty guys run out of the willows up there. I didn't kill anybody because it could've, I might have killed somebody that was innocent too. It broke it up for that time. John's had some trouble with his boats several times since then.

Q: That would be pretty dangerous if somebody took a shot at you when you were in a difficult spot.

A: Now I don't know of anything more about the Bays. They had all this, let's see I think they owned a boat called the *Henry M. Stanley* too, at one time. Gordon Greene eventually owned her, and she hit a dredge called the *Oswego* up at Gallipolis Island. She was laying there one morning in the fog and she come down through there and hit that dredge and sunk her, sunk the *Stanley*.

Q: I wonder, I don't think we ever established what year you were born in, Captain, that's kind of important.

A: December 11, 1886.

Q: 1886. Gee. That's a long . . .

A: I'm pretty near twice as old as you are.

Q: Yes, that's right.

A: How old are you?

Q: 34.

A: I'm over twice as old as you are. I'll soon be 71.

Q: I'll be darned.

A: Yep. And if I don't live to be a 100, I'm going to be disappointed too, that's another thing.

Q: I think everybody in this part of the river will. You're an amazingly active man. However, you don't know it, but I once saw you carried off the roof of your boat. That was in 1955 and you got up there and somebody took the ladder away and your son had to take you down off of that. At the Launch Club there.

A: Oh, yes.

Q: You finally, you reached a point where you couldn't get out of a predicament.

A: Yes well, I could've jumped in the river, all right, that would've been the next thing. I wouldn't have got hurt a getting off. All them guys they do that, you know, some of them. They have a lot of fun with me, but I have just as much fun with them. There's one thing about it, because none of them, they don't hand me nothing up there.

John Knoepfle

Q: I don't imagine they do. Oh, incidentally, on that *Belfont*, what were you hauling back and forth going up in and out of . . .

A: Well we had, the principal thing we took up Licking River, that was pig iron. We supplied the Andrew Steel Company. Our company sold Andrew Steel Company 50,000 tons of pig iron at a dollar off of the market price. That's a good deal, kept the furnaces running.

Q: What was that?

A: Belfont Steel and Iron Company.

Q: Oh, I see.

A: That, the transportation company was the Indiana Belfont. Indiana part of it was the Indiana Flooring Company and they had a place at Coal Grove, Ohio, where they were making floors and they bought all the oak that they could get ahold of, oak and maple, hardwood flooring. And they had a big flooring mill there and we used to send those barges around into — we'd leave them off at Memphis — and then they'd go, or I mean not at Memphis, but we would take nails and wire to Memphis and then . . .

Q: Tennessee?

A: Memphis, Tennessee, yes. I used to. Maybe we'd take oh, two barges at a time and maybe I'd have forty customers for those two barges, and I'd get off of the boat then and I'd take them and deliver them. The Federal Barge Line'd unloaded them there for us and I'd either load them in cars — see, their cars come right down to the barge — I'd either load them in cars or send them on to the next town, maybe move them to another barge where that they would get them.

Q: Railroad cars, Captain?

A: Oh, yes. Yes. Something similar to that or maybe they'd go to Greenville, which you go right in there by the barge and . . . right in the town. Then when those barges were unloaded we'd bring them back to Smithland and Smithland that's where the Cumberland River comes in at Smithland. I was talking to that guy on the telephone. I got two barges of roofing down there and the damn things been laying there for a week and trying to get them up to Nashville. So we'd send them barges up and they would go up to a place called, one of the places was Lee's Landing. And they would load them with lumber up there, and then bring them out, and then we would pick them up, go to Smithland and pick them up there and bring them back to Coal Grove and they would unload them. Then while they were doing that, why then we would get more nails, and then I delivered nails to Cincinnati. I had a conveyor system, what we called a one-man conveyor system, traveled on a track on the barge and I could set it up in an hour with the help of one man. I only needed one man to get ready to help me. You could set it up by yourself, but I always had one man to help me and it was all done by chain dogs and on trollies where you could move it and swing it around. It laid lengthways of the barge when you were traveling. You picked it up, swung it around, shot it out over the side. I could set up anyplace that I had water enough to get in that I could reach 54 feet, 54 feet from the barge. I unloaded lots of stuff here at Cincinnati. Oh, for H. Bellner funny thing, we had a lot of guys that couldn't read, a lot of the deckhands couldn't read, you know. Well, I couldn't see every move they made so we got so that we put colors on. I'll never forget. We had red for H. Bellner and we had green, of all the things in the world, for Kruse down here, Kruse is German, you know, and a green tag on everything. I had a little square tag put on with a tack, so they didn't have to read the names on them, just use the colors. Well, and then we had yellow for Aufdemkampe, and blue for Kohstall, and oh, anybody that used nails in this part of the country, and we had, and they of them had a different, some of them had white and red, green and blue, and some of them had a stripe on them. Got some of them colorblind. They couldn't tell, they'd mix them up on you. (laughter) They could, they were colorblind and couldn't tell.

Q: So you weren't running a packet, you were running a tow.

A: Yes. We'd bring those barges in, you know, and then set them off, and then I'd get off and my partner on there, then he'd pick up somebody to steer the other watch with him, see. We'd always arrange for some other pilot or something or sometimes when I'd get back on the boat, I wouldn't even start a watch. I'd stand a mate watch you know, and leave the pilots that were on there because it was more change that often sometimes . . .

Q: So you were in a nice little hauling thing then.

A: Yes, for about three and a half years. Then when I wound up with them, they were building a new road that went from Marietta to Fly, that's right straight across the river from Sistersville. And we barged the cement on that. The Dunsweller Construction Company had the lower end of it and Monogahela Construction Company had the other end of it. A fellow by the name of Sam Polino from over around Clarksburg, over in that country. He had the upper end and Dunsweller came from Zanesville. And they, I believe Dunsweller came from Chillicothe, yes Chillicothe. They was a great big concern. So we barged the cement up, the cement that went to the upper end of the job we took from Ironton. The cement for the lower end of the job, I brought it out of Pittsburgh, they just passed each other with the . . . . But we had those landings set up there and I looked after those landings. First thing I did I went to Pittsburgh and loaded the cement up at the U.S. Steel Company, place at Munhall. Got started on that, and then they would take care of the other. That's how John got to fooling around the river. I had him up there and he watched the conveyor and had a conveyor system there to move this stuff off on the upper end and that's where he got to fooling around the river. He parked that conveyor business there. And I fooled with that until, well till they finished up that road. Winter came on, too. Two winters up there, part of three years I did live up there, moved the family up there. And then when I came back from there, why they weren't doing any good. We had a superintendent that he and I just didn't see eye to eye. He did so many things, that wasn't, in fact he didn't know what he was doing. So I wanted to get away from him anyhow. While I was going by here, see, that's how I come to get this job. I was going by here on the boat three times a week and they were building this pier out here to put the crane on. That's for the pier, to get the crane to put up on it. So I said to somebody one day — I don't know who it was — somebody hooked on with a yawl or something I was riding up the river with it, I said, "What are they doing in there?" He said, "They're going to put a river terminal in there, unload barges." I said, "That would be a good place for me to light and get off the river." Guy said, "You'll never get off the river." And I said, "Well, I got off once before and stayed off sixteen days." I went to Detroit to go to work, they were building that big plant for Pontiac up at Pontiac, Michigan. I went over to Pontiac. Had a pretty good job over there, too. It'd been more money than I'd ever made before in my life if I'd stayed there, but I just didn't like it. I didn't like it — so I made up my mind — found out who the people was, who the man was, and I found out by next trip in, a fellow here by the name of Walter Quiggins who was quite a character, river man around Cincinnati. In fact, he coaled all these steamboats for years. He was interested in the old *Hercules Carrel,* and then he had a little towboat of his own that he kept over in Licking River and he sold coal to these boats, coal to them packet boats, you know, while they were loading the freight, he'd coal the boats for them.

Q: Yes. Captain Kelley told me that they used to load the Greene boats, bringing over flats with the *Carrel.*

A: Yes, bring a little flat over or a little old boat over there. I can't think of her name. I was trying to think of it. So I got talking to Walter and asked him and he said, "Yes, I know that guy pretty good." He said, "He's a good guy to work for." So I wrote a letter. I got a letter back from him and he said, "What do you have in mind?" They built for their own use at Parkersburg, West Virginia. Well, this plant was at Parkersburg, West Virginia. They were hooked up with Parkersburg Iron and Sheet Company. And they couldn't, they got to putting the pressure on them and pressure and pressure and pressure until they just couldn't put up with it any longer and he made up his mind to bring the thing closer to home and he got hooked up with Weirton Steel Company, quite young at that time, didn't have too much business. So they was going to just handle their own. Possibly whoever had charge of the job would have to run the crane.

They wanted to know if I was a crane runner. I told them I was a crane runner, but I'm not hunting any job running any crane. Stay where I'm at for that. I was getting $300 a month over there, no I was getting $240 month. And he wanted to know how much money I made, and I told him. But I told him, "I'm not interested in running any crane. If you want any help, I'm interested in you. But I'm not interested in running any crane." I said, "I'm tired of it." I'd drive a crane a long time, different places and one thing and another and I just didn't care too much about it. I just thought I'm going to be plain about it and tell him what not to expect cause he'd expect you to run the crane, get over there and when you're working the plant one thing and another. I just didn't have any idea at the time. So he said, "Well, first time you're in Cincinnati, stop and see me." So I thought, "Well, when we get ready," he said. "Well," he said, "I'll let you hear from me." Well, I thought that's the end of that. Well, one day, he said, he called me on the telephone or left word for me to call him. And I called him, and he said, "We've started our job up down there and I've made up my mind I'm going to give you that job." He said, "When can you come?" And I said, "I can't come for 30 days, because these people I'm working for, I have an understanding with them. Said I'd give them 30 days' notice and they'd give me thirty days' notice." Because, I said, "The fellow I'm working for, he's a hard hitter. And I have the reputation of doing jobs and he made me agree to do that." And I said, "I had to do it." He said, "All right. Serve notice on him that this is the first day of it." I went in the office, I had just come back. I wasn't too satisfied anyhow.

I went in there to talk to him, told him, I figured on making a change and told why and one of my daughters wanted to go to the Conservatory of Music and the Mrs. thought that would be fine. It would be a chance to get to Cincinnati, said we wanted to live here. So he was kind of hostile about it. He said, "Well, by God, don't think because you're going to quit that this job will stop." I said, "I got a little story to tell you about that, Mr. Ryan." His name was Ryan. "I got a little story to tell you about that, Mr. Ryan. I said that this company would never have hired me and if they'd of fired you the first day they did hire you, or not hired you, they wouldn't be bankrupt today." He said, "By God, you can quit right now if you want to." I said, "It's all right with me." So I made the telephone call to Oldham. I said, "Well, I guess I'm a free agent. Me and the guy fell out. When I told him." I told him just exactly what I told you, he said, "Well, that's a good way to get to quit." I said, "Well, he had it coming," he did, he broke that company up because he wouldn't listen. Tried to do some things that general managers didn't do. All wouldn't do. So I got on the train the next morning, that was on the 5th of October 1929 and here I am.

Q: You've been here ever since. The old bird found himself a nest.

A: Well, yes. I didn't think I would stay when I come because I didn't know, oh it was a hell of a mess when I came here. They didn't have, they had nothing. Just this wing, that was the end of the building here. They were unloading sugar and they had oh, I bet they had 25 men and had one guy who was kind of a smart aleck, oh I don't know, of course we got into it right away. I just called them all and told them, "Now, boys, there's going to be a lot of changes around here. This place will never run the way it started out." I said, "If any of you have got any ideas, you better talk about it now because I'm going to start cleaning house. Hell, I can pay you out of my own pocket." I said, "Here it is." Well, one of the things they were doing, they were unloading sugar. I had a boy here, by the way he's in the transportation department for the government, been down to Washington for 20 years, Ronald something. I can't think now. They'd been busting a lot of sugar. They asked him what did they want to do with it. And he said, "Well, take it home with you. You can't do nothing else with it." They brought tubs, they brought lard cans, they brought old broken down Model T Fords — the model A's had just come in in 1929 — and I expect there was three or four tons of sugar. I said to him, "That won't work."

He says, "Well, why?" I said, "Well, goddamn it, I stood down there yesterday and saw them deliberately bust them. Pick them up and throw them down. They take a sack and throw it over the side of the tub and half of it fell in the tub and the other half went out and they pick it up and shake the sack out." He said, "Well, it's got dirt in it." And I said, "That don't hurt it. Sugar's the dirtiest damn stuff in the world. They can at least take it home and make syrup out of it. All they have to do is put water in it and the dirt would come to the top and they could boil it and boil the dirt out of it. Another thing. About half of it's going in home brew." See, they were making a lot of home brew at that time, you had to have sugar. So I said, "We'll just stop it where it's at. If you don't want it, I'll leave it in the barge." Some of them got mad and quit, one thing and another. But we never had any more trouble with the sugar. We handled a lot of it.

We had maize, and wire sheets for in the house. I went to Mr. Oldham in one day we didn't have anything to work with. The damn landing was plumb full of logs right where that sawmill was, sure you couldn't get in close to the bank. I got hold of the government, asked them if they wouldn't take them out, had a very good friend, was afraid they wasn't supposed to do it. They took them out for me and throwed them out on the bank and I fastened them so they couldn't get back in the river again and I eventually lifted them with a crane, sawed them up in lengths, loaded them on trucks and took them out to a country sawmill and got the lumber out of them and used it all around here. That was some of them old Cole Crane logs, you know, left in the river, sinkers.

Q: Was that the *Woodruff* took those out?

A: No, it was the *Iroquois* and the *Mingo*, a fellow by the name of George Wright. I think old George is still living out at Mariemont, out in there some place, or Mount Washington, I think it was Mount Washington he lives at. And he was the brickmaster on there, he took them out. And a fellow by the name of Jim, what was that captain's name on there? Old Jim somebody.

Q: I knew that some of those logs were taken up and dumped in a sinkhole up above Coney Island, somebody told me that.

A: They really dumped them right in below the barracks out there, if they'd stay in there, but the hell of it is they wash out of there. All along up there at Brent and along down in there, lots of logs in there. There was a big one in right straight across the river here, I saw it the other day, washed out and rolled in there and there are four or five down on the bar down there at Ludlow, four or five pretty good looking logs, there.

Q: I suppose some enterprising fellow if he knew where they were could get those logs.

A: Well, you could get them. If I had time, I used to get them. I've got them several times out of there, and you could be doing it. I know where there's lots of them.

Q: I suppose they're still in pretty good shape, too.

A: Good as the day they were dumped in the river. Only trouble they're blue inside. Blue, by golly, as your trousers are.

Q: Is that so?

A: The tannic acid in them and that water mixing together, you know, soaked in there, because that oak has a lot of tannic acid.

Q: What would you use that for?

A: Oh, you could use it for a lot of things. For, I don't know whether it could be bleached and used for a hardwood floor or not, but it'd make good wonderful bill stock or rough lumber, crossties out of it. Switch ties or crossing plank, or boat bottoms.

Q: Well, that lumbering, I guess, is a continuing story as long as someone is willing to go and get the logs.

A: Yes.

Q: Aboard Captain John Beatty's boat. All right, Captain, I dare you to give us a resume of your river career.

A: Well, the start of it all, I am told was before I was born, my father was building a sternwheel towboat called the *Colonel* for the Ironton Lumber Company, and the machinery from that boat came off a little gasoline boat that used to tow logs for the Cole and Crane Company. While my father was building this boat, I understand that my mother spent an awful lot of time sitting on the riverbank watching him. She wanted to be sure that I turned out to be a river man, just like my dad. So I guess that's about the earliest beginning any man could have on the river. That particular boat, just for the record, was the first boat that the Ashland Oil and Refining Company ever owned. She was sternwheel, belt-drive, and she had a 16 horsepower single cylinder gasoline engine, with a pair of 32 horsepower flywheels on it. And the manufacture of the engine was Spooce Brothers.

Q: Where were they located?

A: I really don't know. That's the only engine that I recall seeing that was made by that company. I heard of a lot of them, but that's the only one I ever saw. I followed around after my dad for a good many years, and his brother and his father. At various times, I would get a chance to go on a trip with them. They would go up the Big Sandy River, and the Great Kanawha River and the Little Kanawha River, and they would bring out strings of timber, and then raft them out in the Ohio. And they would float them to the Cole and Crane mills at Cincinnati primarily.

John Knoepfle

And at other times they would get rafts of cross ties that came out of small streams such as the Little Sandy River, which is today, I would say, maybe 30 feet across, something like that. And they would bring those cross ties out all rafted together. And they couldn't tow them upstream, so they would take the raft apart, load them into a barge by hand, and tow them upstream to a place at Ironton, Ohio, called Park's Tie Elevator. The ties were then creosoted, some of them, they shipped green, without pressure-treating them. Of course, they were all loaded in railroad cars. There was quite a number went to the DT & I Railroad, the Detroit, Toledo and Ironton, which in later years belonged to the Ford Motor Company. It's now part of the Pennsylvania System.

Q: Could you dilate a little about bringing those logs out of the Big Sandy? I can't imagine, although I've talked to a number of men who've talked about the logging.

A: Well, primarily, when the logs would come out of the Big Sandy, they would come out not in raft size but in what they called strings. As near as my memory serves me, I believe that it took six strings to make a raft. I'd say the string of timber was maybe 12 to 14 feet wide, maybe sixty feet long. They'd take these various strings and put them together and make a raft. And there were times that we would have as many as six rafts. That would cover quite an area. And we would bore a hole in one of the logs on each end of the raft, and insert about a two inch diameter hickory post, so to speak, as a hinge for our sweep. And a sweep was a long willow pole, anywhere from four to five inches in diameter at the one end to practically one inch at the other end, maybe 30 feet long. And on the end of that was a big board, maybe 16 inches wide and 12 feet long and maybe an inch and a half thick. So in other words, a sweep was just a giant oar.

And sometimes one man would row that raft and point it in the direction he wanted it to go on one end, and maybe there'd be a man on the other end, or three or four men, depending on the size of the raft. And you would travel, depending upon the river. This was going on about the time that they were building same of the locks and dams. I can recall some of the packet boats passing us. And sometimes we'd tie up at night and sometimes we wouldn't. All we had was a couple of coils of rope and a good steamboat yawl, and maybe three men. And we just run the end of your line ashore. As I started to grow up, they'd send me ashore with the yawl. They'd tie the line and give me an ax. And when they'd run out of line, if they weren't stopped, they'd shout to me to chop it. I'd chop the line, and they'd pull it aboard. I'd get in the boat, come back out of the raft and get ready to run the line again. Which was a very crude way of doing things, but . . .

Q: And you'd be coming down the Ohio?

A: Well, what they would do is just tum that stuff loose, and it just floated out of the river like the Big Sandy. The farther you got down the Big Sandy, the bigger you started building your raft. You'd start out and you'd come down by a creek, and there may be six strings of timber in that creek. Well, you'd tie off what you had and go back and pull those strings out and make them into a raft and add it to what you already had. And the farther down the river you got, the bigger the river was and the larger your raft of logs would become. It would just gradually build up in size. And I've seen men coming out of the Big Sandy River, they were just mountaineers, and lots of time, they had the dam up at Catlettsburg, and they just ran a line across the river and tied up the first raft, and the next raft would come down. They'd put them all together, and then when they get all the timber in there that that river could hold, they would throw that dam, cut the line, and it would all come out of there, and rush out into the Ohio River. And men would be in water up to their waists. Winter, summer, didn't make any difference. They'd usually set me in the rowboat, so I wouldn't get wet. And everybody else got wet. But those mountaineers would not ride a raft out of the Big Sandy River. They absolutely refused to go out on the Ohio River. They were scared to death.

Q: They were afraid of the big water?

A: They were just afraid of the big river. That's all there was to it.

Q: It seems odd. I imagine it was more dangerous coming down the Big Sandy?

A: Well, very definitely.

Q: It must have been a rough stream coming down the river.

A: Now a lot of the time, they would build a boom across the river like the Big Sandy. In other words, they would just take 15 or 20 logs and chain them together one to the other, single file fashion from end to end. And they'd just keep cutting timber and rolling the logs in the river. They didn't care where they went. Then they would all come down to this big boom. And after they got all their timber cut and got all these loose logs, this was like a big bunch of drift laying around. They were in all sorts of shape. They would part this boom and bring those logs out of there one and two at a time, and start to build them into strings and then into rafts. Then they would proceed on down the stream.

Captain W. C. [John] Beatty, Part III

Q: I guess it was just too bad if a boom broke, right?

A: Well, that did happen. Once in a while they'd get a little flash flood and the boom would break. They'd spend weeks, sometimes months, going down the river trying to find their logs. And their logs could be tied up behind shanty boats or in the trees. If they found them tied up someplace, they knew that someone in that vicinity had caught them, they'd be a shanty boater, and they'd have to pay, as I recall, they paid 50 cents a log, for catching a log and taking care of it. I'm not real sure about that. And there was very definitely a lot of people that would catch those logs. And they'd take a brick or a rock and deface

John Knoepfle

the brand, which was in the end of it. I remember one brand in particular was two C's, Cole and Crane Lumber Company. One sawmill built what they called a saw boat. They took a section of band saw and hooked it onto a little steam engine and it worked very similar like a one-man crosscut saw. And they'd float these logs down alongside of this little saw boat and throw a chain around them. And they'd start this little engine up. They would saw about six inches off the end of this log. They'd then take the butt of this log that had the brand on it, throw it in the boiler, use it for fuel and destroy the evidence all at the same time. And I've seen many, many logs dehorned, so to speak.

Q: Kind of a wild trade in its day up there.

A: Yes, I can recall seeing loggers with corks in their shoes, same as they do up in the north woods yet today. They had big corks so they would run on the logs. They had special tools. Oh, you'd see two men, they usually worked in pairs. And they'd have their steamboat yawl, as we know a steamboat yawl today, and you could always see about a 20 foot pike pole, as they call them now. They were always "spike" pole in those days. There's usually two spike poles, a couple of rafting axes, which is nothing more than just an ordinary ax, like you see today, except that the head of the ax had all surface on it about maybe two inches wide and maybe four inches long. They used it to drive their chain dogs, which was a tapered wedge on each end of about five lengths of chain, which they would drive into the logs and lay them over a strip that tied the whole raft together. It's quite rare today that you even find a chain dog. I've been looking almost a year for one now. It was one of the things I noticed that had never gotten into the museum at Marietta. And I'm looking for one. We're dredging all the time now, and as soon as I find one, or a dozen of them, I'm going to send them to the museum. They're almost extinct.

Q: Well, I hear that Catlettsburg was a roaring town in those logging days.

A: Well, yes, it was a roaring town. I can barely remember. My uncle came back during the first world war, and he took me to Catlettsburg. And I recall walking into one saloon with him. I was quite a young fellow at that time, maybe five years old at the most. And I can recall walking into this bar on one street. We walked all the way through it and come out on the next block. That barroom was a city block long, and I do know that there was twelve saloons in that one block. And just in the last 90 days, all of those old saloon buildings were torn down to make way for a flood wall.

Q: In this last 90 days?

A: In the last 90 days those buildings were torn down. I was talking to a gentleman that has been around Catlettsburg for 60 years, a gentleman by the name of Alec Lewis, who worked for Ashland Oil and Refining Company for many, many years on their old sternwheel towboats. He was telling me about all the old relics, old beer mugs and stone wine jugs, and stuff like that that they found down in the old basements of those old buildings. They said there was more darn relics, and everybody was just clamoring for the things. But just two weeks ago, I passed by Catlettsburg and it just doesn't look like the same town. Those old saloons are gone. It's a shame, but that's the way it is.

Q: Those lumberjacks were just farmers turned lumberjacks during the end of the planting season, I suppose, up there?

A: Oh, they were just mountaineers. I've seen them with knives similar to what we would call a hunting knife today, carried in a little sheath on their belt. I recall one that was a real bad man. Everybody was scared to death of him, and I can remember his pistol. He carried a 44 pistol. It looked like one of those old frontier pistols, with a great big hammer on it. And he was one of the fellows that I was referring to, who was afraid to come out on the Ohio River. But he didn't fear any man. He was a real rough character.

Q: I imagine the companies squabbled a lot over the timber tracts.

A: Well, there was some squabbling. The Cole and Crane Timber Company some way or another tied up both the timber and the mineral rights. They didn't own any of the ground. They leased those rights. And after the Cole and Crane Lumber Company sawed out all this timber and moved it out, it was discovered then the second growth on timber was not too good. They finally went out of the lumber business. And the end result was that they sold their leases to another company, which is today the West Virginia Coal and Coke Corporation. And that was the coal leases that West Virginia Coal and Coke had, they did not own any property. All they did was lease the mineral rights, or they bought those leases rather from Cole and Crane who had gone in primarily for the timber, and just at the same time tied up the mineral rights for no good reason. And then the West Virginia Coal and Coke Company bought those leases and started into the mining business to get the coal into the power plants, basically to Cincinnati, the Cincinnati Gas and Electric Company.

Q: That would be after Crane went out of business?

A: That is right.

Q: What year approximately, was that when they went out of business?

A: Well, I'd say that Crane went out of business about 1926 or 1927. And Cole and Crane's lumber mills were on Eastern Avenue in the vicinity of, well they laid between Kemper lane and Collins Avenue.

Q: And there were a number of mills down here. I understand that Cincinnati Marine Ways had their own mill. Is that right?

A: That's right. The Cincinnati Marine Ways was located in the 1800 and 1900 block on Eastern Avenue, which is about Lancaster Street. That's at the site where I have my present barge landing.

Q: I didn't know that.

A: That's right. And the old Marine Way tracks, the old timbers, are still in there.

Q: They are?

A: Oh, yes. They're very visible. In fact, we find stuff in there that washes out on the bank every now and then. For instance, just recently there was big crank

John Knoepfle

off of a sidewheel boat. It couldn't have been a sternwheel boat, it was entirely too big. It is about 14 inches in diameter, just the crank pin. There is a shaft and a flange on it. As near as we can tell the flange is going to be about eight feet in diameter. We've tried to lift it, and it's too heavy. We have a 20 ton derrick and we can't pick it up. But I'm getting a little bit away from where I started on the river.

Q: Yes, you are. But this has been an amazing diversion. I wonder though, before you come back, if you could possibly, do you remember any mills at Ironton?

A: Yes, I do. I remember the Whistler and Circe Lumber Company. That was just a little bit east of Clark's Tie Elevator. And I recall when Whistler and Circe Mill burnt, and my father went in and dismantled all the machinery and carted it away to the scrapyard. After Clark's Tie Elevator was gone for many years, I think when I was about 15 years old, my grandfather came up with an idea how we could make a lot of money one summer. His idea was that we would pick up all the nails that had been in these tie strips, that they had nailed these cross ties together when they were in wraps. They had always piled those strips up and burnt them. And down in those wood ashes in this big pit where they burnt these tie strips for years and years were just tons and tons of these big square boat spikes. They were cut nails, I guess you would call them cut nails. They were made out of iron. They weren't steel. And I think that summer we got something like 25 tons of them out of that pit, and carted them off to the scrapyard. And at the same time, in the morning when it was cool, we'd get the nails out of there, and in the afternoon when it got hot, I'd go out in the river and go down on a spike pole. We had a little boat there, and we'd feel around, and we'd feel a cross tie. There was some of those ties that would not float. And most of those rafts were made out on the bank on a flat place, and they'd get them all rafted together out on the bank, then when the river would rise they'd float them in. So when they started to tear the rafts apart, some of those ties wouldn't float, they were so green and waterlogged. And they would lose those sinkers, so to speak. So we got 300 sinkers out of that hole, for which we got 35 cents apiece for them. And I'd do that in the afternoon when it was too hot to pick up nails; I'd go swimming and get out four or five cross ties a day.

Q: What year was that, do you recall?

A: Well, I would say that was in about 1927 or 1928. And I recall that there was a tie yard at that time. A gentleman by the name of Culbertson ran a cross tie yard. And he kept all his cross ties standing on end. They were stacked up, so to speak, and they looked like an Indian teepee. It was just what they looked like. They were big at the bottom and small at the top, and he did that to air-dry them. And after he air-dried them so they would absorb creosote, then he would creosote them. He had a big vat of creosote there that they would put a lid on. Then they turned the steam pressure on it, and drove that creosote right in the tie. Then the next mill below the Clark's Tie Elevator was the Nye Lumber

Company. And that was at the foot of Heckler Street. And that, I believe, belonged to Bill Nye. He had a couple of boys that were in school just a couple of years older than I was. And I used to go over there and monkey around the mill. They had an old fellow there who was superintendent of the mill and his name was Jack Welch.

Q: A Welshman, too, I bet?

A: Well, I believe he was. He had a fellow with him all the time as a helper, by the name of Herner, Poke Herner. I never knew his other name. And they both stuttered. I'm telling you to hear those two guys in a conversation, well, you could go out to lunch and come back, and they still hadn't got to the source of what they were talking about. Golly, there goes one of my boats down the river.

Q: Which one is that?

A: You're sitting here working, and I'm having fun, and making money at the same time.

Q: Yes, indeed. That's pretty good.

A: You just can't beat that, can you?

Q: No, sir.

A: Anyway, these two fellows did all the maintenance work around this mill. And they repaired chain dogs. They'd weld the links back together, broken ones. They'd take broken ones and make good ones out of them. Just anything to keep themselves busy. And they maintained a fire watch around the mill, so that they didn't have fires. See that the fire barrels were kept filled and all that sort of thing. Just a couple of maintenance men. I was watching them one day over in the blacksmith shop, and they were welding a rim together for one of their wagons that they carted lumber through the mill on. They got it real hot and set it on the anvil, and old Jack Welch said, "He . . . he . . . he . . . he . . . hit it, Poke." And Poke said, "wh . . . wh . . . wh . . . where?" He said, "Go . . . go . . . goddurn, it's too cold now!" But they were a couple of characters.

Then there was another mill just below there, called the Faron Lumber Company. And I don't know just exactly what street that was in Ironton anymore. I know that it was very close to a company there called the Ironton Mantel Works. And the only thing that that company made was mantels for fireplaces, wood mantels. And they watched all of those mills, and picked out the very choicest lumber that came out of all of those mills around there.

One more big lumber company there that I just barely remember. And the only reason that I remember that is from the size of some of the boards that they used to come out with. And that was the Yellow Poplar Lumber Company, which was up at about the mouth of Ice Creek. That was almost up in Coal Grove, which was a little bit too far for me as a kid to get away from home. And I have seen boards 30 feet long and four feet wide out of the most beautiful golden yellow poplar that you have ever seen. And they cut that for panels, for wagons, doors for automobiles, and such as that. That was the forerunner of

John Knoepfle

plywood. They used those large boards the same as you would use plywood today. Oh, they were terrific things.

And that lumber mill, as time went on, was bought out by the Indiana Flooring Company, which went into hardwood flooring. They bought their hardwood in the south and barged it up the river, which was responsible for the forming of the Indiana Belfont Transportation Company. They had ten barges, ten steel barges, and a 360 horsepower sternwheel diesel boat built. They combined their tonnage with the Belfont Ironworks Company, who had a wire nail mill and two big blast furnaces. They shipped pig iron to Cincinnati, to Louisville, in fact they even took some of it as far as Memphis. They would take barge loads of nails and wire, barbed wire, fence wire of all kinds, any kind of nail you could think of, staples, and so forth. And they would take the pig iron and the nails south, and they would tow lumber back, rather than return the empty barge, so to speak. The two companies got married in their transportation. And that was the Indiana Belfont Transportation company, which was made up of the Indiana Flooring Company and the Belfont Ironworks company.

Q: You might have heard of an earlier mill there? We taped a man named Tom Wagner and he was from Ironton.

A: There was another big Lumber Company there called the Ironton Lumber Company. And I can recall the big brick burner stack that they had there, where they burnt their slabs. A slab is the first cut off of a log and the last cut. And they burnt as many of them as they could to make steam to power the mill, but they still had some of them that they couldn't do anything with. In later years, there got to be so many of those tie poles, they used to turn them loose, but the government stopped them from turning that stuff loose, and made them bring it up the hill and burn it. So they had what they called a burner stack, which was nothing more than just a big round brick stack with openings in it. And they just keep sticking this stuff in there endways. It was just a giant fireplace, so to speak. And I remember my dad wrecked that mill. And the rails that came down the incline that they hauled the logs up on the little cars, we put those T-rails on a johnboat. And we took them one at a time and took them up about three miles up the river, and pulled them out on the bank. That was quite a job for a man and a little boy to load those rails on that rowboat.

The Ironton waterworks was just below the Ironton Lumber Company, and they had in 1903 put a very fine water system in, which consisted of a 24-inch cast-iron pipe in twelve foot lengths. They had taken six lengths of that out on the bank, and hot leaded the joints, corked it very well with corking irons. They'd swell the lead after they poured it in there. Then they'd hammer it and cause it to expand in the joints. And then they would roll it in the river with pieces of manila line under it, tied on to whiskey barrels. They floated that pipe in position in six joints at a time. And they would cut the first two barrels, which would let the one end of the pipe go down, and the diver would insert the male end of the pipe he was trying to put in into the female end of the pipe he already had in. And he got that all entered, then he'd come back and cut loose a couple more barrels, and go back and feel it until he'd get it just like he wanted it, and then he would cold lead that with lead wool.

That pipeline crossed the river. There is a little concrete tunnel still visible just above the Ironton bridge on the Ohio side, that pipeline crossed the river. It went out maybe 150 feet from the Ohio shore, then it had a big ball and socket flexible joint in it. Then it angled over about maybe a 30 degree angle, over toward the mouth of Bear Creek, which was over at Russell, Kentucky. That pipeline then had another ball and socket flexible joint, and it went straight up the Kentucky side about maybe 150 feet out in the river from what is now the normal pool line. That pipeline went up then to about what is Oak Street in Ironton, which is maybe a mile, up the Kentucky side. And they had some six-foot cast iron pipe on its end in six-foot lengths. And they had 16 welds made out of those. They dug the holes and inserted them. And they had some big screens in the bottom of them. In other words, it was more or less a filter bed.

My grandfather was the inspector for the city when that thing was installed. And they used it for a while, and then it got to the point where they were getting too much iron in their water. And they decided to build a new waterworks, which as a very small boy about maybe six years old, I can remember the tremendous hole that they dug in the ground, in about 1920 I would say. And my grandfather was the inspector on the new waterworks when they built that.

So as the years wore on, for some unknown reason, my father bought that pipeline. The old waterworks was dismantled, I think he gave one hundred dollars for that pipeline. He didn't know what he was going to do with it, had no idea that he'd ever be able to get it out or anything, but he bought it. I guess he owned it maybe ten to 15 years at least. And all of a sudden one day he decided that we better get it out of there. And I dismantled that pipeline in 1940. And we got more than enough money out of the lead in those joints in that pipeline to pay for the removal of the whole thing. And when we got through, we had seven hundred tons of the nicest cast iron that you ever seen in your life, which we sold to the Newport Steel Company over here during the war.

Then getting back to this boat called the *Belfont*, I don't know whether you ever heard about it or not, but the *Belfont* is the boat that had a collision with the *City of Cincinnati*. It wrecked one of her sidewheels and scalded the engineer to death on the *City of Cincinnati*.

Q: No, I didn't know that.

A: Well, it happened below Carrollton at about Notch Lick Light, very close to the little creek that comes in called Indian Kentucky River. There's been all sorts of stories about the thing. I was on the *Belfont*, had been working as an oiler, and my dad was captain. For some reason or other, when we got to Cincinnati on this trip south, the boat was going to Memphis, the company decided that my dad should get off and go someplace else. He was gradually getting away from riding the boats so much, and he'd go to various places and unload these barges. They dropped them off all over the place. And he'd stay there and see that these barges were unloaded properly, and that the customers got what was coming to them and so forth. He was kind of a master of transportation, so to speak, for them. So when he'd get off the boat, I'd get off the boat. We got off the boat in Cincinnati and a pilot by the name of Roy Lee Hughes got on the boat.

They had an unusual situation on that boat. When the engineer would go back in the gear room, which was some 60 or 70 feet from up in the main engine room, always when he'd go back there to grease, he'd step to the pilothouse door and say, "I'm going to the back end to grease." And he did just exactly that. Hughes had never been on the boat before. They hadn't shown him too much about the boat. He didn't know whether she handled with a clutch or whether the engine had to stop and then be reversed, or just exactly how she did work. He'd never handled her any at all. So this engineer, his name was Zeb Drummonds. He was a young fellow about 20 years old. And his father had come out on the boat originally as chief engineer. His father's name was Clarence Drummonds. They were just farmers. If there had been a little dirt on the boat, I would have expected to see several rows of corn growing on the roof, because they were just farmers. Nice fellows, but as I say, all they knew was how a fix a plow, so to speak. So Zeb Drummonds did step to the pilothouse door and say, "I'm going back in the gear room to grease her up good." And Roy Hughes remarked, "Well, grease her up good." And he was going down. The river, nice and dark.

So the reason that the engineer did that was that there was a jingle bell back in the gear room and when you told the pilot that you were going back there to grease, if you were going to have to change the speed of the engine or stop her or anything, you'd reach down and jingle that bell back there in the gear room, giving him time to get up to the engine room before you'd ring the bells for what you wanted to do. There were no indicators, all bells so he rang a bell to stop her. Of course, there was no engineer in the engine room. The man didn't know. He imagined that the engine changed speed or that he was backing, and he changed his rudders to backing position, to back away from the man, which naturally the boat was still coming ahead, and steered her right into him. Well, he knew where the gong bell was, which was the last resort for all the power that was on the boat. Just about that time, the engineer walked in the engine room and he hears the gong bell. And boy he really put it all on her. And they hit the *City of Cincinnati* a pretty good pop. That boat was steering right into her, Just as hard as she could go. It wasn't done intentionally. It was just merely a matter that nobody explained to Roy Hughes just how you operated the boat. It wasn't the engineer's fault. It wasn't really Roy Hughes' fault. But the end result was that the tow knees were knocked down on the *Belfont*, and the barge she had in tow run over her head, upset her pilothouse, turned her pilothouse backwards. And well, just about cut one wheel off the *City of Cincinnati*. And as I said, broke the master steam line and scalded the engineer to death. There's been a lot of stories flying around about what happened on that boat and that is the true story of exactly what happened.

Q: I'm glad to know that.

A: Now there's also another rumor. I've never gotten it direct from any of the people that was on the boat. But I understand there was quite a poker game going on, on the *City of Cincinnati* when this accident happened. And the only person in the pilothouse was the cub pilot. What his name was I do not know. But that was the rumor that went on, on the collision as far as the *City of Cincinnati* was concerned.

I traipsed around after my dad, and one thing led on to another. The first thing that I really got mixed up in was the dismantling of a blast furnace out in Lawrence County, back of Ironton. My dad was working for a company in 1924. It was the R. & J. Stern Company. They were scrap iron merchants. A couple of very fine Brooklyn Indians. But they bought him a brand new 1924 Maxwell touring car. And the idea was to haul the men back and forth to the job. It was some 25 miles out there. Mostly they hauled oxygen and acetylene in the back seat of that car. They made a truck out of it. It lasted about three months, and it was a total wreck.

Anyway, that's the first place I ever drove a Model T Ford. They had a Model T Ford truck. And I can see those men way up on those ovens, cutting the rivets out, dismantling this thing, and they had a piece of rope tied on the back of this truck. My job was to back this truck up and they'd tie onto a sheet. I'd go ahead a little bit and get the weight of the sheet on the rope. And they'd turn it loose. I'd back up, and let it down on the ground. I'd say that I was maybe nine years old around that time, something like that. I was working every day. We worked twelve hours a day. But I wouldn't go to school, so my dad was trying to make me go to school. He was going to make me sick of working. That furnace, after it was all dismantled, was moved into Ironton, Ohio, and added to a small furnace that they called Sarah furnace. They even moved the oar bins in, and all the carriages, and some of the cranes, and just all sorts of parts from this old furnace. They practically built a new furnace out of all this old junk. And that furnace made a lot of pig iron that was shipped on this Indiana Belfont Transportation Company. And they built the cranes out on the riverbank to load it into the barges. They suddenly discovered that they needed some ice piers to tie their barges behind. It would make it a lot easier, to hold their barges off of the bank. So they had then quite a nail mill there called the Kelly Nail Mill in Ironton. And I recall those big grindstones that they used to grind their dies on. Some of the stone were two and a half feet across the face, and maybe nine to ten feet in diameter. And they had grooves and raised places on these stones. The stones were kept dressed to fit certain diameters on dies,

John Knoepfle

where they would draw the wire down to various sizes. Instead of having a complete machine shop, a fellow would just take these dies and go in there and take the two halves apart and hold it on the grindstone and sharpen it up again, put the two halves together and go on back. They had an old left-handed monkey wrench and a ballpeen hammer and a pair of pliers, and a coal chisel. And that's all the tools they had to run a wire nail mill with.

They dismantled this mill, and they decided that we should drill some holes in those big grindstones, and bust those stones up, put them on a truck in pieces that one man could lift. And we'd truck them down to the river, put them on a little barge. And we built a crib out of six-by-eights, something like a cross tie, only about 20 feet long. We piled them one on top of another, about like Lincoln Logs that kids play with today. Just sort of a cribbing. And we put a one inch floor in the bottom of that thing. We'd build it about four or five feet deep and we'd put a few rocks in it. That would pull it down in the water a little more. And we'd build up some more timber on it till we'd finally get it setting on the bottom. Then once we got it on the bottom, we just bailed that whole thing all full of rocks. It couldn't go anyplace. It wasn't going to move. Every so often they'd stick a rod through there, and put a big ring on the end of it to tie ropes into. And that went all the way through the pier and through a timber on the other side with a big nut and a washer on it. That's how you fastened on to it. We built that pier that way. My grandfather had built many of them like that, I found out later on. One of the things that was built like that was this Coney Island dike up here.

Q: Is that so?

A: Yes, he worked for a contractor by the name of John Shipman. And that's where my name of John comes from, John Shipman. He named my Uncle John after John Shipman, called him John Shipman Beatty. And that's where my name of John comes from. He built the Coney Island dike, or I say he built it, he worked for John Shipman, who was the prime contractor on the job, in 1898. And according to my grandfather, he installed the first set of spuds on a derrick boat around 1899 or 1900. To his knowledge, it was the first time there had ever been such a thing as a spud put on a derrick boat. And that was John Shipman's idea. My grandfather was a ship carpenter. From Coney Island dike up here, they went to Kenova, west Virginia and built a dike up there at Twelve-pole, which is just above Kenova. And where they went from there I don't know, it's been so long since he told me these things. He died in 1936. And he was 87 years old when he died. Quite a spry old fellow. During the lapse of time from about 1926 and 1929, this Indiana Belfont Transportation Company got interested in barging material for other people. And they started to boating cement for the Alpha Portland Cement Company and the Superior Cement Company, which were both local companies within a 30 or 40 mile radius of Ironton there. They stumbled onto one real good job, which was a state highway, Number 7, that ran from Parkersburg, West Virginia into a little town called Fly, Ohio.

Q: I have been through Fly.

A: Well, that's quite a town. If you've been up Route 7, all the concrete highway, all of that cement, was barged in there. It was my father's responsibility to see that it arrived on time, to see that it was unloaded. He'd just pull into an old muddy riverbank and set up a little old belt conveyor, and up the hill comes the cement. You'd build a tar paper shack to store it in, and we'd use two or three barge loads a week. Well, still wanting to be around with my dad all the time, I wouldn't stay on the boat in the summertime. So I got a job as water boy for a $1.25 a day. And some place along the line, I don't know how it happened, but my father heard of some real good red whiskey that came from up around Monongahela, Pennsylvania. They were getting that cement, part of it, from up in there, so he just told some of the boys on the boat to bring him down five or six gallons. So they'd buy it and hang it on a piece of wire on the ladder down in one of the barges in the rake and tell him, which barge it was in, and he owed them so much money. Well, it was good red whiskey and sometimes it was just moonshine, but he'd fix that real easy.

Q: This was during Prohibition then?

A: Oh, very definitely. Prohibition wasn't ended until about 1933. But I've seen him just take a piece of red oak and a plane, and make himself a few shavings. And put them in a pie pan in the oven until they char almost to the point of taking fire in the oven, and just put it in the gallon jug. It makes the prettiest red whiskey you ever saw.

Q: Is that so?

A: Oh, yes, you can't tell the difference. But anyway, there was a bunch of, I don't know what they were, Italians or what they were, but they were all foreigners. They came from up around Fairmont, West Virginia. And being a good water boy, I had to carry a few short half-pints, which we called little boys. And we got a dollar and a half for a short half-pint. I think he paid six dollars a gallon for this lightning, so to speak. So we made pretty good money. Of course, I had the chaser with me because I was the water boy. That got to be such a thriving business that delivery by towboat wasn't too good, so we found another source of supply. I had a little motorboat the second year we were on this job. And I'll never forget, there was a detour on this road. This moonshine or good red whiskey, that we were picking up, as I say, was in these ice cream packers. And we'd bring about forty gallons at a time, ten gallons in each packer. Then we'd have our motorboat tied down on the lock wall. We'd pull up on the inside of the lock wall, and go up and get our packers, and put them in the boat. And then we'd go back up to the store and get these short half-pint bottles. I guess they were about six ounces. We'd get enough of those bottles to bottle the forty gallons. And I remember they had screw tops on them. They were metal lids and screw tops, and we would bring that down the river.

John Knoepfle

I'd usually take this fellow that was bottling the stuff and selling it. I'd take his boy, he was about a year younger than myself. His name was Dale Beaver. And I've lost track of him, but I have a sneaking idea that he's a pilot. There's a Dale Beaver up in that part of the country that works for one of the sand companies up there. And I hear him on the radio every now and then. I have a sneaking idea that that's the same boy, because all the Beavers were river people. They had towboats and barges and ferryboats, and they were always mixed up in the river business of some kind. I know we used to come down with this motorboat.

And this Howard Beaver lived right in front of Grape Island. And that's right where we were unloading the cement. As we came around the head of Grape Island, if there were many strange cars, this house was kind of up on the side of the hill, and if there were any strange cars around there, we wouldn't land. We'd go down around the foot of the island and come up on the other side and get rid of our ice cream packers and our bottles and so forth, just set them over on the island, some place where they couldn't be seen. We'd be careful we didn't leave any tracks. Then we'd come over and we'd go on up around the island, just as if we were out boat riding. We'd come down to the house then and tie up. And this onetime, we noticed three very strange cars. We had never seen them before. And since there wasn't any travel on the road, it wasn't open to traffic, the only cars that would be on that road would be men that were working on the job or people that lived in that vicinity. So we knew every car. So there was three strange cars there. We got rid of this load and rode up around the island and come back.

Of course, we bad been posted real well; don't open your mouth; don't tell nobody nothing. We no sooner landed that boat than there was half a dozen men all over that boat, just immediately, wanted to know where we'd been, what we'd been doing, when we left, and what we went around behind the island for and everything. So we finally explained to them we were just boat riding. We rode up to Beaver Town, and we came down and decided to go around the island before we tied up. And that was it. Well, nothing would have it, but that they had to go for a boat ride with us. They wanted to see what we did around that island. They found a couple of little willow leaves laying on the deck, which more or less told them that we bad been next to the willows shortly before that, because the leaves weren't wilted and so forth. They were pretty sharp characters.

So we went around that island and they wanted to pull in one place. And we said, "We can't pull in there, there isn't any water there. There isn't any water there, we'll get aground." They said, "Well, we'll pull in there anyway." But we didn't care, that wasn't the place anyway. We were just sharp enough to throw them off. They said, "Well, that looks like there's been a boat in there some time or another, so let's go in there." We said, "Oh, we might go aground if we go in there." So they pulled in and tramped all around. They couldn't find anything. Where we'd dumped our load was way up on the middle of the island. And we had gotten out of the boat and waded ashore with the damn thing. I guess those willow leaves were hung on our clothes or something and had fallen off on the deck. But they didn't find the whiskey. And the only thing they found was one gallon, which they kept. They had two buckets in this well. And they kept a gallon of whiskey in this one bucket all the time. Good, cold whiskey. What you did was just go out and get yourself a good cold drink of whiskey any time you wanted it.

But that's the only thing that they caught him with was one gallon. He said he had it for his own use, and he got away with it. So we eventually got to keeping some of this whiskey down on the derrick boat after that. And we only used this derrick boat about a couple of times a month, which meant that we didn't build a fire in it. So all we'd do is just open the door on the boiler and just lay all these pints of whiskey in there. And we had a lot of fresh kindling, and we had a fire all set. All you had to do was light it. Anybody looked in that boiler, it looked like the fire was ready to go. But under that kindling was more half-pint bottles of whiskey than you could ever shake a stick at.

But we eventually finished that job at that particular location and moved on up the river. And the next year the whole job was finished. I got a job up there taking care of the conveyors. It was up to me to keep gasoline in the engines and keep the conveyors greased and so forth, which was kind of a dull job as far as I was concerned. And I talked to the boss and I told him along my lunch hour I could grease them. And I could come in a half hour early in the morning and gas them up. And have a couple of extra cans around there, and I could run out and gas them up in between times. So how about giving me a laborer's job, as well? I did both jobs. He was already paying me 75 cents an hour to grease these conveyors. But the laborer's got 35 cents an hour, so I did pretty well. I was holding down two jobs. I was just a kid, and all the men around there liked me pretty well. I'd been peddling whiskey and drinking water to them for a long time and knew them all real well. So they kind of helped me through. I wasn't man enough to carry cement all day long. But I kind of coined money. And I got to the point where I got to be kind of a fancy dude on my dress and so forth. I had more money than anybody. We worked about 18 hours every day in the summertime when those jobs were going on.

Then we, as I say, we finished those road building jobs and in early 1929, I'd say sometime around July, things just kind of folded up. And due to this accident of the *Belfont* hitting the *City of Cincinnati*, the company was just about to go broke. The Indiana Flooring Company folded up. They dropped out of the thing, and then they even changed whistles on this *Belfont*, and painted her name out. They did everything to keep the U.S. Marshall from catching her. He was trying to put a sticker on her and tie her up for damages to the *City of Cincinnati*.

John Knoepfle

So there was some old steel work; they had started to build a bridge at Ironton without a permit from the U.S. Engineers. The Engineers kept telling them to stop. They paid no attention. They didn't get any permit at all. They got the piers built. And they even started up with some of the steel work. They started out in this channel span, they put some false work up and put the first beams on there. And they were going to build both ways from this one pier, build a cantilever span. Just hang a piece of steel on one side, and then a piece on the other side and balance it all the way across the river. Well, just about the time they go on their way right good, the U.S. Engineers came along with a crew of men and some cutting torches. They just stopped in there and burnt the whole thing down, and threw it in the river. Just to prove to them that they meant business.

Q: What year was that?

A: Well, I don't know. But I do know that we went back up to this bridge pier on a Sunday. My dad had rented a derrick boat from the Indiana Belfont Transportation Company. They no longer had a job for him. He was out of a job. So he knew about a little scrap iron and junk laying around here and there, and he had bought this pipeline that I referred to a while back. And he decided that since his little boy was a pretty good swimmer, that he might as well make a diver out of him. And we'd go up and get this scrap iron out of the river. I remember we started out on a Sunday morning for some reason or another about five o'clock. We had this little motorboat. And we were towing an empty barge on this derrick boat. We got up under the Ironton bridge. There was a piece of wood block rolled up from under the derrick boat and got in the wheel of that motorboat, and stalled the engine. And I can remember just as plain as if it was yesterday, going in swimming at seven o'clock in the morning, going under that motorboat and digging that block of wood out of that wheel. We went on up the river.

My dad looked over at Russell, Kentucky, and the city of Russell used to get their water out of the river, and there was an old steam pump down there on an incline. "Well," he said, "I guess we might as well get that pump while we're at it. I'll go over here and find out who it belongs to." So we landed over there next to the pump and he went up on the hill. There was a little house up there that used to be the boiler house, there were people living in it. He said, "Well, who owns that pump down there?" And they said, "The city gave it to the preacher." He said, "Well, where can I find the preacher?" They said, "He's in the church down there, just a few doors down. You'll have to hurry if you want to talk to him because church is about ready to start." So he went down to the church, got ahold of the preacher, made a deal with him on a Sunday morning, bought that pump right there and paid him in cash. I think he gave him $10 for it, as near as I can remember. And he come back trotting up the street, and he said, "Okay, put a line on here and haul her aboard. She belongs to us." So we ran a line out there and pulled her aboard this derrick. I guess the old pump maybe weighed a ton and a half or something like that.

We went on up to this bridge, which was maybe two miles on up above there. Those piers were in front of Amoco Steel's big plant there at Ashland, the rolling mill on the Ohio side; I believe Ironton iron blast furnace was right there. The Barrett Division of the Allied Chemical and Dye Company has a big plant in there now. Those steel beams and so forth were all laying in there in all sorts of shapes. So I started out, got in the water and would put wire slings around them. Some of them the water was only up to my shoulders. Suddenly some of the stuff was a little too deep for me. I just couldn't do it.

So where in the world my dad come up with an automobile tire pump I don't know and a little piece of hose. He gave me a five gallon paint bucket and he turned that upside down and wired this small hose up in the thing. And he tied a great big shackle, must weigh about 15 or 20 pounds, on to the bale of the bucket. I can remember having that bucket over my head and this bale under it, and that big old shackle on there. He's up on deck with an automobile tire pump, pumping air, and I'm breathing the air that's in the bucket upside down. And we got all that steel. I guess we got 50 or 60 tons of steel out of there. That was my first taste of diving. I've been around divers at various times, and had held their lines, got to talk to them on the telephone, and I thought that was wonderful.

Q: I just want to pause here to identify that background noise, which is a tow going down.

A: Yes, that I believe is the, I thought for a minute it was the *Liberty*, but I don't believe it is. I don't recognize the guard lights. It sounds like the old *Lin Smith,* which is now the *Cincinnati*. She belongs to the Mississippi Valley Barge Line. That's what she is. I recognize the exhaust and those lights.

We got that steel out of the river; as I say, that was about in July of 1929. We dropped back down to the Ironton bridge and started to work on this old waterworks pipeline. We found it, took a water hose and jetted a hole under it, and got a sling around it. We eventually broke it off and got started to go across the river with it. We were going to take the whole thing up at that time, or at least we thought we were. But we only had a 5 ton derrick boat. It started coming out in six lengths at a time. Each one of those weighed 15 tons. We just weren't about to get them out of there. We abandoned that job. We took the equipment back that we had rented. I think my dad paid 50 dollars a day for the use of that equipment. And the way he had it figured, we had it one day and we got, oh, $500 or $600 worth of scrap iron for $50 expenditure. So in times that were starting to get real tough, that was pretty good, especially since my dad had gone into a little private enterprise of his own.

At one time, I guess when I was about ten years old, he'd gotten away from the river and started a sawmill of his own. And I used to carry water up there to the boiler for the mill out of the creek. And he kind of cornered the

John Knoepfle

market on wooden lathe for houses, plaster lathe. The only thing that upset his deal was that he got ahold of some timber that had been in a forest fire that had burnt all the trees about six foot up from the ground. And it made beautiful lathe, basswood most of it was. Some of it was poplar. It was very fine lathe, sawed nice, good and straight, until you put the plaster mud on it. And when it got wet, why it would just twist from one end to the other and kick the plaster off onto the floor. He had that on 35 houses before he discovered it. He felt obligated to give the people their money back if they paid for the lathe, and to pay for the expense they'd gone to of putting it on, and also for the plaster. But he eventually paid that out. About four years after he left the town, he eventually got all these bills paid. But he came to Cincinnati in October 1929 and went to work for the Cincinnati Sheet Metal Roofing company. And he's been there as terminal superintendent ever since.

Q: Was he with Cole and Crane before?

A: Well, he was kind of an independent contractor. The only time he'd work for companies, like when he'd go captain on a boat, was just in between his own enterprises. While he was trying to think up a new idea, something else to get into, why he'd go out and go to work for some big company. I started out seriously to go to school when we got to Cincinnati. Of course, I'd been kind of going to school kind of spasmodically. I'd gotten through the seventh grade math. I had some first year high school subjects, but I wasn't too smart. I wasn't doing too good. I was always fascinated by electrical energy. I was fooling with high tension coils, and I just wanted to know more about it. So about the time we came to Cincinnati, I decided that I was going to be an electrical engineer. I'd seen a lot of hard work and had done a lot of it, and it just didn't make sense to go on and do it, because I just took one look at my dad.

He had worked like the devil all his life, and all he wound up with was debts. There were a lot of times we didn't have too much to eat. And the fellow says after working like he did, I mean he'd get right in the water and roll these logs and find the end of the log sticking up out, and the other end being . . . he'd get right in the river and roll it out of there just by brute force. The fellow worked hard. He tried hard, but it seemed like every time he got to the point where he just had it made, something happened. He was a very thrifty individual. I think one of the things that was against him was he'd see a chance to make some money by doing a certain job. As soon as he'd get that job, he'd go out and canvas all the scrapyards, and pick up all the old junk, and make the tools to do that job with. But by the time he got those tools made, he no longer had use for the tools. The job was gone. And if he got a breakdown on something homemade, he'd put a bunch of gears together and build himself a hoisting engine or just anything. But if it broke down, he couldn't replace that part. It wasn't a stock item. And that's the way he lived. Take nothing in your two hands and make something out of it. And he is still that way. That's one of the things that he and I discuss. We never argue, he says, "Why, jiminy, down in the scrapyard there's a hoist engine down there that will just do that job. What do you want to buy a new engine for?" I say, "Dad, a hundred years ago that was all right. But today, you buy something that you can replace."

And that's the way we have to do it today. He doesn't understand that. He'll sit down someday, and he'll take, for instance, a deck chair off of his pleasure boat. And he'll go down and he'll spend as much money on tacks and canvas, and varnish the woodwork all up on that chair and make it look like a new one. But he has more money invested in the thing, than he could go buy one factory made. He could run down here to the yachting store and buy one in five minutes. And maybe he'll work two days on it. But he saves money. He doesn't count his time worth anything. Well, that day is gone. It's definitely gone. There's a man to me, I would say anybody that can hire that man, you take attorneys and different professional men and so forth, they're quite proud of the fact that they're worth 30 dollars an hour, I've seen that man just sit down and work 15 or 20 hours on something that he could buy for five dollars. He has the patience of Job and he'll just work and work and work. And it's his training. My grandfather was the same way. And I understand that my grandfather's father was the same way. But he's a wonderful guy. He's a peach.

Q: Well, come back on the river now.

A: Well, I started school here in Cincinnati, the old Electrical Trade School. They bounced me around from one department to the other. That just suited me fine because all I wanted to get was the basic fundamentals, and then the rest of it I could get out of a book. I duplicated some of the books they had, which I don't know whether that was smart or not, I probably should have gotten some different views on the thing; all of a sudden one day I decided I was going to quit school. I knew all the answers. I think by then I was about 16. I came home one day, and Dad said, "I understand you've quit school." And I said, "Yeah, that's right." He said, "Well, you're going to have to work." I said, "Well, I'm looking." "Well," he said, "you're not looking very hard." He said, "I'll tell you what. When you find a job, you can start eating around here again." I found one pretty doggone fast. He announced that at breakfast one morning and by noon that day I had myself a job. It wasn't much of a job, and it wasn't what I felt that I was trained for. I got a job down at Eighth and Main Street, at Schnittger's Drug Store. I was playing nursemaid to a mop. I got nine dollars a week. I was jerking sodas, running errands, serving lunches, and mopping floors. Nine bucks a week. I kept that job for a good while. Nine dollars a week was pretty damn good in the depression, especially for a sixteen year old kid who's lucky to have a job.

Well, the Greene Line boat and the *Betsy Ann* were going to have a race. It was going to be on Saturday afternoon. I went to Mrs. Schnittger, and I said, "Going to be a steamboat race today, and I just got to see it." "Well," she said, "you can see it all right, if it's after five o'clock. I'll let you off a half hour early." I usually worked till 5:30, six days a week, nine bucks. And I said,

John Knoepfle

"Well, Mrs. Schnittger, I just got to be off at noon. I'll stay here and serve lunches. That steamboat race is going to be about 1:30. And I can run down to the river from there, but I got to see that race." "Well," she said, "it's either stay here and take care of your job or you won't have one." And I said, "Well, maybe you don't understand, but the steamboat is more important to me than all the drugstores in the world. I just got to see those steamboats race. That's all there is to it." "Well," she said, "You don't need to come back Monday." So that was the end of my soda jerking.

Well, I fooled around and fooled around, and finally my dad said, "Look, when are you going to get yourself a job?" Now he was all in favor of my going to see that steamboat race. I explained to him that I was going to lose my job. And he thought that Mrs. Schnittger was very narrow-minded that she'd make a boy that loved the river stand up there and jerk sodas and scrub floors when there was a steamboat race going on. Wouldn't let him off just a half a day. So he was all for me blowing that job, to see the steamboat race. He's an odd character, but that was one point that he got across. That race was important. "Now you get out here and see it." Anyway, I went down to him one day, and I said, "Pop, I just can't find a job." "Well," he said, "I'm short a couple of men today. Get down there in that barge of nails and barbed wire." He said, "I think a couple of days of that'll do you good. Maybe you'll look a little harder." Well, I guess I did a pretty good job. I was down there with him fourteen years, in the nails and the barbed wire and the sulphur and the pig iron. We used to get down there, twelve men would unload five hundred tons of sulphur. We'd shovel it with number six scoop shovels into big buckets and the crane would take the buckets up and dump them in a railroad car.

Twelve men as I say would shovel that. And we'd unload 500 tons in ten hours with scoop shovels. Then we started getting a lot of pig iron in there and there would be 16 of us in a barge on pig iron. Every five hours we'd unload 700 tons, and handle every pig by hand, stack it in these skiffs and the crane would take it up 16 tons at a time and dump it in a railroad car. I got to playing around with the crane, the operator there, he'd show me how things worked, and so forth. I'd roll the machinery over for him so he would grease it. One thing and another, I eventually got so I could handle a crane. One Saturday at noon, the fellow went home to lunch, said he'd be right back. And he just never did come back. And that's, oh I guess 20 years ago that that happened.

So my dad said, "Do you think you can run that crane without tearing it up?" After all, it was a $100,000 machine, and I was just a boy, so I said, "Well, I think I can." So for the next five years I sat up in that crane. Seems like I graduated real quick from 35 cents an hour, I got a steady job 30 dollars a week. I was king. Then they gradually got into the river business with derrick boats and barges and so forth. They put me out as the operator of that stuff. My dad and I built a towboat and started into the towing game on our own. I got to a stopping place. I just couldn't advance any farther. I had a good job. I was making what I thought was pretty good money. I was practically my own boss. But there was something I didn't know, which was how the people do business uptown. I probably at that time owned one white shirt to my name, and a couple of neckties. The rest of the time I was in a sport shirt or work clothes.

So I announced that I was going to go look for another job and that I'd like for them to get someone to take my place. They said, "Well, we're not going to replace you. If you leave here, we're just going to quit all this outside activity, and so we're just not going to replace you. Anyway, we don't think you're going to leave." Well, lo and behold, I came up with a job. And it was a pretty good job. I was getting 44 dollars a week on the job that I had had. My starting salary with a very liberal expense account was $5,000 a year. So I took the job as a marine surveyor for Neare Gibbs and Company, who are marine underwriters here on the rivers.

John Knoepfle

Evan Bone, August 26, 1957

Question: This is Mr. Evan P. Bone who spent a good deal of his younger life working on the present dam system on the Ohio River. He was telling me before we began this tape that he was present at Hockingport about in 1904 when they were trying to decide whether to build ice piers on the river opposite Hockingport. Would you care to talk about that, Mr.Bone?

Answer: That was a rather unusual and interesting experience. I was going to school at the time and got a job up there on the Ohio River and being outdoors and it looked like a very nice place. The Corps of Engineers at that time had designed a system of icebreakers, ice piers they called them. They had selected the site of Harpers Ferry directly across the Ohio River from Hockingport because it would have made a fine foundation for ice piers due to the rock ledge, which occurred there. Well after that was started, the pilots, well I don't know just how, it developed that the old time pilots, of course they had stood very high on river traffic, and some of them were a little doubtful about the new improvements, which the government was proposing for the improvement of the Ohio River.

But it happened that in this particular occasion a little personality came into the picture in that one of the prominent pilots on the towboats at that time had formerly lived in the town of Hockingport. His family lived there at this time and he came back occasionally, and it seemed that they thought it would be quite an advantage for the town of Hockingport, which was about two hundred inhabitants I believe, a very pleasant town to live in, and spend the summer. But if they would move the ice piers across the river on the Hockingport side then it might make a little business for Hockingport because the boats would come to tie up behind the ice piers.

So the organization of pilots, whatever they were, made a protest to the Corps of Engineers of the location as planned, using for one reason that due to the sharp bend in the river at that point that it was hard to steer a heavy tow around the bend and avoid the occasion of sheer, which occasionally happens with steamboats, we understand. Well the only reason the government decided to have it on the opposite side of the river from Hockingport was that it made a good foundation. So when they found a protest from the pilots what the government did, they just said, "Well, we won't make any ice piers at all." So we all lost our jobs and the whole project was abandoned.

Q: Kind of a disaster for your first experience on the river?

A: Well that give a little insight to the beginning and the situation of things as they were. Of course as time went I got sort of fascinated with the river and got permanent work after graduation from school. One of my first jobs was on the Fernbank Dam below Cincinnati, that's dam 37. One interesting thing about how experiences, the dam being a rather new feature, this character of dams because they were like any new project. It was actually pioneering, and a lot of new innovations had to be installed. Well one reason, one objection, which the rivermen had to the locks and dams system was that they might constrict traffic at the sites of the dams. Usually they have a navigable pass of about six or 700 feet wide. I wonder if I should try to explain the system of the dams?

Q: Well that would help.

A: Well to go back a little bit, the system of the dams designed from Pittsburgh to Cairo, there was to be 52 of them I believe, and in order to try to make them so they could be used in slack water periods, which is usually about six months of the year, but still not restrict traffic during the other six months when there was sufficient depths of water for traffic. Anyhow, they installed these or designed the moveable dam, which is nothing more than a big leaf that is propped up in the river, rather a series of leaves across the river, which forms the dam, and then when the water stage of the river becomes sufficiently high so that navigation could be carried on without the dams, then these moveable dams, the leaves, wickets are dropped in the bottom of the river, just laid down in the bottom of the river.

Well now then, the stretch of the dam where the wickets are was usually 600 to 700 feet wide, but the pilots and steamboat people were a little afraid that that was not enough, and of course that was all new to everyone and they objected somewhat to the obstruction even though the dam worked, the wickets were dropped down to the bottom of the river during high water periods, still it might obstruct traffic. So at dam 39 it was decided that, best try to make a good little extra measure, so they made the dam. I believe the pass was 900 feet wide and they also decided to make the sill, which is the bottom of the wickets, make it lower and decided to make it three feet below the normal bottom of the river.

Well thereby it turned out to be a serious mistake, but nobody of course saw it at the time. The reason was this, when the dams were lowered, then the high water coming along and of course the river, a lot of silt carried in the water, and it being a wider cross section of the river, the current would flow a little slower and the silt would drop. Then of course that would fill up the wickets and when the time came to raise the wickets in the spring when they were needed, they were hard to get ahold of. So then they found that that was a mistake and so the designs from then on, after a little more experience, they made the sill a little higher than the normal bottom of the river so the current would go a little swifter through the dam and really scour the mechanism of the dam and keep it clean. So that was something that was found just by trial and error.

They even went so far as in the upper river where the first dams were built, they weren't bothered with silt so much at least and they even designed one dam to have a tunnel underneath. Someone thought it would be a wonderful idea to have the dams so one could walk through, get across the river by going under the dam like a subway. Well what happened I forget, which dam

John Knoepfle

was built that way, but what happened that immediately filled up with silt and there was no way to get it out.

This problem with silt was a problem all the way through, especially as they would get farther and farther down towards the source of the river. It was a very serious problem and still had to be worked out by trial and error because the locks at first were made of a what they termed a roller gate, roller lock gate. That is the dams were about a hundred and ten feet wide and that's as wide as the Panama locks, used to sort of boast of it at the time, 600 feet long. But of course didn't have to be so deep, the draft was only, well it started out with nine feet draft and then increased to eleven feet draft. But that meant that the lock gate were made the regular lock gate, this is a standard that has been handed down from structural locks for years and years, that meant that the lock gate had to be very long in proportion to its height, taking a terrific strain on the hinges. So it was thought it would be nicer to make the gate so it would just roll back and forth on a track, just like a regular railroad track was built. The railroad wheels to run the gate back and forth.

But then they found out the old man, the trouble with silt came along again, because in the gates when they rolled out away they had to have a gate recess and that's where the gate would, to get the gate out to not obstruct the entrance into the lock, that recess would fill up with silt, the same thing, problem again. Then the gate was made with a lot of lattice work, a good deal like the construction of a bridge, steel lattice work. It is very difficult to get those cleaned out. So what happened finally they had to go to the miter gates, which was standard the first time.

Well about half of the first dams were made with the rolling gate, the half of the Cincinnati district at least. Then they found out the difficulty with the roller gates; then they had to go with the miter gates. So about every other dam is made with roller gates and the other half with miter gates. The difficulty with the miter gates, they had to have such a terrific weight, a monolith to get enough counter weight to hold the long gates up. So it was more expensive, but we got rid of the trouble with the silt.

One sort of innovation was put in effect during World War I. The system of dams as originally started, the plan was to build every other dam, that is the dams with odd numbers, they were numbered from Pittsburgh down, would be installed first, and then we would come and put the intervening dams to complete the system. Of course to complete the system meant to have so that during slack water period to have a sufficient pool to give a nine foot stage at least all along the river. Well when World War I came along they started a system of making use of the other dams by causing artificial rises in the river. That is they would, the great problem was, getting coal down the river, was a terrific problem at that time during the war when it was very critical, so they would get the fleet of coal towboats on the upper river in one of the pools and then they would lower the wickets and let the water flow down, start down the river and all the towboats would follow along on the crest of that little rise.

Then when that water would reach the next dam, which was built, then the wicket for that dam would be lowered and that would sort of accelerate as it went down the river, each dam would contribute its pool, so they would have time to get down the river a piece. They would get a pretty good little rise and the boats would all go down on the crest of that rise. But one dam, dam 35, an alternate dam, was not yet completed, it was just under construction, that was the dam at New Richmond, Ohio up here. So I happened to be put in charge of that job of trying to get the wickets installed.

Now the wickets as you know are hinged at the bottom so they can be raised on that hinge until they stand upright in the river. Then there is a prop behind the dam, which holds it behind the wickets, which holds in place against the head of the water. Well ordinarily at first those were installed while the dam was being constructed, when it was all in dry by means, the reason of the coffer dam built around it. But often money was slow in coming. Congress would appropriate money not as fast as the constructors of the dam would like it. So they would leave the wickets to be installed until after the masonry was completed, and that means that it had to be done by a diver, which was a very expensive and more difficult work. But now it came in the fall, during the war, it must have been about 1917.

I'm not quite sure, that there was an emergency to get these wickets in at dam 35 at New Richmond. So I happened to be reading at that time Henry Ford's system of mass production on the production line, how automobiles were built. Of course that got to be very popular at that time. That was just being introduced, this thought occurred, why couldn't it be done with installing the wickets. So I might say ordinarily they had a crew to install the wickets and they would get the parts and they would have to assemble the leaf and the props and the horse, so called. Then take them out in the boat and have a derrick boat to lower them down, and then a diver would have to go down and adjust what you call quoin blocks, which form the hinge for the wickets to work in.

Then we would come back and do it all over again, but according to a mass production line the idea was each job could be done by a separate crew by itself. So I got that all planned, had the system on the bank for installing the wickets for the men who could work well. Load a bunch of them on a barge, and then tow the barge out to where the work was going on; then they would, the divers crew and the derrick boats, would lower the wickets into the water and install them. Then to facilitate that, a lot of the hard work, was the diver had a little short shovel that he had to use to dig out the sand and silt, which would collect along the hinges on the bottom, so we had installed a little pump on another barge, a centrifugal pump, which is worked not as a pump but to work as a hydraulic dredge to pump or put suction right at the place where the diver was going to be next to try and pump it out clean.

John Knoepfle

Well like anything else new, it was a little hard to get that organized and when we first started we only had about, this was late in the fall and the system before, they had established the schedule of installing six wickets a day. Well now at New Richmond that would take over a month to get all the wickets in at that rate. Well this was getting late in the fall, and high water might come along anytime and cold weather, and there was a question very doubtful that that could be done under the then current system, unless we could make our production line system work. Well we weren't too sure about that but in starting out this seemed to be so important that the division engineer and the district engineer in charge of the Corps of Engineers both came to watch the work.

After it was all done, after we had worked a day, then the division engineer, which was a big top boss, called me and said, "Now how many did you get in today?" I had to say one. "Oh!" he said, "that would never do, that can't be." In fact they reported back the next day that I had better stick to doing it the way they had been doing it and not fool with any new ideas or anything. Well anyhow we got a night crew and after we got the system going a little better we happened to go to, my family, my wife and I, to the picture show up at New Richmond. They had about two nights a week there'd be a picture show. So before the picture show was over, well to go back, we'd load up on a barge enough wickets assembled, get them assembled by an assembly crew on the bank and load enough on a barge for the night crew to work on. So we had 15 loaded on a barge, which seemed to be plenty.

So in the picture show, long before they started the second show, here were most of the gang that were on the crew installing the wickets came into the show, and I thought, "Oh-oh, something has gone wrong here, some of the machinery or something that in those days so often did." So just as soon as I could get to some of the boys I asked them, "What happened, what broke down?" Well he says, "We got all 15 wickets in, so we just knocked off." So from then on we got along pretty well and got the dam installed in good shape. But it was a good example of how things don't go right at first until you get organized. From then on we used that system.

Well you know sometimes they would have difficulty in getting a force when doing government work because it all was supposed to be done under the civil service. Well for instance in getting a fireman that had to keep steam up on a temporary boiler and out on the coffer dam. On one particular occasion I remember when the wind was coming from the southeast it was very difficult to get a fireman who could keep steam up. That steam had to be piped quite a distance for the dredger, the pile drivers and things of that kind at the dam, which are changing and leakage in the pipes and we would ask for firemen, stoker they would be listed. Well according to civil service system we would select one of the three highest on the list that had the highest grades when taking the civil service examination.

Well then these men would be sent up to us from Cincinnati, perhaps a very good fireman working in an apartment building or an office building and keep up steam he would be all right. But when he would get out there in that bad weather and everything and no protection he wouldn't be good. So we complained quite a good deal to the central office about that. So the division engineer, I mentioned the division engineer, of course they are the army engineer, you understand the officers were usually colonel, sometimes lieutenant colonel usually, but the division engineer had such a deal about the appointment from the civil service organization. So he said, "Well I think I can help that some by putting all you fellows who happened to have charge of work on respective dams and put you on the civil service board, then you can get together." It all has to be done according to civil service, that's the law.

At the same time we have to get work done so you can get together and try to see that the right kind of men get on the list and will get the appointments to do the particular work that you want to do. So that seemed to work well, of course the civil service was a fine thing to avoid, preclude any favoritism things of that kind, give every fellow a chance to whether he is known or not. But at the same time it is very difficult to get it down on paper, the various kinds of jobs, pile drivers, stokers and things of that kind that occur on a dam.

But one particular instance is rather amusing in a sense. We had a crew of men down and digging out the mud in one of these recesses or gates that I was talking about. It was a nasty miserable day and they had to work with hip boots, and they couldn't get aclam shell bucket in there to dig it out automatically, so it just had to be shoveled by hand into a skiff, and then hoisted out. Well the foreman came up to me about the middle of the morning he said, "You know the crew is all quitting, they are walking out on me down there." So I went down there, and I couldn't blame them because of this miserable work. So there is just one man left digging down there. He was all by himself.

Well of course it didn't pay to run the derrick and everything for one man, but I thought a fellow that has guts enough to stick to it like that boy has, why he deserves something. Well as it turns out he didn't have too much education, in fact he couldn't have made out a civil service form by himself in any event. Anyhow I gave him a job as night watchman on the fleet. So each morning I had it fixed so the night watchman would make their reports if anything happened during the night. So one morning he reported, said, "Had a fire on derrick boat 7 last night," and he said, "I took the," now this is quote, "the, For use turn upside down and put the fire out." Of course he had read on the fire extinguisher and he thought the directions were the name of the extinguisher.

Well then he went on to say, "Now the, For use upside down is empty and needs to be filled. again." Well it turned out that the fellow was burned a little bit and of course was very creditable that a fellow would catch a fire like that and know how to put it out whether he knew how to spell fire extinguisher,

John Knoepfle

or not, the fellow was going to get a rating in a civil service. Well they would ask him a question and he would write it down, "Yes Sir. Instead of saying yes, he would say, "Yes Sir." We got him, fixed him up with a lot of aid to get this paper in. So we got him a pretty good job. To me it is very interesting that so many men we can find can do a certain job, but they just can't put it down on paper and get a grade or rating. Of course that had to be done.

Another experience, if I'm not boring you, one time this pertains to government relations, now I don't want to look like I'm slacking about government relations or anything of that kind because it has to be. We do hear a lot of criticism about government work, which the critics don't really analyze and realize what the situation is. There are plenty of faults yes, but they are not so easy to rectify as you might think. One night the telephone rang about two o'clock. They called me about two o'clock in the morning and the night watchman over there said the river was rising fast and was within, I believe a foot, from the top of the lock wall.

Q: What dam was this?

A: This is dam 35 again. We had no warning whatsoever from anywhere, usually get a warning from the central office or the weather bureau. I knew then that if it had risen so quickly as that it would be over the top by morning, so I called some of the men on our side of the river, New Richmond on the opposite side from where the work was going on and asked them to go from house to house and dig out everybody they could and to telephone to try and get them, ring them, tell them there is an emergency down at the dam and get down to the dam. We got a boat so we could get across, and also I told the watchman if he didn't have enough steam on the derrick boat, one of them, to get steam enough to blow the whistle and blow it for emergency for help.

Well that worked fine because a lot of the boys were out on the hills of Kentucky back there and were very sincere and take a responsibility in their work and things of that kind. So before daylight we had a pretty good crew down there. So we got to salvaging the stuff, a lot of lumber was piled up, a lot of machinery, and also the steel company was putting in a lock gate at that time. A lot of their men got out and before the morning was over, those boys worked right through up until I guess about ten o'clock in the morning, had no breakfast whatsoever. It was just like putting out a fire, were saving it and they did save thousands and thousands of dollars worth of stuff that might have been lost and at least a lot of it damaged.

I thought the least we could do is to get sandwiches and coffee down there, hot coffee down there for the boys since they hadn't had breakfast. We got some sent over to the hotel, which was at New Richmond, got two of these great big coffee pots that keeps it pretty hot and got the fellows fixed up with some sandwiches. They got them down to the dock and by that time the river was pretty well over the wall and nearly everything was saved. Well then it turned out that, I hadn't thought of it at that time doesn't make much difference if I had or not, but on that particular dam there was no authority for subsistence that one didn't need it. But I put in the bill anyhow, but it never was recognized. The sum about 12 dollars and a half. So I had to pay that individually, but that's the rule and it has to be they couldn't change the rules very well of course without my making a whole lot of trouble, so those things do happen.

Another funny thing at the time we were working putting those wickets in I was talking about, we really didn't have enough barges and we would get coal delivered by one of the big wholesale coal people on one of these enormous barges and although there would just be a little coal in it. But everyone, all the river people were shy on barges. Well when that barge would be left there, an empty barge, it would be, oh the thing was about 300 feet long and when it was empty it was way up out of the water about twelve feet or so. Then we had a little gasoline launch and we would tow the barge out to the works in the middle of the river from the bank. Now we didn't use this all the time, but that would help out with our plans.

Well one day though, it happened that a little wind came up and the wind got ahold of the bow of that barge just like a sail and it took the barge down the current and down the river, gasoline tow and all. So, you know there was a clam shell bucket digging on excavating, and these clam shell buckets they can really navigate themselves in a sense by walking. That is the operator can get the bucket to swing by manipulating the boom so that the clam shell swings out, and when it's out at the farthest point he will let it go, and then it will grab and anchor itself down the river a piece. Then he whirls it up to the hoist and it draws the boat up to it, then he swings it again. So I asked the operator to catch that boat if he could.

So he went down there, he got about two miles down the river, and then when he threw the bucket out once, well one of the lines, the wire ropes, you know broke. Then he was left down there that was still worse. Well finally about six or seven miles down the river the wind blew the barge up or grounded it up on the Ohio side. Of course I was in bad because if the government knew we deliberately borrowed a big barge that belonged to the coal company and were using it, they would frown on that very severely. But of course the war was going on and we considered it an emergency and we would just do it anyhow. So we got two lines on that and got this little barge boat and another one and tried to pull the big barge off. We couldn't even get the lines off, one of these big lines were about three inch lines I guess.

We were down there working at it the next morning. It looked pretty hopeless, but lo and behold, we saw the smoke of a government towboat coming down the river. They used to have the towboats to tow these different dredges up the river, I forgot which one it was. So we hailed him in. They put a line out there and started to pull that barge. Well the big line just snapped, it was that much I guess. The river had fallen a little bit during the night, so it did look like we were in bad. Finally we got wire line out there, a wire rope and got

John Knoepfle

it made fast to the sturdy timberheads on the boat. They got it pulled off, towed it back, and as far as the official records shows that was the end of it, but it was quite an experience at the time.

You know speaking of the war we were under pressure to try to get a much better navigation. Of course no one knew at that time when the war was going to end and the shipping, which at that time shipping wasn't done by water, anything like it has grown to be now. But they were turning to the river more and more and here the lock and dam systems were just about half completed then. I was really touched sometimes about the boys, the workmen there, how they could serve us at that time, you know one year at the time when there was that big flu epidemic went through the country and with work like that with exposure and damp, rainy and wet.

In one particular job I remember a fellow had to run a pump to pump out the gates before the steel people working on the gate could get to assembling the steel. But the water was always leaking in there of course and had to be pumped out. Well that kind of a pump, it just sprays the water all over every place and the fellow gets all wet. One after another those fellows would drop off sick and you wouldn't have the heart to ask or tell someone they had to do that, but you would be surprised how they would volunteer. I remember the last fellow, he volunteered, he got pneumonia and he died. Several of the crew died by the way, some of them in the hotel there without any physician, didn't have the facilities at that time. But I often wondered, now there's fellows they were fighting for their country just as much as soldiers in the line of battle.

Ordinarily they don't get any decorations or anything for it, of course I don't think they would want it. They just felt like they were doing a job and doing it for the country, but if anyone gets in touch with those kind of things you do think about that. You know, dam 39, as I said I'm not going this in sequence of time, but this was just about the last job I was on. Before that we were sent down to dam 39 and that's the Markland dam, which is now soon to be obsolete because of new dams going up. It was a very peculiar sight because half of the dam was built on piling and half of it on rock. As far as I know it was the only dam on the river, I may be mistaken about that, which is of that kind of construction. Of course the piling if you put the structures on piling, they will settle a little bit, you expect it to, and you allow for that. When it's on rock that is more solid, and it stays in place better. So they had a lot of unusual experiences to think about on that particular dam.

The funniest thing, they had so much trouble with coffer dams breaking occasionally, and they decided, which turned out to be a mistake, to make a big coffer dam, a high coffer dam. We thought we could hold water out, otherwise it would be flooded, make it a little higher, build the dam just right. Well most of the contractors when they were better organized they would go on the policy of getting in quick and out quick. Well as the government we were more cumbersome and had to work slower and we weren't as experienced as the contractors who had been at it for years and we were pretty green at it then. So we couldn't handle those things so quickly. So we thought we would make the coffer dam a little higher, of course make it broader too, thought it would be stable. But anyhow it didn't hold up, and no fault of the designer or anything, but it just happened that conditions were such. Well, happened to remember one time that they had a rise and it was coming along and it was almost up to the top of the coffer dam, not quite, but we thought it wouldn't go over, so we didn't open the sluice gate to get it in.

Usually coffer dams you know closes a portion of the bed of the river. This particular one closed the whole lock, which is 900 feet long and width of about 200 feet, from the bank to the outside edge of the coffer dam. Well all that had to be pumped out, but then when it was going be flooded had sluice gates in the coffer dam that could be opened and let it get filled up, but that would take quite some time, maybe several hours. So we just couldn't wait until the last minute. We thought perhaps it wouldn't come over the top this time and some of the boys happened to be in a derrick boat just outside tied up along the dam and they were speculating, said, "Oh, this wouldn't break, this coffer dam wouldn't let go."

It happened all at once that coffer dam happened to let go right where those fellows were on that boat. The boat and all went right through, when one hole breaks through well then it soon get wider and wider the more current get through. Those fellows got off that boat all right. Anyhow the boat did go right through the coffer dam. It's a little Niagara Falls in miniature when it goes through. The steel hull hit right on the edge of one of the piers of the monolith of the lock wall and knocked a hole in it, enough to make a pretty sizeable leak. One of the colored ship's carpenters went down there and he built a temporary bulkhead where it was leaking through and kept that boat from sinking.

All those bolts and rivets, rivets rather, not bolts, down there and angle iron make it very, you know how steel construction is, but he'd get around there and caulk it up and get it tight enough, it was pumping all the time. Another thing at that same time another boat came in, this was a pump boat and we had about half of the sections of the wall built, they go by order one monolith is so called about a length of a day's work is built, while that is setting hardening, with the forms left on, then you just skip one, and then when they go back and this section is hardened, they take the forms, strip the forms and put them up to the alternate place. Well this particular pump boat went, floated. Now the pump boat got a little rise and didn't go through the coffer dam, the pump boat was inside of the coffer dam and is on piling when it's dry. This is so designed that whenever the river, the coffer dam does flood, the pump boat will float. So sure enough, of course, when the water poured in there from the break I was just talking about why the pump boat floated. It went around a regular whirlpool.

From the end where it broke it is one way, and then the current would flow way up about 600 feet, and then around towards the bank and it was just

John Knoepfle

like a whirlpool. Well this boat went along with it. The first thought would be that boat would surely hit one of those concrete monoliths and sink, it's wooden hulled. Oddly enough the current so take it that it just dodged those as pretty. So it never did hit any of the monoliths. It went around the whole place up perhaps about four or five times before it finally came to rest.

There was a foreman down there who had played football at Center College at one time. I think he studied law down there. So he got his gang of about four selected men and they got there with a line with a bowline in the end, when this boat would come around up there, it was going wild, why they decided to try to throw, push each other, all four, and try to get it over a timber head. The first throw or two, of course they would get soaked each time. They never did catch the boat. Finally the water filled up and it came to rest.

Q: Now this is at Fernbank?

A: Yes, this is at the Fernbank Dam when it was first being laid out. One of the problems of course was with the surveying instrument to sight across the river out into all the way along the river to look at the point where the wickets should be placed so that when it was constructed it would be a straight line. It turned out to be a nice straight line where the water falls over the top of the wickets. It happened to be my job at that time to sight that transit. Well one day I made a mistake and it cost the contractor quite a little bit of money to fix it up and I felt pretty badly about it. When they got on to how I felt well all of those fellows, they were a pretty rough bunch, those guys that follow the river and even the contractor himself, he was quite a husky fellow, had a lot of fun.

They told me well my job was gone, I was through and everything. So then when the boss did come down from the central office they told me they would help me hide and maybe he wouldn't see me after all. Well when I got so worried about it, Mr. Sheridan who was Sheridan-Kirk Company, he said, "Why, don't worry about it. I make mistakes every day. You know the only fellow that never makes mistakes is the fellow that doesn't do anything." Well coming from him of all people you would think he was the roughest and toughest boss there was. So that was a funny experience for me.

Q: Well we are getting toward the end Mr. Bone, now when did you do your last job on the river? We ought to get our dates straight when you came on and when you finished.

A: Well my first job was at Fernbank, that is the first dam, I had worked a little on. Well to go back a little further I had forgotten that I was on the ice pier up at Hockingport, that was my first job, but it blew up in a short time. From then I got a job out of school with a contractor on erecting ice piers at the same time at Maysville, which were built then. From then I got on with the dam work at Fernbank, I was working then for the contractor, and I saw the government engineers around, and it was pretty fascinating, and I got a job at Fernbank, and then I was all through there. That dam was completed, I guess, in about 1910, 1912 or 1911. Then I was sent up to a dam at Ashton, I forget the number right now, 27 I'm not sure about it. Anyhow while that was going on then I happened to be appointed to this job. I was then assistant to the engineer in charge, then I was appointed to this job at dam 39. I was there for two years and I got so much worry and I was just about ready to quit, so then they said well I could go up to dam 35. Well that turned out to be still more worry, but still it was exciting, and it was good. Then I did want to quit, I was pretty sure I wanted to get in other work, but for a short time I was sent up to 34 starting in the odd numbers, but I was only there just a few weeks, and that was about 1919, that's when I quit.

Q: Well that is quite an interesting period of river history you covered, Mr. Bone.

John Knoepfle

Captain Brasher, June 19, 1957, Fort Thanas

Question: This is the 19th of June 1957, and I have come to Fort Thanas to the home of Captain Brasher.

Answer: That's Brasher with a long A sound.

Q: Brasher, we're going to do a little more river lore. Maybe you can tell us where you are from?

A: Well, I was born in Rising Sun, and reared in Jeffersonville, Indiana. My dad was on the river all his life, and his two brothers, my uncles, were also on the river all their life. They were on the packet boats. My Uncle Jim, which was my father's older brother was pilot on the *Admiral* at St. Louis when he passed away about two years ago. Yes, Uncle Jim was 82 when he passed away. And he piloted up until his death. Most of their lives were spent on the old packetboats, that is the *City of Louisville*, the *City of Cincinnati*, the *America*, the *Queen City* and boats of that era.

Q: Let me hold a moment and let you . . . today you're being made immortal.

Mrs. Brasher: Those things are really remarkable aren't they?

Q: When did you first go on the river yourself?

A: I went on the river when I was in school. I spent my summer vacations on the river. I worked as a clerk, and then later on I worked as a steersman.

Q: What boats were those?

A: That was on the *Cincinnati*. That was the boat after the *City of Cincinnati*. She is now the *President* at New Orleans.

Q: And what year would that have been?

A: That would have been back in about, in the 20s, I can't remember the exact year. Back in those days, a steersman got seven dollars a week. That was your salary. So then I also was on the old *Queen City* and the *John W. Hubbard*, but only for a short time. Then I left the river and wasn't on it until after I came out of World War II. During World War II, I was in the Coast Guard on an LST, and then I went back to the river at the end of the war.

Q: Where were you on the LST? Just a side question.

A: I was in the South Pacific, all over.

Q: You were? Well, anyway, you are back from the war now.

A: Back from the war, yes. Then I went with the Greene Line. I went as purser on the *Delta Queen* with Captain Tom Greene. And then I went, after being purser on the boat for a couple of years, then I went as mate. I served as mate for a year, and then I went to captain of her, up until two years ago. Since then I've been on towboats. So that's about the extent of my river to the present date.

Q: You're on diesel tow now, aren't you?

A: Yes. But I do believe the steamboats will come back in existence. However there is, as you know, there is not too many of them, but I believe with the atomic age, why I think the steam will come back into existence again. They say history repeats itself, so no doubt it will. I do believe this. I believe that when atomic power comes into existence, I believe that you'll see your boats, similar to your old-tine packetboats, put themselves in existence again.

Q: Well, I had heard that boat propellers aren't much more efficient than a good sternwheel up until a few years ago.

A: Well that is true. There is a lot of arguments even to this day in regards to the sternwheel and the screw, that is as far as pushing goes or towing of barges and so forth. But one has its advantage over the other. The beauty part about the old sternwheel is the fact that you could make repairs on it without dry-docking your boat, where in the majority of cases with your screws, you can't. And your sternwheel boats with your wheel, you could go a lot of places that you can't go with your screw boat. However, I do believe that they claim that there's a loss of fire somewhere around 40% with the wheel against the screw. But frankly, like I said before, I believe that in time to come that you'll see boats over here similar to what they have there in Europe, or on the Rhine and some of those rivers. You would call them self-propelled barges. Because it is proven, there are statistics that show that river transportation is still the cheapest means. I may be wrong but at least that's my trend of thought.

Q: Well, let's go back to that early river and talk about that a little bit.

A: Okay.

Q: Anything you could say now about the falls, and your uncle might help us, since I have no information at all on the falls in the river.

A: Well, as you know, what founded the city of Louisville were the falls in the Ohio River. The boats back in the early days would come down as far as Louisville, and then the only time that they could go over the falls was during high water. The other portion of the year the boats would bring the freight as far as Louisville, then they would have to make a portage around the falls, and then the boats below the falls would take it on through. They would have what we call the falls pilots that would, when the river was at a stage where they could run the boats over the falls, well, they would take them through. Then they would go on through. But later on, they built the canal at Louisville and of course, that did away with the transferring of freight. Then they built the, or it was after they built the canal, I'm not sure about that, but anyway, they built the dam there at Louisville. Then later on here in around 19, around the 30s I think it was, they put a top on the old dam, which made it higher to back the water farther up the river. Now I believe they're going to put in the new lock there at Louisville and from what I understand they're going to cut away most of the present canal.

Q: You lived then above the falls?

A: Yes, when I was a boy, we lived above the falls in Jeffersonville and the, of course at that time they were using the canal instead of going over the falls; however, they would still go over them only when the river becomes high enough at Louisville.

John Knoepfle

Q: I'd like you to tell that fish story.

A: Would you? Oh.

Q: Nobody will believe you, but . . .

A: Well, I can remember when I was a boy, we lived there at Jeffersonville. I can remember twice men walking up the street with fish that were large enough that they ran an oar through the mouth and the gill and two men, one on each end of the oar, carried it on their shoulder and the fish drug on the ground. That is his tail drug on the ground. And then they used to use there at the falls, they had a wheel mounted on the end of a small barge. This wheel was, similar to a paddlewheel on a boat except where the bucket planks were, they had wire netting similar to poultry netting. They would work this barge out into the current by the falls and the current was strong enough that it would turn this wheel and as this wheel went around in the water it would dip up the fish.

Q: Is that so?

A: And throw them back into the barge and I know several times that their catch was so great that it would tear this wire netting right off the wheel. That's really something for around this part of the country.

Q: Yes, indeed. Well, those long fish that you saw, they weren't cats?

A: No, as I recall they were not catfish. What they were, I don't know.

Q: That's probably deep water fish then.

A: Yes, several places around the falls that, at that time they had never been able to find bottom, they claim they caught some fish in there without eyes. The same type of fish that are in Lost River, Mammoth Cave. So those are true stories. They're not fish stories. (laughter)

Q: Very good, very good. Wonder if you could tell us something about those early boats you were on. Better still tell us about your grandfather and the . . .

A: Oh, and the flatboats?

Q: Yes.

A: Well, my grandfather's name was Ward, and he used to run flatboats through to New Orleans. Back in the early days, why there was so much piracy and thievery going on and even the men traveling on the steamboats at that time, it wasn't safe for them to carry any money. They would be robbed before they reached their destination. So grandfather had a slave whom he had raised or reared, and he would always take Pete with him on these trips to New Orleans. When he would get down there he'd sell the produce or whatever he may have aboard. Then he'd also sell the boat, which they did back in those days. Then he would come back with passage back up the river on the steamboat. He'd give this slave the money and old Pete would put it in a carpetbag and naturally, being a colored man, why he'd walk back. Well, no one would suspect that he had any money or anything and therefore, he would get through without any trouble whatsoever. And that was his method of getting the money back up to this part of the country again.

Q: Could you tell us anything about your father on the river?

A: Yes, my father was captain and pilot on the river. He was on the old *City of Cincinnati*, the *City of Louisville*, the *Loucinda*, the *John W. Hubbard*, and the *Kentucky*. Then he was on the steamer *Indiana*, and later the *America*. He was captain on her after she, the *Indiana*'s name had been changed and she had been made an excursion boat. He was on her for several years. He was on quite a few of those boats back in those days, but I can't recall all of them.

Q: I never heard about the *Loucinda* before. I wonder what kind of a boat she was.

A: Well, she was, I can't tell you whether she was a sidewheeler or whether she was a sternwheeler, but she was quite a noted boat back in those days. And he spent most of his boating between Cincinnati and Louisville with the White Collar Line and later, the Louisville and Cincinnati Packet Company. In fact, I have somewhere around here a copy of, the *City of Louisville* was considered one of the fastest boats, and I have her log here; she only made one trip to New Orleans. She went from Cincinnati to New Orleans in five days and she came back from New Orleans to Cincinnati in five days. She going down, according to her log, they just loped along as you might say, just a slow bell. But that was the reason it took her as long to go down as it did to come back. She only made the one trip. As I recall, it was five days, five hours and 41 minutes. So that was quite a record. In fact, I don't think they have a boat today that would equal that time, that would make that time.

Q: Well, I'd like to hear about your earlier boats now, any details now.

A: Any details, well as I said, my first boating was on the *Cincinnati*. She was a sidewheel boat. She was the sister boat to the *Island Queen*. When the L & C Packet Company, they built hulls. They're going to name them for the old *City of Louisville* and the old *City of Cincinnati*. They started on the *Cincinnati*'s superstructure before they did the *Louisville*'s and it cost the company so much money that they were forced to sell the other hull to the Coney Island Company, which they built and named the *Island Queen*. So therefore they weren't able to complete the boats. They were only able to complete the one. I don't recall what her dimensions were or anything, but she was quite modern for a packet boat in her day. And I guess, in fact she was the last little packet boat ever built, and she was very pretty. She had rather graceful lines and even to this day I don't think even the *Delta Queen*, which was built later than the *Cincinnati*, she wouldn't come up to the *Cincinnati* in design or structure either one. And of course, she wouldn't come up to her speed. Of course, the *Delta Queen* is a sternwheel while the *Cincinnati* was a sidewheel. The old *Queen*, that I spent a short time on, she was a sternwheel packetboat. As I recall from the older men saying, she was about the fastest sternwheel boat that was ever built. She had a lot of speed and was a good handler.

Q: Now you said you were a steersman?

A: A steersman.

Q: Could you describe the duties of a steersman?

A: Well, a steersman is the man that's learning to become a pilot. So that's the same as a cub pilot. Some call them cub pilots and some steersmen. In order to become a pilot you have to be a steersman or a cub pilot for three years before you could go up for your license. And that's what I did. And then I also clerked on the boats. In fact, I even stewarded the boats. You could say I have done a little bit of everything.

Q: Do you remember some of the men that you were under as steersman?

A: Well, yes. I was under my dad and uncle. They were the pilots and I steered under them. Back in the packetboat days between Cincinnati and Louisville, they ran what they called "Meet the Boat" trips. One boat would leave Cincinnati in the morning and the other one would leave Louisville in the morning. And they would take passengers and they carried an orchestra on each boat. The boats would travel until they met, which was generally around three or four o'clock in the afternoon. Then one would land and the other one would land along side of her and they would transfer their passengers. And the people that got on at Louisville would get off and get on the other boat and the ones from Cincinnati would get off their boat and get on the other boat. Then they'd come on back and they'd get back to Cincinnati around nine or ten in the evening, that same evening.

Then on the *America*, I remember my dad having Sy Rinehart and his band from Louisville. And as I recall, I think Sy wrote "Sally from our Alley," or something like that. That was quite a noted song back in those days, I'm quite sure that he wrote that. There was quite a, Louisville at that time was a jazz center, I guess you would classify it as, something similar to New Orleans of yesterday, you might say. But then they bad the calliopes on the boats back in those days, which are just about gone. And Sy, as I recall, was very good on the calliope. He could play it just like a musician could play a piano today.

Well, those "Meet the Boat" trips were quite popular back in those days in both cities, in Cincinnati and also in Louisville. And then the boat that would leave Cincinnati, she would also pick up passengers for this "Meet the Boat" trip as she would go down the river. She would pick them up at Lawrenceburg and Aurora and Rising Sun, even down as far as Patriot and Vevay. Of course, if it was the north-bound boat, the boat leaving Louisville, there wasn't any towns for her to pick up anybody at, any towns of any size. So therefore she didn't make way stops other than just her freight stops.

Q: It's an interesting note. I've never read this anywhere.

A: Yes, it's rather strange. It was a strange thing to me when I was on the *Delta Queen*, we naturally came in contact with people from all over the country even some foreign countries. It was most remarkable how well the *Island Queen* was known.

Q: Oh yes.

A: She seemed to be known all over the country. People would come aboard, and they'd ask, people from California and places from way away from here, "What ever happened to the *Island Queen*?" She was a well-known boat.

Q: It seemed like a personal loss.

A: Yes, she was a well-known boat.

Q: Now you were on the *Queen* too?

A: Yes, I was on the *Queen City*. Back in those days they ran what they called their big boats during summer time, and then during the fall and winter they ran their small boats. That was due to the fact that they didn't carry the number of passengers, and they devoted most of their efforts and so forth to the handling of freight, where during the summer season they handled both passengers and freight.

Q: I see.

A: So they had what they called their summer boats and their winter boats. When they would lay the summer boats up, then they would bring out the smaller boats, which had very little passenger space were mostly all freight space and they operated those. Back before that time, that was before they had the locks and dams in the river, they had their high water boats and their low water boats. Most all the companies that operated at that time would have their big boats that when the river was high they would run, then their shallow-draft smaller boats, most of them were sternwheel, that they would run during the low water season.

Q: Which category did the *Queen City* fall in?

A: Well, the *Queen City* would come under the larger type because she was, well I guess at that time in her day, she was the largest sternwheel boat ever built. She was quite fast, and she was quite large for a sternwheel boat. She was a wooden hull boat as most of them were back in those days.

Q: All right. Maybe you can name a few of the parts of the wooden hull boat.

A: Well, there were your hog chains. The purpose of the hog chain was to keep the boat from breaking in two. And it was fastened in the hull towards the bow of the vessel and it would come up through the decks clear beyond the roof of the boat, back over the boat, and then down and the post at the very stern that these hog chains rested on was called the sampson post. Your hog chain went over the top of it back to what is known as the fantail, which supported your wheel at the stern. Then there was a stanchion, a timber that is a vertical timber that gave support to your decks, and then there was your deck beam that supported your deck. There was your breasthook, that was at the bow if you have a model bow that held the stem, that was the very tip of your hull. There was a rod that ran back, and then it branched out in the shape of a Y and fastened back to your stanchions on each side. Your hull planking was called streaks, and then the one that seemed rather funny was a rosebox. A rosebox is what we would refer to today as a screen, which back in those days they didn't have electric pumps, or pumps, they had what are called siphons that run from steam.

John Knoepfle

And a rosebox was just a box affair around the end of the pipe, of your siphon, which prevented anything clogging it, and that served the purposes of a screen.

Q: Can you talk a little bit about the crown again?

A: Oh yes, the crown. Well, the crown of the vessel is the upward sweep or downward sweep, whichever you want to call it, of the decks. On your main deck, which was your freight deck, it served two purposes. It served as drainage to drain any water that might fall on the deck and also to carry or support the weight. On your upper decks, its sole purpose was for drainage there. Then your wheels, they were made up, the shaft was the center part of the wheel, which was generally was made of iron. Back in the old days, it was quite common for a boat to break her shaft, and then your wheel was built around your shaft. You had your wheel arm, and then your little wedge pieces that went in between the wheel arms were called cocked hats.

Q: Cocked hats?

A: Cocked hats. Then you had your circles, which supported your wheel arms, and then the rocket plank, which dipped in the water, which shoved your boat along. There's quite a few of them I can't recall offhand. The frames, some people refer to them today as ribs, they were called frames. There were your floor timbers and your bottom planks, and then your streaks on the sides, which formed your side planking. You had your guards on your boats back in those days, which was the deck overhung out over the water. Today they don't build boats with guards. Back in those days all boats had guards on them.

Q: You could catch a guard in a lock, couldn't you?

A: No, not necessarily. Your guards were, your main deck was down low enough that your guards, you had what they called a rubbing streak on the outside of your guards, they were low enough that they wouldn't override the lock walls.

Q: How do you spell a streak?

A: S-T-R-E-A-K.

Q: That's odd. I would, that's the speech then.

A: Yes, well some refer to them streaks long E sound, and some refer to them as streaks, long A sound. So that is the old-time ship carpenters, that is river carpenters around here, that's what they would call them. They would call them streaks long E sound. Maybe the proper name was streaks long A sound. But they called them streaks. And then your other item was a ridgepole, they used. What it actually was, was a beam that ran fore and aft, which supported your deck. They called those ridgepoles.

Q: Now, you have your, this must have been your exam book when you went up for your exam.

A: Yes, well this was data that I gathered from the old-timers, you might say, in regards to the construction of the wooden hull vessels. And in the hull was the codwad, which was a timber that ran the top of your frames, you might say, or the top of your hull that ran fore and aft. At the bow you had your stembands, which was a metal band that took shape and formed the same shape as the stem itself. And the reason for that metal band, these boats would go in along the river bank and make landings. And this iron band would strike any hard objects such as stone or anything, and it would absorb the blow instead of the, where wood could not withstand it. Then there was, as you said, the rabbet. The rabbet was notches cut into the stem where your streaks or your planking would fit in and make it flush.

Q: Oh, I see.

A: Then another thing in the hull is limber holes. Do you know what those were? They were holes between each frame to let the water flow through. Then there was the, do you want to mention about the bell system back in those days?

Q: Yes, we could talk about that.

A: There was the bell system that ran from the, it was the communication, the signals that the pilot passed on to the engineer down in the engine room. They had a cord that led up overhead in the pilothouse, that ran over just above the steering wheel overhead and down each side. That was the back and slow bell, and then right in front of the pilot wheel, they had what they called the bell board. On each side of the bell board, they had a line that came out each side with a handle on it and that was the stop and come ahead bell. Then mounted on the front of the bell board was the gong. They rang these bells from the pilothouse and then the engineer would, by the way the bells were rung, why he would know what to do in the way of working the boat and how to work the wheel and so forth. It's something that I doubt if there's a boat on the river today that has the bells; they all use the newer type of communication.

Q: Could you tell us what the mat the signals were?

A: Well, to come ahead slow you rang the, well first of all the gong was used as a ship up, back in those days they had to ship up those engines before they could open their throttles, as to what they wanted to do. First you would ring your gong, then you would ring your come ahead bell on the bell board, once. Then you would ring the overhead bell once. And let the engineers know that you want the wheel to work so that the boat would come ahead and at a slow speed, and then for half-ahead, you would ring the come ahead bell and tap the gong once, and then for come ahead full, you would ring the come ahead bell once. Then for extra speed, in other words for extra power, if you needed it, why you would ring the come ahead bell once and tap the gong twice so that the engineer would open the throttle all the way. Then to back slow, you would ring the back or slow bell, which was overhead, you'd ring that twice to back slow. And for half, you would ring it once and tap the gong once. For full, backing under a full head of steam, why you would just ring it once, to back it full ahead. So the pilots that I have talked to that have been on boats with a bell system and the other newer type of communication, they seem to like the old bell system the best. However, lots of times, so I understand by talking to various ones, there were quite a few accidents caused by misinterpretation of

John Knoepfle

the bells between the pilothouse and the engine room, which with the newer method of the electric type, they don't get that. There's no problem there.

Q: When you got up all this material, you had to go around to the real old-timers to find out.

A: Yes, to find out. I think I canvassed all the old carpenters that were still living at that time. That is how I was able to gather most of what I have here. I just jotted down some of the things that didn't seem to stick with me. Other things did, I didn't bother putting those down. But these others, I don't know, well Bill McClellan was living at that time, and I got a lot of my information from him. He was one of the old boat carpenters. Then there is another one, Bill Harn, now the last I heard Bill Harn was still living, but he's some place up on the Kentucky River. I don't know whether he's still there or not. He built small boats, in fact here's some of the sketches of some of them.

Q: Oh, these are carpenter's sketches that they made up for you. I see in this sketch, oh that's the hull: side, saddle, knuckle, and grub.

A: The roustabouts did have songs they sang all the time they were carrying freight. As I recall, they had one they called "Hay Pile." As the boat would go down the river after the hay was harvested and baled, why they'd hail the boat, and the boat would go in and land, and then these roustabouts would carry the bales aboard. They had a song they always sang as they carried the hay. Down below Madison, Indiana, up on the hill, there used to be large peach orchards there and when they'd harvest the peaches, they would ship the baskets of peaches to Louisville. I know they had a song, a different song, that they sang as they carried the peaches aboard. I remember they sang a song when they would bring barrels aboard, barrels of apples or things like that, that they sang. What these songs were, I don't recall now. Of course, they had a lingo all their own that was hard to understand just what they were saying lots of times.

Q: Did you ever hear them chant the lead?

A: No. There were very few that could. There weren't too many of them. As a rule, as I recall, it was the deckhands that threw the lead, but not a rouster.

Q: A deckhand was in charge of the roustabouts?

A: Yes, a deckhand was over the roustabouts. As a rule, the roustabouts would carry the freight aboard the vessel or the boat, then the deckhands would be there and take it off his shoulders and set it down; there would be what they call the head deckhand. He would be standing around, somewhat of a straw-boss. Of course, he received his orders from the mate and the captain of the boat.

Q: Can you tell us about Joe Bates?

A: Oh yes. Joe was the head deckhand on the old boats. Joe was a great big man, and his roustabouts would labor all day in Cincinnati or Louisville, and soon as the boat would pull out, why they'd assemble back in the deckroom, aft of the boilers, they'd bring out a long table, and one of them would bring Joe's chair out. Joe would sit at the head of the table, he'd take this little tobacco pouch that he kept his money in. He'd open that up, and approximately 30 minutes to an hour, why Joe had all their money. He'd close up his tobacco pouch and he'd walk away from the table. The rousters would then come and take the table and Joe's chair and put it away. The same thing would occur the next day at the other towns. They'd work all day, you might say for Joe.

Q: He must have been a rich man.

A: He should have been. That is about all I can recall. They used to coal the boats, too. I don't know whether anyone ever told you about that or not.

Q: No.

A: When the boats would reach either Louisville or Cincinnati, soon as the boat got in and tied up at the wharfboat, why they would bring a coal flat alongside. It was a small barge loaded with coal. Then some of the rousters would carry coal from the barge over and put it on the boat. They had a box with handles on it. They would fill up these boxes, and one would get in front, and one behind, and that's the way they'd carry it aboard and dump it in the coal bin.

Q: Is that what they called back-and-belly? One man's back to the box.

A: Yes, you know, that's right.

Q: Well, how about wrestling for coins?

A: Oh yes, well that used to be common with the, after the boat would leave port and get under way, why as a rule, after dinner in the evening the passengers would come out on the boiler deck. The boiler deck was the first deck above the main deck, which was where they carried the freight. They would stand out forward and toss coins down on deck and these rousters would get out there and wrassle for them. Sometimes, they'd get over and wrassle, and they would just teeter on the edge of the guard. You just wondered what kept them from going in the river. They could get a nickel or a dime. Well, the *Delta Queen* is the last overnight passenger boat left on the Ohio and Mississippi Rivers, or the Mississippi River system I usually say. She was built in Stockton, California. She was, however the hull was fabricated in Scotland. And her machinery, part of it, was built at the Krupp works in Germany. She ran down the Sacramento River between Stockton and San Francisco, which was also a packet trade similar to our packet trade that we had between Cincinnati and Louisville. World War II came along and they used her then as a troop transport. She would go up the San Joaquin and Sacramento Rivers to the various camps and bring troops out and down to the bay and load them on the big transports. At the end of the war, why the Maritime Commission put her up for sale and the Greene Line bought her and brought her around to New Orleans. There at New Orleans, well in fact to get her around here she had to be towed, so therefore they had to take her wheel off and board her up. Then when she got to New Orleans, why they took the planking from around her and reassembled the wheel. They took her to Pittsburgh under her own power, and there at Dravo's, why they remodeled and restored her back to carrying passengers. They brought her here to Cincinnati. She's been running ever since making New Orleans trips and Kentucky Lake trips during the summer months.

John Knoepfle

Ira Campbell, September 16, 1957

Question: I'm talking to Mr. Ira Campbell who is 85, and has been on Shanty boats and trading boats and worked in the Howard Shipyards at Jeffersonville.
Answer: Forty years.

Q: All right, Mr. Campbell.

A: I worked in Howard Shipyard from the time I was 14 years old until I was 50 years old. My first experience in the shipyard was driving drift bolts, for instance the drift bolt was half inch. We bored the hole seven-sixteenth, that gives the chance of drifting the boat, making the boat much stronger, then the bolt was punched in a certain distance, far enough to put a washer on the inside end and that was my job working with my grandfather in the shipyard.

Later on I growed up to be a man and done planking. When they was building a certain boat, the Howard Shipyard I'm speaking of, the carpenters with their foreman would set up what we called the keel box, lay the keel, set up the frames, put the ribbons on. Ribbons are long pieces of oak that separates the frames of the boat the proper distance apart. Then when they got that all done it was time to start to plank the boat.

The foreman was William Allen who lived in Jeffersonville, Indiana, my home too, was one of the most successful men we called the boss planker. Sometime the planking gang would only consist of four men besides Mr. Allen, sometimes six, according to the size of the boat. Sometimes eight when the boat got big and the timbers would get big and heavy. I have helped and the gang that I worked with big oak boards that would measure four inches in thickness, 20 and 22 inches wide and 52 feet long, which went on the bottom.

Q: Is that so?

A: Yes, 50 and 52. The four inch plank, we would use little boring bits to bore the holes for the spikes to go in through the plank. They were driven by sledges, by mauls, spike mauls we called them. When the bottom was four inches, the spikes was eight inches, on a three inch it was six inches, two inches bottom thickness would be four or possible five inches etc. I remember well of having to plank the Cincinnati Packet called the *City of Louisville* in sixteen days.

To the best of my recollection the *City of Louisville* was 210 foot long, built at Howard Shipyard; I don't remember the year. I could have found some of that stuff if I'd known you were coming. Then the *City of Cincinnati* was built there and the last time I saw anything of the *City of Louisville* and the *City of Cincinnati* was on the wharf at Cincinnati after we'd had a very high river and there they both laid, sunk, on the landing there on the dry ground and they were dismantled and done away with. The *City of Louisville* was a famous boat and so was the *Cincinnati.*

Q: I know, a wonderful boat.

A: Directly after that they used a boat called the *John W. Hubbard*. The *Lucinda* was built at Howards. There never was a boat built by the Howard Shipyards for the Cincinnati Packet Company boat. All the Cincinnati Packet company boats were built around Cincinnati, Marietta, Ohio, and Pittsburgh. When they decided to build the *City of Louisville*, they come to captain Ed Howard and had him to build the *City of Louisville,* the *City of Cincinnati, The Lucinda* and a number of other boats the Cincinnati Packet Company had. Drift bolting, and then my grandfather said to me one day, "Ira, you had better go down." The Howards started quite a steel boat building and my grandfather advised me to go down where they were building the steel boats and learn that business because in a short while there'd be no wooden boats built.

I went down and was a blacksmith helper, driving rivets by hand, then it fell to my lot to bend a lot of the big steel plates to fit the model bow of the boat, I had quite an awful time getting started. It took me two and a half days, to get the first bent sheet in shape that it would fit the boat. I would hear my friend Mr. Ogle say, "Listen at that fellow, whistling and singing." This job was out of the ordinary for just a man to take ahold. Because the other men that followed that part of the job had gone and left and the boss had suggested that I would try my hand. So I did. The first one I bent it took me three days and a half. Then we had an old gentleman by the name of John Worful that planted them sheets to the boat. I said to the boys when I didn't think it would just exactly fit, "Throw it out in the yard, Uncle John will put it up." So Uncle John did put it up. And as I can remember, I'm the only man that never was a sheet called back for alterations. After I'd bent that bad one, I bent ten in eleven days.

Q: Wonderful. Now exactly where did these fit on the boat?

A: Well here's a big steamboat with all the frame work up. Know what that is?

Q: Yes.

A: The width and the length. The mold loft would give you the pattern. That sheet would be four feet wide, ten or twelve feet long and then you'd have to bend it to go around the round part of that boat so it would fit every frame. Now in installing those sheets, this man John Worful, he had a lot of patience and that's what it took. If one of those sheets went out there and it didn't exactly fit, Mr. Worful would make it fit, put some bolts in you know and bore a hole here, pull that part up and then maybe he'd have to bore a hole someplace else until he got it up. It was quite a job to bend them and make them to fit perfect.

Now there was one fellow, I think he's still living, his name was Green; he was a little older than me. He was the best I ever saw. In my experience and the men before me would use the sledge, but Mr. Green found a big wooden mallet was better than the sledge and the flatter because sometimes in using the sledge or the flatter you would bruise the plate. But the wood wouldn't bruise it, then you'd have your templates, little round pieces, you know, and you'd try it on, and each frame has its different shape and you have to bend it so far to fit

John Knoepfle

one here and back here is another one and you have to work with it until it will come around to that template etc., until you get to the end.

Q: Now what was the template exactly?

A: A template is the pattern. We called them templates. Templates are made by some good mechanic in the mold loft. The mold loft is where the boat starts. I don't remember much, about the men who laid the boat off before I got mixed up in that, but the present man that laid the boat on the floor in life size. You take a boat 200 feet or 300 feet. They go in the mold loft, that's a great big long room, oh maybe 50 foot wide and 250 feet long. Nice tongue and groove floor, and then he lays his center line called a baseline, and then all of these bends and these crooks is laid down on the floor. Now I never got that far, the reason I didn't was my education. Mathematics comes in there quite a lot.

They lay the boat down. Now there's only one side of a boat laid down. If they build a hundred model bow boats, they lay one side down, then reverse. You have the pattern for all that one side. There they reversed on the other side, left and right. Then the bevel, where you come around the bow of the boat, every frame has different bevels, and you take a board, they give you that in the mold loft. It's a long board about four inches wide of soft pine and every bevel that frame has, that's forward body, or the after body, that board has that bevel on there for 1, 2, 20, 40, etc. All through the boat.

Then they make templates. A template, if I was going to take the shape of that door, I'd take two strips long enough to go to the top, one across the bottom, and one across the top and maybe one in the middle for stiffness. That would be the size of my door and I'd send it to the lumberyard or some place, and they'd make that door to fit that template, and it will fit that space right there. Now that's what a template is.

Well I can safely say that I done everything but lay the boat down on the floor at the Howard Shipyards in the forty years I put that there. I had an uncle by the name of Barbour, he worked at Howard Shipyard quite a while, then he conceived the idea to build a big shanty boat and go in the rags and iron business. His first boat I think was fifty foot long. He come along home after making a trip down we'll say to Cairo and come to my house.

Mother was a widow woman, there was two of us there, twins. I begged and begged for most a week for her to let me go with him on it. They called them shanty boats them days, now it's all houseboats. And he bought rags and iron, and bone, barrels, whiskey barrels, coal oil barrels. He bought most anything in that line. They was a different price, the price of rags. Now is this what you want? The price of rags, dirty rags was forty cents a hundred, clean white rags was forty-five cents a hundred, good wool was six cents a pound.

Q: Now can you set about the year this was?

A: My first trip was in 1884, I was 14 years old. My first trip was from Cairo, Illinois to Memphis, Tennessee. So on that trip we went to Memphis, Tennessee and the river raised so high that it floated a lot of lumber out of the lumber yard.

I caught it and built me a flat boat to bring back home and in the empty tow, we were towed back to Louisville by the towboat *Alice Brown*. The captain of the boat was Bobby Bowls. When *The Alice Brown* come to Memphis and on her return back uncle Jim Barbour prevailed on the captain of the *Alice Brown* to bring him back and his houseboat and his crowd to Louisville. They made a deal. In those days it cost Uncle Jim $75 for the *Alice Brown* to tow that house boat, known in them days as *Shanty Boat to Louisville*. At that time the captain of the boat would get any of that money that he could pick up a towing a shanty boat from one landing to its other destination.

Q: Now did they push them ahead of their boat?

A: Yes, towed them. On our way up everything went fine until we got opposite Osceola and there was a miserable storm came up and tore our fleet all apart. By that time I had my little flat boat full of Pittsburgh tow boat coal to bring home to make the fire for my mother and my brother. But the storm got so fierce that it upset my little boat and all my coal went to the bottom of the river. The captain of the steamboat and my Uncle Jim got things straightened out and we went on up the river. We landed at Paducah, not at Cairo, Illinois, so the engineers could clean the boilers of the *Alice Brown*. While laying there, they had dropped us off out of the way, to a landing at Cairo, Illinois.

There was two young men that decided that they wanted to go to shore to get something, possible cigars or tobacco, and as they went around the stern of the *Alice Brown*, the engineer not knowing that they were passing behind his wheel, started his wheel up and turned both the skiff and the boys, out of the boat into the river. Then there was me hearing these boys holler, "Save me, save me," and as they passed our shanty boat I took a long line, handy line, and throwed it to one of the boys and he grabbed it and we pulled him in on the boat. The other boy I hollered at him to catch a piece of drift that was near him and somebody would come and get him before he got too far away. We pulled the boy upon the boat and kept him there and the yawl off of the *Alice Brown* went down to the mouth of the Mississippi River, there they picked him up and brought him back home on the towboat. Well then everything got straightened out and they got the boilers clean and everything was ready, and we started up from Cairo on the Ohio River.

Every year Uncle Jim would coal tar the roof of his houseboat; it was a habit of his. Me and my Aunt Annie tried to talk him out of tarring the roof until we got home, but we couldn't get him to stop. He took the wash boiler and filled it about half full of coal tar and set it on the stove and left me and a strange man to watch it. He depended of course, on me because I'd had the experience. The first thing you know the tar, which does all the time when it begins to get hot, it begins to get a black smoke. This strange man, that Uncle Jim picked him and his wife up at Memphis to bring them to Louisville, grabbed the boiler and pulled it off of the stove and tar was red hot and poured all over the boat and set the boat afire and we all had to run to get on the towboat to save our

John Knoepfle

lives. It set the *Alice Brown* afire, but the crew got the hoses out and stopped the fire and cut our boat loose and let it drift down the river, and the captain of the boat took us on to Louisville and to our homes in Jeffersonville opposite Louisville where we lived.

Uncle Jim got a skiff floating down the river with a man in it, and went to the hull of the boat, the cabin burned all off and on this boat we had five thousand gun caps, a fifty pound keg of powder and a half a barrel of coal tar. It spread all over the place and burned the whole cabin off the boat and Uncle Jim saved the hull with some help from the man in the skiff at Pickel and we went on up home to Louisville, Kentucky. Uncle Jim got the next towboat that came up to tow him back to Louisville where he could rebuild the boat and put on a new cabin and start back into the rags and iron business.

Then I didn't see any more of Uncle Jim until the next spring when he would come home, him and his family and his two boys, Clyde and Jim. He went on then and made a couple of more trips, and here he come to my mother to allow me to make another trip with him. The next trip I made with him was from Louisville, Kentucky to Paducah, Kentucky. Then, I was quite a boy, and was homesick, they sent me home to my mother and brother. He went on to New Orleans and come back or made a couple more trips and came back to my mother, prevailed that I would make another trip with him and that time I must bring my grandfather William Barbour, the father of James A. Barbour. Me and Grandpa caught the steamboat *Ohio*, which was with the Cincinnati and Memphis Packet at that time and went to Golconda, Illinois and met Uncle Jim, Aunt Annie and the two boys, and then we turned out and went on our journey to Harwood, Arkansas, which is on the Mississippi River forty or fifty miles below Greenville. That ends my trip. There's more stuff I could give you about these two boys of his.

Q: Well we got into the prices, and then I cut you off. Could you tell me a little bit more about that? The price of iron etc.

A: I didn't give you that. You didn't get the price of iron, then, as I understand you. In rags, iron, bones and anything in that class, barrels, coal oil barrels, oil barrels, common rags was forty cents for 100 pounds, clean rags at that time was 45 cents a pound.

Q: A hundred pounds?

A: A hundred pounds, yes. Old stove plates was forty cents a hundred, good cast iron was sixty cents a hundred.

Q: I guess copper brought a little more?

A: Yes, I think . . . brass and copper was considerable higher priced, which would be 60 or 75 cents a pound. Coal oil barrels was worth $1.25. Whiskey barrels was $1.50.

Q: Were these wooden barrels?

A: Oh yes, oak. Regular old-time wooden barrels, no iron at that time. Whenever Uncle Jim got the houseboat loaded with all that he could carry, his shipping points would be from Paducah, Kentucky or Cairo, Illinois. Then Memphis, Tennessee, when he got down on the lower Mississippi River, Vicksburg would be his place to dispose of his cargo.

Q: Now would he just go from landing to landing to dispose of it?

A: Oh, no, the last boat he had could carry two full cargos of stuff, boxcars, boxcars were 28 feet maybe 30, now they are 60 feet I guess. Then this boy Clyde of Uncle Jim's married the girl, Jennie Hobbs, is still with him, and he married Jennie Hobbs, and they started out for themselves. He built a boat about a hundred feet long and named it after a very prosperous farmer. The name of the prosperous sugar plantation owner was William Kyle. He had the hull built and had the cabin built, but no machinery. By that time him and captain Kyle got very well acquainted and some more of the planters. Captain Kyle asked him in the conversation what he proposed to do with the boat.

Young Barbour, Clyde, was an engineer on the Morgan Line Sugar Towboat Company. He told Captain Kyle, K-Y-L-E, that when he could raise money enough of being an engineer he was going to Jeffersonville, Indiana to Sweeny Brothers to have a set of machinery built for this boat, *The William Kyle*. William Kyle told him to meet him the next morning in Franklin, Louisiana, we're now in Franklin, Louisiana, he would take him to the bank, see if he could raise the money to buy the machinery, which was $3,700 dollars. Young Barbour met captain Kyle the next morning, went to the bank and told them what he proposed to do for this young man Barbour. They wanted to know who was going on Barbour's note. He said, "We don't need no note. We're going to lend him the money and I'm sure he'll pay it back."

Barbour was a hustler. They lent him $500, and $2,700, and he come back to Jeffersonville, contracted the machinery for this little towboat. Sweeney built it, shipped the machinery, and Captain Kyle's bank that he was associated with paid for the machinery. Barbour got started. He afterwards built a small boat. Then after building the *William Kyle* and being successful, then he built the other little towboat, which at present I forget the name, then he built a bigger towboat and named it after his wife, *Jennie Barbour*. Then he used them boats and money rolled in. Oh, he was a money getter. Years later he was successful; when he was a boy he worked at the Howard Shipyards for my grandfather and father in the drift bolting business. His sole desire was to go back to the Howard Shipyard where he had worked one time as a poor boy and have a good big towboat built, which he named after his wife, *Jennie Barbour*.

Q: Now all these towboats were in the southern trade?

A: All of them. This little place called Bayou Teche. All of them little bayous we'd call rivers bayou, B-A-Y-O-U. Well the *Jennie Barbour*, built at Howard Shipyards at the time for $17,000 dollars, would be $100,000 now. When it come time to get a crew together to take the boat down the Ohio and Mississippi into Grand Lake, up Red River into Grand Lake, through Grand Lake into bayou to this river called a bayou. It was my job to hunt the crew. He would

John Knoepfle

come to visit us once in a while in construction of this new towboat. I would write and let him know how the boat was progressing, how the machinery was coming along. The machinery was built by the firm in New Albany by the name of Charles A. Hedgewald, H-E-D-G-E-W-A-L-D, I believe, Charles Hedgewald, Steamboats, they built all the hard machinery for a long time. I recommended for the pilot a young man called Mitchell Smith. I was at home walking through Spring Street, a man come along and said, "Ira, who's going to take the boat down to New Orleans?" "Captain Mitchell Smith." This man said, "Aah, he can't take that boat down there, he ain't been down the river for three years." Well then I recommended Mr. Billie Hinds as the engineer; the deckhand and fireman were Mr. Frank Deptford.

Q: All right, who was he again?

A: Frank Deptford and Balky Leap was the deckhand and fireman. One day my cousin come up to accept the boat, she being finished, wanted to know where my pilot was. I said, "He'll be here." He never showed up. I noticed during those days that I was with him that there'd be a very old gentleman, poorly dressed, would come to that boat every day. Well when we was discussing the pilot, my pilot that I recommended who didn't show up, I ask my cousin Steve Barbour, "Who was that old gentleman that come there every day?" He said, "Ira, that's Captain Jim Pell." He was about 75 years old I guess. I said, "Why don't you give it to him?" Barber says, "I'm going to give it to him."

Well the time come, Captain Pell come, I met him. Our cook was Charles Dunn and his wife Mrs. Dunn. I was a kind of a cub pilot. In times when the river would get very bad, the old captain would say, "Well boy, I'll take her now. The river was getting pretty bad. We had a great big rocking chair, a big woolen blanket that we'd put around us. This time was in October, we'd set in that chair and sleep. Getting back before this, Captain Barbour and Captain Pell on the road down the river got into a big discussion as to when they would get into Red River. Captain Pell said, "A Friday night." My cousin Barbour laughed at him and said, "Oh you can't do that." He said, "If you give me Ira Campbell to help me, I'll put her in the mouth of the Red River a Friday Night." My cousin Barbour laughed at him, but he turned around to me and said, "Ira, you stay with the captain." Then my job was to stay with the captain and pilot the boat as far as it was safe for me to handle it.

Captain Pell would line out the river tell me what I would see, such as hills, trees, sandbars and a clear open river, and then I'd maybe run up to 25 or 30 miles, then he'd raise up, very old and stretch himself. "Boy, I'll take her, it's getting pretty rough now." I'd get in this big chair and wrap up in that blanket, we didn't have any stoves, go to sleep. That went on for about three days. One night about nine or ten o'clock, he said to me, "Boy, get the crew out, we're going to land." "Why, Captain are you at Red River?" "Awful close, awful close." He put her nose into the head of the river, we put out an inch and a half line and everybody went to bed but the watchman. The next morning,

Captain Pell was at the end of his rope, his license went to New Orleans, but we had stopped and was going up the Red River and Barbour's job was then to take it the rest of the way to Franklin, Louisiana. We got pretty well along and finally Barbour found out he was lost and didn't know the way. There happened to be a skiff go across one of these little bayous. He stopped the boat and talked to this man in the skiff a while and the man told him he was in the wrong place, he told him just where to go to get back into the right channel and he would be all right. So he backed around and went down again and in due time we entered Grand Lake, Louisiana, which was twelve miles wide. Young Barbour said to me, he was in the pilot house, "Ira, I've quite a job for you."

"What is that?" "I want you to sound Red River from one shore to the other." Before leaving the Jeffersonville Shipyard I had a sounding pole made, hexagon shaped, each foot had its color, red, white and blue, then I would know how much. So I began to sound the river and I could look up the stairs and talk to him in the pilot house and in my experience of sounding the bottom of Grand Lake, every little bit, quite often I would hit something with my sounding pole that I knowed wasn't the ground, wasn't gravel nor rock and I mentioned it to Barbour, and he said, "Ira, them is cypress logs, this lake is strewed with cypress logs." Then we'd go on and I'd keep a sounding. We finally hit that lake along about as I remember twelve o'clock in the day.

We finished crossing Grand Lake and that night we entered Bayou Teche at Franklin, Louisiana and there we met the town people. My brother, Kenny Barbour, Barbour's wife and they had been looking for us for two or three days and as soon as the whistle blowed on the *Jennie Barbour* my brother knew, being a steamboat man, that that was the new *Jennie Barbour* and they all come down. Had a big time. I stayed with them oh, a couple of months.

But I got homesick, had a nice family at home and some children and I didn't want anything in the south because most everybody I would run into them days were French or colored people, there wasn't many northern people down there then. So I come home, and Barbour went on and become a very, very wealthy man. In him and his wife's steamboat experience with the *William Kyle* they would pass a big wonderful home called Oaklawn Manor. Him and his wife being poor, he used to tell her, "You see that big fine mansion up there?" "Yes." "We're going to live there someday," and she'd laugh at him. It seemed impossible. But they went on, he prospered, the money rolled in to him. He towed the sugar cane and eventually bought Oaklawn Manor, fixed it all up and it partly burned down. He rebuilt it, he was in that kind of shape. Now he had his dear old mother Annie Barbour with him at his home in this wonderful place called Oaklawn Manor. It was a two story affair and he built an elevator to go up to that second story for his mother. His father was still living. His father couldn't make up his mind and know that he was an old man, past a making money, and had that rich boy to support him and his wife, and have him at home, at his fine home.

John Knoepfle

Question: Aboard the towboat *Snyder* in the Muskingum River, and I am talking to Captain Clare Carpenter.
Answer: Right.
Q: All right, Captain Carpenter, would you give us a resume of your river experience?
A: I started on my river experience on a towboat *Leona,* owned by Captain R. J. Hiernaux of Charleroi, Pennsylvania, May the 29th, 1930 at Letart Island in the Ohio River. We was under contract to the government, it was a scow boat tending the dredge *Colonel M. B. Adams.* I stayed on the boat from May the 29th until the following February. They took the dredge boat in for repairs, and then came back out in April. I remained on the *Leona* until November of that year in 1931, and then the boilers on the dredge boat developed leaks and I quit for the year. During that time we did dredging at Letart, at Twelve-pole below lock 28, below lock 25, and below 24, 18, 16 and practically dug the river from lock 14 to Clarington.
Q: That's a steam dredge?
A: A steam dredge and a coal tow steamboat. In the fall of 1932 I started to work for American Barge Line at Louisville on the steamer *Plymouth* and I worked on various boats for many years. Everything from coal passer through to the mate. I left American Barge in June 1941, which actually makes it more than eight years; in that time I worked with Campbell Transportation for a little over a year, quit American and went to work for Campbell for about year. I did the same thing for Campbell, I started in as coal passer and wound up as mate.
Q: What river were you working off at that time?
A: Oh all on the Ohio and upper, not the middle Mississippi, I've never been on the upper Mississippi. I made a trip in 1954 to Woodriver, Illinois, that's as far up as I've been. September of 1941 I started to work for Union Barge Line and have been there ever since. I received my mates license in September 1936, my first pilot license in June 1941. The Masters License about a year later.
Q: What were your duties as a mate on those boats?
A: The mate technically is the second officer on a ship. Actually in river operations it doesn't work out that way because the pilot is really the second officer. If it were to come up to a court trial or lawsuit or something why maybe your mate would be the second officer but it's just the way they operate; the pilot is in second command. As the mate you had the charge of the deck crew, charge of keeping the boat clean, maintaining the boat all over, maintaining the equipment, and the biggest job of course to keep the crew satisfied.
Q: That must have been a big problem?
A: I now have a master license for the Mississippi River and tributaries, I can go anyplace on the Mississippi or on any river that the water flows into, as a

master. As a pilot I have a license for the entire Ohio River, the Great Kanawha River to the head of navigation, the Little Kanawha River to lock 1, the Allegheny River to lock 2 and the Monogahela River to the head of navigation at Fairmont. In the very near future I'm going to have to go into the Mississippi River probably to Memphis, maybe to New Orleans.

Q: Well moving those big tows must have posed some difficult problems of piloting, do you remember any experiences where you had to pit your knowledge against the elements?

A: Oh we always had that, wind, and rain, fog.

Q: You're not on steam tows now are you?

A: Our company doesn't have a steamboat anymore.

Q: So you're here on a diesel.

A: All diesels.

Q: I guess there's a vast difference between piloting a diesel and a steam tow?

A: So far as handling your tow or steering, it's altogether a different proposition. On, shall we say, between the diesel and steam when you consider the steam it's a paddlewheel boat. Now they do have some steam screw-wheel boats with the panel and operate practically the same as your diesel boats.

Q: I guess you can stop a diesel tow a lot easier than a sternwheeler?

A: I don't believe that it would be noticeable if you had two boats of equal horsepower. That is one of the strong points of your diesel. You can take the small hull and put lots of power in it, where with steam and due to the weight of your boilers and machinery and extra equipment that you have to have for steam, why you take a hull that you might be able to get three or four thousand horsepower of diesel, you probably wouldn't be able to get over a thousand in steam. So it just cuts your power down, you just don't have it.

Q: So it's really a matter of concentrated power.

A: I guess the biggest accident that I've ever been involved in, we fished a boat out of the Mississippi River one time. When I was a mate on one of the Campbell boats, well we run this boat aground in the Mississippi River, and the water was falling real fast, and twelve hours after we hit bottom why they was sitting out high and dry. There wasn't any water around it. It finally fell out, the bottom of the boat was about eight feet above the water level, and we had to carry water to wash our face in probably a quarter of a mile. We was up there I believe ten days and they finally got a big government dredge to dig us in.

Q: When was that, Captain?

A: That's a pretty easy one to remember, it happened on my birthday, December the 27th, 1935. The cook wanted to know what kind of cake I wanted for a birthday cake and I told her I didn't like cake, I wanted peach pie. We went aground at 11:30 a.m., and when I finally got time to eat or look for something to eat about four o'clock that evening the pie was all disappeared. Read every once awhile in the "Waterways Journal" where some man had

John Knoepfle

boated so many years and had been on over 40 boats; just recently I counted up and I counted 37 that I've been on.

Q: Can you name some of those now?

A: I can start back in and name the company's boats that they've got now and according to the way our radio schedule goes, *Peace, Neville, William Penn, Reliance, Lehigh, Cornell, Pennsylvania, Liberty, Southern, Eastern, Western,* those are the boats they have now. Then when I started there they had the steamboats, the *Reliance, Sam Craig, J. D. Ayres,* the *C. W. Talbot, Jason,* they also had had another diesel boat called the *Beaver.* Then during World War I they had the *Monongahela* and the *Allegheny* chartered from Carnegie Steel.

Q: The *Monongahela* must have been a wonderful boat?

A: That *Monongahela* was the best sternwheel boat that I've ever been on. She didn't have as much power as the *Jason,* but a much better handler, just a general all around boat to work on.

Q: What made the *Jason* hard to handle?

A: Some defect in construction, she didn't back too much good.

Q: Did that ever get her in trouble?

A: Yes, I guess so. Luckily I never got into trouble with it more than hitting the bank a little bit once in a while. One of our other pilots near run her clear up on a railroad track down in Cincinnati one time.

Q: He did?

A: Yes, knocked down part of a railroad trestle and the water just threw her up on the railroad.

Q: That *Jason* was an old-timer, wasn't it?

A: The *Jason* was the last steam sternwheel boat built, the last steam sternwheel boat built, she came out in 1940.

Q: I didn't know that, I thought there was a Combine boat by the name of *Jason.*

A: I never heard of it.

Q: She's gone too, I guess?

A: No, she, the Amherst Barge Line or Coal Company out of Kanawha River owns her and they're operating her, they're running her all the time between Point Pleasant and Cincinnati in the coal trade.

Q: Under the same name?

A: No, I think it's *Jones* now. It's *Herbert E. Jones,* they changed her name when they bought her. Then going back through the other boats, there was of course the *Leona* that I started on, and the *Plymouth.*

Q: You mentioned that you were a coal passer. Could you describe his duty?

A: The main duties of a coal passer was to take a wheelbarrow and go out in a barge that was usually, we hoped, towed along beside the boat. Sometimes it stuck way out there somewhere, but usually we tried to keep it alongside the boat and load it up with coal and wheel it into the firebox where the fireman would get to it and put it in the furnace.

Q: Did you wheel that over a plank that was laden with flour?

A: No, we never had one with flour on it. I think we used a little lime or something like that a time or two, but the pilots seemed to be getting away from that old idea that you had to have complete darkness at night. Most of them at least would allow a little light out there. We'd take a megaphone and put a light bulb back in it and point it straight down the runway so it wouldn't shine up or anything; we would just shine right down on the plank where we worked.

Q: How many hours did you work a shift on that?

A: Six on and six off.

Q: It kind of back breaking after a while, wouldn't it?

A: Well some of the boats it probably did, I might have been lucky, and I was usually on one, usually stayed on those that didn't burn too often.

Q: What did a coal passer make? That would have been in the thirties when you were a coal passer?

A: Our pay was a $1.66 and two-thirds cents a day or $50 a month. No time off.

Q: I understand some of those passers would miss the plank sometimes and put the bucket in the river?

A: I don't recall any going in the river but a lot of them fell off of those boards in the bottom of a barge upside down and would go down and dig it out and start all over again. But I suppose there has been some of them went in.

Q: Did you actually work on the dredge that you mentioned?

A: No, I was on the steamboat that towed the stuff away from it.

Q: That must be an interesting operation trying to dredge the channel out.

A: Well I don't know how interesting it was, with us it was just a job during the depression where if you had a job you were lucky. It was a good job then, we used to make $75 a month on there for that job. On that job we worked eight hours a day and because we were working for the government and usually was around town some place. Over the period of almost two years that I worked there, the same crew practically, everybody would come up with an automobile. You always knew where you would be, when you got off and went someplace you always knew where to go back to work. More or less like working on a shore job and had a lot of fun.

Q: Well do you find now as a Master, the responsibilities are pretty pressing with those big diesel tows?

A: Oh true you have a lot of responsibility, we have all of our book work to do, we don't have a clerk and that will average possibly an hour and a half a day. You have to take the typewriter, but all in all, we have pretty competent mates and our pilots, most of them do relief master's work part of the time. So they know pretty well what to do unless something get out of hand pretty bad, why it's not too bad.

Q: Well I guess even in your span, the river itself has changed quite a bit with all the government work on it. I wonder if you could comment on any of that?

A: You mean the channel or the actual river, the physical character of the river?

Q: Yes.

A: I would say that the Ohio River hasn't changed too much. Tom, I'm stealing it all. (laughter)

Tom Kenny: Go ahead. He can give you the information. He's a real riverman.

A: And I think it's for the better. I think it's better than it was fifteen years ago.

Q: Well we've talked quite a bit about dredges and coal passers.

T: I'm not in the school with Captain Carpenter, I came as they say AC, after Carpenter. I came on the river in 1942. In fact the first boat I worked on, the first trip I made, Captain Carpenter was on the boat as the pilot. And we got talking about it in the pilot house one day on the *Peace* and he still remembered the fact that at that time when I got on the boat, the first trip I ever made on the river I made it on the boat that he had been on.

A: It was on the *Peace* not so long ago that we were talking about that?

T: I do believe that the modern river towboat today is much more of a job I would say. Wouldn't you say that, Clare? I mean the fact they move the tonnage more efficiently and they move more tonnage than they did in the old days. What do you think?

A: Oh, I agree with you.

Q: Probably more routine too?

T: Yes, I would say much more. Well you have a routine in any job, but I would say in the profession of piloting the unexpected is always your bad fellow. It gets up with you and comes on watch and you go down and go to sleep and it may get up out of bed and arouse you. I've seen a couple of cases of that.

Q: What cases for instance?

T: I could sight you a couple of goodies.

A: I could tell you one too.

T: Just to show you how things can happen so readily. One night on the *Reliance* passed Homer there at Clusters Island and everything was going along fine, and we were making pretty good time and we came down to Lock 9. I stopped the boat because the *Paul Blazer* was in Lock 9. And when he pushed out of the lock, they signaled me to come down into the lock chambers and at that time they were about a trap and a half of water, which meant that there would be a pretty good draw at Lock 9 on the guide wall. So I sort of headed the tow up a little on the inside of the wall figuring on that draw to compensate and pull the head of the tow out. I started down toward that wall and the stern of the boat was out in the river a bit, and I started to back the boat, and I started to pull the stern of the boat toward the shore thinking that the head of the tow would come out and miss that wall. But the unexpected someplace came in, and the stern of the boat went in toward the shore, but the head of the tow never came out. Before I could feel sorry for myself there was an empty gas barge, it was 60 feet up on the end of the wall and it was permanently stuck. And as I say the unexpected, it happened so quick I couldn't even feel sorry for myself.

Q: You're lucky you wasn't loaded.

T: If it were loaded I don't think it would have climbed the wall so readily as it did. So we had to tie the tow off, broke the boat loose from the stern of the tow and we went down and looked it over and here's a pin on top of the wall had been driven underneath a cross frame in the barge and that's why we couldn't pull it off the wall. So we broke the two barges loose on the head and we took the boat and just pulled them out of the river and when we did why we just took the whole top of the wall off and put it in the river. We got the barge off in about ten minutes. It came off very nicely; it brought the pin and the end of the wall and everything with it.

But that just goes to show that with the size of tows and the tonnage and this enormous weight. In fact the enormous inertia of a tow that you are really playing around with that can be very costly and can do a lot of damage. And as I say the unexpected is with you all the time. But I guess maybe that's one of the reasons why we enjoy piloting. I think piloting is a very competitive job in this respect. You compete not only with the river, but you compete with your competitors in the towing industry. We all will sort of welcome a race for a lock and we'll do everything that we can in reason, and which is fair in order to beat that fellow to the lock and whenever we are beaten, why we accept it gracefully and say, "Okay partner, you've got it." But we really do try and it's one of the things I would say about it is being competitive. Of course, any job that's worth anything why, you do compete. That's one of the spices of any industry is the competition that you have, and the competition that you meet.

Q: You mentioned an experience, Clare, you were going to tell.

A: Tom talking about hitting that lock wall up there, I never did know who did that job.

T: Incidentally I put in my diary, I've had the greatest one of them all, in it about knocking down the lock wall. I was on watch. Somebody sent me a clipping out of that "New Cumberland" paper about the *Reliance* taking the end of the wall off so I just pasted it right on the diary page for that date and back in the back of the book I put a great big red line under that date so I would remember it.

A: Sometime in the past six months we were going into Lock 14 on the *Eastern* or the *Western* one, and going up everything was flat again the wall, just as perfect as could be and evidently we was about fifty feet below the outside wall being clear. Everything was in such good condition that I turned around to look at something else and when I looked back we was out in front of the wall.

We hit the wall and about the same thing that happened to Tom, there was an empty barge clumb way up on the wall and when it came down, why the end of it wasn't there. I wondered why the watchman out there hadn't put a line on it to keep it in. He didn't say a word when he came back, and I didn't either. But that night sometime 12 or 14 hours later, he came into the pilot house and I said, "All right, Dan, What happened?"

John Knoepfle

They went to put a line on it and when they started out to put a line on it to pull it in, and one of the deck hands that was out there helping him, got the line around his leg, so the only thing to do was turn loose or wind that man around there and cut his leg off probably. That was the only possible thing to do but that's your unexpected again.

The other instance that I thought about. We came up below Gallipolis one night. I went to bed and along about three o'clock in the morning. I about half woke up and I suppose in a few seconds the door to my room flew open and the pilot said, "Come up here right quick, we've sunk a barge." I said, "Huh?" He said, "Get up right quick, we've sunk a barge."

By that time I'd woke up enough to realize that we didn't have anything but gasoline. I thought, "Oh boy, if we've sunk about 400,000 gallons of gasoline out here in this river things will pick up right." So goes dashing into the pilothouse and blinked my eyes a couple of times and all our barges was out there and I said, "What did you sink?" He said, "There it is." He turned the light around a little bit and there was some bubbles coming up where the air was coming out of the barge that he'd sunk. It was a coal barge that had broke loose and was floating down the river, and it was raining, and in the dark he didn't see it and ran into it. That's your unexpected.

Q: Well I think we are about at the end of the tape and it's been good to talk to you and we didn't identify you on the tape, will you give us your name?

T: My name is Tom Kenny. K-E-N-N-Y. All the Kenney's in England or Ireland, with the Church of England put the E in between the N and the Y to denote that they were Episcopalian and all the Kenny's who remained Catholic spelled their name K-E-N-N-Y. I don't quite belong because some place along in the shuffle, I ended up a Presbyterian, but I still spell our name the Catholic way K-E-N-N-Y.

Q: Well, thank you.

John "Dud" Chamberlain, April 16, 1957

Answer: I'm Dud Chamberlain, John W. Chamberlain. I come from Marietta and I'm 65 years old and been a newspapermen practically all my life.

Question: Can you hold now just a second?

A: This is a rather interesting point I have not discussed with you. I don't know whether we'll ever be able to get the real answer to it. When our first founders came to the river, there was a good salting among them of maritime seamen, shipbuilders from the New England seacoast. We were extremely conscious of the river. We came by the river and it was our sole contact with the outside world, we were thinking in terms of the river. These shipwrights, carpenters, started building boats right almost from the beginning.

It started very briskly because of the Indian Wars in 1795 and 1796, and we began building boats in earnest. They were all designed along the lines of a sea-going vessel, the deep-keeled boats, which were the kind these fellows knew how to build, and they were the only ones. Well, they were not adapted to the shallow draft of the rivers. And I have never found out just exactly that transition came or who was really first responsible for the design of the shallow draft steamboats, the boats that ultimately took over the river traffic. Now that was an important transition when we abandoned the deep sea-going type of boat. The fact of the matter is we pretty nearly had to wait until those old shipwrights died off, before the new type of shallow draft boat.

The Indians had been navigating these streams from the beginning; they did not have big boats. When we started to haul heavy freight, the old keelboats, the first boats that navigated the river, had keels but they did not draw a great deal of water, when we started to haul what you might call heavy tonnage, we developed a new type of craft, that was unique to these parts and a truly new development. Now that same type of boat may have been in existence in other parts of the world, I don't know. For our purposes here, for all practical purposes, it was a brand new development.

Q: It spoke of genius.

A: It spoke of genius. Because I haven't been able to find anything specifically about it, I don't think it was a lightning bolt. It was a transition. A series of adaptations, but it happened pretty rapidly. It was done in about ten or 15 years in there. They had gotten away from the old type of deep draft boat with a keel to what is still the present flat bottom boats. That is just a footnote. Sometime, some bright young man might be able to run that thing down and find out just who were the leading men in that transition. It was a rather natural one, I imagine. It's intrigued me. I've worried and asked about it, who first adapted the thing? I don't know the answer to it. Oh, I think we were talking about, the other day, the shipment of potatoes from our farm there. It did happen.

Q: Where was the farm?

John Knoepfle

A: Well, the farm that I was raised on was my mothers' fathers' place, five miles up the Muskingum from Marietta, just below Dam 2 in the Muskingum, that's Devols Dam. We had a big farm there that was divided about equally between bottom ground, which was for general farming, and then an upper flat above all floods, which was gravel, and later became that type of level, that type of soil in there became a rather famous truck gardening area.

When I was a lad, we were still raising on that upper acreage, practically all of it was devoted to sweet potatoes, primarily because of the ease of getting to the market. And that was the southern market for those sweet potatoes. Now my grandfather, who was operating the farm then as a younger man, had made a lot of trips down the river on flatboats, as his neighbors, father, cousins did every fall, taking their produce to the valley to the southern markets. He knew those markets. He went both before the Civil War and after, the war had restored that commerce.

Incidentally, I've called your attention to the fact that the very important correspondence between him and his wife has been preserved and is now available in the "Quarterly of the Ohio Historical Society." Their early produce that they took down was everything, from salt pork, apples, potatoes, apple butter and even butter itself. They like to I think a point was made I don't want to repeat this because it is in type, but I know they liked to take the pork and hold that pork until they got into the deep south from Memphis on down, because they could sell it there to the darkies. They would buy it without insisting on having the salt washed off.

Q: I didn't know that.

A: They wouldn't sell it before Louisville because the upper ports along there, why, the white people wanted that salt washed away and wanted the meat. When they get down south, why the darkies were satisfied to take anything as it came along.

Q: Would you dilate a little bit on the different temperaments of the men who went down? I know your grandfather was a rather cool man.

A: Well, yes, he was. Well, they were about the same temperament I'd say as they are today. Every one of my people, men, there were the serious hard working fellows that saved their money and there were the playboys. That brings up what to me was the most interesting human element out of that mass of letters that were exchanged between this boy and this girl, to whom he was engaged, and then later he was married. There is a great mass of those letters. They have been sorted out. And the jist of them appear in the state part of the articles. First apparent was the lack of detailed information that you would expect to find.

Then the preponderance of this information, which to me is the heart of the whole thing. Now those letters between that boy and that girl were just exactly the same letters that a traveling man would write home to his wife today. Just exactly the same thing. Now Grandfather did not tell her too much about his adventures on the river. His letters would read like this, "Here I am sitting here keeping the fire going because we don't want the potatoes and the apples to freeze. And all the boys are off gone to town to get drunk. Cousin so and so, and so and so, and I'm miserable and unhappy and all I am thinking about is my little girl back home. And if I could just be with her and I'll never go down this blankety-blank-blank river again."

And she'd come right back at him and say, "No! You are never going down that river again. I'll say you're never going down that river, again. Here I am frozen up here. The hired man has been gone for three days and the cows are down here with the epizootic E-P-I-Z-0-0-T-I-C. That's not epidemic, it is epizootic. Well, I don't know what to do." She didn't know whether it was time to cut the ice on the river or should we wait a little bit longer, and so on, and so on. It was that same theme over and over again.

Then he would say, he would describe some instance on the river, or she would have a little something, a piece of news about the farm. Generally, they were just personal notes between a man and his wife or a man and his girl. Well, all that was over long before I came into the picture.

When I was a little boy up on the farm, we were still selling our produce from those upper acres, not corn and wheat and things like that from the lower acreage, but potatoes from the garden land and selling it to the same dealers down the Mississippi at Memphis and Vicksburg and clear on to New Orleans, contacts that Grandfather had made 30 and 40 years before down there.

We had an itinerant cooper that came and lived with us for a few weeks every winter at which time he occupied our cooper shop, a special building. And he made up, out of our native lumber himself, he fashioned enough barrels to take care of our oncoming crop affairs to ship south. And the barrels were stored there in the cooper shop waiting for the crop to come on. Then we'd load the barrels and take them down to the Muskingum River, which was five miles above Marietta, to our own little landing there.

Now it was not a formal dock of any kind, but just a river bank with a little shelf on it that the packets could drop their gangplanks on. We would have six, eight, ten, maybe as low as two, maybe as high as fifteen or twenty barrels for one shipment to go to Vicksburg or to go to such and such a produce house in New Orleans. Then one of the Muskingum packets, in my time either the *Sonoma*, or the *Lorena* would pick it up and take it on to the wharfboat at Marietta where it would be transferred to an Ohio River boat to be again transferred at Cincinnati for a Mississippi boat.

That passed out of the picture when I was still a little fellow, but I remember it all very well, from the making of the barrels. I'd sit out in the shavings and watch old Bill Ack. A-C-K that was his name. That's all I know about him, an itinerant professional cooper, with his draw knife shaped those barrels and then the storage of the barrels, how they were dried, and then the shipments. But that was all gone after the coming of the railroads and the passing of the packets. And that whole business, that whole thing changed.

Q: I imagine barrel making must have been a major industry along the valley.

A: Well it was. The only cooperage that we made was for that one specific purpose. As we moved on into the truck gardening business, or fancy vegetables, why then and we still do have at Marietta, a fruit package and lumber company who make tomato baskets and cucumber crates and things like that, corn crates and so on. Although, then again tomatoes still have to be packed pretty carefully, but cucumbers, corn and melons and things like that, they go right into the beds of trucks. And don't need any packaging anymore.

There's one little thing that I was thinking of those packets coming downstream and stopping to pick up a single passenger at a fare of, oh it couldn't of been over 25 cents, maybe just 15 cents for that five miles to Marietta. But they would stop that boat to pick up one barrel, whether it was one, or two, or three, or four crates, to go to Marietta. As they came downstream, before they could make that landing, they had to turn around, turn clear around so that they were pointed upstream when they would drop that gangplank. He could not come down parallel, with his wheel to the current, and successfully make landing. He had a complete U-turn in the river and come up there to drop his gangplank on the shore. I just was reading a paperback book. The fellow had a good deal of fairly accurate Mississippi lore that he probably picked up out of Mark Twain or someplace. But he described in detail a couple landings there and I know darn well that he did not remember them, and that those boats would have to turn around before, always have to head upstream.

Q: I did not realize that myself, but come to think of it I've never seen them any other way.

A: Yes. Of course, these big modern tows, they do not do it. Fact of the matter is, they don't land, I mean, they don't come in. But the old packets, they always, now you take when we would have two, three, four or more packets tied up there at the wharfboat at Marietta, they would all be nosed upstream just like a herd of cattle or sheep. They would all be heading the same way.

When they would tie at that old wharfboat, the old *Hornbrook* and best wharfboat there at Marietta, they would be tied up two boats abreast right alongside each other out in the river. Then maybe another to the rear, maybe another one tied on to that back there, waiting their turns. But there would be two on the outer side of the wharfboat right alongside each other, parallel to each other. They would load the second boat across the deck of the inside boat. That stuff would be trucked clear across sometimes. That wharfboat, as *Hornbrook* as has probably told you, had a little deck on top, similar to a Texas on a packet boat, with living quarters where people would put up overnight. There would be comfortable quarters there for women to retire to while they were waiting for the next boat or something like that to come along.

Of course, the thing that impresses me now, is the very, very rapidly changing character of the river. You take in ten or fifteen years things are moving so fast that there is hardly any piece of equipment that is the same as it was ten or 15 years ago. There are two or three things, one particularly that they have never been able to improve on. Brownie, you'd be interested in this. It is the manila hemp on the hawser.

Q: Oh yes, indeed.

A: Some of the old timers will talk much more correctly about it than myself, but the long steel cables that we use now, but we don't use them to make the contacts. It's the hemp itself that is needed to tie that tow together and to pull it in. And it is the thing that they need for docking or going to a lock, going through a lock. Your steel is inflexible. You do not have that give. And one of these big tows would call up hundreds of dollars' worth of that hemp and it is awfully expensive anymore. It is nothing for one of these big tows to have several thousand dollars' worth of that hemp.

Q: They couldn't get it at all during the war. (WWII)

A: Nylon doesn't quite do it. They are trying to. One of the big towing companies I know was experimenting with one of the cordage outfits with having them weave a hawser with a special identification on it in an effort to cut their costs, to keep other boats from stealing it. That is still the same as it has been for many years. They have not been able to improve on it. Then these little winches, buckles, turnbuckles, which they use for the tightening the tow together that hasn't been improved on. There are a number of improvements in the buckle, but not great. The principle is just the same as it's always been. But otherwise, everything is gone.

Everything that was there 20 years ago, it's superseded now and 20 years from now it will be superseded again. I'm thinking particularly of this new development of Ormet Corporation, that big aluminum plant that's just going in fifty miles up from Marietta now, just below Clarington in Monroe County. One of the biggest aluminum plants in the world. They bring their crude bauxite, comes in from South America, Guiana or one of those countries down there, comes across the gulf and up the Mississippi to roughly around Vicksburg, someplace up there. They had built a great dock installation there. That bauxite is taken ashore and goes through its first processing. It is turned into what they call alumina. It is brought by boat again from there clear on up the Mississippi then on up the Ohio to this plant.

Q: Well, let's come back up on the Muskingum.

A: All right.

Q: How about describing as accurately as you can some of those Muskingum packets?

A: Well, the only two that I know about personally were the *Lorena* and the *Sonoma*. The *Sonoma* was a comparatively small boat, perhaps 120 feet long maybe. It was a packet though with a, it did not have a Texas, the pilothouse

John Knoepfle

was the only thing on the third deck. Nothing like the big gorgeous Mississippi River packets, but it did have staterooms. It made a daily round trip originating in Beverly, 20 miles up the Muskingum, and came down to Marietta every day and turned around there at Marietta and returned, every 24 hours.

The *Lorena* made a round trip out of Zanesville, from Zanesville to Pittsburgh, Zanesville down the Muskingum to Marietta then up to Pittsburgh and back once a week. And I've heard that at one time, I did not experience this myself, but I don't doubt for a second that it is true, the fare of that round trip from Zanesville to Pittsburgh to Zanesville, including your berth and your gorgeous meals and whatever entertainment there was on the boat, and usually there was some music of some kind or other, was $7.00. Seven days for $7.00 and that included everything.

The boat that I was most familiar with was the little *Sonoma* because we used it quite a little bit. Our roads were so poor that we still used it to go to Marietta occasionally, not too often as a passenger ride. But if I should by any chance be in town and want to get home and I knew she would be leaving at two o'clock in the afternoon, why I could ride up on the boat that five miles. But they hauled a lot of, all that truck produce went out of there by boat, everything that was shipped. It was picked up and every big farm had its own landing for a docking place all the way along the river.

I don't think the *Sonoma* had set any table, served any meals, except for the crew, because that passage was too brief. Of course, I don't want to get to talking about the meals on the big boats, that is another story and it's a really gorgeous story in itself. But the *Sonoma* had its little stateroom up there on part of the deck, the salon deck.

About 1900 when I was eight years old and my baby sister was four, my mother and some other lady from Marietta took us to Pittsburgh. And I think we made a round trip from Marietta to Pittsburgh and back on one of the big Ohio boats. I think it was the *City of Pittsburgh*, but I'm not sure. I was pretty small. But those were glorious things. I had a number of trips as a boy on some of those big Ohio River boats, both down and up. But they all passed out, the passenger traffic was reduced by the time I was old enough to really know much about it. The passenger traffic was reduced to local traffic. When I first started to work on newspapers as a cub reporter around 1910, I had a daily stop every day. One of our must stops was down at the wharfboat there at Marietta.

Q: What paper were you connected with then?

A: In Marietta? I started on the old "Journal," which is long departed. We had three afternoon dailies in competition with each other when I started working. And none of them made any money. All of them starved to death. Pretty pathetic expressions of journalism. But the river was still then a great, very vital factor in our life. I know my father as a businessman in Marietta, based his business, the Crescent-Mathye Company, which is still in business.

Q: How do you spell that name?

A: C-R-E-S-C-E-N-T. That was the general supplies of one kind or another, building supplies, every material of one kind, we shipped an awful lot by boat. Got an awful lot by boat. It was still a very important factor in our lives, but it was fading out by the time I came on into the picture. One thing that I noticed as a little important note on it, we had a newspaper in Marietta very early in 1801. And I have quite a number of those papers. McCoy's has a splendid file of the Marietta papers. A thing that interested me was these New Englanders came out and they knew what they were doing. They were not illiterate pioneers in the more generally accepted sense. They were settlers and Marietta was from the beginning not a pioneer town. It was a settlement that was picked up bodily from New England and brought on and deposited there. They turned their back on the civilization of the east and they knew why they were doing it. And it was a brave new life and all that.

But as late as 1810, along in the teens there, after they had been out into this country for 25 years, those little weekly papers were still carrying columns on columns of maritime news. To me as a newspaperman, it is fascinating. Here was the gossip of Lisbon and the gossip of Liverpool and the gossip of Rio. Captain so and so has come in and he saw captain so and so. So and so, and such and such a ship is going to such and such a point, that's our mail. And these people well, it was a fact that while these fellows had turned their backs said good-bye forever to the seaboard and all that the seaboard stood for, this smart editor who knew what they were interested in, he would pick up copies of the eastern papers and copy that stuff, set it by hand, just column after column of it because they had relatives and they were a long ways from home with bear tracks all around them. But that was all gone by 1820 or 1825. That news just drifted out of the papers.

We had a new generation coming on who had no roots back in there, and who had turned to the rivers completely. Well, that is a, you pretty near have to get into those early documents to realize our dependence at that time on the river. They were everything, just everything to us. And I want to make this point right now, my hobby for quite a number of years along with a lot of other people now has been the Civil War and particularly the role played by our section of the country, especially Ohio's role in the Civil War. Then more immediately, the role of my own little corner down there, and the position of the rivers in the Civil War.

The war would never, it would not have been the same anyway if the Mississippi River hadn't run north and south. If the Mississippi had been east and west, it would have been another story and I don't have any doubt at all in my mind but that we would have been two nations here. It wasn't so much the generation that fought the war as it was their fathers and grandfathers that had been dependent upon that Mississippi. That had been their lifeline. They had been really fairly conscious of the empire that they were chopping out here and building, they were also aware of the fact that that empire was dependent upon

John Knoepfle

that river. They were not going to see the mouth of that river, the lower end of that Mississippi River, in the hands of an alien, unsympathetic government.

Q: That's right.

A: And when our Ohio boys finally took their foot in hand and we went to war, took Vicksburg and we opened up the river. And henceforth, it was from one to the next to the sea. The war should have ended right there at Vicksburg when we opened up the Mississippi. Of course, those down south did not have sense enough to see it and they had to take two years more of bad ripping. That was not the sole factor, but when I think of this country from 1800 on up to 1850, a lot of those people, what they were thinking about, what they talked about, what was built into their blood and bone of those boys and their fathers and their grandfathers, they were thoroughly conscious of that river.

Q: Speaking of that, you had an anecdote about Sherman's brother. Do you want to tell that?

A: Oh yes. That's a nice little story. That was John Sherman. By the time they broke up down at Lancaster, as it was broken up, they were a big family of those youngsters. But the father, Charles Sherman, was one of the first members of the Ohio Supreme Court, and incidentally, we get pretty confused about that Sherman family. They had seven generations of New England judges back of those boys. But he died, Charles Sherman died a comparatively young man and left this big family. They, as was the custom in those days, they were split. William Tecumseh became the foster son, not the adopted son, but the foster son of the great Thomas Ewing there at Lancaster, and he was raised by Thomas Ewing and married one of Ewing's daughters.

But his younger brother John, the great Senator Sherman and Secretary of the Treasurer and the author of the great phrase, which is still true, "The way to resume is to resume." That was the special payment. He went up to some relatives or friends in Mansfield, I think, and was raised up there. His first job was working as a boy on these Muskingum dams. And because of his unusual ability and he had it, John Sherman was a great man, he lived somewhat in the eclipse of his more spectacular brother, but he was a great man in his own right. And contributed a great deal to William Tecumseh's success, too.

He rose very rapidly. He had a supervisorship, sort of a foremanship. He worked at both Lowell and at McConnelsville. And he got fired from the job back there for political activities before he could vote even. But before he got fired, and this is the story I think that you want, here he was, a vigorous, smart, shrewd youngster. He was on the make at 19, 20 years old. And he heard about an acute salt shortage at Cincinnati just at the height of the meat packing season down there. So, he put two and two together and a few $100 he saved, could wrestle up; he got himself a flatboat, a couple of fellows to help him and a load of salt from Muskingum salt mines. He headed for Cincinnati.

He hit that bad rock ripple, those rapids, shoal there at Luke Chute, and hung his boat up. No water, could not get it off. He was held up there with his couple of helpers, and his load of salt for several vital days. He got the boat off, on down the river to Marietta, on down to Cincinnati, and by the time he got to Cincinnati the shortage was over. The salt was a drug on the market, and he had a total loss or more on his investment. I've often thought that that was the first and the last speculative enterprise that John Sherman ever indulged himself in. He lived to be an old man, a great, fine man.

I wish I could, my own experience actually on the river was confined to my own little activities and my own little boats and the news and so on. I had very vivid experiences there in Marietta at the time of the 1913 flood. I will never, I have written this, we'll never again have that kind of a disaster at Marietta, or probably in any of the other river towns. That's not so much due to flood control as it is to communication. The trouble in 1913, we were completely isolated. We were helpless. They could not get supplies in to us really. Of course, we had no telephone lines, and had no railroads, and no radio. We were just, when that water went down, we were in miserable shape. Railroads were gone and we were just sitting there in the mud and there was one great section of Marietta apart on the other side of the Muskingum River, the little Harmar division over there . . .

Q: It's on the south side.

A: Well, the west side. The water mains had broken, and they had no water to clean themselves up with. Our wells, what wells existed, they were all contaminated except those on the high ground back up on the hill. They used those for drinking purposes, cooking purposes, but there was no water to wash your places out with, or anything else. We were, oh that was a pitiful condition.

Q: You saw the bridges go out.

A: I saw them go. They went the way the thing happened so darn fast. I was working on this little newspaper located on the 200 block on 2nd Street there. Our shop and plant was in a big four story brick building, but we occupied one-half of the ground floor, which sat about three or three and a half feet above the sidewalk. We had our paper storage in the basement. Our little offices and shop were on that one street floor. Now we had a flood in 1913 in January of that year. And a pretty mean little flood. The water had been up on the streets and in the basement there. I had my canoe down already. This Wednesday in the last week of March in 1913, we had no flood warning and we had a big story that day on the flood at Dayton, which was a major thing. And rumors of the flood here in Columbus. I know when I got down to work, I was still living on the farm and came down on the streetcar in the morning, got there at six o'clock. We called up the National Guard to go over and help Dayton. This was Wednesday. The Guards' headquarters were on the top floor of the building where our shop was fortunately for us as it turned out. They called the boys out the night before and they were all there in uniform waiting to get a train out of town to came over to Dayton. They never got out of town, thank God, they didn't! They couldn't get out.

John Knoepfle

But we were not worried at all. We put our paper out that afternoon at half-past two or three o'clock in the afternoon with no real hint of any flood for Marietta. I know after we had gotten the paper out, and were all through, I was very conscious of my girl down in Parkersburg, West Virginia. I was a little bit afraid that I might be cut off from communication from her, so I took the personal precaution of calling up forecaster Howe of the U.S. Weather Bureau at Parkersburg, who at that time was our old authority on river stages. He knew more about them than I think any man has since. He was an older man, very conservative and accurate.

I called him about three o'clock that Wednesday afternoon. I asked him about the river. Not with any thought about my end, except that possibly the streetcar line could be cut off. I wouldn't get to see my girl for a day or so. Howe said, "Mr. Chamberlain," I'll never forget what he said, it became quite important later on, "You are going to get at least 45 feet." I said, my God! That's about seven or eight feet above our flood stage. "Yes," he said, "I don't know how much more. You are going to get that at least and you are going to get it immediately." I said, what do you mean? "That's right. And I can't tell you how much more, Mr. Chamberlain." Well, I thanked him and hung up.

I said, after all, that's just Howe that made that statement. He was pretty much our god, so I took a page of our bulletin paper, wrote out the forecast of Howe's promise to us of 45 feet, on the typewriter. Jumped on the old company bicycle, rode up to the corner where we used to post those bulletins and stuck it up. Loafers came over, looked at it, laughed their heads off, until the end of the time, they kept quoting the river would only get 45 feet. Well, that is the year we got 61 or 62. Howe didn't say that. I always think of it. I decided I'd better get down to see my girl anyway.

So I went up to see her, had a new carload of paper, a brand new carload of paper in our basement down there, and that meant life or death of that little paper. So we decided maybe we better take care of it. Before I left we found a vacant room on the top floor of a building next door across the alley with a freight elevator. When I left the boys, they were starting to roll that paper out.

Well, I got back up at 11:30 that night, there was water in the gutters and the basement was half full of water. Leonard Whiting, a reporter on the paper had decided to spend the night there at the paper with me. I often spent the night there. I come back up from Parkersburg and I would sleep there on the exchange table. Unfortunately, Leonard lived over in Williamstown. My best man wanted an excuse for a night out so he said he would stay with us too, just in case something should come up that we would need to tear down those linotype machines in the morning. They were there, those two fellows, when I got there at 11:30.

Our basement was half-full of water and they had a yardstick on a pole through a trapdoor down onto the basement. They were just breathlessly taking that stage. That water was coming a foot an hour. It kept coming a foot an hour.

It just kept right on coming. We walked around at one o'clock in the morning, we walked around Front Street that is the principal business street there, and a few of the merchants were trying to get their stuff out. But most of them still weren't aware that there was a flood in sight. The big trouble with us we're so far away from the headwaters of water down there, we always had two or three days warning. And this time we just didn't get it.

We just got caught, literally just caught. And then we started at one o'clock to move out. We decided we were going to have to move our whole shop out. We called what members of the staff we could get to help us move. I know a friend of mine that lived just two blocks away, put on his high top boots and by the time he got down he got water over the top of his boots getting into that place. At ten o'clock in the morning, we had everything out with the help of those militia boys. We saved everything, but we were waist deep in there just floundering around in that cold water.

I still had my canoe and the boss told me, says, "Well, we can't do anything more. We've done everything we could. Do you think you can find some whiskey?" I said, "I can find it if there's any anyplace." Well, I got in the canoe and went to the one bar that was still open. Now we closed them just the minute there's any further water at all. But they were closed at rule of the operators in those days. And this one fellow was still open. He had about six inches of water on his floor. That was on Fulton Street. I went up through the old train shed in the canoe, tied up to the back door of his saloon, waded in and got a couple quarts of whiskey. I still swear that guy cut that whiskey, worst I ever drank in all my life. We took that down, drank it. Of course, we'd been up all night, wandering around in that cold water. It never fazed us. Just like water off a duck's back.

Then I went up to a house up on the campus to get cleaned up and maybe get a little rest. I hadn't any more than gotten up there than, that was noon on Thursday, and there came emergency call from some merchants on Front Street that they wanted help to move from their second to their third floors. This was Thursday noon. So a few of us went down and started to move a jewelry store and a bookstore. Just bushels of miscellaneous items that had been scooped up from the first floor and dumped onto the second, just like that. We grabbed them, carried them on up to the third.

Some fellow that was working with us lived uptown and the telephones were still in. His wife called him and a big old abandoned factory building on the upper edges of Marietta had cut loose, was coming down the Muskingum. We knew what that meant. We dropped everything and ran up to the roof. On the top of the third floor of a brick building right across from the Chamber of Commerce, across from the Post Office in that main block there, I ran out the parapet in front and there it came down the, this big plant down the, floating the Ohio like a steamboat, right down the middle of the Muskingum.

John Knoepfle

It hit the Putnam Street bridge. Went through it like going through pasteboard, picked up the central span, carried it a hundred yards downstream, dropped it down on the dam. All the debris that was back of that rushed through there and piled up against the big railroad bridge below. The bridge had been weighted down. It was a better bridge, weighted down with a trainload of coal and gravel cars. It held for perhaps not more than a minute or minute and a half, but to us looking down on the top of it, it seemed years when that Muskingum River dumped right up at the center of it. At the time that bridge went out in the middle of that Muskingum River, I'll bet it was two feet high. When that railroad bridge went the whole thing went, just like that. The whole stretch of it just laid down. I said, "Well, that is the end of it. No point in going ahead and doing any further work or anything else, we were lost anyway." So we just sat there in that bright sunlight and watched that Muskingum go out. She was something to see. She really was something to see. We had an interesting little aftermath on it. I have not given you the river stuff particularly.

Q: That's all right. This is good.

A: Just the more sinister aspects of the river. There is one little sideline on that it meant a great deal to me. We had two Marconi wireless sets for experimental purposes in the physics lab at the college. I was out of school, of course by that time, but I messed around with it some. They had a range of just a few miles in Morse code, that's all just beginning to play with it. Near the crest, there was a relief boat that came down from Pittsburgh with medical supplies and blankets on it. We had things under reasonably good control. We didn't want the boat to come into Marietta, because of the waves from the paddlewheel would break windows. And we also altruistically, figured that there were people down the river that needed help really more than we did right then.

So I've heard that they communicated with that boat through this little Morse outfit while it was still upstream, although I'm not real sure about that. I wasn't in on it. But anyway we told them to keep on going. We didn't want them to try to get into Marietta. As it passed under that big Ohio River bridge at Marietta, I can testify to all of this, some thoughtful person tossed a roll of Pittsburgh newspapers up on that bridge. They were close enough that they could make that toss. Anyway, the roll of papers landed up there. They had refugees that were living up on that bridge and somehow I got ahold of that roll of newspapers. I don't know how I heard about it, but I did, and I got them, and that was the first communication from out of town that Marietta had for days.

It had some real news. Jim Cox had declared a moratorium on the state of Ohio for the emergency. Comforting news for everybody that had a note coming due downtown. And there was an account of Andrew Carnegie's funeral, from which I judged that he must be dead. A couple of other things that were of major news importance to us. So I got down to our plant on the next floor where we had our little stuff we had stored, and I got some of our old "Journal Bulletin" paper. I rewrote that front page, "Special to the Journal." I posted those bulletins at our landing places around town. And I really scooped the town. I didn't say anything to the boss about it or anybody. I didn't tell anybody for weeks after it was over where I got that news. But the Journal really had a scoop!

Q: I'll be.

A: Jim Cox's moratorium and the death of Andrew Carnegie. It's almost impossible to put yourself back to that period of when you could be so completely isolated. Now we were not only isolated from news, but we were isolated. We couldn't get any supplies. The Red Cross couldn't, oh they did get in ultimately over the hills and they helped a lot with blankets and guns and other things. But at first, we were just helpless, that's all. I told that story to a less great speed to which that water came. We were just 24 hours, it was almost like a flash flood. And it really caught us. We were still, all through my boyhood, we were still rafting logs down the two rivers, both of them, the Ohio and the Muskingum for processing and woodworking plants in Marietta.

Q: Oh, is that so?

A: Yes. We had two woodworking plants, one major sawmill right in downtown Marietta just two blocks out of the business district, on the Muskingum where often in my boyhood there were log rafts in the Muskingum there, that had been brought down the Muskingum to be cut up.

Q: I didn't know that.

A: Yes. Then we had a lot of West Virginia wood that was processed in Marietta that came clear around by the Monongahela and down the Ohio and was taken out of western Pennsylvania and of the timberland in West Virginia. It came down that whole way around in there. In fact, I think it was largely the basis of the founding of what was one of our major industries for years, the Marietta Chair Factory that manufactured cheap chairs.

Q: The Marietta Chair Factory?

A: Yes. They are now using the big factory buildings, they have been converted into a dormitory at Marietta College.

Q: Is that so?

A: And quite successfully.

Q: Oh, yes. I think I saw those last fall. I was up through there.

A: The last time you were down there, did you see the monument beside the library building? It's a rather large stone monument with a battered bronze plaque on the front of it, a historical plaque. It's of no particular importance. Always to me that stone will be the marker of the high water mark of the 1913 flood. The flood just lapped the base of that stone, covered the front of that campus there.

Q: Well, that was high. I remember that now.

A: Yes. This story is second hand. It's not from my own personal experience, but the fact that I didn't know about it myself until comparatively a few years ago, I think it should be saved. And it is true. I have confirmed it with a number

John Knoepfle

of the older pilots. That is the story of what they call dog bark navigation. When a man in the old days would be lost in the fog or impenetrable black night, when he couldn't determine his position as to the channel on the river, he would know, of course, where he was on the river so far as miles go. But whether he was fifteen or twenty feet to the port or starboard of the channel meant an awful lot of difference to him.

One of the methods of finding that location was by a method that antedated radar and was exactly the same principle. Still they believe that sending out electrical impulses and waiting for the echo and timing the time it took for the echo to come back. He would stop his wheel and wait for a complete silence and then he would honk! Honk! Once or twice on his whistle. Well, he would know approximately where he was on the river and he would know what hill was off to either port or starboard and approximately how far it was. And he would just listen, timing by his ear for the return echo from that hill and he could tell within a comparatively few feet, which side of the channel he might be on. It gets its name from the bark of the whistle. Now just below Marietta the hills come into the river there on both sides and some of the older pilots still will test their ears and their whistles against the echoes of those hills.

Q: Is that so?

A: There was another adaptation of the same thing, which was even more subtle in a way. If he didn't have any hills to get an echo from, he would stop his boat and he would wait until there was complete stillness in the middle of this fog at night. Then he would rotate his big paddlewheel, not a complete turn, but he would turn it so that the paddle would hit, two or three different paddles, would hit and send waves to the shore. Then he would wait for the return of those waves to come back and he would time the round trip and that would give him a fix on his relationship to the channel.

Coming down on the *Snyder* one of the most colorful things in connection with that whole memorable trip, that was when we brought the *W. P. Snyder* down from Pittsburgh to make it a permanent part of the river museum in Marietta. It was one of the last of the old paddlewheel steamboats, and the gala celebration we had two years ago. Of course, the highlight of the trip were the farewell greetings from all the river craft during that. They all knew the *Snyder* was going to the graveyard and they said good-bye to her and would honk back and everybody would stand up and wave in that traditional river salute. We would cry and have a grand time. I know Fred Way said we sent more steam out that whistle than we did the pistons on that trip the whole way down.

Q: That's right.

A: They crossed at Gridding and went on the Monongahela up there and see, we brought her down the last 30 or 40 miles of the Monongahela and it was just constant with boats everywhere. But at one of the big chemical plants just above New Martinsville, well the name slips my mind, it's on the West Virginia side.

One of the men in an executive position with that plant had a good deal of river background and through Fred he was able to get ahold of one of the old steamboat whistles that had been abandoned and they put it on that plant.

Q: They did?

A: And on the Ohio side, immediately opposite, there is that big cliff that comes down there at Powhatan Point. When we came down, they started to blow that whistle over at the plant and we had a time. The echoes from that cliff for three miles down that river, the air was just full of the blast from the plant and from our boat and the echoes all from that stone cliff on the Ohio side. The old pilot of a boat, from which that whistle was taken, was with us. He sat out there with some tears, and heard his old whistle for the last time. Those things are moving, you know.

And it would get a new skin that was one thing that all of us would remember about the trip, and these other boats saying good-bye to the *Snyder*. That was one of the many, many nice things we had on that trip. We had a loud speaker system. Often, one of the old river men would get on the speaker and say, now we are just about to meet such and such a boat. You'll see such and such characteristics of this boat. And she has got a load of coal, has ten flats or 15 flats and so on coming up, and it is such and such a packet boat and such and such a line. Then at different times, somebody would get on and talk about various historical passages along the river. Then some old river man would come on and talk about a wreck that happened at this point or somebody would describe some feature of the terrain, that it was a dangerous point or this or that or something else in connection with it. Oh, I'm just sorry that I haven't any more of the material that you really want.

Q: Well, you mentioned about paying the roustabouts. I wonder if you might repeat that.

A: I have not got enough on that, I have a vivid memory of them toting bales. I think of it as they would have sugar, maybe from the south they would be unloading at Marietta or they would be picking up sacks of wheat. At the wharfboat there would be a great pile of sacked grain wheat that was going someplace or maybe some other grain. It would be a 100 or a 150 of those 200 pound sacks and there would be six, or eight, or ten, roustabouts, usually colored boys from the deep south, and the mate. And they would just run, not so much chain, they would trot back and forth across the gangplank. And sometimes, they would chant, they would sing. But those songs never got themselves organized with me. They were spontaneous and just work songs and words largely. I can't help you any with those. Maybe if you get somebody that's had a more spontaneous life than I had, they might have picked up some of those lyrics. But I just don't have them myself.

I do know that twenty years ago when I took my first trip on one of these modern towboats, all through my boyhood when a fellow got in trouble at home and had to leave town overnight, one of the first things he thought of

John Knoepfle

was getting a job on a towboat, a job as a deckhand and taking off. In fact, some of my older friends visit, and I'll tell you a story about that in a minute, but that was one of the escape passages. It was like catching a ride on a freight. You get a job on a towboat and go off down the river and get out of trouble.

In 1930, the late 30s, when I came back to the river again and took a rather long trip on one of the big tows, I was deeply impressed with the change that had come over the roustabouts. There were not any roustabouts. Those young deckhands were very carefully selected and lord, they might remind you, oh I know one of the trips on the boat, see those clean-cut fine looking kids string out along those, for locking at night, they would come out there in their yellow jackets and go to their position. It is just like a basketball team. They look just like a team. There wasn't anything loose about the organization.

We had a guy on that one trip in 1939 down the river that was taken with acute appendicitis and that was the Union Barge Line trip. Just a youngster. Well, they flew a plane down and picked him off that boat and took him back up to Pittsburgh. Then while I was on the boat, until I got off, the crew, that is the officer's table, the officer's mess, were still debating among themselves what lad they were going to get to replace that kid. They had a rating list of likely looking guys and there was one youngster that seemed due to get the job because primarily he could play guitar. (laughs) That's changed altogether, the personnel of those boats, just altogether. Of course, the passing of the coal handlers made the changing of the nature of the freight. We don't load and unload at the different ports the way they used to. And there is no coal handling anymore. Used to be wood handling.

I know there is one story won't go in type, although I think I have, got it in type. A famous old steamboat race on the river. This may be fairly new. There was a great race and they both had a whole lot more steam pressure than they had any right to. This conversation was supposed to have taken place over the loud speaker system between the chief engineer and the pilot. He calls down, "How's your pressure holding up? He says, "I still got her up there, sir. She's right up on the safety valve. I'm holding it." The Pilot says, "How's your fuel holding out?" "I ain't got no more. Went through the last cord of fuel there ten miles back." "Well, how about that cargo?" "We got that rack of bacon back there. We are through up to the last row of that bacon right now."

Q: So Captain Savage, he said I think, on the *Island Queen* that he threw a bunch of dead hogs in the middle furnace.

A: I wouldn't be surprised. Oh, they do it. That's why they blow the things up, you know, too. Well, that day has passed, too. They wreck them just the same. Even these new diesels, they get themselves in trouble. We had one, it might have been a big wreck just a comparatively few years ago. Coming up around that big bend just across from Parkersburg, had a big load of steel on, and there was a barge buckled right there in that bend and went down with a whole load of steel right in the channel. That was just across from Parkersburg just a couple years ago. It was a wonder they didn't tear that whole tow to pieces.

They got it cut loose though and saved it. What caused that is the same thing that would cause an old wooden flat car, gondola, to collapse on the curve in the railroads in the old days. And they sandwiched them in, and they had a defective barge in there, loaded with 50 tons of steel or a 100 tons of steel. Coming around that curve, because there was just enough little extra pressure on that barge as tightly as it was integrated in there, it gave way. You know, they now have a new type of barge coming on into the picture now, what they call integrated barges that they tie in together. You keep in touch with me because I possibly may think of something else you should have.

Q: All right.

A: Although I'm not too good of sorts. I am sorry but . . .

Q: Well, supposing I leave you my home address.

A: When I started, I've been writing this weekly column for the "Columbus Citizen," the editorial page column, for almost twenty years now. It's very personal and it covers everything. Politics, local history, and valley stories of one kind or another. Meantime, for quite a while I worked fulltime for the "Citizen" as a feature man and have done some political correspondence and this and that, but I am practically retired now and am not doing very much of anything except this one weekly column.

I lived in Marietta all my life in spite of the fact that I worked fulltime for the "Citizen" here for a while. I ran that column. What other work I did, I maintained residence there in Marietta. I'm here with this attack of tuberculosis. It showed up seven months ago, and I've been in this hospital seven months. I expect to be here a few months more, and then I'll go back to Marietta.

Q: You went to Marietta College?

A: Yes, and Columbia, first year of its existence. My eldest son is news editor of the "Citizen," not through any connection of mine. He came in round about through one of the other Scripps papers. My daughter is a reasonably successful novelist. She has had two novels published in the last two years and has another that will probably be on the fall list, with Bobbs Merrill, although that is not determined yet. And a third child, second son, is with Westinghouse here in Columbus. I had a paper of my own in Marietta for a number of years, which I edited and published quite successfully until we sold it into consolidation about 30 years ago.

Q: Well, fine. I think that will give us that information. Thank you for letting us talk to you.

A: You are entirely welcome.

J. Harvey Coomer, September 17, 1958, Louisville, Kentucky

Question: Mr. Coomer is an old-time mate and Captain on steamboat packets. I know that you were on the Cumberland River, Mr. Coomer, and that you did some logging in your earlier days. Can you tell us about that?

Answer: Burnside, Kentucky is the head navigation of the Cumberland River and the people, their mode of life was cutting timbers, ties and logs thrown into a dry creek, and then when the spring and fall rains came, that washed into the Cumberland River. They floated into Burnside where the companies had booms. Regardless of the time of day or the condition of the weather, people were called out to work on the booms to get these logs, put them in behind the staves so they would not go on down the river. If they did not have the lumber and the staves, there wasn't any work for the people. We'd walk those booms at night with the river rising, the Cumberland River rises a lot of times six and eight feet and more because when that tremendous rainfall comes into the mountain, it all comes into the river at once.

At one time Burnside was called Point Isabel, there where the South Fork River and the Cumberland meet. General Burnside had his headquarters there. They changed the name from Point Isabel to Burnside. In this particular fort where the Cumberland and South Fork met, the river was tremendous deep. The old legend is that there was no bottom. In summertime these staves had to be taken out of the banks of the river. When the river would fall these logs, and staves and ties on the river bank had to be put into box cars and barges, and ferried into the railroad tracks to be loaded onto boxcars. At Burnside there were maybe 50 or 60 carloads of staves, lumber and ties, chicken and eggs.

Chickens and eggs came into Burnside by riverboat. They were shallow draft 10, 12 inches draft. Empty of course when you load them down. You could load them down to four or five feet depth. By riverboat out of Burkesville and Celina, Tennessee out on up Cumberland River to Burnside, which was a shipping point. There was 40 counties back in there that had to be supplied with soil, fertilizer, and commodities, similar to that. They had to put it in, in season just only when the river was up, you see.

Q: Couldn't run in low water up there?

A: In the summertime, the river was real low, it was just more of a branch, which we had small gasoline boats and real small shallow draft barges. We'd load a lot of groceries, canned goods and stuff, and haul down the river in the summertime in that. A lot of times we would have to drag over the shoals by laying a 1,200 foot hawser and tying around two windlasses. We drug those over the barge and up.

Q: Was that a power windlass or did you do it by hand?

A: No, we did it mostly by hand on the gasoline boats, but on the steamboats we had the regular steam windlass.

Q: I'll bet that turning that hand capstan must have been backbreaking work.

A: There have been two or three people that I know of killed by the makeshift windlass. That is the type that you go out and cut a log, you see, and anchor it down and bolt some timbers to it, and you don't have dogs on it or anything to keep it from backfiring if something gives a sudden jerk. Usually they put those on barges to just drag a couple of barges over a shoal or something.

Q: A line like that gets caught.

A: Yes, it tightens it up automatically, well, if that pole gets slinging why . . .

Q: Is that so? Well, anyway, let me ask you two questions about the logs. How were they loaded into the car?

A: They weren't loaded into cars, the logs themselves, it was the staves and ties that was loaded into cars. Logs were rolled into the river when the river went down, they had conveyors, which came down into the water. You sluiced the logs up where a dog would catch it, and then they would go up into the sawmill. And this particular sawmill that cut the big timber was a double saw, a saw was going and coming with a carriage, which would cut three hundred logs a day. Now some of those logs floated 52 inches out of the water.

Q: Boy.

A: Now that was real timber. That was mostly yellow poplar, white pine, and red oak. They were brought up, dried and put out in the yard to be put in the boxcars and then shipped into Cincinnati, Ohio or something like that.

Q: Was that a particular railroad line up there?

A: Yes. It was Southern Railroad. It was the only railroad that went down through there. It had to supply these counties I am speaking of. This freight had to come out of Cincinnati and Louisville, dry goods, shoes, see people had to buy themselves oil. Summertime around these, we handled lots of oil, just old lamp oil — you needed it to make light with — and what you handled then, wire fencing and your fertilizer. Something, it was an absolute necessity down in that country, because nothing would grow unless a tremendous amount of fertilizer was used on that land. And they raised a tremendous lot of corn.

Now the boats ran mostly from Burnside to Nashville, Tennessee. Now going down as far as Celina, our cargo would consist of general groceries, hardware, plows, plowshares and raftsmen's rope, and dogs, and things they used to wrap logs with. And then we would start to pick up corn and stock around Celina and take it on into Nashville, Tennessee. Maybe we would pull into Nashville, Tennessee with a 1,000 coops of chickens, 700 or 800 cases of eggs, and 300 head of hogs, and maybe 400 or 500 head of cattle. And then we would discharge that. Then at Nashville we would load the boat up again with just general commodities, fertilizer, salt, sugar, groceries, clothing, dry goods, oil, fencing, and go back up the river.

Q: Now we have not identified any of these boats yet. You might do that.

A: The boats were *Burkesville, Rowena, Celina, City of Burnside, Patrol* and the *Crescent.* That's the end of the list of boats that was on the Cumberland

John Knoepfle

River between Burnside and Nashville, Tennessee.

Q: Now about what year was that you began on these boats?

A: Well, my father was a steamboat captain and he was a town marshal in the summertime. He seen the sidewalks were cleaned and repaired — they used wooden sidewalks — and the stock run clear, and of course, the roads were just mud roads. And there would be just mud in the roads where it had rock hauled in and broke up with small hammers. He saw that the kids would be sitting around doing nothing, and he would just dictate, he just went out and said, "Come on here, boys. We got some work to do." And he took out there and made the roads without paying them.

Including me and my other brothers. He wouldn't even let us alone. Some of them were sitting around whittling and twiddling at girls, nothing to that. The town had to be kept up and he was the town marshal. Finally, the steamboats went out of existence through good roads being built in that country back through there. It was just impossible to get anything through the country without going down on the steamboats, and put off on the landings, and then maybe hauled 10 or 15 miles back away from the river, to those groceries and settlements back in there.

Q: I'll just make some notes and take it down as we go. I think at this point we ought to have a few vital statistics on yourself so that we can set the time.

A: Well, I was born in 1894, officially, but actually I think I was born in 1892, which would make me about 66 years old the day, this last July, the 28th was my birthday. And officially, according to the doctor's records here, I am 63 years old. I started on the steamboats as a night watchman. There was nothing to do. My father would not let me do it. But I insisted on doing it. If I could not get hired on the boat, I would just sneak aboard and when the boat would pull away from the landing, why there I would be. He had to put up with me. So finally, he just said to me to quit school and go to night watchman. Of course, the night watchman is the most important officer, unlike the officer aboard, because you have got the fire condition to look after.

You are supposed to keep good fire, and heat in your pilothouse fire, and your engine room fire. Your hull is the main thing, you have got to watch the water because these boats are made out of light material, mostly pin oak, quarter-sawed and everything is made light, so it doesn't draw so much water. So you have got to watch your hull. If you didn't have a good mate that knew how to load and unload a boat right, why you'll spring leaks in it, and you are just liable to go to the bottom. Now the cargo has to be placed where it can be got at and discharged without straining the boat whatsoever. So in getting a good night watchman, it is very important, because you have got to go through that hull, at least every half hour and in fact the business, you have constantly got to keep looking in that hold.

These wooden hull boats just spring leaks awfully easy. So that was a very important job, and then his job was filling about 40 lanterns every evening when we got up out of bed, why the first thing to do was to clean his lanterns up good, fill them with oil, and he assists the mate. Now when you pull into a landing, where there was maybe 2,000 or 3,000 sacks of corn to be loaded, why the watchman took the hill and the mates stayed on the boat. He would keep the rousters stirred up at the top of the hill and loaded up so they could take a load of corn back down to the boat, you see. And they had to look at the landings. Then when they run into a landing where there was stock, maybe there was 40 or 50 head of cattle out there for a mile and a half. The mate stayed on the boat and the night watchman if this happened at night, the night watchman had to take the rousters out there with the necessary lanterns and equipment to drive this cattle into the gangplank to get it on board.

Q: There was some pretty wild cattle up there, too.

A: Oh, we ran cattle all night sometimes. And then, if it happened to be a bunch of hogs maybe 70, 80, 90, 100 hogs you had what you call a seine. Now this consisted of about 60 feet of heavy canvas with about every six foot, with a wooden pole, with a spike in the bottom of it. Then you had a roustabout at each one of these poles. You just made a corral. You just went up to the gate where the stock was, and you drove the stock out into the seine. And then you tied those two ends together, and then each post had a roustabout at it. And you just had one man over in the seine driving the hogs, and then you just keep the seine up till maybe you would bring them in for a mile or a mile and a half to the river. And once in a while, one of the roustabouts would be bored to death, but they always are. (laughter)

He would go to sleeping and the hogs about time they would get quick, and then every damn hog goes out. Then you got to corral them up again. Eventually you get them back in the seine again, and then bring them back to the boat and you open it up, and oh, you take rubber hose and nail it to sticks about foot and a half, and then you hit these hogs across the back, and you can usually make them move along on the boat, you see. If they stop on you, just slap them across the back, the piece of rubber doesn't hurt them or anything. And that's about the end of loading stock on the Cumberland River.

Now, about the horses, the saying is that you should never load a white horse — I never did see any difference in color — and never haul a preacher aboard the steamboat. I always took them and never even thought nothing of it. But the only way you can probably get a horse aboard a boat across a gangplank is to lead him up to the end of the gangplank and if he walks on okay, and if he doesn't, you have to throw a rope under his tail and across his back and under his stomach and out through his front legs and have rousters drag him. He'll usually before you get down, why he'll start just scooting. Once you get him aboard you are okay. Now you could turn the horse around in a lot of cases, you could turn this horse around and back him on very easily. At any time a horse will back around where you can't lead them on.

And there's occasions where we've handled stud horses and that is

John Knoepfle

really one of the tragedies of hauling stock aboard a steamboat with the wooden hull — you take a stud horse and put him aboard a boat and let him pass a field where there might be some mares — he gets a whiff of a colt or something in the field, he'll go to stomping. And he'll stomp and stomp, and then nothing you do, except just put one of your rousters back there in the pen with him and chew on his ears. That's true.

Q: Chew on his ears?

A: Chew on his ears. It seemed to pacify him, and he will quit stomping, otherwise he would stomp holes right through the deck.

Q: Is that so? We missed your father's name. Can you tell me his name?

A: Well, my father's name is John Clemens Coomer. His grandfather was born in around Palace, Kentucky about 25 miles below Burnside, Kentucky. My mother's name was Charity Elizabeth. She was born in around Mammoth Cave, Kentucky. Her name was Noe, N-O-E.

Q: That's good. All right. I would like you to tell me little more about mating on the Cumberland, and if you can, tell me the problems in navigating that river.

A: Well, I went from night watchman, I finally convinced my father I could be a mate, and so he gave me a second mate's job, which was unlicensed. You didn't have to have a license. You would have to have some knowledge as night watchman in order to be a second mate. So, the second mate's duty is to assist the captain and the mate stands watch by himself, and he has the duties of navigating the boat, and unloading, and discharging the cargo, and stuff like that. This cargo has to be placed aboard the boat so it can be discharged and not throw any unnecessary strain on the timbers or the hull because those boats are built of light materials, which you can throw a leak in them very readily. It is a knack of a good mate knowing when there is any strain in the boat by just walking up the deck. He can feel it under his feet.

It is just inner knowledge that when you walk up the deck if there is a little strain in the boat, you will feel it or if the boat is careened over a little bit to the starboard or port side, you will feel that the head is a little too low, or the stern is too low, or something like that. You just have a general feeling walking up your deck. It just comes under the heading of experience.

Navigating of steamboats on the Cumberland River is unusual from what it is on the Ohio River because the river is so swift. There are places where you take a boat a 150 feet long, 32 foot beam, only drawing 14 or 15 inches of water. There are places on the Cumberland River that are so swift, that it will not stem through these particular spots, that is move forward. So in order to get this up through these swift spots, you have to pull into the landing, and take a man and drag a hawser up the bank and throw it around a windlass. And this was operated by steam. Now after you get up above the swift part of the river, you just land in again and pick up your men. Now there is a hazard too, on one of these hawsers tied like that that sometimes you will be a going, and the boat will all move, and first thing you know you hit a rock and that rope with that power there will snap, and that rope will snap back and sometimes break a man's leg or something like that.

Q: I've heard of it killing a man.

A: Well, I was very fortunate. I never got very many men hurt. I was always constantly watching for danger. But there have been men that have had legs broken in windlasses, and they get them over and they step in them, and it goes around their limbs and it breaks them in two. That's the thing.

Navigating steamboats on the Cumberland River is unusual, it does not exist on any other river, which I've worked on. It is eleven rivers I have been mate and captain on in the United States. And we would be leaving the Burnside with maybe three carloads of barbed wire fencing, general fencing. Oh, naturally, barbed wire and wire fencing does not float, but your current, being acquainted with the nature of the river, your current is very swift. And in order to get your boat lightened up so you can get off this particular shallow spot where the pilot got out of the channel a little ways, why maybe you would throw 75 or 100 rolls of wire fencing into the river, and the current would carry this right down into some spot where we would pick it up with spike poles.

It would wash it into a kind of a spot of its own down below the shoals. Now we would just reach down with spike poles and keep count of the wire fencing we had thrown over, and then we would just hook spike poles in that to pull it back up and load it in the boats. And sometimes coming upstream we would use the method of ferry boats. If there were shoals all the way to the small town with a ferry crossing, we had a ferry boat come down too, we would adapt to load cattle and stuff like that aboard a ferryboat and take it ashore.

If it wasn't too hazardous, why we would just drive the hogs and the cattle right over board and they would swim ashore, and then we'd get out and corral them up again. Maybe there was only 50, 75 feet, we had to go until we were in deep water again. Those are some of the things that you have to do and so many others, that like, maybe if you were loaded too heavy with fertilizer or something like that, or corn, why we would just have to ferry it ashore till we could get the boat lightened up enough to go on above, and then carry the corn from where we unloaded it to ahead of the shoals and load it up again.

Q: Could you identify some of these bad spots on the Cumberland?

A: Well, just the Cumberland River, the Smith's Shoals is at Burnside. That is seven miles long. Now that is the end of navigation. The only time you could get a coal barge up in that county, full and full of coal, they tried to barge that coal down on high raises. Now the Cumberland Falls is 40 feet high, and when the river gets up 40 or 50 or 60 feet, they used to try to barge coal in, in just regular coal barges made of just boxes. They'd bring it into Burnside, and then unload it. But so many of them sank on the shoals that it just was not profitable for anybody. So, that coal is laying in the Cumberland River now in the form of round shiny nuggets. The coal is round and shiny, and that river is full of coal, the way that stuff washed out of these mountains. Also, some barges

John Knoepfle

would try to float it down, you see.

These things would hit these shoals and tear apart and that stuff would roll and roll and roll. And the first thing you would know, why it just lays in the river. At the Smith's Shoals, which is seven miles long, just step-by-step, now there has never been a steamboat went up over these because the river never got that high, but South Fork River is only about three miles up South Fork. And then we'd leave Burnside, you run into a very bad one. And if the boat is not loaded too heavy, and the pilot stays in the channel, you have no trouble there. And then you go on down to the Greasy Creek Shoals, and the Wild Goose Shoals, and Bellnap Island, and that is where you run into your swift water. The river is narrowed down to the point so it makes it swift, for a boat coming upstream cannot stem, in other words the pilot will not push it through the swift water. You have to assist it with a rope.

There are so many other shoals on down the river that I just don't recall. One particular worst place I know of is what you call Wild Goose. Wild Goose is a shoals where the river is wide, the government came in and built what they call wing dams, which had been done on the Ohio River. And water is very swift in this particular spot, and it looked like when you are going down through this shoals, you just have to drive full ahead at one of these wind dams, just like you were going right across it. But just as quick as the bow of the boat gets up within ten or twelve feet of this particular wind dam, why the current is so swift that it hits the bow of your boat, throws it out, the water hitting the other side of your stern throws it down till you just slide right down to opening the of the river. Crazy thing, why, it would scare people to death to do it.

Q: I bet it would.

A: And that is the worst one, so the others on the river are mostly islands. Where the water is really so swift, it goes along, and there is places where sometimes the pilot would get out of the channel, and he will stick on this. It is mostly all rock bottom. All the Cumberland River is mostly all rock because I think I waded from Nashville to Burnside. On many a cold chilly night I have been laying out there — trying on those gasoline boats — trying to get them loosened up a little bit, or edged over a little bit, where they would get in deeper water.

Q: I wonder if before we leave the Cumberland, you mentioned that there were white roustabouts up on the Cumberland.

A: Yes. Over on Cumberland River, roustabouts consisted mostly of colored people, and these colored people mostly they came out of Nashville. In Burnside, there was only two or three men that plied the steamboats roustabout work. This was just a form of existence. Now these people would come out of the mountains, hills to the river to ship up with, mostly always needed them, and then make four or five weeks aboard a boat and could make two dollars, which two dollars in those days was a tremendous lot of money.

Now they use this money to buy some calico, or gingham, or maybe some salt, or pepper, or sugar, and commodities they could not raise back on their little plot of land back there. That is the only way they had of getting hold of ready cash. Now we classed them and treated them as regular river roustabouts, which was pretty rough. And today I am actually ashamed of some of the things that I have actually done in the way of working people beyond humanity, that is the only way you could put it. And of course in Nashville, Tennessee, why the roustabouts just followed the river as a regular life, they enjoyed it. They liked it as well as the captain, the mate, or the pilot, or the engineers, or clerks, or anybody. They were just part of it. And they had their little ways of getting more money like if they seen the boat was loaded down with all fertilizer, which was going to be carried off the boat ashore.

Maybe it would be pouring down rain, and that fertilizer would get on the neck till actually blood would come out of necks. And this fertilizer off the boat, if it happened to be a rainy day, such thing as bargaining, now the mate that could not ship a crew, you would have to say, a dollar a day, grub, and a penny a sack. And they would go for that for every minute. That extra penny they got for every bag that they carried off the boat. They got an extra penny with that besides their dollar a day, which was 24 hours work.

Q: How was the *Lee Burnside*?

A: Well, wait a minute now. I had to run second mate on these boats for three years before I could apply for a mate's license. I had very little schooling. I didn't know how to read and write very readily. I took the book of rules and regulations, everything governing steamboats, and I memorized all these big words at heart that I was going to have to spell out.

The inspector, the boiler and hull inspector used to make visits to Burnside inspecting the boats. I felt like I just was not going into total strangers. Coming from Burnside to Louisville, Kentucky on the train, which was the first time I was ever aboard a train, was a kind of a shocking deal. And then getting into the Custom House, which wasn't very old with all them fancy things and not knowing too much about reading and writing, I was just kind of lost.

I sat down for three days and wrote out and answered every question they put at me. And so after I got my license they came to Burnside and they told me that I had a very good rating. So I came back to Burnside, and I went as first mate on the *Rowena*, and then on one of the other boats, which a lot of times we would have to ship on account of one boat drawing more water than the other. We had to manipulate like that. And the *Patrol* and then back on another boat called *Celina*, which she was a scow boat, and a very shallow draft boat, so she could carry a pretty good load, but still would not be drawing as much water as one of the other boats would be empty. I got ambitious and some guy came through Burnside and he was telling me about boats from St. Louis, and I got ambitious and I was wondering what there was over in St. Louis, and Cincinnati, Ohio, and Louisville, Kentucky.

I got myself a $1.50 together and took the train out of Burnside for Cincinnati, Ohio. You could come to Cincinnati and back for a $1.50, which is

John Knoepfle

185 miles. I sold my ticket for 75 cents to somebody that was going back to Burnside, and then, when I pulled into the hotel and got a room for 75 cents a night, I had spent half of my wealth. So, I looked up at the tall buildings in Cincinnati and I was a little bit scared of them. I could not see where they were going to stand up. So, I got enough courage to go down to the wharfboat where they had 20 or 30 great big fine steamboats, tremendous large boats compared to what I had been seeing.

I stayed out on the levee and watched them working and listening to the mates and the manipulation, and what they was doing, loading the cargoes and stuff like that. So finally I got up courage and I went in and asked a fellow named Walter Quiggin, he was a good man Walter Quiggin, about a job as a mate, and he looked me over and said, "Well, we got to have tough ones. You got to be tough around here. You are too small." I only weighed about 130 pounds and I was only about 19 years old. I had to claim on my license I was 21 before I could apply, but I was really about 19 or 20 years old. And I was pretty tough because you had to be tough in the Cumberland River in order to be mate on a steamboat. On any water you have, you have to be tough. And he told me that I was just too small and did not look like I had experience. I said, "Well, you just give me a job and I'll show you how tough I am." So he introduced me to the commodore.

Q: Now Mr. Quiggin took you up and introduced you to Commodore Laidley?
A: No, he didn't do that. I talked to Mr. Quiggin and he told me I was too small a person and he said those boats carried 70 and 80 men as roustabouts and it was pretty rough. Of course, I was a little scared myself because it looked pretty rough. And he said, "Well, you come up here." And I went up in the office and there was a fellow named Eddie Ogeman, a nice person, too. He was in transportation. He said, "You come up here," introduced by Eddie and Eddie talked to him. So Eddie Ogeman talked to me and he turned around real quick and said they need a second mate on the *Corker* that runs between Cincinnati and Madison and a fellow named Al Shanks, now he was nice man and a good one. And so I got the job. $8.75 a week, seven days a week and my board.

I was second mate coming back in on a couple of trips, it was Commodore Laidley, which happened to be the commodore of the old White Collar Line and the Mail Line. This was under the heading of the Cincinnati Packet, Louisville and Cincinnati Packet. By the time I went to Cincinnati, the Mail Line had been out of existence. He saw me, and thought I was doing something that wasn't right. He said, "Come here! Come up here!" He wanted to know who I was, and where I was from, and what kind of training I had had that I could do something in that method, you see. And so he gave me a going over, and I went back to work, and I don't think he ever spoke to me after that. I don't think I ever said anything to him. But whatever it was, I corrected according to the way he believed, because he was the commodore.

Q: He was a tough old river man.

A: So it wasn't but a couple of months till I got the first mate's job aboard the *Corker* in the Cincinnati and Madison trade. Then the next boat that I worked on out of Cincinnati was the *Kentucky* and the *Andes* and the *Lucinda* and *Hubbard*. And then I quit this line and went to work for the Greene Line out of Cincinnati up at Pomeroy and Charleston. Of course, I worked on up to Pittsburgh loading in cargoes and things like that out of Cincinnati. You did not have to watch on those rivers as much as you do here. But you had the seasons where the water was shallow, and the boats had to be loaded accordingly, and so forth. We finally got the locks and dams in there. The only dam that was in there that I can remember was the Greenville.

Q: That was built in about 1917.

A: Well, it was there by 1914.

Q: It was as early as that?

A: I was there in 1913. And in 1917 I was mate and captain. Well, being mate with steamboats, you have got to have some general knowledge of humanity. You have to know how to work men and get the necessary work out of them, which in those days it was pretty rugged on the mate because you never got to go to bed as long as the boat was in the landing — maybe it was 3,000 or 4,000 sacks of corn out there — or 3,000 or 4,000 bales of hay somewhere to be loaded, or maybe you would run into three or four carloads of lumber had to be loaded. So he had to stay on watch. In those days captain never could get out very much on the bank or anything like that.

The mate's duties were to always see that the boat was loaded, especially kept on an even keel and the freight placed where it could be discharged, and pick up trade, and always keep the boat on an even keel. It just generally comes to you by walking up the deck. You can feel it if the boat is in tip top shape. If you don't get it that way, why you will spring leaks, which causes a tremendous lot of trouble. The relationship between the mate and the pilot is very bad because I think all mates really hate pilots, because the pilot always only stands up there and turns a little wheel and anybody can do it when there is plenty of water under the boat. And of course, then landing a boat is just merely a question of pulling a couple of bells and the engineer turns the paddlewheel, and soon as they get the head line out, why the mate will have to go to work again unloading, loading freight. The pilot goes to sleep. And so there has never been a good relationship between mates and pilots.

The captain is the law of the boat at all times, of course, and the mate stands out his watch from him and when he is asleep, why he feels that he can lay down and get a good rest. He has got a good mate that is going to take good care the boat because you have got a lot of people's lives at stake there. The boat hazards of fire and wind and hitting logs or in case of emergency, he has got a good mate. The captain knows that if an emergency comes up, why the mate can meet it until he gets up and takes over himself. But the mate and the fireman your third clerk, and your roustabouts, are the people that do the work in operating a steamboat. The fireman has got to keep shoveling and hauling ashes, shoveling and hauling ashes, on this ship and it is a tremendous hot job. And the clerk has got to count each and every package of freight that comes to the boat that goes aboard in and know about where it was placed. Because when he discharges that he will have to go on deck and get that freight out and have it brought to the head of the boat where it can be picked up and discharged in the least time spent. So he has a tremendous job.

Your roustabouts have to work around the clock 24 hours, sometimes work 12, 14 hours without any rest, in sleet, snow and rains, regardless of the conditions or the condition of the cargo to be taken aboard or discharged, why that was a hard, tremendous job. For example loading hay, come frost or drizzly rain or the frost on it and it freezes. They have got the hay lifted to their shoulders and they carry a bale of hay themselves right on in down there on the boat and they carry maybe 100 or 150 bales of that hay or something like that, why that just makes their shoulders very raw. The same thing exists with fertilizer and corn. And so it was a very bad job.

Q: Okay.

A: Well, being a young mate off the Cumberland River, naturally being on the big fine steamboats, they were a tremendous size everything they had on the Ohio River, why they kind of thought we were just over there in a little pond. The Cumberland River is harder to navigate than any river there is. I think that takes in the Tennessee, the Illinois, the Kanawha or any other one, the Mississippi or the Missouri. The Cumberland River is the hardest river to navigate, and get your boat up and down stream, because it is so shallow and swift. Now I come to the end of the year and I worked from Pittsburgh to Cairo, and from St. Louis to Cairo, and from Cairo to New Orleans, and I have come in contact with a tremendous lot of steamboat men captains, pursers, and mates and engineers. I have said before, I have always had a dislike for pilots. And I think generally speaking that mates did in general.

They may not have expressed themselves as readily. I mean they get along with them. In my past experience in coming over here, I had it pretty tough. The mates were supposed to be really tough. Around here, why I was the small structured guy, and probably inexperienced in a lot of ways, and I think some of them tried to dog it over me. I proved to the companies and owners I was very efficient in getting cargoes loaded and unloaded with the least expense. I did that regularly with the Cincinnati Packet company. That is getting the boat in and out, regularly getting the boat in and out from the landing with the least time spent.

Mostly when you see some of the old-timers that was born and raised around on the Ohio River, why they maybe were probably a little jealous and I did not get along with them so well. I know on many occasions I was mate on the *Queen City* coming out of Cincinnati and there was a boat leaving Louisville. We had what is called meet the boat trips. We would transfer passengers, and just quick as the two boats would warp together to transfer passengers, why the deckhands on the boat got to jiving with each other, you know, and first thing you know the mate would take it up and if I caught him back in the deck room I would let him have it. If he caught me over on his boat, why he would let me have it. First thing you know we had a little clash. In particular, one guy, that Coleman Pratt. So this Cole Pratt was one of the roughest talking guys, and I think had less humanity about him than any man I ever met on the river. I have met some pretty nice steamboat mates, including my brother Joe, and brother Stafford, they were mates on river boats. And then there were several others in the Cincinnati and Pittsburgh trade I came in contact with, were very nice, and I could probably name off 50 of them, if you could just think of them.

Q: How about the Nobles? Did you know them?

A: Well, there was Lon Noble, I had to mate with him a little bit because sometimes we were a little lacking at Burnside, Kentucky. With three boats running out of there at times, why we would have to transport a mate or an engineer from Louisville quite often to make up a crew for three boats. Lon Noble from Madison, Indiana was one of the nicest old men, he was an old man when I was a kid, and he had an unusual way of getting work out of men without doing a great deal of fussing. I think he was one of the nicest there. And there was Bud, his brother ran out of Madison, they was good mates, and oh, there were so many of them that I can't recall them now.

Q: I have a question now. I read in a 1901 news clipping where it said that mates out of Cincinnati never cussed. Would you care to comment on that?

A: I think I was about the only mate that actually did not cuss. I knew less cuss words. I know more of cuss words today than I did then. I never saw a mate aboard a steamboat that did not swear. I know them as a picture as a whole. They are gone. They're past. They're dead. A fellow by the name of Rich Vanndory down at Evansville, there was Doc Carr, those was rough guys, but they were good guys. The mates out of Paducah, up the Tennessee River, I knew those, and I never saw a steamboat mate that did not cuss. And you made a statement about mates going to hell. What was that you said last time?

Q: There aren't any mates in heaven, is that right?

A: Well, this stuff goes on petty claims down here. There are many things I have done that I am actually ashamed of. And in those days, I thought it was doing the right thing because I was trained, taught to do that. There have been a lot of people talk about these mates shoving roustabouts overboard and stuff like that. I really don't think that was. I have had many a fight, been cut several different times and shot once by rousters. I know that I had to be pretty tough with some of them sometimes. I would ask them down in the hull of the steamboat, maybe they would just work and work till they were just tired out, maybe go hide on you. They would go down there in the hatches and go back, sometimes in the hull back there and lay back there and you just had to go down in there. You would naturally take a little stick or something like that to hit the side of the wall, or a piece of pipe or something to scare them up a little bit, shake them out. Just like flushing a bunch of quails or something. If you get them scared a little bit, they would come on out, without putting up a fight. I found that roustabouts in those days, the ones that would fight me back, would kill you. That is just a fact. They would kill you if they would fight you back. And the majority of roustabouts back in the days that I was steamboat captain and mate, why you stayed pretty clear of them. But, where are we at?

Q: Well, we're getting toward the end now.

A: The last boat, I was captain on the boat that came out of Memphis, Tennessee, a boat called *Valley Queen*. It was a sternwheel boat, the men bought her at Memphis, and I went to Memphis and brought her to Omaha, Nebraska and we ran that season. Pilots were very scarce up there, in fact, there is no pilot in the world that has ever known the Missouri River. The Missouri River is the most treacherous thing because the current is an average seven miles and the depth is very shallow. Now there are holes in it that is very deep that you could throw a barrel and anchorage there and you would build yourself a sandbar overnight. In the bar, quicksand.

So we loaded up after operating one summer, we laid it up under the U. P. Bridge there and came near sinking in the ice. It had 22 inches of ice in around it. So I kept the ice cut around the hull. Sawed each day. I got out and sawed this ice to keep it from freezing and crushing the hull. I would pour water in this particular spot behind the dike was very still, so I poured oil in that so it would not freeze so quick; so I would not have so much ice to cut. My wife and two children and I were aboard the boat during this spell and the gorge broke and the ice broke in the gorge, about ten miles above Omaha. When it let go, that water, a tremendous amount of water came down on us, and ice, all at one time. I told my wife, "You better take the children and go ashore and go to a picture show." I said, "About two o'clock, about three o'clock this afternoon, the thing will be over. We'll either be sunk, or we will be afloat." And I said, "To get that where the ice piles over the side, why it will just sink, there is no way to hold it." I had ropes tied around the dike, around the dike to the wire cables and back through the hull and up into the engine room and had these wire cables in around the engine. So there was no way of breaking it loose.

It couldn't have possibly broken us loose; it would have torn the boat up if by running these wire cables, and then inside in around the engine, why you would have just torn your hull all to pieces where she would not float at all. The river got in about three inches to the top of the dike. We repaired it and came out in the summer season, and all fixed up nice and painted, and quite a bit of repair work. The owners sent over to Cincinnati and got a Cincinnati pilot and he had been on the Missouri River and had a license on the Missouri River at one time. He had not been up there for years. He wasn't familiar with the conditions there as I was.

We had a pilot the year before that from Hamburg, Illinois and I used to work with him a lot, can't recall his name now. We could have got him. Why, that would have been all right. But this fellow came over there and I told them, "Now, if you just go up the river about a mile and a half up there, you will find a nice deep spot up there where we can turn around, and then we head down under the U. P. Bridge and follow the highway side, the outer side and follow that down or stay on the Nebraska side. If you go down through the middle, that is a tremendous big sandbar, and it is only about 22 inches." "All right, all right, I know it," said this old pilot. He did not know a damn thing, you see. So he goes up the river, turns around, comes down full ahead under the U. P. Bridge in the middle of the river, and that thing just busted all to pieces.

So I asked him to lower the gangplank down. I knew that it was going to have a big sandbar, tremendous big. As she hit the head and they tried to turn it around crossways and it wasn't five minutes, it wasn't three minutes, till I got the deckhands down in the hull, and I seen there was no possible chance. A lot of times you hit a snag or log or something, why you go down, batten your hole, and then you are all right, batten it out. But I knew there wasn't any chance. I got upstairs and we had about 375 passengers aboard. I lowered the gangplank on the opposite side from what the current was of the sandbar, wasn't any water out there, but just that quick. So I put them out on the sandbar and got a few lifeboats down, some fishermen were around as we put everybody ashore.

I came back, I stayed over there for about five years, and come back to Louisville, Kentucky. I got a call from the Coney Island Corporation, and they would like to have me go mate on the *Island Queen*. That was in 1939, so I was mate on the *Island Queen*, 1939 I went to Memphis, wildcatting, back to Cincinnati, put in the Coney Island trade. And that was the end of my steamboat career. So I went in the orange juice business.

Q: And you have made something of a success of that, haven't you?

A: And I made a tremendous success of it. Well, up to a certain point, and then after the certain point, I think I made it better success. Because I make a lot of money and spent a lot of money, had a lot of wild parties and threw money away, and helped the relations and this and that. So I got a few dollars.

Q: So you are kind of settled here at Louisville.

A: At Louisville.

Question: I am at the home of Mr. Lewis Crosley on Loiswood Drive in College Hill and Mr. Crosley during the channelization of the river played some part in that as an engineer. Could you talk to us, Mr. Crosley?

Answer: I was born and raised in Cincinnati. Born on Kemper Lane, November 24, 1888 and my father Powell Crosley was a prominent lawyer here in Cincinnati. We moved to College Hill in 1892 when I was about four years old and we have lived in College Hill ever since. While I was attending the University of Cincinnati I was employed during the summers by the Engineer Corps, the Cincinnati office and Cincinnati district to the Engineer Corps, on various kinds of engineering work. In particular I worked under Mr. C. B. Harris who was a well-known assistant engineer here on several engineering jobs, such as a triangulation survey of the Cincinnati Harbor, other surveys, particularly on the river, which had to do with the acquisition of property, the laying out of certain structures such as dams in preparation for the regular channelization of the river, which was in progress at that time.

Q: This was all pretty much a kind of virgin effort I suppose?

A: This was a part of the development of the river, which of course started many years before and had to do with the all-around use of the river, which has played an important part I think in the development of the Ohio Valley.

Q: You were up around Blennerhassett Island in 1908?

A: That's right. We did interesting work there on old records in courthouses in running down the titles and in preparing for backwater dams, things like that.

Q: Then in the same year you came down and worked on triangulation.

A: That's right. The harbor in Cincinnati was being encroached upon by fills and structures, and the Engineer Corps decided to survey the banks of the river in preparing to control the cross section of the river to prevent a build-up in time of floods. The narrowing of the river became dangerous, and I think they felt they had to stop this, and control the situation. So a very accurate survey was carried on and made, and based on the method of triangulation.

Q: I wonder, did they dredge it after that to control that silt?

A: No, I think it had to do with the banks more than the channel. There was constant dredging going on, but this had to do with filling in, building on the banks of the river.

Q: A little later you spent some time you told me plotting curves?

A: In 1913 there was as you know a very disastrous flood in the Ohio Valley and the Engineer Corps commenced in 1915 to make a study of the river, and stream flows in the Cincinnati district. I spent a good deal of time beginning in the spring of 1915 through to 1917 on the setting up of gauging stations on the various tributaries, and developing the flow curves on those rivers, tributaries. Also on the Ohio River in this district and involved curves on the Whitewater at Harrison where a gauging station was set up and on the Great Miami River at Venice, and on the Little Miami River at Newtown, and the Scioto River at Waverly, and several on the Licking River. One at Morning View, which was a cable station, which the measurements were made from a cable up above the river, and two at Falmouth, one on South Fork and one on the main Licking, and one at Farmers, Kentucky, up in the foothills of the mountains.

Q: It seems like there was special emphasis on the Licking for some reason.

A: There apparently was for some reason. I remember it was at Farmers that we saw rafts of logs, quite a logging industry at that time and large sawmills, quite a lot of activity on a relatively small river.

Q: You don't remember off-hand any particulars about those rafts, do you?

A: I remember on one occasion we were working on the L & N Bridge, which had at that time a pier in the middle of the river, and one of these long slim rafts came down with a man, and a sweep on each side of this raft, and the man on the front end decided to take one side of the pier, and the man on the rear end took the other side, and they ended with the raft wrapped around the pier in rather fast water.

Q: That whole area must have been just cut out finally because that logging operation doesn't exist very much anymore.

A: There is quite a bit of lumber comes out of eastern part of Kentucky, lots of poles and lots of rough lumber comes out of that section today.

Q: What were you doing in Waverly? You mentioned plotting curves.

A: At Waverly at the lower part of the Scioto River we worked on a large railroad bridge. It was the L & N Bridge located a mile or two below Waverly, and it was quite a job to handle the gauging meters and records barging on the lower cords working our way across such a structure. Especially with the huge coal trains that were constantly passing on their way up to the lakes.

Q: You were up on the Kanawha too.

A: It has been a well-known fact, a great deal of the flood waters in the Ohio River, a large part of that water comes from the Big Kanawha. At that time Mr. Devereaux who was head of the weather bureau in Cincinnati wanted to know more about what was going on with the storms and run-off. I was borrowed from the Engineer Corps several times to set up gauging stations in remote spots so advance information could be obtained. I remember one time I was working on a gauging station in the head waters of the New River, which is located in some very remote and wild picturesque country. It's surprising how cool the weather is up there in the mountains in the summertime. When it was hot here in August in Cincinnati it was cool enough there to wear flannel clothes.

Q: You mentioned before that you always hired a local crew. What was the Wisdom in that?

A: I didn't want a misunderstanding to arise in view of the fact that I was in the employment of the government. It might confuse some of the natives in that section of the country, so it happened that these trips were all made by a single engineer. In that case I was the only engineer, the only person in the party, and I always made the practice of employing, perhaps four or five young men to help me do this work, and as a consequence the local people knew what was going on. There was never a misunderstanding in connection with it.

Q: I supposed you wouldn't have come out alive if they thought you were a revenuer or something like that.

A: Might have had some trouble.

Q: So then your last big project on the river was in connection with Dam 39? involved in the war, World War I and probably because of the fact that I had been on all around engineering work for several years I was assigned to the job as engineer at Dam 39. At the time the pass and the abutment walls were being put in, and Mrs. Crosley and I lived at the site, there near Vevay on the government property through that year. That winter, the winter of 1917 was one of the most severe winters we have had in this section of the country.

In December the temperature was extremely low throughout the month. The snowfall as I remember was heavy. And when the cook at the camp there, the chief cook or the steward, he was more than a cook, became ill and was sent up to Cincinnati to a hospital, we learned that he was not expected to live very long. They had to serve some papers to him to sign and it was necessary to pick somebody living there to come up who would not have to go back because the snow at that time was higher than a fence post. Dam 39 as you know is in a remote spot, not near a railroad, quite a few miles below Aurora. So Mrs. Crosley and our daughter, Charlotte Jean, were picked to bring those papers to Cincinnati to be signed. Then about two weeks later I left the job to go in the army. I had a reserve commission in the Engineer Corps.

The only way I could get out was a party of us walked across the river on the ice. It was one of the few recent years that the river has been frozen over because of the fact that there were coffer dams blocking part of the current. It was necessary for us to carry long poles as a precaution. I was met on the other side of the river and taken to Warsaw, Kentucky, where I came in on the train. I forgot to mention that Mrs. Crosley and Charlotte Jean were taken to Aurora in a sleigh pulled by a team of horses, and they went across country, across fences and everything, because the snow was so deep that the regular roads were marked out.

Q: I had a vision there for a moment of them trudging through the hills with a wolf pack coming down on them.

A: Well they had quite an experience that night, but they finally made it.

Q: Wonder if you would talk a little bit about that building downtown during the 1937 flood, that you put up beyond the flood line of the river.

A: Think I mentioned the experience at the time I worked for the government was that in time of flood a safe height above the zero gauge mark would be considered to be 72 feet. The 1913 flood and the 1884 flood were both about 70 feet, varying with certain conditions, and the Cincinnati gauge. So in our construction work with the Crosley Corporation, of which I was Executive Vice President for a number of years, we determined that perhaps 72 feet was a little low. So we set our levels at 74 feet for certain buildings that we built. In the 1937 flood we had a building we call building K on Arlington Street, a large one story building with a concrete foundation and floor set at 74 feet.

The flood came along, the Ohio River gradually rose; wasn't one storm or one rain, I think we had rains over a period of about 40 days; every two or three days we would get another rain, as a consequence the river kept rising. During that period the weather bureau revised their forecast on the expected height of the flood many times because of this peculiar weather situation. The river reached a stage of about 70 feet, and the tanks, the gasoline and oil tank farm of the Standard Oil Company of Ohio located across the tracks from our plant on Arlington Street, their tanks began pulling loose, spilling out gasoline and oil, which made a very dangerous situation in that entire neighborhood.

Sunday morning, Black Sunday in February, I believe it was about the 22nd, an electric wire near the B & O Roundhouse ignited the oil and gasoline on the flood waters, and this fire spread across the valley, and ignited many buildings including our building K, in which the water was then just entering at a stage of 74 feet. The water went up to 80 feet so that building after the fire had a total of six more feet of water on the floor.

Q: It was pretty much of a loss.

A: It was one of the biggest fires in Cincinnati, a very disastrous fire. It happened to be a fire that I heard that Barney Houston, who was chief of the fire department in Cincinnati, made the remark it was one fire that he took one look at and would like to go home.

Q: I bet a rough cold day for that. Well fine, Mr. Crosley, are there any other details that you might be able to think of offhand?

A: I think that's all and thank you.

Q: Thank you.

149   John Knoepfle

Mack Davis, July 3, 1957

Question: I have come down to Greene Line wharf with Mr. Mack Davis who is a very ancient riverman, and he has known every captain I've ever heard of. **Answer:** That's right.

Q: And seems to have been on every boat that I have ever heard of.

A: That's right.

Q: I wonder, Mack, if you would just give us a little resume of your own life so we can place you?

A: When I started on the river I started from a dishwasher, I worked up to cooking. I went some to be a cook. I was cooking on the *Betsy Ann*, in the summer I would come up and act steward. That was Captain Fred Way. I was on the *Betsy Ann* before he bought it. That was a man from Gallipolis named Fred Gill at the time. Captain Freddy sold the boat to Captain Gill, and I still remained on with Captain Freddy Way at the time. I was cooking. In the summer I was cooking all the way through, we run from Cincinnati to Pittsburgh until ice would cut us down. We only have two months to lay up in, and we would start out again. After he sold the *Betsy Ann*, why then rather he laid the *Betsy Ann* up and the *Queen City* come up at the time, that was in 1929. The *Queen City* bought right of way from the *Betsy Ann*.

I shipped me over on the *General Wood*. The two boys, they were stockholders in each boat, the *General Wood*, she was running from Pittsburgh to Charleston. I went over there as cook and steward and I stayed on the *General Wood* until she was sold. After I come back off the *General Wood*, I came on the *Cordill*. John W. Hubbard owned her and the *Queen City*, both of them was operated out of Cincinnati to Pittsburgh. After the *Queen City*, I was steward of the *Queen City* at one time, she went into the hand of a receiver, and that was the end of that. I come over on the *Tom Greene* with Captain Tom Greene, and stayed on there until the time that he bought the *Gordon Greene*, I went over on the *Gordon Greene* with him. Then I was headwaiter on the *Gordon Greene*. We changed from the *Gordon Greene* over on the *Delta Queen*. I stayed there until he died. I left the river then. I felt there wasn't no more for me. I was done for anyone because he was a great friend of mine. That was the career of the Ohio River. That is I've steamboat on the *John K. Speed*; she had a nickname, the *Longfellow*. She was so long so it took a towboat to turn her around. She was running to New Orleans, so I made two or three trips on her. I got off at New Orleans, over on a big old sidewheeler they called the *St. Louis*.

She was going out of St. Louis to New Orleans. After, I made my home around St. Louis, and I was practically on every boat the Eagle Line had. I was on the *Spread Eagle*, I was on the *Bald Eagle* and I was on the, except one boat, I was on the *Alton*. She belonged to them and the *Bald Eagle* belonged to them and the *Spread Eagle*, I was on those. The last new boat they built was the *Peoria.* That was the end of that. Well, she was cut down during, all these boats during that ice in 1917, the hard winter we had. All around here, and the St. Louis boats used to come out of St. Louis and lay up in there and down in Paducah, what they called the Duck's Nest, oh, 25 or 30 boats were there laid up around there. I was on the *Quincy,* and I was on the *St. Paul.* Where we run from St. Paul there, from St. Louis to St. Paul. We were the two regular passenger boats then. It was good old days then. At that time those two boats were running just the same, $25 round trip, all you want to eat, three meals a day, and was seven days round trip. Now it would cost you a $100 and up to make a trip up to St. Paul.

From St. Louis to St. Paul. After that I was with the Massengale Line. The boat, she was named *St. Louis,* a sternwheel boat. I imagine you don't remember. In my career I was on boats around New Orleans. I forgot to put that in too. One was named the *St. James.* She was what you called a coastline boat. She run from New Orleans to Baton Rouge hauling sugar, rice, stuff like that. I was on that for three years; I was quite a young man. My story now is 72 years. I come on the river when I was 14, and I remained on until a few years ago. Another boat I was on around there out of New Orleans, that was a boat they called the *Late Natchez.* Well, there was Captain, Billy Duke and Joe Duke, two brothers. The regular owner of that boat was old Miss Leathers. She was the owner of the old *Natchez,* and so this was *Late Natchez*; she built that boat. Why, she was a boat where she could carry 5,000 bales of cotton.

Q: An awful lot!

A: She run from New Orleans to up above Vicksburg, Mississippi, what they called the bends and they had a boat they called the *Bends.* Then they had another boat I was on that, the *America*; she was another sternwheel boat. They was what you called, the only two boats that running up there, they was called bend boats. She was an awful large boat, but she wasn't as large, her carrying what the *Natchez* would, because she only carried 4,000 and the *Natchez* carried 5,000 bales. They carry 75 what you called hill men. That was a lot of men in those days carrying. Sometimes they'd stay at a landing five, 12 and 14 hours loading cotton, and cotton seed. So they had to have a big bunch of men. Then again, I was on a steamboat all of my life, I was on a boat running from Vicksburg to Greenville, called the *Belle of the Bends.* She was another side-wheel boat, all old wooden hull boats. Wasn't any steel hull boats anywhere much. Wasn't but one steel hull boat, and I'll get to that pretty soon. Well, I run around there for a good couple of years and I changed over, and I went in the Lee Line. I guess you have heard of it?

Q: Yes, I have heard of it.

A: They had twelve boats and I was on each and every one until they went down. When I went that line, the Lee Line, they had boats running down to Friars Point, to Vicksburg and the first Lee Line boat I went on was a small boat running from Memphis down to Vicksburg called the *Sadie Lee,* next boat

I changed over on the *Jim Lee*, she was a great big old sidewheeler, old wooden hull. She run from down to Friars Point, Mississippi. Then I moved up and the next Lee Line boat I was on was, the first steel hull boat I were on, the old *Ferd Herold*. She was a great big boat too, she was running from Memphis to St. Louis. Next boat, I was on the *Pete Lee*. They had boat travel up here, carry whiskey out, we'd come to Cincinnati, the most we'd get out of this river would be down Henderson, whiskey. That was the *Pete Lee*. They had two boats up here, the *Pete Lee* and the *Georgia Lee*. They had another boat I was on, but she didn't come up here, she went to St. Louis that was the *Stacker Lee*; she was a great big old sternwheel boat. The next boat I was on, the last boat with the Lee Line, was the *Rees Lee*; that was the boat that Nolans built, and couldn't make a go down there because she was too fine a boat in them days. She was to be down in that part and well, they bought her from the Nolans. They went broke right then. They sold it to the Lee Line. Her maiden name was *S.S. Brown*, that was the Nolans when they had her. Then when the Lee Line bought her they had all their boats named after family you know, *Rees Lee*. That was the last boat I was on with them. That's about all the boats I can think of.

Q: You said earlier that you were up in the Tennessee.

A: Oh yes, I told you about the Tennessee, from St. Louis to down the battle-field at Shiloh. That's where these boats go that stop there. At that time I was on the *St. Louis* and the Massengale owned her. Captain Massengale out of Paducah owned her. We brought ties, corn and peanuts. And carried an awful lot of passengers during the summer season. Well then out of St. Louis down to the battlefield of Shiloh, that was as far as we could get. The passenger rate was $14 round trip, seven days. All you could eat. Now I want to say this food was fitting to eat, course the service wasn't as great as it is now. It's a little more equipped, you see, and they knew more on the boats. Well back at that time the main thing was storage, but it's not. It's God's heavens truth usually a passenger would set down, have five side dishes besides his meat, ice cream and cake as desert afterwards. Five side dishes; $14 round trip out of St. Louis to the battlefield of Shiloh. You couldn't get it now, $90.

Q: That have must have been a hard push up that Tennessee?

A: It was, pretty hard. You see that river was so, that boat just barely could turn around when she get down that far. She was a pretty large boat, almost as large as the *Queen City*. You heard of that? They had a hard time getting down there. When the water was up she could go pretty far, it was only once a year, when the water was up. I went back down there on the *Gordon Greene*. I was surprised, oh dear Lord, yes Sir, I hardly could believe that was the same river down there. You could have wade across it.

I have been knowing Mr. Lyle for quite a number of years when he was an agent, he was once agent for a boat I was on. That was the *Betsy Ann* and the *General Wood* passenger agent. I think he was a great man at all times, and he's still fighting a battle for the river business. Captain Bo Allen and I, all of us steamed the boat together, that was on the *Chris Greene* and the *Tom Greene*. One time on the *Tom*, he'd be on the *Tom*, one time on the *Chris*. After those boats played out, the two boats, *Chris Greene* and *Tom Greene*, then he come on the *Gordon Greene* as a we always thought he was a great pilot. We always called him Bo Allen. So we thought he was a great pilot, all us boys. Course that's all, times, I think and really believe from my heart that Captain Greene was the best *Tom*, Captain that I ever worked under in my life. He was a man was missed around this river when he died. He was a man was missed as much as President Roosevelt, and you know how we missed him when he died.

Captain Freddy as a young boy, this is Captain Freddy Way, Captain Freddy was so devoted, I knew him from a kid. He made a trip in 1918 from Pittsburgh to St. Paul on the *Joe Fowler*. That was the first boat ever known out of Pittsburgh to make a trip to St. Paul. This boy was so devoted to river life, he would always worry me about looking at the wheel. Every meal I'd wait on him, he would want me to carry him over to look at the wheel. His father, as I come to be acquainted with him, in his older days, he come here to be in the steamboat business, his father told me the boy worried him so. He always wanted to be a steamboat man. The first chance he got, he bought him a boat and that was the end of that.

Q: Can you tell me about the rousters who went along with nicknames and nobody knew who they were?

A: We had several fellows, one was named Louse, his name was Baily. They really wore that name so long until they hardly knew their real name when it was called. We had one called Wing, his name was Joe. On the old *Cape Girardeau*, Lord I forgot that old boat, it was Captain Buck's boat. He was a wonderful guy, too. The fellows used to go over, they'd expect to stage a strike, you know, they'd come down and look; this is very interesting, when those guys, the rousters, come down and look at those boats. They had a pilot, what they called a pilot, they'd send one down. You don't know who he is, the boat would be loaded. They'd want more than $90. If they want $90, they'd come back and say she was worth $90. Captain Buck knowed all those guys, those rousters by their nicknames; I bet if he was living today he could call one, named all nicknames. Wing, that was his right-hand man, Wing. He'd say now, they'd go back, when they'd strike some, well, the boat was there every other day in town. Two dollars a day was about as high as they could get, sometimes three dollars top price. Well, Captain Buck, he'd agreed with them to take them up, a ship on for $90, that's three dollars a day. We'd have more fun out of Captain Buck. He would stay all night riding those rousters about it. "Hey you, come on you here, Wingy. Damn these fellows wanted $90, and all day in town. Come on here." It was a whole lot of fun to see that stage and you couldn't come up on that stage unless you had that reel with those fellows. Because 60 men coming a going, it was awful, and that I never in all my steamboating. I'd wait until they'd get almost loaded before I was to come on that stage. Because you'd get thrown off in the river. That stage had a spring in it. It ain't like these stages now. This would go up and down, like that, you know.

Q: They'd sort of shuffle?

A: Yes, so Captain Buck, we'd have more fun out of him. That was a great friend of Captain Tom, too. He would come over and Stogie White was there, Captain Stogie, we used to have a lot of fun out of Captain Buck and talking about those rousters round the *Cape Girardeau*. Now that was the old *Cape Girardeau*. Well the *Gordon Greene* was Captain Tom and them bought her she was named after old *Cape Girardeau*. Well when they brought her around here they named her *Gordon Greene*, and rebuilt her over. They made a great boat out of that boat. I think she was the most popular boat that ever been in river. Everybody missed her too when she was gone.

When I first started cooking, it wasn't so very much recipes out then. It wasn't no fancy cooking it was just plain cooking. New recipes, I didn't know very much about them. I was once on a boat, different boats, you'd see different ways, you know. It's according to the steward. And in those days each steward wanted to see who could be the best steward, who'd feed the most. So we would have, such as different vegetables, we'd have mashed potatoes, and string beans, and corn on the cob. That would run from dinner cause we fed two meals heavy, dinner, lunch what we call nowadays was just the same as a late dinner. Now lunch is very light, the late dinner is heavy, but we had two heavy meals during the day and a breakfast was of course light, but two dinners were heavy. So it was just plain cooking, nothing fancy.

Q: Did they have a meal toward the evening too?

A: No, in those days we passed coffee, we would have two waiters to go around all over the boat and pass coffee and doughnuts. We didn't have no between meals like we do now. But we would have tea and coffee and doughnuts every day, afternoon. What you call afternoon. In fact, if you wanted a snack sandwich, you could come back to the pantry and get it, but we wouldn't have no regular meal like have a lunch after dinner. Well now like on the *Delta Queen*, she's giving the best service ever were on this river right now. Well they don't have a, just you can come in, you can eat all day as far as that is concerned. In the pantry coffee, sandwiches all day.

When I was on the Kate Adams, she was running from Memphis to Arkansas City, she was carrying the mail. Wasn't very many railroads down there. That was a, three boats that carried the mail, there were two boats rather. There was the *Jim Lee* she was a mail boat, she carried the mail from, they all had, from Memphis to Friars Point, Mississippi. She was a big sidewheel boat. And the *Kate Adams*, she carried the mail from Memphis to Arkansas City. She was owned by a man out of Pittsburgh called Captain Rich Lee. She had a very fine, popular captain there. He was the most popular captain outside of Tom Greene. Of course he was old then in those days, I haven't seen him. His name went down in history all around there, Captain Bob Agnew, he was right from up here at Pomeroy, Ohio. He come from off the *Queen City* and he was made captain of the *Kate Adams*. He was a great dancer. He really liked to dance and put on an awful lot of parties. He made that boat become very popular for passengers on there. Well now you could make a round trip on that boat for $12 round trip. So you would have three days out and she was a very fine boat. It was very nice, very nice on there. Three meals a day, all you want to eat.

They would have dances and Captain Agnew danced half the night. He was a great lady's man. Captain Tom was the next man to come to be popular on a steamboat out of the, Captain Tom Greene, he made everybody like him. He had friends from all parts of the country who traveled on a steamboat. He was the greatest man I ever knew in my life, but he'd be a young man. There never will be another one, there will be no Tom Greene's out there. I can't see, looks like all our good river men died young. Captain Chris he was fine, but he wasn't a mixer as Captain Tom was. Have to be a mixer on a steamboat, he mixed with the public and everybody liked him. Not a soul had anything against that man. And he'd do most any favor for you. I could come down here. I was a great man about going out and playing the racehorses. I could come down here. Get broke. He'd say, "Well, Mack, what do you want now?" "Captain Tom I want 20. I want 15." So he'd tell me, many a time he sat right in that office, and told me, "What are you going to do when I die?" I really did suffer for it; I just snapped out it, I was getting old, and all that kind of stuff. I got away from it. I really did miss him for years.

Q: Speaking of racehorses, there's a track on an island in the lower river, do you remember that outfit?

A: There is a track there now, Dade Park it's called. Kentucky supposed, I don't know how that is, it's on an isle. It's supposed to be in Kentucky. Oh yes many times we went there. Weekdays, we'd come back, coming up on the *Delta* Captain Tom would take the passengers out. "Well Mack, come on you're going out today." Yes we would go out and we'd get there, at Evansville at one or two o'clock right after lunch, and we would go together, all the passengers would all flock out there together every trip. That's Dade Park. I know all about it, I guess. I lost a lots of money if the truth were known about it.

Q: I don't know whether you would know about this, but I have heard that a lot of the cotton planters come up on the Wabash to gamble.

A: No, I don't know about that . . .

Q: Did you ever get up on the Kanawha River?

A: Oh yes we were on the Kanawha River, when they bought this boat the *Gordon Greene*, and they rebuilt her over, she had the run she would go up here to West Virginia, New Martinsville, and come back, stop at Marietta a while, and come on back, stop at Point Pleasant, and then go up to Charleston, clean on up to Montgomery. Talking about people that boat was, if she was a boat the size of the *Delta Queen,* and could have got up there, she would have made a mint of money. That was a seven day trip. We would come in here Friday night just like the *Delta Queen* is coming in here. Friday night at midnight, and we would leave Saturday evening, eight o'clock. That was our regular run until Captain Tom, they was making so much money, so they saw this boat and they could go out and get it for a song, so they say, this boat out of California. So he went and got this *Delta Queen*. He would have been much better off if he had of left that boat stayed here, kept the *Gordon Greene*, these two boats he had running from here daily out of here to Louisville carrying automobiles, and all that market out of here.

Q: I suppose you got up the Kentucky, too?

A: Yes, we went up the Kentucky River on the *Betsy Ann* where those big boats like, they couldn't get no farther in there, they got that little dam up there, but the *Betsy Ann*, wasn't small, quite a distance up that river. We used to take an excursion out of Louisville up there every Sunday. So she went a pretty good ways up there. It's a small river, but there is plenty of water up there.

Q: In talking to Norval Horton, he said that's a lonesome river up there.

A: It is. (chuckles) It's deep up there.

Q: Did the *Betsy Ann* haul any freight out of there?

A: Oh no she didn't haul freight just excursions and passengers. Just running with passengers. She would at times carrying automobiles, anybody wanted to have automobiles come out of Pittsburgh. We run them out of Pittsburgh down to Louisville at that time.

Q: I don't suppose you ever ran up into the Monongahela?

A: Oh no, I never did go up there. No farther than Pittsburgh, that's on the Allegheny. They say they had boats run up there to Morgan City and boats running out of Pittsburgh, but I was out in this part.

Q: Now as the steward I suppose you bought the food for the boat?

A: I bought the food.

Q: How would you go about that?

A: Well I would make my list out as to how much to buy, and buy almost all my stuff in Pittsburgh. After the boat gets to town, I could tell just how much I had, that boat could only carry 90 people, and I could tell just how much to buy according to my people, you see. See if the boat had 90 people and 25 in the crew you see, cause they all ate the same. When I was on the *Queen City* I would do the same thing. Anyhow you have to know something about cooking, you know, to be a steward. You have to know a great deal about cooking to be a steward, to be a steward that has to do the buying. I did all my own buying, would run around 200, 250, that is out of Pittsburgh. Out of Pittsburgh to Louisville, then I would stock up in Louisville coming back. The same amount I would buy out of Pittsburgh. Course I would buy heavy in dry stores, but I could buy enough of them to last a month or two. Flour, baking powder, meal and canned goods. But fresh vegetables I would buy just enough to get on to Louisville, then I would buy at Louisville. Then I would have to buy my meat the same way. I couldn't buy my meat there, I would have just enough to get down to Louisville. The meat, see I would have pork loins, would have fresh hams, sugar cured hams, fish, and we'd have stew beef, so much of that. If you were a cook you can always do that because of the passenger list, you can always figure how much to buy. It's a very easy thing to do. But if you don't know, from the cookhouse, you waste a whole lot of stuff. If you're a good cook you know exactly what to do according to your passengers.

Q: I guess that was a skill handed down from one cook to another. There was no books on it or anything?

A: No, no books on it, no that's right. I came up with some very good old cooks though. That's where the stewards come from. You can't take a steward, make a steward out of him if he don't know nothing about the cooking. What does he know what his cook wants to bring up, what does he know what his cook uses.

Q: Who were some of those cooks and stewards, do you remember?

A: Why I know all the old time cooks, and the old time stewards, they all dead now. My steward from when I was a cook was Harry Keeler. He was what you call one of these tip top stewards. He was steward on the big boat, the *Cincinnati*, and he was over on the Lee Line boats too. Great man. He was a cook and a steward, he come from the cookhouse. Another old fellow that we called Bow-legs, that's Bill Sampson, he lived across the river here. He was a cook, baker, and steward, all around man. There was another fellow, Bill Garrison, Captain Tom had him over here, he was on the *Gordon Greene*. He liked Captain Tom, and you know Captain Tom could cook a little. This man Bill Garrison learned him and showed him. So after Bill Garrison didn't come back from St. Louis, Captain Tom would do his own steward, you know. He were good. He was doggoned good. There was an old steward and a cook, a colored fellow from up here in New Richmond, Warren Miller. He was a steward and a cook. That's where your good steward come from, cooks. If you put a steward on a boat that don't know nothing about cooking why he would be buying a whole lot of stuff, and he don't know where it's going, and it's hard for him. That's what we always called, we always called that a percentage steward, know how to buy, this time you would buy so much and never give out of nothing. That's called a real good steward.

Q: A percentage steward?

A: Have to be, and have to come from a cookhouse to be a percentage steward.

Q: I guess if you had a bad steward on board the cook was pretty unhappy?

A: Yes it would, he would have to be. You take a real good cook, you can't just take a man, just like these dining car stewards, see they are not stewards, they are dining car stewards, they are. Now you take one of these dining car stewards, put them on a boat like the Delta, and he's got a good cook down there, well, all right. What we're going to have if the cook makes out his list, and carries it up to the steward, and when the steward gets ready to buy his big supply the cook done made out his list, and all he's got to do is cut it in to where he is going to buy it. He won't go wrong. There ain't no way now for a steward

John Knoepfle

to go wrong, as it was before, like in the old times, you know, you'd have to, well the steamboat people, company, they couldn't afford to have pick up any, you know, steward, to put on there didn't know what he was doing. They couldn't afford to do that. Now just like the Lee Line. They were a funny type of people, five brothers of them, all made captains. Every captain we had, were made, come from a mate because a mate knows from the bottom to the top. That's like, steward that these men had come out of the kitchen. Had them come out of the kitchen. They wouldn't have, they didn't think you would pass. Same way with the mate. The mate you'd have to be, nowadays you take a pilot, and make a captain out of him. They wouldn't do it. He'd have to be a mate, know how to load a boat and everything, know what to do.

Q: I didn't know that.

A: Every captain up there on the Lee Line, cause they had 12 boats, and practically every, one was in the Mississippi River up in that part belonged to them outside the Streckfus boats. That was the Diamond Jo Line that Streckfus bought there before the railroad. The Diamond Jo, a line had the *Quincy*, the *Dubuque* and the *Sidney*. There wasn't no railroads up in that part like there is now. And there was another class of employee: you had to come from the cookhouse to be a steward; you had to come from being a mate to being captain. Those boats would carry a lot of freight up there too, at that time. Wasn't no trucks. Wasn't no such things as trucks back in those days. 12 boats, I don't see 12 boats, doesn't matter what I think about the boats after the railroad coming and trucks coming, all the boats had to go out of business.

Well Captain Hornbrook was a great captain. He was captain of the *General Wood*, captain and owner of the *General Wood*. And they had another man that was great friend of his was Hoyt, he was on there as a purser, and Captain Hornbrook was very popular on the *General Wood*. She was a small boat; wasn't a fancy boat. But he was a great popular captain with the ladies and passengers. That boat was a very well kept up boat. She ran from Pittsburgh to Cincinnati, she used to carry a great deal of passengers. That was $25 a room, trip too, from here to Pittsburgh and back.

Q: You boated with Captain Wisherd too.

A: Oh yes, I should say, I was on the *Washington* with him. I was cooking on the *Washington* with him. He's a fine fellow, Captain Wisherd. He was captain on the *Washington* for a long time. He had an office in Pittsburgh. I worked for two seasons on the *Washington*. She was very popular around Pittsburgh, too. Carried plenty of passengers out. Was on the excursion boat, she was one of the Streckfus Line boats if I'm not mistaken. I think Captain Wisherd had a charter. Was a charter boat. I'm sure he didn't own her, he had a charter.

Q: Think the war finally knocked that boat out?

A: Yes that's right, couldn't make it.

Q: I guess you were an old buddy of Captain Hughes, too?

A: Oh, my Lord, Captain Hughes, I should say! You know I wanted to ask you about him when I was coming down in the car. Someone told me you were talking across the water someplace.

Q: No, he is up in Massachusetts with, I think a sister-in-law.

A: Is that so? He was one of the greatest around here at all times. He was a great backbone to the Greenes. He out, Captain Gordon Greene died, everything went into Captain Jesse. I tell you one of the greatest old ladies in the world ever were, that was Captain Mary B. Greene. She was the sweetest, couldn't been sweeter. Poor old lady she didn't do any harm for anyone. She was about the best steaming boatman. I knowed two on the boat. That was Bank and Mr. Levers. But she was pilot of the, because Mrs. Greene could pilot a boat as good as any other pilot she had. She didn't ask nobody for nothing. If a pilot wanted to quit, she'd say, "I'll go up and pilot." Or if the Tom, we'd go up the river, that was before Captain Tom got his license after his father died, we'd go up the river, she'd go up and take that boat on out.

Q: Well you were on with Captain Schletker too?

A: Who?

Q: Schletker was on the *Guyandotte*.

A: Oh, my Lord, no I wasn't on the *Guyandotte*.

Q: The *Greenbrier*?

A: No I wasn't on either one of those lighthouse boats. I was never on one of those lighthouse boats. I was always on tow boats or either the packet boats. I was on the old *Ben Franklin*, I was on that cooking and steward. Well the cook had to answer to the steward, you see, because he did all the buying and stuff. Well I was on there with, what's the name of the old fellow that got killed out here? He wasn't a captain, but we all called him Captain Kirschner. I was on the *Ben Franklin* cooking, steward with him, and then he bought the *Arthur Hider*, which was a government boat, which you call willow boats down there in Mississippi, on the Mississippi River. He bought the *Arthur Hider*. He was doing a very good business with the old *Ben Franklin*. He'd have trips from Pittsburgh up here and they had all those pontoons up there when they were doing that dam up at, and after he bought the *Arthur Hider* I went over there on the *Hider*. She was a steel hull boat. Don't know after his death, his son, how he got rid of that boat, that I don't know, I think he had to sell it because he wasn't able to buy any barges. At the time, these fellows had the boats that were coming in that had barges. He couldn't lease anymore barges, this boy couldn't.

Q: That's a private owner?

A: Yes that's a private owner, he couldn't lease any, these big companies like the Campbell Line always coming in with their barges. They had their own set of barges, and stuff like that. They drove that boy clean out of business. I think the old boat was dismantled down across from Louisville there. That was the old *Arthur Hider*. That was only two towboats I were on.

Q: You were on the river a long time?

John Knoepfle

A: I have been on the river, 1872, ever since I was 12 years old. I started when there wasn't very much earning you could get in those days. I runned off from home, stowed away on an old boat, a big old sidewheel boat, the *Providence*. She was running out of St. Louis to New Orleans. I went on there. Running down to the river, I never will forget, they had an old steward on it an Irishman called Mahaffy. After I showed up, I asked could he give me a job. He said, "What can you do, boy?" I said, "I can do anything, wash dishes." (chuckles) So he took me, carried me back in the pantry, and turned me over to the pantry man. I stayed on that old boat clean until the ice cut us down, at least they had to lay up one night. Run all the summer, had until November. Then they'd leave, and come and lay all those boats up down in the Eagles Nest, they called it. That's a place down there at Paducah. There would be over 50 boats be laid up there. But these boats never did come that didn't have no trouble with ice. The only time they had any trouble with ice was in 1917 when they cut them down over here. But all the St. Louis boats, and all these boats would go around there in the Eagles Nest and lay up. But that year of 1917 they lost every boat. The Eagle Packet Company lost their boats. Except the *St. Paul*, I don't see how the Streckfus Line managed to save those boats. They would get in and move those boats. That was the *St. Paul*, that was the *Sidney*, and there was *Dubuque*, and there was the *Quincy*, all down in there. But the ice coming out of Tennessee River, they had their boats above, and at the time the ice come, it cut them down. I imagine it the other time, you know, sat them apart, and didn't do these other four boats any harm. That's the way they claimed that they saved their boats. Otherwise all those boats would have been cut out.

Q: They say the *Peoria* went out in that ice with her wheel turning and her lights on.

A: Yes sir. These boats that were over here, they cut all them down. They cut the Greene Line boats down. They had only one boat left, the old *Greenwood*, after they built these two new boats, the *Chris* and the *Tom*, why then they dismantled her. The reason they dismantled her because we had a charter on the *Betsy Ann*, broke her shaft at Gallipolis Dam, and the old man, Gordon, was on watch on the *Chris Greene*, and backed into this old boat, sunk her. They say they did it on purpose, but that I don't know. (chuckles) But I know she sunk right after. This wharf boat, the old Mail Line boat, that was where I first met Mr. Lyle. He was a passenger agent for the Mail Line boats, too. The wharf-boat was the same spot this wharfboat is. It was the end of the *Greenwood*.

Q: You were originally from St. Louis?

A: That's right.

Q: That's quite a bit you've told me here.

A: When it comes down to talk about the river in the old time back, I can tell you pretty far back.

Thomas J. Reynolds, Richard Lawwell, William Moyer & Sid Dawson

This collection of four memoirs consists of Captain Thomas J. Reynolds, who is captain of the Hiram College Showboat *Majestic*, and discusses the running of a showboat; J. Richard Lawwell, who discusses the 1913 Manchester, Ohio flood and his grandfather, Captain Prather; William J. Moyer, who discusses the 1913 Dayton, Kentucky flood; and Sid Dawson, who is the leader of the Riverboat Ramblers Band, and discusses showboat musicians and music. David Arnold and June Ashweiler, Interviewed Captain Reynolds.

Captain Thomas J. Reynolds

Question: [David Arnold] We are aboard the Hiram College Showboat *Majestic* at the foot of Market street, Public Wharf, Cincinnati, Ohio. (Whistle blows) We have here with us the captain of the *Majestic*, Thomas J. Reynolds of West Virginia. Say hello, Captain.
Answer: Hello.
Q: Well you get no more than you bargain for Captain, how many years for you in showboating?
A: Forty-two years.
Q: And how many years have you been with the Hiram College bunch?
A: Seven years.
Q: How do you like working with the college kids?
A: Fine.
Q: Do you think they put on shows like they used to in the old days?
A: A good bit like the old days.
Q: How about the crowds, do they change much?
A: Well no, not too much, some better I guess it is.
Q: Captain, you used to run this boat by yourself, that is your family used to be the show; you used to do some of the directing and acting, isn't that right?
A: Yes.
Q: What are some of those old shows you used to do, "Lure of the City," and some of those oldies?
A: Yes, "Lure of the City," "St. Elmo," "East Lynn," all those old plays.
Q: "Ned Albert." Good old shows. Your first boat was what, and what year did you start out?
A: It was the *Illinois*, I don't remember the year.
Q: That burned down in Foster, Kentucky, right?
A: Yes.
Q: Was that when you built your first boat, the *America*?
A: That's right, built the *America* after that.

Q: You built this boat when?

A: Built this in 1923.

Q: And what happened to the *America*?

A: Sold it to my brother.

Q: I see. Is it still afloat anywhere?

A: No. It's on the Green River, they built a summer home out of it.

Q: Captain, tell us what it was like back when there were a lot of showboats on the rivers. What were some of the names of them?

A: *Cotton Blossom, Sunny South, Greater New York, French's Sensation,* fourteen in all.

Q: That's a lot of boats. Do you happen to know what happened to those?

A: Yes, they either sank or tore up in a wind storm.

Q: You were telling us a moment ago about the professional actors you had on, maybe you have some significant incidents you might like to relate or about your family in the show? I know that you have told me personally some pretty humorous ones, perhaps you can remember some of those now?

A: Well my family took quite a part in the show and the actors, I had so many of them I don't know much about them now.

Q: I'd like to introduce our business manager June Ashweiler, who has been with the Hiram College group for five seasons. She perhaps would have some light to throw on this. Maybe she can get Captain to talk about the old days.

J: [June Ashweiler] Hello. Captain just said he had a lot of good ones and a lot of bad stories. I remember once he was telling me something about during the slow times when people would come down to the river and bring potatoes and things like that along to pay for the show. Is that right, Captain?

A: Yes, that's right.

J: Is that all you have to say about it?

A: Yes.

J: We had to keep the showboats going one way or another, didn't we?

A: Hard times.

J: In hard times people would bring down potatoes and chickens too sometimes, didn't they? And butter, anything just to get on the boat. They had to come and see the showboat show in one way or another.

A: That was in Hoover's day.

J: Captain, was it your daughter that used to play the calliope.

A: Yes, Catherine.

J: Your daughter Catherine played the calliope, and your son Tommy did some dancing. The two of them did some dancing on the boat?

A: That's right he did dancing, drumming, anything you wanted him to do.

J: He was also advance man too, wasn't he?

A: Yes, advance man.

J: In other words Captain's family took care of the whole show?

A: That's right.

J: How do you keep the boat going this way in such good condition?

A: Well working with Hiram College I guess.

J: I guess I asked for that one. What do you think about these college kids, Captain? Do they run the show as well as some of the professional groups do?

A: They do a very good job of it, yes.

J: Did the old shows have the melodrama, the candy sales, the vaudeville acts much the same as we do now?

A: That's right, the same way.

J: I read some stories about the vaudeville acts being spliced into the melodramas. Did you ever do it that way?

A: Well yes we did. We would run an act of the play and an act of vaudeville to change curtains you know.

J: So that's what, you used vaudeville in that way then. How long has the calliope been on board now?

A: About thirty-four years.

J: About thirty-four years. Is this the biggest one on the river?

A: Yes, it's the biggest one and the last one that Nichols made in Cincinnati.

J: In Cincinnati, Ohio? It was made right here. Do they make calliopes any longer, Captain?

A: Not that I know of.

J: Because we have tried to get parts for ours and we have had a rough time doing it.

A: This the only calliope on the Ohio River.

Q: Made by Nichols.

J: Made by Nichols. I guess the *Avalon* still has one.

A: They don't have it.

J: They don't have it any longer?

A: I heard they got rid of it, I don't know.

J: We can hear this calliope for what is it five miles, Captain?

A: Supposed to hear it four miles all away around.

J: Four miles all away around. It takes a lot of pressure, doesn't it?

A: Eighty pounds.

J: Eighty pounds of steam coming out of those keys. Takes a lot of muscles to play it too, doesn't it?

A: That's right. Look at this boy right here, see those big muscles?

J: Captain's son, Johnnie now plays the calliope on the boat along with David Arnold whom you were talking with before. It takes two of them to hold those keys down these days.

Q: Could just tell her we do twice as good a job that way don't you see. Four hands are better than two.

A: Neither one of them can play a tune by themselves. That beats all.

Q: Captain, I have heard some stories about sometimes you tied up in high water someplace and got stuck in the mud. Is that story true?

A: I don't know much about that one.

Q: You must have been there?

A: I was there. Give me another one.

Q: Did you ever have serious trouble with any of your professional actors?

A: Yes, I had quite a bit of trouble with them drinking.

Mr. J. Richard Lawwell, March 8, 1958

John Knoepfle, Interviewer.

Question: We are at the Ohio State Museum. I am talking to Mr. J. Richard Lawwell who was director of the Anthony Wayne Parkway Board; he was born and raised in Manchester, and has a few reminiscences to tell us about.

Answer: I was born on the Ohio River at Manchester and have a number of recollections of the 1937 flood, but not in Manchester, at Cincinnati. My recollections at Manchester are of the 1913 flood. I was very young at the time, but I do recall that our home on Second Street in Manchester became completely engulfed by the flood. That the entire family had to move out of the second story where we had moved, and they emptied into the rowboats and were taken to the country for the duration of the flood. I also recall there were two floods 1913 and the terrible mess, which was the result of the flood and having to clean out the home and so on.

My grandparents were W. W. Prather and they were also residents of Manchester and my grandfather was known as Captain Prather. He moved, as our family did, from Manchester to Cincinnati in the period following the Civil War, and became a pilot or captain of a river steamer, and was in the trade on the Ohio River. He was connected with a tin ware company, and he had a small boat, which he called the *Katie Prather*, which he plied up and down the Ohio peddling tin ware. He would start at Cincinnati with a load of tin ware, go up the Ohio to the Kanawha, up the Kanawha to Charleston peddling his tin ware. After the disposing of his load, would take on a load of crockery, and then peddle the crockery back down the Ohio.

So, that was his business for a number of years, I don't know how many exactly. The *Katie Prather* was named after his youngest daughter Katherine who had four daughters, one of whom was my mother, and a son. So, there was a very close tie there with the name in the family. In later years he sold the *Katie Prather* and went into what was known as the commission trade. He would, the boat would, go up and down the river picking up poultry and livestock of various kinds to bring to the commission markets in Cincinnati. There is a very interesting story about the *Katie Prather* that has become more or less, much of, the lore of the Ohio. It is said that the *Katie Prather* had a load of turkeys to pick up on the Ohio Brush Creek and that the crew headed up the Brush Creek from the Ohio; it was around Thanksgiving time.

Q: Where was the Brush Creek area?

A: Brush Creek entered the Ohio just above Manchester, it's a fairly good sized stream at its mouth where it enters the river; it was navigable to small boats for some distance. This farm where they were to pick up the turkeys was located up the Brush Creek. There was a riffle that had to be navigated in order to get to this farm. They found that the Brush Creek was falling, and they just managed to get over the riffle. So, they got up to this farm, picked up their crates of turkeys, and headed back down as fast as they could because they knew they might have some difficulty. They got to the riffles and lo and behold the water had fallen to a point where they couldn't quite get over. So the crew of the *Katie Prather*; however, was equal to the situation as the story unfolds.

They had a mate that was quite able to meet the many circumstances, which are encountered on the river. So he ordered the crew to take the turkeys out of the crates. Which they did and he then ordered them to fasten the feet of the turkeys to the deck of the boat, and at a command he ordered the boat to go full speed ahead. He shot a blunderbuss over the heads of the turkeys. They attempted to fly and escape from the shot, of course, and it was just enough to lift the *Katie Prather* over the riffles of the Brush Creek, and they got down to the Ohio, and down river to Cincinnati, and got their produce to market in the proper time. Now that is the story, as I say, of the *Katie Prather*.

Q: An amazing tale.

A: And of course, we hear many stories like that associated with the river and sometimes you wonder whether they are true, or whether they were not true. The *Katie Prather* I know was a registered boat and my grandfather was the captain. I happened to ask Fred Way about the story one time, and Fred immediately began to laugh, and tell me that he knew of the story, that it had been on the river many, many years and that all the old timers knew it. In fact the "Waterways Journal" had printed it not too long ago. So I think, I'm sure there is a basis of fact, and it may be, of course, stretched to some degree, but that is the story of the *Katie Prather* that has been told to me, and that many, many rivermen know about.

William J. Moyer, April 7, 1958

John Knoepfle, Interviewer.

Question: Mr. Moyer lived near the river in Dayton, Kentucky during the 1913 flood and during the ice jam, which followed a few years later, and he is going to talk about those events.

Answer: In the 1913 flood I was in about the third grade in school, and we lived on Lower Third. The back end of our house actually opened up on the river; although, we were a good three or four hundred feet from the river, we could look out our backyard right down over, through our field, into the river.

We spent many, many a day on the river because we had a canoe and we liked it. During the1913 flood some of the things that I remember that the water got up to within two inches of the second floor of our house.

Q: How high was the water then?

A: The river came up to about 69 point some odd feet. It didn't quite hit 70.

Q: Was that in winter of the year?

A: That was in the spring, I don't recall exactly the date, but it was in the early spring of 1913. I'm trying to think of some of the things that were most vivid during that. I remember afterwards rather than the beforehand because going to school, why we wasn't interested in the river, and after it got up right in the front of the house, and kept us from coming in that way, we could always come in the back way. But after it once got surrounded why you were trapped. Dad always had a barge he always kept down in the back lots and whenever high water would come up, why that was our ace in the hole, to get anything out that we had forgotten. All the heavy stuff always went out first, the piano.

In those days we didn't have furnaces, no cellars, it was a big blast stove. A square one, it sat in one room and heated the whole house. And that was still up I know. It was in early spring and dad had gotten out all the heavy furniture and moved all the other furniture upstairs and just a week before that my youngest brother was born. Well the water kept coming up and coming up and dad got a little worried. Finally when it got about three feet on the first floor and he was transporting back and forth to get groceries and so forth in a boat or a john boat we called them in those times. Those great big flat things could put an enormous amount of people or weight on them. They got a little bit worried, so he took mom and my youngest brother out over the back roof, the kitchen roof, was about like a summer kitchen we had, and got down in the john boat and took them uptown, my mother and my youngest brother uptown to my aunts. I vividly remember that thing, when it was all over, walking into our house, and everybody in that neighborhood, they called it Dutchtown at that time. I don't know there maybe were a lot of Dutch people living up there. Most of the grown people all had hip boots on, every property owner, and I'll never forget, dad bought us, my brother and my mother, (I mentioned he was three years younger than I was), a pair of knee boots.

We went down with him after the waters went down and stepping into that house and seeing the plaster off the walls and off the ceiling and mud about two inches thick all over the place where you used to have your carpets and furniture and so forth. It was sort of a sickening feeling. But it didn't seem to bother dad or any of them, any of the people down there, all got busy, cleaned up, got the hose out and scrubbed it down and got the mess, and we cleaned the thing up and dad of course had to leave it dry out.

One of the things I might mention too, when people down there knew that they were going to have a flood, they would prepare their house. They took everything out of it and bore holes in the floor to keep it from buckling. They'd prop up all the windows, take off the doors, just let the water have a full sway of the house, so no buckling or anything would take place. Then when it was over, why you would scrub it up and all your water run down through those holes underneath, you had no cellars and there was nothing in there. Only dad did have a dirt cellar and one back room he always used for storage for fruits and vegetables. He was in the fruit and vegetable business. We used to have barrels and barrels of apples and potatoes and things of that sort down there, but you know we got that out first. That was about the situation of the 1913 flood so far as I remember.

1917 that was a different story, I was around 12 then. I remember going to school that morning and there was no sign of any water coming up. It had the ice gorge, and up in the river, there was talk about it. No radio or anything in them days, why it was extras out every hour or so in the day that would give you information. That's the only way you could ever get any information as to what was happening on the river there outside of observing it.

Q: Was that the "Penny Press?"

A: No that was the old "Commercial Tribune," and of course the present "Enquirer," "Post," and "Times Star," that we had. We used to have four papers. There used to be the morning paper, the "Commercial Tribune." It was always the "Enquirer," But all of them was coming out every once in a while with information on the river, and any ice stories.

I remember it was just a solid mass of ice, it was like one chunk of ice would come up and slide up on top of another and then freeze. Another one would get on up top of that and climbed higher and freeze there. I saw cakes of ice bigger square than this room and maybe it wasn't quite that big, but me being a youngster, they were two or three times higher than I was. But down in back of our place there was about a row of old barges in the river about a hundred foot from shore and between the barges and the shoreline that river froze just like a lake. It was smooth as glass, and boy, we kids used to have a wonderful time skating on that every evening after school. That morning as we were going to school that river down there was within its banks and we were planning on going skating when we got home from school.

Oh, I come home at noontime, I thought I could see the old muddy water coming up the gutter in front of the house. Mother was all excited and everything, and dad was at work and she didn't know whether to let us go back to school or not, but we did. And it was coming home from school that we couldn't get, I couldn't get, in the front of the house. The water was already up in front of the house on the sidewalk. We were coming along a little grade like up from Berry Avenue, started at Third and Berry and started coming on up the upper end of Dayton, so we ran back up the street and cut through somebody's yard and went through the alley and got back there, and dad was home then.

I could see the horse was in the stable in the back and the wagon was back there. They were getting ready to get out, and I remember him saying, "If they don't dynamite that pretty soon," he says, "we are going to have an awful gosh-darn flood around here." Later on the afternoon, I don't particularly recall what time it was, but I heard them talking about dynamiting. Well, it was the next day then, that they dynamited at some time.

That river went down just about as fast as it came up. It left a lot of ice behind. When it went down there was just everything that went down. There were houses that were jammed up the river further in the ice, boats, everything, I seen these barges. Another thing that I remember, that scared me so. These barges in the back of our place that were 400 or 500 feet down, and 100 foot out from the shore, were tied upon shore with these big barge ropes two inch in diameter. Hemp rope, and they were tied around great big willow trees, around, oh, I guess, two to three feet in diameter. When that ice began to move out, it tore those barges right out of there and snapped that two inch diameter hemp line like it was a piece of string, and didn't even budge the tree, but it just pulled the rope right smack in two. The barges were just trapped in the ice.

I wasn't there at the time, but that was the time when, what's her name, Ruth, when one day Ruth Niemann was found. I recall Dad talking about it, as they were standing down there watching some of this ice and rubble going down, and there was a house on top of a house coming down the river, sticking up and frozen in the ice, and there was a basket on there, and they could hear crying from a little baby. They went out, and one of the men went out and grabbed the basket and got back safely. There was a little baby girl. They were never able to find that child's parents and the Niemann's had never had any children, so they adopted her, raised her and today she is married and has a couple of children. She was a product of the 1917 ice gorge and flood. That was all about the situation that I think that I remember. I remember seeing pictures, but later on here, had to be during the war when the river froze over, and of course we were down there then, but we wasn't living near the river.

Dad, in the summer time he had a confectionary stand down at the beach. There used to be the Queen City Beach, the Primrose and the Manhattan Beach. Everybody from around here on a sunshiny afternoon or a Sunday, they went for an outing they either went to Coney Island or they went to those three beaches over here in Kentucky. There was as many as 5,000 to 10,000 people in swimming there on a Sunday afternoon. We had a stand down there during the summer months, one of these knock down affairs. You could get them up in the summer time, and when the season was over you would fold them up and throw them in the backyard somewhere. We actually lived down there.

Old Omar was the one that taught me how to swim. I was about 14, 13 or 14 years old, we were on the river one early morning in the summer months when there was nothing doing down on the beach. I had to watch the stands, dad was working. He would be down there on weekends. When nobody was around he would close up, and lock up. I decided that morning I was going to get the canoe out and go for a ride. It was such a beautiful calm morning. I was taking a wave in the back of the old Qmar, and about the third one back was a big white cap and over I go, canoe and everything. I had to swim or drown, holding the canoe and paddles. I finally made it back all right. From then on the river never bothered me in the least. Dad drove the horse and wagon in 1917 before it started to gorge up. There was several places where people would drive their horse and buggies, and horse and wagons or walk straight across.

Q: Guess it was hard on the bridge monopolies in those days?

A: There wasn't the traffic that there is nowadays. You hardly realize the difference in what 30 years, 34 years will make in progress. Looking back, you saw one or two horse and wagons in ten or twelve squares around here. There wasn't much traffic. People have all moved in the last 30 years, 20 years, more rapidly right along. Why it was nothing to spend an hour and a half or two hours walking from one end of town to maybe Dayton down to Newport, and go to a store or to see somebody. You would take an afternoon stroll. If you were rich enough to have a horse and buggy, then you would get out the buggy, hitch up the horse, and take a ride that way. Many a time we went on the streetcar to visit people right out here in Delhi and back in Cincinnati. That was an all-day jaunt. Now it is 20 or 30 minute drive from your home to there.

Q: Of course that's thirty minutes at the risk of your life.

A: Oh yes.

Sid Dawson

John Knoepfle, Interviewer.

Question: This is the band room of the Grand View Inn, and I am talking to Sid Dawson who is the leader of the Riverboat Ramblers. He has been on the Missouri and Mississippi on the *Goldenrod* and a few other steamboats and I hope he will be able to carry the ball from here.

Answer: I don't really know where to begin. I suspect that being a St. Louisan or being raised in very early childhood in St. Louis, like everyone else that grew up down there came in pretty close contact with riverboats either through actually working with them or just actually seeing them on the river. My first recollection of the steamboats were the early excursions, and I can't remember the name, it was either the *President* or the *Capitol*. Perhaps you will remember, in about 1935.

Q: It's still running I think?

A: Yes I think it's still down in Dallas, or no it's in Texas somewhere Galveston, I suppose. At any rate that was the forerunner actually of the *Admiral*, which is the big excursion boat in St. Louis today. About the most vivid recollection I have of the, which one was it, the *President* or the *Capitol* on the Streckfus Line? I remember seeing Fate Marable playing calliope when I was about eight years old, something like that, I was pretty young. Playing with the plugs in his ears about 7:30 or eight o'clock in the morning, hurrying all the people on for the daily. They had an all day excursion, I think, and an evening cruise. That was I believe just before Fate. When did he die, in 1939 or 1938? Well, he was, as I was saying, playing on this boat. I saw him very early in the morning, I know, I was pretty young. It was part of actually what later was the beginning or inspiration for this idea of the Riverboat Ramblers. I mean the fact that Fate Marable, and subsequently other people we worked with. Both Frank and I played with what I guess would be one of the greats of riverboat jazz, Billy Jackson. He was called or considered the king of riverboat jazz, Billy's heyday in the twenties, 1926 and 1927. I recall Billy saying it was an all day job. They used to start out in the morning, and they played, well like at noontime, a couple of hours, and they played in the afternoon for dancing in the salons or saloons. They called them saloons, didn't they?

Q: This was on the boat?

A: Yes, on the boats out of St. Louis, and out of New Orleans, Cincinnati, and Memphis. Then they did the evening session, and then the night dancing. All and all, the bands would work about ten or twelve hours a day.

Q: It was a pretty grueling operation.

A: The pattern they set then is pretty much followed by the few remaining excursion boats today; when they hit a port the band marches on the gangplank and plays. More or less ballyhoos the attraction of the excursion on the boat, they take the local people out. They might hit, for example, I remember playing in Redwing, Minnesota on the one trip I made on the *Gordon C. Greene* when we went up as far as Minneapolis, I got off in Minneapolis. We got off at Redwing and played on the gangplank and got back on, and the people got on and we took them up to Minneapolis. Then I suppose the boat brought them back. But I got off in Minneapolis. I think my real interest in riverboats first came from a man by the name of Wendell W. Gardner who lived in my home-town of Ferguson, Missouri, a suburb of St. Louis. Wendell Gardner had, I don't know, he passed away a few years back, but I grew up with his son, his son and I, in fact we are still very close friends, had one of the largest collections of steamboat pictures. Perhaps you have come across his name?

Q: Yes.

A: In fact he had a very highly valuable and fine collection of steamboat pictures. Wendell had been at one time a riverboat pilot and had served in various functions on riverboats. He knew Samuel Clemens, Mark Twain, very, very well. He was from Davenport, of course that was upriver from Hannibal, Mark Twain's original hometown.

Q: Did Wendell have any stories about . . . ?

A: Yes, he had an endless store of stories. It's pretty hard to remember any actual details in the stories of fires and going aground and various things. I recall more than anything, since I did grow up practically neighbors, and practically in his home as much as in my own, his walls were lined with pictures of all the various, the *Clairmont*, and most of the old packets, the *Eagle*, the Eagle Line. So he used to take us down to the river on Sunday afternoons a great deal to see, the Model A Fords, it was in the middle thirties. Go down and look at the old boats and talk to some of the captains. Captain Billy, one of them I remember very well. In fact I think Captain Billy is still running the *Golden-rod* if I'm not mistaken.

Q: The Missouri side is pretty foreign to me. I have taped men like Captain Wisherd who worked out of Missouri. He brought the *St. Paul* over here.

A: My personal feelings about the riverboats were that they were instrumental almost as much as anything else. In fact I would say more than anything else in spreading jazz or the gospel around. Louis Armstrong played his first major engagement on one of the riverboats with Fate Marable's band. Fate Marable was undoubtedly one of the finest or best known of all the riverboat jazzmen. He had fine, very elaborate, very large orchestras, violins, and everything, the whole works. As I say Louis Armstrong first came upriver out of New Orleans. His first time away from home was on the riverboats playing well as far as St. Louis and I think he went further up to Davenport. Bix Beiderbecke, he is renowned and an inspiration for all jazzmen today, in fact all popular musicians, actually learned and got his first experience from hearing the riverboat jazz bands when they hit Davenport, Iowa.

Q: You were playing a Beiderbecke favorite there, weren't you?

A: We do play quite a few of them. But were it not for the riverboats probably Bix quite possibly would never have turned to jazz as his medium of expression. Again my own personal experiences beyond the trip with the *Gordon C. Greene* were about 1944 or 1945, I don't recall which, I played an engagement on the *Goldenrod* showboat, the "Old Melodrama." I don't remember, they were doing "Orphan Nell," now or something. I've seen a great number of these melodramas of course they are quite overdone and the hammier the better. The audience encourages and hollers.

Q: Saw these in St. Louis, I suppose?

A: That's right on the *Goldenrod*. In fact, John, if you go down on the levee in St. Louis, you'll just see a mile or so of nothing but old river packets, and even some sternwheelers still in existence. In fact I saw one about, it's been a few years ago, going upriver, a fine old sternwheeler still chugging along. I don't recall the name of it, *Fulton* or something, I do believe. I think they are still in existence, I don't know for what purpose.

Q: There are still some big sternwheel tows on the Ohio operating, and the *Monongahela* is a tremendous tow. That's on the upper river, but the packets are gone now. I think the *Gordon C. Greene* was the last of them. They used the *Gordon*, they used the *Gordon* in the "Kentuckian," if you saw the picture.

A: No, I didn't see it.

Q: They had a tow on the outside. You couldn't see that, of course. They took her out of retirement as a restaurant.

A: Well I played on the, my first of course was on the *Gordon C. Greene*, but then on the *Goldenrod*. Then later on the *S. S. Douglas* with a jazz group from St. Louis. As far as I know it is still there, it was a tavern at a dock and everything is done up very much, like the old early riverboats were with the ornate deck lamps and ships bell and fishnets and what have you. A very picturesque, dressed boat. Then later the *Fort Gage*, which actually turned out to be quite a thing. We took the job originally on more or less a percentage basis Just for the fun of playing on the river. A bunch of us who liked the river and sort of felt strongly attracted to the fact that jazz and the river sort of went hand-in-hand all the way through the history of New Orleans jazz. So, we went on the *Fort Gage* with the idea of playing maybe one or two weekends and all of a sudden overnight it was almost a national success.

The "St. Louis Dispatch" ran a large spread on it in the "Sunday Rotogravure." The people of "Today Magazine" ran about a three page thing of "Jazz on the Mississippi." Which, was important in that the Mississippi was so awfully important to jazz. It brought the folk music considered the only original American art form or a contribution to the art form upriver where it could be heard by so very many people. Eventually from St. Louis it spread to Kansas City and Chicago, and of course, to New York, and then all over the world. So, especially after the people of "Today," and the "Post-Dispatch," then why, we played to capacity crowds. Well the boat couldn't take the vast number of people, and the ship's architect just happened to be a passenger, and a customer got up and made quite a stink about the boat was going to capsize unless people stopped clapping their hands and stamping their feet in time to the music. So, from then on the *Fort Gage*, that was the last cruise except for once when it broke loose from its moorings in a storm and had a considerable amount of damage. In 1951, I believe that was.

Q: You were on there in the forties I guess.

A: Well 1949 and 1950s, the late forties and it was shortly after that I got the idea, when I knew I would be forming my own group, a group to travel; if you wanted to leave St. Louis I couldn't think of a better idea than with the Riverboat Ramblers. So, consequently our uniforms were that of the old riverboat captains.

Q: I can see on here the lapels . . .

A: That's essentially how the Riverboat Ramblers started, but it could begin because I had quite an impression of riverboats. In fact, about the most fun I ever had was playing on the river. I did another stint, although this was not a riverboat thing. I had a band when I was in college, and we were at Lake of the Ozarks on an excursion boat. We played, in fact, we were on the lake practically all afternoon and all night and we had about five hours in between, in which to sleep and eat. And so, up until about 1951, I had practically lived on the water of some sort or another.

Q: That's wonderful.

A: Essentially that is the whole story.

Q: If we had more time I could perhaps tire you out, but I know you are wanting to get upstairs.

A: Well there is so much, and I have a lot of pictures and things, but I just don't, it's so hard to remember so much of what you know.

Q: Where did you go to college?

A: University of Missouri. I was an English major there. Journalism.

Q: I'd better take up something. A teacher's wage is not happy one.

A: I know, in fact I had a semester in education, and then I found out what teachers made.

Q: Well we have a good time going around taping people, as you can see.

A: Yes, I imagine it's quite interesting. I wish I could remember more. I've been on so many boats. On the *Goldenrod* we had our publicity stills made. In fact, one of them is around the wheel that's on display on the *Goldenrod*, and they were taken on the gangplank, we are marching down the gangplank and everything. If we had more time, I don't have them with me, they are down at the hotel. If you will leave your address with me I'll send you a set of them. You might get a kick out of them. One of them is pretty good, you can see Eads Bridge in the background and some packet, I don't remember the name of it now. It was docked directly behind it.

Q: Well good. We'll take it off at this time.

John Knoepfle

J. Emory Edgington, July 16, 1957, Lancaster, Ohio

Question: What are batwings?

Answer: Batwings, that's right, a wheel on the outside with a long shaft across it from one side to the other and a belt connected with the bullwheel. It was a big wheel, they called it a bullwheel. When he bought the boat the boiler on it was a thresh machine boiler with the engine up on top of the boiler. That's when I first went steamboating.

Q: That *Katie Prather* is kind of a famous legendary boat?

A: I supposed you have heard that legend about what became of her. That Bill Kropler was mate on the Louisville packet boats and his father was too, and afterward he was mate for the Greene Lines. Then there was a boy by the name of Jake Chaney, a third cousin of mine, they was decking and my brother Arch and himself and Kropler and Jake were all deckhands and cooks and in between everything you could do. Brother Arch would go to the pilot house, and steer and so would I. That's the first piloting either one of us done. We had no license. Father told us what to do. One time I was setting up in the pilothouse below Manchester light and there was a sandbar up there. I was sitting up on a high stool, steering you know, a little old pilot wheel, I didn't know the sandbar was there, and I didn't pull over in the channel, and hit that sandbar, and went over into the pilot wheel. It was hand power, of course, didn't hurt me any.

Q: Well I heard those batwings could walk over a sandbar?

A: You know the last one that ever I was on, I wasn't even working on them, I was working for T. J. Hall, and the river was down dead low. Matter of fact the gauges were a foot and nine inches below the zero gauge. It was that low. All the bar were way out, so Captain Hall, he asked me if I didn't want to, I was working for the *Iroquois* at that time, asked me if I didn't want to go up, and look at the river when it was down so low. I said okay. Well I took the train and went up as far as Ashland, and then used the streetcar. Understood that a little boat called the *Guyandotte*, was the last one of the batwings too, and she used to run up Guyandotte River, and at this time a man by the name of Murphy owned her at Catlettsburg, and he was a produce man. He handled calves, eggs, chickens, anything, way of stuff, produce. I think even calves. She wasn't big enough to handle any cattle outside of calves.

I understood with an inquiry this little boat *Guyandotte*, which was a batwing was down the river below Ashland, below Ironton rather coming up the river, and I went down to see Mr. Murphy, and he told me about where I could catch her if I would go down to Ironton, and she would be coming up, and just go down and hail her and they would land and get me. Captain Ed West was the pilot and captain on her at that time and a man by the name of John Wilson was the engineer. However, I went down to and seen her coming in at the old Campbell place. Campbell was at that time a mansion. I got off right there and went down the river and went down out on a bar halfway across the river, dry shod, and hailed her.

She came in, she only drew nine inches. I got on, we went up the river. The river was so low up above Catlettsburg, this Davisdon Shallows was there. You had to go up over that, there wasn't water enough for her to go straight and when we got up to the, there was all big rocks too, of course, none of them were out dry, but the boat would run up one on this side and we'd take pike poles and shove her off of that, and she'd come ahead and work slow going ahead and run up on another one on the other side. We would have to take and shove off that one. Done that there, worked up through the shallows, went on up.

Q: You walked over the shallows, too?

A: I got off at Huntington. She went back down the river. I went on and took the train. I bought one of these Allegheny skiffs. I started down the river rowing and I had my notebook. I made and estimated heights, bars, drew sketches, so forth and so on. I went down as far as Portsmouth and this little *Guyandotte* she came down the river. I hailed her and got on her down as far as Maysville on her in that low water. I was so familiar with the river below Maysville that I didn't think I needed any, so I took the train and went back to Cincinnati. And we had a rise shortly after that too, so I had to go to work on the boat, I had to take the boat out. I was working by the year at that time for Hall.

Q: You didn't mention the names of your brothers. I wonder if you could tell us something about them.

A: The one next to me was brother Arch; he was a captain and a pilot. He died just about three years ago. The next one was brother Fred, he died about six years ago. Brother Drew was the fourth boy, and he's been dead about eleven years, perhaps a little longer than that. Brother Roy was lost on the *McBride* here at Cincinnati when they struck that bridge pier, the L and N Bridge pier. I was the youngest one. Brother Ernest who I spoke of a while ago was nine years old when he died in that Good Samaritan Hospital in Cincinnati. He was only nine years old at the time. He would have been a livewire steamboat man if he had of lived. As a boy he was a livewire. Really that's what killed him from the fact that he was on one of our boats at that time, *Charles B. Pearce* I believe it was. He was scuffling with his brother, and he run and hit the corner the table. Right here. Caused an abscess and he died from that. Had two sisters, one sister's now living. The other had died 25 years I guess.

Q: Did your brothers ever combine in an operation?

A: Oh, father and my brothers and myself. My father, the first steamboat he ever owned was a half interest in a boat, a little boat called *John Kyle*, a local packet. He was half owner in her. Then he bought the first *Handy*, the *Handy 1*, and he owned that for, I was seven years old, owned her at that time. Then he sold out part of it to the Redden boys at Vanceburg. They owned a farm there just above Rome right where dam 32 is now. And he and the Reddens didn't get along very good so they traded him that farm for his half interest in the

Handy 1. I was nine years old at that time, between eight and nine. My father owned that first *Handy* when I was seven years old. The reason I remember that, we lived at Vanceburg, see he run the *Handy* from Vanceburg to Maysville, a round trip a day. She was leaving at five o'clock in the morning and getting back around eight or nine, ten o'clock at night. We lived there and of course we always stayed at home every night. I was in the back yard of the house, and I run a doggoned rake through my, between my big toe and the next toe, it come clear through. I was only seven years old that's why I remember that particular time. Next boat he bought after that was the *Katie Prather.* That's when I went to work.

Q: You mentioned the last time we talked about a *Sandy Gyper.*

A: That's a batwing. He rebuilt the *Katie Prather* after he owned her a couple of years. Put a bow on her, a regular marine bore, put on, bought an engine, think the size of that engine was 9 by 14 inches. It run the wheels the same way on that bullwheel. They put that on the deck. Fastened it to the deck, then they run that to the pulley from that engine. That made her a faster boat. She wasn't very fast even at that, I think the best she could do was six miles an hour.

Q: Well did he get that from Captain Prather?

A: Yes, Prather first had the cabin and hull as a Sandy boat type. He used it to peddle tinware and he would tow upriver and then float down river and sell this tinware. He conceived the idea of putting this thrashing machine motor on there and the wheel on there, and loading it down with tinware and going up that way. My father made one trip with him up the river and back down. In one instance there, at that time the coal mines up the Kanawha River, they was a slack coal, they would dump over the river bank, there wasn't any sales for it. And he told me about up at Raymond City, they didn't have to buy any coal up there, because all they had to do was run the head of the boat into one of those coal dumps and run the coal on the deck, and then take and wheel it back next to the boiler where they'd use it.

Another thing he said at that time, he said he got up, there was only the two of them on the boat, me, Prather, and my father, and got up one cold morning, up the Kanawha River there, and where they'd had tied up after they had got the coal on at Raymond City, put a head line and a stern line out. Said he got up the next morning to build a fire in the cook stove and get their breakfast, he went in the wood box to get some kindling to start the fire, and he picked up a darn snake. If I remember right he called it a copperhead snake. He said he turned loose of it mighty quick.

There were so many interesting things in life. I was speaking of boats. My father built the *Silver Wave.* He sold it to Captain Joe Webb. Turned around and bought the *M. P. Wells.* These boats were single deck boats, no packet boats. They operated them between Portsmouth and Cincinnati. In short, for instance, trades between Portsmouth to Manchester, and then from Vanceburg to Maysville. Then from Augusta to Maysville. Two round trips a day. And finally they went too. That business got so low, we decided we would go in the Cincinnati to Portsmouth trade, which we did. So we then put the cabin upstairs, made a double deck boat out of the *M. P. Wells* and also out of the *Silver Wave*. However, I'm ahead of my story there.

Webb, he took the *Bellevue* and went to, he bought the *Bellevue*, and he went to towing from Moscow to Cincinnati with stone and carrying stone and brick from Maysville to Cincinnati too. He decided he wanted to trade back in packet boat again, so he and pa traded the *Silver Wave* for the *Bellevue*. Finally my father, he bought the *Silver Wave* again, he owned her three times. So she finally burned at Higginsport, burned down to the main deck. He rebuilt her, then a single deck boat and called her the *William Duffey*. Then he kept her quite a little while. He had the *Duffey* and the *M. P. Wells* both at that time. I had gone west, was west three years, and when I came back why he had done all that so far as rebuilding the boat. So I went in charge of the *Duffey* and I operated her. He operated the *Wells*. The old packetboat business got bad, and so he couldn't do anything, so he went to towing out of Cincinnati, the local harbor work in the daytime, and at nighttime we would go up the river and take up barges as high up as Buena Vista.

Q: Coal barges?

A: No, be freestone barges, they used to tow freestone from Buena Vista to Cincinnati. There were mills there, Millers and Haydens. They had barges, flats rather, we'd call them now. They were river barges. They would load that stone and tow it to Cincinnati.

Q: Where did they put that in there?

A: You mean . . .

Q: The barges when they brought them into Cincinnati.

A: Just below where the power plant is now, just above Mill Street, between Baymiller and Mill Street there, you see. Wait a minute, Baymiller is below Mill, anyway it was just above where the power plants sets on the lower end of it. I think the Ohio River Company has their elevator on part of it. They made sidewalks out of it. There are some of them in Cincinnati yet, I think. They do not operate those mills any more. We used to carry that free stone on the packet boats too. In small lots, you know. If somebody just wanted just a few, for a walk in a small town, used to carry that as freight on a packet boat.

Q: Were they already made up?

A: They sawed it. They mined the freestone up in the hills there back of Buena Vista, run it down, they had a mill there, they sawed it. Let's see there was Chadins and Miller and Stewarts, they had one above, no below Rockville, just below Buena Vista the Stewarts did, and they had one up at, I can't recall the name of that mill, about three miles above Buena Vista. They didn't ship by barges, they shipped by railroad, hauled too. They were small concerns those two, the Stewarts. That one up at, I can't think of the name of the landing.

Q: Well, it must have been around the turn of the century you were doing that?

A: That was from 1890-1895, 1894, up until around, pretty close to 1900. As a matter of fact, it was larger than that because I was married when I was 19 years old, and we done this towing with the *Bellevue* and the *M. P. Wells* after I was married. I was married in 1889. Around the 1890s up until about 1900, just about that time. However we, I'm ahead of my story. My father also bought the first *Kentucky*, was the Kentucky River packet boat. They built a new one. They sold the old one and he bought it, and he rebuilt it, and called it the *Charles B. Pearce*. He run her from Portsmouth to Cincinnati at the same time we run the *M. P. Wells*. She was double deck at that time, we run her from Portsmouth to Cincinnati. But father had traded at that time to Jim Duffey at Marietta, Ohio.

He was a brother of William Duffey at Higginsport. So he sold her then, Duffey did to his brother at Louisville, which was the Duffey Sand Company down there. They're still in existence, the sand company is still in business. The last one I knew is not living now. He has been dead a couple of three years, I think. They kept running those boats until they wore out, those Duffeys. We got into a fight with the White Collar Line. In the freight business. The C & O Railroad together, and we broke the White Collar Line. The C & O Railroad and ourselves broke the White Collar Line up, and they broke us up too.

Q: There was a rate war going on then.

A: Yes, a rate war. You would carry passengers for ten cents from one point to another. Freight for five cents a hundred pounds. Sometimes wouldn't get anything for it, in order to keep the White Collar Line from getting it. They did the same thing for us, too.

Q: The Bay Line was also fighting White Collar.

A: Yes, they had the *Urania,* and the *Lizzie Bay*, the *Minnie Bay,* and *Henry M. Stanley,* and had that *Louise,* and *Hibernia*, she was the one in the collision on the upper Ohio River and drowned so many people.

Q: No, I didn't know about that.

A: Drowned about 165 people. The pilot, he was drunk, and they had a lot of drunk women up in the pilot house. The way I heard it, of course I was too young to know very much about it at that time. The way I heard it was the pilot, he was trying to pilot the boat, and the woman was on one side, and the other women on the other and he met the, can't remember the other boat now. He met her, and the women blew the whistle; some of the women blew the whistle, they was drunk too. And there was a mix up, and they got together, and they sank one of them maybe both, I don't remember now. At any rate the *Hibernia* had the excursion on her. She belonged to the Bays at that time. Drowned about 165 people out on that excursion. Well that's all hearsay from me, but I think that is just about right.

Q: Well I guess things got pretty touchy on the river with everybody running into competition.

A: Yes the White Collar Line had an operation, from Cincinnati to Madison, Cincinnati to Louisville, Cincinnati to Pomeroy. John Barrett, he bought two packet boats. He run them in opposition to the White Collar Line. I think he run them, one from Madison to Cincinnati and one from Cincinnati to Louisville. Seems to me like he run one of them above Cincinnati, up the river, but I am not positive about that now. Been quite a while ago.

But thinking about *Katie Prather*, I wanted to tell you, a while ago I started to tell you about Bill Coffer, a story that he made up, this is all make believe. My son and Captain Carney's Sal was on the *Henry M. Stanley*, I believe it was, coming from Cincinnati up home. Captain Carney's son was on there to make the trip, they were both about seven years old, six or seven, maybe not quite that old. However, the son was always interested in knowing the *Katie Prather*. He would ask more questions about the *Katie Prather* than you could shake a stick at. However, Dewey he got my son on one side of him, up on the boiler deck, after he left Cincinnati, and captain's boy, Joe I believe it was, on the other side, and the son asked Bill, they got talking and Bill told that his steamboating was on the *Katie Prather*, which it was, and the son then wanted to know what became of the *Katie Prather*. So Bill Coffer, he told this story, his wife, she was sitting back a little piece behind, she heard it all.

He told the boys he said, "I was on the *Katie Prather* up by Brush Creek up to Vanceburg, and some man up at Wagner's Riffle, which was about five miles up Brush Creek," and father did have the *Katie Prather* up Wagner's Riffle come on high water. Took her up to get some corn or something like that. Bill he made this story all up as he went along. He said some man had thousands of turkeys up there. He wanted to ship them out. He come to Captain George, that was my father's name. Said, "Captain George, take the *Katie Prather* up there, load them turkeys on the *Katie Prather*, and take them to market."

And he said Captain George took her up there and tied her up to the bank, put out the plank, didn't have any stages then, put out a stage plank, you know. Here came the turkeys down, driving the turkeys down to the boat and filled her up downstairs and he didn't have room down there and he took them up on the roof, commenced taking them up on the roof. When he got them up there he was afraid they would fly away so he took staples and a hammer and drove a staple down through, between their toes and fastened so they couldn't fly away. Said them boys got them all on, but one great big old gobbler and he was a great big gobbler too, this was Bill's story, and he said they nailed his foot down, and one of the boys, he said he didn't know it was Dave King or one of the others, drove the staple a little bit too far in, he said he hit the hammer a little too hard, and it went down and hurt the old gobbler. He said the old gobbler made a gobble noise, raised his wings and flew, and he said all them turkeys raised their wings and flew, and he said up in the air went the *Katie Prather* and that was the last of the *Katie Prather*.

I was on the *Delta Queen* last year. I was going on a trip to Pittsburgh. I was one of the pilots. Not Pittsburgh, but to Parkersburg, we didn't get quite up that. We turned around at Mustapha Island. And McCann, the clerk on the

Delta Queen, he announced different things over the loud speakers from down there broadcasting and telling them about they come to Brush Creek there, and says the legend is the little boat called the *Katie Prather*, and he went on to tell the story, but he had it all mixed up a certain sense, adding things to it wasn't the story, but he tried to smooth it out you know. But along the same lines.

Q: Shot a gun and got them over the ripples.

A: How was that?

Q: Shot off the guns, so the turkeys took off, and got them over the ripples?

A: No, Bill didn't tell it that way in those days. They've added that to it, you know. They have added a whole lot to that story since. You heard it that way did you? No she was below the riffles, she was just up to the riffles. That's the way Bill told it. Said the turkeys all raised their wings up when that fellow, drove the staple too hard on the gobbler's toes, and he made a gobble noise, and they all raised their wings, and went up in the air, and that was the last of the *Katie Prather*, never seen her anymore. The old "Waterways Journal" published that there thing too, once.

Q: I heard that. You mentioned that those early boats went up the Guyandotte Creek. Do you know how far up?

A: That was the Guyandotte River.

Q: The Guyandotte River.

A: No, I never was up the Guyandotte River myself. It's very narrow, and she only drew nine inches; of course, she could go a long way up there but it's narrow. I don't know, I never heard how far up she went, but she went as far as she could, I guess. Of course, after they built the railroads up the Guyandotte, why that was the same thing on the Big Sandy River, she built up there, why that broke that up.

Q: Did you ever get up the Big Sandy?

A: No never above the locks. I have been up just below the locks.

Q: That was a nasty . . .

A: It was very shallow, that was shallow. That was an awful busy stream. They had batwings of course, and it would get awful low. They had the boat out. I had the, father and I, had the *J. C. Hopkins* chartered one season. Another season following that I chartered them myself. My brother Fred and I chartered it. Captain Jim Sanford, he went in with us too, about three of us had a charter we run up from Chilo to Cincinnati in low water. She only drew 14 inches. The river got so low then we could just barely get her over the New Richmond bar, we had two flats, and we towed them ahead of her. We put our freight on that and held them with the boat. Didn't carry any passengers because it was too slow, just carried freight. We had the *Andy Hatcher* chartered one time in a low water season, too. We run her the Vanceburg-Maysville trade.

Q: All those were Big Sandy boats?

A: Big Sandy, they were sidewheel boats. I believe we started to charter the *Fairfield* but didn't. She was accurately named *Yost*. By the way the *J. C.*

Hopkins, she had two engines on her, we had to carry a striker and an engineer. She was a sidewheel boat all right, but she didn't have that shaft across the hull. Had an engine on each side. She only drew 14 inches too.

Q: Well, they all hauled molasses out of there?

A: Yes, sorghum, molasses, chickens, eggs, calves, all that sort of stuff. Carried whiskey on the boat as freight. I expect they did carry a lot of it for their own personal use. They'd come down here at Catlettsburg, lay overnight and most of them would get drunk. At that time Catlettsburg was a lively town.

Q: I heard as much.

A: Yes, all front streets was a levee there and was about two squares long. That was all saloons along there and mostly restaurants and one hotel.

Q: West Virginia was dry, wasn't it a dry state?

A: It was at one time, but it wasn't at that time. It was dry for a long while.

Q: Could you talk some about the logs that came out of there?

A: Yes, Crane and Cole, they had three sawmills here at Cincinnati and they got their timber, they floated that out of there in rafts, you know. And Ironton had three mills above where the bridge is now, sawmills and they got their timber out of Guyandotte and out of Big Sandy. They held rafts down at the mills, and then they held on both shores below Catlettsburg on the Ohio side, principally clear down to where dam 29 is now. Sometimes below that. They had the *J. O. Cole* and the *Crown Hill* towing those logs down.

Q: I understand sometimes the boat would break up in the Big Sandy?

A: Yes, and they'd come out and the people along the river that had a skiff would go out and catch those logs. Then Crane and Cole would come along, they had their crew come along, they had their brand on them, and the Ironton people had their brand on them, too. These men would come along and gather these logs up and pay the people I think 25 cents a log for catching them. They were rough and tumble people, too. They would try and beat the people out of as much money as they could counting the logs; they'd claim they wasn't their logs and say, "Oh well, we will take it along, if you don't want to hold it or bother with it," something like that.

Q: I hear that as many as 90,000 logs would get through some of those boom busts up there?

A: Oh, I expect there was that many anyway. I don't think I ever heard that, but there is no doubt. They'd have those rafts up the Sandy River, and up Guyandotte River, and then would come that flood.

Q: I have heard a lot of comments on the logging and apparently the Cole Crane people were pretty rough to deal with.

A: They themselves were not, but the men they sent up there, they were people out of Sandy River and log people. Of course they'd be half drunk and all that sort of thing. I tell you they killed a man up there at Logan's Gap, just above Logan's Gap, Henry Griffiths. He had some logs and he got into an argument, and they got into a fight, and they killed him that one time. That was the only time anybody was killed that I heard of. I knew Henry and knew when he was killed. Of course, Henry drank, and they were drinking too. Who was at fault I don't know. Some kind of argument over logs.

Q: Norval Horton told me that, I guess it must have been after the mills were gone, the *Guyandotte* dredged out logs from the banks there below Eastern Avenue took them up above the dam at Coney Island and dropped them in a hole up there. Do you know anything about that?

A: I never heard that, but Crane and Cole before they went out of business, instead of bringing logs down by the river, understanding at the time was the timber was so far back from the Sandy River, that they loaded them on cars from the C & O Railroad, brought them down and built a derrick just below Brent and above the Cincinnati waterworks there. Put a crane on the top of the hill, I mean on top of the river bank and switch in there and unload those logs with this crane, put them in the river, and then they had one boat, I think the *J. O. Cole* at that time. I don't remember now whether they had sold the *Crown Hill* or not. However they were using the *J. O. Cole*, and the other boat and the logs from there down to the mills as they needed them, wanted them sawed up. Of course, they didn't tow them down in as big a rafts as they could.

I was pilot on the *Princess* in the Coney Island trade one season. The *J. O. Cole* came down the river with a big raft full of logs. I was coming up through there in low water too. Just barely water enough to get the *Princess* up over the Crawfish Bar. It was the *Island Queen*, they'd tie her up. She couldn't get up over there. Bringing the *Princess* up I'd have to come ahead on her, two licks dead slow, and she'd hit bottom and stop. Then I would stop her, and that suction would catch up with us. I would come ahead on her again to get up over Crawfish Bar. To get her up. Didn't have any trouble getting her down because the water would back up behind her, and float her over going down.

However, I was starting to say the *J. O. Cole* was coming down above Crawfish Bar. Up there where the boat club is now at the foot of Sara Avenue, and I was standing up by the Gas Works. Well, I come ahead on the, had water enough to do it, come ahead the *Princess*, half head instead of slow bell like I had been coming up over. To get up before she got any in there, she couldn't, current in the river, didn't have any lock and dams then. She couldn't stop of course, and I didn't want her to catch me in there with the *Princess*. Because there wasn't enough room for both of us because of the logs and the *Princess*.

Well, I come ahead with a half head, and I seen I wasn't quite going to make it that way, so I come ahead on a full head. Then she carried a swell behind her, and the launches, and everything at that boat club there at the foot of Clair Avenue. People were down there, the owners of them, they come out and they called me every name they could think of. (chuckles) But I couldn't do anything else. So it didn't do any particular damage, only put some of them out on the bank. It was an emergency, I couldn't help it. So it made me sore, and when I came back down, I came down and I opened her up full head again.

Wasn't a one of them showed up at all. Not a one of them. They didn't call me anymore, son of a bitches.

Q: I'll be darned. Well, I guess they, the *J. O. Cole* was backing down her tow. Didn't they do that?

A: Yes, she was backing it down, that's the way they guided them. They didn't tow them any other way but backed down. That was pretty difficult piloting, too. They had to know their business, had to know the river, where it set up a trench, you know, and get the raft in shape so it wouldn't hit the banks and sticks. So lots of times this would stick all night. But they done pretty good piloting. In fact, they did good piloting, good piloting.

Q: You went up after a while into coal towing?

A: Yes, I packet boated up until 1910. I went to work, the first tow boating I done, that is, I mean outside of what we done with our own boats prior to that. I worked for T. J. Hall and I was pilot at that time on Chilo packets, the Chilo to Cincinnati packet trade. Dan Morgan who was Hall's brother-in-law was hunting a pilot to help Captain Kirk Culver take the *Douglas Hall* up the Kanawha River, and bring out a tow of coal on the rise up there. They wanted to get her up there loose and bring the coal out, the coal was already loaded. He couldn't find, I had been uptown, and I was coming down over the levee, and met Dan coming up the hill, he stopped me, wanted to know if I knew of any pilots he could get to go up and help Captain Culver up with the *Douglas Hall*. I couldn't think of anybody, in fact there wasn't anybody that I knew of.

We talked a little bit and he says to me, "You couldn't possible go, could you?" I said, "I'm a pilot on the *Chilo*, no I couldn't go." He started up the hill and I started down and I just had to think that I had a steersman on the *Chilo*; Jim Barry, a very good pilot, but he didn't have any license. I thought perhaps Brother Drew, who was captain of the *Chilo* would lay me off and let me go on the *Douglas Hall* to help out, and let Jim Barry do the steering on the *Chilo*. So I called Dan back and I says, "Dan, wait a minute, maybe I could go if Drew can let me go. He can use Jim Barry." So we both went down, and I talked to Brother Drew about it and he says, "It would help Dan out," he says, "if you will give me your wages on there, why I would do it." He wanted my wages and his own too. I said, "Okay." I said to Dan, "I'll go and make this trip up." And I says, "Now I don't know about towing coal, I never towed coal down the river. I towed barges all right but never coal." Well he says, "Kirk Culver will help you out, whatever you can do. The main thing is to get her up there and get the coal out."

So the boat came up and we started out. Went up all right and when we got to Ashland, why here is Captain Hall and Dan Morgan both up there and got on the *Douglas Hall*. They was there, and we had to stop and get coal and fuel. So I could see Captain Kirk Culver and Dan Morgan and Tom Hall with their heads stuck together right out in front of the pilothouse down there talking. After a while I hear all three of them come up to the pilot house and got after

John Knoepfle

me to quit piloting on the *Chilo*, and working on there with Kirk Culver. I was getting $2 a day on the *Chilo* and the *Douglas Hall* was paying $5 a day.

I hesitated though, I said, "I don't know anything about towing coal," and Kirk says, "Captain, if you come on here, I'll learn you how to tow coal. I'll help you out every time you need me." He says, "I don't think you'll need me very often, but if you do, okay. I'll get up anytime and help you out, and if I think that you need me without you asking me I'll stay up in the pilothouse with you anyway." He says, "Now there is only one thing I will ask you." He says, "You know my failing, which was getting drunk once in a while." He says, "If I do, I only ask you to simply to stick with me. Don't run away from me." I said, "okay." So from then on I went to towing coal.

Q: You never towed for the Pittsburgh Combine?

A: No, I never worked for them. I worked for Island creek Coal Company twice, about nine years the first time and about four years the last time. Between that, I was in an accident; the first time, I worked for them I went with the McBride, I towed with McBride for about a year and he broke up. I did make a few trips while I was working for him, when the boat was laid up, why I made a few trips for the Ohio River Company on the *E. D. Kenna*. As soon as McBride broke up, why Mr. Morgan came after me to go pilot on the *Kenna* at Ingersoll, the Ohio River Company. So I was with them about five years that time. Then I went back to Island Creek and I was there for six or seven years, something like that. I don't recall exactly.

So they changed their superintendents and another man who is there now, he had favorites up the Kanawha River and he managed to let me go to put him on. Then I went with the Ohio River Company again and I stayed with them until I retired from the company. My wife was sick for about 14 years and she'd have first one stroke after another, and finally her mind went bad from that. When I quit, why she would know me sometimes, and sometimes she wouldn't when I was home. So I decided I would quit, and go home and stay with her as long as she lived, which I did. So I never went back to any regular work outside of the *Avalon*, and even before she passed away, I was on the *Avalon*. The first time they couldn't get anybody else and I went and the next year I was with them, and in fact, this last year would have been the sixth year that I have been on the *Avalon*.

That's a vacation for me. I've been working for the Standard Oil Company of Baton Rouge, *Esso Louisiana*. That was on the boat *Esso Louisiana*, that's Esso Standard Oil at Baton Rouge. From Louisville too, those pilots and captains, they didn't have any license above Louisville. They didn't know the river up there. Well they would get two pilots, and Louisville up the Kanawha, knew the river up there and put on there to learn them the river. Clayton Davis and Captain Ed Young and myself and Captain Troy Young too. We would be on the boat, the two of us would be on there about anywhere from 11 days to15 days from Louisville up to Boomer on the Kanawha River and back to Louisville. So I had about 11 months of that.

That is, about 15 days out of the month up there, and they would learn the river, so they could get your license. Of course, that's over with now that they've all got their license. All but one and of course, he learned the river with them now. But he was on them most of the time, he knew it all right the last time when I was on there, but he hadn't got his license. I talked to one of them at Louisville this summer on the *Avalon*, off the *Avalon*, when the *Louisiana* passed. He told me all the important news. Boy they were a fine bunch of men. Those trips were really vacations for me. Would only be 15 days out of the month, and sometimes I wouldn't catch them every month. They had a couple of other fellows to make trips on there. They made four or five trips. There was about four that I wasn't on. But I enjoyed that. Lots of good eats and all that southern stuff. Those southern cooks, you know.

Q: They are cooks, Captain.

A: Well, I don't know anything else much that I can tell you that you want to know, unless there is something you want to ask.

Q: You had begun to talk about towing coal. I wondered if you, well just in the beginning, talk about the problem of towing coal and fog on the river?

A: Okay. Well, I've had quite a great deal of experience running in fog. But I never have taken any long chances. On towing coals, I have run upstream with empty tows in fog and taken chances. But downstream, I have never taken any chances on towing coal downstream, because you have got too much tonnage there ahead of you and if you see anything you are getting into unexpected, you haven't got time to take care of it. So the best thing to do is to tie up to the bank and wait until the fog lifts or the atmosphere clears up so you can go safely. That's always been my experience. Now they have radar, and the government won't stand behind the pilots. Take his license away from him if he stays out in the fog and gets in trouble trying to run fog when he should be tied up, and could have tied up. The companies won't stand behind him and if the insurance people gets too hot they pay you off.

Q: Were there any parts of the river where fog was more difficult than others?

A: Every few miles or several miles where big creeks and rivers came into the Ohio River, you are more likely to find fog than you are a place where those rivers don't empty into the Ohio. For some reason the fog generally raises in these small streams and blows out into the Ohio. And very often the difference of the temperature of the water out of the small stream into the Ohio River will cause a fog. Then the weather conditions will cause fog. We have what they call rain fog, that's one of the meanest fogs there is because once in a while you think you can go, and I have and started out, and others have started out, and went a little while and we would run into a batch of fog that you didn't know what was coming to you. You just had to guess at it and get into shore and tie up again. That's for downstream work. Upstream work you don't have much trouble about landing, like you went into a bunch of fog you just stopped and run dead slow and tried to find the bank and do find the bank eventually.

Q: Harder to stop going down.

A: For instance, you got 20,000 ton of weight ahead besides the metal in your barges. I'm speaking about the coal. You take these Pittsburgh boats that are towing steel and such as that out of the Pittsburgh district south, they have got the number of barges, they usually tow about 20 barges, they don't load their barges as deep. Four and a half to five and a half feet usually is about the depth of their barges. For a coal barge, it's loaded down to 11 foot side and it's loaded down to eight and a half to nine feet. That's anywhere from 950 to a 1,000 and ten or 15 tons of coal in one of those barges. When you've got 20 of those barges, take the *Omar* and the *Orco*, which used to be the *Campbell*, the *John W. Hubbard*, which was the *Dorrance* or the *Dorrance* was the *John W. Hubbard*, and boats like that, and the Island Creek boats, well, with the Island Creek, while I was with them, we didn't tow more than 20,000 ton.

We towed around 14,000, 12,000 to 14,000 ton. With the *Stan P. Suit* and the *Catharine Davis*. *Catharine Davis* didn't tow as much as the *Suit*. But the Ohio River boats, those three boats I mentioned there, their usual tow, open river was 20 barges. And quite often, pool stage, they'd tow 20, also. There were some pilots that would take chances more so than others. But in my opinion, it's always been very foolish, and I think I've always made just about as good as a time with a tow when I was on the watch piloting as my partner did, or some of the other company boats did. At least I haven't had any smash ups, so in the long run I've made better time. (chuckles) I don't think that I have, ever have sunk in all my towboat experience.

I've only had one barge, no two barges to sink on me. One of them hit a log, and the other one, in getting it out of the landing when we went to make the tow up, and I worked on watch when we done it. Knocked a hole in the rake of the barge, and it was slow leak, and we started down the river with the *Omar*, and after night in the high stage of water, and the water had filled in that bulkhead of the barge to put it down far enough and running at that speed the water came over the end of it. It was after dark and I couldn't see it. First thing I knew that there barge, why I heard the lines break on the far end of it. I immediately stopped her. I just happened to have the search light on looking down the Dam 15 bear trap here, to locate that, and I threw the light down on the end of the barge and I seen it, the upper end of it going down. So, I immediately stopped the boat and went to back her away from the barge. So when it came back, it wouldn't hit the side of the boat and tear the side of her out. Then it just did, missed the side of the boat. The end of it was up out of the water, she went out on down, that was the first one I sank.

The second one, I run over a log on a bar. I didn't know the log was there. That could have been avoided if everything had of been right, but everything wasn't right at the time. I had requested a change in hooking the barge up on the head of the tow, different from the way it was. And the captain of the boat, Issac Faar, Captain of the boat, he said, "Wait till we got below Dam 33." While he was out there at the telephone, I was going to make that change then. Making the change, the watchman hollered back and says, "This barge over here is going to sink on us I believe," and I threw my light down on it and it was just almost, and I immediately backed her over on the bar. But it filled up all right before I got away from it. The sides of it didn't go out of sight, but that log had raked that barge on the bottom from one end to the other. Must have had a knot on it and it didn't do anything, only just sprung the rivets in the bottom, just enough that they all combined made that siphon couldn't hold it. Matter of fact, we had a siphon in it before that, pumping it out. Water had just accumulated in it.

Q: These were steel barges.

A: Steel barges. Yes, they were both steel barges.

Q: You started out I guess with the old wooden barges.

A: Yes, and the first steel barges that I ever had anything to do about towing was two the Island Creek Coal Company had. They were duplicates of some steel barges that the J & L, the Jones and Laughlin people at Pittsburgh made. I think Island Creek and J & L people were the first people who had steel barges, coal barges. Wooden were the principal barges at that time, but a matter of fact, the first time I was with Island Creek they only had those two steel barges, the balance of them were all wood. The next lot of steel barges was ten they ordered, and that made 12. Then they made ten again, then five again, then ten again. Now they haven't got any wooden ones at all. Those two that they originally had, they are gone a long while ago. A whole lot of the others that they made are gone.

Q: Those wooden barges were leaky things too, weren't they?

A: Yes, they were leaky, but you know it's a funny thing that they didn't lose as many of them as they lose now with steel barges.

Q: Is that so? I didn't know that?

A: Proportionately. Proportionately, they didn't lose as many of the wooden barges as they do with the steel ones now. The reason now is they figure that the steels were too safe, more safe than they really are. A steel barge won't sink if there isn't a cause for it and neither would a wooden barge. A wooden barge was something you had to watch all the time. The steel barge you ordinarily don't watch that there unless some condition comes up to call you to mind to watching it. That's the way I figured the thing.

Q: Coaling out of the Kanawha, I guess it was, that operation cast off wooden barges along the way didn't they, to the smaller towns?

A: They had smaller barges some, to take to small towns, they had what they called flats. Flats would hold about 3,500 to 4,500 bushel, not ton, bushels and they would drop them off at little towns around 2,000 population or less than that. For a country landing that had a coal elevator. At that time if you take a town like Maysville, which is about 12,000, and Portsmouth, they would. A standard wooden barge at that time was a 135 foot long and 26 foot wide and had eight foot sides on them. Well they would load them down to seven feet, six and a half to seven feet, and that would only leave them about a foot to foot and a half, the top of the barge above the water. And when they lost very many barges of that sort, in that way, they could be caught out in the river with a wind storm, which makes swells so much that before you could get into the landing to protect them, these swells would swamp them, run over the sides of them.

That didn't always occur, lots of times it would. Of course, if you run into conditions of that sort you would immediately stop your boat shoving and go to backing up. When you backed up you got the current going away from the tow so swells wouldn't sink it near as fast as it would the other way unless it came over the side. But you had to get into shore, you would have to have a flanking way on the inside. Especially if you got close to shore. Those big swells come up and they'd funnel between the shore and the barges sometimes and go over the side that way. Had to be careful about that. So many tricks and turns in that sort of thing. It's all a business in itself. Be like running a truck or on automobile on the road. You've got things you have to guard against. It takes experience to learn it, too. It's interesting work of course, my first steamboating was the packet boat business. I liked that. I was on the *Princess* in the Coney Island trade. I liked that too. That's lots of people there, you know.

Q: Will you talk about hauling all those people up to Coney Island?

A: The *Princess* was a nice boat. So was the *Island Queen*. Although, I never, I rode on the first *Island Queen*, I never rode on the second one. That work on the *Princess*, I enjoyed that as much as any because she was a good staunch boat; she wasn't as big as the *Island Queen* of course, she wasn't allowed to carry as many people. I forget now what her complement was, but I think around 2,500 or something like that. She was one dandy boat to handle, pilot. You know my life on the river, I loved the work, I would rather pilot a steamboat than to eat. Even in some difficult conditions, as long as I didn't get into too much of a jam or didn't do any damage.

But that *Princess*, I could handle her. The *Princess* landing at Coney Island, there was just simply knowing what you were going to do, and how to do it, and doing it there. Then you would land at the wharfboat at Cincinnati. I've landed that *Princess* at that Coney Island wharfboat, turned around and landed and had the head of the boat within ten feet of the wharfboat. By the time I got her squared around to land I'd have her. So I just stopped the inside wheel and come ahead, turn it to the outside wheel, straighten it up, and it was easy. It wasn't much more than mashing an egg when she hit. That's a little bit long and drawn out story. She wouldn't land hard at all.

Q: The ice finally got her.

A: Yes, sunk her just below the Kentucky River, below the big Kentucky River below Carrollton. She was a dandy boat too. The Coney Island Company had the sternwheel boat called the *Island Maid*, a sternwheel boat, she was a good handler. I didn't run the Coney Island trade, but she was out on tramp excursion trips like the *Avalon* does now. I was pilot on her a couple of seasons up the river, up as far as Pittsburgh, Pittsburgh once, and a couple of times after that. And up the Kanawha River two or three times and handled her just as about as well as I was telling you I could handle the *Princess*, because she was a good steering boat and a good backing boat. She answered her rudders and in most and all conditions. You take a boat like that it is a pleasure to handle them.

Q: Kind of cantankerous then?

A: They were kind of loggy, kind of sluggish about answering the rudders and answering the wheels, the big wheel, the water wheel. They carried too much headway. You take a boat that handles real good, why she was able to kill her headway pretty quick. Well you can't do any of that instantly, but then if you know your boat, why, you know what to do. That's the one thing I always try to learn when I get on a boat is to know what she'll do, under certain conditions.

Q: We should talk about some of your ducks and geese.

A: I have had a lot of fun in hunting geese off the tows. It's pretty difficult to get up on a bunch of wild geese on a tow. I would be coming downstream, why it wasn't so much trouble because they don't go, the water under the head of the tow don't make so much noise. Upstream there's just noise enough so that they hear you coming before you get to a duck. He's taking longer chances. He will get under a willow and hide; a goose won't hardly ever do that. He stays out in the open. Of course, now it's against the law to shoot ducks or geese, either one, off a tow. For instance, you take a motor boat out for some hunting ducks and geese, you've got to tow a skiff and yawl along with them. They go to shoot those ducks they've got to get in there, then slip up on the ducks in the yawl, and shoot from that. Any vessel with power you are breaking the law.

Q: You caught them at night.

A: Well after night why that's something else, nine times out of ten you are breaking the law when you shoot out of a boat. At night off the tow.

Q: Well I guess it wasn't always deliberate was it? You could turn on your search light and lo there would be some.

A: You turn your search light on and see the geese, if somebody on the boat a deckhand, watchman or mate without watching for geese wants to shoot geese, why I'll tell you though most rivermen or boatmen are sports enough not to want to kill them after night. You take like that to those swans, for instance the geese I spoke of some little while back. We threw the search light on. Not hunting for geese or blue swan, your light happened to come on and you could switch your light out, but I don't think very many people do it. Lots of times I would hold light on a flock of geese or ducks, and just to see them fly.

So I throw the light around just to keep them kind of worried a little bit, not any intentions of killing them or anything. It's like a fellow getting out and playing baseball or hunting a rabbit or something like that there, and taking his dog out, and leaving his gun at home, don't want to kill him just wants to

John Knoepfle

hear the dogs run.

The people that are still running the stuff that I liked best during my early steamboating was low water. I always liked to run a difficult place. I had a feeling of accomplishing something particularly if I got through it safely enough to not be getting stuck or anything like that. I first went to tow boating, towing coal, with those wooden barges we had to load barges light, up to about four and a half feet, for instance when they was building these locks and dams. You would have a narrow or an out of the way channel to take that stuff down to get around the coffer dam. For instance, one place, Quick's Run up here when they was building 34, or not 34, but 32, you had to cross the river in a channel over a rock reef in above that coffer dam, then drop in underneath of it with your tow of coal and get around the coffer dam, and then come back in underneath of it again and go on down the channel on below. That was washed out some to a certain extent, but if you knew the stage of water you had, if you had four feet you would load your barges to about three foot eight or nine, and four and a half feet, you would give yourself about a four inch clearance.

Sometimes your tow would be wide enough and long enough not to make that turn quite quick enough. I have got many a thrill about bringing tows down around dam 32 coffer dam, several times. I know that's a rock reef there because I have seen it out two or three times. That's the one running from the channel over to the Ohio side. That's like anything else, if you like that line of work regardless of what it is, if you're interested in and like it, and like to accomplish the thing, that's where you get the pleasure out of it. For sometimes the pleasure amounts to as much as the wages you get for it. (chuckles)

Q: We were talking about using a hand capstan before, can you explain that?

A: Yes that's a barrel. Quite a while after the *McBride* sank, my brother was on, I lost him on that, and I couldn't understand why he allowed that to happen because he had been with me. I had learned him, particularly about that M and W Bridge, or L and N Bridge, and about the current setting on that pier. Well, a little while after that, probably three or four weeks or a couple of months, I came down with the *Sam P. Suit*, and I had four barges abreast, and one length, and one of the Ashland Oil boats with propellers, they was coming up stream. Well, he whistled for the same side that the *Peace* did for the *McBride*. See instead of the *Peace* coming outside and blowing one whistle, the *Peace* blowed two whistles for him to take the port.

Well that put him going up around the point this way and in order to steer that, if he was steering straight through that bridge, he'd be this way. In order to bring himself around in the river's current he had to steer this way. Well that threw his stern, his propeller wheel, current in his propeller in a circle out like this you see, that threw the water out against the pier. I didn't realize until I seen that what caused the *McBride* to hit that bridge pier. Well, I was the thing I done, when he whistled what I would be two whistles, I stopped the *Sam P. Suit* and started to backing and I whistled him down and made him take the other side. Made him take the one whistle side.

I backed up, killed the tow, until he got up through there. When he come up through there I seen the wash from his wheel, from his propellers, come right out, just rise and come out and went down the other side of that pier. Showed the piece of wheel wash throwed the head of his tow out toward that pier, and the word that I got from the two people that were saved off of there, two deckhands, they both told me, they said that he blew, that Roy blew the whistle and backed up. Actually backed up until he thought the *Peace* was above, and you thought it was safe to go down. And when he went down he struck the side lash. The guys didn't say that was what caused it. But they said he stopped and backed her, to throw her heaviest tow, which was two or three lengths, I think. To throw that away from that pier. Then he stopped her and went to back her the other way.

Well, when he done that there the head of his tow had already past there. He caught the wheel wash right alongside just about the time that the head of his steamboat was just about on the pier. Well Mr. Long, the engineer of the Ohio River company told me, says, "Captain see, she had the fuel flat right alongside of her, on the port side, and that was the fuel flat." Mr. Long told me, he says, "Captain, the fuel flat showed where it drug on that pier forty feet before the *McBride* turned around." The mate who wasn't on the boat told me that she was down, he had stopped off for something, and another man was mate. So she immediately went down there and see, the *McBride*, she turned over on her side this way and it showed her wire lines on the side that was out of water, showed it hanging up on the hook where they always carried them. They didn't have anything, only rope, manila lines on the face, the face line, one on each side. That's all they had on, didn't have those wire lines on there. If they had the wire lines on there, chances are she wouldn't have broken on that side and went around sideways.

She went around sideways. I don't know if you know that current, with a 30 foot stage of water in the river, that current was so swift that it come up on the guard of her. She just went down this way, sunk sideways. The fuel flat and the boat right against the pier, that didn't go down. I seen about half the length of the boat. The roof was out dry the next morning. That day when I went down there that was dry. If brother Roy had of gone out the pilothouse window and went back on that roof he never would have been in water at all.

And here is another thing, just this summer I was told at Portsmouth, Ohio, by my cousin that an inspector at Cincinnati, a Green inspector at Cincinnati told him personally, he says, "I don't believe and never will believe that Roy Edgington was in the pilot house on that boat when she hit that pier." He says, "I think the striker pilot was up there," and this man, the inspector at Cincinnati was a pilot, and a captain, and a mate, and a deck hand, washer and everything else on the boat. He had been practically all his life on the boat, and he based his opinion upon the fact that Roy didn't have all his clothes on. He had his shoes on, he had a nightshirt on. Didn't have any trousers. It looked like he had just got out of bed, to him, that's what he told this cousin of mine. I don't know. As I started to say a while ago, this mate wasn't on there, he was a regular mate, he told me them face wires wasn't on that boat at all, they ought to have been, they should, too. But it's all over with and can't be helped.

Q: Maybe it was kind of mercy.

A: That's just one thing that I hadn't showed Roy, my brother, about letting a boat take that side of him. He did know about the set on that pier, and that 30 foot stage of water in Cincinnati harbor is one of the worst stages there is. To run those bridges.

Q: The current is swift down there.

A: Well it's very swift and it's treacherous. You take a bigger stage of water, the water that was on the shore further up this way and there isn't so much side set on it. In the first place the bridge isn't built square across the river, it's built this way, instead of being cross ways. The Bellaire Bridge, Ohio, is the same way. The B and O at Bellaire, Ohio's right that way. Had more sinking's and more coal and steamboats, and lives lost on that Bellaire Bridge up there. It's only a 325 foot span.

Q: It angles.

A: Yes, it angles, that left hand pier there, when you come down with a tow you have got to keep the head of your tow on that right hard pier until you're very near down to it, and then you have got to straighten her around to keep from hitting the sides. Here not very long ago there was, I believe an American Barge Line boat come down and sunk two barges. One stayed on the pier and the other one sunk down below, over at the creek about 500 yards below the mouth of the creek.

Q: Funny they didn't make all the bridges suspension bridges.

A: That bridge was Ma Greene's, Greta Greene's, she owns her estate, of course she's dead, her estate owns them, owns the Bellaire Bridge, owns the Parkersburg Bridge, owns the Point Pleasant Railroad Bridge, owns the Kanawa Bridge. Her estate owns them. They pay so much for a ton of coal, so much for passengers, for everything, new that's just what I've heard, for every ton and every passenger goes over that bridge in one way or the other, so much per. They tried to sell her, buy the bridges I mean. She wouldn't sell to them, and I don't know whether her son is living yet or not but he wouldn't sell either.

But whoever has the estate now, I don't know about that, whether they will ever sell or not. These doggone bridges are so doggone dangerous that they ought to make them make wider piers or change the doggone bridges lined up with the current. But it wasn't so long ago, when the government as a matter of fact, when those bridges were built pilots wouldn't take them. They would tie up before dark at night, and wait until daylight to run on bridge. That is with a tow I mean. They wouldn't run them after night. They didn't have any electric lights either then. You see, they wasn't as particular about narrow spans then as they are now. I suppose at that time there was protest made, but the government didn't take as active part in it then as they do now, and perhaps the pilots liked to sleep all night anyway, and rather work in daylight. I don't know what under those sort of conditions are when they didn't have electric lights. I would like to go out and see. (chuckles)

Q: I imagine down here at Cincinnati trying to run those piers now with all the pleasure boating creeping up, it must be a double hazard.

A: You just take this, for instance, the pleasure boats, it's their business to stay out of the way. For a downstream tow because as I said a while ago you can't stop these tows ordinarily. I never tried to take any tows down through the bridges larger than I thought we could handle properly. I've taken as high as twelve barges down on a tow at times through the bridges. But I knew the set of the current on these bridge piers, and there is a difference in the set at different stages of water. I never took any chances, I run the size that I would run in extreme water; I run the same size when the conditions were not so extreme. I knew them see, and I think most pilots do. Of course, you take the steamboat business, like everything else, take right on the highway here, why a dangerous point comes up, take right from this road out to there, take out on this farm some place things can come up there that is dangerous. It's not perfect in anything, but if you learn a trade, and know what it is regardless of what it is, whether it is steamboating or anything else why, the more you know it about the more adept you are and less liable to have something happen, and yet quite often something happens.

Q: Did you ever pilot coal in the lower river below the falls?

A: No, I never did. I've gone down as far as New Albany. Taken barges of coal down there. I don't know anything about the river down below Louisville. I have been too busy. I've often wished that I did know the river down there. I've been too busy from Louisville to Pittsburgh, and the head waters of the Kanawha River. I've always been working, until I quit, semi-retired, don't say I'm semi-retired. I've always been too busy up here to learn it down there.

Q: I suppose you went up on the Mon or the Allegheny?

A: Never been above the Smithfield Street Bridge in my life on Mon River, and I've been up to 16 miles on the Allegheny River. I didn't pilot up there. The fellow that took her up there didn't have a license. He went by map. That was his responsibility not mine. I told him I didn't know it and I wouldn't do it.

Q: Before we close off I wonder if you could describe some of your activity on the government boats that you were on for a while?

A: Yes, they built the *Guyandotte*, the *Miami* at Cincinnati, all at the same time, about 1912. The Cincinnati Engineer District selected me as one of the pilots and captains, and they wasn't finished yet, I was down at Lawrenceburg when they sent me word, I went up and went to work on the boat. They didn't have them all finished, all fitted out, they asked me to go ahead and get them ready to go out, which I did. Some things didn't exactly suit me at the time when I

John Knoepfle

got up there, so I got that straightened out, though. So, I went out in 1912 along in June. Maybe, don't remember, June or July, I was on about seven years.

We dredged the channel out in the river at different places and worked around the locks and dams, dredging. Of course, what I done with the towboat, I was just on the towboat all the time, we towed the scows and dredges around. Come winter time, we would be in winter quarter, we would pick up a whole outfit for winter. As a general thing, the *Miami* and the *Ohio* and the *Guyandotte* and the *Oswego* were always together. These four outfits were usually in one spot. Every once in a while it wasn't that way, but generally it was that way. Well, they had one inspector who was, Harry Peters. So I was there pretty close to seven years. Before I went to work for the government I thought when I got a government job on the boat I would be fixed for life. After I got there I thought I would be fixed for life if something went wrong.

Q: You must have got on the *Guyandotte* just in time for the 1913 flood.

A: I was at Marietta. We were in there and laid up for the winter for repairs. They had me in charge of both steamboats. Laid there with the captain of the other boat, didn't keep anybody but the engineers, and cooks, and firemen, and watchmen on both boats. I had charge of repairs on both steamboats. The dredge master of the *Ohio*, he had charge of the two dredges. We jointly had charge of the whole fleet. The fuel flats, the scows, and all that there. We was all tied up at the mouth of the Muskingum River. I had the main steam lines of the *Miami* tore down for repairs and that flood come. Not having any steam on her and couldn't get any steam on her because her steam pipes were down. We did have steam on the *Guyandotte*.

The river kept raising, and raising, and raising, and coming up. Houses kept coming down the river, and get down about the mouth of the Muskingum River, and start floating back up the river a piece. There was so much water coming out of the Muskingum River, you know. Matter of fact the river got six feet above 1884 flood stage at Marietta in the 1913 flood. Two bridges went out above us. I had 27 lines out on the fleet on to the shore, around trees, and that was all there was to fasten it to was trees. Then there was some deadmen in there, a deadman is a log set down in the dirt, you know, with a chain coming out about eight to ten foot long. Dig a hole down about three foot. Then you fastened that chain, well that's what they called a deadman. That's for a check line. So, it was all right until Lowell Bridge, which was a wooden crib bridge across the Muskingum River, part of it way up there by Lowell, wherever Lowell was, I never was up the Muskingum River only about five miles. It washed out and it come down and there was a little bit of the first bridge up the Muskingum River from the Ohio River across over to the other side.

There was a little of that left on this side. The other side had gone out and the bridge above it, that had all gone out. Steel, and it collapsed in the river, of course. The old bridge was wood, and it came down the river floating right at the height of it. It came down that side where we was laying, right ahead of us, and it hit the part of that steel bridge that was left, took that out of there, came on down, and that darn Lowell Bridge collided onto the head of our fleet. When it did the end of it swung around this way, and lodged there onto that fleet. The first thing I knew the lines commenced breaking, trees commenced falling that we had tied up to on the bank. There on the farmer's side and out in the river we went. The whole business, boats, barges, steel flats and dredge boats right out into the Ohio River.

Well I had steam on the *Guyandotte*. I was laying on the lower end of it too and had about 27 or 28 flood refugees on the boat too, we had taken out of the houses when we were on the west side. One was my wife, and a young sister-in-law, and Clyde, my boy, and we had an engineer, on the boat, of course. Didn't have the engineer up on the *Miami*, we had no use for him over there. Well, out we went, and the *Andy Williams* was laying up with the wharf boat, and I commenced blowing the distress whistle, and she backed out and come down there to us. Wanted to know where I wanted him and I said, "Get down on the head of our tow, ahead of the fleet, and keep coming ahead on her and shoving in her toward the Ohio side. If we get in there with the timber on the shore we could lock, get the line out and could tie up."

Well, the river was so darn high that we weren't any ways near the shore. We was over the top of the bank, you know, way up. Well, I'll tell you, there was a great big, down at this head of Muskingum Island, just above it were some, great big cottonwood trees up there. And the water was right up in the top of them. That's what stopped that fleet. Us a coming ahead with the boat, the *Guyandotte*, the *Williams* on the upper end shoving the head in all the time. Got a line out onto the trees, but the trees were what stopped the fleet and the whole business. We tied up there.

Q: You were lucky.

A: I had made up my mind if we went on down, that is if we couldn't get them stopped before they got down to Parkersburg Bridge, I was just going to turn the boats loose and go ashore with what I had. Let the balance of it go. Go below if I could and salvage what I could. That was in 1913, March, and the Navy and the Army, the Navy came there and took charge by appointment of, no wait a minute, the Army came there and took charge of the outfit, except the steamboats. The government after the Army took charge, why the Navy took charge of the steamboats. I can remember that Major Whirtenburger from New York City, he had charge of the New York Harbor at that time. An awful nice old fellow too, and he took charge. He told me what he would like to do with the boat and wanted to know how soon I could get the steam up on her.

I said, "Just as soon as I can get everything together, that would be as quick as we could possibly do it, and if work goes swiftly." Well, we got her out and took steam on in a couple of days. Meantime I was going a run from Parkersburg to Marietta, carrying supplies, food and stuff like that up to Marietta and Williamstown. They'd bring it into Parkersburg by rail. Supplies for the flood area. So after we got steam on the *Miami*, I started her opposite me on that run and through Whirtenburger, and the Army they would bring supplies in there for the flood relief on below downriver. So Whirtenburger asked me if I thought we could go down the river with supplies. I said, "Yes we can go as far as we can at any rate, if we could get under the bridges."

Well, he said, "You put somebody in charge of the *Miami*, and crew of her, and have her run, and let her do what you are doing here now. You go to Parkersburg, and we'll load two flats with supplies for downriver." Which we did, that's when I got so I didn't like salmon anymore. Carry a case of salmon in on them barges and instead of laying them down or setting them down they'd throw them off to the shore. There were so doggone many of them, you know, and they would bust one open they would go on the deck and some fellow would tramp on a can of it and that juice would run out and I could smell that yet. (chuckles)

Then we lit out for down river. However, I'm a little ahead of my story there. When I went to work, clearing that fleet up, taking one barge out at a time, one dredge out at a time, getting drift all out of it, and getting rid of all that old Lowell Bridge, the last doggone thing I touched was the Lowell Bridge, which was on top of it, that was the store flat, store boat. She was stopped under that there and I had lines out to everything else so as to hold it and come back. I got that thing out in the river, trying to run that thing out, and I couldn't budge it. I would back and come ahead, that thing wouldn't budge. I was taking backing on a slide and swing and couldn't do it.

Go down to the head of the Muskingum Island I saw the tops of trees over there, so I decided to just take it over there and put it into that. There was an apple orchard over there, took the tops out of every darn one of them apple trees and still that wasn't under there. I seen some great big sycamore trees over on the west inside of the island and there was eddy enough in there that I could back it over there and get a swing on it, and I hooked one end of that darn thing into one of them sycamore trees with a downhill pull and got it out. The next place I saw that darn bridge was down there at Bethlehem, 16 miles below Madison in a lot of big sycamore on the shore. I went down with them supplies down the canal to Louisville, and put off what I had left off down there and come back up the river. I didn't have but about three nights sleep in that whole business. When I got back to Marietta, by george, I didn't hardly know myself. I was in bed three weeks.

Q: It was rough water then, wasn't it?

A: I had just exhausted myself, that is all there was to it. But of course these things are all in a lifetime. You know, my daughter-in-law runs a party house here now. Did she tell you anything about it?

Q: Not yet.

Charles Harrison, April 26, 1957

Question: I'm at Florence, Kentucky at the residence of Mr. Charles Harrison who operated, I suppose you could say, the Dayton ferry.

Answer: Okay, well you want to know about logging back in Crane's.

Q: Well, better give me a few details on your life here.

A: Well, when I started out, my dad run the ferry there at Dayton ever since I guess about 1895 up to practically his death. That was up in I'd say about 1940. Then my brother took over the business, and of course I worked with him, but when I got married I went to Springfield, and left the river.

Well, the original story, up there was a fella named Lory, I think was the founder of the ferry. You know like before cars there was no street cars, there was just like horse cars. That was the means of transportation to get over in the East End, or to the Marine Ways, and over to Crane's saw mill, all Fast End activities. That was even before the gasoline engine was even invented, you know, or going. They used to row them across in skiffs. So when my dad took over, why they had to row them back and forth. Then as things came along, well my dad had really the first gas boat on the river. It was a one-cylinder Watkins motor, I think it was, scow type, you call it. It was a sailboat originally. When the wind blowed, it had like a flat type boat, you know, like a scow, but then they would sail it across. That's how they ferried across, and rowed, but then when the power boat came in, why then they started using that until things advanced. He just kept getting better boats all the time, you see, and so that's when I started in the river business as a kid, come down and just helping in the boats and stuff. I was just maybe only about ten years old I could just about turn the motor over. Why I could even run it then, you know, I knew enough about it. So then we got bigger motors and everything like that. So then we used to do, you know, like ferrying them, we'd do towing and stuff like that, and excursions, dad had a big excursion boat.

Q: What was that called?

A: The *Lorelei*. And he had that and would run it out. This other boat we did the towing with, the ferry, you see. We had always two, an extra one, and it was mostly more powerful.

Q: What was the name of the other boat?

A: The ferry boat?

Q: Yes.

A: Well, they called that the *Valley Gem* ferry boat. The Dayton Ferry and Canoe Harbor, is what it run under mostly. That was the name of it, that was the harbor boat, you know, or the name of the business. But this boat that we used for ferry, every boat had its own name, but it was always *Valley Gem*, from there started up about I imagine about the 10th or 12th or something like that. I don't know how many we did have, but we had quite a few through that

John Knoepfle

period of time. But then this other boat, the *Lorelei* that we had, that's when they got a little better. And people, that's one pleasure they had, they'd go to Coney Island. Across from Coney Island, in Silver Grove, was a picnic ground, something like these woods, like these different places.

My mother, she was kind of one of them that always went in for a lot of training. Why it would have I imagine about 100 people, or 75, something like that. We'd have two boats of that type and we'd go up there at Silver Grove. I'd have these Indian outfits on, you know we had these war whoops, all that down, the dancing and everything to perfection, see. So we'd go up there and we'd have like our picnic up there. When we'd get done, why we'd go over to Coney Island, they'd give us free admission. We'd go on the dance floor and we'd put on our war whoops. People would throw money in to us. And then the management, I don't think Schott owned it then, but anyhow, they'd give us kids tickets, you know. We could go on anything, and the ice cream, and stuff like that. We thought we was living high. But we did put on a good show, and we had really good costumes, and we had everything done to perfection.

Q: What year was that?

A: Well, that run back as far as about 1908, up to I'd say about 1916, 1917, along up in there.

Q: Who taught you the Indian routine?

A: Well, my mother and other women, different ones, they seem like, there wasn't, shows or anything that there is now. They had to do something. They had parades, and they was always training you for something. And we'd have about 30 or 40 of us kids, and we would just train. Over in Cincinnati, when this Butternut Bread came in, we was in one of them big parades over there when that was introduced. And my brother, he had a Buster Brown outfit on, and Mae and I. I had some white outfit on. I was on one of them floats that had a fountain on it. I was hot as the dickins. I can remember that. I was only just a little kid then, but I was so hot, and we couldn't get a drink, and everybody was hollering, "We want a drink." They wouldn't let us little kids drink out of the fountain; it was on the float. It was just like on the boat there. Why we'd go up to Coney Island, and we just would have the time of our life. We'd have about three or four of them trips a year, practically. And this boat, my dad would rent out. He had men, it took two men to run it. There were brewery companies that would have their outings and they'd go up to Coney Island or New Richmond and Silver Grove, and all the places just make it a day of it.

Q: That was the *Valley Gem*?

A: No, that was the *Lorelei*. The *Valley Gem*, was the ferry boat. They didn't very seldom take that away, only just to tow, then the *Lorelei* would tow. This Hall Sand Company, had a boat there, too. We used a lot of their sand barges. They don't do that anymore. I don't remember them towing any sand down now. But that was the source of gravel and sand. The *Fred Hall* was there, and I think they had another one at that time, the *Grubbs, J. M. Grubbs*. It was a little boat. A littler boat than the *Hall*. When they was busy they'd go way up the river. They'd get different types of sand, and we used to tow that, too. It would take us oh, like from East End up there around the bend, it would take us to down around Baymiller. I think where they had their place, it would take us about an hour, two hours, something like that.

Q: Had a big terminal at Baymiller?

A: Yes, I think it was somewhere down there where the yard was. We would take that full one down; we'd tow the empty one back. See, this *Lorelei* . . .

Q: What back?

A: We'd tow the barge back, the empty one. They had four or five, oh maybe ten or fifteen barges. We'd take two barges down and load. But one coming back was our limit, because towing back was a little harder, and this *Lorelei*, it had two motors; it had pretty good power.

Q: That's a gasoline boat.

A: Yes.

Q: Well, you were coming up with empties.

A: We'd tow them back up there, tie them up; we'd come back bring the boat to harbor and just leave it. We got $25. It was to tow a full load down or bring it back up this way, just one way. But that was pretty good money in them days. That was about 1910 to 1915, along in there. I think it was about 1917. We tore that boat up because it was old, and it was bigger than the type he wanted. We didn't want people to give that much money for it. My dad just tore it up and used the motors in the ferry, and got more out of it. We used the *Lorelei*, when Crane's run over there, we'd go up there to Brent. It had rafts already made up, and we used it or the ferry, either one. We had to take two. It all depended on how many logs they wanted. If there was only 500 logs, we'd take one boat, and have another for when they came down, we could bank it to the side.

Q: Now Brent was the rail terminal.

A: Yes, that was where they jumped them off, at Brent, off the railroad cars into the river. They had a big derrick there. They had men up there. As soon as they dumped them off they had what's called tie-poles, I think it was called, it was like a tree, only it would be about two. It would run from two to four inches in diameter, 20 feet long. When they'd come across, as it got long, they'd lay them crossways and put them about ten feet apart, and then they had dog chains that had two arms that were spikes and chain between them that would go over the tie-pole, and then they'd log them together. That's the way they kept them. They'd zigzag them logs so they would be like welded together. It would be just one long raft. They wouldn't have them right together. They keep logging them up, but if the river was high, they would run them logs in smaller rafts. You couldn't shove too fast because you'd submerge them. They had these sinkers. Some logs when they're cut why they got sap in them. Maybe they'd break that pole and they'd drop down. Sometimes you had to cut, they'd stop

John Knoepfle

you altogether, you know, if they hit bottom, or if they cut the wrong way. You had to cut them clear loose.

Q: You'd have a snag.

A: Yes, but if the river was low, like in a pool stage, you could run 500 logs to about 2,000. I imagine about 2,000 in a raft would be about a limit. And even the *Crown Hill,* didn't bring much more than that. Or I doubt whether they brought more than 2,000. I know these boats we had, the two that I know, at one time we brought down 1,200. And that was pretty near an all day job because we'd leave there in the morning about seven or six o'clock. It would take about an hour to go up there with a light load. We'd just go up light, and then coming down, you just almost floated. You see, you just used the boat for steering purposes, practically.

Q: Will you describe that a bit, that coming back down?

A: Well, when you come down, where you almost floated with the current, and as the bends turn, you see, why you'll flow to the outside bend of the river; any drift or anything will always flow to the bend here, like the channel, and the idea is to just keep the logs out there. We'd be in the back shoving, just shoving fast enough, just to kind of steer a little bit. And if we seen we was going to maybe start dragging ashore, or getting too close to any harbors or anything like that, why we'd run right on up to the front and get ahold of it, and shove the front out. Or we'd run up halfway and just get right in the middle and push sideways out. Just like the old time boats that had paddles, that same principle. You paddle it anyway you want.

It was just to have enough power but not too much, too much power, and then you'd start submerging. That was the trouble with the *Crown Hill* and the *Cole,* a lot of times they'd start backing so hard that that current from their wheel would submerge them. And they had to lash them up awful tight there to keep them from submerging. And we would really do as good a job with a lighter power boat than they could, if you knew how to handle a tow right. So it would take us an average of say about six hours, or from four to six hours coming down. Then we got down there, why oh above the lumber company, they knew we were coming in, and the other boat would come out and hook on so that we could handle it the way we wanted.

Then they had a rope in the river bank there, they had trees or posts, and they'd be about two to three foot in diameter. Two or three of them right together, way down in the ground, just like a telegraph pole, they'd buried, then they'd have their line they'd put on, tied up, and then this coil. They'd have it coiled right at the water level. Then as we got down there they'd have a skiff, they were at each one of them practically, and then this guy would get in a skiff, and he'd throw it out and sometimes they'd have that reefed on the skiff, you know, the rope was, see. Then they'd come right out, and then they'd timber hitch it. When they'd come down, why they'd have this tie-pole going across there. They could throw a hitch right over there. Sometimes they would even burn a rope, there'd be so much pull on it. And you'd have to slip it. But it would be what you call a slip knot or timber hitch you called it.

You could release or tighten it, you wouldn't burn your hand either, but it would be too fast, just like a brake. Then if you run out of line, or we didn't make our fastening, they had that next one down so that we could catch posts. If we got down below there we couldn't get back up. We couldn't tow in the current. Those big boats if they got, missed because even in high water they had to finally tie wherever they could, and then break that up into small rafts, and then maybe when the river come down lower, then they'd come back, they can only shove about two or three miles an hour, see coming back.

Q: They'd be unhappy about that.

A: Yes, but that was very seldom that ever happened. Well we landed. Let's see, there's one mill, the first mill was right where the ferry landed, right on Eastern Avenue. They had their logs right above our landing there at the foot of Hazen Street. See their logs extended out in the river 200 feet sometimes. They'd run maybe two squares long a raft. Right below there sometimes they'd have a short raft in there from, the Marine Ways didn't have a lot of steamboats there, but if they had steamboats in there wasn't no logs from Hazen street to right below the Marine Ways there. Well that would start in at, I forget what the name of that street is there, but that's at where Beatty's harbor is now, just right at the lower edge of that.

They had rafts from there clear down to the last mill. There was three mills there, the last one was down where that sheet metal is now, was logs all through there. So when they tied them up, they would take an axe and sometimes they'd cut these tie-poles with an axe, and sometimes they'd just knock these dog chains down. They had a railroad track come down there then, they had this log car come down and it had spikes in it, and it was of pretty heavy constructed, and it was weighted so it wouldn't float, and they'd come down, and then this raft with the lumber. When the raft boss was there why, they'd signal down to him all the types, in the office, what they wanted, so many oak, so many feet long, or poplar logs, whatever it was he knew it.

Then they had this saw boat with power on it, they'd drop that log down, and they'd chain it up, and this saw would just saw it what length they wanted. Then this other boat was right there where the track come. Each log would float there, and they could pull about two or three logs, at a time up, and as soon as they started out of water why these spikes at the crossways would catch the logs, see. They didn't even have to tie them or nothing. They just almost stayed right there, they very seldom ever rolled off. They'd just take them right up the hill and when they got up in the mill, they had their cutter, or the track or the traveling car, the bandsaw, they all used bandsaws, and it would come down. And then, see over on this car or truck, whatever they had, well then they'd saw the lumber. They'd just go back and forth, and these men rode that car, where they had handles, and they rode, and they just sawed it and that old board would fall off.

Then this other track, there was more rollers on it, I think it rolled out on power, like a conveyor belt, and they'd slice another one off, it would fall over, and go out into what they called the yard. Then these fellows out there had teams. They didn't have their trucks and their cars like they do now. They would just take wet lumber right on up, stack it to season it. They used scrap in between it so it seasoned. Then they'd take it up there in their yard and they'd store it. If the logs kept drifting out, you know, in their float, or when they come down if you got needing more, why that's when they was getting more in.

But they'd run that raft out pretty well, and they'd only have maybe 100 logs there. Then they'd have this other raft figured to pull in there at about that time. They generally had three openings, but when the river was low, and then the Marine Ways started going out of business, why they started using above there, where we landed with the ferry, from there, from Hazen Street down that was about two squares, why they filled that in. So they run quite a bit longer than the Marine Ways. One time I remember that when they had this fire, I guess a lot of people don't remember either, but they had about every engine within Cincinnati there.

They had a fire for three or four days or maybe a week, at Crane's there. And the fire really started between Hazen Street and the old ship yards. They started out, see and they had these steam engines in to pump, you know, you didn't have pumpers like they've got now. These steam engines they was pumping water, and that, it was really a fire, so in order to smother that out, and you couldn't get too close because of such a tremendous heat. In fact, we didn't even run the ferry in there for several days there was so much smoke and heat, you know, on account of it. And them firemen they was there just night and day just squirting, and I imagine that they was a pumping. Whether they was pumping out of the city mains, or whether they was pumping some out of the river, I don't know. I know that they had an awful lot of steam engines there. They had about every available apparatus that they could spare, in the city.

Q: When was that fire?

A: I think that was around about 1910 or 1912 along in there, someplace along in that neighborhood. I tried to get ahold of my sister today, we had a lot of pictures on that. But in this 1936 flood, that was the first it ever went in our house. We lived on Dayton Avenue. Dayton Taxi Cab was one square down from where the ferry was. The river had come up. It got in our cellar, but it never did get up on the first floor. Well my sister, I'd been married then see, and so then my sisters was home, a couple of them, and so they decided it wouldn't come up, so they moved everything into the attic. The water come up and went on up through there, and all these pictures and everything was up there. So they finally cut a hole in the roof and took out. And now I don't know whether they got them, but I was talking to my nephew and she was supposed to come down from their place, they retired in California. I know I've seen a lot of pictures of that flood. I think they got some of them old ones. They may have pictures of that logging, or of the Crane Mill. I know on these pictures it shows the Marine Ways, and the steamboats being pulled out on dry docks.

Q: Those are very rare pictures.

A: Yes, and all, I bet you we had 200 of them, there wasn't no little ones, they was all them big ones, real nice pictures. In fact, I'd give $100 if I had them myself, but I know that Sis had them and was keeping, but now in that flood they could of got lost. They had some of these Indian trips, you know, where they had us on there, and then pictures of some trees, and then Mother cutting cakes, and they had tables, and then the Marine Ways. I know there's a couple pictures there. The old *Island Queen* there when they was building it, the *Queen City*, and remodeling them, oh, a number of them boats, they'd have four and five of them big steamboats out at one time, a working on them.

Q: Exactly where were the Marine Ways?

A: Well, that was just about a square below Hazen Street. That would be about 1800, about 1700 to 1600 to about 1800, Eastern Avenue, that's about where, right at where Beatty's is, at the lower part, where that gas station is, and where Beatty is. Gas station there now. Well, that started out was about the first part of the Marine Ways, that was from there down. I imagine it was about 1,000 feet long, I imagine, and they had five, six, seven ways there, what they called ways, they was like skids made in . . .

Q: Ways?

A: Ways, they called it "The Marine Ways," is what they called it, but this runway that they had was made out of wood with steel plate on top of it, but it was anchored down and fastened, you know, secure in this rock, they had like a rock base there, see. In order to pull them, they had like a wedge truck like, see. They had their steam engines with a winch on there. They could pull them separate, or they could pull the one boat. They could pull all of them together, you know. As long as the boat was, they'd just put so many wedges under there, that would be the cradles they called them. They would be wedged according to the slant of the bank so the boat would be leveled when it come out. Then if the boat was 300 feet, like the *Island Queen*, I think it would take about five about five of them.

Why, they'd lower them in the water, and then they'd float the right over that see, and then they'd start coming in and they had the ropes on the *Queen*, too. They'd keep pulling it in until it, they'd come up just right under, and then start raising, and then as soon as she'd start raising, why then they'd all have to pull even, see. So they wouldn't twist the boat or anything. They'd go there, a lot of times them chains would break too, but they'd fix that right away. It wouldn't cause any to go back in the river, but if one wasn't pulling, or one was pulling to fast, it caused twisting, like a house it cracked. Then they'd pull them up, when they got them up there, if they had another boat, if

John Knoepfle

the river was low, and they wanted to put, they had it clear up to the top, or where the main building was, why then they would take and jack that all up, put cribbing under there, what they call, like blocks, and then they'd lower them down, and pull up another boat. They'd pull up another one by it, and maybe they had three of them just stepped right down the hill at one time. That way they could pull out five or six boats at one time. I know I got pictures or did have them. I know there were four or five of them, big ones.

Q: Your father worked at the ways?

A: Yes, he was a sort of a boss over there. My grandfather he was a boss of some kind over there, and he was one I think him and Anschutz, I think was the one that built the old *Island Queen*.

Q: Anschutz.

A: Anschutz, he was a boss over there. And I think them two was the most in the building of the wood boats.

Q: They were old time carpenters.

A: Oh yes, they were ship builders, what they were called. My dad, he kind of, well everybody who, you either worked at Crane sawmill or the shipyard over there. See, that was the main help along in Bellevue and Dayton. Then they'd just row across the river in them days, and that's the way they made their living. Marine Ways at one time it handled a lot of men. It handled really more than the sawmills, I believe. They'd have steamboats, see they'd be building them. Oh, they'd have two or three of them building all the time, see. That took quite a few men in woodwork and pipefitters, and Frisbie made all the steam engines, they was the most noted. There was other ones made them, but they was the most, the *Island Queen*, the *Cincinnati*, the Greene Lines, all the Greene Line boats had Frisbie on there, see.

Then boiler makers, that handled quite a variety of men, and electricians, and different things like pipefitters, they had caulkers, and different things like that. He was a good caulker and a planker, and I know that when the old *Island Queen* was planked the last time, why my dad was working over there. I was running the ferry then, and I was running the ferry a lot of times while they'd go over there in the daytime, the work, you know business wasn't too hot. It wasn't making the money maybe it was making now, but you know it was good money then, it was just easy money, and he could go over there after work hours. Like they'd give him a little better rate over there and he'd go over about 8:30 see, had his business over, and then he'd work until about 3:30, then our business would start going and they'd quit about five, or before dark, for their time was slower than it is now. About 5:00 it was or 6:00 it started to get dark, you know, so he'd quit about an hour or two ahead there to help tend to the ferry, too.

In the rush hour we had generally three boats running then, for Crane's, and the shipyard people. All them guys walked then, they didn't ride or nothing, had to walk it. That made it better for the ferry because we could just make trips fast enough that we could just keep them going. They wouldn't be there all at one time like in a factory right now, everybody runs out at the same time. Why you'd have so many you couldn't handle them. So that way it give us a chance. We'd be running there for say an hour real big in the morning and an hour at night, from them three alone. And so, he worked there quite a bit. And this Anschutz, he was an old time boat fellow. Well there was a lot of them boys and old men too, they were all boat builders.

My dad, or my grandfather, he was in there all his life, that's all he did was just ship building. And I know in the Civil War something, I don't know just what it was there, I never did get it straight, a couple times I didn't remember real good, but he was either a captain that shipped stuff for the Civil War from here down the river, or they made connections, or else he was in charge of the boat, or the carpenter works, or the ship builders. But I know they fixed some of them, they made it so that they would be like gun proof, put steel on them and things like that. He was a ship carpenter or ship builder. Why I don't know whether he was in charge of that or was like a captain or a mate, he might have been first mate or something like that, but I know he was pretty good. Well, he's buried in the cemetery in the Navy plot out there.

Q: What was his full name?

A: Henry, Henry William, I believe.

Q: Henry William Harrison?

A: Henry William Harrison. My dad's name, that was Llewelyn.

Q: Must have been some Welsh in your family.

A: Yes, my people all came from England and Scotland, mostly. My mother's side of the family, they dated way back in the sailing days, and some of her relations, they had a sailing ship, came from England over here. Sargeants or something like that was the name, I think. And they was pretty well, you know, like a pretty well-heeled affair, and I know it was only several years back, I imagine about 20 years back, the last of them died, they settled that estate. If my grandmother would have been living she was way up in her 80s or 90s when she died, that was on my mothers' sisters' side. We was the real direct heirs to my grandmother. My dad was living, too then. Well my dad was the only what you say direct heir. Then if she would have lived, why I'd of wound up with $100,000 or better out of that.

Q: You would be in Florida. You wouldn't be interviewed here.

A: I imagine so, or something like that. I don't know, but at one time they was supposed to have ships sailing back and forth, that's how they come from over there.

Q: Well, supposing we come back. I'd liked to ask you to explain this business of those logs backwards down the river.

A: Well, the main thing is backing down. If you're using a steamboat, or a sternwheeler, you've got more chance of flanking them because you can take your rudder and with your wheel turning you can flank it any way you want.

John Knoepfle

With the current in the river, why where the steamboat is on is like backing all the time, it's just practically like pulling it away from shore, floating with the current. But it's practically floating. If it would float with the current, it eventually would drag into the bank, you know.

Q: You wouldn't have any steerage.

A: Yes, but that way is to get the main part in backing down is just for steerage alone, but as far as the pushing, a lot of time when they was out in water where it was not necessary, you know, steer just shove a little bit, then they would push. But you couldn't push very fast because then the front of your tow would start submerging, see, and then that was harder to tow, and you couldn't handle it. And that was one reason they did that. And then when it got down close to where they wanted, why then they kept backing and keeping in close. There was very few boats there generally, where they landed, and you could drag real close to the bank, and if it was necessary, why you could just pull your back in by backing. That would be really the front of your raft, and you could swing that in until it started dragging it on the bank. The pressure of the current and the weight of your raft would automatically shove some of them logs. Even on the ground they would drag hard and that was used as a brake.

The higher the river, the more you'd want to brake it and the harder you'd throw her into the bank, and I've seen many a time, running the ferry they were backing, they had the *Cole* and the *Captain Hill*, we even helped help them too, land them with the ferry. I've seen that a lot of times where they had made three or four jabs before they stop it, and they like to tore up everything coming through there, you know current behind. They only have 500 to 600 logs, but that's behind, that's all they could do. When they'd bank them in that way, with these lines, why they just finally got them in. When the river raised, and the drifts was running heavy, why it was awful hard to hold them. Then they generally cut them, then they'd cut, if they was 200 feet wide or out in the river, from the bank, they'd take and cut that off 100 foot, make it longer. And drop them in, they started sawing a little faster and they run a little longer time, and get rid of them.

Q: All that driftwood piling on . . .

A: Yes, in front of it, that would make it awful hard to hold them. The more drift you've got up there, the more the current gets running too fast. It starts to submerge them a little bit, and banking them in close. A lot of times they was 25 logs wide, and maybe they'd had 100 of them wide or better, several hundred wide in dead water, or they'd go to the river channel. Three mills there run an average of about ten hours a day. I don't know how many feet of lumber they would cut. As much as any modern factory of today practically.

Q: Where did it all go?

A: They kept a weeding that away and I know after they closed, they had lumber up their way, I imagine eight or nine years after they quit business. They closed the mill. It was that long before, and if I'm not mistaken, they sold some lumber to a company in Cincinnati and they moved the balance of it. They started building this here steel plant down there where they unload that steel. And then Captain Beatty bought part of it. Then that Dreses Machine Shop bought part of it. They had on quite a few men, and like all of their deliveries, from the mill, why they had all horse and wagon. And they would come over here. They had to go way down, come across the bridge, that was an all day job to take a load of lumber over in Dayton.

But then a lot of times their old lumber, they had what you call a flat barge, something like these sand barges, they was decked over, and then they had a top or a railing around them, you might say, about a two or three foot rail. A lot of times they'd take that lumber, and then they had a derrick and they'd put it on, and they'd move that barge and then tow it. We'd tow that right ahead of our harbor, and then they had a team of horses would come down there. It was like a wharf there at that time and they'd just haul that lumber over in Dayton and Bellevue. It would be a lot quicker, see. And it's different than it is today as far as boating that way. Then right at the ferry where we landed, that was another source of transportation, not only going across the East End. And then there was the wharf that the city had built.

It wasn't cement, but it was stone, cobblestone, whatever you want to call it like the Cincinnati Wharf was at one time. They could drive a team, or that was all it was mostly then. They'd drive down there, and then they'd could load anything. Then they had the steamboat before the streetcars started to run. Then they had a steamboat run from the foot of Dayton Avenue or Berry Avenue, down to Broadway where the Coney Island boats is, see. They had a steamboat run like morning and night there that took people to Cincinnati, and that was their transportation, and then in Bellevue, at Taylor Avenue they had one, I think they had one, I think that was the *City of Bellevue*. I don't know what the name of that boat was in Dayton.

But the *City of Bellevue* run there at Taylor Avenue, I remember that boat. And people in Bellevue, instead of taking the streetcar to where you'd come out, why they'd just go down to Taylor Avenue and get on this boat and they'd take them over to Broadway, see. They'd have to walk up where they wanted to go. They had another boat at a ferry there at Newport, it came in at Monmouth Street. It was back and forth. Before the bridges. The Suspension Bridge was the first that was built, and then the old steamboaters, they had a lot of argument about that thing, too.

Q: A big fight over . . .

A: Yes, they didn't want no piling built in the river so it would interfere with traffic. They couldn't hold up on the bank, that was a job to build that bridge, you know, without putting any support under it they couldn't hold up anything. The only reason they did get it built was on account of the Civil War, they had to have that done to get across, and that's what really put that through. That's why it come to be a suspension bridge, they wanted to put piers on it, or build one with piers, but the steamboats was the big sort of transportation. They couldn't use that because they said the piers would interfere with the boats. They didn't want piling. Piling makes it a lot easier. They didn't want any interference. There was a big squabble over that.

But I think the war is what caused that to really finish. When they come off of that, like that first pier, the suspension, why that was an awful drop there, the original one, they've changed that about three times now. The first one that come over there, that first pier was planted right down by, come in there on Front Street, instead about where it does now. It comes in there about Third Street. But it come right off of it, come so low, it had a hard time, you know, to come up there. You had to come almost like that, and then you come out right on the regular crown of the bridge. Then later on they went up another square. That took some of that slant off of it after they got over their fighting. They went up another square. Now you're almost on a gradual slant. I had three different pictures of that bridge at one time. I noticed in the first one, when you come off that first pier, that was like going up a pretty good incline. It was a pretty steep jerk there. Then they started building these others, and they built them all with the piers.

I think the Suspension Bridge was the second suspension bridge, on the Ohio. I think up the river somewhere, at Parkersburg or Marietta or somewhere up in there, they built one, but this was the biggest bridge built of that type, under the conditions in the world at that time, it was a pretty measure of a piece of work at that. Then this here bridge too, although this other one was a suspension, and I think it was built before, but this one is the only one that spans the Ohio. That's the only bridge on the Ohio that spans the Ohio today because according to their government markings, why each pier is above low water marks. But this one up there at Parkersburg or Marietta wherever it is well, their piers, one of them, is in what they call the low water mark. That would be in the water, even though the river was down below that mark.

They have a low water and a high water mark, but the Suspension Bridge, the two piers are up above, and this is really the only one. I know when I was getting my steamboat license, why they asked that question, just a tricky question you know, you start a figuring how many bridges span the Ohio all the way down. But I was wise to them, my dad told me, on a couple of them. I was too slick for that one. But you'd start figuring them all out, and that's true, the only one that spans it. It's different like that, and then they'd ask you heights of the currents, and your lights. There is a lot of tricky stuff.

Q: What did you go up for when you took your exam?

A: Well, I went over to the courthouse, or the government building was over there, they had steamboat license exams. I have my license here some place. I let mine run out a long time ago.

Q: All right. Did hog chains prevent the boat from hogging up in the middle?

A: Yes. If it hogs up in the middle, why then, that causes your bow to be down, that causes what you call a head strong boat, why that would cause it to weave. But if it's got a turned belly, why that would cause it just to run straight. You would steer 100% easier. But if they hogged up in the middle, then water dropped up the front and the back. They always leaked a lot when they run, the wooden boats. The steel ones didn't leak as much as the old ones. But they leaked quite a bit, with that situation, why there would be a lot of trouble with steering. Then on this stalling why they, of course they would rot out the nails maybe a little quicker, but eventually they overhauled them so often, or replanked, that they would keep the ribs in such a shape they wouldn't rot fast.

These old steamboats, the real old ones that they used for coal and stuff, they had to hog them up pretty well. They used these here knuckle ratchets to hold their tows together, they used them a lot. On the towboat originally why they weighted that one, and they used all iron in the bottom, used tons and tons of iron, where a boat was, say, five feet in the center. When these steamboats, in order to steer, they had to be weighted in order to hold their course and tow good. They used to have to weigh in what they'd call a draft of the boat. Why it would be, say about five or six foot, the hull, the sides would be that high. But they'd have them weighted down to only be about three or four inches. The water would be from three to six inches above, the deck would be three to six inches, from sinking. They had that much iron in them.

The wind could come up, with that weight in them, then they'd handle the tow. The barges wouldn't sink. But if they was light, why then this boat would just slide with the wind. So they used the hog chains, it was important on a tow boat because they had awful big paddles for those, the buckets were big. They had a lot of vibration, and they had to have two or three different angles of hog chains going in different ways to take that vibration out.

Q: That's why the *Sprague* was . . .

A: Yes, it was one of the biggest boats built to my estimation; the new *Ashland* boat has three motors on it. It's got three eight-foot wheels. It was the most powerful in the world. I've seen them, was on both of them. The *Sprague*, had buckets 52 feet, and five-foot wide. The wheel was 42 feet in diameter. That's a lot of wheel, a lot of push. That would be five by 52 feet shoving the water with these propellers they got. I've seen the *Sprague*; it was in Cincinnati twice. The first time it was here they had a pretty good tow. They took automobiles from here down. When they stopped back they had a good tow.

I had a motorboat at that time, and we was out along side of the boat, when they landed there, it was at the foot of Baymiller Street. We went down there with the boat, and they let us go through it, and the engines was so big, instead of sitting flat like most of them, they sat on an angle. The engines on the *Sprague* had a six foot bore on them. I don't know what the stroke was on it, but it was tremendous. It was really the largest boat that was ever built. The *Island Queen*, was 80 wide by 300 feet long, but that was figuring her extreme

John Knoepfle

out, the overhang (the guards). The *Queen*, I don't believe was over 40 to 45. That would be a lot of boat. I forget how many barges they had on there. It's down on the Mississippi, they got a nightclub made out of it somebody was telling me. But that was sure a lot of boat there, I'll tell you.

There was an awful lot of people from Cincinnati, when they come in, went down to look at it. Of course, we had a motorboat then, and we just went down to joy ride around there. When they came back down, they had a couple barges of cars. That was about the first load of cars, I think they took them to New Orleans or down that way. I knew a lot of people was there watching, something different, and Lord it sure was a big outfit. It didn't seem, though, going up the river, when they were towing, it wasn't as bad on the harbor boats, as the *Island Queen*, and the *Queen City*. The *Queen City* and the *Island Queen*, they'd give you more trouble. The old *City of Louisville*, they didn't bother us because they were down below.

The *Island Queen* and the *Queen City*, oh, and there were a couple of others, boy, they'd give you a rough time. They run so fast, that they'd just suck all the water out of the river when they'd go along. And then, they'd cause an awful strain on the boom and break your line and your spars and everything else. But the old *Island Queen*, when it was light, you know, without a load, they'd let her go. And that *Queen City*, brother, they wasn't any boat around in the harbor, but the *City of Louisville* I think was the fastest sidewheeler ever was on the river, and the *Queen City* was the fastest sternwheeler. I don't know, which one was the fastest between the three. The *Island Queen* I know was a lot faster than the last *Queen* as far as that goes.

Why, when they'd ball the jack why that river would drop as high as, they'd drop it two foot and that would run out on the bank, that would run, oh down eight, ten, 20 feet sometimes, you know, just pull water. And there would be nothing there, and then it all swept back just like a tide, you had your lines awful tight or you'd bust up. This here captain I was telling you about, he was up there on this trip last weekend, and he asked me if I knew him. I said, "Yes, I know you. Yes, and if you knew how many time I cussed you all the times you was going up and down. You almost made me sink every day." And he laughed. He said, "Yes, on that last trip, we used to barrel coming down there and we'd watch you jumping around, and we'd give it all power."

But it did get my old man who used to get so mad at them, boy he'd want to kill them. Butler though, he was, my dad and them, he was more friendly than them others. We'd seen him more at Cranes, and he realized that it was hard on the boats. He'd generally always come down on the *Queen*. He run the *Queen* for a while, but when he come down he swang with the current. In that way it throwed all of the rollers to the Ohio side. There was no boats on that side, see. If that one's a gentleman, there's two of them, and they used to run the *Princess* a lot, too. And he'd come down, and man, as soon as he hit that there waterworks up there, he'd head right for the ferry. And then he'd give it a little swing, then straighten up again, and all them rollers just come right in there. And they'd roll for two or three minutes in there, and the water was shallower over there too, and that made, boy that sure give you a fit.

But that *Queen City* though, it was an extremely fast boat. It was well designed, run like it was a trim running boat. Awful fast. Now this *Chris Greene* and the *Betsy Ann*, now this *Chris Greene*, my brother's got now, he made a bar and a restaurant out of it. They raced for the fastest boat between them. There were packet boats, but as far as being a fast boat, it was a long way from being the fastest boat on the river, although it was racing. But the *Island Queen*, the new *Island Queen* was right behind them, coming up there and even this here captain, he was on then, and we was talking about them, why I told somebody at that time, the *Island Queen* could easily run over them. And they had a pretty good load on the *Queen*, for everybody watching the racing. And he said, "Yes, we was run on about two-thirds throttle."

But they was on different type boats, but a lot of people they seen the race, see. I guess they took for granted that was the two fastest boats on the river. But they was just matching their speed, but it was just a race between the two of them. But how they come to get in the race was they got neck and neck or something and they hit each other or come close or rubbed each other up there and they got kind of feuding between themselves, you know, and one tried to outdo the other one. And I think they kicked the steam up a little heavier than they generally do, and then they made a public thing. It did make more interesting boating you know, steamboating at that time, and people got more interested, and you know, it caused a lot of talk.

Now my brother, he was striker on the Cincinnati, that's the same as the oiler, then the assistant engineer, and then the engineer and on up, he was learning to be an engineer. The *City of Cincinnati*, that was the last one they built, it was like the *Island Queen* you know, that and the *Indiana*, they raced from Louisville to Madison, and so they took on, and he was telling me they had their steam up and everything. And they started out and it got so much weight on there. Had so many people on there, pushing her pretty heavy, and they all steams out, they couldn't get her back up, so this *Indiana*, why she started to walk away from them.

They was both sidewheelers. He said finally they had to cut down on the throttle and he started steaming her up pretty heavy, and they was fired by coal then, not oil burning. They started throwing stuff in there to pick her up. Finally they got the steam back up and they caught them. At one time they was about a quarter of a mile behind. They finally caught up, and beat them. He said, "Boy, that last one, when they were coming, that old engine sure was a challenge. They had everything she'd take on that last run. You ride out there where that wheel vibrates." It was pretty good experience, though. But them two boats were mated.

John Knoepfle

The older *Louisville* was called *Louisville and Cincinnati*. They were about the same type boats; this old *Louisville*, it was the fastest boat of any of them to tell the truth about it. I rode on it once or twice. When it was running, why the engines every time they'd stroke, you could feel that jerk, the push. But a lot of times they wouldn't be going out to kill. But it was just like on the *Island Queen* when they made that last trip, when they were going down, they were wanting all to get home in a hurry, and man they'd really barrel that.

Q: You used "ball and a jack" before. Did that have a special sense?

A: Oh, they all used that. They just mean that for speed. The ball and jack means that you're doing about everything you can do. That's just old slang we used on the river. Well, during that ice there they had over at the shipyard, that's about what ruined the shipyard, that last one. And the old *Greenland* was the last one that was up there. That ice took it out. That about ruined it.

Q: The ice just knocked out the yard itself.

A: Yes and it just kind of run in the bank up through them to a certain extent, the *Greenland*. They lost two or three boats, but that was the last one in the ice, packed up so heavy that it was coming into the boats they had about half planked. It just jammed in there and jammed in, the whole lower deck was full of ice clear up to the second deck. That just floated on out in the river, just floated with the ice. It didn't even sink. It wasn't even planked off. And it floated way down the river. And Captain Wes was there, and he was the night watchman. He had to watch it at night, in the daytime that's when she floated off. When it took off it went way down river a long ways before it sank. It was way down Lawrenceburg where the ice jammed. Everything jammed up, and my brother and I we was on that.

Q: Could you talk about fishing on the river?

A: On a V net you make your openings round on top, and then straight on the bottom just like a V, and you can run from one, so when the fish run in there you want your first throat a pretty good size, so they'll go in there. The bigger your opening is the more fish you catch, then it just tapers back. You can have from two to three throats, and three is about as many as they ever put in. Then on the last stages the end of the net, why you have what they call a drawstring in there; you can loosen it up and take the fish out as you roll the net into the boat. That makes it easy. You don't have to cut the net or try to pull them out. Yes, it's like a string. You can loosen it up.

After you have rolled the net into the boat, you just open it up and the fish come out. With a straight net they are allowed to use today it don't have wings, or you are not allowed anything like that, and it has to be a certain mesh. Years ago you could make it any mesh you wanted. You could start out with a big mesh in the front and little mesh in the back. The littler the more little fish you would catch. If you wanted to catch bigger, you had bigger mesh. On this wing net on the outside, your drop wing would be about from five to 20 feet long. It may run five feet, six feet deep. There would be cork on top and lead on the bottom. Then the wing going to shore could run according to the current, from 25 to 100 feet and that's to run up the river. Or starting from the net, running up the river against the current as much as possible. Fish all swim up the river. They are always battling current. They very seldom drift.

You notice that when the river is clear. In the boat harbor you could see them. They'd always go up the river. When they hit something why they generally float, then back a little bit, and then start out and go around. That's the idea have your outside wing long enough, so they don't swim clear down below. If it's pool water why you don't have to have it quite so long. That way you can catch any fish that comes up the river, then they put their doughballs in there. It was a good bait like cornmeal you put in the mesh in the last throat for flavor that would go down the river. That bait would attract them. Then they'd start following smell. When they got in they couldn't get out. The way the throat's made tapered back why you could keep tapering down just like a horn. The fish would go through, he'd feel it in the gills. Yet he'd give a flip and go right on through and keep going on back, and go clear to that back throat before it would stop. There was space to turn around. After he got in he couldn't get out. It was like a mouse trap.

On a drop net they used a pole and it's generally square, two poles and a rod of wood of any kind. You can use pipe or anything to make them. Pipe is pretty good for it will sink and you can make them in a hoop or a half round. That keeps the four corners out, and then you put a rope in the outside of your net so that will be tied. You want the net part kind of baggy in the center so when you pull it up it will make a funnel. You put bait in the center of that and you set there, and you just have to take a chance of raising it, or if the water is clear you can see the fish in there. Then you just take this pole, you just lift up, when you lift it up, why then you got them; then you swing it over and you take the fish out. Now years ago you was allowed to use the wing net. There was no law again that, or again the mesh on a feather net, that is for small fish, say of about, under a foot, see like for chubs, they're real little fish, and small catfish. Now there's two-throated nets and their mesh runs from an inch to a half inch. It's getting real little.

There's law that you are not allowed to have them certain times. Years ago they had them; you could catch an enormous amount of little fish with them. Then this seine, that's on the out of a wing, they run from 50 foot to 300, 400, or 500 feet. One or two men stand on the bank, and then they take a flat boat and two men generally row it. They coil this seine up, keep putting it on top so it will unravel. They would start out at the bank and those two guys with seines they go as hard as they can right straight out in the middle of the river. When they get out to about the end of that line, then they start to coming down and rowing in. The seine is coming down with the current the guys rowing keep a pulling it in, and keep it kind of stretched. The guys on the bank, they've got the bottom line, and the top line to the seine, and they keep pulling that in.

John Knoepfle

Finally you get this in, and it just keeps coming in and the bottom drags the bank. The fish are there, and they can't get out. You've got them hooked, and then after you get in with the rowboat then you start pulling in and there's no possible chance for them to get away. You just keep pulling in and pulling in and you catch whatever is in that body of water wherever you went.

Coney Island used to be an extremely good place, and right across the railroad from the gas tank in Dayton. Up on the Coney Island we used to go up there at night and they had some fellows used to furnish the boats, and nets if you wanted to go up just for the fun of it. They would guarantee you so much fish, and if you didn't catch any they would give you some. Charge you like a dollar or something. You could help them row. You'd get all the hard work practically, and they did all the bossing. But you would have fun! You know if you never went on, just like these dude ranches, they let you do all the hard work, and you just get the fun out of it.

You could go up there, they had you start out there at the lowest part of that dike when the river was lower. It's higher now than what it was then. They'd start there that was a dandy place. Every time they'd run out with that net, or seine, they'd catch a pretty good bit. I've seen them catch as much as a barrel of fish. You couldn't even get them in a flour barrel. Just one haul! Some hauls maybe they didn't even get only just a couple. They always had plenty of fish there. Up on the Dayton Bar, that was pretty shallow water up there, kind of swift too, in a way because it was narrow. Quite a few would fish that, but everybody had to take turns. If you had a seine, you had to wait your turn. Up on Coney Island there was generally these two guys I knew of that always did that professionally. A fellow runs the ferry up there going across, he would know who they are. So they generally ran it most of the time, had the equipment, anybody was practically entitled to use it for a couple of bucks, you might say, and fish, and there were no arguments about who was to go out first.

At the Dayton Bar there was about three or four fished professionally. When dad run ferry we used fishing as a side line. We sold fish on the side too. He had one or two men working. If there wasn't boat work, he always had about 10 nets out. We didn't do much seining, but we did a lot of free net fishing. Dad caught one cat I know it weighed 85 or 87 pounds. It was the biggest catfish I have seen in the Ohio. We caught a buffalo in the 60s. There's a number of fish we caught up in 40s like spoonbill cats and eels. We caught one eel that was six or seven feet long and three or four inches in diameter.

Q: They are rare around here.

A: Yes, they are pretty rare. They cooked that, I ate part of that one. They skinned that one and used the hide to make wrist bands for watches. One catfish they caught, this big one, why this Glenn Martin had a saloon there at the top of the hill, on west Third and Burns, that house that used to be a saloon; they had like a summer garden there. He bought the fish and had a fish fry and it was just like steaks. Boy it was a big one.

Q: What kind of a cat was it, a spoonbill?

A: No, it was a regular black cat or what they call a shovelhead, mudhead. I think it was sort of blackish like a mudcat. This eel we caught, we was having a big fry down at the boat harbor that night. They had a lot of fish and guys got drinking a little bit and some of them said, boy they wasn't going to eat any eel. We Just sliced it off and didn't tell them. As long as they didn't know it. A funny thing about eel, you can cook it and it tastes good, but it seems like to me it had a taste of vinegar to it. Like you had seasoned it just a fraction. You cook that, let it get cool, and put it in a skillet, you got to cook him again because it goes raw. You have to cook it over again, or it will turn raw. I never knew that until a long time afterwards, too. But somebody told me. Then these sturgeon, there was a lot of them in the area at that time, but now they're scarce. I was talking to a guy who was on the river years, did never see one.

Q: Now what did they look like?

A: More like a shark and kind of round headed, flat nosed, pretty long, they got a mouth underneath, a sucker mouth. White underneath and brown on the top, and scaly, and back where their tail is, fins just like a shark. This fish has a pretty good size tail. It springs out, but it's a pretty good size too. The only way you can get that scale off, you either have to put him in red hot coals or scalding water. That just falls off them, cracks and falls right off. After you get that off there's a vein right in the center like a creek. You take pliers and pull that out. That's all there is outside of the intestines; it's just solid meat, just like a piece of ham, or sausage. Just regular meat, no bones in it. Then the gar that's a longer fish. It's a bigmouth fish. It's a killer. It kills all the other fish. They tried to get rid of them. I have seen those gars six or seven feet long. I don't know what they weigh. I imagine it would be about six or seven inches in diameter, through the center. Fishing one time, of course everybody boasts about fish. I know one time, over where we landed the ferry where Beatty's is right now. Used to be a place that was real deep in there, and they had so many fish one big net couldn't haul them in or put them in the boat. The two fellows would have to roll them in the flat boat, and those guys couldn't hardly roll them in there. They had to get some of them out of the nets and in the boat before they could roll the nets in. There was that much weight. It must have been 400 or 500 pounds.

Q: What year would this have been?

A: It would be about 1915 or 1916, in buffalo, there was quite a few of them caught. A lot of them caught on lines. They used to roll and jump a lot. In the morning when we were on the ferry it would be daylight about five, the first trip I guess that noise from the power, and boy a lot of time you would see them jump. And I imagine some of them would be three or four feet long. You could see them in different places, but in Buffalo they had a habit of jumping more, like ocean fish, marlin or porpoise. I think it is porpoise, they like to jump too.

One time the most fish that I ever did catch, we had this harbor boat out of the beach, we had a place, on the bank, you would put in when the river fell. Why it came down on trestles like bridging we had. That year the river didn't raise, so the boat house was out on the bank, that's the picture, that one I showed you. So it was down below our harbor or regular dock, and they had to come through these weeds, the willows, they only had a path about five foot wide down to the boat harbor. The cruise net had a line with a pulley that goes down to the river. So finally a pop raise comes along, and some guy had an old net there that wasn't much good. It had lights on it. He says, "Just put a net in there, in this here trough there, be the same as a wing net. Put it in and we will catch some fish." I said, "Oh, I haven't got time."

I knew the boat was leaking too, coming apart, although we had caulked. They'll leak a lot anyhow before they swell. So he says, "Well, let's put it in." So we put that thing in, and I bet it wasn't in there 20 minutes. It was right in this path. The river was raising so we had to move in just a little bit, or move up. This net was in the way and we didn't want boats to get on it and mash it. So I say, "Let's get everything out of here so we can get moved in," never expecting to catch a fish. We raised that thing and I swear I never saw so many fish! All them jack salmon and catfish, I'd say about a foot long, from about a half a pound up to about two pounds. Perch, and every kind of fish you could think of, and man, we were so startled we didn't know what to think. So we pick the fish up, and get the boat set, and we threw in there. And boy we were catching fish like that all day long.

And this guy went up and got another net. And his boy come and put in there, and we fished and three of us were making fish boxes to put them in. We was selling fish for five cents a pound, ten cents a pound, anything you wanted to sell them for. That day we caught fish for about ten hours that way. Finally, the river was raising fast and we had to pull up to our other place, and do you know, they couldn't catch a darn one after that. But it was kind of in that one place and they were just in them willows there, the horse weeds, they call them. It was up high enough and I guess fish just had to follow that when the river was high they stay right to the bank.

They must have just followed that groove up there, but that was the most fish I ever did see caught, or ever caught. I'll bet we had 2,000 or 3,000 pounds of fish we caught in ten hours. None of them was very big, over say about two pounds. I guess was about the biggest one we caught. It got to be a problem taking out. I mean that drawstring bag you would pull up there and take it out, and boy, we had the time of our life. We had some old scrap wood there, you know, all around the harbor, and Wes making them cartons and putting the fish in there so they wouldn't die. And we'd sit around my brother and all of them, anybody that was there, we'd sit around selling fish. We'd take whatever we could get. We'd get fifteen cents, or ten cents a pound. If he only had a nickel, we would take a nickel.

Q: What did they usually sell for?

A: Oh, about 20 cents was an average. Years ago all the big fish we caught, this catfish, we got 10 cents a pound for that one. I remember that well. That was a fair price then, too. But you could always get ten cents, but as the years went by, I think 20 or 30 cents. I knew the last time I was around where there's fish, why it was about 30, 35 cents you could get, you know, a pretty good collection of any kind of fish. Down near Aurora they caught a lot. Along the Big Miami, along in that neighborhood there's a lot of fish. A lot of fellows made their living on just fishing there. Up at the waterworks, used to be a good bet, and trout line, used to be a lot of fishing. I have caught one turtle on a trout line. Turtles are hard to catch on a trout line. We've caught a lot of them in the nets. I know we've caught several turtles that weighed ten pounds, maybe I don't know just exactly, but they would be about that big around.

Q: You would get a special price on those, I suppose.

A: Yes, then that depends, too. There's several different types, soft backs, hard backs, thin, and some thick. There are a lot of different types of turtles. The first time I ever caught an eel though, on the line, he's about two or three feet long. I went out there and pulled that old trout line in, tracing it out, and I saw that eel pop up, and I thought it was a water moccasin, the first one I had ever seen! I was a kid about ten or twelve years old at that time. Boy I got that line and I come in there a hollering. My dad, he was running the ferry, and I told my dad there is a snake on the line, a water moccasin. This John McGowen that worked for him then, he had his revolver. He told me, "It isn't a moccasin, that's an eel. We'll eat him." That was the first eel that I ever saw.

Water dogs now, they used to catch a lot of them. I haven't seen a water dog for a long while, but I have seen them a pretty good size. I have seen them weigh as high as a pound or up to five pounds. That's a fish that can live on land or water, and it's got feet. In the lizard family really like, but it's more like a catfish. The skin is real slimy and slick, and it's got a wide nose and the mouth across the front end. It can walk on the ground or walk in the river, and they are supposed to be poisonous. They are no good to eat; I've never heard of anyone eating them. Carp, was supposed to be the worst fish to eat; I have eaten carp. It was real good. They'd clean them, and took the mud vein out, and soak them in saltwater overnight and they're good. I have eaten carp that was really delicious; and then I have eaten them, and they wasn't no good. I have eaten good fish that was no good to eat that way.

Q: The Romans thought they were very great delicacies, but they were cooked with steam not fried.

A: Carp, they call them sewer bass, that's a nickname for them. Then there is the skipjacks and tooth herrings, there's quite a few of them in the river, but they are awful boney. Skipjacks you can eat or tooth herring either one, but there are so many fine bones in them, why you go nuts getting the bones out of them. Perch is a good eating fish, and there is quite a few of them being caught in the river. I was down at my brother's the other day, and Fred workman, this

John Knoepfle

fellow drove last week, we had a trip to go out for him to drive for them. His kid was there waiting for him and he throws the line out, and goes up to my brother's, and the line wasn't out I bet you two minutes, and he was jumping around, doggone he's got a fish all ready. I though he was kidding. He had a perch there about two pounds on it, and he said, "Boy, that kid's going to have to watch his line." I was surprised he caught one that quick. They have been catching quite a bit down there and perch is a real good eating fish. I think the biggest I have seen of them is about five or ten pounds, I imagine ten pounds is about the limit on them as far as I know. White horse and black horse, they get pretty big, and it's kind of coarser meat too. There is a spoonbill cat, they have a big long bill on them; they're like a catfish only they got a real longer snoot on them. And there was a lot them on the Mississippi River, but up here there wasn't too many. Up here they were smaller. But they say down in the Mississippi they were running as high as 80, 90 or 100 pounds.

Q: Used to be known. They were legendary.

A: Well if you're over there by Crane's saw mill, they claim old Jack Hayes and a couple of those old timers, well he was there with the Marine Ways a long time, I've seen a lot of them jump too, they claim that there was one that used to jump down there, and they claimed it weighed over 100 pounds. I don't know if it was some big cat. They had it named or something. But it jumped, and I have seen a lot of them early in the morning when we was making ferry trips, once in a week especially when the river was low like in a pool station. The noise of the propeller going across there just upset them, and they would jump. I have seen some pretty big ones jump. It just seemed like a man jumping, jumping in the river, make a big splash.

Q: Is Jack Hayes still alive?

A: No, he's dead. He would be, I guess, passed 100 years old by now. He was awful active at the Marine Ways, sort of a boss there for a long time. He was awful active. I know when he was in his 80's, and I think he'd get around as good as you would expect. He'd even file saws. He had a little machine shop, and his boys were good designers; they could make any gasoline part for a motor, or a gasoline engine, in fact he would design them. He did get a lot of lathe work. Even at that time, he was around 80 or 85, and he'd file saws, file them good, too. He was real active. He was a little fellow, he was a spunky old devil. He did a lot of fishing over there. They fished a lot of nets, and on the Ohio side there they did an awful lot of that fishing there with nets.

Q: It's an odd thing, as much as we have talked to people, this is about the first time that we have gotten a detail account on that.

A: Well I don't know just how many fish would be in this river, but I don't think there is too awful many because I think about 20, if I took time to remember about 20 is about all I can really, think about.

Q: Well the ferocious bluegill is all around now.

A: Yes and there is quite a few bass too. There is about two different types of bass and they come fairly good sized too.

Q: How about muskies?

A: They didn't have any around here. I never did see any around here.

Q: And the legendary crocodile that . . .

A: No, it might have been one of them big water dogs. Some guy might have a drink too much and they looked bigger. One time we was at the Kentucky River and went up there, and we had a speed boat, and coming back why we was going to do some fishing, and we were going to do a lot of things that we didn't do. Coming down, and them guys years ago, they had a habit of shooting fish, and this dam was cement instead of wickets like ours. They were cement and they slant up, and they've got a long drag in the back, and the water would only be a couple of feet deep there, see. But the river would be deeper, but I mean where that cement would taper off, they'd come out and they couldn't go any farther you could just see them, they would be just about a foot underwater, and those guys would just shoot them and sell them.

Q: That was up on the Kentucky side?

A: Yes that's it. So we knew we was going to make it home that night, and so they had one catfish I believe it was, and it was about 20 pounds. I ask this guy what he wanted for it and he said, "Well, I'll tell you what, if you will give us a ride in that speedboat we will give you a fish." I said, "Boys you've got a ride." This is a boat we had that would run about 25 miles an hour or 30, and that was fast I guess then. That was fast, I guess oh, about 1922 along in there, and that was pretty fast you knew for them days. There was about four of them there, so we gave them a good ride down, and they gave us a catfish. They were cooking some fish there too, and they gave us some cooked fish because we were camping anyhow. They had give us some coffee and stuff. We had a pretty good chat with them, and we took off. Well, we kept the fish, wasn't really killed, it was shocked, but it was numb enough that they got it. So we put a rope on him and put him in a big tub of water, tied him so he wouldn't fall out or jump overboard if he would toss around. We left there and came on up the river until we got up here, why we showed them there, but we was slick enough, we didn't let them see the hole in the head when they shot him. We told them we caught them and anyway we was going to have a fish fry. We called up some girls and was getting some beer and stuff. We had cleaned this fish and then as the guys arrived, why we cut his head off. They never did knew that we didn't catch it. So we had a fish fry out of him.

They did a lot of shooting up there. I think they have barred that now, they are not supposed to do it. Up here on the dams they used to fish a lot, good fishing too. But on account of the war they was afraid to let anyone in there. It got to be where they took too much chances, and people might have got around those wickets and bear traps and stuff. They can get so much current there they might be drowned if they are not real experienced on the river.

John Knoepfle

George Hayhurst & Harry Louden, August 22, 1957

Question: We are in the Rare Book Room of the Public Library in Cincinnati, Ohio and I've come here to talk to two rare rivermen.

Answer George Hayhurst: I'm terribly new, on this river as far as the rareness goes because I didn't start until 1937, and I started out as cabin boy, and made big wages, $75 a month, and board. Let's see, I started down to take another job in a yard down at Fernbank there at the old marine repair station, and I was going in to take this job, and a fellow came up, and told me they needed a cabin boy on the steamer *Scioto*, an old towboat the engineers had. They asked me if I wanted to go out, and I said it don't make any difference to me I was looking for a job. We left that morning about 10 a.m. for Marietta, Ohio to pick up the dredge *Harris*, and bring it back down to Fernbank. I was on the *Scioto* from that time until the war started, and in that time I went up to watchman. I went from cabin boy on to the deck, from the deck to force watchman. Let's see, I left in December of 1941 into the Navy. I had to go in the Navy because I opened my big mouth and said if there is a war I'd join the Navy. I never did think there would be a war. I had to go to keep from being a liar.

Q: Where were you in the Navy?

A: Let's see I started out on the *Lafayette*, and it burned in New York harbor, and after it burned and sank I was fitted out duty on the battleship *Indiana* at Newport News Shipyard. After we left there on a shakedown cruise, we went to Norfolk for just minor repairs and to straighten it out after a shakedown cruise. We were going out on another shakedown cruise I forget the year, I think that was in October of 1942 and the next morning we ended up going by Cape Hatteras for the canal, so we went through the canal over in the Pacific. Then I was over there until 1944. Then we came back to Bremerton, Washington, for repairs. I got transferred to shore duty in Long Beach, and I was in Long Beach on a YR, that is a yard repair ship. I was an Electrician First Class until the war ended. Then I came back to the *Scioto*. I got discharged in October and went back to work the 4th of November on the *Scioto*.

I worked on the *Scioto* up until June of 1946, then till I got hurt in a mishap down in between two barges. I was in the hospital for five months. Then I didn't go back to work no more for the government. Well I had trouble getting around and walking because I had a crushed pelvis. Then a fellow I knew by the name of Bence Eddington come down to the house one day, and asked me if I wanted to take a ride to New Orleans on a boat, and I said well I wasn't doing anything so I might as well. So I went on the *Delta Queen* and let's see, who was captain? Tom Greene was captain on there and Butler was the pilot's name, and Kelley was pilot, and a fellow by the name of L.D. was mate. I went on there and stayed until 1949, and then I went on the *Gordon C. Greene* as mate running from St. Louis to Minneapolis and St. Paul. I was on there until she quit running until 1952. After they laid her up sold her, I went on the *Queen* as mate up until, let's see, it's just been a year two years, I've been off of there. In June I went back to work for the government again where I am now.

Q: Are you down at Fernbank now?

A: Yes. Working at the dam there.

Q: Now you never identified yourself or gave your date and place of birth.

A: Oh, sorry. Well it's George Hayhurst and I was born in Cincinnati in 1915.

Q: Now maybe we can get your friend to do a similar . . .

Harry Louden: I'm not near as good a speaker as George. I know a lot of good steamboat lies I could tell about him, but he probably wouldn't like that.

Q: Would you identify yourself, sir?

H: Yes, I'll give you the best I know how. I'm Harry Louden, and I was born in Boone County, Kentucky the 19th of October 1906. When I didn't have any job other than playing around on the farm, which I wasn't doing any good. Why, when I was 20 years old I came to Fernbank looking for a job on one of the boats. They had a pretty good fleet there at that time. Captain Shelby Chandler gave me a job as cabin boy on the *Scioto*, and I got in the pilot house a little later, that fall I believe, this was in May when I went to work, and in that fall he took me in the pilot house and learned me what I knew at the time he left. Which, if I'd been a little more apt, I could have learned a lot more because he had the ability, and probably I couldn't swallow all of it as much as he could dish out. At any rate in three years I got my license, and then Captain Chandler went into the Division Office, a Director of Navigation, and just left me the job.

I more or less inherited the master's job on the *Scioto*. I worked in the government fleet here with such as Captain Emerson Moore, Shelby Chandler, and J. R. Chandler, and Captain Jim Steward, and all those fellows. They are all topnotch operators. Finally by the skin of my teeth I got far enough along where I could kind of get along. We tow, we do open channel maintenance work, went on then till, oh I don't know up until well we operated the Cincinnati District, but in the meantime I had struggled along. And had managed to get my license from Huntington to Louisville. In 1937 I had a lot of leave owing to me, and I prevailed on Mr. George Burdorf, our chief of operations at the time let me take leave. At that time Captain Tom and Chris Greene was leaving, and they let me ride on the *Gordon Greene* for nine weeks that they put in at Pittsburgh, tourist trade.

Captain Jessie Hughes and Wilsie Miller learned me what I know about the river at Pittsburgh. They treated me awful nice, and it goes along until about 1946, and they had a big reduction. The government abolished our district, and I was transferred to Louisville. I went to Louisville on the 12th day of May in 1947, and did the same kind of work down there. I was on the various towboats they had down there, and put in about three or four years on the dredge *Jewett* with Captain Hawley, Captain A. R. Monk, and I worked with Captain Jim

Wallace, Captain Paul Underwood, Captain George Pickering, now deceased, and oh, a nice bunch of fellows like that, and then they finally sold our dredge.

We used a dredge out of St. Louis to do our maintenance work, and that was the last job I was on, the dredge *Sainte Genevieve* with Captain Cleo Miller from Metropolis, a very fine man. I understand now that she's gone back to St. Louis for the season, and incidentally I'm the man that hired Mr. Hayhurst here, and also the guy that pretty near killed him. When they pulled him out of the scrape, I expect to get him the next time. That's about all, I don't know too much to tell you.

A: Well, the nicest thing about river work is that in nice weather you have a nice ride. You don't do nothing but ride, and clean up the boat. That's all, you have all your bad, hard work in rough weather. You take ice and when it's foggy and rainy, and high water, that's when you have your rough going on the river.

H: Yes, that's when it don't look so good.

A: That's when you'd rather do something else.

Q: And you would be working on the *Scioto* during high water, fog and ice.

A: Oh my lord yes, one time we went up to Huntington and got five barges of coal and ice got to running.

H: Sunk one.

A: Sunk one setting away from Huntington. We didn't sink it, the *Omar* backed her stern up agin it and baled it full of water for us.

Q: Was that a steel barge?

A: Yes, it was a steel barge, had it loaded with coal. We had five, didn't we? We had six come down with five after we lost one to the fish, and then we got down to 35 and a big ice flow shoved us out over in the front of the bear trap. They had the dam up, and we were in there backing trying to back them five up out of there, and she wouldn't do it. The ice was cutting the wheel up and every time you was backing, you was backing more ice into it, and it was just chewing it up. There was ice jammed between the boat into the bank, and we tied them barges off in front of that trap and took them out one at a time.

H: Wasn't so hard, was it?

A: I got over on the bank with a line, I just thought well, this is just a good place to stay. I went on up the bank, and we tied them off up at New Richmond late that night after we got them all out of there. The next morning we went down, and they had locked chamber of ice, and then a barge and finally we got through there, and that was on the 24th day of December.

Q: What year was that?

A: 1945.

H: About the last ice I remember us having that amounted to anything.

A: The ice got so bad they couldn't get the dams down, so we went down to Fernbank and got down there on Christmas Eve, and left on Christmas Day, and went down and knocked 38, didn't we?

H: Yeah.

A: With a barge. They couldn't get out to get the wickets down, and the ice was jamming up and breaching the wickets. In other words there was so much pressure up above that it was the wickets lay flat and letting the water out too, and just getting ice jammed up against it. We took a barge and went underneath the dam, and you'd run up against the wickets and knocked the props out from under them and just back off and let them fall.

Q: Oh I see, that's not the safest kind of work in the world is it?

A: Not when there's ice, no. That was on Christmas Day, and then we laid up that winter didn't we, beached the boat after we got back from there.

H: went to 33 and knocked that down.

A: Yes.

Q: What happened to the dam?

H: We went to 33 and knocked that down right after we got through with 38, don't you remember?

A: Yes, that's where it was, 32 that those two locks men drowned in that ice. I know they went over to operate a trap and they got caught in the ice flow with a skiff, and both of them got drowned in it, turned the skiff over. It's bad all the time. Like one time we were down at Louisville and a storm was coming up, so we were going to land, and we had a roustabout on the boat, he was called Little Willie. Little Willie was about seven feet tall and weighs about 350 pounds.

Q: Was this a Greene boat?

A: Yes, the *Delta Queen*. And the wind got up, and Little Willie was out untying the heel to the stage, and the wind got ahold of the stage, turned it around and knocked Little Willie in the river. He never hit the river, he hit in the forks of the anchor. I thought he went into the river. I looked over the side, there come Little Willie climbing up the anchor chain. I had to laugh because you've got to know Little Willie to appreciate the story. He's a big guy.

Q: Let me take you back just a little bit, Mr. Hayhurst. You started out as a cabin boy, now the *Scioto*, was this a government sternwheeler?

A: A government towboat.

Q: What were your duties then as a cabin boy?

A: Oh, you started out in the morning helping the cooks fix breakfast and after you got everyone up you cleaned up all the boat, that is all the staterooms, and made the beds, and changed them, and then you rotated around, like washing windows and polishing brass. You had days to do that, the worst place to do that is up at Ashland, Kentucky at the Semit Galway Coke Company. They put out a sulfur acid gas, and you can polish brass and go around, and in five minutes it's turned red.

Q: Like polishing it on a battleship.

A: Yes, this sulfur really turned it red and no more than you got it done. Then after you got that done in the morning, you usually got your work done in the morning, you had to help cook, fix lunch and wash the dishes, and in the

John Knoepfle

afternoon while you was resting you usually stringed beans and peeled apples, or something like that.

H: Peeled potatoes.

A: Cabin boy and cook's job, on a steamboat isn't too hard a work, but it's long hours. It's not hard work, but you start out so early and you get finished so late. Then you take on there we had every other weekend off. We worked from on that *Scioto*, on this particular boat you was off Friday noon, and you never had to come back until Monday noon every other weekend. So I was on there, a young boy, and I was going to be a big shot and go home one time. So come Friday and noon I was going to get off, so I grabbed my big bag, and started up the river bank through the cornfield, and I never walked so far through corn in all my life out to the bus. That was up there around that hundred mile house, up just below Portsmouth, big cornfield bottoms up there.

Q: Yes, that is a wide bottom in that area. Well I'm curious about, I've talked to rousters, and I've talked to clerks and wharfboat men, but I wonder if you remembered on the packets, such as the *Greene*, even in late years what the mates did, how they ordered the loading and things like that?

A: Well your loading is usually taken care of by the clerks. See they have a mudclerk that goes out on the bank, now that's in olden times, and he would see where the freight was destined for, and he would keep it all together. But the mates would actually load the boats. In other words to see if the boat was loaded level and properly so that it would make the best time. In other words you wouldn't want all your heavy stuff all on one side no matter whether it's all going off at one time because it makes your boat lay over on that one side, and you couldn't steer properly, and you couldn't get the best time out of it.

Q: Somebody told me they misloaded a *Greene* boat down there at the public landing and turned it over, was that before your time?

A: It could have been, I've never heard about it.

H: Certainly, you can take a packetboat mate, he would give more orders loading three sacks of flour than they'd give in Washington, they can give lots of them.

Q: What kind of orders?

H: Oh, nicknames he'd call them rousters, and hurrying them up, and all that stuff. And you'd got to hear it to know and appreciate it.

A: Like for instance there was different freight they was loading different ways, they'd holler at the rousters if it was as sack of flour, they'd yell, "Belly and back it," or "Wing it," that meant carry it under each arm. Like sacks, they'd carry two sacks at one time, and they'd say, "Wing em," They'd have to carry one under each arm and there'd be two guys throwing them up, and one man carrying them. And you take your roustabouts, they usually only carried the freight on and off, and each boat had its own deckhands. That is they'd have a head deckhand, he would probably be the one that would whip the rest of them, that's the reason he was head deckhand.

H: Took his cut out of the crap game and everything like that.

A: He'd usually run the crap game, now that was something that always beat me is why they'd let one guy cut the game and he didn't do nothing but own the dice. The same way with a card game, every time they'd play cards he'd bring out the cards and lay them down, and he wouldn't do nothing but just set in there and take so much money out of each pot.

H: That's for letting them play. You say he's a tough guy and he'd do that.

Q: Joe Bates used to play with them though, didn't he? Do you remember Joe Bates?

A: Yes, they used to have quite a few mates that would get his cut of them.

H: That was the mate's racket.

A: He would take and get the money out of card games, too.

Q: I understand now at the time that you were on the *Greene* and starting your river a lot of the working conditions had improved. But I know there are tales of the older mates that were tough and fierce men, have you ever heard any of those stories?

A: Yes, but I don't know, you hear tales like that, but I can't see any human being mistreating someone else. I think they was just tales and that's about all.

H: Well some of them were pretty authentic. I've heard some pretty rough things about some of these old tough, I'll tell you an authority might give you some ideas along those lines, Henry McGarvey.

Q: Henry McGarvey, he's down at the . . .

A: He's in Louisville.

H: No, I don't know where he's at, he was steamboat inspector here for a while, and he retired out of the coast guard, and he used to run mate on the old *City of Cincinnati*, and all these old packet boats between Louisville and Cincinnati.

A: You're thinking of Max McGarvey down at . . .

H: This is Henry McGarvey, M-c-G-A-R-V-E-Y I believe, and he lives over at Newport, I think, you'll find him in the telephone book.

Q: Mates have a way of disappearing.

A: Now old Doc Carr, he's down there.

Q: Yes, I've been trying to catch him and he's hard to catch.

H: I'll tell you another fellow that you could interview and give you some stuff is Harvey Coomer.

Q: Oh is he in Louisville now?

H: Harvey Coomer runs these orange juice stands around Cincinnati here,

Q: The old, the father?

H: He runs them himself. He was one of your little tough mates and he wasn't very big, but he was loud. You see them on the street here, Coomer's Orange Juice. Where he lives, I don't know, but Harvey Coomer's . . .

Q: He's in Louisville now, I found that out the other day.

H: Oh is he in Louisville? Well I didn't know that. I tell you why I said that. There was an article in the paper not too long ago about him, showed how he came from over on the Cumberland River, and got a job on the Cincinnati to Louisville line, and they considered him too small to handle the rough elements, but what he made up for lack of size he was pretty loud, and he got away with it. Then he bought into this orange juice company from some fellow over in Kansas and finally bought him out and he made a fortune at it.

A: About handling a boat, you go into a landing with roustabouts, I don't care how many times you make the landing, you can make it three times a day if you don't get up there and tell them where to put the lines they won't do it. I don't know why they just don't. Well now I'll say, there are a few of them that are pretty good. So why they don't do it I don't know. The same way with throwing a line out on a lock wall. They can have an heaving line on it and the boat will be rubbing the lock wall, and they'll throw the heaving line out, and they won't ever pick up the line.

Q: Could you describe the *Scioto* for us?

H: 148 feet overall. Well she was just merely a good old high pressure towboat, pool type boat, built in 1912 here on the river front. Charles Barnes built her, and she was 14 and six feet that was the size of her machines, high pressure. In fact I don't know of any high pressure boats running today. I believe there is one over maybe St. Louis somewhere.

A: *Avalon.*

H: Yes, well I guess the *Avalon* is high pressure. The old high pressure tow-boats are all gone; they got rid of them due to so much trouble with the boilers. They use raw river water in those boilers, and they all gave way to condensing boats, so that they used the water over and over and it was treated, and they didn't have any boiler troubles. They didn't have to wash boilers so much.

Q: That's right, Norval Horton told me that they used to have to stop about every two days in the Mississippi.

H: That's right and up here in this river ordinarily eight days on a double cruise boat was about as long as you could go. We used to go two weeks ordinarily. But of course, we didn't run but 15 hours, but that all gave way to condensing boats, now they've about gave up the ghost with diesels.

Q: The *Scioto* is still on the river in one form or another, isn't it?

H: I'm not sure.

A: The last I saw it was over in St. Louis.

H: Went to St. Louis, over there the Menke showboat people bought her. When we sold her here at Fernbank, they sold her to that Nugent and Company in Louisville, and they operated her a little while. Then this showboat outfit bought her over there, and they were going to use her for quarters and store boats hanging on behind. The last account I heard of her she went to Bayern country for something, I don't know what she's doing today.

Q: Maybe we can talk a little bit about the men. You mentioned Captain Shelby Chandler, can you tell me anything about Captain Chandler?

H: I can tell you a lot of things, all good. I can tell you where you'll see a picture of him in that handbook, the Ohio River handbook if you've got one of them.

A: He's out in California now.

H: He's retired in California and he was one of the old timers. He came up in the Cincinnati Louisville packet line in the latter part of the Combine towboat days. You can find out more about him the handbook than I can tell you.

Q: Just an off question since you mentioned it. Do you know when the Combine folded up?

H: Not exactly but it was along about 1914 I'd imagine, maybe a little later. I saw these old barges with RC on them when I was a kid.

A: They had a tornado down in the lower end of the Mississippi that kind of cleaned them out. They lost I don't know six or seven boats and about 100 and some barges. In fact, you can still see the barges down there. They wash out of the bank every once in a while.

H: I'll tell you what mostly done the Combine. The railroad company bought the controlling interest and just tied them up and let them bust up.

Q: You said you could see RC on them.

H: River Combine. See I've saw a few of the old boats, but that's before my time, and all I know is what I've read and heard about it. You know different coal companies, like the Diamond Coal Company, and Pittsburgh Coal Company, and Walton's, and all that outfit all went together and formed a huge Combine. And oh, I don't know how many coal companies were in it, and they operated all those boats, and they towed the coal to New Orleans.

A: See the *Sprague* belonged to that.

H: The *Sprague* was built in about 1902, was it 1902 or 1905? It was 1905, wasn't it?

H: And the *Wakerobin's* down here as a landing boat.

Q: Now you were on the dredge *Harris* too, you mentioned.

A: No, I never was on that dredge.

H: We went to Marietta and brought it in.

Q: Well dredging must be a rather intricate operation too, isn't it?

H: Yes, we had one over at St. Louis, a big steam dredge, a 20 inch pipeline dredge.

A: There was a difference between the *Sainte Genevieve* dredge and the *Harris*. The *Sainte Genevieve* is a self-propelled dredge where the *Harris* wasn't.

H: You had to tow the *Harris*.

A: The *Harris* had to be towed, it was a suction dredge same as the *Sainte Genevieve*. It had a pipeline for the discharge out on the bank somewhere, or out on a bar that was already formed.

H: It was what was called a box dredge.

Q: Well what's a box dredge?

H: Well a box dredge is one that you have to tow; it's not self-propelled. See she wasn't this *Sainte Genevieve* was a big sternwheel dredge.

A: I hear you could walk those dredges a little bit.

H: You can walk them over this way or over that way. Or you walk them ahead in the cut, but you couldn't walk them no distance.

A: Well, when you set a dredge in the cut dredging, the surveyors mark out the cut for you and buoy it, and then you place anchors up stream at an angle out from the boat with cables on them, and then you have spuds on the dredge that holds you in the cut. Then when you want to move you just let out on one anchor cable and pull in on the other one and that sets you over in another cut.

H: If I had a matchbox, I could show you.

Q: Now explain this for me again.

H: Well, it will probably get worse as it goes along, a lot of things I don't know about a dredge boat, of course but this particular operation here, you just walked your dredge and this cutter running all the time.

Q: That's the ladder in the front of . . .

A: That's the ladder, with the cutter that goes up the ladder and works off a series of gears right there. You cut like this see, she's on this spud, she'll cut over here so far, you drop that spud and pick this one up, go on over there a little bit further till you get to the edge of your cut, then you start back. You start back cleaning out, then back here drop this spud, pick that one up. You just keep advancing in the sand, into the bar or what you are taking out. She walks herself down the river. Ordinarily she'll advance 250 feet on a walk we'll say in eight hours.

Q: You are making that turn by pulling on the anchor?

H: That's right, you are pulling across on these swinging wires, see you advance so far, and your anchors have to be moved down.

A: See, your cutter head hits a log and then you've got to lift it out and cut it.

H: Yes, lots of times you have trouble that way, you get into a log or some rocks or something. If they dig, oh, say advance 300 feet more digging, now the more face you've got the deeper, like you are digging in an eight or ten foot face, you don't advance, it takes tremendous yardage out of there, see.

Q: Did you say a fish, an eight or ten foot?

H: If the face of your bar, say you're digging here, and you've got only four or five feet of water, and you want to make twelve feet, you've got an eight foot face. Well the more face you've got the slower your advance because if you're only digging three or four foot face that's more or less a sweet job and you can step right on down. Maybe advance 300 feet in eight hours easy enough.

A: On high water, whenever you have high water, you are constantly working downstream, and your current will pick up the head of the bar and move it down below on the tail so naturally it fills in. Now you don't have that very much any longer on account of your screw wheel boat sets deep in the water. If the water gets down, say you only have three foot of water over pool stage, which is if it's dammed far enough, and they aren't locking any them boats that stay in the channel. They will keep that channel pretty well dredged out themselves on account of loaded barges, and the screws down there. They'll keep it dug out. But you take a quick rise and a quick fall, it will fill in an awfully lot especially on the lower river. Now from Cincinnati on up to Pittsburgh, you don't have that because it's more or less of a stationary rock bottom here. You take from well, from Evansville, Evansville is about the first from there on down you constantly have a lot of sand and silt down there, and with eave in banks, but then it fills in down there.

Q: I know the Wabash is forming a big bar now.

A: Well.

H: We just got through cutting it.

Q: You did?

A: They had all that rain up there in Indianapolis, and in through there, and it run out terrible. Well you haven't got much room normal down there because there is Wabash Island right at the mouth of the river. It's the same way down here at the south of the Big Miami River, it's constantly moving upstream.

Q: Were you down there when the *Delta Queen* stove in her wheel a couple of weeks ago?

A: She tore out five wheel arms.

H: We went in there after several boats had trouble. We made a 300 foot cut there, this dredge was going to make another temporary deal there of some kind. I don't imagine, there wasn't anybody sticking, we had the channel buoyed around it and falling down, George made a crossing, and we had it buoyed off. I sounded every day and if the river had of gone down to pool, the water wouldn't have been there.

A: Like I say from there on down, the same way at the Evansville bend; it keeps filling in there in that wide bend too. Diamond Island is another one.

H: They were digging there when I left the dredge.

Q: So you mentioned earlier that you were up in the tourist trade in 1937 on the Greene Line boats, can we come back to that a little bit?

A: I started on the *Delta Queen* as watchman on there.

Q: Well what does a watchman do?

A: On a passenger vessel that is, on river passenger vessels have or on all old packet boats too, they have cabin watchmen. They have a fear of fire on them naturally because most all your boats all burn up, that is old packet boats and passenger boats. They aren't the fire hazard anymore, but they were then. The law required that they have a hall watchman, and two cabin watchmen, and a roof watchman, which is still the law, and they have to carry them. Now you're roof watchman he didn't do nothing but just sit up and watch for sparks to fall out of the stacks on the roof, which is something they don't have anymore.

The main reason they have such high stacks on steamboats is because they burned wood and pitch, they made a lot of fire, and they had high stacks so the wind would carry the sparks off the boat. That's the reason they had such high stacks especially on old cotton boats on the lower river. They hauled a lot

John Knoepfle

of cotton. They put them big stacks and them big feathers to break up the spark so they wouldn't fall right away. And the wind would carry them off of the cotton bales into the river. Another thing that's the reason they had such wide guards on those old cotton boats. If anything would happen then they would roll over, and the bales would fall in on that side, and then the weight on the other side, she'd roll over and tip them off the other side, and right the boat up. Most of those boats would sink coming out of an eddy on the lower river. You take on the real sharp bends there, underneath the bend at a point, there is an eddy running upstream. They would get in those eddies to make time. They wouldn't get in the current, they'd stay in the eddy, the eddy going upstream, when they'd get to the head they'd switch to the current right quick, and they wouldn't straighten up soon enough, they'd take water and turn over.

Q: The old Miss is a tricky river to navigate in, isn't it?

A: Well not so much the Ohio, there is bad places in it, but it isn't as fast and as treacherous a river as the Mississippi. On the Mississippi you can tie up in a fog and if you don't have a watchman out there the water will wash the bank away and you'd be floating down the river. I've saw boats go by there and a bank would fall in and break up their tow, make enough waves to break up their ratchets and wires.

Q: Is that so the bank is continually caving in?

A: Continually caving down there, that's the reason they keep cutting the pulp wood off of it because you never knew when it's going to start caving into the river.

Q: Could you distinguish between the duties of the various mates on boats, say there was a 1st mate and 2nd mate, I suppose?

A: Well on all boats there is two watches called the forward watch and the after watch. The forward watch is on from 6 a.m. until 12 noon. The after watch comes on at noon and works until 6 p.m. then the forward watch comes back on from 6 p.m. until midnight. The captain stands the forward watch, the daylight watch, and the mate takes the after watch. If there's a 2nd mate he stands watch with the captain. A long time ago, the captain never stood a watch. he was available all the time. They had the roof captain and he never stood a watch at all. The 2nd mate would stand the forward watch, and he was up all the time then, usually. The 1st mate would stand the after watch. The mate is actually second in charge to the captain, but there is rules and regulations on a boat. The engineer can say whether a boat goes out or not, and so can the pilot. A pilot can refuse to take a boat out, and an engineer can refuse to turn her loose. A captain can turn her loose but he's strictly responsible for her then.

Q: Did you ever refuse to take a boat out, Mr. Louden?

H: Well I don't know, not in a case like that, like he's referring too. He's referring to bad weather or probably engine failure, or something along that. The law says that due in bad weather if the pilot doesn't want to go out, why he doesn't have to or due to engine trouble the engineer can do the same thing. If the old man wants to go, he can go, but he, it's up to him then. No amount of care, in case of anything happens, excuses him in that case.

Q: Well I imagine it must be pretty rough if you are working in a channel with some tow, and dredges around, and the wind comes up or a storm breaks out.

H: We always have, when a dredge boat is working in a channel, we have radios, and they talk back and forth, which side to come down on, and very little trouble. You have to get the dredge out of the way. Always do that, set the dredge out of the way, set her right back. We were doing that on the last job, there's not much to that.

Q: Mrs. Powers, do you have a question? (Remembered as the librarian).

Mrs. Powers: Do you know when the Combine began?

A: Golly no, that was a little before my time.

H: You'd have to see Jessie Hughes to find that out or Emory Edgington.

Q: Everybody's vague about the Combine, very vague.

H: Well they were around at that time, but I tell you, Hughes . . .

A: Jessie Hughes would know.

H: And Edgington would know, he was around at that time. He's 112 years old. You'd find out a lot about the Combine in that river handbook there. It has a good picture of the Chandler in it. Not too much about it, but it mentions . . .

A: I tell you a fellow that would know if you could ever get ahold of him is Captain Gene Hampton, he's down in Memphis. He worked for the Combine. In fact, he was captain on the *Sprague* when I laid it up. Pure Oil had it. He was on the *Rees Lee*, he was on Lee Line boats. He won't tell you how old he is.

P: When was he on the Lee Line boats?

A: Well he was on the *Kate Adams*, the *Rees Lee*, the *Kate* . . .

H: The *Stacker* probably?

A: Yes, he was on the *Stacker Lee*.

P: Was that between 19 and 1920?

A: Yes, ma'am, he started in 1902.

P: Well, I meant with the Lee Line.

A: Yes, ma'am he started in 1902, I know, he and a fella by the name of Harry Fitzgerald who is captain of the *Lady Linda* now.

H: Now you ought to interview Bruce D. Edgington, too.

Q: He won't talk, he claims that he was just a little pup in this pound.

H: Worked for me for years.

P: Do any of you know anything about the *Memphis*, the *Arkansas City* and Rosedale Company that the Lee's owned and anything about the changeover from the Valley Line?

A: Yes, ma'am. Both of these Captain Fitzgerald and Captain Hampton were both working for that company.

P: When they combined and formed?

John Knoepfle

A: I don't know about there, I often heard them talking about being on the strike, and they quit, and Hampton went on the ferryboat at Plaquemine, and runs the ferry.

H: You tell Bruce Edgington something about him and he'll talk.

Q: What's that?

H: Just anything, just little nasty things. Oh, he's a great little boy. He worked for me for about 12 years, and he really read my pedigree several times.

Q: Just let me ask you an offbeat question. When you were on the boat you must have heard rousters singing a lot? Do you remember anything they sang?

H: Well they would make it up as they went along.

A: No, I don't. There's a lot of those old rousters hanging around those wharfboats down there.

Q: It's hard to get them to talk. I've taped two of them.

H: Which ones did you get?

Q: Leslie Souther, the old original hoghead, and then Bee Hines, he's been everywhere.

H: Is Pittsburgh down there?

Q: Kentucky is there.

A: Kentucky is there, but he's the wharf watchman now.

H: I saw one up on the levee, had a little brass cowbell around his neck.

A: There's Iron Jaw if you could get him out of the workhouse long enough.

Q: Is he in the workhouse?

A: He just gets out and back in, he didn't stay out long.

Q: That would be ideal, I could go to the workhouse and talk with him. What is his real name?

A: I don't know, they don't have any real names.

H: You have Iron Jaw, Pittsburgh.

A: Now there's Sam Jenkins, now he's an old rouster. He's been down there, but he's out on the boat now. Sam is a fellow he'll work on a boat until he saves up a $100 and then he's gone until that's gone.

Q: Is he on the *Queen* now?

A: Yes, I saw him the other night on there when they went out.

H: Have you got ahold of Horace Lyle down on the wharf?

Q: Yes, he gave me a good interview, and so did Bob McCann, and I haven't been able to get the Underwoods.

H: We don't want to break up a good thing but them people are going to run off and leave us.

A: Yes, you got the money?

H: Oh, we can eat.

A: They ain't going to run as long.

Q: Well we'll ring off then.

Question: Let's talk to Mr. Norval Horton who has spent a long part of his life as an engineer on packets and towboats.
Answer: That's true. I started out on the ferryboat that went to Madison, Indiana and Milton, Kentucky.
Q: All right, tell us about that ferry again.
A: The ferryboat was between Madison, Indiana and Milton, Kentucky, and the biggest part of the trade was farm trade, bringing tobacco, fruits of all kinds over. And then from there, I went on the *City of Louisville,* big sidewheel boat that ran between Cincinnati and Louisville.
Q: All right, I would like you to talk a little more about that ferry. Your father ran it, didn't he?
A: My father was engineer on it. He was chief engineer on there for years, 34 years, in fact, up until the ferry quit business altogether when the bridge was put in down there. It was long hours and seven days a week and twelve hours a day, and then when there were any repairs to be made, why that was all thrown in free. They didn't pay for it. I got kind of tired on that. I had the opportunity to start out on a sidewheel boat *City of Louisville* with the White Collar Line. I ran striker on her for about a year and a half. She tied up for low water. That fall, instead of going back on the *City of Louisville*, I went on the *J. B. Finley.*
Q: What year was that?
A: That was in 1912. She ran between Louisville and New Orleans towing coal. We used to meet the *Sprague* coming up the river with empties, and the *Finley* going down. The *Finley* would have anywhere from 42 barges to 56. *Sprague* would be coming up with 60; you would wonder how they were going to pass down in that river someplace where you would meet them. I put in that winter on there, then I went on the old *Island Queen*. That was the first *Island Queen*. I ran striker on the *Island Queen*, and the *Princess*. I made my license that fall after the Coney Island season closed. I went on a boat of the Greene Line called the *Chilo*. While we were laying up at Ripley, Ohio, the steam hose burst and I got scalded. I was in the hospital for about a month. I just kept going from one boat to another, wasn't ever satisfied. You want me to call these boats off?
Q: Well, we will catch them sooner or later.
A: Yes. Well, then I went from there to the *E. Stanley Holland*. The Bates and Rodgers Construction Company were installing Dam 33 up there at Maysville. One night we were backing down through the pass, and felt like a big log rolled under, and knocked a big hole in her 20 feet long and about four feet wide and didn't have much time to do anything but just run to the high side of her and jump overboard. They had a black cook on there and he could not swim a lick; he begged me to save him. So I told him, "Don't grab me and I will hold you

John Knoepfle

up." He used sense and I held him up until they came to us with a yawl, although I would never have been able to pull him ashore.

Q: What was his name? Do you remember?

A: I don't remember his name anymore. It has been too long. Well, then we raised the boat and went to Madison, Indiana, and put her back in shape again. I got wandering fever again, and I went on the *Plymouth*, a boat that went up the Kanawha River towing coal for Hatfield Coal Company. And then I was on quite a few boats up in there. I went from her to the *D. T. Lane*, and from the *D. T. Lane* to the *J. T. Hatfield*. I finally wound up on the *Robert Gillham*, spent seven years on the *Robert Gillham*.

Q: What was your position there?

A: Chief engineer. One of the records we set there at one time was for six straight weeks we landed in Cincinnati with 22 barges of coal, and we would take 22 empties back up the river. That was the record for a boat at that time of that size. We never had any breakdowns whatsoever, had beautiful weather, and we put coal in continuously week after week.

Q: About what year was that?

A: That was around about 1923. I got off of her, and I moved around on excursion boats like the *East St. Louis* and ran in the Coney Island trade, and then she went to Pittsburgh. They were offering more money on them Carnegie Steel boats, and J. and L. up there. I took a job on the *Clingerman*; it belonged to Carnegie Steel. I got homesick for Cincinnati again, came back down here, and I started to packet boating a little bit on the *Hubbard*, and several boats that summer and fall. Then I went on to the, what was it I went on after that? The *Hubbard* ran between here, Louisville, and *Tom Greene*. I was on the *Tom Greene* right after she first came out.

Then in the meantime in 1927, I was working for Campbell's Creek Coal Company, I was on the *Robert P. Gillham*, and they transferred me over on the *Eugene Dana Smith*. They chartered her out to a Huntington concern to tow steel pipe down to New Orleans and Way Points. We stopped at Burnside, Louisiana, and several places on that trip. That was the year of the greatest flood on the Mississippi. Never was known to be a flood that immense before. They made that spillway right after that at Cairo into the Gulf to eliminate that kind of trouble. We went on to New Orleans, started back up the river, and we came up there to Greenville, Mississippi. The governor of the state was appealing for boats and barges to rescue people. We had five empty steel barges, so we put in down there and lowered the yawls, and took people out of trees, then run into Memphis with them. In the meantime, we sunk a fuel flat and we had just about enough coal to make it into Memphis. Then I was glad to get away from there for the simple reason that the governor was figuring on confiscating us and sending us back down in there. At that time it was way off the river, you were back over in them bayous. I remember one instance, it was a boat and light in Arkansas, and we come up the levy right after it broke and drowned 21, and there is one thing that is outstanding in my mind was a little white church set up on a knoll. That was the only thing that hadn't disappeared. It was there. And I can still remember that.

Q: That was pretty pitiful down there.

A: Oh yes, that was terrible. They had deer, all the wild game, just come to the levy and you could see herds of deer swimming from across the Mississippi trying to get to dry land and there was not any dry land outside of the levy for miles and miles and miles. Just as far as you could see with binoculars, why, there was water and just the top of trees. Well, we came back up on the Ohio then, and I went back on my other boat, the *Robert Gillham*. And all in all spent seven years with Campbell's Creek Coal Company. Well, then I got off of there and I started to go back on the packet boats again. I was on the *Greenwood*, after they put boilers on her, and they didn't fix the pipe or anything to take care of the higher pressure. And as far as I went was right up above Coney Island. I told Captain Greene, that was Tom's daddy, I said, "You either turn the boat around here or I'll take her back to Cincinnati or I'll get off right here." We stopped five different times to put in joints when they let go. And she was loaded down with perishables and everything, but there was nothing we could do about it. You could not go and you could not get any water in the boilers. It kept blowing out of joints and all this kind of stuff. So we finally put back into Cincinnati and that was the end of that. And the reason I took that, I happened to be home on a vacation, and I was the only eligible chief engineer around. They come out to the house to get me to make that trip. But I only made it above Coney Island. (laughs) Never did go all the way.

Q: They put in new boilers at that time, didn't they?

A: Well, they wasn't just exactly new, they were secondhand boilers but they were allowed about 75 pounds more steam than what the other ones were. And they didn't make provisions to take care of that. I happened to be on the *J. T. Hatfield* at that time. We were up there at Gallipolis, were overhauling the boilers there. And I had a vacation and was home just to rest up when I thought I would do them a favor by taking the boat to Charleston, but I didn't make it. Then I went into government service on a boat by the name of the *Cayuga*. That was along about 1932 or 1933. And I was with the government then about five years on different boats, the *Cayuga*, and the *Guyandotte*, and the *Miami*. In the meantime quite a few years back, that was in 1916, I was on the *Scioto* when they were building that dam down there at Markland, Dam 39. But then they transferred the boat that I was on to St. Louis, a boat by the name of *Guyandotte*, Cincinnati engineers down there, and I wouldn't stay at St. Louis. So that terminated my work with the government. Then I went on a boat by the name of the *Henry C. Yeiser*, which was the old *Robert P. Gillham* and that was the last of my steamboating. My wife had kept after me for years to get off the river and get a job at home, so I went to work for E. Kahn and Sons Company, and I have been there ever since. It will be 24 years this fall.

Q: Good. Now we are going to tow some coal out of Louisville.

A: I was on the *J. B. Finley* and we used to take coal from Louisville to New Orleans. This coal would be transported from Pittsburgh by smaller boat; and three boats, the *Sprague*, the *J. B. Finley*, and the *W. W. O'Neil* would handle the coal from Louisville into New Orleans, after the tug boats put it through the canal and made it up down below Louisville. Coming back up the river after delivering our tow of loads into New Orleans, why we would pick up our empties and have a tow of empties.

To siphon the water out of the barges coming up, the wooden hull barges had a 2-inch plug in the bottom of them, and the deckhands would remove that plug and put a split funnel in there. It was a funnel about two inches in diameter at the small end, and about four at the top, and it had about an inch opening split in it all the way through. They put that so the split was behind the flow of the water, and that would take every drop of water out of those barges after a rain or anything like that. We had to be making a speed though of three miles or better against the current. And lots of times, we would be tied upon the Mississippi River for low water and would have to wait till we got more water to go on. And the channel of the Mississippi River at that time, and I guess the same thing like today, the sand shifted from day to day. Where you were at one day, the next day why you would stick. And it felt funny to be stuck right in the middle of the river. And all they would do would just be lay there up until the sand cut out of the barges, and then we would start going down again. And that was my experience between Louisville and New Orleans.

Q: Now this was all done when the rains began in the winter and you . . .

A: That was the fall rains, after the fall rains got the river up. The Ohio River was practically impossible those days. That was before the completion of the locks and dams. And it was practically impossible to navigate in the summer months. There was at least three to four months every summer when all tow boating had to come to a complete stop unless we just happened to have a rainy summer, and that was very seldom.

Q: So any barges you didn't get out before low season just had to stay there.

A: Had to stay right there at Louisville up until we had more water in the river to transport them on into New Orleans. That was even in later years before the dams were completed. I remember a time I was on a boat by the name of the *Eugene Dana Smith* and we spent two months right here above Coney Island with a tow of empties, couldn't even shove empties up the river between Coney Island and New Richmond. That's a bad stretch of river anyhow. That is before the dam was completed there at Coney Island. And we laid right there and laid our whole crew off. You always kept the chief engineer, and the captain, and the cook. They were the ones that stayed on the boat. And so we lay there that summer two solid months and never turned a wheel.

Q: Well, tell me now about how many barges they could get fleeted down there at Louisville.

A: Well, I have seen as high as 400 to 500 barges waiting till water was high enough till we transport them in. Up above the waterworks right above Louisville, it was nothing but barges lined up all the way through. Same way up here in the Kanawha River when I was working for Hatfield Coal Company. We would have to wait for what they call a splash rise. That is when they would — these storage reservoirs they had up on the Monongahela River, and the Allegheny River — they would open up the storage water, and put it in the Ohio. And we would all be laying there waiting till that water came, and then we stayed right with that surge of water till we got here in Cincinnati, and delivered our tow. Then the pickup, empties that is what I was doing on the *Eugene Dana Smith* that time, when we picked up that tow of empties and started back up. Well, the water got away from us, and we only made it to Coney Island, and that was where we stayed all the rest of the summer. It was all according to the amount of water they had in the storage reservoirs up on the Monongahela and Allegheny River, and how much water they would put into the Ohio to have them splash rises. Locks and dams have overcome all that.

Q: How many barges did those bigger boats tow below Louisville?

A: Well, the *Sprague*, she was the biggest, she could handle around about 66 both ways; the *Finley*, she would have around 44 to 52 both ways. When these boats would meet down around the oxbow or in some narrow part of the Ohio River, you wonder how they were going to get by each other with that many barges in tow. It actually looked funny to see that many barges in the Ohio River at one time and the whole river would just be barges. (laughs)

Coal at New Orleans at that time was put aboard what they call tramp ships and exported to different countries. And it took, well I'll say in the neighborhood of about 40 boats that the Combine owned at that time to keep things moving in the coal business from Pittsburgh to New Orleans. They only had an operating season, I'll say, seven months was the most of any year. And the other five months they were idle.

The coal in the wooden barges at that time, they would have to have a helper to help them through the bridges, and they would tie up to Coal Haven, which was up there around about where Coney Island Dam is right now, and they would deliver, they would move the coal through the bridges with a helper on the front of the tow. They didn't have steerage way enough so they had to have a steamboat, and she would be locked in front of these barges, and she would back and come ahead, and just keep them, all this boat had to do was just push ahead, and she would steer them by reversing, you see or going ahead. Then they would tie the tow of coal up down at Ludlow, Kentucky, till they got the tow through, then they would pick it up and go on into Louisville. Lots of times when the water would get low, why hundreds of barges would be tied up at Coal Haven, and also over here at Ludlow, waiting for some more water so they could move that coal.

Q: Now I have a feeling that at Coal Haven, they were on the Ohio side.

John Knoepfle

A: No, Kentucky side. Yes, it was on the Kentucky side. There over right below Silver Grove.

Q: I see.

A: And that was a good landing for them. When you were bringing coal down the river, any size tow at all, why, you didn't have any control over that tow. The current had control, and they had to pick these landing spots, and I have seen them run as high as three check lines to check them in. The deckhands would go out with big 2-inch hawsers and tie up to trees, and then other boys on the fleet, they would check it, just snub it. And that was an art that had to be learned, that was all there was to it.

Q: Kind of dangerous, too.

A: Was very dangerous if you didn't know how to do it. And they would, smoke would come off of there, off that hemp line, and just be very tight. If they check it too quick, why they would break the line, and then they would miss a landing, and then they had to go on for miles till they found another landing. These pilots knew all these landings on that kind of stuff, and when you would start to make that landing in Coal Haven, why you start to backing up about five miles above there just to check it going through, and then start to flanking in to make the tie.

Q: I guess these helper boats were harbor boats?

A: Harbor boats, that's what they were. Here at Cincinnati used to do a lot of it, and then they had their Hatfield Coal Company. They had a boat by the name of the *Plymouth*, she used to do quite a bit of it.

Q: They would be backing down in front of the tow.

A: No, they would be lashed right across the front.

Q: Oh, I see.

A: And just . . .

Q: And then they would back.

A: And then they would back or come ahead just to shove that tow, whichever way they wanted it. And the other boat all she did was push. That's the only way they could make them bridges.

Q: Well were there any other places up river where they fleeted barges too, if they gave out on a splash flood?

A: Yes, there was several places along. One of them was up there at Vanceburg right, well right there below the big bend at Vanceburg in the Ohio River. That was a good landing spot. And oh I guess between Pittsburgh and Cincinnati there was approximately 20 places that the pilots all knew and would go in for the simple reason of the easy landing. It always was under a point you know, and would have an eddy. If you could make it. If you stopped farther up the river and start to backing in flank and they would get these check lines out there why they could check right at the eddy, and then you were all right.

Q: The eddy would pull them in.

A: Yes, the eddy would pull them in there, and there was always deep water in the places where they picked. On the Mississippi River when we went down on a non-condensing boat, why you had to clean boilers every three days at the most, sometimes it would be every other day. The Mississippi River was so full of mud and sand that the boilers would get fouled, and it would actually get to foaming, and you did not know where your water was in the boiler. I have actually dipped a glass of water out of the Mississippi River and let the sediment in the glass settle, and it would be a half-inch deep, measured by a ruler. That water constantly going in the boilers wasn't doing them any good unless you got rid of that mud and sand.

Q: So you would still be running, but you would shut off certain boilers . . .

A: No, we would have to tie up.

Q: You had to tie up.

A: Tie up and take anywhere from 12 to 18 hours to clean boilers.

Q: Oh I see.

A: That is how dirty and filthy that was. Then they overcome it in later years by having condensing boats you see, and use the same water over and over with just a little makeup. And the makeup water that you used was put in through filters and filtered that sand and mud out. Then you didn't have to clean boilers only open them up maybe every six months too, big improvement when they came up with that condensing filter.

After the Combine went under, why I was on Kanawha River boats and we would tow out enough coal to make up three or four big tows to come into Cincinnati through one of those splash rises. The reason the Combine went out of business, why the steel mills bought up all the mines up in Pennsylvania and utilized that coal up there in their mills. Kanawha River coal, then was what people around Cincinnati and Louisville, and these towns between Point Pleasant and Louisville relied upon. That was another very interesting thing. We'd be coming down river with a tow of coal, and we would want to leave a barge of coal at Manchester or Portsmouth or anything like that. They would never land a barge with a steamboat. They would run a long check line out and the boys would take, checking that barge into that coal harbor where we was at. That was really worthwhile watching. And while we are talking about it, I remember one time down on the Mississippi River, I can't recall just where it was anymore. One of the big rises lifted a wooden hull barge that was at least every bit of a half mile away from the river, and they ran a big hawser line out to it, and just let the steamboat, and her tow of empties, the current of the river taking it down, all at once that barge jumped, looked like it leaped. That line got tight, you know once she brought it right on in and picked it up as tow.

Q: Now I suppose that even when the Combine was running they let certain barges off on the way down the river.

A: No, they did not do much business that way. They would leave it off at Cincinnati, then they had these pool boats that delivered to these towns. They didn't do like the Kanawha River boats did. On their way down, why they would leave a barge off at these towns that ordered coal. But the Combine didn't fool with that, they would deliver either to Cincinnati, or Wheeling, or Portsmouth, or wherever was that and they would send a whole tow of coal there, and then their pool boats would deliver from that point. Hatfield, here at one time had that same setup. They had a boat by the name of the *Reba Reeves* from Carrollton, Kentucky, and she would come up here and pick up five and six barges, and then deliver them at way points down like Lawrenceburg, or Aurora, and Rising Sun and so forth.

Q: Could you go over that business of checking that single barge out again? What did they do? Get the line onto the shore and the people who were interested in getting the barge . . .

A: Yes, well it was our barge. It belonged to the Combine. The barge belonged to the Combine and here it was stranded way out here in this marsh is what it was. They ran this, well they pulled this hawser out to get in on that barge. They took what they called handy line, which is half-inch line, and they ran that out first, and that is the way they pulled this big hawser out to that barge to make the hawser fast to this empty barge. And when that big two-inch hawser tightened up, why the tension on it was so great, it was like a rubber band, and when that barge did let go, it looked like it jumped 100 feet. (laughter) From then on, she just kept coming on in the river.

Logs would break loose, when we came in there in East Denham, and we would have to go as far as Louisville to pick them up, and we'd stop when we'd see a fellow that had a bunch of logs, and even if some of them were unbranded, by the time the crew who were picking up the logs got through walking on them, well they had brands on their shoes, and would be branded. And at Indiana one time, they all got together one time, and they come out with shotguns, and they wouldn't even allow us to even land. That was a very crooked business at that time. (laughs)

Q: In other words, there was a difference in the value of the log if it was unbranded?

A: Yes, they had to give us 25 cents for a log that was branded, and then five or six dollars for a log that was unbranded. And another thing, when I was on the government snagging outfit, we run from Pittsburgh to New Orleans, I was on a boat by the name of the *Miami*. We was towing the derrick for Cincinnati engineers that took care of wrecking these barges, you know, and so forth and so on. And we had been up here at Sturgis Landing, I don't know what it is there at the east end, where they handle those motorboats, you know, and unload them barges and everything there.

Q: Yes Beatty's Landing it is now.

A: Well we had to clean that landing out. Now some beautiful walnut logs and oak logs were actually down in there, and the government wasn't allowed to sell that stuff, so we had to take them down here right above Fernbank, there is a deep hole there about 80 feet deep. I can't think of the name of that creek that comes in right above Fernbank and right under there is about 80 foot of water.

We would take whole barges of the beautiful lumber like that, which was water soaked and all, and was in perfect shape and just throw it away down there. That was really throwing a lot of money away. The government was awful wasteful on anything like that. We would wreck a steamboat or something like that, just a barge with a shimmy, they would not even sell it for scrap iron. It would all go into a deep hole someplace. Throw it away.

Q: Probably a lot of it still there.

A: Yes. A fellow could go down in that hole, have a derrick, go down there, he would get all kinds of machinery, logs of all kinds, and everything else.

Q: That's up above Fernbank.

A: Yes. Have to get the name of the creek that comes in there, but right under that creek is about 80 foot of water. And we used to take barges, we had flat barges that were full of walnut and oak logs and just roll them off in there, and they would go on down, you see.

Q: Oh, my.

A: Beautiful lumber. The same way with machinery. We wrecked quite a few boats that sunk, we would take that, like the *Goldenrod*, she used to be old light-house boat, and we wrecked her and her machinery all went in there. This thing here, this lamp, part of it is the *Homer Smith* and part of it is the *Goldenrod*.

Q: Is that so?

A: Yes this goose's neck on here, that came off the *Goldenrod*. That used to hold the oil cans in a tray. And this other thing here, and that was off the *Homer Smith*, she had coal oil lights up in her cabin and those were some of the receptacles that held the lights.

Q: So you made a good brass lamp out of it.

A: Yes I made a brass lamp out of it. Same thing with the bottom there on, the same thing. Buy the remnants in a wrecking of the boat that I saved myself, and then built them up into a lamp. Before I put it in the lamp, I used to have this thing on the boat and instead of having a shade here, this held a oil pan with the oil cans on it, brass you know. And then when I quit the river, why I brought it home and made a lamp out of it.

Q: Well what else did you do on that *Crown Hill*? Did you go up for tows too, on the *Crown Hill*?

A: We would go up to Catlettsburg, Big Sandy River, and they rafted logs out of the Sandy so we would tow them into Cincinnati. All we did though, we just, with a log boat, you just went with the current. You couldn't make any time with them, just handle them so they would keep them out of the bends, and so forth and so on till we got there.

Q: You never went up into the Big Sandy, I guess.

A: No the boat wasn't, that is the locks wouldn't take this boat. The boat was too big to go through.

Q: Stogie White told me that there were 21 saloons along the wharf under Catlettsburg.

John Knoepfle

A: There were. That's about all there were saloons, little country stores. Even part of the country stores was a combination saloon and store at that time. And these mountaineers would come in there with them logs, they was really hard, too. All they knew was the knife, to cut and oh, they had a lot of fights, cutting scrapes and everything, just get full of that whiskey you know, and get mean. I didn't do too much playing around up in town, I stayed on the boat. (laughter)

Q: I imagine not.

A: Because an outsider, they didn't have much use for him. Same way with Kentucky River, that was the same thing there. I worked on the *Gregory*, she belonged to the government over at Frankfort, Kentucky, government engineers. And we did the snagging on the Kentucky River and we, I remember one time at Lock 11, at Irvine, Kentucky, and we had a big snag to take out of the river. They put off 200 sticks of dynamite to wreck these snag and fish rolled up by the wagon load. Farmers came from around different farms with two horse wagons to haul the fish away.

Q: A real bonanza.

A: Oh, yes. We had never dreamed it would do anything like that, never dreamed there was that many fish around. And they really rolled up. I was up on that boat. Oh, that was a lonesome river, I guess it still is. I could only take a year of it. Just like being in jail.

Q: Is that so?

A: The little old towns along the way and we were stuck up there at Heidelberg one time. The boat broke down and we had to wait for a part for two months before it was ever delivered. That was during World War I. And all we did was just hunt and fish and just lay around for two solid months. Didn't do a thing. Roll the wheel over every day to keep it balanced. See, those wooden wheels, why if you did not keep them wet all the way around, why they get out of balance. Part of it would get heavy, and then you would have a run in it. The engines would, and you had to keep rolling every day to keep the whole wheel, that is you didn't have to keep it continuously rolling, just roll to a certain point, and then tie it. Then the next day roll it over a little bit more, and just keep that up so you would keep the wheel in balance. Another thing, if it dried out, why they used to have what they called gibs in there, and wedges to hold these wheel arms and buckets, and if they dried out on you the first time you did start up, why you would throw them all out, and there you were without anything.

Yes, and during any ice on the river on those sternwheel boats it was really tough for the simple reason that the ice would accumulate and actually you had to came to a stop and take hot water. The ice would get to rubbing against your bearings, outboard bearings and all that. And I have seen pitmans even ice up where they would be going in and out, you know, on a zero night, and that wind would be blowing, and it would ice up till they would, well the back end, that is what it would do, when it come down, you know, and we would have to stop and melt the ice off. It was a tough life, ain't no kidding.

Q: Yes, I understand the old river was no place for children.

A: That's right. Then I was on the *Val P. Collins* down here at Sekitan during that 1917 and 1918 cold winter and that was the coldest experience I ever had on the river. It was 18 degrees below zero that one morning, and the wind would be coming in there, and actually freeze up the pipes in the engine room. Although we kept steam blowing through the engines to heat it up and all that, but it was that cold, you couldn't cover them pitman holes you know, enough to, we kept the ice broke up around that fleet down there up until we finally had to give it up. We tore up two wheels, backing over it, and it froze in, and then when that ice, oh that was terrible, when that ice let go, why we were actually free of it up until that big gorge came down there at Sugar Creek, and backed the ice up, and it shoved us in against a bunch of trees. And then that ice just shoved right through our hull. She couldn't, there wasn't any give, you know. And she was buoyed up for every bit of 15 minutes with ice all through her hull, before she finally went down. We all had a chance to get off her because it was right in there at the bank, you see. The ice shoved us right in. Nobody was hurt or lost their life or anything, but it was a crime after all the pains that we went through to save her, and then to have a gorge take place about 50 miles below you and back it up there till it got to the point, well they even had flood water down here at Cincinnati. I guess you have heard about that.

Q: Yes, I know that.

A: That shoved that ice right through our hull, a wooden hull boat.

Q: Now where exactly did you take care of those barges when that ice hit you? I think I missed that. Where were you?

A: Well, down here at Island Creek Coal Company at Sekitan. That's down here below Fernbank. And Island Creek used to always have a big fleet in there, and that's where they unloaded the coal. They used to put it in railroad cars, and even go to the lakes with it from here.

Q: Sekitan, is that what you called it?

A: Sekitan, that's right below Addyston.

Q: How do you spell it?

A: S-E-K-I-T-A-N.

Q: Oh, I see.

A: See, Addyston was the first town, and then Sekitan was right next to Addyston. And Island Creek had their tows tied up down there. They had two steamboats up there at the time, and both of them went down, too. The *Reba Reeves* done the same thing. And Island Creek lost all their equipment. There was only one thing was saved, a big steel unloading tipple. And that ice shoved it out on shore, but it was steel hull and all the rest was wood. Wooden barges and wooden hull steamboats, and the ice just took everything.

Q: I understand the *Princess* of Ralston, Kentucky, was lost.

A: Yes, she was lost down there at the mouth of the Kentucky River. That was during that big ice. And the *Island Queen*, when the Kentucky River ran out, why, the *Princess* went down right at the mouth of the river, and the *Island Queen* pulled her here right above Louisville before they ever got her out of it. But they saved the *Island Queen*, that was the old *Island Queen*. I ran on that *Princess* one season up here at the island.

Q: What kind of a boat was the *Princess*?

A: She was a sidewheel boat. She was allowed 1,500 people, a pretty good sized boat, just about half as big as the *Island Queen* then. The *Island Queen* was allowed 3,000. Used to make alternate trips. The *Princess* would leave at 9:30 down here and 11:00 o'clock, and 1:30, I believe it was, then 4:00. The last trip was 7:00. Then the Island Queen was an hour later on everything.

And then that was another thing, on those excursion boats going up to Coney Island at that time, they had Mike Mullen's Day, and Irish Day, and tremendous crowds would go up there. They would have 30,000, 40,000 people there. And then they would have to run extra boats to get them back. And one time, I was on the *Island Queen*, it was on Irish Day up there, and somebody started a panic by telling that was the last boat, although there were three extra boats. Well, those Irish came out of Coney Island just like cattle and cops couldn't stop them or anything, and the only way they had to cut the ropes on the boat to get her away from there, or they would probably just kept loading on there, and stuff, and sunk her right there at the pier. People are harder to handle than animals in something like that. Well, that was a very enjoyable summer. I enjoyed it. Homer Denney played the calliope.

Q: On the *Princess*, was he on that?

A: No, he was on the *Island Queen*. They had a fellow name of Hickman on the *Princess*. And Homer and I were pretty good buddies. You have met him, haven't you?

Q: Yes, he played on his electric organ for me, but he wouldn't talk. He is not much to talk.

A: No. Well, he is hard of hearing too, you know now, and wears that hearing aid. He always was kind of backward about that talking.

Q: I wonder if you remembered much about Ironton. I knew there were . . .

A: No, I never was around Ironton to amount to anything, just by passing there. I was on a boat there one time, *D. T. Lane*, I believe it was and we sunk three barges of coal right in that bend right below Ironton. We had a fog come down on us before we could make a landing, and they did not have radar at that time. By the time we got these things checked, why three of them piled up on them rocks right below Ironton.

Q: Fog must have been a terrible hazard in those days.

A: Yes, fog was really tough, or wind. You take coming down the river with loaded barges especially when the water was up where they had them loaded within a foot of it being out, and all at once a wind would come up before you even had one of these landings, and they had to put splash boards up, and everything else to save them. A lot of times they would lose a bunch of them. The waves would roll over right in them and right down they would go.

Q: In other words, they would put the splash boards up higher.

A: Yes. They would put splash boards up on the side of the barge and nail them up there, you see, to keep the water from rolling over in the barge.

Q: Course that put you more at the mercy of the wind too, didn't it?

A: Yes, that's right. Another thing about it, you take a barge of lump coal especially in a wooden hull, and when that air rushes in there when you knock a hole and that water pushes the air out between the coal, big lumps of coal fly up in the air as high as 20 feet, lumps that big.

Q: Is that so?

A: Yes. Right up in the air. Right above the hole.

Q: Pressure?

A: Yes, pressure. And there was one time up here at Dam 33, we were locking, double-locking coal, and a double lock meant we had too many barges for one locking, and then you had to lock half of them through, and then the other half. At first locking going through, there happened to be a big old stump in the lock chamber and they didn't know anything about it. And they let these barges down, and here come that stump up, and down went the barge. (laughter) We were up there about three days till they got a derrick up there, and dug the barge out of there so we could lock through. Had everything tied up. And I never will forget that. I happened to be up in the pilothouse at the time, and it was on the first locking, we were watching them lock them down and all at once we saw this big old stump come up right through the coal. (laughter) And the skipper says, "Uh oh. We're hooked here." And we were there three days till they got a derrick boat up there, and another barge, and dug the coal out. Well, they wrecked the barge, just tore it out piece by piece. That was a funny experience to see something like that out there.

And I was on the old *City of Louisville* one time and we were coming up the river. It was down here below Carrollton, Kentucky, and the Kentucky River was running out a little bit. And the right boiler in the engine room, it was a sidewheel boat, a tree came out of the Kentucky River, and came right up through her outrigging, and went right on up into the cabin. It stood right on edge, big tall tree, you know. And when the *City of Louisville* hit it, it must have been pointed like that, and it started putting that tree like that, and I guess the stump of it hit the ground, and it went right on up.

Q: It snagged right up there.

A: It snagged right up there. I guess it did a couple of thousand dollars of damage. At that time when poles came out through your outriggers, and on up into your cabin, why you were lucky somebody didn't get killed.

Q: Well, tell me what boat was that that sunk the barges in the fog below Ironton?

John Knoepfle

A: *D. T. Lane*. I was on the *D. T. Lane*, and fog around Ironton doesn't give you any warning. You would be laying overhead, and all at once it just comes down. And before the pilot could ever get straightened out, he was lost when the fog came down, they didn't have radar or anything like that at that day, and we hit the bank right below Ironton, and all them big rocks in there, and lost three of our barges.

Q: I suppose when that coal began to pop in the wind, it was rough for any deckhand out there on the barges.

A: Yes. Whenever the wind started blowing and they were out there getting them splashboards up, especially in the wintertime, why them deckhands would come in all iced up. They would just have ice all over them when they put them splashboards on, you know. Then when waves would hit the side of a barge, and then bust up and come over and freeze on them. They had a rough life, there is no kidding about it. Then when they didn't have anything like that to do, why they would either be rolling coal into the boiler room or, that was out of the fuel flat, then going up the river with empties, they would have them out painting the boat. They would have to scrub and paint her.

Q: Well, they were rousters, I guess.

A: No, they were deckhands. A rouster was on these packet boats that carried freight.

Q: Well, were these fellows colored boys?

A: No, they were all white. I never saw a colored deckhand. On all the steamboats that I was on, why they all had white. Well, that's really a rough time in them days. I got a brother now that's on the river. He's with this American Barge Line, been with them now nine years, chief engineer on the *Guadalcanal* I believe. We used to have to work, chief engineer of a boat, he could put in a 100 hours a week or a 150, have a breakdown or something like that, but now they work a month, and they are off a month. And they really got a nice breakup. In them days, we worked the year round. Well, the chief engineer was kept on the payroll year around. We didn't work in that low water or things like that. And just had to be there. That is about all I . . .

Q: That's plenty. That's wonderful, too. Now, could you say a little about where you are from?

A: I was born and raised in Madison, Indiana, at 117 South Walnut Street, and I had my education up until I was about 16 years old, and I left there in the *City of Louisville*. I remember on the *City of Louisville*, the big wharfboat they had down there at that time, a White Collar Line, and in that day they didn't have trucks, they had horse-drawn wagons. I especially remember the brewery trucks coming there right before the boat was supposed to leave, and they had six horses to a wagon, and unload barrels of beer. They would put that on the boats, and then they put a block of ice on each barrel, and then put a tarp over it to hold the cold up until they could get it down here to Lawrenceburg or Aurora, Madison, Indiana and Louisville.

Q: Fine, you remember any of the other kinds of freight offhand?

A: Well, practically everything that was manufactured here in Cincinnati at that time. That was about the only means of transportation outside, it was cheaper than trains, therefore they ship steamboat. Another thing about it they had, we leave here at 5:00 o'clock in the evening, we would arrive at Louisville around about 1:00 at night, and there was the freight right there on the wharfboat for them to pick up next morning at Louisville. When the trains would pick it up, they would have to be shifted around, and it took two or three days. But they would put it in there overnight. Yes, there was a lot of freight of all kinds.

And I remember when a deckhand would be coming up the river on those packet boats, the old *City of Louisville*, and the *Indiana* and *Cincinnati*, and down here at Norris landing, we would stop there, and pick up hay; and they would have as high as 1,500 to 2,000 bales of hay to come on. I remember them roustabouts, them colored roustabouts, they had a song they would sing. "Oh, if I knowed this old boat, I'd sho stayed in port. Oh, oh my." (laughter) But they would carry hay there, hour in, hour out, till they'd load all that stuff on there. Didn't have much freight coming up from Louisville like we did from Cincinnati into Louisville, especially in the hardware business from Cincinnati and machine tools and all that kind of stuff.

Q: Where exactly is Norris landing?

A: Norris landing is right below Rising Sun. It's about four mile, I should say, right below. And it was all hay country, and they used to ship all the hay up here to Cincinnati.

Q: Is that the song they used to call "Haypiles?"

A: Well, I guess that was. When they would see a big pile of hay, then they would start singing. A roustabout on those packet boats had an awful life, too when you think about it. They never had no regular hours. When you make a landing, they would wake them up, and they had to carry freight. After that they would get to sleep on the freight, didn't have any beds or anything, they just had to sleep around on the freight. And when they fed them, they fed them just like you feed dogs. One guy would dish it out of the pans, the cook would sit out there, and each one of them had an individual pan and fork, and he had his own cup and they would pour him coffee and they would holler "Grub pile!" and here they would all come, and then these guys would dish it out to them.

Q: Grub pile?

A: Yes, that's what they called it, grub pile. But the passengers and the crew, they were treated royal on there. They had the best eats of all kinds, and that *City of Louisville* had a beautiful cabin. She was longer, I think she was 310 feet long, and this cabin must have been at least 200 feet, and I can still see it. She had the chandeliers, and all the, they had electric lights on there, but the government at that time required coal oil lights too in case of electric failure. It wasn't very reliable, on electric. So they had these brass chandeliers all through

John Knoepfle

there, and when they had the tables all set, and all decorated, all this brass on the side overhead on these chandeliers, it was really a beautiful setting.

And they fed the best, they had the best of grub. That was back in about 1912. I was on in 1913, that was a pretty good thing. We were doing a railroad trade between Cincinnati and Aurora, and the 1913 flood, you see, that was the one that came out of the Big Miami River, and caused all that damage, and knocked the railroads out, dam, railroad, bridges, went out and everything else. So we did the railroad trade between Aurora and Cincinnati. And we came up to Miami River when it was running out, and before we could ever get by, we would come up on the Indiana side, and we would be plumb across from Kentucky. That current was coming out of there that fast it would shove you plumb across. Those big sidewheel boats were fast and powerful, but they would be shoved plumb across the river before you would ever get by it. And that was a tremendous trade they did there with that railroad. You would be surprised how much freight that railroad would be travel, that is carry. And of course, we would pick it up at Cincinnati, and take it to Aurora, and they had these trains there, and they would load it right in those cars and leave Aurora. Well, you could not, Miami River down there, those bridges over Miami River, they were all washed out, railroad bridges and all. In fact that one bridge is lost, and they don't even know now where it ever disappeared to. They claim it went in quicksand; and they call it Lost Bridge. The bridge they replace it with, they call it Lost Bridge. Still call it that.

Q: Where is that?

A: That is down here right below Cleves. It's on the old road. It isn't on that new Route 50 that they put down through there. It is on the old road where you go out of Cleves the back way. And that is Lost Bridge that goes over there. Well, that was replaced there when it went out in the 1913 flood, and they never did find any remains of that other bridge at all.

Q: I'll be darned. Before we close, I wonder if you could, do you remember the names of some of the roustabouts? I know they had all kinds of strange names.

A: Well, not offhand. There were so many of them that, and I remember several of them that would get full of cocaine, and their action, and they would hide their whiskey and cocaine when they were under the influence of it. And then when they would sober up, they did not even know where to look for it. I used to point it out to them. I would say, "Well, here it is. Way up there." They would climb way up in a little hole of some kind and stick it away. And I remember one case, they were feeding them when they were coming out of Louisville. These two colored boys they had a disagreement, and this one guy went out on the head of the boat and got an axe and he started back, and this guy saw him coming, he just went in there someplace, and he pulled out a big gun and he started shooting and I thought I take a dive and get behind the, (laughter) . . . .

Q: Well that's fine.

Question: We're here with Captain Jesse Hughes. Can you tell us how you began working on the river?

Answer: Well I'll tell you I came from up in Washington County, Washington County, Ohio. Lived up in the country there with my grandmother. My mother died when I was a little fellow, and I lived with my grandmother. Lived up there in the country and all you could see was the steamboats. There was nothing else up there to look at except the trees, and the farms, and one thing and another. So I lived there until I got to be 16 years old. Watched the boats and went down when the boats landed. I got acquainted with some of the fellows on the boat, and after a while I got a job on the boat.

Q: Same thing happened to Captain Hornbrook, he was a farm boy and . . .

A: Well I knew he was, he lived up here above Powhatan.

Q: Do you remember the first boat you were on, Captain?

A: Oh yes. The first boat I was on was the *T. M. Barnsdail*, she was a little packet that ran out of Marietta. Round trip every day. I washed dishes on there, I worked all winter for nothing, for my board. In the spring they gave me 50 cents a week, and I thought I was doing pretty well.

Q: You were sixteen when you went on the boat?

A: I was 16 yes, and I was on there two years. I got to be steward, head cook, had charge of the cabins, and a whole lot of things on there. I was making four or five dollars a week then.

Q: Where did you go from the *Barnsdail*, Captain?

A: Well, after I left the *Barnsdail* I got a job on the boat called the *Sunshine*.

Q: The *Sunshine*?

A: She was a great big steamboat, and she belonged to Captain Mack Gamble. Mack Gamble, his son is the *Waterways Journal* correspondent now from up there at Clarington, and he is just the very image of his dad.

Q: Well the *Sunshine* was a famous boat.

A: She ran out of Cincinnati in later years. She was a fine boat, yes sir. I was on there quite a while, and then I went over from there over on the *Courier*. She was a smaller boat, but she belonged to the same man, and I worked for him for two years. I stayed with him until he sold his boats and didn't have any job any longer. Then I figured around, and got a job with Captain Gordon Greene.

Q: What year would that have been?

A: That was 1896. I left the *Courier* in 1895, or she left me; she was sold and went away. In 1896 I went to work for Captain Gordon Greene, and I put in 55 years there. Just ended up here in 1951.

Q: That's a long span on the river, Captain. You must have many experiences.

A: Yes, you are bound to have. You can't get along without it. Of course I didn't have any thrilling experiences. I wasn't in any accidents or disasters of any kind. I never had any accidents on the boat. My piloting on the boat, after I got to piloting, I was fairly successful because I got along all right and never had any mishaps. Everything was very commonplace.

Q: When did you first go up on the Kanawha River?

A: I started in there in 1896, when I went to work for Captain Greene.

Q: We were talking about, you saw the salt furnaces at work. Could you tell us something about that?

A: The salt furnaces, I couldn't tell you anything very intimate about it. It's just a lot of stuff there. They have those great big sheds where they have those great big pans and you pump that salt water. It's a brine. It pumps it out of the wells, and they pump it into those pans, and it evaporates. It goes through a certain process, I don't know just what it is. After a while it gets in a grain formation, and then they put it out in pans, and it kinds of grains. Gets dry and they also extract those bromine, and other stuff from it. That leaves it a kind of a white looking salt, looks like a great big pile of snow. They throw it up there in that big shed, and it stays there and the water drains out it. It just looks like a great big snow bank.

Q: That was shipped by steamer?

A: That was what?

Q: Shipped by packets down the river.

A: Some of it yes. They shipped more out of Pomeroy than they did out of Kanawha River. Kanawha River, I don't know how they shipped theirs. Part of it by rail and some of I guess they used right around there where they made it. The salt furnace business used to be a great industry in Kanawha River, but it died down now so it doesn't amount to anything. At Pomeroy it has changed a great deal too. This granulated salt that has come in has replaced the other kind of salt. the Pomeroy salt was course grained. More for the curing for meat; this other kind of salt they have now is for table use. It's granulated, and fine, and white, and flows freely. It has replaced the other to a great extent. But the other is still used for the curing of meat.

Q: What else did the boats haul? What other commodities in those days?

A: We handled everything there was that anybody wanted to send. We handled cattle, stock, and produce of all kinds. Hay and corn and potatoes and anything a farmer had to ship. Why he would haul it down to the river to the landing, and get out and wave his handkerchief at us, and we would go in there and land. Tie up and put a stage down there, and get everybody out and we would carry it on the boat. Take it wherever he wanted it to go.

Q: Is that what the bullrail was for?

A: The bullrail was to hold the cattle on the boat, yes sir. Bullrails were just ordinary pieces of 2 by 6. They were sawed the proper length to go in between each one of the stationaries on the side, and they were all removable, could be taken out at a minutes notice. But they were solid enough to keep the cattle and things on the boat. We would sometimes have the boat loaded with cattle.

Q: They bunked the passengers up above and the cattle below?

A: Kept them upstairs yes. Well I tell you our trips were never very long, you know. It was 220 miles from Pomeroy to Cincinnati, and about half of that distance would be the average journey of the shipments that we would get. We would load them on the boat on the afternoon or the evening, and next morning we would be down here at Cincinnati. We'd be unloading and driving them off the boat. Drive them out on the wharf boat, and the stock miller was there, and they would drive them out to the stockyards out back of town here and that was all there was to it.

Q: You mentioned that you piloted the *Cricket*. When were you master of the *Cricket*, captain?

A: Oh, I was there about, off and on about four years.

Q: What year?

A: 1900 and 1901, 1902 and 1903.

Q: The *Cricket* towed a showboat and also a water circus I understand?

A: Sure that was at times during those four years. In winter time I would take the little steamboat and go up the Big Sandy River with it.

Q: What did you do up there?

A: Carry freight and things up there, you know. The Big Sandy River was a great place for the light draft steamboats, because there wasn't no railroads up there and everything had to go by the boats. Everybody had to buy stuff. Whenever the river would raise, why then the merchants would all order their stuff so they could get it delivered on the boats. Everybody was always busy about that time. It wasn't a question of getting business, it was a question of how much your boat would carry. You would get down there at Ashland or Catlettsburg, and lay there at the wharf, and just load your boat down until she wouldn't carry anymore, and whenever she had all she could take, why you would get out of there, and go on up and deliver it. It took about three days, day and night running with a double crew. Three days was the usual length of the trip from Catlettsburg to Pikeville, Kentucky. Pikeville was the head of navigation up there. It's still up there. The little town is quite a town now, but it was just a little country village then. We ran there whenever there was water to run on. Of course, after the season was over, along in March or April or sometimes May, why the river would get down so low that boats couldn't run, and we would have to stay out. Then we would run on the Ohio River, and that was the time when I towed that showboat and towed that water circus. I towed anything that I could get a job on. I was just looking for employment. I towed logs out of the Big Sandy River.

Q: Can you tell us a little about that logging operations?

A: The logging operations is a thing that I wasn't concerned in very much, only in the towing. The logs were all fastened together with chain dogs, and saplings, and poles and one thing and another, into a raft, and the raft was floated down to Catlettsburg. And then when it was arrived there, why then it was ready to

John Knoepfle

be towed to wherever they wanted to ship it. And the trips, they usually went to Cincinnati or to Louisville. The farthest of them went to Louisville and the next was Cincinnati, and then we sometimes would take a trip to Levanna up here where the boatyard was. They was all used for boat building. They had their own sawmills, and they would saw up their lumber and build the boats.

Q: Building boats must have been a tremendous trade along here.

A: It was a big trade. It used to be in years ago if a man could run a sawmill, he was never out of a job. Because he could run a sawmill, he could saw lumber, and he could run a boatyard, and he always had all the business that he could tend to.

Q: I imagine the valley must have been full of excellent wood carvers.

A: It was. It was full of lots of good timber too at that time. Some of the finest trees that you ever saw come out of, them logs come out of the Big Sandy there and Guyan. They had poplar logs there that was five and six feet in diameter. Wonderful, just straight as a lead pencil. But it's all gone now. You couldn't get any timber up there if you had to. Everything is cut down, and they'd make a railroad tie, and they have to wait now until some more grows before they can cut anymore.

Q: Can you tell us something about the actors aboard the showboats when you were working the *Cricket* towing the showboats?

A: The actors were a crew that was hired on there by the man that owned the showboat, and after he got his actors and performers, then he would get up his play, whatever he was going to produce for his audience. And then they would rehearse and fix it all up the way they wanted it before they started out. Of course, they had to have a change in the program ever once in a while, and they had to be prepared to give more than one kind of a show. That is more than one title, and sometimes they would be pretty good and sometimes they would be just moderate. It was always interesting.

Q: Did the audience ever become angry with the actors for a bad show?

A: No, I never knew of that.

Q: Always an appreciative audience.

A: They was always good enough to be satisfied, everything was always very nice.

Q: The actors liked to cut up a little after shows were over I suppose.

A: Well that was the part that the public never saw. They would put that on after the show was over, and everybody had gone home. Then they'd put on that part for themselves.

Q: Would you like to describe that?

A: Well there was nothing special about it. The performers were used to being out in front of an audience where they would talk for the peoples benefit, and they liked to have people enjoy it, and they liked to have people notice it, and give them applause ever once in a while. I don't know, I kind of lost my place.

Q: They liked to put on the dog. Did this come in conflict with you trying to get the boat underway in the morning?

A: I never had any trouble with them about that, but I would hear their complaints. They'd growl and kick to another you know. At the breakfast table they would be fussing and fuming about that because they'd say they waked them up too soon. Of course, that was part of the business, and it was my part to get the boat out of there, and get her to the next stop wherever it would be. Sometimes you could make it before breakfast, and sometimes we couldn't.

Q: Why did you have to get the boat out early?

A: On account of after the sun comes up in the morning the wind usually raises, and blows a great deal stronger during the middle of the day than it does early morning. With a small steamboat, with a big showboat why you had to get out in the early morning before the wind raised if you wanted to get very far. Because you couldn't shove that boat against that wind if it got to blowing real hard. I've been in places where I would have to tie up, and have to stop and lay up during part of the day, and wait for the wind to lay. At sundown the wind lays just like I spoke of here. It's always easier after the sun goes down and the wind becomes quiet and you can get along better.

Q: Well fine. How about the water circus? That must have been quite a project on the river, towing a water circus.

A: Well, it was a good thing, but it wasn't nothing extra. The man never made any money out of it. Well, I'll tell you he went down the river, we followed the river down here, made all the river towns aware, that there were any justified to stop at. Got out of Paducah, and after he got to Paducah he decided he didn't want to go down the river any farther, he wanted to come back. He lived at Ironton, and he didn't want to get too far away from home.

Q: What was his name?

A: His name was Newman, N-E-W-M-A-N. So he came back up the same way he came down, what they called backtracking, and he didn't do much business. He lost his shirt. (chuckles)

Q: Did he have a lot of animals on his boat?

A: Not a great deal he had a few, but not very many. He managed to sort of get along without them because they was too hard to handle and too hard to acquire. They'd liable to get loose, and eat up some of the audience.

Q: Guess he had a lot of performers though.

A: He had a lot of performers yes. He had trapeze performers, and he had the fellows that'd do these cartwheels, and all that kind of stuff. They'd get up, and swing around on the trapeze, and turn flip flops in the air. Oh they had a lot of things there. Had a couple of fellows under a great big old blanket and get them up in a certain way and made kind of an animal out of it they called a jocko. It was a kind of ridiculous looking thing, but it sure did bring the house down. They made a hit every time they put it on. Didn't mean anything. You've seen two men under a blanket I expect. That's about all it was, but it made a hit. Another thing he had was an imitation of an automobile. At that time there was

John Knoepfle

no such thing as an automobile, hardly. People had heard of them, but nobody had ever seen them hardly. He had a thing there on the boat that had four wheels on it and it was supposed to represent an automobile, and boy there was a crowd around that thing all the time looking at it. It wouldn't run. They had to pull it around when they wanted to move it, there wasn't a engine or anything, but it made a hit. Just goes to show how things were changed since that time.

Q: Yes, indeed. Tell us about the Greene Line, something about the Greene Line, Chris and Gordon Greene.

A: I went to work for Captain Greene in 1896, and he and his wife lived on the boat. They had no family, and there was only just the two of them. They only had the one steamboat. Later on they got a second boat. A smaller boat and they kept her for a long time. After they sold her they built the *Cricket*.

Q: What was the name of the second boat, do you recall?

A: The second boat was the *Argand*, A-R-G-A-N-D.

Q: A sidewheeler?

A: No a sternwheeler. A small sternwheel boat. I could show you a picture of her in there. She ran from Parkersburg to Pittsburgh. I worked on there two years. I got my license about that time so I could pilot on my own hook, and that was the beginning of my work.

Q: Then he bought the *Cricket*.

A: And then after he sold the *Argand*, he wanted a light draft boat so he could carry the stuff off the *Green*. You see the *Greenwood* ran to Pittsburgh and she had what they called a huckster trade. Huckster trade was a lot of produce. A man that bought produce along the river, and all the stores along the river would ship that produce on the boats to Pittsburgh to the markets at Pittsburgh, and they were what you called hucksters. Every week they would have a lot of eggs, and chickens, and calves, and all stuff of that kind they'd buy up in the country. And they had to be in there at a certain time for market. If they didn't get in there at market time, why it wouldn't sell, and be left on their hands, and it's perishable stuff, and they couldn't keep it. Had to get in there on time. There was times when the river used to get down so low up around Pittsburgh, below Pittsburgh, between there and Wheeling, that the *Greenwood* sometimes like all other boats had trouble getting up there. This little *Cricket* was built with a light draft so she could go in there on very scant water.

Q: What was the draft?

A: She drew fifteen inches. Just about that much, and that's what she was built for, and that's what we used her for, and that's why it came out just exactly the way we planned it. And if you have seen those pictures or drawings that I have made, why you would see it right there.

Q: A farmer crossing with his wagon in front of the *Cricket* with water up to the hub of the wheels.

A: Yes sir, the water was just up to the hubs of the wagon. He drove across the river ahead of us, and we had to stop to keep from running over him. That all sounded kind of funny, like a tall story, and it does yet. Because people can't realize just exactly the conditions that existed at that time. But it was really a true occurrence. If I was up there I could show you exactly where the man drove down the river bank, farm landing up there below Matamoras. The conditions then were much different then, than what they are now. Anybody that knows anything about the river will know that whenever the dry weather comes on — the rains quit — why the river soon gets low. The longer it lasts, why the lower it gets. Used to be when the water was clear, before there was so much sewerage in the water, you could stand in the pilot house on a steamboat, and look down in the water, and see the gravel stones on the bottom of the river just like you see the floor in your house. You could see broken dishes, and see all kind of stuff in the bottom of the river. It was just that way.

Q: You could drink that water then?

A: Yes, you could. In those days they didn't make any fuss about it. Everybody drank it and liked it. Do you want me to describe what they did last night?

Q: Yes, tell us about the water barrel.

A: Don't know whether that would be so good, maybe that wouldn't be a good thing to do. Seems so unsanitary.

Q: Oh well that's the way they all drank it, you might just as well describe it.

A: Of course the people in Cincinnati here drank the water that come out the river, and they do yet as far as that is concerned. They drink river water here and like it.

Q: Probably more unsanitary now than it was then?

A: Oh yes, but of course they have a purifying process they put it through that improves it a great deal that they didn't have then, I guess.

Q: Tell us about piloting in high waters, that would be interesting.

A: The high water situation is just the same as it would be now as far as that concerned, when the river is high, why it's high. Used to sometimes get, I've been out on cases on floods where the river would be so high we'd have to land up against the people's houses. We had to stay away from all the towns where they were because the waves of the boat would break the windows. The waves roll in on just the houses, and the waves of the steamboats would break the glass, and break the store door windows, and everything. Always had a lot of damage on that, and that was very unsatisfactory. People were very indignant about that. Not only that but they would get out and shoot at you.

Q: Shotguns?

A: Yes, they had shotguns. Oh boy, I've seen them come out wholesale, just like moonshiners would. Yes sir, I know one night on the *Argand* we was going up past West Wheeling trying to get into Wheeling to lay up, and some old fellow came out with a shotgun there in the dark there right at West Wheeling, and he cut loose there, and I heard the bullet hit the corner of the pilot house, but he didn't break any glass. (chuckles) That was about the closest call that I ever had. But there were a number of cases where boats, that they'd shoot through and through them. The cabin was light built, you know, and they'd just shoot bullets clear through them. There have been cases where people have been killed that way. I know of a case up there at Moundsville where they had high water. They had a pretty serious time up there about that. They like to took the matter into court. Every time the river gets high the people are very prompt about coming out with a shotgun. They'll flourish it around, and point it at you whether they shoot it or not. I've seen fellows come out with a shotgun in shanty boats that would float, and wouldn't hurt them at all. But simply because the river was high.

Q: They didn't like the wake.

A: No and one time I remember in particular, I think it was in 1910, they was a kind of a flash summer flood they had, and was on the *Cricket*, and we had a boatload of chickens, and a boatload of eggs taking them to Pittsburgh. A whole boatload of stuff going to Pittsburgh, and had to get there, and right on top of this flood, come up there to a place called. Murraysville up there below Parkersburg, and dark came on us evening, and after it got dark we started. The electric light plant of course, and at night a steamboat that has a light plant running on her looks twice as big as she does during the daytime when there is no light running on her. This little boat, she was a little thing, but when she was lighted up at night she looked so big that just the minute they turned that light on people would all come out, and they figured that she was a great big boat, and she was going to move awful fast, and she would throw some awful waves, and they thought they would shoot at her. And boy they came out along there from a little town across the river on the other side called Long Bottom. Every house along there had a shot gun, and they were shooting too. It got dark and I couldn't tell how close they was going to come to us, I sent word down to the engineer to shut his light plant down, stop his lights, and just the minute the lights went out they all raised a big cheer in Long Bottom. Heard one fellow holler, "Hey I got him that time, I shot his lights out." (chuckles) I took the hint, and knew very well the best thing we could do was to tie up; we went in there, some big trees right alongside close there, and tie up there and laid there until morning. They quit shooting then, and the next morning after daylight, we turned loose went on to the river, and nobody ever said a word or pulled a trigger.

Q: Piloting could be dangerous?

A: It was dangerous, of course nobody knows what direction they were shooting. All you could do was wait to hear something. It turned out all right. We didn't do any damage, or didn't hurt them any, and they didn't hurt us.

Q: Do you want to talk about the Greene Line?

A: Well the *H. K. Bedford* was the first boat that Captain Greene had, and he ran her very successfully, and after he had been operating her about ten years, he built a boat called *Greenwood. She* was built at Parkersburg. She was slightly larger than what the *Bedford* was. She ran in the same trade, and did the same business. She was a wonderful old steamboat. They built her in 1898, and she lasted, I don't know how many years, but she was finally wrecked down here at the Suspension Bridge at Cincinnati. She wrecked here in 1927. She lasted all those years.

Of course, you could repair a boat, and renew her, and keep her going as long as you wanted too, if you didn't have a fire or something of that kind to destroy her. As long as it was ordinary wear and tear you could repair that, and make her last as long as you wanted her to. Used to be some old towboats up around Pittsburgh that were 50 to 75 years old, and they kept them repaired well, and they lasted as long as they wanted them. Of course, they are all gone now. Everything is built out of steel now. You couldn't get enough wood to build a boat if you had to. You can't get any oak timber anymore. That's one thing where they had to have so much of it was for the wheel. The water wheel was made out of oak, and it was all made out of arms, and planks one thing and another that you shove on the water, and it took a lot of timber to make a wheel. It has got to the point where you can't hardly get any timber for a wheel. That's one reason why the steamboats have gone out of business, because they couldn't get any material to renew themselves.

Q: I didn't know about that.

A: Yes, spoke timber is very scarce, hard to get. You just can't get it, that's all.

Q: How about the other boats besides the *Greenwood*?

A: The *Greenland* was a sidewheel boat, she came in the picture along about 1903 and she ran for 15 years. She lasted 15 years, and she was lost in the ice down here in the winter of 1917, spring of 1918. She was wrecked in the ice, and went off down the river a total wreck. She settled in that ice gorge down there at Mill Creek, and went down out of sight and nobody ever knew where she went. And the next spring part of her was found down on the Kentucky shore down across from North Bend, Indiana. Part of the hull was there, but the cabins was all gone to pieces, and it scattered out, nobody knew where it went. The boilers they were lost in the river somewhere. Nobody ever knew. The machinery was still on, and they saved it, and put it on another boat later on. But they never used it very much. That was the end of the *Greenland*. Then after that, well conditions changed on the river, and the business didn't justify any more boats being built. Captain Greene still wanted to build one, and he ordered a boat pattern of fir wood lumber from Oregon to build a hull, couldn't get any more oak, and then after he got the order placed for the lumber, why he got to studying about it, and I talked to him about it, and other people did too. And he kind of decided he wouldn't build any wooden boat. He built a steel boat. After that was decided, he made his contract and he built the *Tom Greene*. That was the first steel boat we built. She was 200 feet long, and 38 feet wide. She was a pretty good size boat. She was a very successful boat. She ran here for years, and she ran here until they couldn't run her any longer. The labor conditions got so bad you couldn't get a crew on her and the mining conditions changed, and you couldn't buy coal for her anymore. The labor organizations come in, and they organized everybody and nobody wanted to work any longer. You couldn't get any deckhands to handle any freight, and they just had to quit.

Q: What happened to the *Tom Greene* finally?

A: Well they just laid her up. They couldn't run her any longer. They couldn't get coal to run her. Laid her up down here. They finally sold her. Some people dismantled her and made a barge out of her. She was over at St. Louis the last time I heard of her. They was towing automobiles on that barge. That was the end of the *Tom Greene*. The *Chris Greene*, she was almost the same size boat, just slightly smaller. They built her two years after they built the *Tom*. She ran for 16 years in the Louisville to Cincinnati trade. She was one of the most successful boats they'd ever had down there. Everybody liked her. She was always on time. She wasn't what you would call a real fast boat, but she was a good boat. She was always reliable. She would always get there. She ran until the conditions got the same, that they couldn't get coal for her. They couldn't get a crew to unload her, they couldn't get people to work. They had to quit. Both boats were dismantled about the same time. The *Chris Greene* was sold to a man over here at Dayton. He took her over there and dismantled her, and made a motorboat harbor out of her. And he has her over there now.

Q: Still there.

A: She lays right over here at Newport.

Q: They have all the bunting and flags out on it all summer I noticed.

A: Have you been over there?

Q: No but you can see it driving down the parkway.

A: Well that was what become of the *Chris Greene*. She was a good little steamboat, and everybody liked her that ever worked on her.

Q: The steamboat fire caught some of Greene's boats too, didn't it?

A: The only fire he ever had was the fire that they had down here at the wharf in 1922. The Coney Island Company had two steamboats down there, and they lost both of them, the *Island Queen* and the *Morning Star*. And they was all tied up there together, the water was low, and the boats laid up, and crew down and tied them up, the crew had all gone home. And they was painting on them and fixing them up for the fall of the year. This was along in early November, and there was a fellow heating some paint on a kitchen stove to fix the roof on the *Morning Star*, and it was kind of a coal tar preparation. It boiled over on the stove and set the boat afire. After one boat got afire, and it wasn't long until the four of them was burning.

Q: They couldn't get out.

A: They couldn't get them apart. You couldn't get them separated. Captain Greene lost two boats, and they lost two boats. The little *Chris Greene* she was laying there, and she was the smallest one of the bunch, and she was laying on the outside, and they thought they could get her loose. They chopped the lines loose and before she floated away the heat from the other boats ignited her, and she floated out in the river in the harbor here, burning. She floated into the shore over there at Covington, there below the Suspension Bridge, and the fire department came down there, and played the hose on her, and put the fire out. They saved the hull, but the cabin all burned off. That was the end of the first *Chris Greene*. The second *Chris Greene*, of course was a larger boat that I just now spoke about. But that's the only fires that the Greene Line ever experienced. But there were a lot of others that they didn't, they weren't concerned in and that was the end of a good many boats.

Q: Captain, maybe you can describe the old days when they used to haul coal down on the little barges from Pittsburgh at the spring floods.

A: Yes sir, I can remember that quite well. The coal business around Pittsburgh was a wonderful thing. It came out of the mines on the hills up around the Monongahela River, and there is nothing else up there but coal mines. They had lots of timber up there, and they built lots of barges to haul that coal in, and they'd bring it down the Monongahela River and have them keep it around there at Pittsburgh until there would come a raise in the Ohio River, and then they would all make a grand rush to get down with it on that rise. If the river would get up to as much as eight feet at Pittsburgh that was what was called barge water. Barges would draw about six feet, not over seven. If the river would get up to eight and a half or nine that was what they called coal boat water. That was in common river terms that was called coal boat water because you could take a tow of coal boats down on that stage of water. The coal boats were built heavier, and a big coal boat would carry 25,000 bushel of coal. They were very light built, out of thin lumber, and very easily wrecked. They would hook them things together. They would start down the river whenever it would get a raise. Anything over eight feet of water, why they'd send coal out of Pittsburgh.

Q: I guess that's the reason they wanted to get out first, because there would be so many wrecks that it would make everyone . . .

A: Yes they all came in a bunch. I've seen them when they would be going along and they wouldn't be over 100 yards apart. It was a very risky thing to do because the man in the lead, somebody had to go ahead first. The first man if he happened to hit bottom with some of his barges, it wouldn't take very much of a lick to make them barges leak. They'd get to leaking and get water in them and get down a little bit lower, and lower, and lower, and pretty soon one of them would go down. Then that thing would settle. He couldn't stop his tow, and he would just drop down out of his tow, and he would go on with the rest of it, and leave that laying there right in the channel and there that would be. The next fellow come right along, and he would run over the top of it because he didn't know it was there and he couldn't see it in time to keep off it. He would sink one on top that, and then he would go on with what he had left, and here come the rest of them. And by the time they would all get by, the river would be full. Now that was the way it happened, and there was hardly ever a raise that came out Pittsburgh in the old days, but what there would be some boat sink something, someplace, along the river. The upper river, most of

John Knoepfle

it was above Wheeling. But I have seen some awful spills down river, way down below there. I remember one time when I was a schoolboy before I ever went on the river, they had a wreck at Marietta and they sunk, oh there must have been 20 to 25 boats sunk there. They just sunk and piled up there until the top of them was sticking out of water.

Q: That was coal boats?

A: Piles of coal one on top of another. Yes sir, it was an awful riskful way to do, and they wouldn't think of doing it now. Because they couldn't afford too.

Q: Do you suppose that's why the sand along the river is still pretty black?

A: Why they say the river is full of coal now. There hasn't been any coal sunk for a good many years to speak of, but in the old days when the river would get down low you could get down on the shore and you could take a skiff, and roll your pants up, and you would wade along the river and get a skiff load of coal. The finest coal in the world. It was nice clean coal, and burned up, there wasn't any ash to it. That Pittsburgh coal couldn't be beat. That was exactly why it was that way, and since they got the locks and dams in the river, the river never gets low, only down to a certain stage. This coal that's under water there never shows up anymore, and you never find any. But it's there covered up just the same as it was. Because there hasn't been more than half of it ever picked out. If the river would ever get down, they would put the wickets down in these dams here now, and let the river get down as low as it would go, why you would see it the same way as it used to be. The wickets to these dams if they were put down and allowed to stay down, they river would drain out, and get so low that you could wade across the river just like it was in the old days. Getting back onto that coal subject. That coal business, they used to ship that all the way to New Orleans. And the southern markets were the big thing that they had to figure on. In later years things commenced to change, and they commenced to getting more of these big steel mills up around, Pittsburgh and up in that locality and they commenced to have more of a market at home for the coal, and they didn't want to send it south because they needed it right at Pittsburgh. I remember one time there was a boat called the Oakland, a great big steamboat, she started down river with a tow, and she grounded two barges on the head of Montgomery Island. That's 36 miles below Pittsburgh, and they couldn't get them off, and they just had to let them stay there, and they went on with the rest of it. It wasn't more than two or three weeks after that thing happened until a strike come on at Pittsburgh. And the coal had all been shipped out from Pittsburgh, and the coal miners went on strike, and they wouldn't dig anymore. And there was an awful shortage at Pittsburgh. The first one they ever had up there. So they went down there. They got a lot of men around Pittsburgh there, and a lot of wheelbarrows, and a steamboat, and towed the empty barges, and come down there to Montgomery Island, and laid boards across that gravel bar on the head of the Island, and everybody took a shovel, and all of them big old Irishmen went to work, and they wheeled out two barges of coal across the head of that Island. Wheeled it over and dumped it into another barge, and towed it back to Pittsburgh. That sounds like a tall story, but I can show you the place where it happened, and I can give you the date.

Q: When did that occur?

A: That happened along, well I would have to study a minute, I don't know just exactly, but it was along in the late 1890s. It was after I went on the river. It was after I went to work for the Greene Line in 1896. Yes sir, I remember well when that happened.

Q: You mentioned much earlier that you were on the river until about 1951.

A: I was on until 1951. I went on the river in 1891, and I was on the river until 1951, just exactly 60 years.

Q: What were you doing at the end there, on the river?

A: I was pilot on the *Delta Queen*, the last work I did. I was on her 3 years.

Q: Is that so? I never knew that.

A: She came here in 1948. I made the first trip on her. Took her to Pittsburgh and brought her back. First time she was ever up there. I made all the trips that she ever made around here until 1951. Then I thought I had been there long enough, I got off and went over and lived with my daughter in Honolulu. I lived there until 1954, that was last year. I came back last September.

Q: *Delta Queen* must have seemed a hard boat to handle because of her size?

A: She is, she is a very particular boat and very peculiar.

Q: Can you tell us something about that?

A: I couldn't tell you anything that would be of great interest because it pertains to little technical things that pertain to the piloting profession. I don't know if it is hardly the thing to discuss exactly because oh, I don't know, steamboats are like people. There is no two of them that's alike. Piloting a steamboat is like driving a car, you know your own car, and you know what you can do with it, and you can do it better than somebody else. Piloting a steamboat is a little on that order. There is some things that a steamboat will do readily, and some things that she will not do. As a pilot you have got to know what she is going to do, and make her do it. Whenever you get in a position where you have to do something that a steamboat won't do, why you are going to fail. There are certain things, and certain ways the wind blows, and certain conditions that the steamboat comes in contact with that it makes it difficult to make a proper landing, to make a correct landing, to make a good easy landing. Sometimes you just can't get her to do what you want her to do, and if you try to land you are going to do some damage. The bigger the boat the bigger damage would be. A big boat will hit mighty hard, and you won't know it. A small steamboat you can hit the bank awful hard, and feel like you're, sound like you have wrecked the boat. You go down into the hull and she is not hurt a bit. It's on the same thing as a skiff. You take a wooden skiff, you can run it up on the shore as hard as you want with a pair of oars, the bow upon the bank, it will scratch the gravel, make a lot of noise, won't hurt the boat at all. You take a great big boat, that

John Knoepfle

has weights in her, if she hits the bank hard enough to make that kind of noise, you are going to tear the bottom off her. So that's the laws that governs that.

Q: What were you doing prior to piloting the *Delta Queen*?

A: I was on the *Gordon Greene*, the *Gordon C. Greene* for 13 years. They bought her in 1935. The Greene Line, Mrs. Greene, Tom, and Chris, and myself. We went over to St. Louis.

Q: You were on then with Mary Greene?

A: Yes, I used to be on the boat with her a good bit. In later years she was one of the main part of the show on the boats there. She made every trip, and she was always the social hostess. She helped with everything. She had great popularity and had lots of friends. Lots of people rode on the boat because she was on there.

Q: She was quite an institution on the river.

A: Yes she was an unusual person. We went over there to St. Louis bought that boat and fixed her up, changed her name, and I piloted her back here.

Q: What was she at St. Louis?

A: She was the *Cape Girardeau.*

Q: Oh that's right. You didn't know a deckhand named. Zugelter, did you?

A: What was his name?

Q: Zugelter.

A: I used to know a boy that used to be on the *Gordon Greene*; he's a priest now isn't he? Why, I know Zugelter.

Q: Yes, he's a friend of mine and he talked about knocking the top of the pilot house off one of those boats when they got in the Ohio.

A: (chuckles) Do you want to record this?

Q: Sure he won't mind.

A: I know him he was a captain watchman on the boat at that time. He used to come up in the pilot house there and I used to cut up with him. Used to tell him tales and one thing or another. (chuckles) If you would ask him, mention my name, he'll know it. Yes sir, I remember Zugelter. He was a nice young fellow. He is a priest I guess by this time, ordained or something. I haven't seen him for a long time. He was kind of, I think he was an orphan. I think his father was living, but his mother was dead. I don't know how he got on the boat there. He would come on there as a cabin watchman. You know they have to have what they call bellringers. They have stations all over the boat where you have to punch a clock. He was a clock puncher.

Q: Now just what was the clock punching routine about?

A: The clock punching outfit is a thing that you, you have to walk all over the boat, and have to keep on walking all during the night hours as a watchman. On boats that carry passengers you have to have a clock puncher all the time. Every night, and you've got to have a record of their punch. The thing itself makes a record on a piece of paper, and if you miss one of those clocks, or one of those stations anytime during the night, why that will show it. If you don't have a clear record of a morning when you turn in, your name is Dennis. That's where the clock puncher came in. It's a very trying job to do. You have to walk upstairs and downstairs, and upstairs and downstairs, punch that clock and go 100 yards, and you would punch another one, go downstairs three or four squares, three or four flights of stairs punch another one, run back up there to the top again and punch one up there. That's the way it was. But they have those in all factories and everything.

Q: Is this a safety precaution to make sure that the watchman makes his rounds?

A: Yes sir, it's one of the restrictions that the inspection service puts on steamboats that carry passengers. That's the only thing that's put on.

Q: If you had a chance would you go back out on the river?

A: I don't think I would now because my vision isn't as good as it was. I wouldn't try to trust myself to piloting a boat anymore, not after night. I can see pretty good, but still at the same time my vision isn't as clear as it was. At night it makes a vast difference. Makes a world of a difference. I used to be able to, I didn't care how dark it was, I could see a little bit. But now when it gets dark I can't see at all. That's the greatest difference in the world. So for that reason I wouldn't trust myself to try to work anymore.

Q: You are living a leisurely life up here now?

A: Well, I guess it would be. It's about the only thing I can do. I have no choice.

Q: You are quite active. How about mentioning your projects at the historical library. That would be interesting.

A: Do you want to include that in this?

Q: Sure.

A: I don't know just exactly what I will do with it when I get it all done. But I was over there and got a lot more today. I worked there until they closed at half past four, and I was the last one out. (chuckles)

Q: How far along did you get on this?

A: Well I went about a month.

Q: You are at 1894?

A: Yes in 1894, in the early summer of 1884 rather. I have a good many of the details of the 1884 flood there, and a lot of records of things.

Q: So you are systemically copying the information from the river columns of the old "Enquirer?"

A: Every day I am taking a little bit off of it.

Q: You have gotten four years done?

A: I have got four years. I'm going in on the fifth year.

Q: This is quite a project.

A: It is and I don't know, it's a bigger job than I'll be able to complete I expect. I don't know because I just kind of feel in my bones that I will be interrupted before I get done. But maybe not.

Q: With what you've got it would make a scholar's delight to have that.

A: The only thing is that it will have no commercial value. I couldn't sell it for anything. There is the satisfaction of having it. That's where it comes in.

Q: Sone people will know its value, whether it sells or not.

A: I will be able to make a very interesting talk on the subject.

Q: Well it's interesting as a fact that you have just shown me this huge box of books that represent a diary that you kept since the time you were 13, and which is complete and up to date.

A: Well the first time whenever I tried to keep a diary I was about 11 years old, and I picked up a lot of bills on the street, handbills that had been scattered around the street. I had a bunch of them, and after I got them I didn't know what to do with them. So I sat down and started writing on the back of those things. I would write a little every day on one of them, and then I'd lay it aside, and write on another one. But I didn't keep it up very long, and I finally threw them away. But then about a year later than that, after things had changed, my mother had died, and I had gone up to live in the country with my grandmother, why I took a notion one day that I would like to keep a diary. And I didn't have any book to write it in. So I had some white paper, you know a long time ago the bakeries used to wrap up the bread in white paper. They wouldn't wrap it up until they would sell it to you. If you would go into a bakery, and buy a loaf of bread, they'd wrap it up and give it to you. And I used to save the wrappings on those bread from the bake shop. I had some of that white paper saved up, and it was nice to draw on, and I used to use it for that.

I took some of it and folded it up very carefully, got me a needle and thread, and sewed myself up a book. That's what that book is in there in that envelope I showed you. I have a three year diary in that envelope made out of paper I sewed up with a needle and thread. Then after I got on the boat, I got interested a little bit more. I got off the boat down at Marietta, and I was in a bookstore, and I saw they had books with dates in them. Diaries. I saw one there that was about two years old, and asked the man what he wanted for it and he said 15 cents. So I just said I'll take that one. So I took a pen and ink and changed the dates on all of it. Corrected it up to date with the year that it was at that time. That's one of those that I have in there now. It's written full, and been in there all these years. That started me, I got started then a little bit better, and every year I bought myself a new diary, and I was 13 years old when I started it. And I've got all of them in there in that box there now. I have the dates on the back of them. You can tell what book you're getting just by picking it out.

Q: Well with you painting, and sketches, and your diaries, and this new project you are on, you are going to leave quite a legacy, Captain.

A: I don't know it will be a legacy or not, whether it will be worth anything or not, but it will be interesting to some, of course.

Question: Well, Mr. Keller, you said that you would start to talk from way back. I think you were born in 1880 something.
Answer: 1888.
Q: 1888. Can you tell us something about your early experiences?
A: Yes, when I was a boy going to school I started to fish in what is called Mud Lake that is below the Allied Mills, and Barton Mill. Mud Lake was a clear lake, and then there was a ridge, and then there was long lake on the other side of that ridge. We used to wade across the slough there, and we would catch some fish. Then we would take them big fish, take them out on the ridge, and then we would build a fire. We would wrap them up in mud, that black mud. Then we would put the fish in the fire and we would have baked fish. See when you would remove the mud, the skin would come off, so that you would have a plain fish. Of course, later on we went as far as to the river, and also fished there. But then we quit the fishing down here. We wanted to go onto the river, and so we made a boat. This boat we built, we put the motor in the boat, and in place of putting a propeller under the boat, we put it right out with the back corner. So what we had was just throwed the water up in the air and didn't go forward. That was a failure. So then we went, and got another boat, and built another boat rather, I should say. Then we went and returned the motor that we had bought from the Weber Brothers in Pekin. They were building motors at that time, so we bought one of their horse and a half motors. Well then, from there on we took this boat. And we used to travel by boat down the river because that was about the only way you could get down there in those days. Because cars they didn't travel in the sand because all those back hills were all sand in them days. The sand, if we had a storm, the sand would, I saw a time when the sand would blow as high as the fence, that is just like snow. We used to have to lay down horse blankets to get across those places. But the trouble was the farm wagon and the horses, they would go into a track, and your horse will step right where the track is, and that keeps the thing all cut up. So we went by boat and we took a trip down, one of our first trips, to the lower end of Spring Lake, or the upper end of Clear Lake. This is on the Mason County line. In them days there wasn't any dike around this levee, and we could run right into the lake. We went into the hills by the sandy. There was an old man that had his cabin there by the sandy hill, and we pitched our camps on the side of that hill.

So we were going out hunting. So we went over to the river or the lake, I don't remember just exactly what the name of the lake was, but it was, I think it was Slim Lake. We went over there and put out our decoys and we hunted. So on the way back, the firewood along the bank was scarce, so on the way back I decided I was going to cut some of that firewood that we were passing. And I got up and took the axe and I was going to chop. I missed the limb and me and the axe went out. The axe pulled me out in the water, and it was measured afterwards, there was seven foot water there. So then we decided that we ought to get that axe because I had an idea that with a wooden handle the axe would be standing straight up. So we threwed an oar lock out there, and we went around the ring, around this place, and we just kept going around and around until finally come up with the axe out of seven foot of water. (chuckles) So then we went in and the old man was telling me about the upper lake there. So the next morning when we went out, we had left our decoys out all night, so next morning when we went out to hunt we had no decoys. There was only one there, and the rest were all gone. Now I don't know where they went to but nevertheless, we hunted all over that country, but we never found the decoys. So then we give up and we come back.

And in the meantime, the old gentleman on the hill, he told me that in early days that the stage, when the river was low there, the stage from St. Louis came up along the water's edge to almost where we were at there, about a quarter of a mile from there I should judge. And they would cut up over on top of the hill to go to Chicago. And you still can see that cut in the hill down there. Of course, I was relying on what he said. Later afterwards we went down to the head of Clear Lake, and we did our hunting mostly, and also fishing along the edge of Clear Lake and in the backwaters. Then afterwards we went on down to the main lake, and we fished in there and we hunted in there. Of course, it was a club and there was only these certain places that you could hunt. They would let you fish, but finally they stopped everything. Then we went out and we took our boat in the river. We went down the river with a cabin and we were on our honeymoon, and I was going to spend the two weeks down and around the lower end of Clear Lake. Well when we go there Clear Lake was all full of ice, and so we had to take, there was a little slough that run down along the river between the main part of the lake, and if you went in around the back, there was a kind of a shelter. We pulled in there. And at night we woke up, and we heard this crunching noise, and all the ice in that lake went through that cut that night. The next morning the lake was clear.

We started and we pulled in through the lake, and went down into Havens Slough on this island. We was on this island and we left the cabin there. On the way in with our launch, which was 27 foot boat, the winds were towards us and we had to quarter them. In other words they hit the side of the bow and we had to do that in order to get to where we wanted to go. The right side of was nothing but stumps, and we couldn't go in there. There was great danger if we got in there, it would have upset the boat. So we went on and of course every time the wave would hit the bow it would throw water in the air, and it would accumulate, and hit the boat until it began so the flywheel started to dragging in the water and throwing the water. So I tried to keep the motor running. And finally it was just running on one cylinder, and by that time the canvas had come off of the boat and was dragging in the water and holding me back.

Well I got to the point where I was going to turn onto the lake to go to the Havens Slough, and that was as far as I got. So the wind was so strong that it carried me the rest of the way, and the next morning the launch was out on dry ground. That's how strong it was, a wave just picked it up, and washed it right outside on the ground. Of course, we stayed there. The cabin boat, the hull had kind of dried out, and the water was a raising see, and as it raised we couldn't keep the cabin boat afloat. So the water started getting higher and higher and the island was all under water. The only way we could hold the boat was we cut four big poles, and we stuck them down through into the floor outside of the cabin boat because no ropes would have held it. As the waves took this boat up and down, it would pull a pole down, it kept us busy running around the boat pushing the poles down so we wouldn't be over in the swamp and drown. (chuckles) So that went on all night and of course in a condition like that I was outside, but Mrs. Keller got awful sick, seasick from being inside. She was so awful seasick. That was the event of that particular time. It went on, and of course we hunted down there, and we done a great deal of that hunting. There was an old man on that island by the name of Tucker. I think he was from Kentucky, but what amused me, it was awful cold weather that time, and here he was out in the water. I was dressed up in a Mackinaw, and he was in the water without any shoes on. And he had an iron ring, not an iron ring, a brass ring on an ankle, and another brass ring on the wrist. And I says to him, "Mr. Tucker, what are you doing with those things under water?" He says he has rheumatism, and he says that's why he's wearing them. (chuckles)

Q: Now you mentioned that you had pushed for various men in the duck hunting season. Could you talk about that a little bit?

A: This man he had some kind of material that he would sell to the railroads and in place of, taking and, oh I don't know just exactly how to explain this, they'd pay him for it, and he would give them a shoot on the ducks. So I would take these men and take them out, and then we would shoot until about 12 o'clock. I remember that I pushed for, which takes care of controlling the shooting in the blinds, for the vice president and his son, of the B & O, and also at the same time there were the general manager, and the master mechanic, as far as I can remember. At various times we'd change. We followed this rule, but at different times we would change, and we had men from the different roads would come in. Most all of that shooting was done down on the Sangamon River, and there was fellows I remember in particular, oh I think Mississippi, come up there, a sheriff, and oh, I don't remember what the other ones were. I remember the shooting of the sheriff. He was so fast, I never saw a man shoot quail so fast, and kill three out a bunch when they would rise. He was a terribly fast shot. We continued later on of having this place.

When I was pushing in this blind, and controlling, we had thousands of ducks. If you would stand off in a distance it would look like a funnel. Every duck in the country would see that funnel, and come down in there. So we had

John Knoepfle

an awful lot of ducks, and we had to try to take care of them. The idea was we sometimes would maybe have several thousands ducks in there at one time. They would come back in there, as soon as we'd drive them out they would come back in there, almost like rain drops, by the thousands. Well we couldn't shoot ducks that way because if you'd go to work, and shoot when a big body of the ducks were there you scared all the ducks. So we would try to go to work, and break these big amount of ducks up into small bunches so they would come back in a small bunch because then we would only scare maybe five or ten or maybe a dozen ducks. So the men that time I was pushing for, they looked at me and they didn't know what, they had come there to shoot ducks, and they didn't know why I was trying to scare them away, well that was the reason. Finally we broke these ducks up, and then when they come back in smaller bunches we would shoot. We would only shoot till 12 o'clock, and then all shooting would stop. Then we had this lake that we shot on that was a very long affair. So we could reverse, and then we could go down to the other end of the lake, and then we could shoot tomorrow. As we shot there, then the duck would go up in the upper part, the same as they did when we shot in the upper part they went to the lower part. So that's the way we shot them.

I fished Spring Lake and enjoyed it. It was one of the best lakes around the country that I knew of. The water was so clear that you could drop anything on the bottom and see it, and also the fish could see your fly. Well, I used to do a great deal of fly fishing. I enjoyed it, because it took a little bit of experience, but I would take the fly and make a long cast, and in them days I would see fish come at least 20 feet to where the fly was coming down, and he would have that fly, and he would never stop, he would keep jumping and jumping. I have had them where they'd jump and complete 180 degrees, a half circle, and land on the other side, all in the jumping process as they went. It used to be in earlier fishing that when you go to throw a fly in there see, the fish could see it. And the fly fishing then, of course, there was a lot of moss, and there were moss holes. Usually these holes is where the big bass laid in. In those days the holes were deep. I know of places where the holes were five or six feet deep. These bass would lay in these holes, and you would have to fish according to how the wind was. Because if the wind was from one direction, whichever way, the fish would lay up in the opposite direction. Because if it was a dragonfly or whatever was there, it would carry this up to the other end. Usually there was scum and moss seeds and the like that would form on there. That's the place that the fish would be. But that wasn't the way you should fish the hole.

I have started at the nearest edge, and then fish there. Then keep working around your right and left edge as you are going on. Because you may catch fish, and if you would have made the cast up where you knew the fish would be, if you caught a fish, then he drove all the rest of the fish out of the hole. My method would be just as I explained. You always worked, which ever direction the wind went because whatever fell in the water it would go to the opposite side of the hole. Now I have fished and I remember as high as eight bass out of one place in the moss just by using this kind of a method. Another thing, your moss, a lot of the places that people thought there wasn't bass under it, you had to know what your moss was like. In other words by the color and all, and beneath it may be hollow under, and that's where your fish would be laying. Of course, a lot depended on the weather, or the temperature and so forth. If the water was exceedingly warm, they would go to these spring holes, and that would be the place to fish.

I can remember one day when I fished from morning until about 4 o'clock constantly, and I caught one bass, a little bass undersize about six inches. So then I went to another place that I thought the fish would be. I went to this place where there was a running spring water coming out. There was big hole in the moss, oh I would say it was about 15 foot in diameter. I laid six casts in that hole, I got six bass straight weighing around two pounds out of that one hole. So that gives the method that I used some, the way I fished. But you have to take also the sunlight. If you are fishing with your back to the sun, especially when it is getting late in the evening when the fishing should be the best, why it will cast a shadow way out there maybe half way across the lake, and then you will scare the fish out. Another method I would use large bass seldom make a second pass. If he's a large fish, he'll make a pass at that fly once, and I could maybe say that maybe a half a dozen in my time that would of made a second pass, but that's all. From then on you have got to use another method. But I marked this place where this bass was, and just went away and left him. Then go back just as the sun was going over the hill and when there is a shadow on the water, then make that cast. But you have got to have accuracy because you only have one try and it's got to be good. That was the method on that. But a lot of these fish would lay way back in this spring water. It doesn't matter how much noise you make, you can make all the noise you want on top of the water, all of the talk, and people don't talk and all that, that doesn't. What scares fish is if you bump anything. I have seen it when I carelessly happened to drop an oar on the side of the boat, as I was rowing, I saw bass jump out of the water because they feel that through their scales someway, I don't know just what it is. They don't hear it, they feel it. They used to feed back in water, they couldn't swim in it hardly. But to catch them in there, that was a problem because I used to throw around a 100 foot line, but it still didn't do you no good because the minute they heard any noise you could see them plowing out to the deep water and there would be, maybe, a spring hole. There was one spring hole out there, I don't know how deep it was, but it was a terrible big one, and it was awful deep. Well there they laid down in there, the big ones lay on the bottom. Another thing that happens when you are fishing that way, sometimes you saw a big fish. You know there are big fish in there, but the big fish didn't take it. You come in expecting one when a fish strikes you are getting a big fish, but a big fish didn't strike, you got a little fish. Because they get everything they want

John Knoepfle

if they want it. But it used to be there was time, which is all passed now that if you would go to work and you'd throw that fly, which I knew this moss seed, and all that would float in there, the underneath was all hollow, and there was a time when I throw that fly on top of that, and from then on you had to be awful careful. We all fish too fast.

You have got to fish slow if you want to catch fish because everything is alert. If you are fishing, and there is a big fish, he looks out, he watches you, and everything, every move. So the best way I used to do was to throw it in there, and leave it lay. Then after it laid there a little bit just pull it a little bit. Just like it was a bug creeping. Then lay around, pull it a little bit. Then if sometimes those bass would come around there, you'd think a dynamite was in it. They'd come up there sometimes that high, just come straight up, and have the bait in their mouth, and turn over and back down, see. That's a lot of the ways that I fished. But here's what has happened. Now maybe the wash, they used to be what I'm telling you about, that was serious deep holes clear down there that always had fish in them, but since the wash from the hills, and it's getting so that it has finally filled all of it up. One place where I was in the upper, I went there always and I could always catch fish. I could of took a dime and threw it over the bottom in five foot, between five and six foot of water, and seen it just as plain as if you had it in your hand. But that very place today, I can't even push a boat through it. That's all full of silt and wash from the hills. That's the problem we have all over. Now in our other lakes, the minute they go to work, and they put a dam in, why then it seems like that it gathers all this silt in the bottom. There's places I know I could take, I got a pole, you could push a pole down, you might go through three, four feet, then you would hit the actual gravel and the sand. Now that's what is happening to the fish.

I was fishing in the lower end of Spring Lake, and I had first experience of seeing a 300 pound hog swim in deep water. I saw this hog swim across, which I thought wasn't possible. And all that I could see was the tip of the ears and the nose of this hog. He swam across there and on the other side there was a swamp there, that the depth of it I do not know because it was nothing but swampy black mud. They would come through this place, and they would feed out there. I never could understand that, but this particular day I was fishing down there. And my wife insisted the dog, I heard the dogs barking, and she says, "Let's go up and see what those dogs has got." So I went back in there, the only way I could get back is through the little channel that he had to get to the shore. I went back in there and here these dogs had this hog out in that mud, and they was tearing it to pieces. There were some on the front of the hog and some on the back. I couldn't get to them with a boat, and I couldn't get to them walking. The only thing I could do was try to scare them away, which I finally succeeded in doing. In the meantime the owner happened to be coming home from fishing. So I told him about the incident. He didn't believe me.

I had a new paddle. I broke the paddle trying to get the dogs off the hog. I thought that he ought to pay for my paddle. That's beside the point. While I was talking to him the dogs started barking up onto the hill. They were after his other hogs. That give me the experience of seeing how those animals get over that swamp when a human being can't. I had a little boat with a cockpit, I used to be able to push around and jump ducks. And I would shoot those ducks as they jumped out of these various different places. Now we had at that time some piles of logs and so forth, that these ducks would get in and they thought that they were so secure in there that we would actually have to get up and take a paddle or pole or anything to beat on the logs to get the ducks to jump out of there, because they used to feed on these Spanish needles in there. Well that's the way I would go along push and jump the ducks as I pushed through where the timber was. But out in the open water if you work it right and know how to do it, you'll get mighty close to the ducks. When there is a big bunch of ducks, I used to try and get exactly in the line with the sun on my back, so they had to look through the sun at me, and of course you can't lift a paddle or you have no oars. Nothing but, I had a little scuttle, in other words a little paddle only about two foot long. You don't dare lift your oar or paddle up out of the water. All that you do is scuttle, you know, and scuttle that because you dare not move, you got to sit just like something, a stump or something. And I could do that and I could get close to the ducks by that method because I used the sun, used that method of jumping ducks. For years I have never used nothing, but when I went fishing was fish basket. I have one of those old Hawkeye baskets.

Q: What is a Hawkeye basket?

A: Well that was the make of the basket. I used to use that and have that ice in this basket. Many a time I would almost give anything to know how many fish in the number of years was in that basket. My method always was never to drag a fish on a stringer because you take and drag a fish around all day in hot weather and he'll die, and then he's really of no value as far as I'm concerned when their gills turn white. But turning back to this fish basket, the minute I caught a bass I would take and break their neck. That is I would take my two fingers of one hand, and then my forefinger and thumb of the other hand, and pry the head back and break and snap his neck off. Then he was dead and I would put him on ice. I didn't believe in dragging fish around, and making them suffer because I thought to much of the fish. And I still do. When you had a fish, you had a good fresh fish. If you want to know when you have a fresh fish look at the gills, that is the first thing. If you get a gill has pus like that, then your fish has started to spoil. If I take these fish when I bring them home, their gills are just as red, and that's one reason why I always done that, and carried a fish basket and I still do. I never go out without that.

This is mostly in the wintertime. In the wintertime the fish they have a coat on them to protect them against the cold and so forth, as far as I know. But when you go to work and you take your dry hands and you touch that fish, why they will get sores where they break this coat, see. I suppose people up north in

John Knoepfle

the winter, when you have fish you can take, and the water after you wash them and you can pull it up almost you'd have to wash and wash them to get that off there, but that is what I call a coat. You should always wet your hands. I always did. Another thing if you catch a fish in the gills, when you tear that one gill, why he is a dead fish. There is no use returning him to the water because he is going to die. Nothing will kill a fish quicker than that or water temperatures.

What I mean by water temperatures, fish are accustomed to living in one degree. Take for instance minnows, now even today if I am fishing with minnows I temper my water. The water you get them in may be different than the water you fish in, and if I would take that bucket, and set it that warm water, they would all be dead. You have got to step them up to temper them or detemper them, whichever way you want to. You have to step them up or step them down to get the degrees. I do it right now when I went into ice, in the lake fishing that I've done this year. Now the water I get here is colder than the lake water, but if I go to work, and take and put that minnow, if I was fishing with minnow, and I would put it on, see the fish in the lake, he is not tempered, and he will be just stiff, he's dead, so what use is he? If you want to keep them alive you have to get the temperatures between the two exact or you don't have good fishing. That's the reason I take them out, pour out of there, then I put a little lake water in, and then I take and poor out some more then in this process, and pour in the other way again. And that's the way I temper the water. Then when you get that minnow out there in this lake water he is used to it. You can take your bucket, and sit it out in the lake. Then he is used to this lake water, and then he is lively that's meant by tempering the minnow.

Q: With all of these tricks that you have learned, you must have caught many fish. Can you tell us something about your record catches?

A: My record catches, I don't know, I had a few that I don't think, with the fish the way they are now, would be broken. In fact I can't back this up because the book I had I haven't got. But I used to catch, the first of the season, that was way back in 1938 or somewhere in the 30's, an average of 100 fish, bass for the first ten trips, and I did that for about ten years. I averaged it up, and the average showed that I had caught around eight, and some percent of bass in that time for the number of trips against the number of fish. I can recall one time I went out at what they call a pile hole where this boat, and all that I was telling you about where the marine railway was, I started out there. It was early in the morning. Mrs. Keller was with me, she had a lot of importance in this fishing because she would push my boat for me. It takes someone who knows how to push a boat to push for a fly fisherman. Because if you don't push right you are liable to get a fly in the back of the ear or something because you can't stay straight. A good pusher will always turn the boat on an angle so that when the fly travels back and forth it won't be going past your head, you'll be over here, see. Well we started up this lake, it was early in the morning, and we fished clear up to what they call the spillway. That is where the water is let out of the actual part of Spring Lake. So, we had no bass, and I says there are sure no bass biting today. We had to go back down, the only reason why you would fish back was with, I had to go back because it kept that boat in the lower end. So in as much as we had to go back down, I said, well I was halfway, but I says I'll try it anyway. That was one o'clock. So I fished from the spillway, back down over the same waters that I hadn't caught a fish. We started out at one o'clock, and the time I got to the pike hole it was three o'clock, and we had caught 18 bass, and at three o'clock they stopped, just like somebody turned off the clock. You could have fished the rest of the day and you wouldn't get a fish. That's the habit of it. If they stopped there, they stopped here. They worked. I don't know sometimes I think they carry clocks with them.

Ducks, you could take, I've often wondered when I was hunting ducks, there seemed to me that they must have something that tells them. I know that I was always pretty good at sneaking up on them ducks. But when I knew that I was absolutely good, they never knew there was no one around, but still you can tell by the action. Whenever ducks starts to stretch his neck up, you know, stretch it out, then he will start doing this, he starts to squirm on the water. They know somebody is around. How did they know that has always been my wonder. How do they know these things? I feel a lot of times they are gifted with a lot of stuff that we don't know about. Take weather, I saw the ducks, if it was going to be a bad day tomorrow, I saw the ducks come in today. They have already got that warning or the feeling, whatever you call it. I don't know, I've seen them start and start to flying down. That of any value to you?

Take wild pigeons, for instance, my dad told me that when he was young that the wild pigeons were so thick that they would shut out the sun when they'd fly. And I also boarded with a colonel at that time from the Civil War. He was a colonel in the Civil War, and he told me the same story about the wild pigeons being so thick. If they had a particular place to roost, he told me that the droppings under there would be deep. I'm showing you with my hand just about four feet deep. He said that they got so, if I remember correctly, that netting them or some way until today, we have not one wild pigeon.

Q: Yes, they shipped them by the barrel from Louisville up to Cincinnati, and sold them for meat. Just gutted them out. You have some photographs here of a wrecked steamboat, I wonder if you could comment on that?

A: I'd like to but I don't know just what date that is.

Q: Doesn't matter.

A: It was after July, this excursion boat at night going down the river, I think most of the people on that boat was from Kingston Mines, well they somehow or another they must have hit something in the river. I don't remember that part, but they hit something and it upset this boat. Well, I just don't remember just how many was drowned. But of course I had a launch up the river about two miles from there. So I went up there and got into this launch and I went down; and I saw them as they were taking people out of the boat. Now I just don't

John Knoepfle

remember what year it was, but it was way back there. I would hate to say.

Q: Well, it made a mess out of that steamboat. I can see from your pictures here. You mentioned I think a levee breaking too.

A: Oh yes, we forgot that didn't we? (chuckles) Usually on the first day of bass fishing, I had a boat, always kept the boat in the lower end of the Spring Lake down by the Marine Railway. And at this time I took the boat down, it wasn't down there then, I took it down on a trailer. It was a year when the water was so high, the water was I think about four foot, four or five foot from the top of the levee on the outside. I should judge it the bottom inside have been about 18 foot through 20 according to the height of the levee. Well, I got to the bottom of the hill, and the first thing I did, I drove my car over the levee and down into the drainage, and parked it in there the way I usually do. Then I walked back and I was going to go to work and I was going to pull my boat over and down into the lake. As I come back, Mrs. Keller was standing on the levee, and as I come back up these three fellows come there, names . . .

Q: Louis Heckler, Maurice Hoff, and Amie Daniels.

A: Yes, they had pulled a flat boat across right where I was standing, so as they pulled the flat boat across, they were going to put it down in the lake too. And as they pulled down the side of the bank on the inside and as they stepped there, why all at once all I could see was just water and sand come out of the ground or out of the levee. A fountain oh, as high as this door. It kept boiling, and first thing the whole thing opened up. Then Mrs. Keller, she was standing on the levee petrified watching them you know. She couldn't move. I went to work, and I could feel it in my feet what was coming, and I felt just like a ripple in the water. It come from the outside towards the river. I could feel this ripple in the sand, I said, "Run!" I said, "Run, run, because it is going to cave on us!" She ran, and I got over there, we got off of it just as the whole thing came out. The other one fell down in there, and as he fell down in there it all went down, and these fellows were buried, and then they were up and they was down. I couldn't take time to see him. I was trying to save myself see. So they got out of it all right. I am getting so hoarse. (After a short break in the interview).

Q: Now we can finish the levee boil.

A: After this I had to go down into the drainage. I went around, there was a boat, got over there, went down into the drainage, and got my car. There was some pretty bad places due to the pressure of the water. I managed to get through. I run it awful fast, I managed to get up, and back on the old road again.

Q: Now we are going to talk about the older river.

A: When I was young I used to fish in the river. I would go down the Kickapoo Creek bank, and I would walk down to the river. And there they used to catch catfish, used to catch them. Nice strings of catfish; they weren't very big but oh my, the carp. The carp was immense size. I can remember one time, that my first fly rod that I bought years ago, and it was the first trip I had with this fly rod. I walked down there, and went clear down the river right where the mouth of the Kickapoo Creek goes into the river. I went to work and I started to fish in there, and, my oh my, I never fished but just a few minutes, and I had no fly rod. Them carp was so big they broke it. And I sat down on the bank and started crying. A kid, you know, they had broke my fly rod. There was carp in there you couldn't land them in, they was thick. And so I used to walk down the river and sometimes we would fish in the river with a throw line. That is a line with three hooks on, and a weight that you threw out. I can remember that I threw out this throw line, didn't know, I thought I was snagged on something so I began to pull in, and when it was getting towards the bank I could see I had an immense carp on. The carp had a hook in his mouth, and the other hook he had in his tail, and he was doubled in a U shape. And I got him about ten foot from the bank where I could see him good, and he saw me, and flop, and away he went. (chuckles) And that was that.

Q: What did you use to fish for catfish? What kind of bait doughballs?

A: No, just a pole and worms. Just common worms.

Q: You said you thought those carp must have gotten large because of the brewery. Could you explain that a little?

A: Whatever came out of there I don't know, we use to call it slop beer. It's a byproduct or something of what they use. I don't know how they do it now, maybe they use that stuff. But in them days they would run it into the creek, where they used to haul all the dead horses and cattle, and everything from around. They had a whole big yard, and it was all laying out there, and my you could tell a long time before you got there, and a long time after you passed it, and you couldn't hardly stand it when you would get passed.

Q: What would they do with those carcasses?

A: Oh they ripped them up, and I don't know what they really done with them. Made soap out of them or skinned the hides I guess, they shaved the hides off.

Q: Fertilizers too, I guess.

A: Oh yes, I forgot that, they probably did that too.

Q: Did you ever do any hunting besides ducks?

A: Yes, I hunted deer.

Q: Around in here?

A: No, out west in Colorado. I have hunted grouse.

Q: Let's talk about pecan trees.

A: Years ago when we would take the river ridge and along the lakes there, there were those big pecan trees, but nevertheless I saw trees that I would say 12 to 14 inches that were cut down just so they could pick the pecans off. It ruined the tree by cutting it down as it was an easy way to get that. That's how they destroyed the stuff, they had too much stuff.

Q: That seems to be the history of the country, wasting everything. Well now I see there is a mention here of a beer wagon.

A: Well you will have to go over there to see all that stuff.

Q: You mentioned though that you yourself hauled railroad ties.

John Knoepfle

A: I hauled railroad ties from this camp I showed you. I hauled it to the railroad.

Q: This was in the west now?

A: In Colorado and I also worked in that apple ranch there. They call them ranches but they are orchards. The remarkable thing about that is, and always puzzled me, I saw trees right on big rock, the only things holding them is the cracks in the rocks. The roots go down in there, and that is the only thing that supports them. But it's a different climate. When I got out there, here we perspire and out there it is a burning just like if you had opened the furnace door, and the heat come back out. It is a different kind of heat, and you might walk right over there, and I suppose maybe you experienced that, you walk right over there in the shade, and you are cooled off.

Q: Tell me in this area what kinds of work did you do in those early days?

A: In this area I was the automobile man. They sent me all over the country you know. Them days they didn't have the garages, and everything like they have today. I worked out of the factory. They used to send me, I've went to places as big as the Cat over there and fixed cars. I remember one time that they had a car, that they didn't know, I think they even took it to Chicago. They got so many different parts for it, they got tired of sending it to them. So they sent me over to see what was the matter with it, see. So I went over there and I took a look at it. Of course, it was from my factory experience that I knew in 15 minutes what was the matter with the car. Because you see it had a spiral gear. When you run a gear against another gear, this gear sits this way, and this gear sits this way. The teeth are half around there. Well the minute this gets in play you see, it lifts this here, whatever this other that is running, which happened to be in this case the timer. And then I lifted it up, let it fall, and you just stand that tooth and down it goes. The next tooth brings it down and lets it fall. Well it just sounded bump, bump, just like if you had a loose bearing. Everybody thought it was a loose bearing. Well it had two bushings in there with holes in them and one bushing, they were threaded, and one bushing would push up, and the other push down. That way by spreading them you could take all that out, and the noise was gone. Just like a magician, but it was my factory training and experience from working in the factory that I was able to determine that.

Q: What factory was this?

A: This was the factory in the Heights in Peoria.

Q: When did you go to work for them?

A: Maybe you should know when Halley's Comet was around. (chuckles) That was when I went to the back door and looked, oh Halley's comet, you know it only come in 100 years. I used to work nights see. I was working in a machine shop. Another job that I didn't like, I was working on this high speed grinder, a steel grinder that you put sandpaper, or emery cloth discs on. It traveled at a terrific speed, I think about 5,000 revolutions per minute. In fact, it did get loose once and went clear through the factory. So I was always glad when I got off of that thing. Because I was grinding the cams for the camshaft. That was a different system, in place of having the cam on the camshaft they had it over a kind of a lever, and it would raise that, see. That happened to be my particular job then. But then later on I went to the shaper. It's a machine that if I wanted to make this here level, see I can set my tool, and it goes back and forth like this. I worked on that, and then I worked on a broaching machine. Before that time I don't remember, but I went out west, I was so sick all the time and I thought about that time was when I went out there.

When I come back I think I went back to the repair end, and it was a remarkable thing how we handled gasoline in those days. Gasoline was I think about six cents a gallon, and we used to run and wash the floor, this greasy floor. We would wash this floor with gasoline, and of course it would run down the sewer. If it ever got ignited it would probably blowed that high. So it did one day it ignited, and it was in the winter time, and there was snow on the ground, and they had a big double door, and there was just a little bit of grade that come up in there. We had a big long building maybe from here to the house about a whole row of cars. Every man had a stall where he had his car that he was working on. So I had this car in the far corner. The tool closet was in the corner of the building. So in them days they had the cylinders what we called, it isn't like now, we had a metal crankcase that supported the crankshaft. In other words, you took your cylinders off the top of this and you took your bottom pan, as they say, off that. You still had your crankshaft in there. Well, I had a whole bucket full of gas, and I was washing off the oil so I could see, and I had set the mag, which was all my fault, I had set the mag on off, but you see, being tore down, the wire had been disconnected, and made it so it wasn't off. So I washed it on one side, and took the crank and turned it over.

And wham everything was fire all over. Here I was with a whole bucket full of gasoline, and so there was one sitting on the floor. And this fellow's name was George Reammers, and he was working back behind the wheel. Well, this fellow Jess Ward was coming down the aisle to go get this tool cabinet for some tools. As he came up there toward the tools, why this George Reammers, he had this bucket full of burning gas, and he was going to throw it out. When he came around the front wheel he stumbled, and he throwed it right on the breast of Jess Ward. While he was on fire, I looked around and there wasn't a spot on him but his face was all I could see. The rest of it was just like a human torch. So I said, "Come on let's run to the door." I throwed up the door. A fellow named Harry Rush, he was working on the next machine, and he went out from under the back end of it, and he run too. And I had thrown the doors open, and we got him outside, and in the process of the snow being there, you see we shoveled a big yoke there doubled, you shoveled it on this side and you shoveled it on that side. There was a big pile of snow, we said, "Jess, jump in this snow," he did, we buried him totally that is all that saved his life. That man never had nothing but singed hair. But the guy that stumbled, it burned all the flesh off his arm and everything and he was the one that got it. But you see they

John Knoepfle

had a sprinkler system in the building, and of course by that time the sprinkler system broke. But then I had another experience there if you want to take it?

Q: Sure.

A: I used to take the man out here now wherever. In them days they would get a car, and they would come into the factory to take that car home. Well, there was about three or four of us men that they used to send, we was on the roads, they'd send us on the road for repairs or delivering these cars. They sent a man out to pull this car in. In fact, he was from the Board of Trade down here, but I can't remember his name. But it wasn't far from the factory, it was only out there about a mile. So that night, it was one of those days that was warm, it was warm as it could be, and then it started turning cold. When we got out there, it was mud, and then it turned, it started to freezing. Of course, we got out and we got stuck with that car. So we had to leave it there. Then we come back, and I don't know, we had another car, I think we had two cars up there. We couldn't get there. So this boss, it was his fault, he goes up in there, and he says, "Let's get one of them new ones." When they have a, it ain't like today, they'd assemble this car, and they had a test for it. We would use a test sheet. They'd set it on top, and then they would take the car out and run it up and down to test it and all. Well, there was one up with a test sheet on, but there was an incline to go down from the upper story to the bottom story like this a ramp, which wouldn't have meant nothing if you had a run out there. But when you got at the bottom of the ramp there was a building, and he had to make a left turn. There was nobody who would tackle it. I don't know whether I was simple, or crazy, or what. I says, "I will drive it down." So I went to work and we put chains on it, and of course, I used the system of low. If you want to get down you put it in low, and make it pull the motor. I got down without any trouble and got out. I went out there and finally pulled and we got, by that time the rope that we was towing with was frozen, and the ground was all getting froze. So we finally got the car in, but worked maybe until one o'clock or something. The next day boy did they tear into us for taking that new car out. So that's the way it went on and on. The next morning it was around zero or two below zero.

Q: How long did you stay with that company?

A: I don't remember exactly, possible two years is all. I went from there, I went for the Dodge people then.

Q: That must have been a pretty early company then?

A: Yes, nowadays we got everything to test everything, they have got the tests. When we used to do that our tests were up here, we had to know what we was doing and all that. I can take you down there, and show you or bring it up here, a tester that I made before they had those earliest testers. We'd have to go out and try to find out. See I was with Interstate, and then I was with the Ish Brothers. Then I was with Knox where they sold the Knox car. But right at that point I changed, but nevertheless I know that when I come down, I was on Main Street, and got with Ford. Then from Ford, oh we had Dodge, we had Chevrolet, we had Dort, we had Saxon, a good many different kinds of cars.

Q: How is it in this particular area these car companies started? Was there an easy supply of metal?

A: No because we are getting into later years. That's been a long time ago. We always had to go out, and oh so many different details on trips. One trip I was ordered to stay with a man as long as he wanted. They sent me this fellow, did you ever hear of Grinnell, Iowa where the college there . . . . They make gloves there, don't they? Well, I took this fellow, he was only 15, 20 miles from Grinnell, that was where he was going. By the time he got to Grinnell he thought he was able to take the car. On 4th of July now mind you. There was something wasn't just right on that starter, and he wanted me to lay down in the dirt there, and fix that. And if I couldn't, if he had turned me loose there, and if I would have missed that train see, I couldn't have got another train until the next day. And had a big celebration in Davenport, Iowa up here. So I wanted to get back there. I could have done it if I could get on that train. So I says, "Well, I can't do that, I have got that train coming through here in ten or 15 minutes. I will do what I can, but otherwise I will be laying over here a day, and I can't do that." So I did and the fellow never got of town, I don't think he got five or ten miles, and the clutch slipped off the pins. Then I was glad they sent the other guy. They sent him Harry Rush, one of the other fellows, and he didn't like the place at all. Our idea always was to try to satisfy the customers, which I tried to do. I lived in Indianapolis for a whole week with a banker. Well you know me, and they served dinner in courses, and they were way up there, I felt like a mouse. (chuckles) But I was there for a whole week, and lived with that banker.

Q: Until they learned how to use the car.

A: No, I was repairing a car there. The same way, as I went way down to Industry, if you ever heard of that place. It's in the southwest down there. That fellow was a doctor, and put me up in the barn. (laughter) He was a great fellow, he used to go to work, and if he couldn't start the car, he would just go, and get something to put on the carburetor, and started in on fire. That's the truth. I have went as far as down here to Keokuk Dam. They sent me down there to Keokuk, and that was a most interesting trip because they were building the dam at the time. That was a big process; that was an awful big dam. They showed where some of those fellows fell in, went right in the concrete, and they never got them. Then they had that big stone crusher. They would take the stone right out of the hill there and crush them. It was just like a great big spin on top and the farther down it would go it would get bigger. Never moved much out of place, but it just had grooves in it. That bowl went around just like a big soup bowl only it was as big as this room. That was full of those big rocks. When it got down to the bottom, why they was just a little rock, like that. That thing was awful slick with all that stuff going down and if something would jam, those fellows had poles, they worked around the edge of that, and they had big leather belts on them. They told me, if I remember right, that one of them went down too. They sent me over there to straighten out something with one of the managers at the factory, and that night they had a storm, and the lightning struck the barn and the barn burned up. (laughter) So it goes on, and on, and on. I have been a lot of places, and done a lot of things. I don't know.

Q: Well, you are going to do some more fishing I guess?

A: I suppose if I live that long, I don't think I will live that long.

Q: Well, maybe none of us will the way things are going. Do you have anything you can think of?

Barbara Nauer: We didn't talk about that brewery. Wasn't your family involved in the brewery at one time? Didn't you say your family worked in the brewery, or you did, or your grandfather?

A: No, here is my father, there is my uncle, there's my aunt, all relations.

B: I just wondered how you came by the wooden bottle capper that you showed us that is over there in the barn, and those lights, and those things?

A: All that old stuff and I haven't got it all, I can remember when I was kid there was a rifle, with a big long barrel, and he had that. Downstairs, I didn't show is a muzzle loading revolver, and a derringer. All that has some connection with that brewery up there. The barrel over there, 1822, and you see on the door there is a spring and I think that is a German custom, wasn't it?

B: Where was the brewery located? Was it in this town?

A: Right here. But there was two breweries at that time, and to answer your question that was the first one, and there was another one up here on Dutch Hill.

Q: Well do you have a parting word of advice for fishermen?

A: (laughter) Well, I don't think that we are ever going to have the fishing like we had it because you see, our lakes have changed. Our vegetation has gone. You've got to have vegetation and not too much of it. There is a certain limit to the vegetation. If you get too much it sucks oxygen out of the air, and of course your fish can't survive. You've got to have a certain amount of open air, and the waves that push the air back into the water. I had the experience with that a few years ago with, where the vegetation was so thick, that you couldn't hardly get through it. If you would look back there, there was clear holes, just as clear, but there wasn't a living thing in them because there was no oxygen left in those holes. These fish would come out to the edge where this run was, and you see your outboard motor when it runs through the water it puts oxygen in that water, where I was catching an awful lot of fish, just from where the activity of the outboard motors. So if you get too much vegetation it's not good, and if you do not have any it's not good. When you dam a place now you are corralling all that sediments, like I told you up in the upper end where I could look five or six feet. Now there is nothing but muck. Just that black jelly.

Q: I guess that should take care of it.

A: Do you think you have anything that's any good?

Q: Oh yes, thank you.

Albert S. Kelley, July 27, 1957

Question: This is the 27th of July on a rainy morning at the Greene Line Wharf. I have come down to the Delta to visit with Mr. Albert S. Kelley, the *Delta Queen's* pilot who began his river career on the *City of Louisville*.

Answer: I started on the river in the year of 1916, May 4th on the *City of Louisville*, and at that time Captain Charles Brasher, Sr. was pilot and Captain Ed Maurer. They both of course have passed away a few years back, and I'm still going along on the river as yet. I started steering on the *City of Louisville* as cub pilot, which was and had the record of making fastest run between Louisville and Cincinnati that any boat has ever made. She went down from Louisville in five hours and 52 minutes, and she came up the river from Louisville to Cincinnati in nine hours and 42 minutes, and I think and I'm very sure that record stands good yet. She was the champion of all sidewheelers, I think that ran out of Cincinnati. They had at that time the sister ship to the *City of Louisville*, the *City of Cincinnati*, which operated on the opposite day and they ran here for a good many years. I think the *City of Louisville* came out, was built in 1892, and I think it was 1895 when she made that record run. The *Cincinnati* was a very fast boat, the *City of Cincinnati*, but she never could beat the *Louisville's* record. They ran up to 1917 and 1918 in the ice, and were cut down here at the wharf here in the ice in 1917 and 1918. So after that ice spell had cut down the boats mostly from around here then why I went in the Navy. I joined the Navy in 1918 and served in the Navy four years, almost four years. In 1923 I came back on the river and finished up my time, which at that time required three years as steersman. Then in 1923 I got my first issue of license and Captain Ed Maurer at that time was hull inspector at Louisville, and he issued my first issue of license, after spending two years with him as steersman, then it happened that he issued my first issue of license.

Q: Was you with him after the war?

A: Well no, I think during the war, I think it was 1918, in the fall of 1918, he got his appointment as hull inspector at Pittsburgh, but he wasn't up there too long at that district, I think two or three years then he was appointed at Louisville, Kentucky. So he was there when he gave me my first issue of license. I guess I had it very lucky because on the day I got my license I went to work the same day and that's quick because sometimes you may have to wait two or three months for an appointment or a job. But I was lucky, just went right on to work.

Q: Where was that?

A: Well the first boat I ever want on as a pilot was the old sternwheeler *Kentucky* at that time. That was the first boat that I went on as pilot, then I went from there to the *Andes*, and the last *Cincinnati* they built in 1925, and I was on her in 1925 and part of 1926. Then I went on a sternwheeler boat here they

John Knoepfle

called the *John W. Hubbard* and I was on her a number of times, and also the *Queen City*, which was very famous, especially the upstream boat from here to Pittsburgh; but however, the company bought her, and she did run from here to Louisville, oh I would say two or three years on the opposite day of the new *Cincinnati* run. I was practically on all of those boats, and then I was on the excursion boat the *Princess* and the *America* at Louisville. It ran out of there excursions from Louisville to Coney Island. I was on there several different times you know. In other words, it all belonged to the same company. The Louisville and Cincinnati Packet company at that time.

Q: Was that the White Collar line?

A: No, back in the Louisville days the old steamer *City of Cincinnati* was the White Collar line, but in after that ice, Captain Laidley sold out to Captain Roe and Captain Hubbard of Pittsburgh, they took over then.

Q: Now you were on these various boats and about what year does that bring you up to, Mr. Kelley?

A: What do you mean up to the present year?

Q: Yes.

A: Well right offhand I couldn't say the dates on all those boats, but I can say this much, I have worked steady ever since then. As I say when I got my license in 1923, I've been steady here and fortunately one good thing about it, I haven't been sick or off anytime for disability or like that. I've been around here steamboating out of Cincinnati practically ever since then. Of course, I have done quite a bit of boating from Cincinnati to Huntington, West Virginia, and also the Kanawha River. I have license up to Montgomery, that's 30 miles above Charleston. I have license up as far as New Martinsville up on the Ohio River. I have done some steamboating up there especially on the *Gordon Greene*. I was up there on her in 1947, and also licensed pilot from New Martinsville to Cairo, Illinois, that's the mouth of the Ohio River. And up Tennessee River as far as Eggner's Ferry Bridge. That's about 60 miles from Paducah, and I have license on the Mississippi River as far down as Laconia Light that is as far as the Memphis district goes. In other words, I would say about 150 miles below Memphis.

Q: When did you come with the Greene Line?

A: I started with the Greene Line May the 5th, I believe it was in 1931 and at that time the Greene Line bought over the old Cincinnati Packet Company here. They bought them out and they had the sternwheeler *Tom Greene*, and also sternwheeler *Chris Greene*. Well they wanted to get down in this packet trade here at Louisville to Cincinnati because it seemed like it had held up and the future of it looked better than any other packet trade. So they came here in 1931 in this Louisville to Cincinnati trade in May 6th, 1931. And I went on the *Tom Greene*, my partner and I, a pilot by the name of Charlie Kirby, and by the way, it is probably a record I don't know if possibly way back 50 or 60 years ago, but anyway I'm going to tell you this. We had been partners at that time,

Captain Charlie Kirby about four or five years previous before the Greene Line took over down here, and we were partners all together 20 years and I think that is a long time to be partners with one fellow, you know one pilot. We were on the *Tom Greene* 16 years steady on that one boat and I believe it could be a record, I don't know possibly, but I know one thing sure it's a long time.

Q: Wonder if you could talk a little bit about the steamer *Kentucky* since you are the first man I've talked to who was on that boat?

A: Well of course the steamer *Kentucky* of course originally was the *Levi J. Workum*. However, I know little about her when she was a *Levi J. Workum* but I would say back well maybe along in about 1908 or 1910 she ran from here from Cincinnati to Aurora, and carried whiskey, mostly just whiskey, the still they had down there, Petersburg rather I should have said. But I don't know just how long she ran in that trade but a good many years.

Q: I guess that whiskey must have been a fabulous trade.

A: Of course that was before prohibition in 1919 I think it was, but yes at that time it was and later it must have been a year, oh I don't know, maybe 1914 or 1915, she was taken out on the dry dock and lengthened out, and then named the steamer *Kentucky*. She was a very famous boat, that is she was slow, she never made any fast time, but the management always said, she made more money than any boat they ever had, and after that was said she probably run away more business than any other boat they had because she was slow. You had to deliver the freight on time and like of that, that's what counted. Well the faster boats maybe got a little more business, but they were a lot more expensive. Now the *Kentucky* was a very cheap boat to operate and she was a very faithful boat. She wasn't very fast coming up again a strong current. It used to take us I would say 24 hours to come from Louisville to Cincinnati with a big river. Now a big river, I mean about 40 or 45 feet on the gauge at Cincinnati. However when you turned around and headed downstream, she was really a fast boat. She would go down with the current naturally real fast, but coming up is where she was a long time. I say maybe 24 hours to come up with a big current. The management, they always said that she made more money for the company than any boat they ever had, but she probably ran more business away than any boat they ever had. (chuckles)

Q: I guess coming upstream you had to hug the willows with her.

A: Oh yes it was a very common thing to come in with a boat like that and other sternwheelers too, with a lot of willow limbs on her guard and the carpenter, he would always look around outside. He would say, "Well they have been trimming the willows, because here is the evidence." But you had to do that to get out of the current because if you didn't you just wouldn't make any time. Now the passenger boats like the *City of Louisville* and the *City of Cincinnati* and even the *Delta*, they said you could pull them across on a current across the river like you were coming around a point and want to cut over to the next point. Well you pull them out in the current they would keep going right on, they

John Knoepfle

would still have a pretty good headway, they'd go on. But the *Kentucky*, if you made it straight across, if you fell across the river there, and say just opposite of some house or barn from where you started to cross, why you was lucky if you didn't drop below that before you got out of a strong current.

Q: How about the *Andes*, I understand from Dent Sanford that she had an amazing whistle?

A: Yes the *Andes* had a very pretty whistle I always thought. It was a whistle that you could hear a long distance away. It had a very good tone. The *Andes* was a very good boat. She wasn't as large a boat as the steamer *Kentucky* and the *John W. Hubbard* and those boats, but she was a good freight carrier and a very good boat.

Q: Was she in the upriver trade?

A: Well, yes, she ran upriver a number of years. I believe Pat Morrow at one time owned her, I'm not sure of that, but I think he did, and then in later years she came down here in the Louisville to Cincinnati packet trade. She was a very good boat, and I was on her I would say two or three years, different times you know. Now those boats in those days, the larger boats, they would maybe have to lay them up in low water season, then they would bring out the light draft boats like the steamer *Kentucky* or the *Andes*, you see. Because you didn't have the nice pools of water then as you got now. In low water season, they had to bring those boats out because the larger and heavier boats couldn't run.

Q: Were you on the *Andes* when she was running upriver?

A: No, I wasn't on the *Andes* while she was running up the river, but I do remember one time here, while I was on her here in the Louisville to Cincinnati packet trade, we came up to lock 38 that was just completed, and we came in there one morning I would say about 7:30 and the lockmaster told us, said, "Well, you are the first boat that has gone through this lock." At that time I don't know just what year that was, it must have been around 1924, I believe, 1925 or something like that. But I know he was telling us that we were the first boat that went through lock 38.

Q: How about this *Cincinnati*? You mentioned that was the *Andes* before.

A: You mean the last *Cincinnati*, I suppose. Well the *City of Cincinnati*, the old *Cincinnati*, called that the *City of Cincinnati*, and this last *Cincinnati* that was built was the *Cincinnati*. She was built and came out in 1924. I believe the Mardi Gras at New Orleans was her first trip, but right off the date that she left here, it must have been in February, I would say in 1924. But I didn't go on her until long in, let's see I think it was June of 1924, and I was on her until about the middle of September of 1924. You know they'd run those boats here in the Cincinnati-Louisville trade through the summer months on account of they would get more people those days. But long after the, in other words, say the first of September, school would open up, why they figured they wouldn't carry as many people. And they would lay them boats up and bring out their smaller boats the fall and winter months. Because there weren't enough passengers in those months to justify them and run them because they were very expensive, those boats to run, and you had to get a good many people on them to make a go, and they figured through the summer months, why they could do that. And she was very popular boat here for, I would say up until 1929 or 1930. And people over at St. Louis bought her and made an excursion boat out of here. That's the Streckus Line. She's now running out of New Orleans, named as the *President*, an excursion boat.

Q: When they laid a boat up did they moor it or take it out of the water completely?

A: No, not unless they was going to clock the boat. If they were going to clock for some repair to do on her hull or something like that they would dock them, pull them out on the ways or dock, either one. But just to lay the boat up for the lack of business or just repairs to the engine room, something that the engineers could do or the machine shop, no they would usually drop them down below the wharfboats and do that down there, you see. But if they had to go to the ways, some hull work to do, then they had to dock them or pull them out on the ways, either one.

Q: Getting back to that *City of Louisville*, I was told by Norval Horton, he was an engineer on her, that they used to load it up with beer and take it down river. Do you know anything about this?

A: Well, yes, not only beer but all kinds of freight. I have seen them laying at Carrollton, Kentucky and put on several hundred cases of whiskey and barrels of whiskey, and places like that. In those days, of course that was before prohibition you know. They carried quite a bit of whiskey and also stock. Now I have seen them load stock at Louisville and bring to Cincinnati market, and they would drive them down in those days. I have seen maybe 200 head of cattle and maybe hogs and sheep. Of course, they had a regular deck space to put them on the lower deck. It was right funny of a morning, they'd usually, you didn't have to have an alarm to wake you up, there would be some cow bawling or a pig a squealing down on the deck, you know wake you up.

Q: How did they ever get that livestock up the public landing here I wonder?

A: They drove them. They'd just drive them. They didn't truck them in those days. They just had regular men to drive them out to the stockyards. Of course, you couldn't do it now because of traffic, but back in those days traffic wasn't too bad, nothing like it is now, and they would drive them. There was men that did that all the time and they knew what they were doing. They would take certain routes, you know, where it wouldn't be right through the business part of town, and they got along fine, and probably got them a little quicker than the trucks do now.

Q: I guess you were on the *Princess* with the excursion trade up to Coney Island weren't you?

A: Yes, some, but mostly out of Louisville. I remember one summer I believe it was in 1927 she ran out of Louisville down to Sugar Grove, a little amusement park they had down there, in other words, a picnic ground, about 20 miles below Louisville. We ran out from out of Louisville down there, and also picked them up from New Albany, Indiana, and sometimes we would have colored trips too, you know, and we did pretty well with her. I don't know just how many people she could carry, I forgot now, but she was a very fast boat. She was a side-wheeler, the *Princess* was, and a very good handler. I always liked to handle that boat because she really was a good handler.

Q: Could you talk a little bit about, you say the *Princess* was a good handler, why?

A: Well the *Princess* as I said was a sidewheeler, a high pressure boat, and she wasn't, she had good power for the size boat. I don't know just how long she was or how wide she was, but I always thought she was just the right size for the power she had, and she was a very good handler. Now a sidewheel boat, you know can twist them, what we call twisting is we would come ahead on one wheel and back on the other, and I always said she could turn around out in the river on the length of herself on a dime. You could just twist her right around. She was a very good handler.

Q: So some of them weren't so responsive I guess. Some of the boats.

A: Some of them, yes. But back in those days, I don't know, the riverboats then, and especially the sidewheelers that I knew about were all very good handlers. Now you take the *America*, of course it was formerly the *Indiana*, and she was made an excursion boat in I think around the year 1923, 1922 or 1923 was called *America* and she ran out of Louisville to Coney Island there for a number of years for excursions, and I was also on her several different times and she was another good handler and a very fast boat. She was a high pressure boat, a sidewheeler and she was a very good boat and I always thought she was one of the prettiest boats I ever saw, a sidewheeler, because she sat up on the water and looked like a duck. She was a very proud looking boat.

Q: I've seen pictures of her and she had that.

A: Yes, that's right.

Q: Now we are going to talk about the upper river.

A: The upper river trade, I was only on the packet boats the *Tom Greene* and the *Chris Greene*. We ran to Huntington, West Virginia, so we did quite a bit of way business like Maysville, Portsmouth, and Ironton, Ashland, and up through Huntington, West Virginia. We would carry soap by the carload. Lots out of here and just all kinds of freight, and I remember especially at Ironton, Ohio, you stopped there and loaded up with kegs of nails and staples and barb wire fence and all kind of fencing out of Ironton.

Q: What did you do in Portsmouth?

A: Well Portsmouth was generally made on a Sunday morning going up and we would stop there to give the people a church stop, go to church you know. We would arrive there, say around five or six o'clock in the morning and we would stay there until I would say eleven o'clock that day, but we would carry just all kinds of freight out of Portsmouth there and to Portsmouth, soap, and just a general run of freight.

Q: Household things.

A: Household stuff, that's right, stores and others.

Q: You mentioned Ashland too, how about Ashland?

A: Ashland ran about the same, about the same freight I would say that Huntington or Portsmouth would, about the same kind of freight.

Q: They were still doing some logging up there then, weren't they?

A: You mean raft logging?

Q: On the Big Sandy.

A: Well yes, once in a while you would see rafts of logs come out of Big Sandy but not so much in those years. I think that was about played out at that time I was coming up there; but however, I did get to see a few rafts come out of there on rises when they could get them out.

Q: Did you ever stop at Catlettsburg?

A: Not very many times, I believe I maybe recall two or three times that we landed at Catlettsburg. At that time Catlettsburg, the packet boats wasn't doing so good out of there then. But Huntington was a very good town for packet boats at that time. They had a wharf boat there, a nice new wharfboat, and they did a wonderful business out of Huntington.

Q: What were they shipping up there?

A: There would just be the same run of business you would say the other towns. It seemed like cigarettes and soap as I can recall was our heaviest freight. we used to carry a tremendous lot of freight out of soap especially from Proctor and Gamble out of Cincinnati, up river and down the river. We would get a lot of groceries too. Canned goods and stuff that wasn't perishable, up the river.

Q: I guess you were with the Greenes up on the Kanawha.

A: Yes I made several trips up the Kanawha River. We used to go up there on the weekends, because that was, through the summer months especially, that was a very good run for passengers. The freight business at Charleston was fairly good. It wasn't anything to brag about at that time, but the passenger business was really good. Now we would leave Cincinnati on a Saturday evening, at three o'clock I believe was our leaving time, and we'd get up to Charleston Monday morning sometimes you see, with our stops. It was a very nice trip up to Charleston, West Virginia.

Q: A beautiful river up there.

A: Oh beautiful, and especially after you get above Charleston. I never ran on the *Tom Greene* up above Charleston, I did on the *Gordon*; however, but you take from Charleston up to Montgomery, that's where you go through those mountains between there and it's really beautiful. The river is kind of windy, in other words, I would say crooked. Sharp bends, it's very pretty up there. We used to try to make that run in daylight to give the passengers time to see that.

Q: That's called the Hawk's Nest I think.

John Knoepfle

A: That's on farther up, we never could get up as far as that. Montgomery was about as far as we could get with our boat. Montgomery, West Virginia because above there it narrowed down and it was a little bit too treacherous to try in above Montgomery.

Q: We haven't spoken about the *Queen City* or the days on *W. Hubbard* yet.

A: The *Queen City* of course was a very famous boat. She was built in, I don't know in just what year, but I would imagine around 1904, something like that. I wouldn't say I was right about that, but however she ran Cincinnati to Pittsburgh for several years in that Pittsburgh and Cincinnati packet trade and the sister ship was the *Virginia*. The *Queen City* was a very big sternwheel boat. In fact, she was one of the biggest sternwheel boats in this upper end of the river until the *Delta Queen* came here. She was a very fast boat and I always thought she was one of the prettiest sternwheel boats that was ever on any of these rivers. She ran in the passenger trade here for several years up to Pittsburgh and I believe it was around about 1923 the Louisville-Cincinnati Packet Company bought her and brought her down here and ran in to Louisville. In this lower trade, and she ran on the opposite day that the *Cincinnati* run. She was a big fast sternwheel boat and she made good time and she had one of the prettiest cabins on her I believe I ever saw. She had a lot of mahogany, her door finishing was, and all of her what we called gingerbread work in the cabin was very beautiful. She had a very beautiful cabin on her and her staterooms were very large. They were in fact built large and roomy, and they were very nice. The furniture was nice and in those days of course, you could get that stuff a lot cheaper. It would cost a lot of money now to buy that stuff now, but she was a very fine boat and a very fast boat.

Q: How about the *John W. Hubbard*?

A: The *John W. Hubbard* was built and ran on the Mississippi River, she was the *M. A. Burke* when she ran down there. Now I couldn't say just what town she run out of, probably Vicksburg. She came up here in about 1922. A Louisville-Cincinnati Company, of course when he took the steamboat business over from Captain Laidley, they didn't have many boats left to run and they built this boat and brought her up here. She had cotton guards when she came up here, but they remodeled her and changed that because naturally they didn't need cotton guards up in this country. The *John W. Hubbard* was a very good boat; she was one of the best handlers, sternwheelers I believe I was ever on. She was cost compound, her machinery, she was very fast and she made good time here in this Louisville-Cincinnati packet trade. She went and come on her schedule and she carried passengers too. She had very nice rooms on her and she was a very pretty boat. All except when she first came up here, I remember taking a look at her, she had those cotton guards, and naturally I wasn't used to boats that looked you know with those cotton guards on her, and see I thought she was the ugliest boat I had ever looked at. But after they remodeled her and fixed her up like the Ohio River boats, why she was all right, a very good boat.

Q: I remember last week we talked a little bit about coaling the *Greene*. You counted the coal boxes coming on. Could you discuss that a little?

A: I believe I would call that coaling, and back in those, that was on the *City of Louisville* now, and I was steersman then, and of course they didn't pay the steersman any wages in those days. I was a single fellow of course, but I needed a little change for laundry and maybe a package of cigarettes once in a while. But anyway they gave me a dollar a day to check coal. Now I am talking about *City of Louisville* because that's the only boat that I ever checked coal on. The *Hercules Carrel*, a towboat came out of Licking River over here and brought the coal over to us in a flat. They'd land along the outside of us when the *Louisville* would be here early in the morning and they would usually come over about eight o'clock and start coaling the boat. The *Louisville* was a coal burner and she burned a lot of coal, and I would say she would burn maybe three or 400 boxes of coal a roundtrip. Now those boxes maybe would hold two and a half to three bushels and the colored fellows would put that on and one would be in front of it and one behind, in other words there was handlebars they called it carried it on. I know I would have a checker being out checking that coal on. Usually it would take us about two and a half to three hours to coal the boat of a morning, most always in the morning.

Q: I know this is a foggy old river, do you remember any problems handling boats in the fog? Are there different kinds of fogs you had to contend with, and things like that?

A: When I started out I started out of course, handling fogs on occasions, and do yet. We never get through with that. Of course, now a days the boats have radar. We don't have any, but radar is very good they help you out a lot. But one thing about those radar is they don't pick up the bridge pier and that is the main thing. They don't exactly live by them, the dense fog, they lay up too, with radar. But as far as fog experience we've had quite a bit of it here just lately, and we usually try to get along as far as we can. We maybe have to stop, float, and run slow and get into as close to shore as we can and get our bearings that way. And if it gets too bad, why we just go in and tie up in what we call choking the stump.

Q: Choking the stump.

A: Yes, choke the stump or tree or something, but you can't do any good in heavy fog. You've got to see something, you have to get a bearings to run on. You just can't do any good in heavy fog. While we do run through what we call a little patch of it once in a while maybe it will be a little rough for five or ten minutes, and then you get someplace that gets better. But usually around these hills and hollers where these creeks come in is where you get your heaviest fog.

Q: How about wind on the river?

A: The wind that is one of our greatest difficulties of course, in the pilot in handling the boat. One thing about the wind, of course, ordinary wind doesn't bother you so much, but you take a strong wind, and especially if it hits the side

John Knoepfle

of your boat and if you are trying to make a landing in a close place, it does have a great affect on your boat. Well you have to go according to that, you've got to come up to say if you were going to make a lock or any landing the winds on shore. You've got to come up with a little more speed and you have got to hold your boat out in the river a little farther and in the water rather and you have to allow for all that because the minute that boat runs out of headway that wind has got you. And she'll take you in on something, whatever you are trying to land against. Of course, we don't always make an easy landing but we try to make it as best as we can, and usually we do without doing any damage.

Q: You mentioned the bridge piers and I know that Cincinnati has rough piers. I imagine you have taken a lot of boats out of here. Is there any particular trick for getting through these piers when you move a boat out?

A: Of course I have went out of here and it didn't look so good, fog. I remember one particular time I left here on the *Tom Greene*, that must have been around like in 1932 or 1933, and it was what we call a rain fog. A warm rainy foggy weather. We got ready to leave here, it was just about dark and it didn't look too bad around the C & O Bridge down there, I could still see the lights on the bridge. But we had a pretty good stage of water at the time. I would say 35 to 30 feet here on the gauge, and that's the stage that is very treacherous here, you have to be very careful down around these bridge piers. We got down through the C & O Bridge all right, we made it, and it just shut out completely, and I knew there were some coal barges over on the Ohio side there. I got over what I thought was getting pretty close to them and I backed the boat up on a straight rudder and killed her headway up, flipped around and tried to count the revolutions, what I thought would turn her around you see, and head upstream. Fortunately I must have been just right on it because when I headed her upstream with the current I was just straight up with the barges and there was a light showed up was on the barge. Captain Tom Greene said, "Well here it is," and put a line out, that was it we tied up to the coal barge. But maybe couldn't do that in a 1,000 times again. In other words, old lady-luck was with me.

Q: I understand it's awful easy to get turned around in the fog and not know where you are.

A: Oh yes, you can get turned around, and then the distance will fool you. Maybe you think you see something, maybe you think it's trees, and it won't be nothing but a patch of fog and maybe it will be trees and you'll think it's fog. So it is very deceiving on that, and then especially on the water. Yes, you can get turned around mighty easy.

Q: I wanted to ask you if you were ever hung up on the shoals and things like that, shoal water.

A: You mean sandbars I guess?

Q: Yes.

A: Well yes I have a number of times, we have gotten hung up, on these sandbars, especially these crossings. But I wouldn't say that we were hung up so bad that we had to have help to get us off or anything like that. But I have rubbed sandbars. I think I have been very fortunate, not bragging or anything like that, but I've never grounded a boat so bad that you couldn't get off on its own power. Maybe in low water season or something like a crossing or a fill up sand will work in the channel and a lot of time there is not as much water there as you think there is. You naturally hit that reef or rub on it and you have to back and twist them around to get them off.

Q: I've heard it said that often when a boat was hung up like that if they waited overnight there would be enough water, the water would run outside, the sand out from and under the boat and they could float off.

A: That might be true to a certain extent. But in this pool water you have now there is no current much to help you out on cutting out. Before they had locks and dams of those reefs, the current would naturally cut it out. Eventually it would cut out and lot of times help you get over those reefs. But in this pool water there is quite a bit of difference, there is no current to help you out on that, but I can say this much, if you are aground on a sandbar with a boat and the more you back that boat the more sand will pile up under the boat. In other words, you'd more want to come ahead on the boat because that washes the sand out away from you. The wheel backing up throws the water and the sand and stuff right up under the hull of the boat and naturally you pile that sand up and you get harder aground all the time.

Q: Wonder if toward the end now you might want to mention other men that you knew on the river, sometimes little incidents and things pop up in reviewing the men.

A: I've been with a quite a few rivermen but I'll tell you most of them are dead and gone. As I've mentioned earlier, Ed Maurer, and Captain Charlie Brasher, Sr. learned me the river in 1916 and 1917 when I was with them. Of course, that was way back when I was steersman. In later years I was partners with Captain Charlie Brasher, he was Captain of the boat, and his brother Captain Jim Brasher. They have all passed away now. Used to be partners with them on a boat and my first, in other words starting out days, you know. But as I mentioned Captain Charlie Kirby I guess was my partner longer than any other pilots I worked with 20 years with him you see, and that's a long time right there. So of course, Captain Maurer as I said became inspector, and he retired from that office five or six years ago. Oh there are a number of pilots I have been with. Years have gone along and the *Delta*, of course, right now Captain Harris Underwood is my partner and has been for this is the second year with him, and Captain Paul Underwood is Captain, I was partners with him over there for two years prior to that. Captain Jim Butler was on there with me, and oh, I don't know just a number of pilots I've been with, and Captain Lawrence Allen, they are all very good pilots. Some of them mostly retired. Some of them are done passed on. So I feel like I'm about the only one of the oldtimers left

John Knoepfle

around here now. I don't know, you look back and study it over just a little bit and you think they're gone they're gone they're gone so there you are.

Q: You were in the lower river a little bit too I take it, below the falls since you had a license for there.

A: Yes of course we run down there now, you know to Cairo, Paducah.

Q: Guess it's not nearly the problem that it used to be. I understand there was a lot of shoal water in the lower river.

A: Yes, by the way we had quite a bit of this last trip coming up, especially Wabash River. The Wabash River has been out very strong here in the last two months, heavy rains they had had up there, and it seemed like it has washed and formed a bar right in the mouth of it, a sandbar, and there has been quite a few towboats busting up there and grounding there. But however, we got through there all right, but it's very bad down there right now. There are a number of places that the water is thin in places. But the government is getting after it now and dredging and doing what they can with it and I think in the next month or two it will be in very good shape again.

Q: I bet it was a pilot's nightmare around the turn of the century down there to get those boats through.

A: I suppose it was.

Q: You went through the canal I guess to get around the fall at Louisville, right?

A: Yes, we've been over the falls a number of times with the *Delta* in fact, we've been over once this year. I believe it was the third trip we made to New Orleans this spring, we went over the falls. Now going over those falls you have to have, of course a certain stage of water to do this. In other words I would say when you have about 45 feet of water here on the Cincinnati gauge, then you can go over the falls at Louisville because that levels it up, you see, down there and the dam's all down, the water levels up below the falls, why then you are all right, you can go over the falls. We very seldom do that, but on high water we do have to go that because lock 41 is out and you have to go over the falls.

Q: I guess Captain Bo Allen is about the only man alive now that ever went over them in low water.

A: I imagine he is, well you see Captain Bo Allen, he worked out of Louisville and Evansville trade for years down there and of course he had more experience on them falls than I have. Quite a bit more.

Q: The old falls pilots are all gone now.

A: Oh yes, they have about all gone. Captain Graham Varble was about the last one that was a famous Ohio River falls pilot and he died here about ten or twelve years ago. So he was one of the last ones that I know of.

Q: I think you have given us quite an interview, Mr. Kelley.

A: Well I have I have, of course there is a lot of other things that I could talk about, but it would take a lot of time and everything.

Q: Wonder if before we close off you could give us a few vital statistics, Mr. Kelley, where and when you born and things like that?

A: I'm a Kentuckian and I was born in Oldham County Kentucky and the county seat is LaGrange, Kentucky. The nearest town, I'm a farm boy, you know, raised on a farm, the nearest town was a little town called Westport, Kentucky and that was right on the river. I guess it come about me wanting to be on the river and make a pilot, I had a couple of friends that were clerks on this old boat we spoke of earlier, the *City of Louisville*, and they were from Westport, by the name of Carr. There was two brothers of them and they were clerks on the boat, and they were a little older than I was, but however, I knew them and I kept after them and they got me on and talked to the pilots and the management to get me on as steersman on the boats and that's about the way I started. I remember when I was a boy I used to go down the river there in Westport and watch the boats go by and always imagined I would like to be a pilot, especially those big sidewheel boats because one thing about those boats, you could hear those boats coming I would say eight or ten miles down the river. The sidewheel boats always made a different sound from any other boats. You could hear them buckets. Now when I say buckets I mean the wheels paddling the water, and it just looked like it played a tune and you could hear its escapes, they were high pressure boats and they had a different escape noise from the boats than they have nowadays. They were something to see, they would go by and especially in the dark when they were all lit up, they were pretty, and I always sat there and imagined I would like to be on one of those boats. Naturally I wanted to be a pilot. So it finally come about and I got my chance at it and well here I am.

Q: What year was it you were born?

A: 18 and 96, November 5th.

Q: You are spanning a century.

A: Well yes I guess I am kind of rounding it out. (laughter)

Q: Fine, well I thank you.

Horace Lyle, June 25, 1957

Question: Can you tell us about your work on the river?

Answer: I was boat crazy. So I came down and asked for a job and I asked and asked and they kept putting me off. Finally they put me on. Gave me a job as a clerk on the *Chilo*. John Douglas was head clerk on her.

Q: How do you spell the name of that boat?

A: C-H-I-L-0, it was named for Chilo, Ohio, right up the river here, you know, 36 miles. Originally she ran from Cincinnati to Chilo. At that time she was making one trip a week to Huntington and one trip through to Pomeroy, and occasionally we would go on up to Charleston. As I say I found out in later years why they put me off so long about giving me a job. First place it was during the war and help was hard to get. The main reason they didn't want to hire me is because I was a city boy, and their experience had been that a city boy won't stay on a boat. He wants to be in town where the lights are at night. But after I got on I guess the country boy came out of me then pretty strong because I got in it and I stayed in it. I was on the various Greene Line boats at that time for a year or two and then I came into the Cincinnati office with Jim Wirthlin who was their agent at the old Greene Line wharfboat at the foot of Sycamore Street at that time. I was kind of his leg man, I helped him in almost anyway shape and form, including, in those days you didn't mail a lot of the bills, you didn't mail out, you went out and collected them. Now at that time in these bottoms, most of the commission men were in the bottoms. I've often thought about what a little girl up in one of those commission houses told me once at that time, and I think she was right. She said, "Well, you'll never amount to anything as long as you stay in the bottoms." I found that to be true because I've been in them all my life now. I believe she was right.

Q: Well.

A: Well, anyway of course from time to time I did go out in boat service and you will find in the river business, I think almost everyone agrees, that just like in railroading all the activity and excitement and all the of interest happen out in train service. Nothing happens around the freight house or station of too much interest. Although occasionally it does, and being around a wharfboat, of course you see all the boats, too. That's one thing and you get acquainted with all the people, particularly the characters. I think historically it has been my experience at least that the most people rather than being interested in the plain facts are more interested in these little, so called characters, and we had plenty of them. I don't know of a business that has any more. I supposed many businesses do.

Q: Well, you came on the wharf in 1918.

A: Well, I went on the boat in 1918, I came here on the wharfboat with Jim Wirthlin in 1919. Worked there a year or two, and then I at that time at the close of World War I, the Wheeling Steel Corporation, in Wheeling, started a line of packet boats between Pittsburgh and Cincinnati. There hadn't been any packet boats, that is the boat, of course, that carries freight and passengers on the boat itself. There hadn't been one since about 1911 or 1912, I believe, and they did this and I was their agent at Cincinnati, and from that time on until 1933, 1933 was the last year there were any Pittsburgh boats. When you said you talked to Fred Hornbrook, he was in on that, too. We had the little *Ouachita* running here at that time. That was the last season we had any Pittsburgh to Cincinnati service. But for those years I was agent for the Pittsburgh and Cincinnati boats and of course occasionally I was out on the boats for short stretches at a time when they were little bit short or something of that kind. But after 1933 I came back to the Greene Line and their wharf boat here, the one that was here at that time and rated bills for a while and that sort of thing until 1939.

At that time Union Barge Lines started a merchandise division with cargo box barges, which would be a substitute for the packet boat, in which they took package freight on them instead of barge lots, and they would drop a covered barge off at the Cincinnati wharfboat, right here, to be loaded with merchandise freight for one of their regular tows going south and another towboat coming up would pick it up. Well, there was considerable delay in that and there is a rule merchandise is in much more of a hurry than the barge lots are. Although there is still a saying there. Well, it was working out rather successfully, but just about that time World War II came along, and they needed those barges very badly for barge lot service, and they discontinued that. So then I came back to the Greene Line again, and since that time I have been at the Greene Line. I was on the *Gordon Greene* in the season 1941 and 1942 as kind of a general utility man, and then I came in the office as the passenger agent to take care of the bookings of the people. On the *Gordon* we carried passengers only. We had two freight boats Cincinnati and Louisville, the *Tom Greene* and the *Chris Greene*. But the *Gordon Greene* was strictly a passenger boat. I continued in that until Tom Greene died in 1950. And then there were quite a number of deaths around here.

In the first place, you probably have someplace in your records that Mrs. Greene, Tom's mother, died in 1949, in April I believe it was. He died the following July, just a little over a year later. Things were in kind of an uproar then, there were really none of the actual Greenes alive. Tom's widow was trying her best, she had four young children at that time who are now, of course considerably older, two of them married. Mr. Kramer who had been secretary-treasurer of the company died in 1952, and by that time I had been around long enough that the company elected me as the secretary and treasurer of the company, an officer of the company, and I bought a little of the stock, which was not required particularly, but I felt that in that position I should have it. So since that time, of course, Mrs. Greene has caught on and getting better all the time at management, and she is the general manager, and I'm supposed to be

John Knoepfle

her assistant. Because many times as she says, and it is true, when you are dealing with men, men would prefer to talk to a man. There are many things they will talk to a man about concerning business that they hesitate to talk to a woman about. When it comes down to it, though, she has the final say. So, there is no question about that. So that is just about the background and having been mainly on the shore all this time, of course, I have seen many of them come and go. Some of them have gone to other and better things and some of them have died. Of course many of them that I knew to start with were quite old men then, and gone long ago and some of those are in the category that I was speaking of before they were really characters.

Q: Could you mention a few of those old men?

A: Yes we had, this one that I remember, his name was Kiger Dunaway, some of the names were rather fantastic too. He was, well he was the ship's carpenter. No, I'll tell you who I was thinking of that was telling about this radio business. His name was Sam Kanard, and he was from Williamstown, West Virginia, which is directly across the river from Marietta. Radios were new in the early 1920s and this old man was standing watch as engineer and he thought they were calling watch at the wrong time. They were calling it too early so he asked the pilot on the boat when they came to, were sitting down at the supper table. He was grumbling. He said, "They are calling these watches too early, what time you got, Bill?" Bill said, "Well, I got just six o'clock by my watch." He said, "Well, is that right?" And Bill said, "Yes, I just set it by the radio up in the pilothouse." Sard said, "Well that is just a cheap radio, maybe it ain't right." We had, I remember, speaking of Marietta too, across from Williamstown no, that wasn't at Marietta, that was up at Hannibal I believe, there was a fellow named Jake Mackentanz. He was an old country boy, owned a little wharfboat there, or at least was the agent there. Of course, when they put freight off, the clerk on the boat would have bills, and they generally gave the wharfboat man a little manifest showing the freight that was on the boat that he was to get. Then when they would get through they would ask him does he check out the same as they do in case they had forgotten to put something off or in case he has got something that didn't belong to him.

And this tale was told about him. It's probably not true, but it makes a good story anyway. It could have happened, knowing him. One time they had a couple of these little burros you know, little jacks to put off, and they put them off and tied them there and got all through, and asked Jake how he checked out. He says, I'm short two bureaus and over two jackasses. So that sounds like one of those stories though that may or may not be true. But there were quite a number of instances of that kind. I was trying to think about, oh yes there was Uncle Billie Cuppy, he was an old engineer and he had a sears Roebuck watch he was very proud of. He said it kept perfect time and he'd had it for about 25 years. So when you got the true story of that watch, he had bought it from Sears Roebuck, and in about a year or two the works went kind of bad, and he took it to the jewelers and they put a new set of works in it, and then in another year or two the case got all scuffed up and he took it to the jewelers, and put a new case on it. But to him that was still the same old Sears Roebuck watch. It kept such perfect time.

Q: Well let's harken back a little to those Pittsburgh Cincinnati boats. Do you know any other boats in the run ran besides the *Ouachita*?

A: Oh yes, in fact in those days we had the *General Wood*, the *General Crowder*, and we had the *Betsy Ann*. These boats didn't all run at the same time. They ran at various times. To start with, this Liberty Transit Company I spoke of in the beginning operated the *General Wood*, and the *Betsy Ann*. They finally quit and somebody took over the *General Wood*. Did I mention the *General Crowder*? The *General Crowder* was sold down south, and they took her down to Canulette's at New Orleans and while she was down there in the ways, they were going to run her down south there someplace, and she burned up. Anyway they had the *General Wood*, and then *Betsy Ann* came originally from down around Natchez. They bought her and brought her up here. Fred Way operated her and Bill Pollock operated the *General Wood*, although they ran together, that is they worked together.

Then there was the *Senator Cordill*. She originally ran Pittsburgh to Charleston, but she ran Pittsburgh to Cincinnati. Then in the later days we had the *Queen City*. The *Queen City* ended her days, finally after this all played out the *Queen City*, well, she was partly dismantled, and became the wharfboat at Pittsburgh. And Howard Morris generated her there. That was about the last, well then we got the *Ouachita* from down from Captain Prince down at Natchez, and she operated here one summer, very economical operating boat. As long as we had a few people to carry on her she could make it but she was such a small boat you couldn't get enough freight on her to make expenses in winter. So at that time there was company here in Cincinnati called the Ohio River Transit Company, was operating between Cincinnati and Louisville. Actually in opposition to the Greene Line, which was also operating Louisville and Cincinnati. They bought the *Ouachita*.

They run connection with their two boats, which were rather old boats. One of them had been a ferry boat at Louisville. I can't remember their names now. Let's see, they used the *Watterson*, which had been a ferry boat at Louisville as their Louisville wharfboat. Oh, *Froman Coots* was the name of one of their boats. The other one the Greene Line boat later and I can't think what they called her, I mean before she came here. I believe it was either the *Cary Bird* or the I don't remember her name now anyway. Well of course the very last boat to actually run to Pittsburgh was the *Gordan Greene*. She ran up there a season or two after the, I said that was the end of the Pittsburgh to Cincinnati boats, but it wasn't actually. The Greene Line in summertime, when they first got the *Gordon*, I think that was about 1937, they ran from Pittsburgh to Cincinnati, carried freight and passengers. But they didn't run there over one or two seasons and it just didn't work out. First place there is some difficult navigation up there for a packet boat, so many locks and dams and in that there's so many delays. That was before the days of radar, and from Pittsburgh to Wheeling it is 60 miles by highway or rail but it is 90 miles by river and that is a stretch of river where you have a great deal of both smoke and fog, very difficult navigation. So they found it was better to run the Gordon down in more of her home trade here. Of course, they ran from Cincinnati to Charleston and New Martinsville for quite a while there and in later years the *Gordon Greene* in her last two years, she ran from St. Louis to St. Paul in the summertime. That was after we had the *Delta Queen*. The *Delta Queen*, one of the reasons we don't run her to Charleston and New Martinsville is the best reason you can find, that is she can't go through the locks in the Kanawha River because they are too small for her. I forget her dimensions but she's too wide to go in them.

Q: Well, supposing we hold here and give you a chance to light up that cigarette. Now we are going to talk about the business at the wharf here in Cincinnati.

A: Well of course business in those days was much simpler than it is today. I used to kid a good bit about, I just used the old nail keg method. That all the money that came in you put it in the nail keg, and when you paid bills you took it out, but you didn't have any further records. Naturally that wasn't strictly true. But I do remember that when we made freight bills, we didn't do it like anyone would do it today, even the simplest of business would do today. You put down the weight rate and the extension, as they call it, in other words what it is, how much it weighs, so much per 100 pounds and extend it out to the proper amount. We just put down so many packages of so and so, even merchandise, and just so much money. Particularly in those days they moved a great deal of household goods, and they would just go down and look at it and look it over. And a good clerk would say well that moving is worth about, they called it a moving, you know, that moving is about worth ten dollars or that one is worth about five dollars. They would judge it by the size of the pile of household goods, and somewhat by the quality, too. If they saw somebody had some pretty good stuff they'd pay a little more, which is proper in its way because freight weights are really made not only on the basis of weight, but on the value because the party in possession is liable for loss and damage there.

Another thing you were speaking of the way they organized the handling of the freight. On the boats themselves they had the roustabouts and that was more organized than you would think. They weren't all roustabouts, the head roustabout was called a deckhand. He was the boss of the roustabouts, and sort of a colored foreman under the mate. The mate was the actual boss of the roustabouts. The roustabout would work under way, they got paid by the day, at that time about a dollar a day. Of course, they fed them in a tin pan on deck and they slept wherever they could on the freight, under the boilers in wintertime and that sort of thing. Then when they got into town, they'd generally pay off as they were into town, and frequently they would start their crap game and one man generally went up the hill with all the money. Naturally they didn't get high caliber men in those jobs. In the town itself it was customary to have labor, which got paid by the hour, and these various gangs of laborers, they didn't exactly have foremen, but there would be one man and he would have his gang of say six and another man his gang of six. You didn't have to pay them off individually. When they would go to pay them off, whatever they were making would vary. I remember during World War I it got to be 60 cents an hour and they thought that was terrific. Going to break everybody up, but whatever the amount was, there was a man say he had six men, they would just give him in the smallest amount of currency possible, the full amount for all of them. Then he would go with his six up to the saloon right here at the corner of Front and Sycamore, and go in the saloon and get the change. Of course, probably leave a good bit of it there, or all of it.

Q: What was the name of that saloon?

A: I don't remember, it wasn't the Silver Moon, that had quite a reputation and was talked about quite a bit. The Silver Moon was on Front Street between Broadway and Sycamore. But there was one right on the northwest corner of Front and Sycamore and I don't know the name of it. The saloon that most of the white men went to was Charlie Naegelen's, which was up at Pearl and Sycamore and only recently has been torn down to make way for a new expressway. Then after he died, a son-in-law took it over and rivermen still went in there quite a bit. In fact, he had pictures of boats around on the walls. He even had schedules of the *Delta Queen* in there. I don't think we ever got any customer from there, but they had the schedule in there anyway. And then after the son-in-law was gone they were under new management, and they called it the Old Time Café. That was where most of the white crew would stop in, the clerks and the pilots and the mates and all the white folks on the boat. That was their saloon.

Q: Maybe you can go back a little on the wharf and tell us a little more about the appearance and change in the landing.

A: This landing as they know it today was paved in 1920 and previous to that time was simply, it wasn't cobblestone, but it was stones that were just put in, well, it looked like hit or miss. I suppose originally it was fairly good paving, but it was full of very deep chuckholes, and back in 1918 up to 1920 as I knew it then, we had a great many horse drawn drays and that sort of equipment at that time. In fact, trucks were just beginning to come into their own. But occasionally a truck would come down and they would break springs. I used to say if I owned one I wouldn't send them down to the river with freight regardless of the amount of savings in shipping by river because it was so hard on the equipment. But of course, in 1920 the levee was paved and today it's just as good as any street in town. When the levee was paved if you will notice out there they put ringbolts in there, they call that places to fasten or tie to. That was on the old levee too, they had those to tie up to.

Q: Did they have more then?

A: No there were no more, they were just like they are now, just scattered here and there. They're in somewhat regular pattern. Then as far as the business details were concerned, the clerks on wharfboat received the freight that was brought in. The man would come upstairs and pay the cashier, generally there was one man who was both the cashier, the agent and the whole fact totem. Then go down and get his freight and sign for it. The people coming down would bring the bills of lading down and the clerk would sign for the freight, and then the labor would put it on the boat. Of course, the mate superintended the loading of the boat and they were loaded somewhat roughly in station order. So that the first stop you come to the freight would be accessible. That would be the one that would be loaded out where you could get at it first, you know. Outside of that I can't think of anything else. It was not exactly primitive for that day and age, it worked quite adequately. There was no necessity in having any accounting machines or making out typewritten bills or anything of that kind. It was a very simple process. Just like when you'd go to the general store in those days, and get some coffee, and have the man grind it, and pay him for it and walk out.

Q: I'd say that was business by the word I suppose.

A: Yes, a great deal.

Q: You knew that Captain Hornbrook said that he never paid a dollar down on a boat when they were transferred, you know.

A: Yes, a great many of those transactions were simply by word of mouth, no contract drawn up. Captain Greene was known for his integrity, and he could get a loan at the bank on his word, for that manner. If he would tell somebody to build a boat, now there was another thing, today we've often discussed that talking to Tom Greene. They built one of those modern towboats, and this sometime ago, and they said that the amount of money that her plans, the blueprints, the drawings of the plans to draw this boat, I forget the amount of money it was, but I believe it was around $10,000 and they said that was just exactly what it cost to build the *Greenwood*. The way they would do it in those days, there were ship carpenters. There were several places that built boats one time right here in Cincinnati up the Cincinnati Marine way. But frequently the only plans were in the ship carpenters head. They would lay a keel, and they knew just how to go about it, and they knew how to lay the strakes, and the various parts of the wooden hull. Everything was wood of course in those days. Then when they got up to the cabin there was more or less a set plan to follow there. There could be some variations in it, but not too much. It was a very simple task, I don't know now a days maybe you would draw plans if you were going to build a woodshed in the backyard. But this was just like you were going to build some little woodshed or something of that kind and you just have an idea in your mind of what you were going to do, and get yourself the right amount of lumber and just build it, that's all. That's the way they built boats in those days.

Q: I guess there are none of those carpenters around now?

A: I believe that we have one of the last, and he died here just not over two months ago. His name was Henry Stull and he lived up in Dayton, Kentucky for a while, but he had moved down here to Hebron, Kentucky at the time of this death. He was in pretty good health, just a little past 72, and in fact he had been working in his garden that very day. Took a pain and went to the hospital and he died of a heart attack, I presume. Most of them are pretty hardy fellows. There is one too, Bill Horn who is retired, he lives down around Beattyville, Kentucky now. That's where he came from to start with. He was carpenter on the old *Island Queen* for many years. A good ship's carpenter could build a steamboat's sternwheel just by rule of thumb. They didn't need to do too much consulting of plans. They knew of course what dimensions it should be, they knew the thickness that the plank should be, and what the length should be. They had all that in their head and they didn't have to go consult a blueprint, then go and make a piece.

Another thing I have seen so many ship carpenters use is a very dangerous tool in the hands of a novice. I've often wondered how you learn to use it without cutting your foot off, and that's what they call an adz. That's like a very sharp hatchet you stand straddle of it, and you chip towards you with it and in particular hewing out large sticks of timber, there is certain things that you hew on there that you always have to use that tool rather than any other. That was a very common tool for ships' carpenter to use. As I say very dangerous in the hands of a novice; that thing could slip and cut your foot terribly bad. I suspect it has been done, for that matter. A good ships' carpenter could just do pretty near anything of that kind and without following any particular plans except for what he carried right in his own head. There are very few today that could go ahead and build a ships' sternwheel, particularly that, from scratch. Now they could, this on the *Avalon* this last winter, I know Ernie Wagner over there, with some help, helped rebuild the wheel, but the way he did that he would take one piece off that was rotted or something of that kind and make another piece just like it to put on. In other words, he could follow the pattern that way, but if he had to start with nothing ahead of him, I don't know whether he could have built it or not.

Q: Didn't even know what the parts were?

A: That's right, and they all had names. There were the wheel arms, of course, they're the part that go out from the shaft. The shaft was what would be the axle on an ordinary wheel. The spokes they'd go out from that, are called the wheel arms. Then there are keys, which go between the spokes. They call those wheel keys, and the last one down in where the spokes come in close together they call it a cocked hat because it had that appearance. Those U bolts that go

John Knoepfle

through the bucket planks, we call those bucket planks there the paddlewheel part, that is called a bucket. The U bolts that go through there and are bolted on the other side are called stirrups. They have somewhat the appearance of a jockey's stirrup or something of that kind. As I say they all have their technical names, and I imagine quite a number of those names with the passing of the sternwheels are going to be lost. Well there will be no sternwheel boats built, for that matter. Everything is propeller. And furthermore, I believe that a steamboat, almost now is the case, but within the next two or three years, a steamboat is going to be a museum piece, just like a steam locomotive. A steam locomotive is getting to be a museum piece now. Everything is diesel. Well that's the way on the river, in the first place, diesel operation is very much more economical. In our particular case with the *Delta Queen*, it wouldn't be because it would cost so terribly much to convert her to start with, and another thing in our particular case, that sternwheel has a fascination for people and is really a drawing card. Something that brings people to it. Of course, it's called by various misnomers they call her paddle wheelers, and many people confuse the sidewheeler with a sternwheeler. They for some reason, they seem to think that everything that is a sternwheel was built about 1840 or maybe just after the War between the states or something of that kind. Where a lot of them are modern and up to date of course they are not old at all. Another confusion that you have probably run into in talking to people is that many people particularly in the east, and I would say particularly since *Edna*, Ferber's "Showboat," confuse a packet boat or an excursion boat, with a showboat. They are of the opinion that a showboat is self-powered, which has never been the case.

A: There is none left now except the one over in St. Louis that the Menke brothers operate and which never leaves St. Louis. Then this one Hiram College has, you know, this fellow at Point Pleasant has got, I forget what he calls it. *Majestic* I believe. It still goes around a little.

Q: I notice speaking of sternwheels, there is one out there on the river now isn't there?

A: That's not a steamboat. That's a gas boat there, but it is a sternwheel. That's a derrick boat or something of that kind over there. I don't know who that belongs to or what it's doing over there. Frequently Ashland Oil ties in tows there while they take a barge load of oil up the Licking River. They have a refinery up at Latonia, you know. They take one barge at a time up in there.

Q: Speaking of those carpenters, there must have quite a lumber industry around here.

A: Well I don't think so much around here as up in those smaller country towns. That's where you got most of that. Yet there was a lot of lumber industry in Cincinnati for that matter. It used to be a big lumber town, much more than it is now, although there is still quite a few lumber companies around Cincinnati. I can remember too, there used to be a great call for what they called tobacco hoops. They were big hoops that they put around hogsheads of tobacco and up here around Buena Vista, which is about 18 miles this side of Portsmouth, just above Vanceburg. We used to go in there, we'd just get roll after roll or bundle after bundle of these tobacco hoops. They cut the timber out back in there. See up in that country, well about where that Roosevelt Game Preserve is now, that was great lumber country. And up at Rome, Stout Post Office, they always called it Rome, that's up above Manchester a few miles, back in there around Wamsley and Blue creek there was a great deal of timber, second growth timber, I imagine. We used to pick up an awful lot of tobacco hoops up in there. That seemed to be the thing that was prevalent there. I don't know what that would be made from, something that would bend, but probably from poplar.

Q: The country went west on barrels I think.

A: Oh yes. You were speaking about the various chants and so forth that these roustabouts used. I don't think they were quite as prevalent as they are said to be in story or song. Although they did, you would hear them, say really kind of sing song stuff, not much of a rhyme, but I have heard them use the expressions, such as, "Come up to me, stick you head out along, tell me what shoulder you want it on." That's when they would be coming up, one fellow would maybe put it on one shoulder, and one on the other, they carried a great deal of weight on their shoulders. Then another thing they would sing song stuff a good bit like when they would load freight on him, they'd say, "Now take it in and talk about Ironton. Come in and take it in, and talk about Huntington." Or they had some naturals too, they always called Louisville, Louisyville, and for some reason, I know Cincinnati is not proud of it and you seldom hear it any place else, but all the roustabouts always did call Cincinnati, Ragtown. Why it was called Ragtown I have often myself wondered and tried to trace it down. There's two things, one thing I do know that in the old days a great deal of paper and rags came into Cincinnati from various points. The paper frequently went out here to Container Corporation, and the rags frequently went to Philip Carey, which they used in the making of roofing and that sort of thing.

Another thing I heard from other sources, a man moved down here from Chicago told me about up there, he said, "Oh you go down to Cincinnati, that Old Ragtown," and they claim it was just the opposite of what you would think. In other words like you call a real tall fellow you call him Shorty. They say that Cincinnati was quite intolerant of any vagrants of any kind. So anybody that was raggy had better get out because they wouldn't put up with them, they had better get out before sundown. So just the reverse of what they say they called Cincinnati Ragtown. But I don't know that would be the true thing or not. Roustabouts always did call it Ragtown, and it's known that way not only on the Ohio River but clear on down the Mississippi. Because in recent years I've been down that way much more than I have here on the Ohio. It's known clear down at New Orleans as Ragtown. I don't know of any towns that have a nickname of that kind. I imagine some of them have, and I don't know about it. I can't think of any particular chant that they would get to singing, sometimes

John Knoepfle

a particular item or a lot of freight handling, they would begin to sing a little chant about that particular item. For example up here, years and years ago you used to carry lots of apples in barrels. They came from the country up between Gallipolis and Huntington, and you could load apples up there just apples, apples. Apples came to all these commission houses in Cincinnati. Maybe some rousters would start singing about those apples, and how they made him tired and this and that and the other. But I honestly can't recall what words they used. They were actually made up on the spur of the minute and I think that is what you would call now that they have imported from the West Indies, Calypso.

Actually, what it is would be a similar thing. Whatever was going at the moment they would make up some little chant about it. It didn't necessarily rhyme, but of course a roustabout did have a peculiar step and swing when he was carrying freight. They called that coon jining and that's been described a number of places. It's a peculiar walk and what it is, as you go out on a plank or a board it will frequently spring under you, you know, and it will throw you. If you get in the right rhythm with it. So they had a somewhat of a staggering walk. It's kind of a swinging walk that they counteracts that swing. They could walk that without it springing them off and away. I'd say that came from that book he told how the coon jining started. One particular colored fellow anyway, the rest of them were going out on the plank, the regular stage had a plank, you know, and they get to going, and it would throw them off, and one of them had this staggering walk and the mate watched him and told him said, "Jin that coon," so they got that coon jin from that, they say. Now I tell you who has that, it isn't Horace Kane, who's the fellow that wrote "Ole Man River?"
Q: Billy Bryant.
A: No, no, Bill Bryant wrote the "Children of Ol' Man River." No this fellow was from down south, in fact, he wrote John Henry, not John Henry "The C & O Man was a Steel Driving Man," but this John Henry was a roustabout. That was in that particular book. I can't think who wrote that, it wasn't Horace Kane, it's the same fellow that wrote the one they made the play from. *Old Man Adam and His Children* was the name of the book, and the play was where the colored folk went to heaven, and had the fish fry and all that sort of thing.
Q: An Irish name, I don't remember now. Now let's go back to the wharfboat men.
A: We had some on the wharfboat that I guess the reason they were on the wharfboat, they didn't have sense to steamboat. Anyway some of them were quite characters and some of them were quite intelligent. I don't know whether quaint is the proper term for them are not. I doubt it. But they were original to say the least. Some of them were surprising well informed. This Bill Bedilion was one that was Fred Hornbrook's brother-in-law incidentally. Bill was a fellow that was crazy about Bobbie Burns, and if you start almost any subject he could turn it to Bobbie Burns, and he would be quoting "Tam-O-Shanter," to you, the whole thing, and you couldn't stop him when he got started on it

either. He would always get the subject around to that. He had some pretty good original sayings of his own. One thing he said, "There are three things that are just a damn nuisance except when you need them, that's a lantern, an umbrella, and a woman." He had several things, and that's the only one I can recall at the moment. He had quite a number of sayings of that kind. It may not of been original. If they weren't original, they were at least new to most of us who heard them. He would come up with some pretty good stuff every once in a while.

Then around these wharfboats, we had one here on the old Louisville and Cincinnati wharfboat that was really a character. He was an old time hard-boiled mate. Oh, I want to tell you about another mate down, Pappy Lou Brown, around Memphis too, before I get through. But anyway this Dutch Henry this was, Henry Schmidt lived over in Dayton, Kentucky and he talked with quite a broken German accent. He would come up with stuff just innocently funny. Everything with him was, "by God, by God," he put that right in the middle of everything. One thing tickled me once, we had down here at Patriot, Indiana there was a lady owned a drugstore on the wharf there. She sent up to the Cincinnati Wharfboat, wanted some watermelons. We cut the watermelons in here, and ate watermelons and put the rinds, in those days they had great big old potbellied stoves out in the middle of the office. They put the rinds there, we had seeds on the floor and I don't know what. Dutch Henry came that night and looked around and he said, "Looks like a by God smell." (chuckles) He was peculiar, he was very hardboiled. On the other hand, he was crazy about animals and cats. He kept the wharfboat full of cats and it was a good thing because with cats around a wharfboat you didn't see any rats. Rats won't stay around where cats are. You know he would start over the levee at night all those cats would up the hill to meet him. The reason was that he would always stop in the butcher shop and had cat meat and they knew they were going to be fed. He fed them regardless of the fact that they said a well fed cat won't bother rats. But there wasn't many rats around the old wooden wharfboat when he was there.

Q: They were usually a bother weren't they?

A: Yes. Oh, I want to tell you about this Pappy Lou Brown. He was quite a character. I've heard of him but never saw him. He was a Memphis mate and an awfully hardboiled one. These various pilots that are down there today ran with him, but many of those men are older men now. Pappy Lou only had one arm and he was very proud when he got off the boat. He dressed in a silk shirt and that sort of thing. One they tell of him, in Vicksburg he had a high yeller girl, so he went down and he bought a half dozen silk shirts and he had this gal slip off the sleeve, you know, because he had one arm. He came down and opened them up and she'd cut off the wrong sleeve and he said, "God damn I'll kill that N word slept on Pappy Lou's arm all last night and didn't know, which arm it was." Oh I guess he must have been quite a character, awfully hard, awfully hard. They had a strike of the rousters, even in those days, one time down at Memphis. Oh I think they had been getting $1.00 a day and they wanted

John Knoepfle

$1.50 a day. So he went up and he got the ringleader of the gang and he said, "Now, I'll tell you what." He said, "I'm going to make you kind of my foreman. I'm going to give you $2.00 a day and get the rest of these back down here at a $1.00 a day. You are going to be Pappy's right hand man." They got it settled and this fellow came down and he was getting $2.00 a day and he was Pappy Lou's right hand man. Well, he began getting tougher and tougher on Pappy Lou's right hand man. He made it so tough on him that finally, they called up and they had a great big box of, I believe it was bacon or something, it weighed 500 or 600 pounds. He had four men raise it and said, "Now come here Pappy Lou's right hand man," he said, "Put it on his back," and they put it on and just flattened him out. Killed him deader than a mackerel. This was in the old days and he was hard. They were going down the river, and he just pushed him over and kicked him the river and said, "Well, there goes Pappy Lou's right hand man." He says, "Which one of you other boys wants to be Pappy Lou's right hand man now?" They tell that on him, but it could of been true, may of been a little exaggeration in there. He was hard and it wasn't unusual for a white mate to kill colored people at all. They didn't think of it, down south in particular. Of course they got the very lowest of ones, they couldn't even pick cotton I suspect.

Q: I heard that the mates were very colorful.

A: The mates were always very colorful characters. In fact, I would say that they had more of what you call color about them, and I don't mean colored, but color, than any of the other licensed men. There was more occasion of them to have because they were actually the foreman of the roustabouts or the colored crew. A good many of them, there was Walter Lanham, he had a handlebar mustache. I suppose the colored folk could understand, but he cut or clipped his words off very short. He said, "Roll barl, roll barl," instead of saying, barrel, it would be roll barl. He would say le-i-com, le-i-com.

Q: What is that you were just saying?

A: Let it come, let it come. They'd clip their words off, and they were always in a hurry. We had some of them, I don't know how they got a license, but there was one of them around here who couldn't read or write, and we had a good deal of business from Belknap Hardware in Louisville, and of course you would have a big Belknap on there. He could recognize that as being from Belknap, and they'd come in with a great big carton, one time he had had lamp chimneys in it, and he said, "What you got there?" He looked at it and said, "Oh, hardware, throw it down." They threw it down all right, there was glass tinkling all over the place. "Hardware, throw it down!" It was from Belknap. But that fellow too, he came from up here at Chilo. I'm trying to think of his name, I know it quite well. Maybe I had better not mention his name because he was a little bit on the ignorant side, although he's dead now. He used to have a number of wives. Somebody had told him as long as you married them in a different county you didn't have to bother about getting divorced from the one before.

He had three or four that I knew about and they were pretty nice country girls. Dennis Taylor, that was his name. Denny Taylor, he came up from around Manchester someplace.

We had some of these wharfboat men, as I say, there was up at Manchester, he was a Holy Roller preacher on the side. Uncle John Shelton, and later he went on to Ironton. There was one from the upper end, even in later years, he had a long beard that came about to his waist. Real tall thin old man, can't remember his name now, he came from up around Bellaire someplace. Alex Shaw, I think I mentioned him, he was the one when we would get tied up in the fog he would say, "Well, we might as well be here as where we are at." He used to have some expressions probably considered corny now a days, he would say, "Well, we will soon be in sky-hoppity-doodle-burg," and oh things of that nature. For a mate he was rather a jovial fellow, most of them were pretty sour. At least the clerk would think so, because they used to say they would try to run over a clerk. Actually a mate was frequently judged, particularly in town, where labor was paid by the hour, the faster he could get the freight on the boat and the faster he could get it off why, of course the less the expense was and a better showing he would make. He unloaded the boat of so much freight in such and such a price. They wouldn't consider the fact but you make mistakes and not let the clerk sort that, and you could lose stuff that way that finally would cost far more than the actual saving in labor of handling it. Of course that wasn't their department, their department was to save money.

Q: I guess they weren't too gentle with it, either.

A: No, no, they would run over you whether you would check it or not. Some of them would unless you would just make them wait on you, which was sometimes pretty hard to do. You had to get orders from headquarters to do that sometimes, and then they would be champing at the bit because it made it that much longer unloading the boat and that made it cost that much more, and then they would be liable to be called on the carpet, saying that the cost was so much to unload the boat. They'd say, "Well, that clerk held me up. I had to wait until he could read the marks on it and get it sorted out right." I don't know of anything else I can think of right at the moment of too much importance.

Q: There's a lot of details that I wouldn't have known.

A: I suppose a great many of these men will never go down in history, they will be anonymous at least, and their names will be forgotten, but in their day and age they were probably known from one end of the river to the other. Just as this Pappy Lou Brown that I was speaking of was known at the time and his name is probably lost to history. And quite a few others the same way. There was an old man, possible you have heard of him, from Manchester. The name was Pres Ellison, J. Preston Ellison. Did you know him? He lived to be past 90 I think. He was clerk on the Greene Line boats for years and years. Head clerk and he was quite a character. He was a single man until he was about 75 or 80,

John Knoepfle

and then he got married. I don't know what he did in later years. I presume nothing at that age.

Q: The Ellisons must have been a big river family.

A: Yes, he was of the same Ellison family. The Nolls around Marietta too were quite river people. In fact, I think Fred Hornbrook was in business with Mark Noll at one time. Years ago when the old, old Louisville and Cincinnati Packet Company quit business after the 1917 ice, that was when Captain Laidley had the Louisville and Cincinnati Packet Company. Probably there is a great deal on him. But this new outfit came in and there was Captain Noll and Captain Billie Rowe. This Captain Noll was quite a sage, I would say. He had some excellent advice, particularly for a young fellow. He used to advise us around here. Of course, that was before the days of Social Security, and he used to say, "Now you boys watch and see that you are not one of the 99." He says, "You know what that is, don't you?" He says, "At the age of 65 there is only one person in 100 that is not dependent upon on somebody else." He says, "Children or relatives or somebody." So of course, Social Security has kind of killed that advice. For that matter, but he had had quite a bit of experience in his time. He was a man who had went bankrupt when he was 50 years old, and came back and made more money than he had ever made before. One time he owned the ferry boat at Marietta. When they built the bridge at Marietta over to Williamstown, in some way in that building, of course, they got stock in the bridge for their ferry stock, and made an amicable settlement on that. But he talked one time about them at Marietta. He said they were talking about building a glass factory, and he said some promoter came in and got me and two three other old codgers, and he said we went out in the field, and he said he looked up and said, "Wonder which way the wind blows here?" We said, "We didn't know what way the wind was blowing with the glass factory at that time." After he left town we found which way the wind was blowing. We lost our money. (chuckles) He used to tell that on himself.

Q: Was he a relative of Hod Knolls?

A: No, this was N-O-L-L. Orville Noll was a nephew, and he in later years had a wharfboat at New Martinsville, and before that he had owned a little excursion boat in Pittsburgh called the *Verne Swain*.

Q: Was this Orville or . . .

A: Orville! Orville was a character. He would knowingly steal from you and brag about it. He told Bill Pollock when he had the *General Wood* in Pittsburgh one winter and Orville had the Pittsburgh wharfboat, Bill told me he said, "I took the typewriter over and told Orville to use that typewriter this winter while the boat was laid up." I said, "What did you do that for?" He said, "Well, if I had of left it on the boat, Orville would have come over and stolen it. So I figured if I loaned it to him that I would get it back." Which was about true. Orville was pretty good about raising freight bills, by that I mean they would come in with freight charges so much, and he would look over, and think we could get a little more than that on it. And he would just raise the amounts on them, and collect a little more and of course he didn't give that to the boat that was his. He told Fred Hoyt once and it made Hoyt so mad because Hoyt had been so particular to get the right rates on it, and not to overcharge these people to keep the business up. So after the boat laid up there one time he told, he said, "Fred, you were easy picking." Of course, that made Hoyt insanely mad. Hoyt was in with Hornbrook, was a kind of a partner. Hoyt was a clerk for Hornbrooks for quite a while, and I imagine Hornbrook mentioned something about Fred Hoyt. Well he was a character in himself. He's retired now and still living in Marietta. He's quite well informed and quite well educated, mainly self-educated. He has a terrific command of English or as he used to say on the *General Wood*, "We only speak two languages on the *General Wood*, English and profane." He said, "Now over on the *Liberty* they are a little more accomplished than we are." He says, "They speak English, profane and obscene." (chuckles)

Q: Well we are getting pretty close to the end.

A: Yes, I expect I have been going on like a windy Jim about long enough. Probably many of the things that would have been most interesting I've forgotten, temporarily at least.

Q: Maybe we will get together before summer is out and talk some more.

A: All right.

Q: I want to thank you for talking to me.

A: Well that's perfectly all right.

Curtis Marshall, May 20, 1957

Question: Could you give us a few vital statistics on yourself, Mr. Marshall, before we start?

Answer: I was born in April 1883, so I'm 74 years old now and my early school days were in Gallipolis, but afterwards we moved into Hocking County for a few years, which I'll mention in here, then we went back to the river where my father took it up again. I lived here up until 1901. I spent some time in the big machine shop in Hamilton, Ohio and in 1902 I came here. Been here ever since.

Q: What did you do in Columbus then?

A: I make layouts and drawings for traffic lights all over the state.

Q: Traffic lights.

A: Yes, all these traffic lights is my work. I'm the fellow that they cuss. My father, George C. Marshall, was born in North Lewisburg, that's up near Bellefontaine in 1851. He was left without a home when he was about ten years old, that's just the beginning of the Civil War. He and a younger brother, who was just eight years old, and he was ten, they started west. He finally ended up in Terre Haute, Indiana and later on he was on a steamboat on the Wabash. Then on the lower Ohio and still later he was running out of St. Louis. I don't know how many trips he made between St. Louis and Kansas City, not very many, but I think in about 1872 or 1873 he was in Cincinnati where Captain Jonathan Hamilton up on the Ohio River was trying to raise a crew to go down to New Orleans and bring a boat back. So, they got the crew, they traveled by boat to New Orleans and they brought the boat, which was the first screw propeller on the Ohio River, and that is still claimed to be the fastest boat that was ever there. The boat was named the *Wild Gazelle*.

Q: Was that so? I didn't know about that.

A: I don't know how long he was on there, but he was on several other boats, and then he was on the steamer *Telephone*, which was written up in the telephone company's advertising a bit. He was engineer on there, and which that ice cut down in New Year's Day of 1885. He saved a man's life, here in town and never forgot it.

Q: A man here in town.

A: He used to be here, he's been dead quite a number of years. He left the river then, early in 1887, and went back in the mining district. But then we went back to Gallipolis early in 1890. Then he was with Bay Line, there was two brothers George and William Bay of Ironton. They had several boats, one was the *Minnie Bay*, the *Lizzie Bay*, the *Louise*, *Chevalier*, *Henry M. Stanley*, and the *Greyhound*. The *Lizzie Bay* for quite a while was in the what they called the trade between Pittsburgh and Charleston, West Virginia. Came down to Gallipolis and the *Louise* ran opposite from Cincinnati to Charleston. Well, he made several trips on the *Lizzie Bay*, but after it was changed over to the *Louise*, that was the boat he was on the longest. Now there was the biggest line, the best-known line was what they called the Cincinnati and Pittsburgh Packet Line in the early 90s. They had several boats named the *Scotia*, *Keystone State*, *Andes*, *Congo*, *Tacoma*. Now, the *Andes* was known for having the greatest collection of whistles. There was over seven whistles in one. But they was all tuned musically. That whistle now is in the museum down at Marietta. You see their one whistle was probably that big around and stands as high as a barrel. The whole thing was a high as you could reach.

Q: How did they blow it without letting out all their steam?

A: Well, it did take enough to slow them down. The packet boats, that what you call passenger boats, all had their whistles tuned musically. The towboats were not so careful, they had more of a growl or a groan. But the packet boats were all tuned. It was a pleasure listening to them. Later on, there was in the same line between Cincinnati and Pittsburgh was the *Queen City*, the *Virginia*, and the *Iron Queen*. It was quite a competition there with them, which had the nicest boats and the best accommodations. The *Virginia* was all finished in beautiful cherrywood inside just like a piano polished. The *Queen City* everything was just spotless on it. For quite a while, those two had quite a competition who had the best orchestra. People would go down there and listen to the boats just to dance to the orchestra at that time. The *Queen City* had an orchestra of three fellows from back in the mountains of Tennessee. One of them played the large harp, you know the string harp, and the violin and the flute. And you could hear that sometimes over that water for miles.

Q: I wonder who those men were.

A: They were black, I never saw, well at that time it was hard to mix in the blacks and whites, but they were there. Somehow, I don't know where this fellow learned to play that harp from down in the mountains there. You know down close to the water, that sound will travel for miles. Where it wouldn't up on land. And at Gallipolis, the *Queen City* came up to Cincinnati and arrived here on Sunday evening. Oh, sometime between seven and nine o'clock in the evening. Most of the young folks would go down there just to listen to the music. The *Virginia* came down from Pittsburgh on the same evening, but sometimes they would be a few hours apart. Later on, the boats got the sort of a ride idea, they sold what they called a ticket to meet the ride. Paid a quarter for it and got on the first boat and you rode till you met the next one and they would bring you back again. Sometimes, he'd maybe hit 15 or 20 miles each way, sometimes it wouldn't be near that far. Depended on, which one got there first. Now at the time, those packet run from Cincinnati to Pittsburgh, a round trip took one day less than a week. You had part of a day layover in Pittsburgh, and that round trip with all meals, berth and everything, was $14.

Q: That was out of Gallipolis.

A: No, that was out of Cincinnati.

Q: Out of Cincinnati.

John Knoepfle

A: Cincinnati clear to Pittsburgh and back. All the packet boats, there was quite a race, which had the best cooks and the best meals. There were very few hotels I served anything like that. Now the fare from Gallipolis to Cincinnati was 200 miles, and took about two days and one night, and was five meals, that was three dollars. The White Collar boats from Cincinnati were sidewheelers, what we call the White Collar line. Up on the smoke stacks was, great big white bands painted, was their ornament. Most boat lines had some kind of a mark that you could distinguish them for miles. That's what they had. The White Collar Lines were all sidewheelers. While up in the northern part of the river, there was mostly sternwheeler, that's where the wheel is directly behind. There was only two of the White Collar boats that run up north. There was the *Bonanza* and the *Bostona* and they only went as far as Pomeroy. The sidewheelers never seemed to do so much good in the upper Ohio.

Q: Too shallow up there, I guess.

A: It wasn't that, the people just didn't like them, they didn't patronize them very much and they were slower. You see, one thing about a side driven boat, they could go ahead up and back in there, they could turn on a pivot just like that. They didn't make a big circle like a sternwheeler would. But there was another, oh yes, this Cincinnati Packet Line, they had the *Bonanza*, the *Bostona*, the *City of Vevay*, the *City of Louisville, City of Madison, City of Cincinnati*. Most of those ran south from Cincinnati to Louisville and to Cairo. One time, they built a big sidewheeler, a very beautiful boat called the *City of Pittsburgh*, and it came to Pittsburgh. It didn't make more than two or three trips. It was a business failure. After that it was sold to people up in St. Louis. That's the last I heard it was on that river. But in the summertime, when the Ohio River got kind of down, there was little bits of sidewheeler used to run up the small river. Used to say they could run on a heavy dew. (chuckles) The wheels were not even cased in, just sticking outside. It was told about them if they come up to a sandbar these wheels would just crawl over it and get on the other side.

Q: Is that so? Called the batwings?

A: Well, I never heard it called that. They called them guttersnipes because they could run up a gutter. Or, they could run on a heavy dew. That's what they used to sort of slam at them. I know, at one time, when there were several of us boys were out wading and the river was low and one of these boats, called the *Whisper* passed between us and shore. I forget. There was the *Little Sandy* and several of the names I didn't know.

Q: But *Little Sandy* was one of the boats out of the Big Sandy River.

A: Those boats were all flat bottomed and I don't think any of them needed more than a foot of water to float in. But you see, in the Ohio, when it got low and the other boats had to lay up, why these came out and they were the passenger boats there. There were quite a lot of towboats, oh hundreds of them. Many I have forgotten, but there was one they used to call the *Iron Line*, because almost all their names begin with Iron. There was *Ironsides, Iron Age,*

Iron Duke, and *Iron Cliff*. Then there was another, a Brown Line, which had the *Sam Brown*, *Jim Brown* and the *Luella Brown* and a little bit of an old boat they called the *Henry De* Bus. We always remember, it passed here so often. Now the *Tom Dodsworth* was another old boat that, oh it wasn't very nice to look at, wasn't a wonderful boat, but they had the boards and signs off that boat down at the museum at Marietta. Have you ever seen the museum there?

Q: I was there last fall.

A: Did you see a steamboat exhibit?

Q: Yes.

A: Well that to me is very interesting. Then there was another line of towboats out of Kanawha River, was the Marmets, *Otto Marmet* and *Sallie*, and I forget some of the others. Now so many people mispronounce that name they call it Kanowah and everything else but Kanaz is the name they call it down there. Just like Gallipolis, they call it Gallipolis and everything, but Gallipolis is the French pronunciation. There were two giant boats though, towboats, the *Joseph B. Williams* and the *Sprague*. Now that *Sprague* took a cargo of 54,000 tons of coal at one time. That's bigger than any cargo ever crossed the ocean and it covered more space than the statehouse yard up here. Those towboats run about ten feet deep and each one holds from 800 to 1,000 tons to the boat. That *Sprague,* I just read a few days ago, is down at Memphis, Tennessee now. It's anchored there, just sort of living quarters for poor people. Now, in Gallipolis we had quite a, oh a good many of the families that had someone on a steamboat. Hardly a boat passed there wasn't somebody was interested on it.

There was quite a race between the children, particularly among the boys, to learn different boats by the whistles. We could tell over a 150 boats without ever seeing them just from the different tone of the whistle. When a certain boat passed that town during the day, and that boat whistled, why the children, if their father was on that boat, was excused. Always had to get up and fly to the river. Go down there and see dad for maybe for a little while, sometimes maybe an hour or so. The mother would generally take the smaller ones and meet them down there. Of course, that was our only connection, you might say, with the big cities. Now, an odd thing you probably hadn't thought of, and in my days then we never saw an orange or banana, only at Christmas time. There was no refrigeration, no way of keeping them, so our father would go to Cincinnati and bring them back from there, and that's all we ever had.

We recognized many boats by their whistles and there were certain other marks. We could see a boat a mile away and tell what its name was before it got to us. Lots of them had some kind of ornament up between the smokestacks, and others just by the shape of the boat, there was ornaments on there, now the White Collar Line was one of them, and some others has things like that. The cabin, what they called the Texas and the hog chains. The Texas was the place where the crew slept, and the cabins where the passengers slept. Now the hog chains was, they had great big iron braces that held the boat in shape

John Knoepfle

from that twisting and turning, the boat had a bend to it, from bow to stern, and that's what carried the strain from the load. And on that one boat we called the *Kanawha,* that had sort of like leaves all around the top of the smokestacks. Prettiest leaves, cut out like oak leaves. They were made out of metal. I suppose they were great big things. On the Pittsburgh towboats many of them had smokestacks that were hinged, to let them down this way because the bridges were so low. See the bridges were low, and they went under there, and sometimes in high water they would come down with their stacks let down.

Now among the boys, we played a game we called broker merchant. It was based on steamboats. Two boys would get off like they were going to sell a certain boat, they would just give you hints that you would have to guess by. Well, they might have said it had an anchor between its stacks. And if someone happened to know, they would guess what one it was. Or sometimes, they would tell about the hog chains, or the Texas, or the load or things like that. Supposed to govern the sale of, which wasn't no sale, it's just a game we played. Those games we used to play, more or less kept every boat in mind. Now, in the early 90s, hardly a day passed that there wasn't at least five or six packet boats pass here a day.

Towboats now in weather like this, would make a big raise in the river. They'd be towboats passing here 24 a day, for maybe two weeks. One right on the sided of another. Then they would go south to wherever they would end up. When they come back, they'd come back on less water. It was told that time, that they could tow coal from Pittsburgh to Louisville for 18 cents a ton, take the boat back empty. Now there was another lot of boats we called the daylight boats that didn't have accommodations for sleeping in it. Maybe around 35, 40 miles, make it down the river and back in the afternoon or evening. One in particular was called *Capitol City*, that ran from Charleston down to Cincinnati. Another one called the *Columbia*, the *Neva*, the *Claribell*, the *Carrie Brown*. The *Carrie Brown* and the *Klondike*, ran between Huntington and Gallipolis and the *Columbia* ran to Pomeroy and Gallipolis. The *Neva* and the *Claribell*, they went up the Kanawha River, not quite to Charleston.

Q: You know I have never heard the name of many of these boats?

A: Well I say many of them have slipped my mind, but they were just 100 years ago. An odd thing, we was making a trip one time, on a boat going south, and down there at Greenup, Kentucky, what they used to call stop the boat on hail, somebody would run out on the bank and hail this way. They would generally load on some freight, or usually livestock, or things like that. But, this particular time, they had come down field with maybe ten or 12 cattle, one of them was a great big bull, and they let down the stage plank. It would reach as far as the garage out there, and they put the sides on it because when it was those cattle, there was always some kind of excitement, and generally three or four roustabouts get knocked in the river. This time, they loaded on these cattle, but this bull, they only get him to the end of the stage plank. He would throw his head this way and a couple of the roustabouts would fly in the river, and he run back up in the field, I expect at least four or five times he went back and forth before they got him. The last time, they brought him down and the captain just took that big line, about a three inch rope, and slipped it over his horns, and put the other end around the capstan, with the steam power you just dragged him up with his feet skidding this way. (chuckles) So they dragged him on with it. Lots of time on those hail calls, the roustabout would have to go up and take that rope off of the tree or whatever they had it tied to. They didn't wait on him, he took ahold of the end of the rope and the boat started out and dragged him out, and he crawled under the boilers to dry off. Those roustabouts had to sleep among the freight, I don't know how they got a man to work, but they did.

Q: Must have been a pretty hard life out there.

A: It was for those fellows. Otherwise, the crew got along pretty nice. Some of those mates were absolutely brutal, they had these big ox whips, as long as from here to that wall, they would cut those fellows if they didn't move enough. I've seen boats stowed, these ordinary old iron cookstoves, they would only let one man to a stove and two sacks of wheat was an ordinary load. See, that was about 150, 160 pounds. Now, there is a couple of little amusing incidents here that I think would be what I had in mind. This boat they called the *Columbia*, was a small cabin boat and the local band made her to use for a trip, that boat up Pomeroy and back. There was a charge fare, I don't know how much, but then they raised money, that's the way they bought their uniforms and music. As we were going up the river, a storm came up, nobody seemed to know the difference. They got to dancing and having such a good time, nobody heard anything. Well shortly after the storm stopped nobody thought about it, but we was just standing in the cabin, there was a fellow named Joe Anderson, he was quite a joker in the town.

Q: Bill Anderson?

A: Yes, Bill Anderson, I don't know what became of him. But, he was standing back towards the, I guess you know how the boats were made, a cabin run down the middle, the staterooms outside, and then the promenade deck was clear off of that, the only light in the cabin was above like these transoms you see in streetcars, that's all the light, the daylight they had in there. Well this Bill Anderson stood over inside, I happened to look up at the transoms and a pair of girl's legs was hanging down the front of it. Something we never saw in those days, you know nothing like today, like this you could see them swimming. She was sitting, I said, "Look at there, Bill." He said, "My Lord, I have never seen anything like that," he went over to the chair that was generally sitting along the side and he went over there, of course everybody knew him as quite a joker and began watching him, but he wouldn't give it away and he got to fumbling with one of the lights, and shot his hand up and grabbed one of the girls, she let out a shriek, you could hear it echo from West Virginia clear across to Ohio. This broke the light, and somebody started the story that somebody fell overboard. They stopped the boat and they come around and asked who was missing, who was gone, and things like that, and nobody knew. Even turned the boat around, took the searchlight and searched the water for a mile or two. Never found out, but after a shriek we went through the door and I saw a couple come running downstairs, she was a girl I knew in school. But anyway, they never said a thing, nobody said anything. The papers down there carried the story, said there was a mystery who fell overboard. (chuckles)

There was just one other story. I left Cincinnati one time on a boat called the *Avalon;* it's not the *Avalon* that's up at Pittsburgh now. But, I saw one up there a year or so ago. This was an *Avalon,* we left there I suppose five or six o'clock in the evening. It was weather something like this with these thunderstorms coming along. The boat started out there, everybody was having a good time, but among the passengers there was two good size young ladies. I imagine they were 25 or 30 years old and they were husky, wasn't heavy. They had their mother, a little bit of a dried up woman, didn't look like she weighed 100 pounds, and we started north on the river, why everybody began to listen to the music and sitting around talking. We got up there farther when the storm broke, the little woman went into one of these staterooms and shut the thing tight. You couldn't get in there, the girls coaxed to get her out, afraid she'd smother. It was hot in there, you know it was summertime. They couldn't get her out, coaxed and begged and argued, and they finally called the captain, and he coaxed with her for quite a while. But couldn't get any response from her, and finally he was leaning against the door talking, and she opened that little transom with the top of an umbrella, and nearly beat the top of his head off, before (chuckles) he knew what was coming. So, they coaxed and begged and argued and finally he gave orders for the mate to break the door. Well those mates were great big husky fellows, you know big enough to handle it. The mate rushed the door and caved it in and grabbed that woman. She came out of there fighting, clawing and biting and it took those two mates and the captain to hold that one woman. This little bit of a thing, they got her down in a chair, and held her like this, and her heels were going like that, and she was shrieking mad. And we went clear as far as New Richmond, which is about 12:30 in the morning before we got there, and they had to go up and get a doctor to come down and give her an hypodermic. Of course, she was going clear to Charleston. I think that is about what I have here in my notes.

Q: Mr. Marshall is going to describe one of the roustabout songs that he heard and then when he watched them on the gangplank.

A: They usually had a song, there was quite a lot of them, but when they were working, it was more or less in time with what they were doing. One of their songs in particular, when they were carrying loads, was "Oh hard labor, oh oh hard labor, oh oh hard labor makes a man, oh."

Q: That over and over?

A: Over and over and they would keep that going. Another one was "Old John Henry." "Old John Henry, where you been so long," but I have forgotten the rest of that of that one.

Peggy Knoepfle: They used to sing Old John Henry.

A: Yes, that was one of the old river songs.

P: Well did they stomp their feet or anything?

A: No, they just hunched their shoulders, because they generally had a load on their back.

P: Oh I see.

Q: I guess that was to ease the load.

A: Well it was just a matter of doing it in time.

Q: Did they make a kind of shuffle on the plank?

A: Well actually they had to keep going pretty lively and they did their laying down after they got through the load.

Q: The mates really prodded them.

A: Oh yes, and strange to say, the meaner the mate was, the more they wanted to work for him. They thought more of the man that roughed them up once in a while.

Q: Imagine that. What kind of things were shipped in and out of Gallipolis, do you remember that?

A: Well there was lots of stoves.

Q: Stoves, there was a manufacturing plant.

A: Yes, they were made there see, we had five foundries in Gallipolis. In certain times, in the late fall, it was apples. Apples were not put in baskets, only in recent years, they were all barrels. They would get those barrels rolling up there, just one right passed the other, just a continual parade then in the fall, later it was tobacco and livestock. Ever once in a while a farmer would move, why he would load his horse and cow on there and all his household goods. One trip we made, an old man, I guess we was coming up the river, he left somewhere down in Kentucky and he was going up to West Virginia. Well he had to go down ever so often to feed his horses and cows and look after things on it. Then there was an awful lot of baled hay and stuff like that they shipped. That's what the roustabouts usually liked because they crawled up in that baled hay to sleep. All the sleep they got was between towns. They didn't have any time off.

P: Where did the roustabouts come from, down south?

A: No, they were from all along the river. You would be traveling on a boat, and come up to some little town, and some old black mammy would come out and put out her hand, the old man would put the money in it maybe, and the next time there would be a couple more or something like that. They were just strung along, they didn't seem to come from any one place.

Q: They didn't sing when they rolled those barrels, did they?

A: Oh yes, well it just depended on somebody wanted to start or not. Another odd trip, I was speaking about this *Avalon,* The last trip I made up the river with

John Knoepfle

it, the river was low and they had what they called a lighter. It was a barge hung along. They'd load the freight on the barge to keep the boat from getting too deep in the water. I think it was very long after they left Cincinnati, from there clear to Gallipolis there was a crap game. The roustabouts, and when one man would lose out, why some passenger would stake him and he would go back in. It went on for a day and night. I don't think there was very much money in it anyway, but the passengers had as much fun watching the roustabouts.

Well from up the river when they had a flood, a lot of those little streams, people had logs that were branded, and they would wash them out and down the Ohio. If we would catch one and tie it up, why we got 50 cents a log. That was big money in those days. We would tie it up until someday the lumber company would come down and pay us the 50 cents and get them back again.

Q: I guess they would just send agents down to search along the towns for logs.
A: Yes, but most of the time they found somebody because any log that had landed, somebody had it. The others that went on down landed someplace else. But, when you think in that day and that time, I speak about a boy worked 12 hours a day for 50 cents a day. That's my wages for about two or three years. A man's wages for a family he got $1 a day. So, 50 cents for a log was a big day's work.

Q: Indeed. Tell us about swimming the river then.
A: At that time, the early days I speak about, a boy never said he could swim until he had swum a test clear across the Ohio River, which at that time was probably well over a half mile, between a half and three quarters of a mile. When he crossed, a boat would go with them, they could, five or six, make the trial at one time. Just like Indians would. After that, you were a swimmer.

P: How old were they usually when they did this?
A: Oh, sometimes nine, ten, sometimes 12, 15. One little boy that lived up on the hill, he was hardly old enough to go to school, he could paddle that far. They were French people by the name of Blanc.

Q: Well it's a fine beautiful old town. I was through it last summer. I noticed there is kind of an inlet, now maybe it has been dammed or something, but there is considerable body of water moves in.
A: That's where I say we used to learn to paddle before we tried it out on the river. That's what backed that water up. Before that, the creek used to go clear dry in the summertime. But now it makes practically a lake out of it.

Q: A lot of boating in there now.
A: I don't know I haven't been there much, but I imagine slack water would be a nice place for canoes or rowboats.

Q: What was the name of the creek?
A: Chickamauga. It runs, oh it comes out this way pretty well out in Gallia County. Another reason I remember in 1884 flood, which was a biggest they had down there, it practically left the town sticking up on a point of land. My father was on a little boat called the *New Era* that came out in the country this

way, as far as it could, and way out near Kerr station. They hauled food supplies in, the railroad couldn't haul in there because the rails were under water down towards the town. It was a little bit of a boat, I don't know how big it was, I never saw it, I don't remember. She hauled it back there to feed those people.

Q: Back to Kerr Station.

A: Yes, around Kerr station, somewhere in there. That's probably five or six miles this side of Gallipolis, but there is quite a valley out in there.

Q: I guess they remembered the 1880 flood with a vengeance.

A: 1884, they always talk about the 1884 flood, but since that time they had a bigger one. I think it was in 1937, and I think it was bigger than that.

Q: Is that so?

A: Yes.

P: It was changed by the glacier.

A: Yes, the glacier changed it and that's what started the Ohio, the glacier slid that far and the water running around the edge of that big mass is what started the Ohio . . . . (pause in tape).

The Marshall family, the first record we have, was John, was Marshall of Ireland. Originally, they thought the name came from Germany or at least it was on the European continent. But the English after they had conquered Ireland, appointed this man John as Marshall of the Ireland. That's where the name came from. And the English ruled over there for about 400 or 500 years, and in the early 1600s he migrated to Virginia, down near Yorktown. And the old Virginia Marshalls were you might say, the first of the family here. Now John Marshall, the Chief Justice is in direct line of that John Marshall of Ireland. Odd to say some time ago, a lady wrote me, from down in Mississippi that she was trying to trace the line. But most Marshalls just left here and there. They have a hard time connecting the line. We had a mayor here years ago, and he didn't know anything about his family, and like my father left up there when he was about ten years old, and he didn't remember much about his.

P: Your father came from Virginia?

A: No.

P: Your grandfather?

A: Well yes at the time this state was early laid out, over west of here was what they called the Virginia land see, this all belonged to Virginia, seven states were made out of what was Augusta County, Virginia. And they gave these grants of land to any Virginia soldier that served up here in North Lewisburg, because he served one term for himself, and his son was drafted, so he served a term for his son, so he got the two grants of land.

P: That was in the Revolutionary War.

A: Yes and the Marshall name is quite common up through that Miami Valley, clear down to Wilmington, Xenia, Springfield, and Bellefontaine and up that way. But they were more or less all connected from the Virginia line.

John Knoepfle

Q: Now that brings me back. Maybe I can prod another song out of your memories. You've never heard any songs that are older than those 19th century ballads that your father might have known.

A: Of course, back in the old days, the songs that my father used to sing were not necessarily connected with the river.

Q: What songs would they have been?

A: "When You and I Were Young, Maggie" and that goes back 100 years ago.

Q: There was a quite a settlement throughout the state, wasn't there? Worthington, those people were all Virginians.

A: Now the people from southern Ohio, they came through up the Kanawha River Valley. My mother's people were among the first settlers down there, and the first one of her grandfathers, well there was forty Revolutionary soldiers living in Gallipolis in that county in the early 1800s, and Daniel Wigner was one of them, which my mother traces right back to. But those people came down through Old Virginia, and then they followed the Kanawha River down to Ohio here, and in that way they happened to settle in Gallipolis. Of course, their settlement in Gallipolis was after the French had left. But the Welsh people of Jackson County was another story of that. They came overland by teams and over what is now Wheeling, through that way. See this is what we call Route 40, old national road was a buffalo trail, and it was laid out by the buffaloes long before the white man ever got here But the Welsh came over and came down the river and I think that they said that they got caught in a flood some-where and their horses drowned, and they lost everything they had. And what little they had left somebody stole from them, so they started from Gallipolis to walking out, and then they got into Jackson County and said those hills reminded them so much of Wales that they just settled there.

P: What did the Welsh do? Did they have a particular trade?

A: Well, mostly merchants or something like that. Mostly, they were Welsh farmers. But the Welsh are pretty near the leaders in musical awards. There was a group here, we was down in Jackson several times for the Stedvalks Compe-tition, and they don't think anything about a $100,000 for a prize. But their Stedvalks includes everything from little kids up to six and seven years old, recitations and speaking, writing, all school work.

Q: They still do that in Jackson County.

A: Well they sort of wore it out a few years ago, I don't know whether they've started it up again or not. And up in Van Wert County is a lot of them up there. So, practically all these Welsh in and around Columbus came either to Jackson or Van Wert.

Q: Well you've given us some nice things.

Robert McCann, July 27, 1957

Question: We are at the wharfboat of the *Delta Queen*. I am going to talk to Mr. Robert H. McCann who was purser on the *Delta Queen*, and I'll ask him to begin by recounting his river career.

Answer: I started in on the river in 1927, well in a couple of weeks it will be 30 years ago. I started in on the *Betsy Ann* in the Pittsburgh to Cincinnati trade as a clerk. A mud clerk they called us because we were the ones that got out in the mud sometimes. At a bank landing we would get out in the mud to receive freight, that's where the term mud clerk came from. I worked on various boats in the Pittsburgh trade. There were several different companies that used to run there. One would run another out of business. There were five boats: the *Betsy Ann, General Wood, Queen City, Senator Cordill* and *Liberty*. I worked on all five of them and I worked for most of the different owners that owned them at different times for about seven years. Then in 1934 I came to the Greene Line, and have been here ever since. On the Greene Line I have worked first on the *Chris Greene*, made a trip or two on the *Tom Greene*. I was on the *Evergreene* even when she was the *Kiwanis*, and later when she was the *Evergreene*. Most of all I was on the *Gordon C. Greene*. Now I'm on the *Delta Queen*. That's practically all the boats that they've had since I have been here.

Q: You mentioned that you were in that trade, up river I guess it was, with all those boats, could you tell us something about the *Liberty*?

A: She was the smallest of all. The was a boat about 142 feet landing and she had been built originally for a short trade between Wheeling and Clarington. Later on she branched out and ran from Wheel to Zanesville, and then Pittsburgh to Zanesville. Then when the Muskingum River filled up with mud so much that the *Liberty* couldn't get up there, she went in the Pittsburgh and Wheeling trade. She was the first boat I ever spent the night on when I was a boy in high school. And later on I worked on her at different times in the Pittsburgh and Wheeling trade, and in the Pittsburgh and Charleston trade, which was the last trade she ever ran in. The *Liberty* was the last boat that ever ran as an actual packet, carrying both freight and passengers on a regular schedule. She wound up her days in the Pittsburgh and Charleston trade in 1936. I believe she was the last absolutely true packet in a packet service that ever ran anywhere in the Mississippi River system.

Q: I heard that. Somebody has a packet on the upper Mississippi now I understand.

A: Well she wouldn't actually be a packet because packets have to carry both freight and passengers and run in a regular trade and there just isn't anybody that's doing that.

Q: The old *Liberty* was the last of them.

John Knoepfle

A: That was the last. Of course, we had the *Tom Greene* and *Chris Greene*, and *Gordon C. Greene* here and they had all been packets. But in their last days they were not. The *Tom* and *Chris* carried only freight in their last days and the *Gordon* carried only passengers. Actually for a little while in 1937 or 1938 we did carry some freight on the *Gordon* with the passengers. You might say from that standpoint she was a packet, but from another standpoint she didn't take everything that was offered, she just carried certain shipments for certain people. She wasn't really a public carrier.

Q: You mentioned the *Senator Cordill* too. That was an ill-fated boat I understand.

A: Yes she was. But I was lucky. I never was on her when she sank. She sank more than any other boats that were ever up there.

Q: Finally got out on an open river and hit a wicket. Captain Hornbrook told me that.

A: That's right. Yes, I was aboard her after that happened. After she had been refloated.

Q: Is that so?

A: But of course she never ran after that.

Q: What kind of a boat was the *Cordill*?

A: She was a pretty good boat. She was a packet. She had a very beautiful cabin. It was a cabin that I would not consider efficient because it didn't have very many rooms in it. The rooms were poorly, some of them were very large, some of them were very small. There was an awful lot of waste space. It wasn't used for anything but it was pretty. She would carry a big load of freight but that was hard to put on her because the way she was braced it was hard to get in and out of her. She was a good carrier and in a good many ways you would say she was a very fine packet boat. But she was awkward to work with because the freight was hard to get to.

Q: How about the *Betsy Ann*?

A: That's the first boat I ever actually worked on. She was a Pittsburgh to Cincinnati packet most of the time that I was on her. She was very roomy. Now she wasn't as good a carrier as the *Cordill*, she wasn't as big a boat, but she had a whole lot more space. It was easy to get to all the space that she had. I'd say that of the regular packets up there with the possible exception of the *Queen City* she was the best of all. Of course, the *Queen City* was as big as any two of the others put together and naturally it's hard to compare any of the others with her. But if you leave her out I'd say the *Betsy Ann* was the best of all. And she had a wrought iron hull. The rest of them were all wooden boats, and she had cross compound convention machinery. She was economical to operate. She had a very nice cabin. It wasn't quite as ornate as the *Cordill* but it was a pretty cabin and she had if I recall 26 staterooms. Her cabin was probably 50 to 20 feet shorter than the Cordill but it had 26 rooms and the Cordill only had 20.

Q: Is that so? You've operated mostly as a purser.

A: Well I've worked in the office as a purser or a clerk. I was really a clerk working under a purser nearly all the time in the Pittsburgh trade until for about three months in the summer of 1933 I was purser on the *Cordill*. But that's the only time I actually had charge of an office up there.

Q: Exactly what does a purser do on the inland rivers?

A: Well, a purser gathers in all the money and disperses it. The purser handles the purse you might say. Passengers pay their fares to him or to an agent. If they pay through an agent he collects from the agent. The purser also pays money out to the people who work on the boat in the form of wages, or the people who supply the boat in the form of payments for whatever they buy.

Q: It could get to be a pretty complicated job at times.

A: Yes you have to keep all the records, do all the bookkeeping and keep account of the money and turn it over to the company.

Q: I imagine on the old river most of that was done out of a fellow's hat.

A: It probably was, yes.

Q: There aren't enough records to go around of anything on the old river.

A: You hear stories about nail kegs and like that.

Q: You then operated more on the upper river than on the lower river.

A: Yes I've never been further down the river than Louisville until I went down on the *Gordon C. Greene* in 1936.

Q: Well I wonder if you could speak about the freight that was carried on these river boats? I had gleanings, I know that at Ironton it was heavy on nail kegs and things like that. But how about some of those other towns?

A: They would carry on stoves too. You got a lot of stoves out of Ironton. We also got stoves out of Portsmouth and various other places. We carried almost everything that you could ship, in less than carload lots. We carried furniture out of Manchester and Marietta. We even carried furniture downstream out of Pittsburgh. Of course, it was mostly steel beds out of Pittsburgh. Simmons Bed Company had a big factory up there. And that was another job we had was rating that freight. We had to figure those freight bills and make the bills out. And collect them. They had agents at all the wharfboats, and we would charge up the bills to these agents, and then it was up to us to make agents pay the boat.

Q: Guess you ran into some difficulties at times.

A: Oh sometimes, some of them were pretty hard, most of them were not. Most of them were honest people. Of course, as business dwindled see, I got in on the end of the deal, as business dwindled the wharfboats weren't taking in enough money to operate on. It became harder and harder for them to pay off because they were paying their operating expenses in some cases out of the boat's money. It was pretty hard for them to stay ahead of everybody. Sometimes they would be real nice to one boat and pay that boat everything they owed, and then they couldn't pay any of the other boats for a while. I think by and large they nearly all paid out eventually. Some of them were a little bit hard to get, but I think they all finally paid out.

John Knoepfle

Q: There were various combinations upriver I understand that boat owners . . .
A: Yes, that's right. That's why you'd work on one boat for a while, and then another boat for a while; some of the boat owners would combine and drive somebody out of business. And one boat would lay up, and if you were on that boat why, you would try to get on one of the boats that forced her out of business. That's how I came to be on all five boats.

Q: I guess you are one of the last men that packet boated up in the Muskingum.
A: No, I never packet boated up in the Muskingum. I guess I gave the wrong impression there. The *Liberty* ran up there, but it was before my time. I had relatives, my father had two sisters that lived on the Muskingum River in Zanesville, and I did take a ride on a little boat called the *Milton* one time, oh I suppose it was when I was in high school, rode her from Zanesville to Philo. The purser on the *Milton* took a paper and pencil to figure how much I owed. There was four of us at 25 cents apiece, and he took a paper and pencil to figure it out. But we just had that nine mile ride up there. But I do remember seeing a steamboat at Zanesville, and it may have been the *Liberty*. I'm not sure.

Q: You don't remember that purser's name?
A: I never knew it. If I ever heard it didn't register. One time, see the *General Wood* ran in 1929 in the Pittsburgh and Charleston trade, and she was a big long narrow sternwheeler. And the greatest business in the Pittsburgh and Charleston trade was produce. We would leave Pittsburgh every Tuesday and we'd leave Charleston on Friday morning. We would be at Gallipolis, Ohio, Friday afternoon. We would start loading eggs and chickens, and sometimes livestock. And as we went up the river we would add more and more to our trip, and also in season there would be potatoes and tomatoes and various kinds of farm produce. And she'd just keep on loading and take it up and deliver some at Wheeling and some at Pittsburgh. Wheeling was usually mostly livestock and a little livestock went to Pittsburgh. Most of the livestock went to Wheeling. But the thing that I just happened to think of was that there used to be a landing called Willow Glen. It was in Washington County, Ohio between Newport and Marietta, and I don't know whether the place is still there or not, but on this particular Saturday night we had landed just about, well I went off duty at six o'clock and went back to eat supper and I hadn't finished supper yet when they made the landing. We went in the landing and started to pick up a load of tomatoes, and we were just about finished loading when the wind hit us. It was a hard rain and a hard wind, and it turned the boat all the way around and she just rode around right under her stage. The stage just rode right around on the nosing of the boat and the toe of the stage never made any mark on the bank except the first one that had been laid down there where they put it down. The boat turned all the way around under her stage. It's the only time I ever saw a boat do it, and the only time I ever heard of a boat doing it. She went clear around and faced down the river.

And the cabin of the *General Wood* didn't have any doorsill to the front door, but there was a big wide crack over the front door, and of course the rain beating in on that ran down against the cabin. The wind was driving it back there and it ran in under the front door, and we'd finished supper with the steward in there with a dustpan and a bucket trying to bail the cabin out. He said that was the only time he'd ever bailed out a cabin. That was something that was rather unusual and exciting. I never saw it happen in any other place. We handled produce on various other boats I was up there on. The biggest produce trip I was ever connected with was on the *Senator Cordill* on the Thanksgiving trip that same year, 1929. We went into Pittsburgh with somewhere in the neighborhood of 2,100 coops of poultry. That was not a record trip but it was the biggest one I was ever on.

Q: Must have been a lot of squawking upriver with all those birds aboard.

A: It was. I was on the *Betsy Ann* one time when we had 5,000 cases of eggs, and of course that wasn't a record either. I believe that was the biggest egg trip I was ever in on. The *Cordill* was supposed to have handled 10,000 cases one time. But I didn't see it.

Q: That's all perishable. What did you ever do if you were coming upriver with a boat load like that and got caught on a sandbar or something like that?

A: Well those things happened before I got into the business. When I came along the locks and dams were finished and we didn't get caught on sandbars. But in the past they would have to try and get to a railroad and reship the freight.

Q: Must have been a serious loss.

A: Well it must have been. I don't know how that was handled, I never was in on it and I don't know that was handled. I've wondered myself.

Q: Well, were there any tricks to loading a boat that you might recall offhand? I know that a mate had to be pretty true. He could foul up if he didn't load right.

A: Of course, you try to send the stuff in so the mate could load it. You tried to send the farthest away freight in first. If you were going up the river you would send the farthest up the river first if you could. If you were going down the river you would send the farthest downriver first, and the mate had to know where the places were that the boat needed heavy weight, and where she needed light weight. But for the most part, as far as the clerks were concerned, all they had to do was to try to send the farthest stuff away first. Of course, if you loaded a lot of freight on at Pittsburgh, sending to Cincinnati first and Portsmouth, then at Ashland, then Huntington, and so forth. Well, you would come on down to Rochester and Fast Liverpool and Steubenville and you'd be picking up more freight for these same landings. Of course they would have to try to load it so that they wouldn't block anything that they'd already put on. You couldn't take freight on for Cincinnati at Wheeling, and load it ahead of something put on at Pittsburgh for Huntington. You would send in the farthest stuff away first, but it was up to the mate to get it on the boat so it could come off.

Q: I suppose the clerk and the mate were often at loggerheads over freight.

John Knoepfle

A: Nearly all the time. Nearly all the time. There was always humbug about. There was always some kind of an argument.

Q: I know Horace Lyle pointed it up. He said a mate's job was to save money to get it on and off fast and a clerk's job was to protect it best he could.

A: That's right. That's a pretty good way to put it. I've had mates say, "Throw it off. Throw it down." And they didn't like to have the clerk try to read the marks either. The clerk was responsible if the freight got off wrong. It was up to the clerk that it didn't get off wrong. Oh, it was wonderful if the mate got into the wrong freight pile. He could stand on the Wheeling Wharfboat and bellow, "Hell, take it back and tell them Parkersburg," about 25 times. Each time he bellowed he yelled a little bit louder. Pretty soon things came to a stop. Everybody had a conference.

Q: The mates were kind of an institution, weren't they? I understand that some of them were pretty rough men to deal with.

A: Yes, some of them were. Coburn Pratt was supposed to be the roughest, but he was one of the easiest to get along with that I ever worked with. Coburn, I've heard, now I never worked with him in the earlier days, but I heard that he had shot a couple of men.

Q: I was told that by, Norval Horton I think told me that, he's an engineer. Said he used to carry a cane with a lead-loaded end.

A: Yes, he did, and he was, nobody ever wanted to walk up behind him either, it was very dangerous. I remember a truck driver came up behind him one time and asked where to put something and there was a lot of noise going on and Coburn was yelling at somebody and making a loud noise himself and the driver just walked up and put his hand on his shoulder. I never saw such a look on a man's face in my life as there was on Coburn's as he turned around there. He was ready for action. I don't think he had his cane with him, I think he had some kind of a little thing, probably a piece of lead with leather attached to it or something that he was waving around in his hand, ready to use if he had to.

Q: You know the river is a funny place. Most of the memoirs and reminiscences are all those sentimental tales. Then you hear about these mean undercurrents

A: Well I liked Coburn Pratt. He was a man. I don't think he was mean. I think he was scared. I think that probably some circumstance that arose in connection with his job had caused the trouble that he got into, and I don't think there was anything mean about him. I think he was really a very kind hearted person. But he was probably was scared.

Q: I had never thought of that possibility but I guess there was a lot of that on the river.

A: You know I think most of these people that you hear about now and then that had something like that in their past, that were always walking around with a gun, or a cane, or something like that, ready to attack if necessary, I think they were afraid because if they had done like that, even though they were innocent of any intentions of doing anything, they always had a feeling that maybe somebody was after them for it.

Q: The river was a widely related clan, I guess.

A: Yes. We had oh, I guess he was waiter or cabin boy or something who disappeared one time off the *Cordill*. Coburn was mate on there and right away there was quite an investigation to see if Coburn could have done anything to him. That it was just because of Coburn's reputation, and later on they found his body under a derrick boat in the river. His skull was fractured and there was suspicion of foul play but they never could pin it down to anybody. I never could believe that Coburn had anything to do with it, and he was kind of a smart aleck anyway. He had same political connection that was important, that was the reason he was on there. He was a fairly good worker, but I don't think anybody ever will know what happened to him.

Q: I knew there was a certain type of mate, because two men have told me this, that some of the mates carried ox whips, and things like that. Must have made it, must have been a very curious relationship with the rousters they had.

A: The rousters were different from what you see around here now too. They were for the most part much less intelligent, and they seemed to expect to be treated rough. It seems that they had to have something like that to get them going. Had to give them a push if you were going to get them to do anything. Of course, they would learn to do certain things, you used to take a roustabout that was good on your huckster boat, could handle livestock and eggs and chickens and things like that, and you put him on some other boat and he might not be any good at all. But conversely a man that was good, say down here in the Louisville trade might not be any good at all in the Pittsburgh to Charleston trades. One thing that roustabouts had to learn, and there was nobody ever taught them, you just had to learn, was how to call out these landings. Used to give a man a box and you would tell him such and such a landing and he had to remember that learning until he got in there, and then tell it. Because you're sending freight on a boat and you send something in, say, "Tell him Parkersburg." Well when he gets in he's got to say "Parkersburg" so the man inside knows where to put that freight. So maybe the next man behind him might have some other learning, and if this man doesn't remember that he's got Parkersburg, the man behind him doesn't know what he had, he's supposed to know he has something for Hockingport or someplace else. The man in front, it's just up to him to know what he's got, the clerk tells him. Well the clerk isn't supposed to remember what each man has. The clerk sends it on, he tells the man what he's got. You take some landings, of course if you have a whole lot of mixed freight, it is probably coming out of a wharfboat, but you take some bank landings, you'd have a warehouse that was 200 feet away from the boat. If you had 30 men and you gave a man a package and told him what it was, if he walked down the hill and walked in on a boat and back to the deck room, he had walked 200 or 300 feet away from you, and if there are 30 men carrying, by the time he got down there you had a good many packages gone by you, and if they yelled, "What's this man got?" You didn't know what he had got. There wasn't any way to remember.

Q: So they'd just find that out themselves?

A: They would just go down and walk in and say "Parkersburg" and take it to the right place. Of course that's how some freight got mixed up by them not knowing what they had. We had a deaf and dumb deckhand on several of the boats, and I adopted the system of giving him a little note with what he was supposed to tell them. I would just write Parkersburg, and I would hand that to him when the stevedores gave him the package, I'd hand him that note. When he took it in he'd hand that note to the inside stevedores and there was supposed somebody in there that could read. Now in the huckster business we had to keep the lots of eggs separate. We'd have so many cases of white eggs, and so many cases of brown eggs. They would all be for the same shipper, and they wouldn't be any particular way of telling them apart, you just had to keep them separate. Maybe the same man might have eight or nine different lots of eggs. Well, you'd send in, this was a 277 case lot, well you'd tell the first man that he had he first of the 277 case lot. You'd tell the last man that he had the last of the 277 case lot, the men in between wouldn't be told anything. They were sent on for that particular huckster. The huckster could call for those lots along the way at different places, and they had to be stored so that you could get out certain kinds of eggs at certain places.

Q: The huckster would stay on board.

A: No, he would go up the river ahead of the boat and meet the boat at each landing, and then he would call for what he had sold. You had to get it out, and of course it was up to the clerk to keep track of what was taken out, and it was up to the mate to get it out. And if you went in, say, I. C. Matlack stopped at Steubenville and sold some eggs, well you would have to get the right eggs out of the right pile, and then you would go on to past Liverpool, maybe he had been there while you were coming up and sold some more. Then he'd go to Rochester, and he'd sold some more, and when you got to Pittsburgh, why you had the rest of them to put off. You had to have them so you could get them, and you had to keep them straight. That was a pretty tricky thing. I didn't realize then how hard it must have been to pack them so they wouldn't fall down and still could get them out and not block the boat off so you couldn't get anything else on it. But the mates must have had a bigger job than we realized. We thought we had a big job just keeping track of it, but they must have a hard job. Some mates couldn't keep the stuff straight. But that was up to them, the clerk never got blamed if the mate mixed the freight up. The huckster would be down, well Matlack's the one I mentioned. He'd be at Long Bottom, Ohio. He'd be there when you loaded. You sent the stuff on straight, and he would be there at the various landings where he wanted stuff off and you ask for it. If it was mixed up when he got to Pittsburgh he never went to you about it. He told the mate.

Q: I have never so far talked to any mates. They are as hard to come by as roustabouts. They seem to have disappeared.

A: I don't know where you would find one either. I don't believe there are any of the old time mates left on the upper river.

Q: I suppose part of your job was furnishing entertainment on the boats too, wasn't it?

A: Well, in later years yes, but when the boats were running full of freight, why the freight was the principal entertainment. Well you didn't have time to furnish much entertainment. You leave Pittsburgh you might have, oh you might have 300 or 400 shipments to get off before you got to Wheeling. It was only 90 miles from Pittsburgh to Wheeling, and the river would fall 78 feet in those 90 miles, and you would make seven or eight landings in between there and pick up and put off freight. And you had to rate your freight bills and enter them in the freight book and make out the freight bill and write it up in the discharge book and check it out for the various landings as you came along. You didn't have time to do much entertainment. You would leave Pittsburgh on Saturday afternoon at two o'clock, and if you were on time you would be ready to leave Wheeling at seven o'clock the next morning and you would have handled anywhere from 200 to 400 shipments.

Q: It was a tremendous job, wasn't it?

A: Why sure and two of you did it.

Q: What were the wages the clerk made for that kind of work?

A: Oh, anywhere from $1.50 a day up to $4.00 a day.

Q: Is that so? Imagine that.

A: I think some of them got less. I think, oh gee I think I have known some of them that worked for, oh let's see, I'm trying to think what the lowest one I did hear of was about 60 cents a day I believe. Of course, the boat wasn't doing that kind of business either. The boat that was, I believe on the *Liberty* in her last days when business had practically gone off and left her, they were getting by as cheap as they could, I think they got down to around 50 cents a day.

John Knoepfle

John W. Menke, September 22, 1957

Question: This is Monday, the 22nd of September 1957, about 1:30 in the afternoon in the harbor at St. Louis aboard the *Goldenrod*. I am talking to Captain John W. Menke who is a kind of patriarch of showboaters. Well, Captain, I knew that you were a Cincinnatian first, is that right?

Answer: Yes, I was born in Cincinnati in 1880 and stayed around there till about 1900 and . . .

Q: Till around 1905, I'll bet you were . . .

A: No, let me see, around 1902. I went to Jersey City in 1902. Stayed there till 1904.

Q: What were you doing out in Jersey City?

A: Well, I worked in a watch factory in Jersey City, my brother Ben and I. For about two years, I guess. Then we built a motorboat over there while working in the watch factory, at night and on Sundays. Took about nine months to finish the job. When we got through, we made excursions around New York harbor, and up the Hudson River, and down to Rockaway, and Sandy Hook and all around. Shipped it by rail to Pittsburgh, and come down the Ohio River to Cincinnati, and that's how we got our first showboat. Got a job with "French's New Sensation" doing the advertising. And we've been every day since, both of us, my brother and I.

Q: What was the name of that boat you were running excursions with?

A: *Cincy*, we called it the *Cincy* on account of Cincinnati.

Q: Well, the Menkes were in Cincinnati I guess, your father, when did you come in there?

A: Father was a jeweler. He worked for the Duhme Company of Cincinnati. He was the superintendent there for 27 years. He died in 1898 just before the Spanish American War.

Q: He was a, I know because I have seen those cards, that there was a Menke in hardware. I guess he was an uncle?

A: Yes, there was a Menke in the machinist business over there for a long time. That was an uncle. Uncle Brent, he had a shop up on Main Street right across, near the old courthouse up in there.

Q: Where did you live in Cincinnati?

A: We lived at 1736 Queen City Avenue, Clermont they call it.

Q: Well, you mentioned "French's New Sensation." The name is pretty well known. Can you tell us anything about that operation?

A: French was one of the pioneers in showboat business. He operated in about 1875 on up until we come in the picture about 1904. We made all the western rivers from Pittsburgh to Cairo to St. Paul, down to New Orleans, all the bayous, used to cover about 15 states on a trip once a year.

Q: Well, they must have been hungry for entertainment in those spots.

A: There were not so many boats. They didn't get any entertainment except from showboats and tent shows and stuff like that.

Q: Well, I don't know anything about French at all, could you tell me something about him?

A: I don't know so much about him. He died the same year that we opened, I guess. His wife ran the business after that and we worked for her. A fellow by the name of John E. McNair was the manager of the boat at that time. We used the *Cincy* for about four years. We covered all the western rivers without in advance doing the advertising, Ben and I. Eventually, we bought our first showboat, the *Sunny South*. And since that time, we have had seven all told, and the *Goldenrod* is the last one. It is the only one afloat. We kept a boat on the Ohio River named *Majestic*, a small boat. It takes out a college troupe every year.

Q: Yes, that's the Hiram College boat.

A: Yes, Hiram College. We came into St. Louis in 1937 with the *Goldenrod* for a two week stop and we have been here ever since. It will be 20 years in October since she landed at St. Louis.

Q: You mentioned that you had some trouble with the city of St. Louis when you got in here. could you talk about that a little?

A: Yes, the city of St. Louis wouldn't let any showboats land at St. Louis. So we went to federal court and Judge Moore gave us an injunction against the city of St. Louis to keep them from interfering with our business and afterwards made it permanent, so we haven't been bothered since.

Q: Well, I was thinking that over. Did you have rights at a public landing? Is that how that court decision was made?

A: The city doesn't have any jurisdiction over boats. A navigable stream is controlled by the government. All there was to it was it was not a building, it was a boat.

Q: Well, this *Sunny South*, now when you ran that were you running straight melodramas on the river?

A: No, they were always, years ago most of the boats carried variety shows, didn't have any melodramas.

Q: So you would have magician acts and things like that.

A: Magic acts, and all kinds of dance acts, and all the acts you had acquired.

Q: When did this, first everybody that ever thinks of a showboat, thinks of the playing of the melodrama. When did that all come into the picture?

A: Only when we started to play the bigger cities.

Q: Is that so?

A: We operated in Pittsburgh with two old time shows, and did the same here at St. Louis. But the melodramas never did go on the road at all. It was always in bigger cities. It was about the same style show they had in tent shows.

Q: Well, how did those little country audiences react to things like a magician show?

A: Oh, they always liked all kinds of variety shows, any old show.

Q: I think you mentioned earlier that your first boat was the . . .

A: *Sunny South.*

Q: What boat were you using to tow that, Captain?

A: *Wabash.*

Q: The *Wabash.* I like to get those things set. Well, how did you do business-wise in those early days with the boat?

A: Well, business was good.

Q: It was?

A: Business was all right.

Q: I know that Captain Reynolds later during the depression, he was running motion pictures in his boat, and farmers way out in the country took their fences down and made parking lots out of them. They made more money with parking lots than they did with their farm. (laughter) We were talking about Daddy Price the other day. When did you first meet him, Captain?

A: About 1904 and 1905, I guess.

Q: What was he running then?

A: He operated Price's *Water Queen*, and then afterwards bought French's *Sensation*. He also owned the *Greater New York*. He had three of them at one time.

Q: He was quite a horse trader of showboats, wasn't he?

A: Well, he didn't do much trading. He just always had somebody run them for him. On the other boats, he would take a man on his boats that could operate them all by themselves.

Q: Well, I've been told by a number of people that he was a shrewd penny pincher.

A: Oh yes. Yes, the old man, everybody said he was tight. But it didn't make any difference, if you were to tear off any part of the boat while operating, going through the bayous of Louisiana, if you would tear off any part of the boat, maybe hang it on the trees, and he would say it was all right, it was rotten and needed a new one anyway.

Q: Well, he must have been a real character.

A: Well, the old man made a lot of money. He was a nice old guy.

Q: How long did you operate the *Sunny South*, Captain?

A: Four years. Four years and we bought her for $26,000 and we owed $6,000 on her when the bank closed us up in 1907. I had a partner at that time by the name of Brad Coleman, and I think I left with a ten dollar bill, and he had the same, busted.

Q: The bank took the boat for sale, I guess.

A: They had a buyer in sight. A man up there at Parkersburg was going to buy it and he backed out and didn't buy it, so the bank was stuck with it. For about three years, it sat there and didn't do anything. Then they sold it to a fellow in Littlewood, West Virginia and he gave them a bum note for it, and they didn't get, he took it up the Monongahela River, and she sunk in the ice in the Monongahela River in the second winter, and the bank was holding the bag.

Q: What did you do? Did you bounce right back into the business after that with your ten dollar bill?

A: I went out in advance doing the advertising for the *Wonderland* showboat. I always had a job, anytime I wanted to go to work in advance, I would go back with one of the boats, keep on a going, save some more money and put it back in another showboat.

Q: I think I read in Bryant's book about the advance agent often wasn't ahead of the boat.

A: Well, that's when Garland Nema got his name, he's down here in a little town called Cave in Rock, Illinois. He got behind the boat a couple of days with the motorboat Something happened with the motorboat, he couldn't get it started or something. He was trailing along behind them by about two days instead of being ahead.

Q: I noticed at your map out there, that you had gotten up to Beattyville. Do you remember making a stop up there in Kentucky?

A: No, that's on the Kentucky River. No, we never played the Kentucky because our boats were always too big to get through the locks up there.

Q: Oh, I see. Yes, you always had these big boats.

A: Yes, we always had the big boats, never had the small ones.

Q: What did you, when you got, I imagine you must have bought back into a boat after you were an advance agent for a while.

A: Well, probably 1911, 1912, 1913, about two years, and I bought the *Greater New York* from old man Price. Had it five days. In fact a strong windstorm came up at Newburgh, Indiana and she was a total loss.

Q: Is that so?

A: She was out of commission. The water went clear up over the top of the jack staff on the roof. So we had all our belongings under a tent at Newburgh, Indiana. That's the same storm that sunk the steamer for Captain Price, the *Robert Dodds*. And I made a deal with Captain Price to pay him $1,000 for the *Dodds*, and the water was in the pilothouse on that one. Just the spokes and the pilothouse were sticking out. So we waited till April, took us until October to get her cleaned up and ready to go, and we left Newburgh, Indiana, and went to Paducah from there with the steamer *Robert Dodds*, and went into the corn towing business. Towed corn out of the Cumberland and Tennessee River.

Q: Were you using barges?

A: Yes, we used one barge, a regular barge built to tow corn with.

Q: Well, let's depart on that a little bit. How did they load the barges?

A: Oh, we carried about 25 roustabouts that carried corn. We would pay them one cent on, and one cent off; we would pay them in pennies as they would bring it on, and as they go off, and that way they all kept straight.

Q: They carried it on by the bushel.

A: By the sack.

Q: By the sack.

A: About a bushel and a half in a sack.

Q: So was it corn on the ear?

A: Oh no, shelled corn.

Q: What was that for? Old Monongahela? Were they making a whiskey out of it or something?

A: No, it was all shipped usually to Nashville. They would load it in cars at Paducah and Brookport, Illinois.

Q: How much of that could you carry on there?

A: We would carry 5,000 sacks on the barge, and then we would sometimes put some on the steamer, maybe 700 or 800 bags.

Q: Load it right down the center of the boat.

A: Well, they would load it wherever we had room. And they would carry it off, and put it in the railroad cars. When we were in the corn business, we were towing corn out of the Tennessee and Cumberland River. Captain Price came up from New Orleans with his showboat, the *Sensation*. He said, "You'll have to buy this showboat from me because I'm getting too old, and can't operate it by myself and my boys left me." He said he had had enough showboating. I told him I didn't think I wanted any more showboats, I had enough trouble with showboats. So I finally made a deal with him, and I bought the boat for $22,000, and he went with us for a season, and I paid him off the second season, all we owed him. From then on things went along pretty good. About two years later I bought the *Goldenrod*. That was December 1923. Then we operated two of them, and I bought the *Hollywood*, and we operated three of them at one time.

Q: That *Sensation* must of been kind of a luxurious boat at $22,000 wasn't it?

A: Oh, she was a big boat. It was in good shape when I got it, and we operated it from then on until about 1931.

Q: When you transferred that boat from Price to yourself, was that just a verbal agreement you made?

A: Yes, it was. No papers exchanged hands at all.

Q: And you paid him back.

A: Yes, we didn't need any papers or anything. That was it. When he got all his money why, everybody was happy. We never had any arguments at any time.

Q: Well, now let's see, you had the *Sensation* and the *Hollywood* and both of these boats came to tragic ends, I guess.

A: Well, one of them got caught in a storm while she was on the Marine Ways at Mound City, and the other one was destroyed in the ice on the Clarks River just outside of Paducah in 1929. And the *Sensation* was wrecked in the storm in, I got some of those dates wrong . . .

Q: *Hollywood* in 1936, wasn't it?

A: *Hollywood* was in 1939.

Q: That's something that can be checked. Anyway, you were in Pittsburgh.

A: In Pittsburgh with this boat in 1930, 1929 or 1930. We were showing here when the *Hollywood* passed out in the ice. One was in 1931, and this was in, well boats are pretty much like people, they just die off of old age. When they get so bad off that you can't operate them, you either got to fix, or let them go by the boards.

Q: I was just wondering if you described the wonderful days when you were, I guess you did that, up here above the city and the farmers were making lots out of their fields.

A: We showed St. Louis in 1931, showed about 18 miles from downtown out on the Missouri River; we turned people away every night. 500 people trying to get on and the boat full, sold out, usually sold out two weeks in advance after the third day we were there. That went on all summer until October, and we moved into the Fox Theater in St. Louis and showed to 23,000 people the first night on Sunday opening night. We done about five shows, I think.

Q: That day.

A: Yes. From St. Louis we went to Memphis with the *Hollywood* showed Memphis all winter. We were up on Wolf River, a little river down there, and we did that, and stayed there all winter. A show every night.

Q: Did you show "Uncle Tom's Cabin" in Memphis?

A: I don't think it would have gone through. (laughter) We did about the same shows we were doing out here.

Q: You don't show "Uncle Tom's Cabin" here either?

A: Yes, we have done "Tom" here not so long ago, about a year or so ago. It went over all right. This is not so much a southern town, I think. Everybody talks about being way down south in St. Louis, but it is far from the south.

Q: Well, it is like Kentucky, there's a line all the way across, the Civil War, and then they met some people from Alabama. Alabamans didn't think that they were southern at all. You mentioned that you had all the scripts for your melodramas. You had gotten them from an actor at one time.

A: I bought a whole trunkful of them, got about 250 scripts in it. We still play them. We reach in there, don't know what we are going to play next week until we get one out and go with it.

Q: I guess he was an itinerant actor, had all those scripts.

A: Well, he was a director, and he would travel all these shows down to seven or eight in the cast. He was very good at that. He did a good job of it. I wish he was still alive, I'd like to have him with us yet.

Q: What was his name, Captain?

A: Fredericks, I have forgotten his first name now.

Q: I had heard that those old shows, men they trimmed them down, they just cut out the things that people originally thought were funny.

A: Well, they trimmed them down to get rid of all the deadwood, cut a lot of the cast out, just kept the lead in the show. Lots of times it made it better than it was in the first place.

335   John Knoepfle

Q: Well, let's go up to Catlettsburg again. I know we missed that.

A: Well, Catlettsburg, Kentucky, we played there, we played once a year always on a regular route. Sometimes we would get there when they had their rafters bringing logs out of Big Sandy. They were a little bit rough but no one ever got hurt, didn't have to kill anybody. They had one whole row of saloons in Catlettsburg right on the river front. Must have been a whole block of them. But they all had a few fights. It wasn't too bad.

Q: Now when you get, now speaking of those loggers, I know they are people from up in the hills. Do they take the shows more seriously, say than a city fellow would?

A: Well, yes, they don't want any hecklers in their shows. They like to hear the show and want to hear the whole story, being they bring their children, and their wife, and their whole family comes to the show. We always gave them a clean show. We never had anything that you couldn't bring your sister and your mother to. No burlesque, we never had any burlesque show. A lot of folks say, "Why don't you put on a burlesque show?" You go into those towns and the mayor, they bring their family, and you would not have been able to get out of town. They would have hung us all. (laughter)

Q: So you played . . .

A: We played for preachers and everybody at churches and all. It was clean, I always kept it that way. Even the girl's show, we used to carry a girl's show, too. We would have about seven or eight in the lineup but none of the girls were allowed off the boat after dark. Not for what they were going to do, but for what they said they were going to. I mean, the town boys would say, "I was out and had one of them show girls out last night." They never got a chance to say that. If they did, when you came back the next year, you would not be able to land. So we kept it clean and the girls, folks that we had were mostly married and the single girls, they were some of them professionals who were used to traveling with the different shows. Why, they thought it was pretty much like going to a convent. (laughter) They couldn't get off at all. They didn't have much fun. But they always, that was the law, and we laid it down to them when they come on and told them if they couldn't go along like that, they might as well go home now. That's the way it had to be.

Q: Did you ever play up on the Monogahela?

A: Oh, yes. We made the Monogahela River from Pittsburgh all the way up to Fairmont, that's as far as we could go. We made that trip every year.

Q: Play the miners . . .

A: Miners, coal miners, we would usually get in there early in the season, March and April. We opened up there about the time they had snow and everything else up that way, cold and a lot of rain. But that didn't seem to bother them any, because they had been housed up all winter and wanted to go somewhere, and we got there why, it gave them an outlet. That was a good river for us. We always did a lot of business up there, it never failed. We did "Uncle Tom" up there one time.

Q: Oh, yes!

A: Yes. We did "Tom" up there and did a lot of business with "Tom." We were up there during 1913 when they had the big flood on the Ohio River. So instead of going down the line, we just played Monongahela River three different trips all that, until the flood waters went down on the Ohio River. Through the mining district up there, we had a lot of foreigners, but they took the show all right. We never had any trouble with them. Sometimes they didn't understand what they was talking about but they got the drift somehow.

Q: I was told that showboating, despite Edna Ferber, was pretty much an Ohio River thing.

A: Well, Edna Ferber's story didn't fit the showboat at all. She was just some, she wrote up a lot of stuff that someone told her on the shore, that was all. The only time she spent on a showboat was on the Chesapeake Bay on the *James Adams* boat. And they well, they did probably the same kind of shows we did, just rep shows, they call them. Same as the tent shows. They used to play a week at a town, and she got most of her story off of there. But she talked about the gambling, I think. Didn't she have a lot of gambling stuff? There never was a showboat that had a game on it, except the crew on the boat that played a little poker once in a while, but no roulette tables and all that stuff. That was just a lot of somebody's dream. Because you would come into it in a bar, they had a bar according to a picture I saw, but if we had a bar, and roulette table, and landed in a town, I don't think we would ever have got out. Those little towns would not stand for that. We had to please everybody in town. There never was a boat had a bar and roulette table, and that gambling stuff on it, all he ever done was show one night in a town and it's time to go to the next one. You had to keep it clean, and they had to be on the up and up all the time, because we had to come back next year. That's the only place you could go was just up, and down the river.

Q: So you have been here in St. Louis a long time and think you might stay.

A: Well, every year I think about making another trip, and every year it seems like I get hold of another steamboat of some kind, a towboat, and decide I am going to leave, and make another round trip. I would like to make one more trip around to see what has become of all the kids that used to pass bills for us on the road, see what they are doing. A lot of them are old men. Some of them come through here, and ask me if I remember him, he had passed bills in this town and that town. I don't remember them, there was just too many of them.

Q: You let them in free if they passed bills, right?

A: Oh yes, they always got a free pass. The kids all got a free pass, and then when they make the parade, we always carried a band, and to make the parade, we would put a red coat on the boys, the kids, and they would carry the banners, and pass bills as they went along the street with the band. A lot of those guys,

John Knoepfle

well, every one of them, I guess, are old folks, they got kids as old as they were when they were doing the job. A regular bunch of kids would always be there pretty near every year, same kids would be on the job waiting for the boat to come, get a job doing something. They would sweep the boat out, carry water, carry handbills and banners. We would always have some banners the kids would have to carry. Someday maybe we will make another trip.

Q: That is quite a grand tour I guess.

A: Yes, do like a farewell performance. (laughter) Make a farewell trip, and come back next year again.

Q: Well, that is a shrewd old gimmick in show business isn't it?

A: Oh yes, a farewell trip. I know the boat could go out and make a lot of money. I believe that she would turn away at every town along the route. Of course, all the kids have grown up, and they have had children, and they have all talked about showboats, when they were kids they used to go. All the folks away from the river don't know about Menke. In a little town we were the only thing come through there to give them any entertainment. Now they can get to picture shows. Hardly any traveling shows get to those towns now. Traveling shows are all through, there were a couple of hundred tent shows operating in the western country. They're all about all through. I think there is only four or five of them operating now. I imagine they are hungry for live actors, want to see something besides pictures.

Q: Yes. I think so, too.

A: I feel like a boat would do a lot of business to make a trip. You could keep going around. But we got kind of used to this loafing here in St. Louis. When you get a little older, you want to sit a little more, I guess.

Q: Watch the river go by.

A: Watch the river go by, yes.

Q: Well, fine. I have kept you most of the afternoon Captain, and I want to say how much I have enjoyed talking to you, and how much I appreciate you making the interview twice.

A: Well, sometimes, somedays, you feel more like talking than other days. Maybe we could have done a better job sometime, maybe later on.

Q: Fine.

John O'Hearn, August 5, 1957

Question: We are in Graeter's Candy Store, in Swifton Village. Can you tell us your name and when you were born?
Answer: John O'Hearn born 1889.
Q: And you lived in the East End is that right?
A: Lived in Cincinnati East End.
Q: Well I would like you first to tell us a little bit about the *O'Neil* you made your trip on.
A: Well I just made one trip on that as a cabin boy. That was to keep the wicks clean, the shades of the lamp clean and oil in the lamp. They didn't have no electric then. It was all oil lamp. That's about all the job consisted of.
Q: Those were reflector lamps, different colors I guess.
A: Well the lights on the stacks, they were red globe and green globe and on the head of the barges there would be a red globe and a green globe.
Q: I see.
A: And on the stern end there was white globes, two white globe lamps.
Q: And then you were responsible for all the other lamps on the boat too.
A: Oh yes in the kitchen and every lamp in the place there. There wasn't any too many of them, about ten or twelve all told.
Q: Enough to keep you busy.
A: Yes just to keep you busy and when you wasn't busy why you could peel potatoes for the cook, help her.
Q: Did they call that a spud cook?
A: Yes, that was a spud cook.
Q: Let's see the *O'Neil* was a coal tow, wasn't she?
A: Yes, she was a tow boat. Plied between Pittsburgh and Cincinnati mostly, and down the river all the way down.
Q: You went on to New Orleans.
A: Yes, went to New Orleans and back and that was the end of my trip.
Q: I see.
A: I was born right there on the river all my life and seen boats go up and down.
Q: Let's see, this was in 1908 you made that time on the *O'Neil*.
A: Let's see about 1908, yes around about that time.
Q: You mentioned earlier coming up to Louisville the boat always seemed to break down, can you explain that a little bit?
A: Well yes, in Louisville they had a beer they called the Louisville Common, that was the only place you could buy it. They'd give you a big water bucket full for a nickel. Well the boat always had to have a little trouble you know. Stopped long enough to get a bucket of beer.
Q: Everybody on board I guess had some.
A: Yes.

Q: Well I wonder if you'd talk some about the coal cranes and the mills there on Eastern Avenue.

A: Well they had two boats there they called the *J. O. Cole* and the *Crown Hill* and they would go up the river you know and send a man up first and he'd buy timber up there, he wouldn't buy the land he would just buy the timber. They'd take all the timber of that land that they bought.

Q: Was Cranes . . .

A: Yes Charlie Crane that was his name he had that job and they'd log them up there in the Big Sandy, and bring them, then they'd go up with the boat and tow them down to the mills. They'd get them down here then they'd cut them up in whatever order they had. Course they used to have a lot of walnut there for a while, but later on they just couldn't just get any walnut logs.

Q: How big were some of those logs they brought down?

A: Oh some of them would be four feet in diameter.

Q: You were telling me about a huge oak there before.

A: Yes I seen them have an oak there one time was about, well between three and four feet in diameter, and I never just saw the size of it. It was all hollow. It was a hollow log. It was all full of water in there and when they put it on the carriage to take it up into the mill, there was a three pound catfish rolled out of it. You ought to have seen those guys with their spike poles trying to get that fish. Finally they got him with their spike pole, run him through and that was the end of Mr. Fish.

Q: That must have been a little side line with these fellows.

A: Oh yes they'd get a hollow log and a fish would get in there and the next thing you know, you'd get to a real steep incline and the water would wash out of there and whatever was in there would come out.

Q: Those men who worked the logs down there, can you describe a little bit of their activity?

A: Well they were just the ordinary rough guys like rivermen are, but they knew what they were doing all the time. All good swimmers, good big strong men and they could do anything with a spike pole, they could really handle spike poles. They'd cut these logs out here and send them down, then the man called the loader he'd put them on a carriage and they'd them take up into the mill.

Q: So the carriage was put down under the water.

A: Oh yes, the carriage was run down clean under, and the water then they would push right in close to the rails and when it would come out of the water, why that steep incline with big spikes on it, they would get ahold of the logs on the front end, and as they pulled out, why the log would just lay right on there.

Q: I see.

A: They could pick two or well they could pick two good three foot in diameter logs up at one time.

Q: Tell me about your own activities if the logs got loose.

A: Well they used to when the high water come up, now and then they would break loose way up there in the Big Sandy, and they would came floating down, wild down the river. Well I was just a youngster then, we'd get a boat, two of us would get in the boat, we used to catch them logs. And the logs we'd see Crane and Company on, well we'd get a quarter for every log we caught. If we caught an outside firm's why that was 50 cents. We could make money.

Q: Fifty cents to Crane or to the other firm?

A: That would be fifty cents to you for catching the logs.

Q: Would Cole Crane pay you that?

A: Oh yes.

Q: In other word they'd pay you 50 cents and got the other firm's logs?

A: They kept the other firm's logs.

Q: You mentioned that you had an eddy up there.

A: Yes we had an eddy right there at Ferry street, and we'd catch them and push them in there and if we got too many in there then we would have to start logging them together.

Q: Guess you could make a fair amount of money.

A: Oh yes, we made more money doing nothing, as the fellow says, than a mechanic could make. While they run, they run, sometimes they'd run all day.

Q: Earlier you mentioned that the Cole Crane boats raced up from the new dam.

A: Well they were down there when they finished that dam at Louisville, or at Fernbank. All kinds of boats were down there you knew celebrating, and these two boats got together coming up. Boy they could almost shake hands with one another going there along there having a race all the way up the river to see who would get up first. They thought more of their boats, some of these captains did, than they did their families.

Q: Who was on the old *Crown Hill*?

A: Captain Butler was on one, and Johnny, the other fellow's name was Johnny, can't think of his name right now. His first name was Johnny I know.

Q: Well, fine. I would like to get back to the coal tows. You mentioned about getting around Cairo in low water. Could you talk about that again?

A: Yes there was a what they call like an island down there and when the water was down low they would have to go way around to get out, but after they would get up to a certain raise you know, and get up over this island they could just cut straight through, they could save pretty near a whole day's work. That was around Cairo, Illinois.

Q: You were talking about wheeling the coal over from the barge to the tow.

A: Well they had what they call a coal barge, you know, and they would have, that was their own coal that they used on the boat, they would have that right up again the boat. Not exactly again it, but then they would put a plank at night, they would put a plank, they would put the plank there at daylight too, but at night they would put that plank there and put flour on it, and they would wheel it in. That was the only thing they had to guide them was that flour, that white

John Knoepfle

line. If you'd miss that, why sometimes the wheelbarrow would go in; and sometimes the wheelbarrow and the guy pushing it would go in. I never did see any of them drown, but they never did get to wheelbarrow anymore.

Q: That's fine. You mentioned an experience with geese up around Louisville.

A: Oh yes, up the river on the front end of the barge. When the barges are empty they're high, way up high. And at night especially, you can't see nothing, maybe a little light half a mile ahead or something, and out on the river it is dark and you couldn't even light a match out there or cigarette or something; if you did you could hear the pilot give you a couple of cuss words for doing it.

Q: It would blind him?

A: Yes, and I was sitting there with a fellow one night, he was gauging the water. They have a pole they run down, and gauge the water as they go along to keep from running aground. The first thing I heard was something go swishhhhhh, boy my hair went right up and down. The old fellow sitting there by me says, "Take it easy sonny, they're only some wild geese." He said, "You'll hit a couple or more of them before we get up there." It sounded like the whole sky came down.

Q: Like the wrath of God.

A: Yes if you wasn't used to it, it would scare you. But the old fellow he never flinched, he just sat there. He was used to it.

Q: Now you mentioned too about the *Hercules Carrel*, and this would take us back into the log raft I guess, no the coal tows that *Carrel* would go up to meet.

A: Whenever they would come down the river with a big tow, you know, right there at Dayton, Kentucky the bend in the river there, a pretty good bend, when they'd wire down what they had coming through with, she'd go up there and help them around that bend, then help them through the bridges. The *Hercules Carrel* used to do most of that, but not all of it, but she done the most of it.

Q: And that's up by the mouth of the Little Miami.

A: Yes just around near there, she'd bring them on down around the bend, down under the bridges. Some of them had monstrous big tows too, behind them.

Q: Well how about the little gaugers you mentioned?

A: Oh yes, they had two little boats there they used to run up and gauge, get alongside the fleet, you know, and they'd gauge the coal, what kind of coal it was, and the kind of maps, and I forget the names of them. I did know them but it's kind of slipped my mind.

Q: Oh, we were talking about little auxiliary tows for the log boom, remember that?

A: Which?

Q: The little tows that would latch on front of the booms coming through here.

A: You mean the . . .

Q: When they brought a log raft down and they would want help from another boat. Could you talk about that a little?

A: Yes they had, well they'd crane boats, they used to come down. When they'd get to the bend they'd cut off from the backend where they were. They'd run around the head of the tow and get around the front of the tow, and they'd come around the bend with it that way, and when they'd get around it, run back to the backend again.

Q: Oh, I didn't know that.

A: Yes, they used to do that, they'd come around, you know, and when they'd get so they could circle her they'd cut off here, and they'd run around that tow, and get to the other end of it and pull it around the bend.

Q: Backing down.

A: Backing yes, they'd back her down sometimes they'd hold or stay that end or delay just a few squares more about a mile and a half and they were there. They've done that lots of time without any help, but you couldn't do that with a big tow without breaking her in two.

Q: Well then they would have an extra boat.

A: Yes, yes.

Q: Or along either ford or along either bank.

A: With a big barge tow you couldn't do that with them. But for logging that's the way they used to do it. Lots of times they'd cut her off and run way around, drag her on down.

Q: Wonder if you could talk a little bit about Captain Henderson who was the skipper on the *O'Neil* on the New Orleans trip?

A: Well he wasn't none of them, he wasn't no real rough guy. He was more of a quiet nice sociable guy. He never found fault with every little thing. Whenever he ordered anything on the order of meat or anything like that onboard the boat, he always smelled the meat first before he'd pay for it.

Q: He would!

A: Yes, he'd pick it up and smell it, you know, and if it was all right, it was, and if it wasn't, it wasn't.

Q: I know some of those old captains and pilots were very flashy dressers.

A: Oh yes, yes they wore spats some of them when they'd leave the boat, you know, and go up into the town where they'd be anchored, you know. Yes, hats on and everything.

Q: Now you lived down . . .

A: Oh yes that other pilot or other captain I was telling you about I forgot. His name was Johnny McGuire.

Q: McGuire.

A: I knew it was an Irish name, Johnny McGuire. He was little bit of a fellow about as big as me, five foot seven about 150 pounds. Just as tough as they made them though.

Q: He was!

A: He was that. (chuckles)

John Knoepfle

Q: Well you were from the East End and the East End produced a number of competent river men. Could you tell us something about those men?

A: Yes, they was a quite . . . I'll name you some of the captains. There was pilots. There was a Doss family down there. Old man Doss the first coal man, he was on the *City of Pittsburg* on and down around near Cairo, Illinois somewhere around where she caught fire, and he was drowned or he died from it. I was just a youngster then. And his son Harry, he was a pilot. He run on the *Island Queen* here quite a while. Now he's got a son now that's a pilot. And I hadn't seen him for so long ago, but I know he's a pilot. There was Harvey Brown, his father had a big hay and grain place down there in the East End, he was a pilot. And there was Captain Butler, one of the greatest pilots. He was a good one too, and a good guy to get along with, but a bad guy to have for an enemy. Yes Sir, he was really tough. And there was another fellow Lou Lepper, he was a captain.

Q: Lepper wrote a memoir. It was published, I understand.

A: They were all nice guys, but they never stood back for nothing.

Q: How about the Marine Ways? Could you tell us something about them?

A: Well they had a pretty good bunch of men there. They had to be husky and strong. They built a lot of boats down there. The *Island Queen*, they built the *Island Queen* and they had a big boss there, was Jack Hayes, that was his name, his name was Jack Hayes. He knew more about the river, than the river knew about itself, I believe.

Q: Well could you tell us about how they tried to save the *Greenwood* during the ice then?

A: Well that was in 1917, the river was up high, and the *Greenwood* was a big packet. She was up so high that she couldn't go no higher because she was up against the marine shed. And they put about six or eight of these three inch cables on her and every now and then they'd dynamite around her. It was all frozen gorges up the river. They was thinking they could save her, but when that river let go them cables just snapped, and zing, you could hear them snapping and first thing you know out she went. Down the river she went. She hit a pier down there, and that was the last we saw of her.

A: She was a famous old boat too.

Q: Yes, it was. The *Greenwood* she was a sternwheeler.

Q: Well this takes me over to the roustabouts.

A: Oh them roustabouts on them packets that used to come up from down in New Orleans and Natchez and them places. They used to get up here and they'd get down in the Silver Moon. That's where the hangout for them was along Front Street there. Guys would be cutting and shooting, every Saturday night, they'd be a big time whenever one of those big boats pulled in down there. Northern roustabouts, and the Southern roustabouts.

Q: They were opposed . . .

A: They were opposed to one another, yes (chuckles) they just didn't like one another.

Q: Is that so?

A: Well they would fight, always a fight.

Q: The waterfront was a kind of dangerous place in the old days?

A: Oh yes, that was a bad place to go. You had to have a lot of protection with you when you went there.

Q: Unless you were that Irish cop.

A: Oh yes, they had a, Jack McCarty was his name. He'd come down there and he'd just walk up to them and say, "Get off the sidewalk." If they didn't go why he'd walk about ten feet and turn around and put the club to them and there they'd lay. "Just leave them lay," he said, "What's the use to even bother about them? Just leave them lay there."

Q: He was from Mt. Adams.

A: Yes, he was from Mt. Adams, Jack McCarty.

Q: Well let's see. Now the rousters always went from Marine way by boat.

A: Oh whenever they'd come up there to have a boat fixed with any roustabouts on there, well they'd want to get down to the Silver Moon. They wouldn't dare to come up to catch the cars, streetcar on Eastern Avenue. They'd get a rowboat off of their own boat and they'd row down to the Silver Moon. Then they'd have that hard row to get back up again. But they thought that was better than coming up on Eastern Avenue.

Q: They must have been incredibly strong men to carry, to carry the weights they did.

A: Oh yes, they were really built. You had to be a he-man to work on a boat.

Q: Well let's see.

A: I guess half of them didn't know how to swim either. Fellows just worked on boats.

Q: I suppose the river got a lot of those men . . .

A: Oh yes.

Q: One way or another.

A: They'd get drunk and walk off the barge, or something at night and that would be the last of them.

Q: Well we were talking before about racing, wonder if could . . .

A: Oh yes, the *Island Queen* and there was a packet named the *Queen City* and they had a sister ship, a sister boat rather called the *Virginia*. One of them was a single paddle, and the other was a double paddle. The *Queen City* was a double paddle, and she could travel. Every time she would be pulling out the same time the *Island Queen* was pulling out for Coney Island there'd be a race all the way up the river to see who'd get there first. Just for nothing. Them guys if you could beat them today you'd have to beat them tomorrow.

Q: (laughter) So they managed to smoke up the East End?

A: Oh they'd throw more smoke out, sometimes you could see the flame coming out of the stack.

Q: Is that so?

A: Yes.

Q: You mentioned about the *Princess* being a ballasted boat, can you?

A: Yes, her hold had ballasts in it. She was set so high on the water that they had to ballast it, 1917 that got her too, that ice.

Q: Did it?

A: Yes.

Q: Right down in the Kentucky River.

A: She was in the Kentucky River at the time.

Q: Well, we talked about whistles too. Whistles and the *Morning Star*.

A: *Morning Star* had a whistle, it was a beautiful thing, and she hit a pier or something down there at the foot of Broadway. And anyhow she sunk. When they salvaged her they got this whistle, and they put it on the *Courier* that traveled between Cincinnati and Pittsburgh. It was the most beautiful whistle, and they tried to make another one like it, but even the people that made that one, couldn't make it.

Q: Couldn't make one.

A: Yes, it was a beautiful whistle.

Q: And people would come out . . .

A: Yes, just to hear that thing whistle they'd come out on the banks just to hear it whistle.

Q: And up by the . . .

A: All through the valley there that whistle just sounded all through there, Walnut Hills, and you could hear it all over. It was a pretty thing.

Q: Now, you mentioned there was the mates that were pretty tough characters, too.

A: Oh yes, them mates on those packets anyhow, they were really rough. They'd take them roustabouts, and hit them with sticks, and everything else, fists, knock them in the river, and everything and keep hollering, "Come on, let's get going here," and was just like slaves, that's all it was.

Q: Do you remember any more of the mate's dialogue, the kind of things they said?

A: Well I would be afraid to say (laughter) anything they say. I can cuss but not like some of them.

Q: I am going to tape the college professor someday who memorized the mates spiel and he won't have any compunction about it.

A: Yes.

Q: Oh you mentioned too about *Hercules Carrel* with cutters.

A: Oh yes there I think it was in 1913 the first they had of it. The river was froze over then because we were skating on it and somebody got an idea about putting steel cutters on the front of the *Hercules Carrel* bow. She was a powerful boat. So they did and they started her up the river and she'd just keep running from here up to about Coney Island, and she would turn around and come back. Just kept the channel open, you know. Of course, no other boats went up there, but they figured that would take some of the squeeze off of the shores, you know, and it would let go.

Q: I see, and then there was the snag boats.

A: The old *E. A. Woodruff,* yes she was a snag boat, she used to take snags and things out of the river, barges, she done that.

Q: How about dynamiting with barges?

A: Oh yes, they used to dynamite. They would have divers go down and set some dynamite and blow something loose down there, and then seen them blow a barge loose there one time. When she came out of there she was like a big whale coming up, just whew!

Q: Right out of the water.

A: Yes, jumped right out of the water. Turn over, you know, and all that coal would go out of her, and whew!

Q: Well we've got to a lot of the things we decided to talk about. I wonder if I can ask you a few incidental questions. Whether you have any recollections for instance of shanty boaters along the river.

A: Just no good. They'd steal everything they could. But they was one fellow down there his name was Brown. He had a little money. He had the hardwood floors in it.

Q: He did!

A: Yes, and an ice box. They'd bring ice down to him, and electric lights. They just had a electric pole down there, and of course, that was on a reel, you know, if the river come up they'd just keep winding it up. Go down they'd let it out. And he had a Victrola in there. We fellows on Saturday night we'd go down there and play a little poker, you know. We'd have some beer and everything like that and have a nice old time down there. Nobody would bother you.

Q: I guess he worked part-time up on the bank somewhere.

A: Yes he had a part-time job, I think he was a shoemaker. He was a bachelor, and you know come day go day with him. Saturday nights would be our nights.

Q: You had a nice little existence there.

A: Yes, we'd play a little nickel, five cent limit poker, you know, and have some beer to drink. Have pretty near the same every Saturday night. But he had it pretty nice. He was a pretty talented fellow, he used to like to read a whole lot you know. Keep books, you know, books that, hell it was first time I seen one of them. "Geez," I said, "do you read these?" And he said, "Yes." "Boy," I said, "I couldn't even carry one of them." (laughter) There were a lot of them rivermen, they were brutal in their working conditions and things like that, but they had a lot of good ideas and things like that you know. They could talk to you on, oh religion or anything.

Q: Is that so?

John Knoepfle

A: Yes, I told one of them one day I said, "Hell you fellows don't even believe in God, do you?" He told me he says, "I know more about God than you'll ever know, son." He says, "There's a God, don't think it ain't." He says, "Because you see it the way we act around here." He says, "Don't believe there ain't a God." He says, "There is."

Q: Well could you tell me a little more about some of your other activities outside of the river, what you did?

A: Well I never did do much of anything I guess, different little jobs off and on. During the war I was working at the, 1917 I was at R. K. LeBlond. It was a machine tool industry. I worked for them for about eight years. It was a nice place to work too. Clean and neat. They were making machines for the government. I guess that's what kept me out of it. I ask for an examination and I was drafted. They put me in 2B, put me in industrial class. So there was nothing I could do, I couldn't even enlist. Wouldn't let you enlist after you had that 2B card. I went there, and then I went over to the united states Playing Card Company and I worked there for about 35 years. Then I retired.

Q: What were you doing for them?

A: I was running machines over there. Punch machines, that punches cards out.

Q: You were responsible for millions of playing cards then?

A: Oh yes, yes many a deck I've punched out.

Q: Did you ever work for the City Transit?

A: I worked on the streetcars.

Q: Did you?

A: That was in around 1910.

Q: Can you tell me something about that, just offbeat?

A: Well let's see, I got fired off that job.

Q: You did?

A: Yes you know, they wouldn't tell you when they fired you. They wouldn't tell you what you were fired for. But you could guess that you missed a fare and they thought you had it or something like that. But I never did play that way. I don't think I ever stole anything in my life. It's a pretty good job if you've got a lot of patience. If you get reported it's bad, like one time there were three women got on the car. It was coming in from Oakley. And they said give us three transfers, oh I can't remember just where they wanted to go. So I punched them three transfers and they sat there and I went to the backend. And finally they beckoned to me to come up again. So I went up and they wanted them changed you know. Well I just punched a different route for them on the same transfers and handed them to them. I went to the backend again. I was talking to a fellow and finally he says, "They want you up there again, John." So I went up and I said, "Do you want me?" "Yes, we decided we want to ride on another route."

So I said, "Okay, just a minute," and I went in the backend, and I always had an extra book of transfers, You was allowed to have an extra book in case anything happened to the others. So I took this extra book and my punch in, and I throwed it one of their laps and said, "When you find a road you want to ride on you just punch it." (laughter) That was a black mark again me. Yes, they reported me. (laughter) They reported me for it and I says, "Well I went down to Robert E. Lee that was the president of the transit company at that time, and he looked at me, and he started to laugh, and he says, "What's your beef?" I told him and he says, "Oh hell, are you the guy that . . . ." I says, "I'm the guy if that's what you mean." He says, "By God," he says, "I couldn't of thought of that." He says, "I should of when I was working on the streetcars." He was working on them himself one time. He said, "that's one for the books." I says, "Well I guess I'm fired." He says, "No, go back and if you get any more of them, tell them the same thing."

Q: I understand some of those fellows on the cars got rich.

A: Oh yes, they didn't have no fare boxes, you know. Well sometimes your changer would get full and you had to put it in your pocket. Yes they didn't pay nothing. Of course, if you got fired off of the streetcar everybody would say why he got fired for knocking down. So you might as well knock down.

Q: Those earlier cars, they were horse drawn, weren't they?

A: Well I remember the horse cars, but I never worked on them. All we had was them little four wheel cars. Then they got those double-deckers. Yes, we had it pretty good, well I think days were better in them days than they are now.

Q: Could be, I don't know.

A: Yes, I would say. You know the trouble today with the people is, take the teenagers, why they blame everything on to them and this and that. I don't think it's half of the teenagers. That's their life, a good life, a lot of them are making good. The only thing I'd say about it is ain't going to live as long as I live. Because they don't get the exercise.

Q: Could be.

A: Yes, damn it if they want a pack of cigarettes they'll go out, and get in the car maybe just for a square go down and get a pack of cigarettes. They got to ride in that car down there and back where it would do them good if they'd of went out and walked. Walk's the best thing in the world. Walk and a lot of good water. Drink a lot of good water.

Q: True they all look like they're tired.

A: They do, they do.

Q: They're already living like old men.

A: They don't want to be bothered with nothing. Like you and I said before they couldn't sit here this long. They'd be up, "Oh got to do this or do that." They don't get no exercise, automobiles are spoiling them. Making them lazy.

Q: Might be, I don't know.

A: Gee, I used to walk two miles to school and back.

Q: Well you're living kind of a leisurely life now aren't you?

A: Yes, yes I am on social security.

Q: And you have a little part-time job here at Graeter's.

A: A part-time job here and I like it. I might as well say my own boss. Nobody bothers me. I do the work the way they want it. So they got no gripe and I got none either.

Q: And on a day like this you feel like a rich man I suppose.

A: Yes.

Q: Good weather and all.

A: I got that social security check coming in, and then I get a dollar from the firm that I work for. I get a dollar for every year that I worked there. I get that every month. And besides my $15 or $20 a week here. That's spending money.

Q: Well I'll put the bite on you or something. (laughter)

A: Well John they ain't no fish in the river now, the Ohio River.

Q: I heard there was some marvelous fishing down there.

A: Oh boy, we used to catch fish, never had to buy fish.

Q: I talked to a man named Charles Harrison and who ran the Dayton ferry.

A: Oh, yes. Oh yes, he and I were buddies. Where did you see him?

Q: Well I went out there in that boat house, which they converted out of the *Chris Greene*.

A: Yes, the old *Chris Greene*, that's what they done.

Q: He said they used to catch sturgeon in the river.

A: Yes, he ran the old Dayton ferry there. Oh God, I thought he was dead.

Q: No, they are very much alive; you ought to drop over there some evening.

A: That's what I'm going to do. He was a character, had an old ferry boat would go across there and that thing would be going like this and them waves . . .

Q: Rocking!

A: When them boats would pass. This old propeller would be out of water and she'd blooooom, and she'd get the water and she'd stop.

Q: He told us that some of the packets threw an awful wave and on purpose too.

A: Oh boy, yes.

Q: He said that Captain Brennan on the *City of Louisville* was always a kind of curious fellow.

A: Yes, I remember him he was on the *City of Louisville*.

Q: He didn't throw any waves like the other ones.

A: The *Island Queen* used to do it.

Q: Did it?

A: Yes. They shot at it, the *Island Queen*, one time some of them people up through there. The river was up high, you know, and that thing plowing up the river there, and them side wheelers throw an awful side wave, you know. They took a shot at the pilot house. I don't know whether they tried to hit it or not. But they scared old Doss.

Q: Did?

A: Yes, sir. Then after that he got out in the middle of the river when he would get high water, they'd get over as close as they could to the bank. That channel was real fast when it was high water.

Q: I know that Charley met Wes Doss I think it was and they were talking about that. He used to cuss at them from the ferry boat.

A: Yes, he used to have a fellow named Wallace, Bill Wallace run the ferry boat for him every once in a while. I don't know where Bill is any more, but he could handle the boat. Last time I heard of him he was some big shot up there in Cincinnati. He got a big yacht down in Florida.

Q: Is that so?

A: Bill took it down for him and I think he's still maybe running it for him.

Q: You know a fellow named Paris or Parish that used to make . . .

A: Pat Parish, yes, he made speed boats over there.

Q: I would like to get in touch with him. I don't exactly know how to do that.

A: Well he's over in Dayton, Kentucky there. I'll tell you how you can get in touch with him. Go down to what's his name's boat house there and ask. Pat lives there in Dayton.

Q: Well, I'll do that then. Well we're beginning to gab off our topic.

A: Yes. He was a pretty rough customer, but just as I said they were all good fellows at heart. Boy, I wonder what would happen if they'd all come back to life again, see the river almost closed down and different things.

Q: They'd be disappointed, I guess.

A: They wouldn't like it at all.

Q: Not so much fun there as there was.

A: In them days no matter what, you'd go in a saloon, now all you see is women laying on the bar, and them days you never seen that. They had the gardens and there you were. If you wasn't 21 years old, you didn't have to have anything to show you were 21, but if the bartender thought you wasn't 21 you didn't get nothing to drink. He'd throw you out of there. Most of the places now a days, they'd give it to you if you're ready to fall down. Them days they didn't. They were that way about their families.

Q: Not so many of the old bars either, there was a kind of dignity about those older bars that you don't find now days.

A: No, they ain't got nothing, you go in there and it looks like going into a funeral home. There's no lights in the places. Those pretty lights, but they don't throw no light. You could go to fashionable places downtown, you could go in there and buy a glass of beer and you'd get a whole dinner. The best of ham, the best of beef and whatever kind of a sandwich you wanted.

Q: There is still a beautiful old bar in Norwood I think, has all that turned wood and tiled floor. Big white haired bartender could just slide a beer down to you.

A: Yes, I've heard of him, but in fact, I never go in a saloon much anymore.

Q: Well this is quite a nice place.

A: Well years ago they had good whiskey, 18 or 20 years old. And you could get a big two ounce glass of it for ten cents.

Q: They shipped a lot of whiskey around here by boat, didn't they?

A: Yes, oh yes, whiskey and beer. The *Chilo* used to go up the river, it was a packet, and she used to go up the river. And this may sound funny, but it's a fact, every fishing camp along the river, if you wanted beer, all you had to do was call up and have it delivered by the *Chilo*.

Q: Is that so?

A: She'd come up the river, and when she'd get near your camp, they knew every camp up there on her, they'd whistle and they'd say, "Here comes our beer." They'd come right in and unload it, back out and go on up to the next camp. They'd do that way all the way up the river.

Q: Is that so?

A: Saturday or Friday night was big night. She run late on them nights. She would be full of beer, whiskey too, I guess.

Q: They brought it on the boat and put ice on top of it.

A: Oh that beer would keep.

Q: Would!

A: Yes, that beer would keep for weeks without any ice. The beer they got now won't. The beer they got now, when they throw it in they got to do like they do ice cream and stuff like that. The one that's in there they have to tap it first before they tap a new beer that just come in. It would sour on them. Used to see some of them old river men, they'd be bringing them empties back you know. There would be lots of beer in them yet you know. They'd take a bucket, they'd drink it and it wouldn't be sour. That beer would be two and three days old.

Q: That was all barrel beer, wasn't it?

A: Yes. Now they, even if barreled beer they can't keep that. When you say the good old days, well there was a lot of bad about the good old days, but I think the people were more sociable.

Q: Could be.

A: Yes. They was always willing to help you even if you were even a stranger. They'd help you in them days. Now they ain't got time to do anything like that. You'd see them, like a fellow would be in trouble with his horse or something. One would come along and they'd all give them a lift. Now if a fellow is in trouble with his automobile, they just beep-beep and get the hell out of the way. They pass you up like they are afraid of you.

Q: Well, I want to thank you for talking to me.

A: Well everything I told you was the truth.

Q: Well fine. If you get a chance go over and visit Charley there. He's usually there on Friday nights.

A: I forgot all about him until we got to talking here. Ain't that funny?

Q: Well wonderful.

A: I thought that he was dead.

Q: No, indeed.

Ellen & Romain Proctor, April 10, 1957

Romain Proctor: We are happy to be here because we have come into Columbus to celebrate the second anniversary of our grandson's birthday. We are over at the Zanger house. Dr. Zanger of Ohio State University. I am Romain Proctor and my wife Ellen is sitting right beside me. Say hello Mama.

Ellen Proctor: Hello Mama.

R: So we are off. We are the proprietors of a traveling Marionette show, a puppet show. We make practically everything we use on show. We build our own puppets. Ellen dresses them. We write our plays. I make the properties, the stages and scenery. We troupe the show ourselves. We work usually in about 36 states a year. We have been in nine foreign countries. Our work has been very interesting because we have a number of hobbies we pursue as we go around the country. For instance, we are interested in the Civil War. So we have visited practically all the battlefields of the Civil War, and studied out the tactics for everything from what happened, where they went after the battle, and so forth, the effects of the battle. We have been interested in beauty spots all up and down the country. We have been interested in especially the Cherokee Indians, and we have followed their trails as we have to go around to make a living. One of the things that has interested us most has been the rivers. You know the very names of the rivers are almost poetry. Like the Oostanaula, the Coosa, the Tallapoosa, the Tallahatchie, the Yalobusha and the Yazoo.

John Knoepfle Question: Where are all those rivers?

Answer R: Those are all Southern rivers. The Coosa starts up in Georgia. The Oostanaula is one of its tributaries. The Coosa and Tallapoosa form the Alabama River. Then over in Mississippi the Tallahatchie and the Yalobusha form the Yazoo, which flows down into the Mississippi just at Vicksburg. One reason we are very interested in these, so many military things have happened on these rivers. For instance, Sherman's march down to Atlanta crossed over through the Georgia territory of the rivers. Of course, one of the most bitterly fought battles was down on the Chickamauga Creek in the same neighborhood. So the rivers have played a very important part in our country from a military standpoint and we crossed them up there, but we were interested in the rivers purely of their own romance and their own beauty. The Mississippi being our greatest river and to us it's a great big huge enormous river; it's just a lovely river. So we followed it from way up in northern Minnesota, not in Bemidji, but short of Bemidji, clear down to where it pours into the gulf. We've gone down as far as the roads go and we've crossed over it many, many places on bridges and ferries. So the river has been very important to us. We've enjoyed it very much, and we have been able to see some of the older vessels that are tied up, for instance the showboat at St. Louis and the towboat at Vicksburg, and we have been privileged to go aboard these boats and visit with the people who used to run them. Of course, with the showboat, we knew the showboat before it was tied up, when it was on the rivers. It used to come up the Illinois and we used to go over to Beardstown and see the shows. Then we were fortunate knowing some of the earlier people on the showboats.

Q: Which showboat is that?

R: That is the *Goldenrod*. Lester Lake who lived in and around Cincinnati became a very well-known magician under the name of Marvello. Lester in his younger days was a professional photographer and he quit in photography to do magic, and the only job he could get was playing leading man on a showboat. He went on showboat to do magic, but he had to play a leading man to get to do magic between acts. You know the old showboats, nearly everyone doubled, not only did they have a soft-shoe dance or could sing a song, but they frequently played an instrument. Now when the showboats would come in for instance, over in Illinois, most of them would have calliopes in the old days.

A man named Ray Choissier, crazy Ray Choissier from Pinckneyville, Illinois was a calliope player. We had an experience a few years ago, we visited a circus winter quarters and they were trying to tune up an old calliope and I said to this man who was working on it, "Do you know Ray Choissier?" He said, "Ah, yes, he was a steam man." So it seems that the steam calliope has been superseded by electric things, but these old men held these things in such an awe and reverence, so Ray Choissier was a steam man. Well the thing that impressed me mainly with Ray Choissier, he had little cards made, little business cards and it said on them, "Hundreds have seen him, thousands have heard him, and millions never will," (chuckles) which amused me no end. They'd play the calliope before the showtime to attract attention. They'd be tied up at the levee, play the calliope, then the band would come out and serenade while the people would buy their tickets. Then the band would go in, and part of them would go in, and part of them would become an orchestra. You would see the piano player suddenly ducking out of the pit and going up and playing a part on the stage as a trumpet player. The plays that we saw, I knew them, were not the old standard melodramas, but more of the more recent things. But between acts they would have different specialties where these people would do their tricks, including my friend Lester doing his magic.

Lester told me a tale. Now this of course is purely second hand, but I believe it is true. It seems when Edna Ferber wrote her story, the novel *Showboat*, she wanted some firsthand information for local color. So she wrote to the showboat and ask permission to join on for a week just to get local color. But the showboat people never heard of Edna Ferber, they ignored the telegraph and put it in a drawer. Edna Ferber went to the Chesapeake Bay area and did see a showboat, but not the type we used on our rivers. Several years later when the book was published and became a huge success old Captain Menke of the showboat remembered that he had received such a telegram. So he digs it out of the drawer, frames it and was hanging when I saw the boat last, it was hanging on the wall, the letter from Edna Ferber. She didn't get to see, but still he was showman enough to exploit that.

The next boat that impressed me very greatly was the *Sprague*, which was the greatest, I'll say was the largest towboat on the river. The biggest ever built. According to the story it moved more, what shall I say, cargo than any other craft in maritime history. Over 100 barges I believe of coal were pushed down the Ohio into the Mississippi by this one tow boat. It was a tremendous thing and the old boat then later belonged to Standard Oil. The *SS Standard Oil* was used on the river, but now it seems a tendency is for smaller tow boats, diesels and smaller tows because of the locks and so forth. The *Sprague* was given to the city of Vicksburg and is now used as a yacht club. You can go aboard for a very nominal fee. So a number of years ago, Mimi Zanger here before she was Mrs. Zanger, and Ellen and I were in Vicksburg. So while Ellen was working, Mimi and I went down to the river just to look at the *Sprague*. We didn't know anything about going on it. We learned later that you could go on by paying a small fee.

But while we were looking an old pilot named Captain Portwood came up and he says, "Look at her, look at her, biggest goddamn boat on the river. Isn't she beautiful. Isn't she lovely. Come I'll show you." So he took each of us, he took her wrist and my wrist and literally dragged us, he was like the ancient mariner to us, he dragged us aboard and there was a man on board to sell us a ticket but not the captain. The captain, that was his right as a pilot to come aboard, and we were his friends and he told them so. "And I'm bringing my friends aboard, my guests." So the thing that threw us was, and surprised us very much, he turned to us suddenly and said, "What's your name?" After he had panned us off as his friends. So he wouldn't let us pay, but I did sneak away from him later and paid the man our admission. I didn't want to freeload on the boat. Then two or three of the old crew of the boat that had been working before it was tied up they were still there and they were acting as guides. But the old Captain Portwood wouldn't let us pay anything and he would take us from one part of the boat up to the other. Up to the pilothouse, down to the engine room, and he would explain to us, and always identify himself with it, of course, because he had been a pilot for many years. And also he found pictures of himself that were hanging in there when he had piloted the boat, which was practically covered with cotton bales. A packet that was so loaded down that you could barely see the boat for the cotton bales on it.

He was a very profane old man, but it was the type of profanity that was so original and so natural with him that it doesn't sound like profanity. While we were aboard the boat there was a sidetrack of a railroad nearby and a train came chugging by and Mimi and I both turned to look at the train, and he grabbed her by the arm and spun her around and said, "Don't look at that god-damn train, look at this boat, look at this boat, you can always see a goddamn train, but not this boat." He took us all over the thing and showed us. He was a

John Knoepfle

very irascible, fiery, very old man, but he was the last of the old river pilots that I ever saw.

Mrs. Hedges who was about 83 years old now and lives in St. Louis was the adopted daughter of Colonel Hughes. He had an interesting background on the river. He started on the Mississippi as a young man. He saved his money and bought him a small boat. He didn't associate with his crew at all. Whenever he came into town and had a few minutes, instead of going to saloons, or the hang-outs with the crew members, the old man went down to the library. He would read and there was some talk that he gained a great deal of information about the world. His line prospered, he happened to have a number of boats, and he got into the ice business. They would cut ice in the winter up river and then they would store it on wharfboats and that would be an ice house. Then in the hot weather they would peddle that ice down the river to hotels and saloons and places of that sort. The Colonel made a great deal of money.

Mrs. Hedges was left an orphan because her parents who were very prominent people went down the river to nurse in a yellow fever epidemic and they died by contracting the disease, leaving this little child, and Colonel Hughes adopted her. She was educated in Europe. Had a wonderful education and she knew the most amazing people. She knew Cosima Wagner, she knew Henrik Ibsen. So with people of almost fabulous reputations, she would give me all kinds of information about them. So once I asked her if knew Mark Twain, and she said yes. She knew Mark Twain, she had been to dinners with him and things of that sort. And said, "Did you know anything about him on the river?" And she said, "Well, he worked for my father for a while, but he was not a good pilot. He ran the boat on a snag or a sawyer or something and piled the boat up, and my father said that he just couldn't afford him. Instead of paying attention on the boat he must of have been thinking up stories." So that is purely second hand information, but that was her opinion of Mark Twain as a riverman.

We have a peculiar type of puppet show in as much as we do many different things. For instance, a little earlier just about a year ago, Dr. Zanger through the English Department had us come to the English Department at LSU and do a talk on, pardon me OSU, I've got the wrong state here. I was down in Louisiana it seems. Did a talk on puppets in relation to folk drama, and tied it in that way. We sometime lecture and do demonstrations. We've taught up at the University of Minnesota for their Continuation Studies. So all of our work is not straight entertainment. But the big part of our work is giving shows around the country, in which we act out plays and do variety acts. At present we offer eight plays, mainly adapted from folk stories or children's stories. For instance, things like *Rumpelstiltskin*, *Sleeping Beauty*, *Jack in the Beanstalk* and *Red Riding Hood*. Plays of that sort that we have adapted getting as much of ourselves into it as possible. Using just the skeleton of the story and building on that. We travel by truck. We have an International Metro, that's a type truck with the body going from bumper to bumper. So it's just like a little house on wheels. We do not sleep in it. We use it purely for traveling and for carrying our equipment and all the excess junk we pick up as we go around the country. We collect many things and by the time we get home it's full of books, antique furniture and just about everything. Shells and rocks and things that interest us and our friends.

Q: Where is your home?

R: We live in Springfield, Illinois but we're seldom there. Our children are now grown. Our older boy is in New York, and editor on Crystal Publications, and he is going to NYU Law School. His wife has a master's in psychology, and she has been offered, they are thinking of going up to Clark University, to work on her doctorate. So they may go up there, and then he will enter Harvard Law School. He will transfer from NYU. Our second boy is at Washington U. working on his doctorate in English. Of course, our baby Mimi is here, wife of Dr. Zander at Ohio State University. I will get it right this time. So our children are all gone, they are all married and flown the coop. So we own this home, which acts as headquarters. It has a full basement and a full attic and they're literally full. We have, I believe, the best library of puppet books in the country. Have an agent in Brussels, I have one in Paris, and two in London to buy books for us. So we have been able to pick up nearly everything that has been written on puppets. It is not complete but it is more complete than any other collection I know. Then we have a very large collection of puppets from all over the world. Shadow puppets from China, and Java and Bali, Siam and Greece. Round puppets from well just all over the world. Hand puppets and round puppets and string puppets, marionettes. So that is our home base and our mailing address. Our mail always reaches us no matter where we go because it goes there and it is forwarded to us.

In traveling we work with superior people. We are very fortunate in working with nice people. Most of our sponsors are colleges, art museums, children's theatre groups, and we work with groups that try to make money for some reason, such as the Junior League will sometimes sponsor us for a project or groups of that sort, they are called service clubs or civic clubs. They are usually the same element as a Junior League would be but in a smaller city you cannot have Junior Leagues. So we work with nice people.

When we go in we have to take in a complete stage. We erect our stage on their stage in their auditorium. We have been in some very, very interesting places to erect our little stage, which I will tell you later. Our stage consists of a bridge on which we stand. A lower platform for the puppets. We have maskings to hide us from the audience and then the scenery, the backdrops hide us so we work over them and can manipulate our puppets in their own setting. We make their properties for them, paint all their scenery. We have a rail going around three sides where we hang the puppets and we can reach out and get a puppet whenever we want it, And then we have a place to put it when we are

John Knoepfle

with it, which is a problem with a string puppet which had from nine to 25 to 30 strings. Some of them are very complicated so you don't just throw them in a corner. You have to hang them up rather carefully so you can use them again.

With our variety acts we have a banjo player, crooner, an opera singer, a piano player. Piano play for years was called Tom DeKays, but since Liberace has become very famous for especially younger people when we'd bring the puppet out on the stage and everybody would say Liberace so we had to change his name. We called him Liber Itchie. Changed his makeup, changed his face rather, so he now looks more like a caricature of Liberace. We have circus acts, many circus acts doing all sorts of things, animals and clowns and such. We have a scene in the graveyard. We have tombstones and skeletons. Have it fixed now so the moon rises, clouds pass through the sky and one cloud rains. Little drops of rain drop off the cloud, drop through the cloud down onto the ground and every time a drop of rain hits the stage a flower pops up. (chuckles) In other words we started out with a skeleton and we have ended up with a whole act built around the skeleton. So now we have three skeletons in the act as well as seven tombstones and all of these other props that go into it. That is the type of performance we give for straight entertainment.

Frequently, we bring in a number of foreign puppets and show the different categories of puppets, how they are manipulated and make it into a lecture demonstration in conjunction with our play. That is the program angle of it. Some of the places we have played that are rather interesting, we had been to Carville, Louisiana where everyone in our audience had leprosy. We played at the Houston Respiratory center where every one of the audience had on some form of iron lung. We played for Sister Kenney's Institute. We played for many mental hospitals where everyone was mentally sick, which to me is the most depressing place because even sick children are still happy. But these people are the forgotten people. We played oh, we played in a lady's bedroom once. We set up our stage once on a stage made of baled hay. We set up stage once on a semi-trailer truck. We used the side door as our proscenium and worked the show in that. So we have been in some very interesting places. If you would be interested Ellen and I will try, although this is not easy, we'll try to do a scene for you. The reason that it is not easy is that the puppet becomes part of you. When you are giving a puppet show identify yourself with the puppet and when you are working you coordinate so with the puppet that to try to do a scene without it, I do not know if that is possible. Let's start with *Red Riding Hood* where the little dog tries to warn her of the wolf. Let us take just before he tells her when she asks, "Do you smell something?" The little dog is running around the stage listening, looking and he finally goes sniff, sniff, sniff.

E: (Ellen as Red Riding Hood) What's the matter, Tommy Tucker, do you smell something?

R: (Romain as the dog) Woof, woof.

E: Woof, woof.

R: Yes, woof, woof.

E: You know it sounded just exactly like he said, wolf, wolf.

R: Yes, yes, wolf, wolf, wolf.

E: Oh I know, you want to play a game.

R: No, no, no, wolf, wolf, wolf, run, run, run.

E: Wolf, wolf, wolf, run, run, run. Ah, Tommy Tucker, come on, we don't have time to play any games, we have to hurry.

R: Ah, good afternoon.

E: Oh, you frightened me.

R: Ah, how are you today?

E: I'm sorry sir but I can't talk to you because my mother said for me not to talk to anybody that I saw in the forest.

R: Ah, but I'm sure your mother would like for you to talk to a nice friendly gentleman like I am. See me wag my tail.

E: You look friendly when you wag your tail like that. I am going to speak to you, Mr. Wolf. How do you do, Mr. Wolf?

R: Ah, how do you do?

E: Mr. Wolf, you know my little dog Tommy Tucker is friendly too when he wags his tail.

R: I don't like dogs. Aaaaaaaaaahhhhheeeee.

E: Oh, what's the matter?

R: Ah, every time I get hot or excited my fleas bother me.

E: Do you have fleas, Mr. Wolf. Do you know what, Mr. Wolf? Once my little dog Tommy Tucker had fleas and you know what my mother did? She gave him a bath.

R: A bath, I don't like baths.

E: But baths are good for you, Mr. Wolf.

R: What do you have in this big basket?

E: Oh my basket is full of good things to eat.

R: Ah and I'm hungry.

E: Oh but you can't have any of the things in my basket, Mr. Wolf. No sir because I'm taking this basket to my grandma's house.

R: Is she a nice plump grandma?

E: Oh no, my grandma is not fat. But, Mr. Wolf, you know what? I betcha my grandma is the nicest grandma in the whole world.

R: Yes.

E: Yes, look at my cape, do you like it?

R: It's beautiful.

E: Oh I'm so glad you like it Mr. Wolf cause do you know my grandma made it for me.

R: She did?

E: Yes, say can you keep a secret?

R: Ah yes, I like secrets.

John Knoepfle

E: Well if I tell you, you won't go telling anybody.

R: Ah no.

E: All right now you listen. It's magic.

R: What is magic? Your grandma?

E: No my cape.

R: What's magic about it?

E: The good fairies in the forest put a magic spell on it and they said as long as I have this cape on nothing can hurt me.

R: As long as you have the magic spell on nothing can hurt you?

E: No Mr. Wolf the magic cape.

R: Ah, you mean as long as you wear the magic cape nothing can hurt you? Hah, hah, hah, hah, hah.

E: Well it's true.

R: Well it sounds like a silly superstition to me. We'll see if it's true. (A chopping sound) What's that?

E: What, that chopping?

R: Yes, what's that?

E: That's my daddy. He's there chopping down trees. He has his great big axe.

R: His axe.

E: Yes.

R: Aaaaaaaaaah, say where did you say your grandmother lived?

E: I didn't say. But if you want to know I will tell you. My grandma lives on the other side of that forest. You know that little house Mr. Wolf, the one that has the red shutters?

R: Well let's go over to Grandma's. I'd feel safer over there.

E: Oh no you can't go to my grandma's.

R: Ah yes, I'm sure she would like to see a nice friendly gentleman like I am.

E: No Mr. Wolf because she's not expecting you. Besides I have to hurry.

R: There is no better way to hurry than to run, come on, let's run.

E: Run a race.

R: Yes we'll run a race come on let's run.

E: I like to run races.

R: Well come on let's run.

E: You just don't start out and run when you run a race.

R: No.

E: No didn't you ever run a race before?

R: Well I never ran one like this.

E: Well you have to run for the money first.

R: I never ran one for money.

E: Oh Mr. Wolf I'll have to show you what to do then. You take your toe and you draw a line on the ground with your toe.

R: You mean just like this?

E: And then we both stand on our line at the very same time.

R: All right I'm on it.

E: Well wait that's not all Mr. Wolf. Then when we are both on the line then I'll say one for the money, two for the show, three to make ready and four to go. But don't you run until I say four to go.

R: All right all right all right I'm on the line come on and say four to go, four to go, four to go.

E: Oh Mr. Wolf, now get on the line.

R: I'm on the line hurry up hurry up yes.

E: One for the money.

R: One for the money.

E: Two for the show.

R: Two for the show.

E: Say Mr. Wolf are you sure you want to go to Grandma's house?

R: Oh yes I'm sure. Oh come on I'm drowning in my own gastric juices. Hurry up hurry up.

E: Well all right get on the line.

R: I'm on the line.

E: Are you ready?

R: I'm ready I'm ready.

E: One for the money.

R: One for the money.

E: Two for the show.

R: Two for the show.

E: Three to make ready.

R: Three to make ready.

E: Say Mr. Wolf, maybe Grandma won't like us to go to her house.

R: Oh let's wait til we get there to find out, come on let's run.

E: Well all right. One for the money.

R: Yes.

E: Two for the show.

R: Yes.

E: Three to make ready.

R: Yes.

E: And four to go.

Q: Wonderful, I've never heard the story before.

R: In the story of *Goldilocks and the Three Bears* as you know you really have just the three episodes. You have the bears leaving home because the porridge is too hot to eat. You have Goldilocks coming in, eating the porridge, breaking the chair and going up and getting in the little bear's bed. Then the other bears come home, which is the third episode. Well we had done the first part of the show and the bears come home. The first one is always the father bear and he said, "Someone has been in this room." A little voice has been in this room and a little voice out in the audience says, "Yes, it's Goldilocks, she has eaten the

John Knoepfle

porridge, she has broken the chair, she's up in baby bear's bed and you had better go up there and do something about it," left me high and dry. Then you could hear a muffled sound, it was her mother putting her hand over the little girl's mouth. I tried to go through, Goldilocks, who is Goldilocks, you know, that sort of thing as if I didn't know. She brought the show right to a conclusion right now. We had one child I remember come to the front of the stage after the curtain was down, the audience was filing out, and this little voice said, "Goldilocks, Goldilocks, come out and play, come out and play Goldilocks." So evidently the puppet was quite real to her. Ellen, can you think of some things that happened?

E: Well, one was when the child wanted to know if the monkey was alive.

R: The puppets evidently create an illusion of being in real life, so Ellen was trying to explain to a child once that this puppet was not alive, she had a little monkey. She said, "Look when I relax the string the puppet just lies there, he can't do anything." The child looked. Eventually Ellen started to pick the puppet up. As soon as there was tension on the string the puppet started to react to the pull, and he said, "Yes, it is too alive." She was never able to convince the child that the puppet wasn't alive. Another child came back stage once and we had a lion. This child came up and very tentatively touched the lion, jumped back, nothing happened, touched it again a little bolder this time. Then he went around in back put his finger up against the lion's mouth and nothing happened. Then he went over and bit the lion on the tail. That was the final test.

Jules Zanger: Can you tell about the effect after the show when you stick your head through the curtain?

R: There is an illusion, yes, the puppets acting on their own stage create an illusion of their being much bigger than they really are. In other words, it's a matter of relativity. We are in the habit of measuring everything, when you go to the store to buy cloth you use a yardstick and measure it. Well we do not give our audience a yardstick if we can help. Everything is made to the puppet's own proportion. So when you see the puppet on his own stage with everything surrounding him in his own proportion, if you are sitting back in a dark auditorium the puppet looks much larger. So as the people sit there for an hour they become accustomed to this puppet on the stage and they think it's real, I mean life size. And to break this illusion at the end of our show, we have a puppet come out and say, "Now we would like to introduce the largest of puppets, Mrs. Proctor." Ellen sticks her head out and being three times larger than the puppet, she just gives the illusion of a giant coming out. We have had many reactions on that. We heard one voice say once, "Why, she looked so large I could see the pores in her skin." Another woman came back once and said, "Are you the only people running this show?" And she acted so funny. After the show she said, "You probably wondered why I was so curious. Why I kept asking questions." She said, "My little girl came home and said you have the biggest woman in the world on that show. The biggest woman I have ever seen," and I wanted to see what it was. So this child did not understand that it was an illusion, she thought that Ellen was much larger than the puppet.

I start with an idea, whether it's a stage, or scenery, properties and start drawing pictures. I visualize everything in sketches. Eventually get it to the point I want, and then I make a detailed drawing same size. I find that the easiest way for the puppets or the properties. With the puppets, I draft this thing very carefully, planning where the joints are to fall, the balance of the puppet and so forth. Then I model features like head, hands, feet in clay. It is a permanently soft clay. After I get my modeling as well as I can I make a plaster cast. I make them usually, say a head I make it in four pieces. So that they can come apart and I can get anything out without breaking the cast. Into this plaster cast I cast plastic wood that you can get at hardware stores or paint stores. I buy it directly from the manufacturer in great big cans, usually 25 pounds because we use a lot of it. It is a good method because you can duplicate your puppets.

Now with a string marionette it is difficult to change clothing on a puppet because the strings are attached. So if we have a puppet that has to change clothes I make duplicate puppets. I'll make two or three, how many changes of clothes I'll make puppets for them. So with the heads instead of making a puppet head, I will make the required number say three for three changes, and will make them all at the same time and paint them all at the same time so they are just as close to identical as possible. The bodies are made largely of plastic wood, especially the chest and hip parts. The lower legs I usually whittle, because wood makes an easier joint and I can cut my joints right in with a bandsaw. So the legs are usually made of wood. The upper arms I make of cloth because they need to be more flexible. So they are a mixed up medium when it comes to the making. Plastic, wood, leather, and wood and cloth. Whatever material does the best job.

In stringing them we usually plan as much of the string in advance as possible because a puppet is made to do a specific thing. A puppet that can juggle for instance cannot tap dance. Or a tap dancer probably couldn't do a hand stand, especially on another puppet's hands. So when we design the puppets we design them to do one thing and the puppet has a personality and a will of his own. He will do it his way. No matter how carefully we plan, when we make the puppet we find out we have to exploit what the puppet can do and do that. Because if we have a puppet that does a trick, say for instance an old traditional puppet like a pole thrower, which goes clear back to the time of Robin Hood who used to fight with quarter staves, we can make a puppet juggle a stick or he can juggle it with his feet, or he can throw it, catch it, things of that sort. But we have tried to duplicate one of those figures to do the same thing. But the second figure wouldn't do exactly what the first one would do. So although it is purely mechanical, the material thing and you work with tools and make it, still its own personality comes through and it does what it wants to do. Another mistaken idea is that we work the puppets. Literally the puppets

John Knoepfle

work us. At the end of the show we are the ones that are perspiring. The puppets simply go back in their trunks and are packed away neatly and we have to lug them out. The puppets don't work. We work.

Q: How did you get interested in puppeteering?

R: When I was a child I lived in Birmingham, Alabama. I was running down one of those red hills when my foot slipped and I fell and knocked a little skin off my elbow. I picked up what was then called blood poisoning, septicemia. It was purely an infection and it attacked the bone of my upper arm and I had to have the bone removed. For two years I was in and out of the hospital with 17 operations. At first my friends came to see me, then they forgot me. The only companions I had were some hand puppets, Japanese hand puppets that my folks had given me when I was five years old. So that was sort of a life saver for me. They knew very little about occupational therapy then. But I stumbled on occupational therapy with the puppets and it not only kept up my morale and gave me something to live for and play with, but also it exercised the very arm that was in trouble. So thanks to the puppets I have the use of this arm.

The arm was shorter, but I make my living with the very arm that was attacked. Then I didn't forget puppets. I didn't do anything with them until our children were about to be born. I made puppets for our first child. Little babies were not interested in puppets, but we were entertaining all the neighbor's children with puppets. Then the depression came on shortly after that. I was doing art work, illustrating books, doing advertising art. People weren't buying it when the depression hit. The crash took so much out of that type of buying. But lodges, clubs, churches, schools, everyone had to have money quickly. They would say, "You give a puppet show for us and help raise money." It got so every night we were doing something for someone to raise money. Suddenly someone said to us, "Why don't we give you a percentage of this," and we had a business. I remember the first professional show we played, the depression had hit us very hard, and we did a 35 minute show and received $35 for it. A dollar a minute, and if I live to be a million, if I had a million dollars I would never be as rich as I was then. That was the most money in the world to me, a dollar a minute. To me that was a miracle. Thanks to the puppets, we have been able to educate our children, we've been able to do things we want and it is rather ironical to me that these little woodenheaded actors could send blood and bone humans through college. So that is how we got started on those things.

Jules Zanger: Tell about your trip to Europe.

R: Well we wanted to go to Europe because we had been corresponding with about 250 puppeteers all over the world. These people are very friendly, in other words we have an in-group feeling, with a profession which is stronger than nationality or nearly anything else. So these people would say, "Why don't you come and visit? Why don't you come and see us?" So we decided finally that we could swing it. So we packed up three cases of puppets and took off. We had bad luck. The man who was to arrange the tour in England for us died just as we got there. But we had enough contacts that we would go into these different places we would do what we would call tabletops. We would use variety puppets and we would stand on one table and work on another. Because of the difference in light, that is electricity and sound equipment, we didn't take our equipment of that sort. We used what they had. And we stumbled into many interesting places. Not only were they nice people, friendly, and as I say we had a very strong in-group feeling. We were dear friends even though we had only corresponded. But one of our friends, for instance has a shop right across the street from Shakespeare's birthplace, which was a pleasure to visit with them. Another man taught in a very interesting school, they call it a Remans school. In England when a child runs afoul of the law, at least in this district around Birmingham, instead of dragging a child to jail or paddling him or doing something like that they send him to this school. The child thinks or is led to believe that he is just going to school, but actually the faculty of the school are studying the child. This faculty is made up of psychologists, psychiatrists different people of that sort. And by the time the child's case comes before the court, the judges, I think they have three judges only, have a full report on this child, his attitudes, his background, his mental state and so forth. They know everything they can about him so when they do make a decision on the child they have something to work with. To me it is a wonderful thing. So with puppets we stumbled on that sort of thing too. We just ran into very interesting people, nice people. Many of these people had written about puppets. Published books on them. They had wonderful collections. So it was a very rewarding experience for us. Some of them were little more than gypsies, playing along the beaches, some were very fine scholarly people who were almost un-approachable, but always friendly when they knew you had puppets.

In Italy I had the addresses of some people, also in Belgium. But not being able to speak the language we would get in some very, very funny setups. We got to a famous editor in Italy and he couldn't speak English nor could any of the people in his office. When we first went to the office he wasn't in and we tried to find out when he would be in so we could get there. They couldn't speak English; we couldn't speak Italian. So finally by pointing to the clock and sign language and drawing pictures, we found out that he usually came in about one o'clock in the afternoon. So the next day I showed up at one. He couldn't speak English, I couldn't speak Italian, but he knew a man who knew all about puppets. So he tried to tell me about this man who knew all about puppets. Well I finally got the address and started out to look for the man. So when I got to the man he couldn't speak English either and we tried with synonyms. I know a few words in German and he knew a few words in French and I finally found out for instance, we were going from Rome up to Florence, that there was only one show in Florence, and that show was run by a church and the operators of the puppets were children. And how that came about, with such words as garcon and fie and bambino and what have you, we finally found

John Knoepfle

out about what age groups they were. So getting information in a foreign country about puppets when you do not speak the language is difficult. We could make ourselves understood in talking about puppets because so many of our terms are universal. We use the same materials and the same tools as they do. Although our actual words may not be same, it is very easy to talk about the puppets. That wasn't a problem, but when you tried to find out somebody that knew about puppets and where he lived and what he was doing, it was a rat race. So I wasted a great deal of time in Europe trying to find people that I couldn't even find because I didn't have the language and no one else seemed to be able to dig out what I was talking about.

Question: I have come to the levee at St. Louis, Missouri to speak with Captain Robert Roehrig who is a long time riverman and has had much of his experience on the Missouri and other rivers. It is now ten minutes to three in the afternoon of a cool day. All right Captain, could you give us a resume of your river experience?

Answer: It happens to be that I'm 76 years old. Will be 77 the 11th day of April next. That puts my birth in 1881. So therefore I'm able to probably go back a few years and tell a few things that may be of some interest. I first started boating with my dad back in the 1890s when he was on different boats at that particular time, working for the Farmer's Elevator Company, which owned two packet boats, the old *Bald Eagle* and the new *Belle of Calhoun*. The *Belle of Calhoun* was built by the Schwartz brothers for their use. As a youngster I saw her being built down at the old St. Louis yards as they call it now. At that time it was called Carondelet Ways. I can yet, by shutting my eyes, hear a couple of hundred caulkers, caulking seams on those different vessels built at that time.

Q: Could I ask you exactly where the yards were?

A: They are at the same location as they are now at the foot of Davis Street. At that time the only entrance to the yard was at the foot of Marsal Street. The old yard, of course there is nothing left of them. At present they are owned by the St. Louis Shipyard Company. Now getting back to my early boating, as I've said, I used to be on the boats that my dad was on because he had lost his boats in the winter of 1892-1893 when he went broke. So therefore he had to work for others. In that particular time I have reference he was working for as I say, the Farmer's Elevator Company, which was owned by the Schwartz brothers.

Q: How is it they had two packets?

A: They had one packet operating on the lower river at that particular time. That was the *Bald Eagle* carrying wheat from the different points below St. Louis, 50, 60, 75 miles into St. Louis. The new boat which was the *Belle of Calhoun* was in the St. Louis and Clarksville packetboat trade. But that's the time when I used to ride those boats and do little things that I could according to my age and not being paid. Was glad to be able to be fed and get a little money for my clothes and such. But in 1899 my dad and Captain Jones from Wagoner at that time Indian Territory, they had the steamer *Gus Fowler* and I went to work on her as a deckhand, roustabout, roof watchman, assistant engineer or anything that they saw fit to put me at. That was my first time aboard working on a boat that I was being paid at. My statement made a few moments ago about being employed at most anything on a boat and stating that I at time was filling the job of a rouster. Well now roustabouts on boats those days were mostly colored. But at times when they were shorthanded anyone of the officers on the boat, let it be the captain, the pilots off of watch, or the

John Knoepfle

engineers off of watch, or even myself, which I said, I did some rouster work. We often would help get freight aboard and that way my time as a rouster on a boat was rather limited.

But the other work on the boat was assistant engineer and even as a cub pilot or a roof watchman. Referring to the loading of cargo on the different packet boats I have a little story to tell that might be amusing. I remember one old roustabout that was on the Missouri River packet boats, they called him Sugar Foot. The reason for that was because he had enormous big feet. He was one of the oldtimers and had rather stuck to certain boats and I remember him very well working on my dad's boats upon the Missouri River. This one particular time I was riding the boat just as a youngster seeing what was going on. At this particular landing there was lot of wheat to be loaded, which in those days was loaded in sacks, a roustabout would carry one sack on his shoulders and sometimes if he was a big fellow he would carry two. Well my dad, it happened to be a cool frosty fall morning, and my dad and other officers of the boat were out shouldering these sacks of wheat on the roustabout's shoulders. That means to pick the wheat sack up out of the pile and placing it on the shoulders of the rouster while he was going aboard. This Sugar Foot as they called him, he was one of these kinds that could just slough along and take life easy and never hurry and they were very anxious to get this wheat loaded and they tried to hurry old Sugar up. But he would just not be hurried. So it happened to be that in picking up some of these sacks of wheat that there was a black snake laying in there between two sacks and being a cool morning why he wasn't very active. So Sugar he of course, climbed up the bank and come to the pile of sacks in his slow motion, so my dad picked this snake up by the back of his head and knew it wasn't dangerous and wrapped it around Sugar's neck and said, "Now Sugar, if you don't hustle the rest of this trip I am going to leave that snake aboard." It happened to be that it had a good effect on Old Sugar and he moved rather fast after that.

A roof watchman's job, so called back in the old days, was usually called upon to sit up on the roof at night on these packet boats coming down the Missouri in particular because they had no markings of any kind, and the pilots to work by and the roof watchman would sit up on the roof and watch for snags or such obstructions as may interfere with the safe navigation of a vessel at night. We might start in with the old *General Meade*.

Q: All right.

A: I like to talk about the Missouri River boats because I have really lived and was born on the Missouri River at Washington, Missouri and my first riding, when I say riding the boats that means as a I would very often during particularly school vacations always spent all my time on boats that my dad was interested in. Now on the Missouri River, that particular stream is a little bit peculiar in that the type of boats that it was necessary to have to operate that river had to be very, very shallow draft and my first recollection of some of the oldtime boats was the old *General Meade*. She was a long slim shallow draft boat that had very, very little cabin with an idea of making her as light as possible. She was built the same as a number of the Missouri River boats at that time to be built at Pittsburgh. The same type of boat was a boat that was being used by General Custer at the time he fought his battle at the Little Big Horn with dire results. The boat that he had made his headquarters on was the old steamer *Far West*. I remember my dad telling about some of his experiences on the Missouri River and amongst them I recollect that he had stated that at one time he was chief engineer on the *Far West* but not at the time of Custer's campaign. But nevertheless he had been on that boat. A number of other instances that may be interesting would be my dad telling about his different trips up the Missouri River all the way to Ft. Benton. Those trips that they usually called mountain trips because they went all the way up into the mountains of the headwaters of the Missouri. But two items that interested me very much was the fact that he had said on two of his different trips up Missouri River, they didn't happen at the same time but at different times, the boat it was necessary to stop the boat to let the herd of buffalo swim across the river. Now that of course means a lot of buffalo.

Q: Could you give us some vital statistics on your father?

A: My dad started steamboating before the Civil War as a young man. Worked as engineer, also as pilot and captain. He was married during the early days of the Civil War and made his home in Washington, Missouri where I was born. My two older brothers were both rivermen. Both have passed on. My dad after the time during the Civil War, was in the so called Marine Service. The Marine Service is nothing more than being employed on boats that were in government service. I can site one instance that was interesting. My oldest brother was just a baby. This particular instance that I mentioned, now dad was engineer on a boat that had been operating around about our old hometown, hauling some troops, supplies, and army goods up and down the river and happened to be at Washington when Price's army, which is a matter of history made their trip through Missouri and were camped up on the bluffs below Washington. And this particular boat that dad was on had a lot of government stores, such as uniforms, and cases, and a lot of stores and supplies. Well going downriver and passing these bluffs they were fired on by some of Price's troops up on the bluffs but fortunately were not hit. But what I wished to mention about my brother being just a baby in arms, my dad placed my mother on the boat behind a lot of machinery, which would of partially protected her in case there would have been a hit. Now that's about enough about dad's past history, which is very slight in that he had a lot, a lot of experience on the river.

One of the things that I do recall him telling about was that there was a certain Missouri River packet boat that he was skipper of at the time, I think it was the old steamer *New Haven*, which was one of the smaller Missouri riverboats, but anyway he told about them taking on a lot of freight, which at

John Knoepfle

that particular season of the year was wheat in sacks, and loading up on Missouri River not very far above the mouth at Black Walnut. After the boat was loaded they backed out in the river in the usual manner and they headed downstream and found the river very low, was unable to get through without getting aground. But this grounding in those days was rather expected, all those boats made at that time were all equipped with spars as they called them. Now those spars were nothing more than big poles hung at the head of the boat on a derrick one on each side with an idea of using them in case that the grounding took place. On this particular case, as I said the river was low, and they got aground and setting these spars to shove the boat sideways or ahead wasn't very successful. They just wore out all of the boat crews. When nighttime came my dad decided then to give it up and wait until morning. So he told the crews, all boat crews to go to bed, but before. So they laid an anchor, which means they take an anchor and attach a line and take it out upriver from the boat so that in case she washed off the bar that she would not go floating along by herself. That had been done, and after nightfall the crew went to bed with the exception of the watchman whom he had told to be sure and hold steam during the night and notify him of anything happening. Dad, like the rest of the crew, went to bed. Sometime during the wee hours of the morning he woke up and stepped out on the roof of the boat, his room by the way is up under the pilothouse on the boat, stepped out on the roof of the boat, and happened to be a low lying fog that was just about the height of the roof of the boat all the way from shore to shore on each side of the river. He was able to see the stars though by looking up and he saw those stars move. Now that didn't satisfy him so he took a sight on one of the stars to one of the smokestacks. Well that star did move, so dad decided that that just could not be. So he went down below and found the watchman sitting on the what they called the bitts, that's nothing more than a pair of mooring posts that are always built on all packet boats, that's at the head of the boat and on these bitts was where the anchor line had been made fast to. Well here was the watchman sitting there sound asleep on these bitts and the anchor line had become untied off of the bitts and the boat was floating down river finding her own channel. Now that was rather unusual in this particular instance, but it was nothing uncommon because very, very often a boat would get aground and if you just waited long enough why the current would wash the sand out from under them and set them afloat again.

I mentioned the act of sparring this vessel off of a bar. Now these poles as I mentioned are nothing more than what you might call today would be like a big telegraph pole with a heavy set of rope blocks, usually about four to five shivs each with the top of this so called spar that we would call the telephone pole lashed with a lashing on at the top end. This one block would be in there and the other block down under the deck on the boat with an idea when this spar is set overboard either sideways or ahead or back depending entirely on which way you prefer to move the vessel off of the bar. Then of course, a line from the blocks would be passed through a shiv or a snatch block to a steam capstan, which is always located on the head of these boats. Now this sparring off of a boat on a bar could never be done twice the same way in that you just got to meet the conditions as they are and set you spar accordingly. That of course today is a lost art because none of that is ever done anymore.

Getting back to my own experience on the river, as I say this first job I had being paid was in 1899, that was on the old steamer *Gus Fowler*. That was one of the Fowler boats that was built on the Ohio River and as I say was operated in this part of the country by Captain H. L. Jones and my dad. My work on the *Gus Fowler* was either in the engine room as an assistant engineer or I also put in same time as a clerk, a second clerk. Now a second clerk on any packet boat means that his job is to check freight, load it on the boat at different landings, and of course, in reverse action when freight was unloaded. Now that clerk doing that kind of work usually it was necessary for him to get to shore as soon as possible after a boat made the landing so as to cut down the loss of time at the landing. Very often he would have to leap into the mud on these different shores to get at to where he wanted to go. So therefore he was commonly called mud clerk. That was a name that really hung to the clerk that was either second or third, whichever happened to be. If the boat was big enough it carried three clerks, which was chief clerk, second clerk and third. But in my case there was only two of us, a chief clerk and myself.

After packet boating for some little time I left the river; steamboating at that particular period was getting to a point where it wasn't very interesting. So being an engineer and licensed I took up work ashore around the industrial plants and construction mostly. Standing watches in engine rooms at industrial plants, which I kept at for quite a few years at different places, such as here in St. Louis, out in Kansas building a diesel power plant, down in Oklahoma rebuilding old worn out plants; Alabama the same thing, and I was also sent down on the island of Cuba in the winter of 1918, and spent three years and a half at that place, back and forth several times each year on vacation. Then in about 1921 or 1922 coming back off the island of Cuba my brother and I bought a little steamboat up on the Missouri River, which he operated part of the time, and I operated part of the time. So that got me back on the river again.

Q: What was the name of that boat?

A: That boat was called the *August Wohlt* built by the old Missouri River family at Hermann, Missouri primarily as a packet boat for the Gasconade River.

Q: How did you spell that last name?

A: W-O-H-L-T, an old German name.

Q: What was this river the packet was on?

A: It was built primarily for the Gasconade River as a Gasconade River packetboat. Rather light and small. These different packet boats that I have been connected with in different capacities carried anything from wheat and corn in sacks, to cattle on the hoof, hogs and lambs. I can state a very interesting

John Knoepfle

happening in that I woke up one morning and it happened to be that my brother Bill was mate on this particular boat. I think it was the old *Benton* on the Missouri River, and I heard some sheep. And on coming out on the deck aft of the cabin, there is always a section in the clear that is called the recess on the second deck, which is so called the boiler deck. Well that happened to be fenced off and here was a lot of sheep up on the boiler deck aft of the cabin. Now other things that you might call livestock carrying was chickens, chickens in coops. They would usually be put up on second deck too, amongst where the passengers would be. Of course, that being light was a type of cargo that could be very easily carried on the second deck. My brother and I had this steamer, the *August Wohlt,* up on the Missouri River several years and finally sold her be used as a towboat to some parties at Glasgow, Missouri that were in the sand business. She was then being used as a towboat to handle the sand barges out as empties to the dredge and back to the shore as loads from the dredge. In 1931 I and Captain Roy Miller bought the steamer *Ralph Hicks,* a steel hull towboat that had been at work up on the Missouri River for quite some years for the Maston Construction Company and being steam was beginning to be a little bit outmoded in this day of diesel power. So they decided to replace her with diesel and at that particular time why Captain Miller and myself bought her and brought her down the Missouri River from way up the northwestern corner of Missouri. You could throw a stone over into the Iowa line. Captain Miller and myself operated her for several years as a towboat; we finally sold her to Captain Charles Drake. He used her for a while, and then dismantled her.

You asked about the *Blue Wing.* The *Blue* was a packetboat bought by my dad and Captain Jones at the time that they owned the steamer *White Eagle,* which was packet boating up on the Illinois River during 1892. The *Blue Wing* was a smaller boat and they had decided to put her up on the Mississippi River in opposition to the Eagle Packet Company's boats. I happened to be riding the boat as a youngster, my mother and I and my dad decided to go through the Calhoun County over towards the Mississippi side and drum up some freight business, and told Captain John Little, pilot on the boat, to proceed on to St. Louis. And if not being in a hurry lay up if darkness caught him, but mother and I went to bed in the captain's room up on the roof. Sometime during the night I heard a crash. I woke up and jumped out and looked out and here was the steamer *Blue Wing* had run on the inside, that's towards the shore side of a water intake tower at the foot of East Grand Avenue. There's where the old waterworks was and still is. It had hit this bridge span that runs from the pumping station out to this tower and knocked it down, had laid across the head of the boat, fouling the boat in that position. Fortunately no damage was done to the hull so the boat was gotten out of there by cutting this big span in pieces and taking the boat back out on her own power. The only damage that was done was to her upper works which had hit the bridge span.

Q: You mentioned before that was a closed in boat. It was a logging boat that was closed in as I recall.

A: No, she was a typical packet boat that was built primarily to use on the Kentucky River and anyone having read any of Captain Billy Lepper's tales of the river will recall that Captain Billy Lepper was a clerk on this particular boat back in the old days of boating on the Kentucky River. Captain Billy Lepper, of course is now passed away. You asked the question of coaling of boats. That's nothing more than getting fuel aboard in those days, which was done by roustabouts carrying a box with a handle on each side both ways. These boxes would hold so called about three bushels of coal. Now the coaling of these different packet boats was done in this manner. In here at St. Louis there was a lot of so called small barges that they called coal flats. They were loaded on the eastside out of cars and coal was carried aboard the different packet boats by these darkies. Now getting back to the type of coal, eastern coal was considered a very good coal. Now what I mean by eastern coal, coal that was mined in West Virginia or in the eastern end of Kentucky, that was very good high grade coal. All of the old firemen on these packet boats when they would see any so called eastern coal brought aboard for the boat, that made them smile because of the fact it fired so easily and didn't require a lot of working of the fire, as the Illinois coal would, which would clinker very much.

One of the Missouri River packet boats that I was on a number of times was the old steamer *Helena*. Had been built to work up on the Missouri River in the vicinity of Helena, Montana. That's why the name *Helena*, my dad and Captain Arch Bryan bought here in 1890. Brought her down the Missouri River to operate out of St. Louis, between St. Louis and Rocheport, Missouri, which was called a short trade trip in that the roundtrip could be made in a week's time. I have one particular remembrance of what happened on the *Helena* was that we had landed at a little town up on the Missouri River, Augusta. And just below Augusta was another landing called Hamburg Landing. That particular place there were a lot of darkies that were still working on the farms up in the hills and they would come down at times and help load these boats when they had the so called wheat pile. That's nothing more than a pile of wheat in sacks. The mosquitos were awfully bad at that particular place. Captain Arch Bryan got to kidding one of these darkies about living up there where the mosquitos were so bad. "Oh," he says, "Captain, they don't bother us." "Why," he says, "I bet you can't lay down on your belly there with your back for 15 minutes and let them bite you." "I can do that, Captain, for a quarter; I can do that for a quarter." So he says, "All right you do that and you'll get a quarter." That the darky laid there and squirmed around once in a while and a mosquito would give him a good bite. The captain saw he was going to lose his quarter, so he went to the firebox and picked up a hot coal and heaved it out on the bare back of this darky and he jumped up and couldn't stand that. The captain said, "I

John Knoepfle

guess you lost your quarter, darky." He says, "No sir, no sir, that was no mosquito, that was a gallinipper." So the captain paid him his quarter.

You will remember I stated that the last steamboat I was interested in was the steamer *Ralph Hicks* and after selling her I opened up a barge terminal here at St. Louis because of the fact that the different towboats are now becoming far more numerous and there had to be places where barges could be moored and exchanged to another tow, which I did here at St. Louis at the foot of Poplar Street. Now that was in the early 1930s and during that time, of course as boating had picked up, towboats became more numerous and were mostly all modern and diesel. It happened to be that the different insurance companies that were insuring the different vessels had opened up offices in St. Louis and one of the leading marine insurance companies was the Hartford Insurance Company, River Marine Department. Being new in the game here it was necessary for them to have contact with someone that was familiar with different types of boats, their construction and the different repairs that were necessary once in a while.

So I connected with them on a retainer basis in that when they had an inspection to make of a boat that they wished to insure, it was my job to write up an inspection and make recommendations as to its valuation and their risks. From that then I stayed on as a surveyor and inspector and also at salvage work when they had some sort of a sinking or loss for some time purely on a retainer basis, and then later I want to work for them alone as a salvage inspector and surveyor after disposing of my barge terminal. Some of the salvage work I was connected with was very, very interesting in that some losses were very heavy. For example in 1941 a barge of scrap was sunk against the dam at Dubuque, Iowa. Now this barge happened to be about a 1,400 ton barge, a 195 foot long by 35 foot wide and 11 foot deep. This had struck the lock wall while in tow of a diesel towboat. Now it hitting this lock wall it was damaged enough that it would fill with water, swung around and hit the piers of the dam and sunk in about 31 foot at that particular point. The interesting feature of that was that because the river was high and work could not be carried on until the river fell enough that the gates at this particular dam would be closed, cutting off the current enough to enable the diver to operate.

This particular diver that we had happened to be from Chicago, his name was Frank Hefflen, a very good man. I like to tell one little story on him, in that I know it is interesting. Now being down in 31 feet of water is just about on the edge of the depth that it is safe to work in and come up immediately without suffering from so called bends, which happen to divers. They go into deep water and come out from under that pressure quickly. Well this particular barge being sunk, Frank went down and put some slings under it so it could be able to make a lift. While he was there, of course we were talking to him back and forth over the marine telephone he was equipped with, and that particular part of the salvage work, which was going on was unloading of this scrap, which had to be done with an orange peel derrick. Nothing more than a derrick, which everyone is familiar with who has mostly would say that the familiarity would be with the clamshell, but the clamshell would not take up this baled scrap so it was necessary to use an orange peel, which is nothing more than if you would slice an orange four ways and peel the points back.

That's why the name orange peel. But back to Frank, it happened to be that we didn't have any need for him down there for an hour or so. So I told him, "Frank you had better come on up, we won't need you down there for an hour." "Oh," he says, "I don't want to come up, just go ahead, I'll crawl under one end of this barge and I'll take a nap as long as you keep that air compressor going, just go ahead I'll take a nap and wake me when you want me." That's what Frank did! I didn't care much about him taking that chance of course. But Frank knew what he was about so I conceded.

In my time on the steamer *Gus Fowler* with my dad, as I stated before, I was liable to be put on anything and at the time that this boat was in this trade between St. Louis and the lower river, inspection time came up, which is nothing more than annual inspection made of all packet steamboats and others by the United States Steamboat Inspectors. At that time were under the Department of Commerce and I recollect at that particular time two inspectors, one was a hull inspector, Captain Arch Gordon, and Captain Bill Corey as the boiler inspector. This particular boat was laying at the foot of Biddle Street. We were living in St. Louis, and dad instructed me now you fill these boilers tonight and warm that water so that when we put the hydrostatic pressure test on them, it was always common practice to warm the water because the cold water on that high pressure is a little bit hard on boiler steel, so therefore water was always warmed. All right, it was my job that night to build a light wood fire under the boiler to get the water warm so that when they hired this steam tug to furnish steam for our boiler feed pumps to pump the pressure up to the testing pressure, which was always 150% of the operating pressure. During the time that this inspector came aboard of the boat Captain Gordon and Captain Corey, why Captain Gordon, by the way, had been at one time quite a rounder, drinks and so forth, but got religion and didn't cuss under any circumstances.

He came down to the boilers that morning, and put the back of hand against the britching, which is the casing around the boilers, says "Kid you haven't got these boilers warm have you?" I said, "Yes sir, I have a fire under them." He said, "It don't feel like it." I just let him go because I wouldn't argue with him but during the time that this inspection was going on, the tug as I stated was furnishing steam to the boiler feed pump. Captain Corey was in the engine room reading the steam gauge over the throttle, which was common practice in checking the pressures and Captain Gordon was standing on some support aft of the boilers reading their gauge, which they had put on the boilers, which is accepted as being correct. I was in the engine room door doing what they called at that time, passing the word. For example, Captain Gordon would call out the steam pressure, or the water pressure, on his gauge, and then in turn I would call out that same pressure to Captain Corey who was standing at the throttle checking the boat's steam gauge. The pressure kept building up and building up and finally something let go. It happened to be that one of the flues collapsed under that enormous pressure, and blew the brick and tile, which is laid horizontally under the aft end of the boiler to the britching, which is nothing more than the casing.

Now this tile in those days was always laid on there with clay, mud and horse manure. Those days they didn't use the present asbestos covering, which is common to everyone today. Because of the fact that clay could be had for nothing and also could the horse manure. Therefore it was a point of economy to use that kind of caulking. But getting back to Captain Gordon, as I said these brick or tile and this clay with this horse manure in it blew up all over Captain Gordon, on his face and so forth, and that water being a little warmer than he thought, it kind of stung him a little bit. You know water at a 170 degrees temperature feels pretty hot to your skin. While it won't boil it seems hot. That was about the temperature of that water, and Captain Gordon kind of forgot himself and said, "Damn it, kid, you have got this water hot," as he was wiping clay, mud, and horse manure off his face and out of his eyes.

Anyone coming to the levee at Front here at St. Louis today would find it impossible to recognize it as it was in the old days because of the fact that all the old riverfront buildings have been dismantled, making way for the park as has been contemplated beautifying this levee front. These stores, buildings, and so forth on this riverfront was one saloon after another, and one pawn shop after another, and one clothing store after another run by people of course that were in the clothing store business those days, which we all remember. The type of levee loiterers was good old roustabouts and such and behind every alleyway it would be possible to find a crap game going on. I remember one time there was a redheaded policeman, they called him Red Reagan, that walked the levee front here. He would very often catch these crap shooters in the doorways, hallways or in an alleyway somewhere and of course in those days they all carried their nightsticks. Well he would break in them quick and commence to kick and use the club on them and they would all scatter in all directions. He would make no arrest but he would pick up the change that was lying handy.

Q: Pretty good job.

A: Speaking about the levee conditions back in the old days. At certain seasons of the year, which is the fall, I like to mention the fact about the amount of apples that was brought into St. Louis, usually out of Calhoun County, Illinois. Which is that narrow peninsula between the Mississippi and the Illinois River. I've seen this levee covered with apple barrels for a distance of three quarters of a mile anyway. I remember one time that we were living out on Warren Street and there were a lot of apples in barrels on the levee and the commission houses, which at that time were up on Third Street all the way from Lucas

Avenue on north up to Biddle Street would come down and pick out what they wanted of the barreled apples and what was left was usually sold by someone. So often it was up to the captain of the steamboat that brought the apples in or the clerk, which I had done myself to dispose of them at whatever they could get. I myself have bought barrels of apples for $1.25, have hauled them out to our home, which give us apples all winter for $1.25.

As I stated before, I connected with the Hartford Fire Insurance Company as a marine surveyor, which took me over all of the rivers, we'll say, from Yankton, South Dakota, to Pittsburgh on the Ohio, and Baton Rouge on the lower Mississippi, Minneapolis on the upper Mississippi, and Joliet on the Illinois. So that meant that wherever there was a river I would sometimes get to for some reason or other. Either from an inspection standpoint on possible insurance or maybe get damages of some sort or possible sinkings. For example, a lot of people have heard about the barge boat of automobiles that was sunk on the Ohio River just below Golconda a number of years ago in December. The salvaging of those particular automobiles had to be delayed because of the fact the river was too high to be able to carry on any salvage work. So it was put off until the following May, and it happened to be that a contractor from Moline, Illinois, a building contractor and a heavy hauler and construction contractor took the job of getting these automobiles off the sunken barge and getting them ashore, which he did. There were 150 cars on this particular barge and all were salvaged off of it but five. A number of them of course had slipped off the top deck of this barge when she listed before sinking.

Now those were all gotten out of the bottom of the river with the exception of four or five and they were in such condition, and in such a position, on the river that it wasn't possible to make this attempt at salvage. Now these cars when they, mind you now, had been in the water in a sunken submerged condition from December to the following May. During this time the river was high and muddy and a lot of debris was carried down the river, and these cars as we got them out, were filled with mud and trash up as far as the top of the seats and under the hood on the front end of the car and under the deck of the trunk in the back. So they all had to be washed out and cleaned as much as possible. The surprising fact that when this contractor got them ashore at this little town of Golconda, he sold them for whatever he could get. Believe it or not there were four of those cars were driven out of there under their own power in that as they were gotten ashore they were cleaned up, the oil was taken out and fresh oil put in, and washed out as much as possible and the battery was charged and were driven away. In fact, one of these four cars towed another car with it. So it means that the building of automobiles today, you can't even sink them for six or eight months and feel sure that they will never run again because they sometimes do. My activities as a marine surveyor have terminated January 1, 1956 in that I have been retired by the Hartford Fire Insurance Company and am on a retirement pension. My hobby of course is still boating and putting in

John Knoepfle

my time now doing an occasional survey job for different people that are interested. Also, I am rebuilding a steel hull excursion boat which I had purchased several years ago. Getting it from a single screw to a twin screw job, and hope to have it operating sometime this next season.

Q: Well now, we are going to close out our interview, and I want to thank you for having taken the time to talk to us, Captain.

A: John, it's been a pleasure to be able to tell a few of the things in my past and I sincerely wish that you can get a lot more of this same type of recording. I also want to at this particular to invite you to our next meeting of the Golden Eagle Club, which is a river museum group that is gathering a lot of records for posterity, which we hope to be able to keep the memory of the old packet boats alive someway. Thank you.

Q: Thank you, Captain.

Dent Sanford, June 21, 1957

Question: Mr. Sanford has a long and distinguished career as an engineer, and we are going to talk this morning about some of his steamboating days.

Answer: In my early days of engineering on the Ohio River I can recall some very interesting happenings. As chief engineer on a large towboat by the name of *B. D. Wood* towing coal and iron from Pittsburgh, we happened to lose a wheel as we were coming down in the Mingo Chute at Mingo Junction. The steamer *Voyager* coming up the river with empties landed her empties caught us with our loaded tow and landed us. Then in about four days we had a new wheel, and proceeded on our way to Louisville. As we were passing Cincinnati the wheel was squeaking pretty loud, about like a new pair of shoes. The barges at Mill Creek Landing in those days stuck out pretty far. Big loaded barges with coal that belonged to the Combine. To make the turn there in the river, it was necessary to give her all the power that you could possibly give her, when the pilot notified you of that effect with two raps of the gong. Of which I received in due time and I gave her everything that we had and again lost the wheel. The steamer *Hercules Carrel* came to our rescue and landed us down below town. Those were wonderful days with Captain "Doggy" Dippold and that type of real mariners. Men that knew the river and how to handle towboats.

Then another experience that I had was on the biggest sternwheel boat at that time, the steamer *John K. Speed*. We were on our way up from New Orleans to Cincinnati and about six miles below Rosedale, Mississippi, about 8:30 in the evening a boilerhead burst, moving the smokestack, called the Bricheling, from the front of the boiler, allowed the flames to go up through and caused the vessel to catch fire, which we were successful enough to keep from burning up. Furthermore, I was the only one, probably fires under the boiler, and I didn't want them to burn up, and consequently I went down with a brand new pair of overalls on to extinguish and put the fire out under the boilers, which I accomplished. Although it happened that I got argyrosis from the blue in the brand-new overalls. I burned the back of my neck pretty bad; the hair never did grow there. Captain Harry Doss was my pilot on watch when that incident happened. We cast anchor there. A mate by the name of Jim Howard from Indiana was a mate on the boat. The big steamer *Kate Adams* happened to come along and picked us up and towed us up to Rosedale where we waited for boiler makers from Cincinnati to come down with a new, we installed the new head, and proceeded to Cincinnati.

As a child, if I recall correctly, my father was a pilot on the steamer *Andes*, running in the Pittsburgh and Cincinnati trade. Was about my first year in school if I recall correctly, and I coming down from my grandparents by the name of Meldahl, up in West Virginia, on daddy's boat, coming home to go to

John Knoepfle

school. As the boat rounded to at Catlettsburg, Kentucky to make the landing there daddy rang to stop the engines, but the engines didn't stop. Consequently, due to the turning around of the boat there to make the landing, it was impossible for him to do anything else, and he started up the Big Sandy River. Of course, the Captain, his name was Muhleman and his brother was the chief engineer. The captain came running up to the pilot house, asked daddy what was taking place. I just don't recall exact words, but nevertheless, daddy said, "Something has gone wrong. They can't stop the engines." Captain said, "What in the world should we do?" Daddy said, "Why, just put the reversing lever in the middle, so that it will shut all the valves on the engine." The captain called down to his brother and he immediately did, and consequently the wheels stopped rolling and the *Andes* just naturally slowed down, and eased herself into the landing until they got the throttle valve repaired, which I afterwards found out. It was a throttle valve that the threads were stripped and they couldn't shut the steam off the engine. It was quite an experience and very good judgement used, because the *Andes* had quite a trip under her at that time.

In the early days of towboating and just prior to my time as an engineer, I would say about the time of the amalgamation of the coal companies up there with two, and with the Consolidated Coal and Coke Company that took over and operated the towboats for a number of years there, the engineers had a pretty tough time of it and went by luck a great deal. A good many of the big towboats blew up. It was caused by the fact if you did not engineer your towboat with steam in excess of that of the law your towboat didn't do the work that it should do. Consequently they didn't want you as an engineer. In other words, the old saying was, "You don't carry steam on the big Pittsburgh towboats according to the gauge, you carry it according to the bank," the way the towboat is taking its empties up the river. I happened to get in on that in the real heydays of that experience and time and I found it to be very, very interesting.

I recall on one occasion of having an assistant engineer with me, the first time he had been an engineer on a boat. Anyhow when he saw the, as we call it down in the flower garden, where it says the name of the gauge manufacturer on the gauge, the needle was pointing right straight down and he looked at that gauge and he said to me, "Is that gauge wrong?" And I said, "No that gauge is all right, it's just we that are wrong." "My goodness alive," he said, "isn't that dangerous?" I said, "Oh yes, quite dangerous." He said, "My goodness, I wonder how much more steam we got than we are allowed." "Well," I said, "look at your steamboat certificate, and then check your steam pressure and you will find out." "Oh," he says, "how come you got so much steam?" I said, "You had some help out there and you put the false weights on according to my instructions, on the safety valves that fit right over the big weights that they had on those lever valves in those days." And I said, "Consequently, it carries more steam." "Well," he says, "about how much more steam do we have now than we should have?" "Oh, I'd say, about a 150, maybe

200 pounds more," and I said "we got plenty, you know," I said, "when you first start out of port with one of these boats before you put these weights on, they are very docile and quiet like a kitten, but after a little while, when they get to rolling their wheel with this dynamite steam," I said, "each time they exhaust it sounds like a canon going off." In those days it was quite interesting. We had some mighty good, even towboat races, and I want to say that in those days I was mighty guilty just the same as the rest of them in carrying dynamite steam. However, many years after that, especially during this last war, I had an occasion twice at sea to either carry dynamite steam or lose the ship with all the soldiers in transportation on that ship.

Q: What ship was that?

A: That ship was the *President Monroe*. There was 6,800 soldiers on her. Another ship that I was requested to do my best with her, because it was matter of getting away from a submarine was the *Victory* and she was a high pressure boat as it was, but she was still a more high pressure boat when I got her safety valves fixed the way I wanted them. We made our port successfully.

Q: Could you explain the flower garden again?

A: Yes, I will gladly. At the bottom face of the steam gauge, practically all steam gauges, you will see a monogram there stating the manufacturer of the gauge, and that was in terms, in those days of calling it the flower garden.

Another very funny experience that I've had, rather queer to sit there and watch it and not be able to do anything about it, but I happened to be in the pilothouse on the *Vulcan* of the Jones & Laughlin Company when the *Voyager* and the *Nellie Walton* were racing for the locks. If I recall correctly, I think it was Lock 3, it may have been 2, but I don't really remember, but I remember the incident. But anyhow I know that the *Walton* was on the inside, and the *Voyager* on the outside of the shore swell, when the *Walton* stopped so as to slide into the lock. The locks were open for them, they had blowed their whistles for the locks and everything accordingly, but the *Walton* being inside made the grade, but she couldn't stop. The wheel stopped all right, but the swell washed her right on down into the locks. She took the gates clear out and went on down through. The *Voyager* happened to be a very powerful towboat and made the turn all right and didn't go down over the dam. But to see that *Nellie Walton* going down through that lock, no train would have gone any faster than she went down through there, and to see the water leaving that lock and see the way it was washing down below the lock was really a treat to behold.

There used to be quite a big towboat here on the river. She was a very expensive, very fine boat by the name of *Cruiser* and I happened to be on the *Cruiser* making a trip to Louisville with coal and iron. It happened so, that we wanted to be in Louisville in the morning, and when we got just above Grassy Flats or very close to them, the pilot on watch, Captain Al Eckler must of dozed off because I happened to look out and I could see a light, being still dark yet, but it didn't seem that the light changed positions, or the boat changed positions from the light. After having the sounding line dropped, I saw the boat was not moving, and was then fully aware that we were out on the Grassy Flats with our full tow. As luck would have it with us the river was raising. The next big problem was what to do and how to do it to get out of there. So, I called for the fireman to come back to watch things for me. She was working full straight ahead or working ahead full power. I went to the pilothouse and sure enough there was the pilot, Captain Eckler, sound asleep sitting in the chair with his hands on the steering levers. The question comes up though, as to what to do with a party of that kind, because when they are in a condition of that kind you never know what their actions may be. So, I hooked the pilothouse door open, so I could make an exit right quick if I had to and I stretched myself and I reached over and woke Captain Al up. And it happened just as I anticipated, he did jump up and was all excited. I finally got him quieted down.

We left the boat working full ahead and we went down and had a cup of coffee. After we had our coffee, I talked to Captain Al, I says, "She is all right now Captain, and I understand that we have a raising river yet." "Yes," he said, "the river is still coming up." "Well," I said, "it's naturally then up to you because you are the man in the pilothouse here." He says, "Well, I think I can make the whole turn here. I think I can make a swing and get her righted up and we will be all right." I said, "I'd just get ahold of the mate after you get her turned around and casually talk with him." Captain Eckler was very much excited, very much nervous yet, and he said, "Please, please don't ever tell this story on me." I said, "Captain Eckler, as long as you are alive, I will never tell this story." He said, "I would be ruined with the Combine, I would never be able to pilot again, if it were found out that I went to sleep at the wheel on watch." I said, "Captain, I'll never say a word until after you're gone," but I can tell the story now because it was one of the things that happened during my time. Well, anyhow we made our turn, we went on into Louisville, and very few people know of the circumstance yet to this day.

I believe I omitted one of the very important parts when I said I had a young man that it was his first trip on duty as an engineer. His name was Clifford Stockoff from Henderson, Kentucky. Cliff was a mighty fine, big robust young man and when he saw this excessive steam being carried and had to work with it, it looked to me like I could see that he began to fail. When we got back to Pittsburgh he quit and was quite sick. If I recall correctly, I think it was in the neighborhood of six weeks after that he died and the coroner's verdict was that he died of fright. They found nothing organically wrong with him in any shape, way or form. I was questioned by the coroner if I knew what could have taken place and that was my answer. I thought the boy not having that experience, you have to grow into that you just don't walk into it, and then master it. Consequently that young man died of fright and fright only.

Q: Just shattered him I guess.

A: Yes.

Bernard Savage, April 16, 1957

Question: We are at the home of Captain Bernard Savage in Columbus, Ohio. The Captain has had a lot experience on the river. He was born in a town on the Muskingum. Is that right?

Answer: That's right.

Q: Now, we don't care how long . . .

A: No, I don't care.

Q: Well, could you just try to give us some of your earliest recollections on the river? When did you come on the river?

A: Oh, my earliest recollections would be when I was between eight and nine years old. I shipped out of Pittsburgh on the *Joe B. Williams*, it was the biggest towboat on the river at that time. They had a big tow designed for New Orleans, and I shipped up to cabin boy. Got $2.50 a week. And went down to New Orleans and delivered the tow. The river was low and by the time we delivered the tow, the river was so low we couldn't get back. We emptied right away. So we had to lay there maybe, oh sometimes we would lay there as much as two weeks until we got a load. We never come back with empties. But on that first trip that was a great trip for a small boy, you know and it equaled a trip around the world for all the farm machines and that junk. When we landed at New Orleans, there was a schooner tied up right below a sailing ship, and there was river pirates. I'd go over there, and my uncle was engineer on the steamboat, and he got in the marine hospital for something, and I would go over there and help them out with them river pirates you know. They'd have fun with me. They would send me over on the steamboat after a couple of buckets of steam, and left-handed monkey wrench, and that kind of stuff. Just having fun with me. So eventually they signed me on as A. B. Seaman, gave me a certificate and everything. Boy, I wish I had that now. I wouldn't take nothing for it. One day, the mate says, "You're going to have to help swab the decks." "No, no," I said, "I'm a A. B. Seaman. I'm not swabbing no decks. I follow the big shots you know." "Oh," he said, "try you for mutiny." "Go ahead." Well, they organized a marine court you know, and tried me and convicted me and sentenced me to walk the plank. And they even had the plank out over the river. So I sat down on the deck to take off my shoes and the mate says, "You needn't take them off. You're going to Davey Jones Locker." "Well," I said, "you're crazy. I ain't going, no. I can swim as good as you can or better." And, about that time, the Captain's wife come out of the cabin and got me by the ear and led me and said, "You guys let that boy alone. You'll scare him." I said, "You can't scare me. I can swim." And my uncle come back from the hospital, the rest of the crew told him, "That boy's over hobnobbing with them pirates." He jumped on me. I said, "What's a pirate?" I didn't know what a pirate was. "Well," he says, "they're

John Knoepfle

robbing thieves." I said, "I had $1.50 and they didn't take that." And, "Well," he said, "they would have took it if they thought you had that much, they'd probably took it away." "No sir," I said, "I shipped up on that boat, A. B. Seaman. I'm going to quit this steamboat." "You aren't going to do nothing of the kind." The Coast Guard caught up with them about two or three years after that and they sunk the ship and killed one or two of them. They sent the rest of them to the pen. There were a lot of river pirates, there are yet on them river towns. A lot of them on there.

Q: About what year was that?

A: Along about 1893 in there, three or four, I can't remember too good anymore. Never could remember dates much. That's about the time 1893 or 1894.

Q: Well, did you stay on that steamboat when you came back up from New Orleans?

A: Yes. I stayed on there for more than two years.

Q: As a cabin boy, I guess.

A: Cabin boy, and then as I got, I was a pretty good sized boy for my age and I got bigger. I felt like I could fireman on them, you know, and I got a fireman's job on them and graduated to fireman and mate. Lock rider and lock trimmer, and then mate, and then first and second mate, and then pilot and chief engineer, cub pilot. You had to cub for two or three years before you got a license.

Q: Who did you cub under?

A: Oh, I don't know now. I can't remember their names. Captain oh, I couldn't tell you now. I can't remember names. But I done most of striker under my uncle. He was chief engineer.

Q: What was his name, Captain?

A: Name was Fisher. I was blowed up on one of them big towboats, on the *Hoxie*. Blowed up in Ravenswood, maybe you know or had some record of that. Since she was blowed up.

Q: No, I didn't know about that.

A: Yes, we was coming up with empties and she blew up there and we was coming close to shore and blew the whole cabin off of her, right over the boiler, landed out on the river bank and the river . . .

Q: What tow was that?

A: Oh, that would be . . .

Q: Did you say the boat was named the *H. M. Hoxie*?

A: *Hoxie*, yes. It blew up at Ravenswood going upstream with empties. They claimed we was carrying low water and high steam, but we wasn't. We did carry a boat that maybe allowed 200 pounds. Sometimes coming upstream we'd carry 225. The river would be fairly swift, you know. Oh, them riffles, we'd have to double, tie up half the fleet, and double up, you know? Some place in the Ohio River got riffles almost like a creek you know. And the river would be swifter in places. We'd have to tie up part of them and take the others over, and come back and get them.

Q: Well, you worked on the workhorses up on the Allegheny River, didn't you?

A: Oh yes, I worked on them towboats on the Allegheny River.

Q: What were some of those boats?

A: I blew up on the *Hawk*. The *Hawk* and the *Oneida*. I was on the *Hawk* when she blew up. *Dick Fowler*.

Q: Were you on the *Fowler*?

A: I was on the *Dick Fowler*.

Q: What did you do on the *Fowler*?

A: I think I was a smoke officer and fireman on her. The *H. K. Bedford*, that was a towboat and Captain Webster bought her and converted her into a packet. *Island Queen*, I made tow trips on the *Island Queen*. Pittsburgh to New Orleans, Pittsburgh to Cincinnati with the *Cassel*. I was on her when I was a kid, you know, and the old *Dick* engineer on her had big long red whiskers.

Q: He did, did he?

A: I was on there one time, and one day I thought I was pretty big, you know. I said, "About how many horsepower is them engine," I'd heard somebody talking about horsepower, you know. "Well," he says "son," he talked slow, he says, "son just depends on the size of the horses." (laughter) The way he said it, I never liked that old guy, and never would do a thing for him afterwards. (laughter) His name was Bunch, Bill Bunch. His whiskers came clear down here and that scared me. I never would run errands for him.

Q: On the *Lizzie Cassel*?

A: *Sonoma*, I built a model of her and I worked on her, the *Valley Gem*, they was packet boats, *Greenwood* and *Bessie Siler*. *Annie Laurie*, that's the one we sold to a coffee tycoon from Brazil. And the *Queen City* and the *Island Queen*, they was both about alike. We got in a race with the *Queen City*. Damn, what boat was that? *Island Queen* from Wheeling to Pittsburgh. And all the passengers was betting on the race. And we landed and took on some hogs, fat hogs, and it was hot weather and three or four of them died and I was fireman on her. Three or four of them died, heat you know killed them. And we heaved them in the furnace in the middle doors you know. We beat them into Pittsburgh about ten minutes and the captain come dawn, I had two skiff oars and two bricks on the safety valve. (laughter) They was allowed 100, around 190 pounds, I don't know how much they had. I couldn't tell because the steam gauge was clear around. The passengers was betting on the race, see. And the steam gauge was clear around against the pin. They traded me off right then. (laughter) I got fired.

Old Daddy Price fired me one time on a showboat. We was up the Kentucky River and I was engineer on the steamboat and he was shy of musicians, and he was going to make a musician out of me. I couldn't carry a tune in a basket. I've not a bit more music in me than a rabbit, but he said I could play a bass drum. We would go out and put on a little parade in them little towns, you know. Said, "Now when they're standing still, why go by the

John Knoepfle

drums see." And he'd shake his head for a little faster or a little slower. He knew I could. I kept him shaking his head all the time and one day Old Daddy said, "We'll get that bass drum and we'll go out on a nice long beach and march up and down the river banks and practice." There was old actors and actorines sitting up on the hill by the showboat, you know, and I got the drum and got out on the front end of the showboat. I whammed the drumstick through one head and flipped her over and rammed through the other head, and throwed drum, drumstick and all into the river. (laughter) Old Daddy paid me off. He had to pay my fare home, from clear up in High Bridge on the Kentucky River, up to Marietta, that burned him up.

Peggy Knoepfle: How did he get started in showboating?

A:Oh, he started with a shantyboat. His wife was a crack shot with a rifle, and he had a roustabout that could play a banjo. And he would get them down in them river towns, you know, he'd get them down to a river landing, just take their picture, tintype pictures, and that's the way he started. He made a fortune. If he had a good season he would buy or three of the other ones out. And if he had a bad season he'd sell them, and borrow it back the next spring. He was a crazy old guy. But he couldn't, he'd take right down the middle of the river and not a sandbar or nothing, he was right down the middle of the river. He thought he was great pilot. He wasn't half as good a pilot as Mrs. Price. *Raymond Horner*, She was coming down one night with a tow of coal and the fall line on the cable was hanging down between the carriers. And a guy was running electric on the cable way. He set the brake all right, he kept a loose clip on the end of the line so if they did get in the towboat, or any boat, you'd take the line off the drum see, and not hurt it and we had to keep that cable way 90 feet above low water. The engineers would read it every 30 days. If it was low we'd pull it. But sometimes the carriers wouldn't space right and the fall line would bang down between the carriers and the *Raymond Horner* coming down there with a tow and they couldn't see it was only a half inch line. They couldn't see it and caught her smokestack. She had boiler line smokestacks. Tore them smokestacks off of her, tore the pilothouse off of her, drowned the pilot and I think drowned the cub pilot too, and then they had Consolidated Coal and Coke Company, I think owned her then. And they sued the Becker Contract Company and broke them up and the government had to take the job over and finish it. *Tom Dodsworth*, I was on her. She was a towboat. Lock 19, towing down there, the river was high and hit a light standard on the river wall, sunk her down with seven or eight passengers.

Q: That was the *Kanawha*.

A: That was the *Kanawha*. I went down in a diving suit and got them out of the cabin. Drowned them in the cabin.

Q: Where is these towboats?

A: Well, I run on the *J. B. Finley* and *Sam Brown*, the *Alice Brown*, *Tom Brown*, they was owned by the Consolidated Coal and Coke Company when they sold them mines to the Steel Trust, along about 1912, if I'm right. And that way then they laid most of them big towboats up. They sold them to the Steel Trust and they would haul coal from Pennsylvania over to the lakes and haul the ore back, see. They made it both ways and they laid most of them big towboats up. Consolidated Coal and Coke Company took over. And they never made any money. And they sold out to the Steel Trust.

Q: How about telling us about that *Virginia*.

A: Well, when she was built, she was the last word in luxurious travel. Then that was the days after the gamblers and big shots on them, but they had some of the best people in the country traveled on that *Virginia*, up and down the river. President McKinley and his wife was on twice. All inside of her cabin was finished in genuine mahogany, crystal chandeliers, everything nice.

Q: What were you on the *Virginia*?

A: What time was I on it?

Q: Yes.

A: Well let's see, can't remember dates too good. I was on her different times, sometimes. I was on her probably two years once.

Q: Were you a fireman or an engineer aboard her?

A: I was an engineer once. Pilot on her.

Q: Were you up there when she got spreadeagled on that?

A: No, no, we'd got off of them before that. We was working on locks and dams. I worked on them locks and dams two or three years before that 1913 flood. We lived there at Little Hocking during the 1913 flood. And it was right across from Little Hocking where she'd cross on the West Virginia side where she got stuck and broke in two. We lived in a little cottage upon a little knoll in an orchard. And the water got up. We could stand on the window and door, and step in the water, but didn't get in the house. Everything went down that river, boy everything went down that river. And I was master mechanic on that job and I had two derrick boats and a sand-digger, and a steamboat, and a dredge boat, and six or eight barges, and I fleeted them all up on the West Virginia side. I had 28 wire lines out to big sycamore trees. And I kept two of them derrick boats at the head of the fleet see, loaded with junk, old shivs and scrap iron and stuff. Kept engineers on them boats night and day. And a house would come down you know. They've have a bucket up you know and they'd drop that bucket through that house and see skillets and pans and everything flying. (chuckles) Yes, everything went down. I rode out to a house and was all flooded up to the upstairs windows. Houses on Maple Avenue in Marietta, the white pine buildings of the fairgrounds, they'd float high, and they'd lodge against them bridges. And took all the bridges but the railroad bridge off Marietta and lodged them against the Putnam Street Bridge. Fairground building threw a current all down Maple Avenue, took every house off on that street, even took brick sidewalks out, and chimney foundations.

John Knoepfle

Them houses all float with the upstairs out. I rode out to a house and we went into an upstairs window and picked up $27 and two gold watches. Had an upstairs mantle with a clock sitting on the mantle. We went out, one baby laying on the bed kicking up his heels. We took that one off. And another had a gasoline boat with one of them going right for them big trees on the head of that island above Parkersburg. There was a man and five kids on the roof of it, and the kids all had the measles. We took them off. And when that house hit them trees boy, it just disappeared. We landed two 60,000 gallon tanks of gasoline. Landed one right below our house, got a line on it, checked it in and broke our line. Got a line on it again and checked it in. Landed right by a farmer's barn. And everybody had any, wasn't much gasoline used then. That was real gasoline too. Everybody had anything that burnt gas, they'd come and get all the gas. And when the river went down, they come out of Sistersville, two tanks and we tied up one lodged on them trees at the head of Blennerhassett Island and put a rope on it and tied it up to a tree. Got $250 for that one. Got $200 in salvage, $250 for the other one.

I landed a building that come out of Marietta. A lumber yard all pigeonholes stuck up with chair-rungs, and newel posts and railings; molding there was a million feet of molding. Everybody that was building a house in 40 miles came and got all they wanted of that. They never come after it. Rest of it burned up for kindling. Landed 150 barrel tank of paraffin right by my kitchen door. Put a wire around an apple tree and checked it in right by my kitchen door. Landed a Standard Oil Company warehouse. Boy, did it have everything in it? They come and got that though.

Q: Well did you save your own derrick tows and things? Were you able to save the boats you were trying to hold on the banks?

A: Oh yes we held them, I had 28 wire lines on big sycamore trees. Yes, we held them. Course they was out in the middle of the river when we got out in the bottoms you know. But I fleeted them up inside the land wall below the lock and dam there. Yes, I held them. They wouldn't allow you out there with a steamboat when them floods you know because if you was on a steamboat, you'd get a steamboat out in them backwaters and them floods and they'd be up in people's houses you know. That house would be setting on the foundation just, oh a bow wave of that steamboat would start it rocking, and they'd shoot at you. They shot me twice above Parkersburg.

Q: They did?

A: Yes out there in a towboat. What in the hell was her name? And the bow wave, you know started them rocking. They'd float off. Maybe taking a chance on not floating off the foundation. Yes, they didn't allow you out. I had a motorboat that I bought off a superintendent of a foundation company that was building that lock and dam, and they went broke. And the superintendent bought a ocean going motorboat up at Schenectady, New York and brought her down there. He got killed there. The *Queen City* come in there with some stuff to put off and they had a flat with A-frames in to hold pump sections. The *Queen City* landed along that flat and shoved it in against the wall, and then fell back and one of them caught him, and we got him in the skiff and brought over and flagged the freight train in eight or nine miles above Parkersburg. We flagged the freight train, put him in the caboose, and he died in the caboose before we could get him to the hospital. And I bought that motorboat off his widow. It was all built of cypress. He built it with carpenters he had in wintertime, see. Boy, it was nice outfit. Had a French made engine, wasn't many gasoline engines then. This was a French made engine, the duty on that engine and the magneto cost $1,200. I bought that off his widow and that thing, it was rigged for, you could step a sail on it. When they shut down he was going down and way up the coast of Florida, see. He got killed there. Could rig a sail on it, and it had tools and stuff I didn't even know what they was for. And I could of made a barrel of money in that 19 flood. Traveling men would get left, you know, from working home someplace and if you get them and get them home they would give you any price you ask, you know. But I didn't put it in the river. It would pull a bow wave, too. The engine wasn't so good on it, you couldn't depend on like you could, you can't depend on no gasoline engine. Anybody that was raised on steam, that's one thing I don't think too much of these flying machines. I was raised on steam. We got gasoline and diesel, and all kind of engines. I don't think too much of any gasoline rig.

Q: Well, how can you say that when it's so hard to stop a sternwheeler on the river?

A: Well, he didn't figure on sailing on the river see, he figured on sailing up around when he got out of the Mississippi, go down the Mississippi and up around the coast. That's the reason he had, he knew the engine wasn't dependable you know. He had it rigged for, put a sail on it. He put a sail up on it. And I finally sold it to a hotel man in Cincinnati. Oh, he had that thing 15, 20, years after that. It was ocean going. You could cook and sleep, you could sleep nine people on it, cook meals and everything. The cabin all had sealed, what do you call them?

Q: Compartments I guess.

A: Yes sealed glass. What do you call them?

Peggy Knoepfle: Portholes.

A: Portholes. I sold it for $400.

Q: Well, let me take you back to steam. Try to tell me something about stopping a sternwheeler on the river coming down.

A: Only way you could land them for fog or we'd run them bridges, see. If you hit a bridge pier and sunk any of them, they'd lose their insurance. We'd run the bridges, but we'd have to land for fog. And the only way you could land would be to put four men in a yawl, a big crawler two inch line and back her stand hard in, hard in as you could, close to shore as you could. They take ashore and take three or four or five turns around a big tree. Then put them on the bits.

John Knoepfle

They'd put that line on the bits and check her see. That's the only way they could stop one of them. You couldn't, like a flying machine, you couldn't back up with them in the big river. But now in them pools they can land one of them any place, you haven't got the current. We had a devil of a current. That was the only way you could land them. The last tugboat I was on, she never went out of Pittsburgh that she didn't kill a man before you got to New Orleans. The last time I was on, had a landing right below Wheeling and the mate on that boat went and got ashore a line around a tree. The mate wound up tight on the bits and didn't slack it enough and broke it. Cut him in two just like you'd cut him in two with a knife. She killed a man, I'd never make another trip when I got off there in Marietta. And I never went on one afterwards.

That big two inch line just wound right up on the bits and held it. Instead of slacking it you know, like you should, the mate, he should have known better than that. Cut him in two. Ooooh, it was awful. Drag on them lines you know. Right in two. They was a lot them drowned. I fished a lot of them out. When they drown they claim they'll float till their gall busts. Cold water, takes about 79 days, not too much. It's when their body begins to deteriorate and them little gas bubbles is what makes them float, cause I know. I've seen where babies would fall in the river and get drowned. They'd probably float the next day. But a man floats face down and a woman floats face up. And I've asked doctors what was the reason of that, and they said the best they could figure out was a woman's liver lays more on one side than the other and that's the first organ in the body that starts to deteriorate. It puffs up and enough on one side of the body, provided everything else is equal, it will gradually turn them. They don't come up on the float, they don't come right up. Maybe in a five mile current, they'll float maybe three miles before they come to the surface, see. That there extra weight will gradually turn them over. And invariably, I've fished a lot of them out of the river and you will find them with their arms folded on their breast just about like a undertaker would fix them.

One day, the day George Hart was nominated, inaugurated Governor here, a guy jumped off the Broad Street Bridge. I come pretty near getting ahold of him. I would if he hadn't pulled his overcoat off. I would of got him. He jumped off the Broad Street Bridge, right close to a pier and the water wasn't very deep. He hit broken stones and stuff in there when he lit. He floated down and by the time the fireman got there with the boat and stuff he was dead of course. Had his arms folded on his breast just about like an undertaker would fix him up. They'll always do that.

I dug one up one time, up lock 15 with a derrick boat. A farmer had come in there and drowned himself. We could see where he went in the river, and they offered $125, they couldn't drag him out, they offered $125 for anybody that found him. I was digging around, come up with him, had him by one foot. He was all covered with sand and I'd boom up and slack off you know. Was going to boom in on the head of the derrick boat and take the hose and wash the sand off him before I let him out of the bucket. And the fireman came out the door and seen him, and he leaped in the river and swum ashore and he never did come back. He had pretty near two week's pay coming to him, he never even got his pay. He never come back.

Well, you get into some funny things on the river . . . diving suit, I went down and got two little boys. Down in the mouth of little Kanawha at Parkersburg, the sawmill was there you know, and they had log rafts, there was sunken logs in there. Two kids was naked and they just rolled over a sunken log and they drag upstream or the log would jump the guide hooks on them and they'd drag downstream. And so I got the diving suit and went down. They was locked together. That's what they do when you try to fish them out. I never try to get one unless he goes down the third time, they're helpless then. Go down behind them or hit them behind the ear, you can stun them. I went down in the diving suit out in Oklahoma in a job out there on the Arkansas River. A shoe clerk and his best girl was in swimming, and she got in a whirlpool went down, and he tried to save her. She locked arms around him, and you couldn't find them for three or four days. So I went down to Ft. Smith and got the government diving suit. I was running a cable way there. Sand and gravel business for a big contractor I sent down to Ft. Smith and got the government diving suit. Went down and got them, they was locked together just as tight. The undertaker took them away that way, couldn't even pull them apart. They'll do that. You never should get too close to one of them, because no matter if they got good sense, they'll still try to struggle you know. Still try to climb over you. Invariably both drown. Yes, I've fished out a lot of them, around them river jobs.

Italians, in them days we hired common labor and get them Italians you know. You'd hire a whole gang, had to hire a whole gang. Hired the boss and he had the gang. Had to build a camp for them and everything. I was towing slows with a towboat up at lock 7 and I had a big stone on one end of the flat. One end was high and the other end was low. There was four of them wops setting on the head load. Well, I kicked around you know and run the lines off. A dredge boat was whistling for the steamboat and the river had been up and the banks was muddy and slippery. The high end slipped right up in that slippery mud you know. Sunk the other end and they just set there. All they had to do in the world was get up and run the length of that boat and jump out on the bank. They set there. And I went back in there and I found her out in the river and put a line on the timberhead. Picked her up and there they was all right. Never even come up. A white man will come up three times. Most of the time, twice anyhow. They never even come up. All they had to do was just run and jump out of the boat. They drowned a lot, drowned nine Mohammedans down here on the Muskingum River. They was fixing a dam there. While I was kicking a boat across the break in the dam mill race. It had some timbers on it, nine of them on it and I was kicking across on two lines. See, slack one and let the current kick it across. One hit that current, rocked up and every one of them

John Knoepfle

jumped in the river and drowned them. Fished them out and someway according to their religion, they never cleaned them up or nothing. They buried than with their feet sticking out. Two or three days and then they took them up and fixed them all up and buried them. But they wouldn't never, those health authorities wouldn't let them. They're buried in Beverly now.

Q: What were Mohammedans doing on the Muskingum?

A: Oh they was laborers.

Q: Is that so?

A: Yes, laborers. Oh, they got them from every place in them days. They paid them twelve and a half cents an hour, 15 was the best they got. Yes, they got them from every place. A good many of them was Italians on them river jobs. You'd hire a boss and he'd have maybe 30 or 40 men. Get right down among them with a pick handle and make them go. (chuckles) I knocked one in the head with a swinging derrick. I couldn't, didn't see him down inside the coffer dam. Gathered him up and took him over. He had a money belt strapped around his leg, $700 in it. The undertaker got that. They drowned one there at lock 18, he had a belt with $1,200 in it, the undertaker got that. I fished him out too, and you know they was going over after supper to clean up a boat with a shovel, couldn't get coal all out of it with a clam shell see. I seen them all standing there jabbering you know, and the superintendent was there. I rode over, had half of the river coffered off see, at the end of the coffer dam the current around there cut out pretty deep. I rode out and I said, "What's the matter, Mac?" One of them fell in there. I could see where he'd splashed on the head of the boat when he fell in. I had a pike pole on the boat and I picked that pike pole up and I felt him. Felt like you was getting the mud see. Got that pike hook in his shirt and pulled him up and none of them wops would help me get him in the skiff. Superintendent and I finally got him in the skiff and got him up on. He had a cheap watch. He'd only been in 15 minutes. They should have brought him to if they had of done it. We rolled him and pumped him and everything, couldn't get enough macaroni out of him. A week or two after that I went home and mother had a dish of macaroni and cheese, I loved that stuff, but I couldn't go it. I looked at his watch, we brought him to though, as much as 28 minutes. I've seen heart action three quarters of an hour after he's drowned. We fished him out. The longest time I remember he'd been in 28 minutes and rolled him and pumped him out. Brought him to. I was drowned three times.

Q: You were?

A: You got it around them river jobs.

Q: Where did that happen?

A: Fall in. I fell off the head of a boat coming upstream. I was drowned that time for finishes. The river was swift and we was coming upstream and I fell off the head of a flat. Had a flat on the head of the towboat. I went under that boat and I'd come up against the bottom of it you know. Tore the back out of my shirt and popped up between the head of the steamboat and the head of the flat and they grabbed me.

Q: You were lucky!

A: Yes, I would have been gone that time. If I had of went under the steamboat I would have been, I could hold my breath for a minute and a half. I can now. I do a lot of deep breathing. If you do that every day, you can hold you breath for, oh I've seen the time I could hold my breath for pretty near two minutes.

Q: This is when you went to Brazil. You took a boat there.

A: Oh, took her to New Orleans and bulkheaded her up the boiler deck. Took the wheel off and pilot house and the stacks. Then towed her out with a deep sea tug. Landed in the mouth of the Amazon River on Christmas night. I think it was either 1893 or 1894. Landed in the mouth of the Amazon River and there was a lot of boats on the Amazon River, but there wasn't much type of boats, the type of boats that we built here, see. Them coffee men thought that would be a good outfit for them. They never done no good with it because it blowed up after we left there. It blowed up. We only stayed there a year to break in a native crew. Oh, I suppose they would get drunk. We was afraid of them at first, when we first went over there. Way up in the head waters of that river they'd never seen a white man.

They was as primitive then as they was five hundred years ago. They was always warring. Tribes warring with each other. We settled a war between two tribes with them search lights. They was great for their kids you see and we made up a scheme. We got so we could understand blather some of their language. We made up a scheme, if they didn't quit fighting, we'd just do it for fun. But wasn't to them you know. We made up a scheme if they didn't quit fighting, they'd lose all their kids and we'd throw them search lights. What you could do with them, we had two of them on a river with low banks. Where real dark nights you see, you can't go by the skyline on the hill, and all of them steamboats had two searchlights; you could throw one on each bank, see. And you know what you could do with them, whipping them around through there. Depopulate one of them towns in a minute. They wouldn't come back till daylight. Little villages. They was all warring at each other. They wasn't just foolish either. They mated their best men with their best women and some of them were perfect. They was perfect physically built. Perfectly built.

They done that like we breed livestock see, to get good warriors. That's all they wanted, all warriors you know. They was always battling with each other. Good country. Yes, we settled that war. I don't know how long it lasted, but they stopped anyhow, made up and had a big pow-wow you know. Oh, probably next week they'd be at it again sometimes. We didn't stay long enough to see. Primarily up in there we'd map them out a channel you know. Of course, those coffee companies figured on expansion like everybody else. They didn't have no plantations up in there. But a man could have made a fortune in that country if he'd had a floating sawmill. The price of mahogany was in this

John Knoepfle

country up; in that country it cost you nothing much to get it cut, saw it up and load it, and bring it back to this country. Could have made a fortune. Mahogany trees there were three foot through. Gee, what furniture and stuff. Them days they used it more than they do now. Yes, could have made a fortune.

Q: What was the name of the boat that you . . .

A: The *Annie Laurie*.

Q: The *Annie Laurie*, yes.

A: George Wallace built her. He had a steamboat in the Muskingum River. Lived, I think he lived in Malta across the road from McConnelsville. Oh he built the *Lorena* too. He built her and sold her. He sold *Annie Laurie*. I don't know, he was mixed up in oh, all his life practically in river traffic. His people before him, I think, was mixed up with river traffic. I can remember when I was a real small boy, my grandad lived to be 98. Had all his hair and all his teeth when he died. Had more hair than me and you and her has got. (chuckles) And they used to build flat boats there on the Muskingum River and load them with produce in the fall and float them. They'd float them down to New Orleans and sell them, and sell the boat and walk back. They'd walk back, him and the neighbors that went with him walked back from New Orleans three times through wilderness, there wasn't no road then. That was before these boats and he come back on that *Robert E. Lee* one trip up to Cairo. She didn't come up the Ohio River. The last trip he made he come up on her. And they had yellow fever all in that southern country them days. That trip he come up on the *Robert E. Lee* and a lot of them died of yellow fever. And they burnt wood on them then. The ship carpenter would make caskets for them. Wherever, they'd stock wood up, they'd bury them what died. When they got into Marietta, he came up on another boat from there to Marietta. There was a Frenchman on there, and him and my grandad was kind of friendly and when he got off in Marietta the captain of the steamboat asked if he wasn't going to take his — the Frenchman died of yellow fever and they buried him — and he asked him if he wasn't going to take his friend's trunk. "No," he said, "it didn't belong to him." They opened it and it had $1,800 in it. $1,800 in them days was a fortune, them days. He could just as well had it because they didn't know nothing. They didn't have the facilities for finding out the purse of anybody them days like they do now. They never paid no more attention to him, just buried him. Yes sir, they walked from New Orleans. That's a long a walk. The Ohio River is 981 miles. It's 1,100 miles from Cairo to New Orleans. We drive down there in two days. Fly down in three or four hours. If they'd had them things then it would have scared them to death though then.

Q: Your grandfather was a farmer.

A: No, he was cigarmaker. They'd make money with that stuff and they'd build a boat then. Produce was cheap then. They'd load that down and float it down, four or five of them would go. A vacation for them you know. But they'd have to walk back. The first one I can remember, I used to pump all the boats they had laid along close to where we lived. I'd pump it out with a hand pump when it would get water in them before they'd start. Didn't have it all loaded yet. But I can remember that. Yes, them days they had it rough what we got now. They lived as long as we do. Some of them longer, my grandma lived to be 98 and she raised ten children of her own and three grandchildren. She did all the work the day before she died. Lived longer than any of them do now.

Q: Well, then you were born up on the Muskingum somewhere?

A: I was born in Lowell.

Q: Lowell.

A: That's ten miles above Marietta on the Muskingum River.

Q: Were there boats around Lowell?

A: They was principally on the Monongahela River. They was short, powerful, built to bring coal out and fleet them up, fleet the barges up for the big boats to take south. The reason the big boats go up that river was because locks. They couldn't lock through. They was bigger than the locks. The boats that took the coal south was bigger and more powerful, they could take a half a dozen tows that the pool boats would bring out of the Monongahela. I ran on some packet boats that went up that river too. They was up there, up at Brownsville. There was two packet boats, one would go up one day, and one down. Sometimes we would have 300 barrels of whiskey. There was a lot of distilleries up that river. Them miners would get down there at night you know and we'd have whiskey barrels all around the barge. They'd just slip a barrel off in the river and swim ashore. There was no railroads up that river then. There is now because I've been on them. All the traffic was carried by steamboat. Crew of the towboats got the coal out and the packetboats carried all the freight. On the bank, half of the river would be up and the bank would be muddy. They'd land and put off freight, just run out a plank and then deck hands would take it out and dump it off right in the mud. If they didn't like, there was nothing they could do about it, there was no other way to get it you know. One old fellow was a saloon keeper in Pittsburgh, and the crew would tap them whiskey barrels. This old fellow brought in three barrels of 35 year old whiskey, and he just figured there was nobody tapped that. He was coming down after it got dark. He got him a board and put it across the bow and sat on the board. That way they couldn't tap it. They'd raise a hoop you know, and bore a hole in and draw out a bucket full and then plug it and drive the hoop back. They'd tap that, and one of the deck hands went down in the hole and bored a hole up through the deck into the head of the barrel. I had two cedar buckets, kept them in the engine room. We got two buckets full and built a plug up through, and of course they had to drive it through the deck into the head of the barrel. Got into Pittsburgh, oh about two or three o'clock in the morning, and when the deck hands rolled them whiskey barrels off, of course they naturally pulled the plug out of that one, and they was all half asleep, never pay no attention to it, they was out on the wharf and just happened to holler, "Let go." The hole was down and run the whole

John Knoepfle

barrel out. Tapped it right close to one edge and run the whole barrel of whiskey out. In them days you could buy a barrel of whiskey for $90 the best of it. Now, I don't know what it cost now. Well whatever it would cost too much. I never generally drank whiskey and everyone was on me to drink whiskey.

Peggy Knoepfle: Can you tell me how many men it took to fire a pool boat?

A: It only took one fireman. I fired one of them myself. I was blown up on two of them. They was generally only two boiler boats. Where the big boats was four or five, and some of them six boiler boats. One fireman would fire them. They was not very big, but they was powerful. They could handle. They was good handlers. They would take six, eight, or ten barges of coal see, where a big boat would take 25, 30, maybe 40, take them south.

Peggy Knoepfle: Were they fired on the coal they was carrying? Is that right, they would just send them up to get the coal from the barges to fire the engines.

A: They'd coal them up at the docks. Some of them, and some of they'd carry a flat. Three different sizes of barges: a flat, a barge, and a coalboat. Well, a flat was about 60 feet long and a barge would be 70 or 80, and coalboat would be 110. Coalboat would carry 10,000 bushels of coal. They'd carry a flat onside of the tugboat and the coal monkey would wheel coal out of the flat into the fire box. Some of them had coal bins in the head of them, in front of the boilers. If you was on that boat in Marietta, you could see. They'd fill them full and they'd fire out of them. Then they'd land at them docks and coal up. Fill that coal box full of coal, that would last them three or four days. Wasn't like the big boats, on a big boat taking a tow south they'd have a filled flat on each side of the steamboat. They'd have, sometimes them *J. B. Williams*, the *Alice Brown*, and the Sam Brown, and them would have four man wheeling coal and two men shoveling it in the boilers, see. They'd be four, five, six boiler boats. *Hoxie*, was a five boiler boat. I was blown up on her down at Ravenswood. Them boats, one good fireman could fire them. They didn't try to make any speed you know. Course it took a lot of power to handle them boats. That river was narrow and wasn't so crooked in some places as the Ohio River.

There was in one of them villages way up in the head waters, they was headhunters. The alligators would catch a kid and they was a lake, a swamp rather, back from the river a piece. We laid there four days one time and dynamited either five or six. I think three alligators and two crocodiles. They'd load up, put half a stick of dynamite in a dead fish and wire it up in the steamboat if they was along the shore. But out in the lake we'd put a fuse in it you know. They'd let the old medicine man light the fuse. He didn't understand nothing like that you know. They was primitive as they was 500 to 1,000 years ago. They couldn't understand. We had two high powered rifles and two or three revolvers. They couldn't understand what them things could do. All they had was blow guns and bow and arrows. Some of them had spears. But they'd poison them arrows and that poison, they'd take the liver out of anything that had a liver in it and put some other stuff with it and let that liquify. Drop of it as big as a bean, and kill you, a break in your skin and kill you in seven minutes. Not a cobra or any poisonous snake, they'd devil him, a cobra would kill anything when they bite, you know. They'd let them bite that liver while it was fresh and get all the poison they could get out of the snake and then let that liquify. Some of them wouldn't use it, they'd kill their own people. Kids would get it you know. They was great for their kids. They took good care of them.

Peggy Knoepfle: Apparently they didn't have any soap up there?

A: No, they didn't know what soap was. Well, we was leaving there we give them all the soap we had. Some of them we thought more of than others we'd give them a whole box of Ivory soap. If they'd of had gold and diamonds, you could of got it for that. It'd do them some good. Them medicine men, they'd do things that our doctors couldn't do, wouldn't even believe it. They'd do it. They had some terrible diseases. They'd take care of them. We'd carry a lot of drugs if we could handle quinine and that stuff. We'd give them that you know. But they'd take that Ivory soap, when some of them would get crippled and cut and stuff. Wash out. We'd show the medicine man how to use it. They wouldn't let them wash with it. When they got ahold of it, they wouldn't let nobody else have it. We'd give it to any of them see. We'd black our self-up and go in swimming with them and wash it off and they would try to wash their black off. I don't know what, we'd give the medicine man, they wouldn't let none of the tribe have that, they'd keep that. They wasn't so dumb as you would think either considering everything you know. Of course we, the guy with me had false teeth and he'd take them teeth out and put them, they couldn't understand that either. He'd take them teeth out and put them back in. They couldn't understand a gun of no kind.

Peggy Knoepfle: You were pretty far up then on the Amazon?

A: Oh we went 2,500 miles up. Talk about the majesty of the Mississippi. There wasn't any more majestic than that river. Of course, a lot of that way up in the head waters was jungle, was all jungle. There was no jungle on the Mississippi. I don't know I never was on the Mississippi, only from Cairo to New Orleans. I was never above I've been up the head waters of it. We went out on an excursion boat. What's them two towns up there one across the river from the other? That's the head waters of the Mississippi.

Q: Up at St. Paul?

A: St. Paul and Minneapolis. I've been there and we was there a couple of times. We went up. Had a boy up there in the show. Mother and I and one of my daughters was up there. We wasn't far from St. Paul, Minneapolis. That excursion boat, that big *Admiral*, big excursion boat. She went out early and we went on a moonlight trip on her. But I've crossed the Mississippi in different places, but I never run on a boat that went above Cairo. Between Cairo and St. Louis. The Ohio river boats, I'd never go above Cairo on the Mississippi. Packetboats, tugboats never did you know, they all went south; 981 miles from Pittsburgh to Cairo. I've seen that old river and all its moods. The 1913 flood,

John Knoepfle

we lived down there at Parkersburg and everything went down that river. First came the pigpens and chicken houses and that stuff you know. Different buildings, and then come houses, barns, we landed a . . .

Q: Well I imagine it must have rather hazardous piloting in the upper Ohio.

A: You had to know the bottom of the river. Any pilot had to know the bottom of the river. Anybody could steer a steamboat, just like driving an automobile, if they knew the bottom of the river. But the pilot had to know the bottom of that river. And of course, you had channel markers, but you had to know where the high and low places was. A river you know is just like a creek. Like a riffle in a creek. There is high and low places. When they built them locks and dams, they built them to make a nine foot stage over them low places, see. High places, riffles, there would be a riffle in a creek. Yes, them packet boats, they ran all the time, except in the winter.

Q: I imagine on some of them rocky ledges up there, up above around Hockingport must have been very dangerous.

A: Well they wasn't no rocky places, most high places in the bottom of the river is sand bars see, sand and gravel. Then after they built lock 18, we took out, that was above Parkersburg we took out a, that was rocky along there. Was all them limestone quarries along there and that stone run out under the river. We went in there with four dredge boats, and drilled that, and took off six feet. Averaged six feet, 800 feet wide, for a mile or a mile and a quarter. Right out of the bottom of the river. Drilled it with steam drill and shot it. Dug it out with them dredge boats.

We dug up a calliope there. One of the showboats, about one of the last of them, the last I had anything to do with them, down the river and the river was pretty high and the lock was done then. The pilot had took the river wall for the land wall, see; and the steamboat, he was running pretty close to shore, the steamboat hit one of them steel timberheads, with powerlines on them, split her wide open. She sunk and sunk down about, oh had about three feet between the ceiling and the floor in the cabin. All the actors and the actorines was asleep in bed, seven or eight o'clock. Never got up till noon. They was all in bed, she didn't sink. She sunk down, stuck on the bottom and we went down there, they was swimming around in there, two or three of them on the bass drum, all the mattresses and doors on a steamboat is life preservers. You can grab a door and pick it up off the hinges, jump in the river and it will float you. Bed mattresses and that stuff will float. We gave them overalls, stuff, and took all them off.

They just got stores in Marietta. You know I got a lard can full of eggs and two big hams and a big sack of potatoes. They just couldn't do nothing with it, water you know. Told us to take, fished up their jewelry, all them show people had to put all their money in jewelry, you know. We fished up their jewelry off of the cabin floors, they had it under their pillows and stuff. Took all their clothes and that stuff. We took them off the showboat, or the steamboat, and took them back up to Marietta. They raised the steamboat. Didn't hurt the showboat see, broke loose, the steamboat when she sunk, broke loose from the showboat. Showboat didn't draw as much water as a steamboat, that's the reason it didn't hurt the showboat. When the steamboat sunk, that broke her loose from the showboat and the towboat coming upstream with a tow empty, they caught the showboat and landed it. They took some of them off the steamboat too.

Q: You don't remember what boat that was, do you?

A: No.

Q: Well I guess I could find out.

A: I think it was the *Raymond Horner*. Oh, they was so many of them. You can't remember all of them. My memory is not too good any more. Things happened last week, I can't remember as I could as when I was five years old. A lot of people that way.

Q: Well, speaking of showboats, can you tell us a little more about your friend Daddy Price?

A: Old Daddy! Well he was the star of all of them. He'd buy them in the spring and sell them in the fall. I didn't see the coming of the showboats, but I seen them go. The steamboats too, just like these old time railroad engineers seen the steam locomotives go. The first showboat there was any record of was on the river in 1813, but they didn't amount to much. One time they had a circus. They had four barges fleeted up and they had a circus on that. A whole circus going along them river towns.

Q: That was about 1900, wasn't it?

A: Yes, that was about 1900. One of my kids was little then, just a baby and I had her down there. Had her up in front of the snake charmer, you know. She was a little monkey. The snake charmer picked up a big snake. I was holding her in my arms you know. She picked up a big snake and wrapped it around, hung it around her neck. She just looked straight, she never made a sound or nothing. I thought they'd scare her, but it didn't. She thought I'd protect her.

Q: I think the *Cricket*, the little *Cricket* towed that water circus. The *Cricket* was the tow?

A: The *Cricket* towed it?

Q: Yes.

A: Could be, I don't remember now. Yes, they had a full size circus. The showboats is all gone now. Old Daddy Price, he was something, little old short guy with sideburns. Always wore a long gold watch chain around his neck, clear down, great big link thing, about like a dog chain. But he made a fortune. He kept it too. He'd get 50 cents for ten, 20 in them days is a lot of gold, ten, 20 and 30, see. And he'd get 50 cents in some of them towns. And a town like Marietta, a town where they would charge him a $5 wharfage, see. They'd charge a steamboat, a showboat wharfage in them towns, to tie up at the wharf, you know. If they'd charge him more than $5, he wouldn't show there, he wouldn't show Parkersburg, he'd go across the river to Bedford. They'd come

John Knoepfle

over, what a lot of them do, they'd come over in rowboats. Used to go up the Big Kanawha. They'd come in up there in buggies and ox carts.

And one woman sent her boy and wanted to know if we wouldn't cut the steamboat, we couldn't get above Charleston, wanted to know if we wouldn't cut the steamboat, let it loose and come up after her and the kids. (chuckles) It was a big job to cut the steamboat loose on one of them showboats. They used to haul a steering line and stuff, bell cords and stuff was hooked up from the pilot house on the showboat. They would have to cut all of them loose and cut the, it wasn't as much to cut the steamboat loose as it was to cut the pilot lines and the bell cords. Oh, they would come in there, they'd hear that calliope you know. You could hear that, we'd get in, in the morning and they'd play four or five on a calliope, and then about an hour or two before showtime of an evening steam up the boiler, play some more on them. They would come in there from miles and miles.

Q: Daddy Price never tried to make an actor out of you, did he?

A: Yes, he tried to make a bass drummer out of me. There was no music in me.

Q: Well tell me, did you know a showboater by the name of Ralph Emerson?

A: Yes, old Captain Bryant I guess he's in Hollywood now. What's his name?

Q: Billy Bryant.

A: Billy Bryant, yes, I knew them all. I knew them when Old Daddy Price, they had one boy, and I was on them when he was a baby. I was on one of them when he run one of them, when Daddy had three or four of them, he run one of them, off and on. I wasn't on them all, that time, but off and on. One time we was laying up the Kentucky River, and come a big thunder storm, the hills like they is down around southern part of the state here, and a big storm, you know water was running right off. We was laying above the dam and right below the mouth of a creek, and that creek ran out and broke all our lines, but one head line off the showboat. And Old Daddy got his money trunk, he always kept his money in a trunk in the steamboat, and he got his money trunk and took that ashore, and then he got his wife and baby and took them ashore, then he got the actors and actorines, and took them ashore, and the ship carpenter and myself. We was sitting out on the head of the showboat and he was pacing up and down the river banks yelling for us to come on ashore. We stayed on. But if that line had of broke it would went over that dam, would have ruined her, tore her all to pieces. Yes, that was a wild place up that Kentucky River, they'd shoot at you if you waved at the girls. Some of them guys would shoot at you. That river wasn't very wide you know, like them steamboat guys waved at everybody they'd see. We'd go up to High Bridge and back.

Q: What kind of audience did they play to up there?

A: Oh, every kind, you know what them hillbillies would be, they was worse than they are now, and they're bad enough now when they get in civilized country. Yes, some of them was wild. But we never had no trouble with them, we always treated them nice. It was good business you know to treat them right.

You could get in trouble up that Kentucky River. Why I was up there one time, there was an old fellow that was up there leasing oil land. I was driving him in a buggy. Had a buggy and he was leasing land for oil and coal. Was driving along a country road, long about dark, and two guys stepped out of the brush and one of them caught ahold of the horse. And this old fellow had a big mole on his nose. One of them took the horse bridle and the other one says, "Mister, I want to feel your nose." And the old man says, "All right." And they felt that mole on his nose, said, "All right, you can go." They knew we was coming; they didn't have no telephones them days. They was looking for revenuers you see. And they knew if one of them had a mole on his nose, he was all right see. That went ahead of us. So we ask them, it was pretty late, and we asked them about where we could get a place to stay all night. They said, "Go up to the second house there. They got six or seven rooms. They'll put you up. We did and they unhitched the horse, fed him, fixed supper for us. We stayed there and wanted to pay them the next. morning. No, they wouldn't take nothing. The old man slipped a couple of dollars under his plate. They went out and they fed our horse and hitched him up, all ready to go. And we was driving along a half hour or so afterwards and I looked around behind me, said, "There is a gunny sack in the back end of the buckboard." I said, "What's in that sack?" He said, "I don't know. I've never see it before." He stopped and got out. A half-gallon of moon-shine in it. Neither one of us drank it. Give it away. (chuckles) They wouldn't take nothing. They're all good people up in that country if you'd treat them right, but you'd better not fool with them. Yes indeed, snuff-eaters. We used to go to the dances up in there, believe it or not they'd set on the edge of a board and put their feet on a, boards were flat, playing a fiddle, a guitar, whatever music could play. Those women in there all chewed snuff, and you know, they'd stop and they could hit a cat in the eye at 15 feet. (chuckles)

A: Now you were in the Spanish-American War too?

Q: Yes, I was in three years in the 1st cavalry. Got up in that mess over there. I went over there with the Rough Riders. That was a lousy outfit, everything: doctors, lawyers, robbers, murderers, thieves, Indians, cowboys, all kinds.

Q: Did you know Teddy?

A: Oh yes, when Teddy was in Washington, we'd all had an invitation anytime we was going through there we could stop, and no matter who was in his office, when they came out, we went in, that was orders. And when we'd go in there you could just see him wilt. He didn't have to keep up on his dignity with us because we knew him when, you know. I said the last time I was about there, it was about, been there for an hour and a half and the whole place was full. A lot of big shots out there waiting to get in there. "Ah," he said, "the hell with them. they are nothing but peanut politicians." (chuckles) He said, "Maybe you haven't got much time, but they haven't got nothing else but." No, Teddy was one of the boys. Him and old Joe Wheeler.

Q: Wow! That's fighting Joe?

John Knoepfle

A: He was in command of the cavalry. He'd put me over, I was on his staff and they had one outfit that didn't have but one 1st lieutenant. I don't know why he done it; it was all contrary to the rules of the army, but he put me in charge of that outfit and I was only about 21 you know. I had four doctors, four or five lawyers, civil engineers, and all them guys. About puzzled me you know, was all that brain and I didn't have brains enough to get in out of the rain. Now he said, "They got a 1st lieutenant," he says, "he'll outrank you but I'll take care of that." I lined them all up and I said, "Now here boys, this is it we are in this mess and you know the rules." You get a handbook, you see, with all the rules. "We're in this mess and we've got to shoot ourselves out of it or get shot out of it." I said, "I'll do the best I can and you guys know the rules." I never had no trouble to amount to. They was all kinds.

Q: Did you get up to San Juan Hill?

A: I sure did. We pulled two doctors out of trenches to take care of wounded. We didn't have nothing then, nothing but a little old first-aid package. A little Jew had 75 of them under a big mango tree right at the foot of San Juan Hill and he was doing the best he could with them you know. One of the lieutenants got his leg shot off and laid down all broke up and he was trying to fix him up. I was down there for something, I don't know what, but I went back up and pulled two of them doctors out and sent them down there and they split that and he set there and held his leg and they sawed his leg off with a hand saw. It was only a ten point-hand saw, no they had no narcotics, nothing to give them there. Of course, we had hospital equipment on the ship but we got in that mess. And it was over before, the whole business only lasted 100 days. It was over before it could get organized. You know how the army is. They do the last thing first and the first thing last. Oh, General Shafter, a Chicago reporter off the "Chicago Inner-Ocean" had a cut in the "Chicago Inner-Ocean" on the front page. We get them there three weeks old, 25 cents, the only paper sold on the battlefield. They had a cut where General Shafter had moved his headquarters to the front and he just swung his hammock around on the other side of the tree. And he took a cow over there so he could have milk for his coffee.

Four of us took a shot at that cow to be sure that we'd get her. And we killed that cow and had to butcher her and everything. Skinned her and cut it up and he made a beef to Teddy Roosevelt, you know. And Teddy said, "If I can find out who done it I'll punish them." He had about 25 pounds of that steak in his tent right then. (laughter) And same way when we took him over pork. We laid there three weeks before we went over and all of them farmers around there raised a lot of hogs. And when we left there, there wasn't a hog in that country we could get. We chased two of them one time, I and a fella named Duke. I was going to get some chickens and he was going to get a pig. I was up an apple tree about nine o'clock right in front of the front door, not 75 feet from the house and had two big Plymouth rocks. And Duke was in the pigpen and he couldn't catch a pig. He'd pulled out his pistol and shot him. Of course, that farmer leaped up, you know, I'd turned the old horse loose and went running with them two chickens. We got all the pigs in that country. And they'd come in, them farmers would come in and bellyache to Roosevelt. Teddy would tell them, "Now if I can catch them, I'll punish them." He'd have a couple of hams in his tent right then. (chuckles) We talked about when he was in Washington when he was president.

Q: Well let's get back on the river if we can. About what year did you come off of the river?

A: I got off the river in 1917. I was on them lock and dams, though, before that. I left the river in 1917, went into camp. World War I was on. Went in there and got in there one day and bought me a house in Nashville. Kids were just big enough to do something, wasn't much. I had chief engineer job in the power house in Marietta. Lock 17 out above Marietta, and lived in a government house. Then one child was born; I think the last one. I had 17 acres of garden land there. I was supposed to put up the powerhouse. First thing that come was the whistle. That was the last thing you put on. That was government for you. I got requested and all I had to do was make out a river report and weather report and answer two or three letters, fool letters from the home office. I couldn't take it. I could work them days. When I couldn't work, wasn't nothing to do, I'd go goofy. So I pulled out of there and moved into camp. The kids all got jobs making $40 a day there one time. Two of them worked in Grueber Hand and Watch Factory. Yes, I got clear away from it and never went back to it.

Q: Did the building of the dam put an end to independent packet boating on the river?

A: No, no, made it better. That made it so they could go all the time see, in low water. They could go, towboats could go nine foot. They made nine foot stage after it was all done of course, it wasn't all done for years. The first one I worked on in 1902, lock 18 above Parkersburg, they didn't build them and number them one, two, three, four, and that way. They built 18 and they built 7, 9, 11, 12, 14, 15, 17, and 18 was done before they ever started some of them. Then they jumped up to 21, up to 26, up to 35. Went down to Louisville, Kentucky, below that riffle in the river there. That was bad place for towboats, Louisville. They had falls in the river there. Had to get a falls pilot when we'd go down there on a big river, on them falls. Then they built a dam below there and backed the water up over them see.

Q: Some of those falls pilots were a lot of famous men, weren't they?

A: They got $100 to take the boat over; $100 them days was something, wasn't $49.50 like they got now. Them falls pilots that's all they done taking steam-boats over. They had a coast guard station there at Louisville. May be there yet.

Q: It is. They have a lighthouse there.

A: Yes let's see, I think that was the last one I worked on. And finished 17, finished 17 and I worked on that one and I took the fleet. T. A. Gillespie outfit that built it. I forgot now who they was, they went broke. T. A. Gillespie bought

John Knoepfle

17 and 18. I took the fleet down we finished that one. I think that's the last one I was on. I can't remember too much now.

Q: Wonder if you can tell me any more about the Muskingum. That's where your earliest memories are.

A: Well, that's the first steamboat I was on. I used to run off from school and go on them steamboats, below the Marietta and back. They made a round trip a day, from Beverly to Marietta. Packetboat. Now they've abandoned that river. That's a shame too. That's a beautiful valley up there.

Q: It is. I have seen it.

A: Of course, we don't pay so much attention to it. We was raised there, see. But people from other states drive that valley, that's a beautiful valley. My father worked on that river when the state owned it. Then he worked on it when the government took it over, them locks and dams. The government took it over. He worked on it then, $1 a day, 10 cents an hour.

Q: Working on the dam for the state, was that it?

A: Yes, the state owned it first. State built them dams first, then the government took it over. Maybe the state will take it back now, I don't know, to preserve it to keep it there. Shame to let it go, they let them dams go out wouldn't be nothing but a creek. Then a lot of them towns around there, you know, depend on it for water supply. They've got an organization now in McConnelsville trying to do something about it. I don't know what they're going to do about it. Spend millions of dollars and give it to foreign countries and let anything like that get it. Of course, it never, none of those rivers ever paid for themselves. They never even paid to operate them locks and dams, none of them.

Q: Last time you mentioned a mate who was cut in two by a line.

A: A what?

Q: A mate that was cut in two by a line when he tried to stop the boat.

A: Checking line, checking the boat in.

Q: Do you remember what boat that was?

A: That was on the *Onward.*

Q: The what?

A: *Onward,* when I got off, I went to the Marietta. I said if he killed a man or drowned a man on that trip I'd never make another one. I never did. I got off of it in Marietta and never was on one after.

Q: He must have had a bad reputation then.

A: He did. Every trip they'd lose a man or two. Oh, that old river eat up a lot of them you know. Different ways, steamboats blow up, drown and fall overboard. Now they make them wear them Mae Wests, all of them crews on them boats, most of them. Them lock and dam crews, they make them when they are working around, they make them wear them Mae Wests. They fall in the river, a lot of them drowned on them lock and dams jobs too. Fall in the river. The river eat up many of them. Bet I fished out 50 or more. Last time I was in a diving suit, I got two little boys down at the mouth of the Little Kanawha.

Q: Can you remember any of your grandfathers?

A: They used to boat produce from out of the Muskingum River to New Orleans. Walk back. Had to there wasn't no, after the first of the steamboats, the packetboats. That was one of them there, two of them there. They'd come up from Cairo on them, and then they'd walk from Cairo. But he walked from New Orleans, five of them walked from New Orleans twice. Through wilderness, Indian country and everything you know.

Q: About what year would that have been I wonder?

A: Oh, it'd be around, around 18 . . . I was a small boy, I remember pumping the boats out before they'd leave, after they'd get them loaded. I was 75, that would be around 1880, around there.

Q: Your grandfather was alive at time.

A: Yes, he died while I was in the army. He was 98 when he died. He was in every civilized country in the world.

Q: Was you father on the river too?

A: Yes, he worked on the lock and dams. When we was all little he worked on them. They used to pole boats from Marietta upstream to Waynesville.

Q: They did?

A: Worked for the government. Walk along on the guard with a pole against his shoulder, set the pole on the bottom, walk around on the guard, one on each side.

Q: Oh, is that so?

A: The river wasn't very high, nor very swift, but there was a current in it. They poled against the current. Of course, they could float downstream. The state had a little steamboat that they took, quarterboat, they lived right on the job, see. They had what they called a quarterboat. Place for people to sleep. They got all of $1 a day. When I first went some on them lock and dams, job laborers only got 12 and a half 15 cents an hour. Now a guy on the river now gets 7 or 800 a month. We got 150 and that was a lot of money. There wasn't that much difference. Of course, you could buy a suit of clothes then for $9.99, if you didn't get it wet and they would give you a set of dishes with it or something. You'd get two pounds of buffalo for two bits and they'd give you liver or enough spareribs if you'd take it. Now we pay 89 cents a pound for liver, seven cents a pound for bacon, and ten cents a pound for butter, 12 or 14 cents for a dozen eggs, 11, 12, and there wasn't much difference as there is now. Lot of differences, but there's not that much. He's an engineer $40 a day. He got 30 men on that bridge job. Cost $100 a day just to feed them.

Q: What bridge was this?

A: Twelfth Street Bridge.

Q: The Twelfth Street Bridge here in Columbus. I wonder if you might talk about those models you have been making. You have been spending a lot of time, steamboat models.

John Knoepfle

A: Oh, I've put in a lot of time on them. Most of the time making them is running around hunting up stuff you know, that will fit on them. When we was out on the West Coast, I bought that showboat for my granddaughter. We hunted in all them gadget stores, all over that country to get little figurines, you know, like to conform to the size of the showboat. You could get plenty of them, but they was either too big, or too little, but we finally gathered up a bunch of them. Run around hunting that stuff to fit on them, hard to find. So it takes a lot of time to make a pilot house or the wheel. If it don't look right, throw it away, and make another one. If you had any plans, but you can't get plans for them.

Q: What models have you made?

A: Oh, I made two of the *Rowena*, two of the *Virginia*, and one of the *Sally Belle*, one of the *Sonoma*, and made one *Johnny Jones*. The *Sonoma*, she was a Muskingum packet. They took her up the Kentucky River, and sunk her up there. Had a Kentucky River pilot on her too and making a landing and hit a stump. Something knocked a plank loose on her and freight slid on her, and sank her and drowned the captain's sister. The captain's sister was a cook on her. Drowned her and two or three passengers . . . sunk there. Verne Webster, oldtime steamboat man, he was a pilot and engineer. He never went down there. I offered to go down there in a derrick boat and take the boilers and engines off her, but he was afraid to go back down there, afraid they'd sue him. He was a native of Ohio. I lived in Beverly. I guess somebody did take it. They built a lock and dam above there, and I could have took a derrick boat and went down there and wrecked her and knocked the super structure off her and picked the boilers up and the engine off her. She was a Muskingum riverboat.

Question: Can you give us a resume about your experience on the river?
Answer: I was born at Front and Carr Street December 8, 1890 in the west end of Cincinnati. I went to the eighth grade at 12th District School at Cincinnati. Started working on the river during summer vacations on the Pittsburg Coal Company, the Combine Landings, at Mill Creek Landing and Ludlow Landing running pump boats. Pump boats are boats, nonpropelled boats that pump out the barges, and they were wooden barges at that time. They'd drop them down from length to length, and then pump out the barges that have made some water overnight or during the day after a rain and so forth. The landing bosses at Mill Creek were Bill Spencer and later Al Fritz on Ludlow Landing and Joe Buck later, and later John Wilson. And I started working on the various harbor boats such as the *Relief,* the *Ranger,* the *Fallie,* the *Delta,* the *Crusade*r and *Fulton* in the capacities of a night watchman, deck watchman, fireman, striker and steersman under chief engineers Mel Leep, Charles Cox, Earl Brian, Harry Charleton and William Shahan, and Captains Charles Menges, James Stewart, Bradford Williams and George Drake.

And as a striker engineer on the Coney Island steamer, the *Princess,* under Captain Emerson Moore and pilot Harry Doss; *Morning Star,* under Captain Clarence Sandborn and chief engineer William Harris. And on the *Island Queen I,* under Captain Jim DePuy and pilot George Bales. Receiving original license first assistant engineer on 27th of September 1917. I shipped the same year as an assistant engineer on the steamer *John Barrett* under Captain Clarence Carter and pilot Harry Doss and chief engineer Hiram Howe. Taking the first load of automobiles from Cincinnati, Ohio to Memphis, Tennessee. I was transferred to the steamer *James Moren* under Captain Clarence Nichols and pilot Harvey McCullough. After a year with the Barrett line I left the lower river and shipped as the second engineer to *Julius Fleischmann* under Captain Albert Martin and chief Walter Martin.

After several months, I went on the steam tug *Silver Star,* which was used to gauge. In other words, gauging coal by meeting the tows up the river and measuring the coal. The barges being level, and knowing the amount of cubic feet of timber, you know under the boat, and the size of the pump boxes as the barge was level. We had a rod and we'd stick this rod down through the barge, possibly eight or nine times and get an average depth, then we would measure for the bulkhead. And then of course after that, that was done for many years until the steel barge came out. And then of course she was all taken by a mean draft at that time. And during the beginning of World War I, I went in the Merchant Marine School Case School of Applied Science with the late Commander Harry Voight and received a raise in grade to a second assistant engineer of 10,000 tons and third assistant engineer, all gross tons of ocean

John Knoepfle

steamers. I returned to Cincinnati and shipped on the steamer *LeRoy* with Captain Wilbur Chapman, was then ordered to Detroit and shipped on the steamer *Maruba*, which was cut in half so it could enter the Welland Canal from Detroit, Michigan to Quebec, Canada, as an assistant engineer. Then for Lake Graphite from Lorain, Ohio to Quebec. I returned to Cincinnati again and shipped on the steamer *E. A. Woodruff.*

Q: What year was that?

A: That was approximately in the year 1919, and was transferred to the steamer *Guyandotte* in July 1919, under Captain Emory Edgington relieving Captain Nelson, the chief engineer Nelson Beare. When Mr. Beare was appointed chief engineer at Lock 16; I resigned from the *Guyandotte* in 1921. I started working for the Campbells Creek Coal Company on the steamers *Robert P. Gillham* and *Eugene Dana Smith* under chief engineer Dana Wright. Then I served as engineer and helped fit out the steamer *Helper*, which overturned at Cincinnati, Ohio drowning Captain E. Burnside. In 1922 I returned to U. S. Engineers as chief engineer of the steamer *Ottawa* under Captains Emerson Moore and Roy Hughes with James Stutzman now Lock Master at Dam 37, as assistant engineer. On December 1, 1920 I was appointed chief engineer of the light house tender *Goldenrod*. And in 1934 to the *Greenbriar*, then a new boat under Captain Leslie T. Hill.

After Captain Hill retired I was married to Ruth Hastings in Neville, Ohio on July 1924. I was relieved as chief engineer by Fred A. Barrows, and then I received my master's license, was master of the *Greenbriar* with Captain Art Shriver, Lee Blagg and Elmer Chandler as pilots. Receiving master's license on June 9, 1938 and pilot's license December 1939 and I have license on the Ohio River from Pittsburgh, Pennsylvania to Cairo, Illinois. And on the Monongahela River from Morgantown to Pittsburgh. On the Allegheny River from Lock Number 8 to Pittsburgh, and the Great Kanawha River from Point Pleasant, West Virginia to Boomer, West Virginia.

During my years on the *Goldenrod* and *Greenbriar* I became very well known to many rivermen and natives in many cities along the route, while supplying kerosene, recharging battery lights, and installing commercial electric lights. Many of the names of notable rivermen were given to the lights and daymarks while I was in the service. Also many notables who visited the *Greenbriar*, such as President Herbert Hoover and Mrs. Hoover, Nicholas Longworth, Governor Lesley of Indiana, Mayor James E. Stuart of Cincinnati, the noted humorist Irvin S. Cobb was also aboard in the Tennessee River. And the noted columnist O. O. McIntyre and many others. When the lighthouse service was absorbed by the Coast Guard on July 1939 I received my first commission as Chief Warrant Officer and took oath the first of April 1940 at Decatur, Alabama. I was promoted to lieutenant commander 1943-45. I reverted back to permanent lieutenant on the first of July 1946 and was promoted to lieutenant commander on the 10th of February 1950. After decommissioning of the *Greenbriar*, I was appointed Aid to Navigation Officer and Assistant of the Coast Guard Auxiliary on the Ohio River and tributaries. Since retiring I have made quite a few trips on the river as chief engineer and as pilot and master. For the last three years I have been pilot on the *Avalon* during the extra trips between Pittsburg, Cairo, Charleston, West Virginia and generally on the return trip. While the boat stayed at different towns I always come home. And I made several other trips, and then last year I made, year before last, I made a trip on the *Claude Tully*.

Q: Was that a tow?

A: Towboat yes. On the Towboat the *Claude Tully*, towing kerosene to Falling View, West Virginia and Pittsburg several times until the pilots got organized up in that area. Then of course I returned and made several trips on the *Lucy Jane Lucas* to Cairo, Illinois.

Q: What were you towing there?

A: Towing coal barges down, fluorspar, sulphur, scrap-iron and coal returning.

Q: Is the *Lucas* gone now?

A: The *Lucas* belongs to the Ohio River Company and is working. She's the smallest of the boats now. Now she works in the upper Ohio River around Powhatan Point to the Tiger Creek Plant above Gallipolis, a power plant. That's the large atomic plant there.

Q: Is that a sternwheel boat?

A: No, no, it's a screw wheel boat. And then early this year I made a trip on the *H. A. Crane* motor vessel, *H. A. Crane* of the Ohio River Company with Captain Clayton Adams to Cairo, Illinois with nine barges of coal for Cairo and Mount Vernon, picking up empties in route. And after arrival to Cairo switched over to empty coal barges and scrap-iron upstream.

Q: What was it you picked up in route? I didn't understand.

A: I picked up empty barges in route. Then we had, finally we left the empty barges; we picked up extra empty barge at Mount Vernon, Indiana coming upstream. I went up the mouth of the Green River and left empty coal barges and picked up loads to come to Cincinnati. And we come on through to Cincinnati straight then leaving the coal down at the Tanners Creek Plant of the electric plant just below Lawrenceburg, Indiana. And just about three weeks ago I got on the *Avalon* and took it to Paducah, Kentucky making excursions in route while it proceeded up in the Tennessee River and out of the Tennessee River. She'll go on up the Allegheny River before returning to Cincinnati in about the first part of May, early May.

Q: Well now you were on the boat before the Coast Guard.

A: Oh yes, I was in the former Lighthouse Service. That's where I started. I relieved Chief Engineer Bill Handley who was the father of Dr. Handley who was a coroner of Hamilton County for many years and he was the grandfather of Judge Daniel C Handley now on the municipal court bench in Cincinnati.

Q: Well, he must have been on the river a long time?

John Knoepfle

A: Oh he was. His dad Dr. Dan Handley, older Dan he learned to be and engineer while he studied for a doctor during his off times as engineer of these big sidewheel packetboats in the trade. And Bill Handley himself is quite a character, the old gentleman. And I succeeded him, on the first day of, I went on the *Goldenrod* the first day of December 1922. Stayed on there about a year and a half until the *Greenbrier* came out. And I was chief engineer of the *Greenbrier* for 14 years; and I was master of her for eight years including the time then when the Coast Guard come here. The work was divided up, and while I was in uniform, I made many changes was assigned to flood areas, flood and disaster areas along the Ohio River, lower parts of the Ohio River and Green River area and along the Cumberland.

Q: Well, could you describe those changes, Captain?

A: Pardon me.

Q: Could you describe any of those changes?

A: In the changes, you know, I was sent here like in charge of a crew working out of a certain spot. Now we would work one year out of Cannelton, Indiana where we had boats come from the lakes. Then we dispatched them with food and supplies to these people in the Green River area, the Green River bottom area. And generally, they didn't want to leave; the natives didn't want to leave. As long as they can get something, some staples, they're all right.

Q: They'll go back to their houses.

A: Oh yes, yes, they go back to the houses. They won't move out of them. It's just like me born and raised over here. Our house is in the flood nearly every year up until the time I was 18 years old just across the river here, and part of the thing, we had to pump out our cellars over there. And it just kept us busy. And of course in years I was in the different parts. I had charge of an aid to navigation business on the Ohio River and I made most of the changes, from oil lights to either battery operated or commercial electric operated lights on the entire Ohio River and its tributaries.

Q: I imagine the oil lights had to have tenders.

A: The oil lights had to have tenders yes. They paid them a rate of about $15 a month, you know, and of course the commercial electric lights were much better and a whole lot cheaper. And so they reverted to that wherever we got electricity run down to the, and in that length of time, I had quite a different time with some of the lamplighters. And these lights are put on, these navigation lights are put on high hills, you know. Like Cave-in-Rock, Illinois and places like that. And some of these lights, you know we had quite a bit of trouble with a man down in Haunted Hollow, below Louisville I sent the boys up to fix, he was sitting on the road with a gun across his knee. I said, "What's this for Mr. Miller?" I said, "The boys have to go up and take care of the light." "You see that sign." I said, "In other words, you don't want me to go up on that hill?" I said, "We have to take care of the light. The light's up there. The light is a government project." I said, It's up there and we're paying Mr. Miller a certain amount." I said, "And if Mr. Miller gets electricity we'll put the light in." And him being a director of the REA in Corydon, Indiana. Of course, he could go a little further than the rest of them. He had poles running out there to that light. And since that time he was all right.

Then again some of the later lights before I got out of the service, I always changed lights. Lights were changed according to the will of the navigators, and the pilots would say, "There would be a good place to light to help us out of a certain place, if we could just come with our towboats out of different locks or along the shores." One of them was on a high bluff called Henry Clay Hill, just below Cave-in-Rock, Illinois. And while I was putting it up there Mr. Starkey, the man who owned the property — when I put it up, there was no sign of any houses, I always asked permission — and he just raised the dickens about it and had me cited for everything that was in the book, you know. So anyhow I finally got on to it and I got that over with, and he come back a second time for vandalism. One of the boys painted his initial on the thing you know. And I says to him, he called me up there and I said, "You see that initial Mr. Starkey? That was just a kid; he wasn't a man; he was just a kid. You know a bunch of boys like we have working here that enlist. And the kid just took that paintbrush and painted his initial, which is not observed, don't bother nobody, but you ought to be tickled to death that thing is there. Because, this kid was one of the first men killed in the battle of the landing of Salerno Beach." I said, "You ought to be tickled!" And before I left that place I had him crying, and then he was just that much better you know. Oh and in different places and along the Ohio River if I could only think of the different things that happened in among the lamplighters and in 1,500 miles of river you'd have something to do because so much of it, it don't seem like $15 a month for a light is a whole lot, but believe me it's coffee and sugar for lots of them, and you see, if they don't use it for nothing else.

Q: Some of them tend strings of lights didn't they?

A: Yes some of them. We have several places, we have men take care of strings of lights, especially Shawneetown, Illinois. They would go from Shawneetown up one day and down the next. Went up to the mouth of the Wabash River, Wabash Island and the names of where the lights were, you know like Brown Island, and Graham Varble and they reached there at the Raleigh Bar, J. C. Warehouse, on down into Shawneetown, Bowlesville Mines and Shawneetown Bend, upper and lower, and then across the Greens Crossing, and now she's last light at Greens Crossing, and then we go down and make a long crossing there to Saline River and on down the shore to Battery Rocks and into Caseyville.

Q: So a man would have quite a job tending those lights.

A: Yes, he had quite a job, and in other words the $15 rate was the base rate. There was always a little extra on that. So no doubt a man he got himself about $20 a month for lights anyhow, you know, which was good pay down in that part of the country in between the extra time.

John Knoepfle

Q: So these were oil lights.

A: These were oil lights, yes. And they're gradually coming out with oil lights. Now for lights on the river, the pilot doesn't want too bright of a light. He wants just something to know the spot there you see, even if an oil light is an awful good light if you can just see it, you see. And a flashing light of course is a little off, but still it's better than a poor oil light. And they work very nicely. They're charged, them about every seven months, with batteries that are charged on the tender, on the cutter that runs in the area for that. Now the Coast Guard has the *Forsythia* that runs from Sewickley, Pennsylvania up the Ohio River and up the Monongahela to lock number 8 and return and down to Ravenswood, West Virginia. Then we had another cutter, the *Sycamore*, based at Cincinnati and it runs from Cincinnati up to Ravenswood, West Virginia and down to Louisville. And from Louisville we have another cutter the *Sumac*, which runs from Louisville to Cairo and recently they had them up in Green River about 80 odd miles putting, since they dredged out and enlarged the locks to bring out a lot of that coal, they've put a lot of day marks up in there. In other words, day marks are a ten by ten board, or a six by six, or a ten by ten, whichever the case may be, and I think on account of the river they were about six by six and they have a mark set up on angle. Some of them call them diamond boards and day boards, you know. They had the markings on them, you know, and the size of the river and they all had reflector buttons on them and reflector tape. And they can be picked up by a boat's searchlight, you know, just practically as good as our regular light if it was there.

Q: Well, I'm a little curious to know why a pilot doesn't want an extremely bright light.

A: It gets back in their eyes, you know. It gets back. Especially the green light. A green light on a calm day had just a tail light from that light. It goes right in your eyes, you know.

Q: Reflects on the water.

A: Reflects on the water and into your eyes. You know when it's dark and no lights at all in the pilothouse, you know. Everything is dark as a stack of black cats. It's just the idea it brings a light, a beam of light. The red lights are not too bad, but after all they are the best, the commercial electric lights. There's no get out about that and they're the most reliable.

Q: They are?

A: Oh, those storms take them out and we've got to look for . . . nothing is such that non-mechanical you know, that will go out once in a while. But now I noticed on my last trip where a lot of lights in the Green River area from Newburg, Indiana, we had a man took care of quite a string of lights there. Something must have happen to him because they've changed all the lights to what you call battery flashing upper and lower Green River and the Green River Three Mile Island, and Three Mile Island, you know. And French Island on down to Crosby, Scuffletown, Vannada, those were all names as we know them as we come down the river from any given point. You know, and it's just one of those things up there when you leave at night, you're leaving in the dark. You're standing the watch. The only thing about it that gets you tired is your eyes. And that means you've got to stand on and get watch and look ahead of you and see where you're at. And many times you use searchlights to help you out in trying to locate buoys and such and markers along the river. But boats go just the same, don't make a bit of difference what time of the day or night, the boats go just the same.

Q: This was on the *Avalon*.

A: On the steamer *Avalon*.

Q: Which you piloted?

A: Yes I was pilot of the steamer *Avalon* with Captain Lawrence Allen having the forward watch and I had the after watch. Forward watch is from 12 to six. After watch from six to 12. I come on watch, we left Cincinnati at nine p.m. Eastern Standard Time, lock 37, 23 and 7/10s feet and stationary. On watch at Buckeye Landing and proceeding downstream moored Vevay, Indiana at 3 a.m. We had trips out of Vevay, Ghent and Carrollton, leaving Carrollton, Kentucky at 1:30 p.m. Eastern Standard Time, arriving Madison, Indiana 2:30 p.m. Eastern Standard Time. On watch in the afternoon trip to Indiana, Kentucky River, day mark, returned to Madison, Indiana at 6:00 p.m. Off watch. Made calls for Captain Wagner, and arranged for fuel oil. At Louisville, I went uptown on March the 17th was a Sunday. In other words, that was three trips, school children trips in the morning was Saturday, and two trips out of Madison, Indiana on March 17th that was Sunday, at 12:30 a.m. departed Madison, Indiana and tied up temporarily at Six Mile Island for an hour and a half to wait daylight to go in the oil dock for fuel. Captain Allen relieved me at the Big Four Bridge just above the oil dock. Then I had the afternoon trio from 2:30 to 5:30 upstream to Twelve Mile Island and returned to Louisville. March 18th, Monday at 12:45, in other words I had the afternoon trip from 2:30 to 5:30 p.m. Had an evening trip, but Captain Allen had that.

And on March 18th, Monday I come on watch at 12:00 and at 12:45 we started upstream with a trip, it was after midnight. I returned at 2:30 a.m. to unload at the foot of Fourth Street in Louisville. At 3 a.m. Central Standard Time proceeded downstream, 22.4 in the lower gauge in Louisville, down through the canal, down through the locks, the large lock at Lock 41 and I got off watch at Fishtown Light. I came on watch at noon at Chenault Reach Light, and off watch at Yellow Bank Island Light, which is just above Owensboro, Kentucky. At 12 on March 19th, that's Tuesday at 12 o'clock midnight departed Owensboro, off watch at the head of Diamond Island Light. Severe storm at 3 a.m. near Dade Park Bridge. I was on watch, I come on watch again at 6 a.m. that morning, or at noon at Goat Hill Light. Dam 51 there's 21.7 falling on its gauge. We landed at Paducah at 5 a.m., and it was awfully cold. I stayed at the Palmer Hotel to get the 5:30 bus to Covington and returned home.

John Knoepfle

Q: You were a pilot during the storm.

A: Oh yes. Yes. We were pilot. We had an awful storm, you know, but not enough to bother us you know, but I called the captain just in case. And he was up with me for about 30 minutes and it blowed over and we went right ahead. Now say this run, as I left Owensboro and got of watch at Diamond Island, see I passed, I left Owensboro and went down through French Island and down through into Lock 47, Vannada, Scuffletown, Indian Hill, Three Mile Island, Lock 47, then Three Mile Island, then down passing Green River, on down to Dade Park Bridge where we had this storm, all the way down passed Evansville, Indiana and going down again passed Henderson, Kentucky and down through the chute at Henderson, Kentucky, and on down passed Lock 48 and down the head of Diamond Island where I was relieved and Captain Allen come on.

On the last trip, on the trip back up on the *A. H. Crane*, we had lots of water and of course we were running pretty good nights and the radar and run a lot of radar, you know where you can just see not even to tie up, but where you can just see enough to help you out. And returning we run radar nearly every night especially in places like there was a bad like we made the cutoff at Cumberland Island through the chute at Dog Island and on through the regular channel. Then of course, when I come on watch the following day, it caught me right at Mount Vernon, Indiana and up past Diamond Island, West Franklin and Cypress Bend, and then into the lock, passing Lock 48. There's quite a cutoff can be made by going on what we call Deadman's Island. Up the shore and right up along the Kentucky shore all the way, you know to the bridge to above the bridge at Henderson, Kentucky. Therefore we made very good time all the way up you know by running these shores, and running these cutoffs. And most all of it was done by radar. And of course by golly, it just happens to be that daylight caught us at Henderson Bridge. Of course the radar we have are very good, but they always show a bridge with a plain view of anything, but it doesn't show piers. You see that's one thing, it doesn't show the piers and the piers is what you're looking for. There for everything we had very good conditions on, very nice trip you know on the whole business.

Q: You made it through the bridge anyway.

A: We made it through the bridge, yes. We made it through the bridge without losing a bit of time. Then of course we got up to Green River, we picked up a barge. No we didn't. I was going to say it was another boat was in at the same time at Evansville at the Mead Johnson Terminal down below Evansville.

Q: Well, I wonder now if we can wind the Captain out about some of the experiences on the older boats. Do you think that would be possible?

A: Well, here's the thing I never run much on the packetboats.

Q: You were an engineer.

A: I was an engineer on them. I was an engineer on some of them, I was an engineer on the old *Island Queen I*, and I helped several times. I helped Fred out on *II*.

Q: Fred who, who was that?

A: Fred Dickow, he was chief engineer there. I helped Fred out and made several trips with him on the *Island Queen II*.

Q: Well what kind of boat was the first *Island Queen*?

A: First *Island Queen* was wooden hull affair, and she had what you call compound engines with the, low pressure cylinder was forward and the high pressure cylinder was aft you know. Independent sidewheel boats took an engineer on each side, and you worked with big arms, you know and the pitmans going around. And you have to watch out so you don't get them on center. If you do by golly she's liable to hang on you there. You have to give them a little more steam to get them off and on center.

Q: I imagine it was, you had to be pretty careful of the, to keep them from setting up a rhythm that would jar the boat.

A: You watched that there. That's all handled through the pilothouse. They tell you how fast they want you to run. They'll give you what they call a slow bell or a half head or a full head you know according to those bells that they ring. In those days they didn't even use the indicators. They used bells. And of course in our time we was always using bells. And all the time I was engineer of the *Greenbriar* I used bells. But later on we got to using the indicators you know, and they finally put an indicator on the *Avalon*. I find them all right but I am so used to bells that I know that when they reach for a bell I know what that means, you know. There's three bells and each one of them has a meaning. One bell kills the other one practically you know, puts you on the other bell, and that's all handled from the pilothouse. But nowadays on the more modern boats it's all handled, even the steamboats some of them are handled from the pilothouse. Pilothouse control and that gets so that if anything happens that the engineer didn't make a mistake all the time, sometimes they make mistakes you know, and they claimed they ring a bell and didn't answer it and such. But that's happened all the time. But now as I say I've been with Captain Edgington a whole lot. Captain Emory Edgington, he right today is 87 years old. And he's a wonder. He stands that watch up around Pittsburg and above Cincinnati. And he's awfully easy to relieve you know. I always relieve, take the after watch, you know from midnight on, and then when she stays in town, then I go home. See I don't stay there because I don't want to stay there. I just like the trip. I just go on there to help them out. They help me out too, of course.

Q: Well would you tell us something about the *Greenbriar*?

A: The *Greenbriar* was built around in 1923, 1924 and . . .

Q: Locally?

A: At Charleston, West Virginia and I was, the last three months, on her construction. I was up at the wharves with the command of the superintendent of construction for the Lighthouse Service at that time. They built three new cutters that year. A sidewheel boat called the *Willow* and a larger sternwheel boat called *Wakerobin* for the upper Mississippi, the *Willow* run below St. Louis

John Knoepfle

to New Orleans, and the *Greenbriar* had the Ohio River and the tributaries. At those times we didn't have no buoys to take care of see. Everything was lights on the shores. And we'd have 18, 20 drums well, besides their tanks full in the hull, and we' go up as far as we go down to Cairo, Cincinnati being our headquarters. We'd try to get there. We generally made three trips a year, two and a half trips a year in other words. We made one complete trip in the spring starting south we'd go to Cairo and up Paducah and up Tennessee River to Florence, Alabama. Come back out of there and go back on up the Ohio River to Cincinnati. Work on, to Cincinnati taking care, just alternate, in the possibly some days we might make ten miles, and another day we might not make two, and then we might make 50. Just according o the work on the shore as we went. We'd have to paint the lights, supply them, clear the brush away from them, chop the brush away.

Q: The brush was a problem.

A: Yes, then these young fellows, you know, especially these Coast Guard boys, in the Lighthouse Service they had men hired for that, of course they were seasoned men and they were all hired for that, these young fellows in the Coast Guard they went, they enlisted thinking they only had to do work on a boat. When they get them out there and cut that brush and paint those lights, that was a hard job. Now our son, we have a son Bob, he was with me for about five years on the *Greenbriar*, and then he started with me. Of course, I forgot to tell you about the moving of the government boats on the river, the LCS's. There was over 150 built at Pittsburg . . .

Q: During the war.

A: During the war yes, and they were generally dispatched out of this office, the Ohio River contingent of them, and there were some built at Seneca, Illinois, which is very close to Chicago. And they had a different bunch of pilots there than we had. Of course, our men would take some as far as Memphis, and then of course, the through pilots you know from New Orleans, would take them up and go on to New Orleans with them, see. The Coast Guard delivered them to New Orleans.

Q: Well those boats must have had a deep draft for the Ohio.

A: Well they would get them as light as eight and a half feet, and of course they was 300 feet long and 50 feet wide, and we never had nothing so big move so fast. And our son Bob was on there now. He was with me on the *Greenbriar* for about five years. Now he worked in town for a while, and then finally got back on the boats, and he's now a pilot, captain of a watch on the *Pat Murphy*, on the tug *Pat Murphy*, which does the principle work for the Mississippi Valley Barge Line.

Q: Let's go back to that, to the *Greenbriar*, what kind of engine did she have?

A: The *Greenbriar* had what they called high pressure engines. They were 15 inch cylinders, diameter cylinders and seven foot stroke. And they were built at Cincinnati by the Frisbie Engine Machinery Company. The *Wakerobin* was a larger boat. She had 18 inch cylinders and a seven and a half foot stroke, and they were also built by Frisbie. And they had the round, they started out with the round cylindrical fire tube boilers, and they were replaced on the *Wakerobin* by water tube boilers, but now both those boats are out of commission. And the last I understand the *Greenbriar* is a suction dredge working at the vicinity at the canal, industrial canal out of New Orleans.

Q: Well, how about the older *Goldenrod*?

A: The *Goldenrod* before it, it was 37 years old. I just don't know how long Mr. Handley was on there. Mr. Handley was the chief, he had at one time, the Lighthouse Service was under the Navy, they had placed on those boats what we call a cabin. We have a large mirror upstairs that I got off her. What we call a lady's cabin, in other words the officer's cabin. And the packetboat they had after the part, what they called a lady's cabin where they carried a lot of men. They were carpeted the same way with part of this back part of the *Goldenrod*. It was carpeted well back, you know and they had special rooms for what we would call the superintendent of the light houses, he would travel.

Q: He would travel in the lady's cabins.

A: Oh they had a special cabin. What they call, in other words, we call them on a packetboat the lady's cabin . . . . During my time we had a lot of navigation lights named after different people on the river. And one of them happens to be named after Lillian Hughes, a young girl, and while she done more favors for rivermen, while she was on the boat, and while she was in charge of the office at the Huntington, West Virginia wharfboats. Everybody knew Lillian because well we have one navigation light, of course, a lot of navigation lights were named, if it did pertain to one certain bar or bend or someplace in the river we would name after river people. And we have one of them after one lady and she was Miss Lillian Hughes. And how it come, I moved the light from Knox Bar up the river about a mile to a place called . . . to the Baden, Pennsylvania Water Works. And at that time the burgess of the borough of Baden was Irvin Earling, quite a riverman and his people. And he says, Irvin Earling says, "What are you going to name that light Red?" I said "Well I don't know, but it doesn't mean nothing particular around here. I could name it after anything, but I thought possibly of Fred Irwin because he lived here." He was an old pilot and he lived here at Baden. So he said, "Why not name it Lillian Hughes?" I said, "Well, you've got something there." Because I knew Lillian, she was possibly my wife's age now you know. And everybody knew her. She was friendly just like my wife knows Captain Hughes and Mrs. Hughes very well. We were all very good friends. Lillian passed away. We named the light after her, and it stuck.

Now we have lights named after Gordon Greene down at the part of the country where he was from. When they changed channels at Brother's Island I changed the name of the light after Gordon Greene Light. And James Rowley down the bend below, an old pilot, down the bend below Vanceburg, Kentucky. And there's several others, Graham Varble down below Wabash

John Knoepfle

River Light, and Les Walston up in the bend at the head of the Ox-bows below Leavenworth, Indiana. And just happens to be the name of the light was quite a thing to get something would be understood by the people you know, and then of course the department sends out a notice to mariners, of course all the changes, they have that.

Q: Well now let's get back to the lady's cabin on the . . .

A: On the passenger boats . . . always had a lady's cabin that was the after part, but to my recollection the *City of Cincinnati* and the *City of Louisville* were big sidewheel boats and they had a bar back there.

Q: Bar!

A: Yes, then of course it was run by, they had guests, they done a little gambling, but nothing I don't think too much out of the ordinary, but they turned loose in among themselves. There were regular people that traveled these boats, and I won't doubt it they gambled a little bit, you know. That was a habit, and a habit that I missed, I never gambled or drank much. I drank a little of everything, but I never drank much.

Q: You were a connoisseur.

A: Connoisseur, (laughs) anyhow there's different times. A lady called me up one time from Carrsville, Kentucky, Mrs. Belle Carr, she says, "Captain is there anything I can do about, my husband gets a check sometimes, on that check they'll put paid every month and he gives them a check, up there at the bank, and you know they'll cash it for him up there and he'll get drunk."

Q: She was a light tender!

A: She was a light tender, yes. She was a light tender at Carrsville, Kentucky for years. I said, "The only thing I know Mrs. Carr is to go up there and beat him to it. That's the only thing I know, of course they know him and I don't know if you can get them at the bank, why don't you tell them at the bank not to allow him because it's in your name." Well anyhow there's so many different things like that there.

Q: Well, tell us about the *Morning Star*.

A: Oh, after the Coney Island boat *Princess* was sunk in the ice of 1917 she sank, she come out of the Kentucky River and sank there at Brooksburg just a little below the Little Kentucky River, in the Kentucky River on the Indiana side. Well, Coney Island was kind of badly in need of a boat so they bought a boat called the *Morning Star* from Captain Walter Blair in the upper Mississippi River, and Captain Jim Dupuy and myself and this, oh Wooden Head, his name was Clarence Sandborn, he was a mate.

Q: Wooden Head!

A: A Wooden Head they called him, yes. He was Captain of her later when he got up. And a bunch of us went down to Cairo to get on her. And I was second engineer with Charley Harris and we had the two brothers, Walter and Stuart Conner were pilots. And somehow or another one of our firemen got sick. We stopped at Evansville and tried to get another fireman and just at that time prohibition came in. The 18th Amendment, the Volstead Act started. Well this fellow said come down and see if I could get a man. I told Captain Dupuy, "Well, I got a man but he don't want to leave today he said on account of too much liquor going on up here to get him coming down here." I said, "I might get him but he wants to go tomorrow." He said, "Well we can't lay over." I says to him, "Come on down." He says, "Let's see if you can bring him down and we'll just put one line out." I said, "All right Cap." I bring him down and see if he could get this fellow aboard. I said, "Come on down. Bring your clothes down. You'll have it all ready tomorrow for when you go to work." I didn't tell him tomorrow or when it was going to be. "And I'll look it over." I said, "All right, that'll be fine." So we got him down there and we got aboard there. All of a sudden I seen the boat going. Charley, the pilot had a voice arrangement so the chief engineer could start his side and back on out of there. And I run over when we got underway and started my side. I mean the engines on different sides. And the colored fellow said, "How far is this boat going?" I said, "Well, you shipped up on it." "Oh, now that's tomorrow." I said, "She's gone now. You don't mind that there." And do you know, he stayed there until those boats burned up; he was a very good friend of Captain Mander Patterson.

Q: You shanghaied that poor fellow.

A: But it didn't make a difference anyhow. He liked it after all.

Q: What kind of engines did the *Morning Star* have?

A: The *Morning Star* had 18 cylinders and eight foot stroke. They were called a lever engine with a California cut off. She had four boilers. Sidewheel boat, they brought her here. Clarence Sandborn and Harry Charlton the engineer had some tar boiling on one of the cook stoves and it blowed up and set a whole bunch of fire, and that fire was Captain Hughes, his boat. That was his boat. That was the *Tacoma* was burned up. They called it the *Tack Hammer*. And that's where his boat was burned up, you know in the fire of 1921 I think.

Q: I think it was earlier than that.

A: No, it wasn't. No. About 1921 because I was on the *Ottawa* at Caseyville, Kentucky when I heard the news about them all burning.

Q: What was the . . .? The *Ottawa* is a boat I'm not familiar with.

A: The *Ottawa*, there were five boats that the U. S. Engineers had around here. The *Ottawa*, the government built three boats at one time: the *Scioto*, the *Miami* and the *Guyandotte*. Built them on the riverbank between Main and Walnut Street. Bill Handley was superintendent and taken off the *Goldenrod* to act as Marine superintendent on that. Then later they built two other boats with a little more diameter cylinders. Those were 15 six. Then they built the two boats, the *Ottawa* and the *Cayuga* there, and each towed a dredge. And that was before the Locks and Dams were in the Ohio River. Then the boats would start all directions in the spring you know to clear out the channels at different places. We had the *Guyandotte*, it towed the *Ohio*. The *Miami* it towed the *Marietta*, then the *Scioto* towed the *Indiana*. It was a suction dredge. It was the first suction dredge they had in this part of the country. It run out of Fernbank there, we had quite a big place there. And Mrs. C. B. Harris was in charge, you know.

Q: I suppose when the water reached a certain stage you just gave up dredging.

A: Yes that's it, then before the dams. Then they had a big sidewheel boat called *E. A. Woodruff* and I was the last engineer on the *E. A. Woodruff*, big sidewheel boat and they had a big polly hook on it like a boot jack hull. Take a big polly hook and just tear those barges to pieces.

Q: Sunken barges.

A: Yes, you know those barges were sunk and then also logs; it would gather logs out of the channels and saw them up or whatever the case may be.

Q: Well the *Woodruff* was built locally I suppose.

A: As I understand she was built in Newport with an iron hull made by the Swift Iron Works on the location of the Newport Steel Works today. Up in there, there's where those plates were rolled.

Q: Did she have any special engines for her work?

A: Yes she had special sidewheel engines. They were what you call a piston valve. Now most of them on the riverboats were either pocket valve or a slide valve. This was a piston valve engine of good size and possibly must have been 17 six something like that. Five boilers I know that. And I had her all ready to go when I was taken off and they decided not to use her anymore. Like the engineers do spend a lot of money on her and decide not to use her no more, and then again I went to the *Guyandotte* at Lock 12 Warwood, West Virginia.

Q: You were on the *Guyandotte*.

A: I was on the *Guyandotte* then yes!

Q: That was another dredge boat.

A: That was another steel hull towboat that towed a dredge boat, the *Ohio* with Captain Emory Edgington.

Q: Oh yes.

A: Yes I was with Captain Edgington then.

Q: Was there a man named Knight?

A: Knight?

Q: He's over with "Waterways Journal" now.

A: No, Roy Barkhav, you know he's from here. Most of those fellows with the "Waterways Journal" were never on boats very much you know.

Q: I think I'll . . .

A: Now it's just like we had packetboat pilots I can remember. I met Captain Hornbrook once or twice. I knew Captain Wisherd very well, and he's still living today; and of course Fred Hornbrook is, but he was from the upper Ohio River and also he had brothers around Evansville, and I met them. One of them was called Birch and the other had charge of the *Erastus Wells*, which is a harbor boat at St. Louis, sidewheel boat. But I was in most of the time when they changed from wood to steel. In my time when I started out everything was wood and gee whiz, we didn't know what it was to see a steel hull boat or knew of one. The *Woodruff* was one of the only ones you know. In breaking ice, we had big ice flows and things like that there when I was a kid. I lived across the street here and I got ahold of some fuses, dynamite fuses and I didn't know what they were. They were blowing and blasting in the river here, and I had some in the toolbox. And when I was a youngster I worked as a delivery boy for a place called Lowry and Goebel Carpet House in Cincinnati and I lived in Evanston. My folks, I was 18 years old when they sold this place and moved to Evanston. My mother had a whole bunch of women folks there one day and I was down in the cellar and I put this thing in a vice to file it and the thing blowed up. And I had like shrapnel in my hands and face. I was all bleeding. My aunt taking me to the doctor. I'll never forget that. (laughs) They tell me about it.

Q: You were lucky you survived that.

A: Oh, I'll tell you. I've had several narrow escapes I'll tell you. Of course anyone in them days had a business will have them. As long as he's able to get out of them. During my younger days in Cincinnati Harbor, I lived around the river, I had one brother of course, he got away and worked in town. He was a printer. My dad worked at American Book Company for 59 years, and then he quit. He walked back and forth to Front and Carr Street many a day. Finally they moved to Evanston. I was on the harbor boat as I say and shoveled coal all night, and then maybe grind valves the next day whichever harbor boat was around. They were single crew.

Q: What was some of those harbor boats?

A: Some of the harbor boats were the *Ranger*, and the *Relief*, and the *Sally*, the *Fulton* and the *Adelle*. I've got a lot of pictures.

Q: They were boats that serviced . . .

A: Serviced at different times the harbor boats. Belonged to what we call what we called the Pittsburg Coal Combine. Then the independent boats at that time was the *Hercules Carrell*, and the *Frank Miller*, or the *George Matheson* in later years. The *George Matheson* and the *Frank Miller* was owned by two brothers, Frank and Phil Miller, and they were characters. One of them couldn't read or write and the other signed his name. One time they were towing with the *Frank Miller*, the river was pretty well froze over. They couldn't get the small boats, the barges in up to Petersburg where they had a distillery in Petersburg, Kentucky. It seemed like about every time they'd make a trip to this distillery and back with a load of corn from the wharfboat at Aurora, Indiana they'd stop and get a quart or pint at that distillery you see. They would drink a little bit, finally they got to cussing one another and they wasn't going to have one brother calling his brother an SB and so on and so forth, so at the landing down at Aurora, Phil throwed a line and made the boat fast to the wharfboat. And Frank, he run downstairs and out of the pilothouse and grabbed an axe that they always had on the side of it, and run up the hill chopping at Frank. A lady heard and she screamed and somebody turned in the fire alarm. In those times, the horses up there that pulled the garbage also pulled the fire

John Knoepfle

engines. And you should have seen the horses run around and around, and then the fire engines and everything. And the police there after they found out what it was, they wouldn't even let them land there anymore. (laughter)

But they were two characters; and I had a good friend was engineer on there and he heard a lot of going on, the woman screaming upstairs and doggone they were both fighting among themselves. They were great big ruffians you know. What's his name came up there, Sam Ellis and wanted to see them, and both of them turned on him. They said, "We'll teach you to meddle in family affairs." Oh, they were characters. They had a boat called the *Frank Miller*. During one of the big ice they had a boat, they bought the hull, the boat was sunk, it was called the *George Matheson*, on the Little Miami River bar. My brother and I was pretty young and we were down in the hull cleaning the mud out, just like sand hogs would, you know. We got money and it was just like playing around for us anyhow. One day Captain Frank said, "What are you doing with that mud?" He says, "Oh, throwing mud overboard Cap." "Oh, don't throw anymore overboard, just keep all that there, we'll just put some rope in there, it's just as good as any asbestos." In other words, if there wasn't any asbestos to throw on top of the boilers, they'd just put mud on it. (chuckles)

One time out there, they was building a bridge at Sciotoville, and I was sent by Captain Regan, the pole gauger here to measure a barge of coal at Sciotoville. They were building a bridge up there. Going down the river this was about at Sciotoville is the upper end of the Portsmouth, passing New Boston and Sciotoville; going down the river I wasn't paying no attention to it, I decided to go back down the river on the boat. It took me practically all day to go by the way of Norfolk and Western to get up there to Sciotoville and take a train up, another streetcar up to Sciotoville, take you pretty near all day. Well I had measured a barge of coal so I decided to come back with them because they would be back the next day, be at Cincinnati the next day practically. And it only had a single crew. The boat was under charge of the Hartweg brothers. They were boys that run boats in this neighborhood, towboats especially, Bill and Fred Hartweg. They kept, there being several others, he was coming down the river and doggone he looked over, "Who is that over there?" Somebody hailed him from the ferryboat at Portsmouth. Had a ferryboat there then. "Oh boy, George Dameron. So he had some weight on the safety valve. God knows how much steam he had and it's the only time in my life I've ever seen weights jump up and down and not break off and blow up. I thought that anything like that would happen. They jumped up and steam was all over the boat. The whole boat enveloped in steam. And here he thought it was, it was George Dameron, he was the inspector, the boiler inspector from the Cincinnati office, and he thought that instead of him it was another pilot they sent up to help him down, Charlie Cole. And when he saw Charlie Cole, oh he just give him the dickens all over and they finally got to shaking hands and they were all right again, but he put those weights on there and God knows how much steam he had you know. You've heard of how a lot of these boats carried steam.

Q: To make better time.

A: To make better time that's it. So by golly, we picked him up and I never heard such steam going in my life, and I was a young fellow of 30 and I was learning the business. And I was wondering what it was all about so I made it my business to see what it was all about. Anything like that happened out of the ordinary. I was always a pretty good swimmer and diver and did a lot of raising a boat that sank you know.

Q: What were some of those?

A: The *Delta* down at the foot of Lawrence Street and the *Fulton* when she hit the bridge at the, I was working in 1915 during the big storm here in Cincinnati. The *Convoy* sank just below the Southern Bridge and the *Fulton* sank. They drowned five or six people on the *Convoy* here. The *Fulton* drowned a Captain Brad Williams, a good friend of mine, at that pier that had the numbers on it, Central Bridge. Hit that there and the storm blowed the barges over and the steamboat went over and hit it. I was waiting at Lawrence Street to go on her to make a trip to Madison. I never had my license at that time, of course I could go on as watchman, you know, fireman, whichever the case may be. I'd help them out whenever they needed somebody. Anyhow they sent me over there. I was getting ready to go and I practically seen her hit there during that cyclone. Knocked the steeple down there at St. Philomena's Church there on Pearl Street. Every time you think of something one thing brings on another. They had an old timer down there, his name was Leo Posival and he was a pretty good Dutchman, and his son still has a place on Pike Street there. Now Leo used to build lights for the Coast Guard you know; he was a tinner mechanic all the way through. He put up four new steeples at St. Philomena's Church, that was the last church that was there. A whole bunch had big doings at the church and Leo went up there and I saw him the next day. He was drunk all over. "By God they fed us beef. They fed us beef." And I didn't know what he meant. I found out that while he was fiddling, him and another bunch of them people in the neighborhoods was fiddling, they had a big turkey dinner and everybody ate turkey and all they had left was beef. They was sorry but all they had left was beef when he got up there. (laughter) And he was mad about it.

Q: Tell me now, you know Irvin S. Cobb.

A: I knew Irvin Cobb and I met him two or three times, but this time here in particularly I was at a place called Cuba Landing on the Tennessee River. We laid up at night on the *Goldenrod*. On the *Paducah*, the packetboat *Paducah*, it landed down in back of us and they would take on a load of ties. And he says to the, the captain, and I walked down to the *Paducah* to talk to Captain Pete Wilson and they had taken on these ties. And he said, "I can't do a thing with these darkies." He says, "This fellow Cobb is giving them money." When Cobb heard anybody talk, that's all he had to do. Nobody can talk like a darkie, I

John Knoepfle

don't care what you say. They've got their own language. They talk their own sense you know. You can't hardly make out what they say. Every bit of it is original. Cobb could think of all that stuff. "Well," he said, "I don't know maybe Red could do something with him."

Q: Why was Cobb giving them the money?

A: To hear them talk let them gamble a little bit you know. If he let them gamble a little bit, give them a little bit of money they didn't have otherwise and let them gamble with. That was always the way with a colored fellow, especially with them rouster type. One of them would have all the money and some of them wouldn't have nothing. That didn't mean how much work they done. They knew they was going to eat and that was just the way they struck you. Never get mad about it. They gambled, they had to pay them off. Like when they were unloading cement for the government at Cairo, they had to pay them off every night like you pay them off on the packetboat. Then they always took quarters and dollars. If they didn't borrow money they wouldn't work. Borrowed money that way. It was funny thing about the old rouster fellow. Anyhow Cobb went up there and says, "Do you think there might be a little . . ." this was during prohibition days. "Do you think there might be a little liquor around here?" I says, "No, I don't know Mr. Cobb, it could be." So I called an old lamp lighter we had. I said, "Uncle Henry, got a little liquor around?" He says, "I don't know son. None around here." He calls me off, says, "How much you want?" I says, "A quart, five quarts." "Oh no, there's nothing like that around here." Then he calls me back and says, "I got some in barrels, in charred barrels." He said, "How about a barrel?" They was the cutest little barrels you ever seen, about that big around, like pickle barrels or something, charred barrels you know.

They was charred all right and by God they'd put this stuff in them and you know, what they'd make back in the hills and over on the mounds, take it up and hide it you know. Somebody come along fill it. Old Cobb says to him, "Can we just try it?" "Yes sir." And he gets a nail and drives a nail in it and puts a weed straw in there. And old Cobb would pull on it. He was petrified you know, embalmed before, I don't think the undertakers had anything to do with him, he was just petrified. He was never drunk, never weaved or nothing, but by God he was just naturally drunk. You know, he would drink anything too. I was waiting there with him and he said, "Go on and try it." And doggone I acted like I was taking a whiff of it, and oh boy, I couldn't stand it. So Henry plugged it up. And they were going to ring the bell when they had the ties all on. They finally tapped the bell about a half an hour before they had all the ties on the boat you know, waiting to go down. So I says, "Well Mr. Cobb I was getting about ready to go." He says, "Well say, what are we going to do with this? How are we going to get that on this boat?" I say, "I don't know." Well anyhow first he paid him and I said, "How much was this liquor?" He said, "Five dollars." Five dollars for a barrel you know. I thought that was an awful price when I seen what size barrels it was; I didn't know what to think. Anyhow

I says, "Any chance of getting that on the boat?" "No sir, I don't know sir." I says, "Five dollars?" And he says, "Yes sir." Put it in a sack you know, and that's the way we paid it. Put in the gunny sack, you know and walk around and you have them put it in a gunny sack back on the fantail. That darkie never had so much money in his life. He had about $15. At one time that was a lots of money down there especially.

Q: What year was that?

A: That was in about possibly 1925 or 1927 something like that. Well anyhow I got back on the boat, well the *Paducah* left. We laid up at night, but the *Paducah*, she left and went on down the river. She left at six o'clock, the *Paducah* every night for Florence, Sheffield and Tuscumbia towns up the Tennessee River. She loaded cotton here, peanuts here, you know lots of peanuts up in this country and so she got in on the, oh when the boat got to Paducah in other words, Captain Wilson called me and says, "Sy where did them darkies get that whiskey?" I said, "I don't know anything about no whiskey, Cap." "Oh they got some whiskey somewhere," he says. "Why?" He says, "I don't know but I've never had this boat unloaded so quick in my life." Of course I didn't know a thing about it. (chuckles) So the day before, he was down at a place and we had an assistant superintendent here, his name was John Hanshew. He had one daughter Margaret. All his life it was Margaret. That was it. Margaret got married and he let her have a big wedding and all that you know. Anyhow Johnny couldn't hear very well. He had one of those ear trumpets. You've seen the kind that put over your ear. Well he was asking some little kid, I guess he must have been about ten or 12 years old, he was walking across from his cotton patches down there in Tennessee River, walking towards the hill. Mr. Hanshew says, "Do you know where so and so lives?" He says, "You'll have to talk loud boy cause I can't hear." And then he says, "Wait a minute." And he pulls that thing around out of there and puts it in his ear and points to the little darkie. As far as I know that kid is still running, you know. (laughter) And the last I seen of that kid he was out of sight. He's still running.

Q: You got into the upper reaches of the Tennessee then on . . .

A: We got in all the reaches there was, what you call meant about ten or 12 days for us. Up and down the Tennessee River 226 miles. Then of course we'd try to give a holiday or something at Shiloh, that's Pittsburg Landing, Tennessee, at Shiloh battlefield, and then around there you know. Lot of people come down there in those days. I got a picture here someplace when we came down on the old *Paducah* . . .

Q: That must have been a rough river to travel wasn't it?

A: It was rough, very thin water and very swift. And around the island here, but since these new locks were put in, see they put in the new lock at Gilbertsville and that's done away, gee whiz all of them low places. Some of the towns of Newburg, Kentucky, Birmingham, Kentucky, and until you got way back up in the Tennessee lands, small towns were all flooded out. See a 65 foot of a lift at

John Knoepfle

Kentucky Dam right now. They had to change the lock. And they had the floating timberheads, you know the boats puts the lines on, goes up and down with the boats. We was going up there the last time and the fellow, sometimes you see his name on there, before they had the pool filled up, but Kentucky Dam was pretty well underway. Course I've been up there since it's been filled, and along many years before, but of course Jimmy Hinthorn, one of my neighbor boys, was with me and that boy is married now. He's a chief warrant officer now in the Coast Guard at Mobile here. Anyhow we just put buoys on dry land you know and when they fill up of course they was right in the channel. I was up there when they first went in the Coast Guard, and when the last ships went up there. There was a fellow named Bodine Henslin. Did you ever read the "Waterways Journal?" Sometimes you see his name in there. He was the postmaster at Newburg, Kentucky and he could write with a fine hand. He had one of them offset pens. Doggone he'd write a fine hand. He wrote me a letter and it was so doggone pretty I couldn't read it. So he made whiskey too. And he was in the penitentiary for a while. They got him out and he was a post-master. I never saw a Congressional Record in my life till then nor since. He says, "While you're going up this river you'll need, want some reading." So he gave me a whole bunch of these, still done up with the paper on there.

A lot of these little country postmasters, they get them more than they do in the city, know more about them in the country places. So I took them down. I kept all open during the time of the transition from the Coast Guard to the Lighthouse Service. By gee whiz I was going through them things and from what I seen I didn't know what they was going to do with me. Because the chief engineer Fred Barrows and the pilot Elmer Chandler were given warrants in Evansville, Indiana. Of course, I never knew what a warrant meant or what a chief warrant meant or nothing in the military service. The United States Judge swore them in at Evansville. Well anyhow, I was going up there I opened up them things. I seen where my name was in there for being first nominated and then confirmed, and later was confirmed. Here I really didn't know nothing about it yet. When the boat gets to Decatur, Alabama on April 1, 1940 there was a registered package, it had my commission in it. It had my commission in it for me, and this fellow Chandler that swore me in he was a warrant then and could swear me in. So he swore me in and from that time I was in the Coast Guard. I jumped right up and when I retired I finally got my final commission.

Q: Did you ever navigate on the French Broad?

A: I been up there. Been on the French Broad, I've been up there but no, they never. These fellows here Paul Underwood or Harris, a pilot on the *Delta Queen* now they have. They're from that country, they're from Knoxville, on the French Broad and the Little Tennessee. They were pilots when they built the Wilson Dam; I never saw so much wrote on a pilot's license in my life. And it didn't mean, didn't mean even 50 mile. They'd go up the Little Tennessee, and French Broad, and Holston. You know, I've been up there just a little bit with a Coast Guard boat. I had to make, in later years when some of the Coast Guard went there, I made a report of the whole district every year, write out the whole thing. I had all my notes. Some of those books up there, all the pilot work in them. That's all I have. This is a pocket secretary, and I've got them for about 16 years or so. When I'd make a trip, I had a jeep assigned to me at last, and I'd take that jeep I'd meet a boat, then I had to ride the boat for quite a while. I would go on as a liaison between the Coast Guard and the Navy and the Army you know. Changes in the river where a pilot would recommend changes and I got to know that river so much. I fell right into it in other words. Course it is just the line of work that I've always done. I don't know nothing else. I had a stationary engineers license for 40 odd years but never used them hardly.

Years ago, just below the mouth of Mill Creek here, up until the 1913 flood they had what they call Shantytown. The whole bank was covered with shantyboats, houseboats and everything. They even had a church. And they had a little old squatty fellow I only knew as Barnett. I'll never forget him. He was called the Mayor of Shantytown. We always had to go through Shantytown to go down to Mill Creek Landing, you see. They had as many as 50 to 100 barges in there, wooden barges. They'd bring them downriver as far as they could on a certain raise, and of course they would wait until they'd get another raise to go on south, and then finally to New Orleans. They had what they called the coalboats, and the barges. The barges were heavier built, was all wood, and they'd leak. That's why they put them back on Mill Creek, so that old sewage stuff would get in there and stop those leaks. That's right that old sewage stuff come out of Mill Creek. Sometimes they would put a boat up at the head and working her wheel to work that stuff underneath, but it would stop the leaks in those barges. They wouldn't have to pump them so much.

Had one big tugboat called *Charley*, had the boilers of the Grapevine; it was sunk up here at below the C & O Bridge in 1917, had the boilers on it. One of the first ones that had a big engine on it working back and forth. And when I was a young man I would take that engine apart and look at it. I remembered, doggone I used to study those valves, work all night, work harder taking those things out and looking at them than I would at my own work. I never had no education. I had to get all my education you see. I had to get it. I had to make my education, what education I did have. I had to make the whole business just by reading and doing things like that. I got to know what things meant, what the valves, what made an engine go. That was always my business to try and find out what made it go, and how it went. I bought certain books. I never read a book through in my life. Another fellow I run to, was Jesse Stuart, he wrote this book called *Taps for Private Tussie* up there at Greenup here. I never met this fellow Stuart but missed him by just a little bit each time I went there. He wrote *The Man with a Bull Tongue Plow*, and that *Taps for Private Tussie* and that is the nearest book I ever tried to read through in my life, but I do like to read newspapers now that I'm retired.

John Knoepfle

Q: Do you remember the wages you used to make on your boat?

A: Well the wages, I do know that in the harbor here, I'll never forget that the captain and chief engineer in the harbor worked for $100 a month. Sam Kay, was mate, he got $75. I got $50. Pretty near all year around, I got $50, a month.

Q: About what year would that have been?

A: I would say in about . . . 1912, 1914. I know that I was running chief engineer for 100 some odd dollars a month. I forget. I got my papers, up there yet with my wages, I went on the *Goldenrod* with. I was paid $160 a month and they was big wages at that time.

Q: I wonder what the deckhands and the roustabouts made.

A: Around $25 to $50. Them rousters see they used a different class of people on towboats and packetboats. Everything was interlocked, but there was so much different. Now like that fellow Fred Hornbrook never done no towboating. One of the finest gentlemen you ever met in your life. Same way with Captain Wisherd. But they were very good packetboat men, excursion boat men and that kind of stuff and that's what I never had a whole lot of. And as fine a bunch of fellows that were my very age Pete Butler, Walter English, they were all pilots and Wilbur Chapman. We was all in the same age bracket, brought up together you know, and one time we had an engineers' association NEVA, and I was president of it as late as 1930. You couldn't pick up a crew around this part of the country for love or money nowadays. These young crews, now the companies are building more men. The companies are building, after you get the license, the wages are now a whole lot better. Gee whiz they work! I never got so much money for in my life, for a job. I got about $50 a day for ten days here. I got the highest rate. Two days I got in January were $45 a month. Nine days or ten days was $50 a day, but that don't happen all the time, now we don't get that. Old Myers, we were always arguing with him about wages. By God he don't pay half that much.

Q: Was that the Ohio?

A: No the Ohio River Company they were different you know. All the big companies the towboats always paid more money than the packetboats. Towboats always paid more money than the packetboats. The thing of it is just do it. I don't know what mate's wages is. Deckhand's wages is a whole lot more than chief engineer or captain's wages were in those days when I started in. And some of these jobs you couldn't hardly get a relief unless someone'd be after your job. Different people after your job. That's the way it always was. But nowadays, by gosh they're training them. They're maybe not so many of them, but they've got it down to a nice thing now. It's a good job but they only pay these bigger wages when they have to like in an emergency see. Then they had a wage set for that. That's a set wage for an emergency. But otherwise I think the pilots get around $23 some cents a day and their board of course. They work 20 days and ten days off. They work 40 days or the equivalent. But now in July it's supposed to be 15 and 15, and those wages go on through all that time. You don't lose. Sick and years ago you were pretty near afraid to get off the boat. But by golly I've seen times like this one old captain, I was a young man, that didn't make no difference on that boat you know. I said, "I'll just jump in the river." I said, "That's all right with me. I'm getting off of here. That's all there is to it." I said, "You get somebody." Me and him had a few words you know. I always considered that the chief engineer had just as much responsibility as any captain ever lived. I don't think he's got to take cn a bit more responsibility. He works a little easier, and there's a whole lot more talk about it. That's exactly the way I think of it right today. Call me if they are in trouble or something like that as far as an engine is concerned, the oldtimer, because there's nobody hardly around now. I could care less. He and Myers come this office, he's the boss of the *Avalon*, manages the *Avalon*. And just like this they have storms and everything else over there. He says, "I've got a plane reservation for you. I want you to go over there and help me out for a few days." Mrs. Schletker she says, "You're not going. He's not going to fly anyhow." So finally, I went by bus but I got there in time at that, at Nashville. And I was engineer on her for two days, and then I went captain on her for a couple of days while Wagoner went home. He had to change a house or something like that. He had to go home for a few days, and I was captain of her for a few days. But that's the way it was from chief engineer to captain, I'm one of the few that can do that, that has license for everything. It's just that I don't do any more than I have to, but I like to do it once in a while. I don't know nothing else, and I can pay the taxes that way.

Q: Well, you've had a long career.

A: That's just one of the things when you haven't done nothing else all your life like my dad; he was with the American Book Company, he was a very faithful employee. And doggone, he'd been quitting as long as I can remember, but by golly he still stayed there. And you know we all think that and certain things come along, we see how much better we've got it than somebody else. We never had nothing just what we worked for. Doggone every day, never had a dime given to us to amount to anything, and I say when I quit I paid for this house, owned a little Ford out there, and got me a little money in the bank.

Q: Yes it's good to end up with it. I hope that I do as well. Captain would you talk about measuring wooden coal barges?

A: At one time we had three coal gaugers at Cincinnati, in my time. One was Harry Rigdon had the *Silver Star*, Scotty Carr had the *Sentinel*, and Willard Grubbs the *Willard*. We'd meet the coalboats, at the upper end of town possibly any place between New Richmond and Cincinnati or below, in the harbor as they'd come down. At that time, the locks and dams were not in. They'd come down in what you would call a flash flood. That was the time of the wooden barges and coalboats see. The coalboat was the larger of the two. The standard barge was 26 foot wide by 150 foot long and ten and a half to ten foot sides. These barges were brought down here and Captain Rigdon had what we call on the boat, we had a rod. It was about a 12 foot rod, numbering rod, and we'd stick that rod down in certain places throughout the barge and get an average depth. Then we would also take and measure the rakes of the barges on account of the slanting rakes; there was always a bulkhead, a watertight bulkhead from the starting of the rake to the deadflat of the barge. Therefore we'd take the measurement of half of that, which would give us approximately a square. Captain Rigdon would take the figures and he sent each company or each individual who asked for it a bill of landing, giving him giving him the amount of bushels, which was in the barge. It was at that time weighed as bushels. Therefore the barge had to be level you know. If the barge was just poured, if it was just poured in like the dumpsters do, but it had to be leveled even if the point of origin or on the way or sometimes here at the delivery point. When the barges were leveled pretty good, therefore he could give pretty good amount of bushel, amount of capacity of the barge due to the measurement.

Q: Now this was just for coal that was coming to Cincinnati.

A: This was for coal that was coming into Cincinnati. A lot of barges for Cincinnati. These coal gaugers were appointed by, worked under the Cincinnati Chamber of Commerce. Therefore I do know that they used the bushel, and it was 2,688 cubic inches to the bushel. That was the factor they used. Now often this coal was purchased enroute. Such places like when they were building the bridge at Sciotoville. I used to go up there and measure coal and bring the figures down to Captain Rigdon and he'd calculate them and issue a bill of lading for that. Now to do that the way it was necessary a barge was built. And as soon as it was emptied the first time, he had a record of all the barges, they were all numbered, he'd take the D depth, the area of the four pump boxes, have to pump out the barge, and the timbers, both the crosswise and lengthwise timbers in the boat, in the barge. That's how he could measure.

Now the coalboats they were larger, and they were more for southern delivery. They were very scantily built you know, and the bottom and the side was two inch timbers, where the barges were more sturdily built with a six inch gun'l, or gunwale as it was called. They were held together by drift bolts holding the barges together. Of course, they were caulked and before the dams were in, they kept quite a lot of those barges in Cincinnati. One of them was above where the Cincinnati Waterworks is now, just below there called Stewart's Upper Landing. Then across from the mouth of the Little Miami River they had Brown's Landing. Below that they had Coal Haven Landing, which the ice piers are still remaining. Years ago when the Pittsburg Combine took over the entire business, of course they took in all the barges and they kept Coal Haven Landing and repaired the piers by encasing them with concrete. Across the river from Coal Haven and downstream a little bit was a landing of the Marmet Company. They operated two boats, *Florence Marmet* the *Lucy Marmet* and the *George Matheson*; there were three boats. When the Combine boats come in they was the large ones. Some of them would prepare to go through the bridges and go on down. Now below Cincinnati, I'm getting ahead of my story. They also had two large landings, one below the mouth of Mill Creek approximately a half mile below the mouth of Mill Creek, below the Southern Bridge in other words. Another at Ludlow Harbor below the point.

Q: What were their names?

A: That was the name of them was, Ludlow Harbor and Mill Creek Landing, yes. They had as much as 100 barges at a time at Mill Creek Landing because it was one of those things they had pumping up there called a wooden man. Just like running across and meeting. Each one of them had a pump box and when a barge leaked, they had such as a pumping out an oil well. One timber would, one boom, would run all away across and it was possible to pump ten barges at a time if necessary. But they would hook barges and drop down to another coupling and pump it out you know according to how much coal.

Q: Which was the wooden man? What was that?

A: A wooden man was the rigging. It was like an oil well rigging. It operates from a steam engine on a pump boat. It went across the barge and it would pump out the water that drained in either from rain or seepage or whatever the case may be. Of course it wasn't (chuckles) about keeping the barge at Ludlow Landing. Down there was the sewage out of Mill Creek you know, so that kept in those barges, you know it wasn't an acid, it was alkaline base, you know and it stopped the barges up pretty well. Of course all these barges and all coal fleets carried extra sawdust and manure, for such things to put in the heads of barges to stop the leaks. If one of them was leaking pretty badly they'd make an effort to stop it, you know.

Q: With sawdust and manure!

A: With manure or sawdust whichever the case may be, which they had the handiest. They could always tell by a barge leaking, the barge needed to be pumped. They'd put so many lumps of coal on the timberhead and that would give the night watchman or the day man, which barges they wanted to pump that night. They'd measure them. The barges were measured at least twice a day, twice a day, then twice at night. The night watchman was supposed to measure them and of course they always, it was up to the main landing men generally to do that work. Then when the time came for a raise to ship the coal south the boats would come to Pittsburg and add to their tows. They'd generally go to Louisville. If they had falls water they'd go over the falls and make up their tow again at Sand Island below Louisville or White City. At different places along down the Ohio River where there was deep water, why they could make up their tow, and then sometimes a larger boat would take care such as the *Joseph E. Williams*, and the *Harry Brown*, and the *John A. Wood*. The *Harry Brown* was a high pressure boat but there was another Brown boat. It was a compound condensing boat. Then the *J. B. Findley* and the *Sprague*. The *Sprague* was the largest. The idea of it is of the building of a foundation place

John Knoepfle

for the boats to handle other barges around that you know. They were not as rigid as the steel barges we have today.

Q: Now is this lock post and dam?

A: Since this system of lock and dams has been put in the barges have always resort to steel barges. The standard barge being 175 long, 26 foot wide, 11 foot sides. That was a standard barge possibly around someplace very close to a 1,000 ton capacity at different depths. And that's why those barges when they started them out that done away with the coal gaugers. Coal then was done by what you call mine weight and by measuring displacement, which was so hard to do with a wooden barge, you see. The wooden barge had so many timbers and stuff like that in it. The steel barge was all practically done by mine weights. They had tables of what the mine weight would be and such. Then it seems like before that time the coal companies in the Cincinnati Harbor, in the harbors here, would yard a lot of coal in case of low water. They'd yard a lot, and then still they had a lot of coal in the barges. Different companies had boats around here what they call harbor boats. Now the Combine, the Pittsburg Coal Company had such boats as: the *Ranger*, and the *Fallie*, and the *Fulton*, and the *Relief*, and the *Adelle*, and the *Delta*. Just boats of that type of what you would call the Pittsburg pool boat type. They would move barges and possibly make a trip to Madison or Louisville, Kentucky now and then, with a barge between if they had enough water. It was always a project of getting over what we called bad places, such as, the starting place below here was Big Miami River, and of course Laughery Creek, Laughery Island you know, and Rising Sun Bar, and Ranty Bar and all down through that lower country.

Q: Shoal water.

A: Shoal water yes, and then we would sometimes have to lighten the barges possibly drawing maybe five and a half and six foot. It was during the construction of locks and dams. There was a lot of coal used those days instead of, nowadays of course, all that stuff is mostly diesel driven cranes and such. Down in Louisville there was a different proposition there and they had a landing what they called Pumpkin Patch and Quart Fulton and several other landings above the falls. In those days, the dam was lower than it is now and they could concentrate these barges up there and they had a fall boat or falls pilots that such as Captain Billy Cook and Captain Graham Varble, the Varble family, several of them, the Carter family, Clarence Carter. Several others that were in that business of going over the falls, taking these barges, and of course, they'd make up at Sand Island and down below for the larger boats. They'd help them, you know, found the foundation fleet so they could help them get together. Then they would get the lines up to a tow properly.

Now with the steel barge, the raising of the canal at Louisville, the heights of the dam, it is increased by about, I'm not sure, but six or seven feet anyhow. That has done away the proposed lock 40, which was to go in possibly someplace around Lonesome Hollow just above Madison, Indiana. Now with the dam raised and the steel barges it gives them more water over the dam and dam water, falls water, now what it's called. The outside way is a stage of 20 feet above the dam, and 50 feet below; 22 feet above the dam that's it: 22 feet above the dam and 50 feet below the dam is considered falls water, safe falls water. Therefore you don't go through the canal, but you go around the outside way through the Pennsylvania, and the Big Four bridges, down through there at Louisville, and then boats possibly might make as much as two trips over there. But instead of having coal nowadays it's more of the finished product, the finished steel products from Pittsburg and vicinity. The boat generally goes right on through, but there was a delay with the older type locks.

Q: Did you ever go through the falls before the dams were put on?

A: Oh yes, I made several trips over what they call, of course that was never down in this falls water because it's always been bypassed by locks of some kinds. There was possibly a two and a half mile canal above the falls at Louisville, and then they had the two locks. One of them was a standard 110 by 600, that is the large lock now, which at some future time I understand will be the small lock when they'll put a 1,200 foot lock in. But then they had a small 350 or 60, which formerly was in two steps. Now it's in one step.

Q: Do you remember what it would have been like to go take a tow through?

A: Well at those times like going over the falls, when they had falls pilots, they had certain eddies they had to keep out of and of course it was more of a rapids, a rough rapids. It could tell by it being a falls only the engineers could tell it by the difference in the gauges, above and below they could tell what the falls was, what the fall was at the time, but it was so hard. Now we could say, falls water, both the passenger boats and the freight boats would take either, they had before this, they had what they had, a Kentucky chute and an Indiana chute. Now the Kentucky chute is abandoned by the Hydraulic Electric Plant that is built on the dam, below it, below the Pennsylvania Bridge.

Q: It's covered up that chute.

A: And it sort of funnels the water up with a certain amount of wickets that can be lowered anytime, and this is in constant telephone connection from the piers out on the dam to the lockmaster at Louisville, and he of course directs the amount of dam he wants raised up or lowered. The amount of the dam that's down is marked on the Louisville waterworks above town so the navigator can get an idea of how many feet it's over and calculate the amount of draw he might have in getting into the canal.

Q: They must have lost boats there coming through the rapids.

A: Very few that I know. The *Wilmot* exploded. Of course there was possibly before my time there's been boats lost, but I don't remember very many lost. I saw *Queen City* sank above the old lock you know, but she wasn't lost, she was raised. It was sank right out there making the turn around on one of the New Orleans trips. She had the turn and of course she settled very straight on

John Knoepfle

possibly whatever the foundation is, which no doubt was rock. It didn't hurt her at all. When they raised her she was ready to go.

Q: Did they use a lot of lead lines in the . . .

A: No, you can't use no lines at all because the water was too swift. You could use no sounding gear practically of any kind outside possibly a pole now and then. These fellows run you so much they knew exactly where to go. Those days with the old dam, nobody would trust anybody, only a regular standard falls pilot, for that kind of work. Because they knew exactly how the land laid and what marks they had to run these different places. Nowadays it's been built up so that the current is not much greater there than it is right in the open river at that place. The only thing you had is a bad bridge below. Upper bridge was not too bad, but you had a bad bridge and a lot of piers below. But apparently I don't know of anybody in my time, I don't remember any boats hitting it. I remember the *Wilmot* exploded coming up over the fall with a tow, the *V. W. Wilmot*. One of the family of Varbles that were fall pilots was killed on there. It wasn't young Dan, yes it was young Dan. And then there was another Graham that was with the . . . he died. He fell off the boat someplace in the vicinity of Memphis. Then he had a navigation light named after him someplace down there, was a well-known fellow.

Q: He fell off the . . .

A: He fell off the *Henry A. Laughlin* or the *Vestry*. I just don't know, which of the two in the vicinity of Memphis. He was a New Orleans pilot. They'd change pilots at Louisville for the trips below.

Q: Did they go straight down to Cairo once they were through?

A: When they were through, they very seldom stopped only in heavy fog or a bad piece of river and they thought maybe they had better sound it first before they'd go through it. Those were the days with no buoys, all they had was navigation lights as an aid to navigation. The pilots if they were in doubt, they'd possibly send a yawl ahead, some men to give them some soundings. They may have land and sound it out you know. But most of the downstream work unless it was out of the ordinary fine weather, they would lay up at night, then run when it was daylight, especially on the downstream trip. Coming up of course it wasn't so bad you know. They could hug the shores pretty well. It wasn't necessary to get right into the channel and oft times they would have bunches of bottoms of coalboats besides being off. You know they had bottoms they would take and rebuild them at Pittsburg and load them out again. Instead of a lot of timberheads they had just a log you know, possibly imbedded in the coal back of the tie, put there to tie the lines to.

Q: This was coal they would be carrying to fuel themselves coming up.

A: They'd carry their own. They'd drop off fuel flats at different places along the line. Of course on the Ohio River we had quite a number of places where different boats could drop off a fuel flat on the way down. We had some at Vanceburg, we had some more at down around Tell City, Indiana, at Louisville and Cincinnati of course the large cities. Each boat would possibly have a fuel flat right here to pick up to go ahead back upstream with. All those boats those days were hand fired and it was a hard job. They had big boats like the *W. W. O'Neil*. I think she was a twenty-four twelve or something of that sort. I have the exact dimensions of those boats upstairs.

Q: Let's talk about the ice gorge on the Tennessee.

A: All right, during 1917 ice, which was prevalent all along the entire reaches of the Ohio River, Cincinnati and Paducah, Kentucky experienced the worst of the disaster. Now at Cincinnati the boats, *City of Louisville*, the *City of Cincinnati*, the *Hercules Carrel*, the *Loucinda*, were cut down in the ice. The *Julius Fleishmann* was over in the Licking River keeping it clear. I get so mixed up. Then at Paducah, the ice in the Tennessee River, which was frozen possibly 100 miles up come out you know, and the Ohio River ice met and took the Eagle Packet Company boat the, let's see it took the boats like the, no the *Golden Eagle* was built later. The *Gray Eagle* was just taken off from the Paducah docks and taken up to the landings inside of Owens Island, what they call the Owl's Nest. Then the boats the *Peoria*, the *Spread Eagle*, and several others were cut down in the ice. The remaining boats, the *J. B. Finley*, on the island side, the steamers *Paducah* and *Alabama*, the *Reefer*, the *John Barrett*, the *Gleaner*, and the *Slack Barrett*. Of course the *Josh Cook* was laying up in the upper arm, she was cut down, she lay opposite the . . . Joppa, Illinois was her wreck. The *Peoria* sank in the middle of the river at Brookport, Illinois.

Q: What do you mean cut down?

A: Cut down by ice just cut down the hull of it. In this case it seems to me like as I watched the *Peoria* thinking there was somebody on it and didn't know for sure. We was in such a place we couldn't get out. It would crush a small boat like the *John Barrett* right down if she attempted it. But the wheel was running very slowly and her lights were burning but everybody got ashore off of *Peoria*, and then she sank crossways in the river at Brookport, Illinois.

Q: Guess where that ice met it just ground them up.

A: Cut them up. There was no raising to them, nothing worthwhile raising. It took the top works off. I was in Cairo later and saw a lot of stuff float down the river. The *Josh Cook* was sunk opposite Joppa, Illinois. She was a towboat belonged to a Missouri Portland Cement Company.

Q: They thought they would be safe in the Tennessee.

A: They thought that was one of the things, that's why the St. Louis and Tennessee River brought all their equipment to Paducah thinking they'd be safe in Tennessee. The only one saved in the whole bunch of them was the *Bald Eagle* and she happened to be pulled out on the Paducah Marine Ways. I watched practically the whole setup. I was down there on a boat called the *John Barrett*, Clarence Carter was the Captain of her and Harry Doss, from Cincinnati here was the pilot, and Hiram Hall from Newport, Kentucky was the chief engineer, and I was the assistant engineer on it.

Q: The Ice must have went out with a terrific roar.

A: It did. Just crushed these boats down. We could see them going down and hear the ice crushing them. The boats that were saved, there were quite a few of them over in possibly a little more shelter. Like on the Kentucky side of the Owens Island where at the upper end was the *Alabama* and the *Tennessee* and the *John Barrett*, the *Gleaner*, *Slack Barrett*, and the *J. B. Finley*, the *Spread Eagle*, *Josh Cook*, *Silver Star* in that gorge. There were also two others up in there, *John L. Lowry* and the *Joe Fowler* were also saved in that gorge.

Q: Now which ones were sunk?

A: The boats that were sunk were the *Gray Eagle*, the *Spread Eagle*, the *Peoria*, and the towboat *Josh Cook* was a large, she was one of the large type of boats.

Q: Did that ice go out at night?

A: It did in this case, in this case it went out at night. It happened to be that I was laying, after the ice went out of the Tennessee River, I was laying on the John Barrett alongside of three barges of rock that we had out of Rappolees Landing in the Cumberland River. We were laying there inside where all these boats had left thinking the ice was out and the boat come down. Some barges got adrift in the upper Tennessee River and hit our tow and I happened to be the only one on watch. I was downstairs so I quick come ahead on her. We was laying with two barges against the bank and steamboat and one barge on the outside of it. The tow hit us and broke us loose and it backed our stern in and knocked the sternwheel out of the bearings. We was going adrift down the river and we were picked up by a boat called the *Clyde*. The *Clyde* was a barge that towed the original barges of ties that hit our boat and turned us loose. Then of course we raised our wheel back in the bearings. That was on the starboard side and got it together so we could use it. Then the ice ran out and of course lot of it sunk being pretty well pulverized and lot of the ice sank and we proceeded on to Cairo to the home offices of the Barrett Line with the three barges of rock. Course they were steel barges.

Q: It was a great disaster wasn't it?

A: It was quite a loss, the biggest loss known at any one time on the Ohio River.

Q: Well this is the *Woodruff* again.

A: Yes sir. I was on the *E. A. Woodruff* and Terrence Stratton was on the *Scioto*. And the *Woodruff* was a five boiler boat and she had a bow. It was sort of a delta bow but it was sort of like a bootjack affair where she run up between two logs and she had a heavy crane that reached overboard. She could pull up pretty near anything she could get ahold of and lift, and then of course on the end of another thing she had was a polly hook. When the wooden barge sank they wouldn't try to raise them. They'd just take that polly hook, and back when they was in a channel I was speaking of they couldn't raise them very handy. They'd take this polly hook and just make a run down through them and just tear them to pieces, barges flying in all directions.

Q: What exactly is a polly hook?

A: A polly hook is just a large piece of steel with a form of a polly hook reaching from an A frame that would get down in the water and we'd back the full weight of that big heavy boat on that. It would tear the things to pieces. A polly I'd say like a polly's nose, polly's beak in other words. I was the last engineer on it. The picture I was showing you this fellow Stratton was on the *Scioto* and he had some molasses on his boat and I had some bread on our boat. We both about closing out you know. Everything about eaten, so we kept on eating to see which one could finish out the molasses and bread. (chuckles) Funny thing about this young fellow Stratton, a very healthy looking young man, he took the flu and went right now. I got the flu so bad myself. I made a trip to Detroit, went on half a ship you know across to Quebec, Canada where they put it together, put it together at Montreal, the part above the water and the other part at Leavitt across from Quebec. I come home from there and I went on a boat called *Robert P. Gillham*, lying here above the landing the first time I ever knew I was so fagged out. I wasn't fit to go on a boat. It was during the flu days that I crawled on my hands and knees up the hill. That's the only time in my life that I ever bought a quart of whiskey. Then after I bought it I give it away. Because I got up here and sat on the corner up here. I didn't live down here. I lived in Evanston then. Picked that thing up and I was just lucky to get home. Barb, my brother's wife, he was married long before I was. I stayed with them. I lived on Jonathan Avenue.

One time I was on a boat here and Captain Albert Martin was master and I was chief engineer of the *Eugene Dana Smith* at that time, owned by Campbells Creek Coal Company. Just like all wooden boats when they'd bring stores aboard or through some other way they get bugs aboard such as cockroaches and bedbugs. And this *Dana Smith* for some reason I'll tell you I never saw so many bedbugs in my life on any one boat. It don't seem like it bothered Captain Martin or anybody but they did bother me. I put two stools in there with a lantern on each stool. I knew where the bugs, I was dead for sleep and I had to get some sleep, the lanterns kept them away for a while. But the Captain thought, "That engineer's crazy. Why, he's got a light burning in there." I said, "I don't know if I'm crazy or not but by golly I could sleep with the lights, but I couldn't sleep with the bugs." As long as those lights were burning the bugs didn't come out.

Q: I guess that was kind of characteristic of the wooden boats.

A: It was. Lots of times it was hard to get rats off of them too. Sometimes rats would get on, and they'd walk around. I've seen them walk along the ridgepoles and get on the bell wires and jingle the bell wires. Especially down in Cairo, places like that you know. They'd sort of jingled the bells. They'd get up in them places. It was awful hard to get them off the old wooden type boats without regular fumigation. They'd get so bad they'd just have to do something.

Q: I guess the jingling bells might have caused confusion.

A: No it didn't cause no confusion it was just the idea when the boat was laying

John Knoepfle

up because when the boat was running they were all hibernating somewhere. Funny thing how they would hibernate . . . . There is so much at different times that happened. In my time on the *Greenbriar*, I had quite a lot of . . . you were speaking about songs. I know songs like "Old Man River," and several of more of them there "Floating Down the River," and things like that stuff that are later. When I was a youngster a bunch of us went down in a little steam tug called the *OK*, it was owned by a fellow named Mose Pickelheimer down at Taylors Port, Kentucky. A bunch of fellows got on there and during the latter part of the trip, they sort of got a little inebriated. My brother and these other boys were pretty well posted on the handling of the boat, which at that time being a steamer required licensed officers. Well we all got to having a good time, plenty to eat and plenty to drink, of course a few were sort of inebriated. And they sang a song "From Taylors Port to Rabbit Hash is 18 mile and from Rabbit Hash to Taylors Port is 18 mile." They just kept on going all through the night till they either got sleepy or we got sleepy. So we laid the boat up and everybody went to bed and we didn't know at Taylors Port or Rabbit Hash either one.

During the 1913 flood we always had a big three oar-lock yawl down at Mill Creek Landing and Captain Menges sent three of us, my brother and I and another young man, we were all good oarsmen, sent us down to Dayton, Ohio to help out to see what we could do about getting those people out of there. Well we could do a little more than they could with an outside motor because we went right up to places and got people out of trees and out of posts and houses that you couldn't even get no other way. Then of course we had quite a few incidents, several boats got away and barges got away through the Cincinnati Harbor. And a boat called *Jewel* was taking some of the boats down river and she straddled the Kentucky Pier, the channel pier of the Southern Bridge down here until the barges got loose. We had a little boat then called the *Ranger* and we shoved these barges in against the bank. Some of them were caught down at the Anderson Ferry by the Kottmeyers who incidentally still run the Anderson Ferry. No doubt that you have met them?

Q: No I haven't.

A: Well, they was quite a family and they had several of the different boats by the name of *Boone*. Now I think the last one was *Boone 7*. They ranged from the horse ferry to the present through steam to the present diesel ferryboat, which they now have. *Boone 7* I think it is, Oliver and Harry Kottmeyer run it, and they were all sons of the original Kottmeyers, which run the ferry. They lived around down there at Constance, Kentucky . . . . One of these Kottmeyers, the elder Kottmeyer by the name of Louie, he owned a boat called the *Alert*. It was a single boiler boat and he done a lot of harbor work around here. He had several independent harbor boats besides boats for the Combine. One of these boats was the *Frank Miller* owned by two brothers, Frank and Phil Miller and they was characters in their own.

Q: Maybe you could talk some about the lumber company.

A: The only lumber company I know of there was the Yellow Poplar Lumber Company up around Ironton, Ohio. Captain Beatty, Captain Campbell Beatty, that's W. C. Beatty, he's John Beatty's daddy, he took care of their lumber for quite a while. Also, a lot of logs and lumber came out of the Kanawha and the Guyandotte and Big Sandy River. They had log runs would happen quite a bit. Then they had the boats the *J. O. Cole* and the *Crown Hill*. They were owned by the Crane Lumber Company, which was just north of very possibly the front of Hayden Street. Then on down too they had two mills up there.

Q: Where were the mills?

A: The mills were on the right side of the Ohio River, just about where Hayden Street is in Cincinnati. One was called the New York Mill and the other was just the plain Crane Mill that I knew of. Finally, logs would go adrift and men like G. Butler, pilot on there, there was another one Joe Butler, later Captain on the *Island Queen* and pilot on the *Island Queen* was on there and Jock Meek; They'd come out of those rivers you know, lots of these fellows would come out of the river when the rivers was real bad. And see, the Ohio River looked too big for them, and jump off! (chuckles) Lots of the lumber was pretty well held together by chain-dogs, fastened by chain-dogs and sapling, either would put a sapling across and a chain-dog to each one of them.

A chain-dog was a two spikes affair like with a chain between them that would hold the log down. Hold them together so they could be towed. They were towed in large rafts and I have also seen them on the Tennessee River. But here at Cincinnati Mill they sawed up a lot of river timber. You know what I mean the good green oak and poplar when poplar was prevalent. There was a lot of that lumber come here to Cincinnati , and they used these two boats, and the last boat was the *Carolina*, was before Crane quit the business and that was the last boat. Butler was Captain of that Gilbert Butler.

Q: They caught logs that was . . .

A: Lots of logs would go adrift, they'd give somebody who'd catch them along the river, give them a little piece of money for catching them, so much a log or so much a tie. You'd go down with these boats and gather them up, then pull them upstream the same as they would in the freight. They'd just line them up.

Q: Crane as far as I could determine was a pretty tough man wasn't he?

A: There were C. Crane and I don't know if his daughter or someone married some nobility or something over there, Carolina Krippendorf, in the shoe business or something like that. I don't remember the way it kind of lined up, but I'm not too very well posted on it. But I do know the two boats. The *Crown Hill* ended up as a towboat to Menke's Showboat. The *J. O. Cole*, the last I heard of her was in and around Paducah somewhere. For a long while she towed in that trade, she towed railroad cars from Golconda, Illinois to Roseclaire to the Spar Mines. There was no way to get out to the main line. But now they have a connecting railroad along there.

John Knoepfle

Sanford Smith, September 16, 1957

Answer: My name is Sandy Smith, I live at Bethlehem, Indiana. I worked on the river or run a boat on the river for 32 years, an 85 foot boat with 100 horsepower diesel engine. Our trade was freight and passengers from Louisville to Madison.

Question: That's fine, now that boat was named the *New Hanover* wasn't it?

A: Yes, our boat was the *New Hanover*. We run trips between Bethlehem to Louisville, the next day from Bethlehem to Madison carrying passengers from Louisville to do their trading one day and the next day from Bethlehem up to Madison to do their trading there. And our crew all lived in Bethlehem.

Q: Do you remember any of the crew?

A: Well, my partner was Jesse Singer and we had a crew hired, of course. It was a small crew, maybe five in the whole crew. We done all the work except in port. When we were in Louisville with the boat, a load there to load out, we hired up to 35 roustabouts who would do the unloading or the loading.

Q: Now you said that these people you carried did their trading. What did you mean by that?

A: Well, there were all sorts of people. There was no automobiles or no trucks at that time, that is at the beginning of that time. They lived in the country. If they didn't have enough freight, they'd go to Madison. They'd buy their groceries and everything.

Q: And you hauled that back and forth?

A: Twice a week. We probably picked up 40 and 50 passengers between here and Madison and they'd go and do their trading, come back home the same day, you see. Next day was Louisville. We carried freight from out of Louisville to Madison, Indiana.

Q: You ran on up to . . .

A: Probably 15 years ago. It would be 1914 until 1947.

Q: You weren't carrying passengers at the end there, were you?

A: Yes, we carried passengers, but the trade run out, and trucks and automobiles took the passenger trade away, and the freight trade away. It run down until we didn't have anything left. Couldn't even pay the men. Finally got down along when wages were pretty high you see. We finally got down to pay them what the boat would make and the crew all agreed to run it, you know, just to divide it up, but at that we was only paying ten dollars a week. So we had to quit.

Q: You must have lasted as long if not longer than anybody.

A: We were the last boat on the river, yes. In addition to that we had opposition lots of times, you know. The Turners, they ran their boat and we run ours, and they would butt in our trade along here. Built a boat and put in there against her, and we run nearly two years; they carried passengers as low down as ten cents a roundtrip. We just finally fought it. We stayed the longest and run the other boat out. The trucks and automobiles run us out. We was the last boat on the river. All the big boats at Cincinnati quit. They ran boats from Cincinnati to Louisville. That's the Mail Line Company. They had packets in here too.

Q: Made landings in here too.

A: Oh, yes. Land here, yes land anywhere, carry freight, passengers and anything. They had packets from Carrollton to Louisville, and then they had the big sidewheelers from Louisville to Cincinnati. One left Louisville everyday about three o'clock.

Q: Did you ever get in the way of those boats on the river?

A: Oh no, the river always has its own laws, and you're governed by that. Now whether your boat is big or little, you are just as big as any of the rest of them. In the signals on the river, if the boat's coming upstream, if they want to pass on the left hand side, they whistle two whistles. If they were passing on the right, they whistled once. The upper boat if they think that's right, they answer their signals according to what they are. Two for the left, one for the right. If they don't want it that way, they blow four short whistles, change the signal the other way. Instead of passing on the left they can pass on the right. It's hardly ever done that way. Sometimes the towboats where they have big tow and think maybe they can't make that, in other words, the boat coming downstream has the right of way but the boat coming upstream has the first choice.

Q: Your run was always from Madisonville, and then Louisville, and then back. You never ran on the other tributaries!

A: No, I never ran out of them. See in that way I didn't come in contact with lots of these pilots that run on the other boats. We never come together.

Q: Well who were some of the rivermen that you did know Captain?

A: There was Cyril Turner, Arron Baker, Ed Turner, Jesse Singer, and Roy McBride, I can't think of all of them.

Q: You mentioned stopping off at landings, it hasn't got too much to do with the river, but I'm kind of interested in it. Ed Taylor, I think he said it was at London Landing.

A: No London Landing on our run, no. There is a London Bottom up here.

Q: That must have been it. He said in 1916, 1917, and 1918, around about then, they were planting a lot of sunflower seeds in this area, and I am just curious to know a little more about that.

A: Well, what they call London Bottom is about ten miles up the river here, about half way to Madison. It's a big bottom like the Bethlehem Bottom here, it's wide and long. At that time they raised hundreds of acres of sunflower seeds and they sold them seeds. They made oil out of them.

Q: Did they raise them systematically like they would raise corn?

A: Just like corn. Drill them into rows, cultivate them just like you would plant corn. They would grow a big hedge 12 or 14 inches across and full of big white seed. They always raised what you called the Russian Sunflower there. There is a white seed, and then there's another kind that has black seed in them.

John Knoepfle

Q: What did they call them?

A: Russian, that was a strain of sunflower seed.

Q: There must have been some profit in it to put the whole bottom in that.

A: Oh, a big profit at that time, yes. It was more profitable than anything else they could raise. They would raise hundreds of acres out here. We loaded our boat a number of times with just sunflower seed.

Q: You took it to the commercial houses in Louisville.

A: In Louisville, yes.

Q: Who was buying it down there, do you remember?

A: No I don't recollect who was buying it at Louisville. Rick Mathews was buying it here. He bought boatloads of it.

Q: I knew the *City of Louisville*, the packet, took a lot of it up to McCullough's in Cincinnati.

A: Cincinnati yes, Cincinnati was a big market for sunflowers too.

Q: But all the Chamber of Commerce reports put that in under the title Other Seeds so you can't tell, which was sunflower and which wasn't, or I would be able to find out exactly how much they were shipping out in a given year.

A: Oh, a wonderful, wonderful seed, cut them, went to the field with the wagon, have men cutting them heads off you know, throw them the wagon. Then you would have somebody with sticks to beat them heads out, beat them seeds out of the heads. They would let them hang in the field until they were dead ripe and when they got dead ripe and dry, why just a few licks would knock all the seed out of the head wonderful.

Q: I talked to a couple of roustabouts in Cincinnati that had loaded sunflower seeds. They sort of liked that because the bags were easy to carry onto the boats.

A: Put them in what you called double gunny sacks; they were great big sacks just like they always put oats in, but they were not so heavy. Several of them double gunnies made a pretty good load on your back. Our small crew on the boat, we had the pilot, clerk, engineer, two deckhands. Everything that was handled along the way all of us had to handle it. We all worked. We got so used to carrying that stuff that I know one time down here we had a fellow working on the boat that weighed about 180 pounds, a big strong man, we was loading mussel shells. You used to catch a lot of mussel shells here. They would break those mussel shells, they are on hinges, you know. They would break them, put them in these big double gunny sacks, sew them. The lot we was putting on down there, we averaged 400 feet a day. We was carrying them on the boat and they put one on Jack Dean. He just stood there and his legs wiggled, he couldn't make a step with it. I was next. I was a little fellow weighed about 130 pounds. They just laid it on my shoulder and I carried it on the boat. But he couldn't carry one of them. But that's like the tale they used to tell about the fellow that lifted the calf over the fence so it could suck the cow. Started when it was born and kept on lifting it over until it was half grown. In years gone by you developed them shoulder muscles when everything was carried.

Q: What were they doing with the mussel shells, making buttons?

A: They had a button factory at Madison and the biggest part of the shells, seem like from here to Madison was the best beds in the river. There were hundreds of people along there catching them shells. We'd do the trimming. We loaded our boat with them just as long as we could carry them going up.

Q: Did they go out in skiffs after those shells or was there any special way they caught them?

A: They have about 12 foot rods, took a pipe about 12 foot long and they would take this heavy galvanized wire and twist hooks. Every hook had four grabs, two on each side just like this, see. Four hooks to the grab. When they'd tie them on that rod with lines, there would be maybe a hundred or more of those hooks on one line. Then they had another line to that and they would put it down and drag it through the bed, you know. Every time one of those hooks went into a mussel shell, they are open down there in the mud you know, they're working on the shells open, one of those things goes in there, and the mussel shuts up on it. You come up and you had maybe a bushel or two of mussel shells hanging on that line. The current in the river and your boat pulled that there bar down on the mussel beds. Then when you got to the end of it you had to pull back up and start again.

Q: Well I guess all that went out when they got the river locked and dammed.

A: When they put this dam in down at Louisville why it just settled mud all over the beds and you couldn't get to the mussels. They were there, but they were covered up with mud, maybe four feet deep. No more mussels. No, that killed the mussel business.

Q: I don't suppose there were ever any pearl bearing mussels in there.

A: Once in a while they found a pearl but very seldom. Of course, when they caught them mussels they had to put them in a cooker and cook them to kill the mussel and get them open. They would break them open and get the insides out. Generally used the mussel part for fish bait. It was a big job to open them up and clean them after they catch them.

Q: I guess those cookers were regularly established ovens here on the bank sometimes.

A: Every fellow had a cooker of his own. He would just take a sheet of metal and throw over the bottom of the frame and put it in there. It was a great business here. There was a fellow by the name of McFarland, he came around from St. Louis and brought a boat and barges around here. He had a crew of maybe 25 or 30 men working for him. The river was real low at that time and up there at Hanover was a big bar on the Kentucky side. It would come out dry two-thirds of the way across the river, that throwed the channel on the Indiana side and all the water had to run through that channel. So the trend of the current was very light, and right through that channel he museled in there. There was a big mussel bed in there. He museled in there one whole summer. Took out barge loads, and took them around to St. Louis. They took out barge loads of

John Knoepfle

mussels right out of that chute, and it was so narrow that when a boat came down through there, why those musselers all had to get out of there, go to shore, you know. We'd go up there when we was on that run and maybe meet the big sidewheeler from Louisville coming down. We would have to lay to below until she got through because it was so narrow that two boats couldn't hardly pass. I recollect one time there was a towboat coming down through there and a bunch of them musselers, of course, was all in the channel and the fellow whistled for them to get out of the way and they all got out of the way, but one. He couldn't get his bars up or something and he jumped overboard and swam ashore and left his boat out there. The barges run right over it.

Q: A big coal barge, I guess.

A: Yes, big coal barge.

Q: Speaking of those coal barges, that was probably a Combine barge that came down. I have been trying to get any facts on that kind of shipping.

A: There was big Combines at Pittsburgh, but still individual concerns too, that owned boats. Where the coal came down the river at that time, they would load them barges up there and they had a place dredged out that they called a pit, and they would load them barges all through the dry weather, hundreds and hundreds of them. It would come a raise in the river, they would all come out at once. I saw times when you could count a dozen here one right after another. They'd get water enough and they would come out of that pit with a big tow, maybe with 16, 20 barges of coal, but you couldn't get out until it rained and raised the river. After they put the dam in then you could come out anytime.

Q: You don't remember anything in particular about those boats on this stretch of the river. It must of been hard to navigate a chute like that.

A: Well, the river at that time got very low, and you had to know the river the same as you would know the paths from your house to the barn, or your garden or anything you could travel in the night blindfolded you know. That's the way you got to really know the river. Because the channel run in certain places, first on one side of the river, and then on the other. If you got out of that channel with a boat of any size at all, why you'd go aground. Maybe run into a rock or something and it would sink your boat. This fellow one time was taking an examination for a pilot's license and he was asked if he knew where all the rocks and snags were in the river. Well he says, "I know where a few of them are that I've hit." You had to know the river then. Even with our boat, you had to know the river by heart, and know where every shallow place was and where the channel went, where a landing was that was deep enough for you to land, and some that you couldn't land, all those things, you know.

Q: How much water was the *New Hanover* drawing?

A: It didn't draw much water unless it was loaded. When it was loaded, around three foot.

Q: Some of those up riverboats didn't draw 12 inches.

A: I know there was some light, but some of these coal barges, they was as much as eight foot deep. They'd load them down to six or seven feet but if they didn't have water enough they couldn't load them that deep. Had to load them according to the water if you was going to bring them out.

Q: It just occurred to me, you say your boat was named the *New Hanover*.

A: *New Hanover*, the first boat was just *Hanover*.

Q: Was that a gasoline boat?

A: That was a gasoline boat, had the type of engine in it that goes chug, chug, chug. Four cycles and hit every other revolution. Big fly wheels on it. That was the old fashioned engine. The other diesel engine, that ran four cylinders.

Q: When were you running the old *Hanover*?

A: Well, it was an old boat when we bought her in the first place; it had been run for quite a while. We bought her and got so we had to have another boat, so we built another one. It got so the old boat they'd say here comes the old *Hanover*. It got to be a byword, here comes the old *Hanover*. So when they built the second boat to block that off, the old *Hanover*, you know I just named the other one the *New Hanover*.

Q: You must have gotten that older boat when you were first on the river.

A: Yes, in 1914 or 1915, that's when it was. Then they got the second boat and wore it out and then built the third one.

Q: Then you had three altogether.

A: Three boats yes. Had two boats, built two boats new.

Q: The old *Hanover* must have been a Kentucky riverboat or something like that.

A: Well it had run up the Kentucky River before we got it. It belonged to Turners. We bought it from Turners.

Q: How did you keep your records straight with all these individual loading trips you were making?

A: (chuckles) That puts me in mind of a fellow one time when we was going to Madison; we had made probably 40 landings between here and Madison. I was clerk and he had been a watching me work. Every time we landed you know, we would get from one to two or three, and maybe a coop of chickens, some bags of corn or something they wanted to ship. All little things. Everything had be billed out. They would tell me where they wanted it to go and I'd bill it up, so it be there when we'd get to Madison. All had to go on the billing, coops, chickens, it goes a certain place. That fellow he had been watching me, and finally he came around and said, "I don't see how in the world you keep track of all this stuff." I says, "A man can do that." He said, "No telling how much he is worth." I always kept track of everything, was all systematic forms. Same thing on the other end everything had to be billed out. We had an agent down there. He stayed there and took care of the office all the time.

Q: Your particular agent.

A: Yes, we had an office and a freight agent there.

Q: Did you say his name was . . .

A: Dave Jones. When we would get in there he would have the freight all lined out. Boat would schedule the levee, you know what day to bring it in there. He'd have the freight all received there just ready to load. We had a warehouse there. Anything come in, while we was gone would put it in the warehouse, we had to carry it down the hill. It was a right smart piece up the levee.

Q: Well I hear everybody gets heart attacks trying to climb that riverbank.

A: We had that. They always had plenty of roustabouts had to do that. They all done the work, you know. It cost $25 to $30 every time they loaded.

Q: Actually I suppose the wages of the stevedores and roustabouts weren't so much less than what a clerk would get. I have talked to other clerks it doesn't seem they were making a disproportionate amount of money more than the rousters were making.

A: Well we always paid them 40 cents an hour.

Q: The clerks!

A: The rousters. We paid them 40 cents an hour. They struck on me one time down there, 60 cents they wouldn't work unless they did get 60 cents. There was kind of a half-breed, anyhow he was a yellow rouster you know, he was part white. He was a head guy of the bunch. He said, "60 cents or no work." I says, "All right, come on 60 cents, but I want to tell you this is the last 60 cents you'll get." I says, "You needn't come down here anymore because I'll bring my help with me." The next trip down I took enough help to handle it myself. Told them after that if they wanted to work it would be 40 cents. If they didn't, why, just stay away. So, they come to it.

Q: Those were men who worked on the levee. They weren't regular boat men?

A: No, just the roustabouts that hung around there to do that work. They would unload the big boats, the Cincinnati packets. Up at the wharfboat, they'd hire them to do that.

Q: What else did you carry around here besides sunflower and mussels, was there any other particular thing?

A: Everything corn, everything imaginable, stock, horses, cows, sheep, all kind of stock, lots of it went to Louisville, just everything. I know one time, although we didn't run on Sunday, a fellow brought in 25 head of young mules and he was riding a gray horse and them mules was all following him. They wanted me to take them Westport down here about six or seven miles down the river on the Kentucky side. We had pens we run on the side of the stage, and run out on the shore, with wings on it. I thought well if them mules don't want to go on the boat I don't know how we will ever get them on. We got the pens all out and the fellow said, "You ready?" He was on that old gray mare, he just rode up stage you know, and every dern one of them mules followed him right on the boat, didn't have to bother.

Q: There was really a problem if the stock wouldn't get on the boat if you haven't got a steam capstan aboard.

A: Well talking about a capstan, on the last boat we had we had a capstan. Oh, I'm a little ahead of my story there. We had three gasoline boats, but when we sold the first boat we bought a steamboat. Her name was the *Alma*.

Q: How do you spell that?

A: A-L-M-A. That was her name. She was quite a good sized steamboat. We had a capstan on that and we went to load a cow one time. Got her up to the end of the stage and she just laid down. I tried every way to get her up and she wouldn't get up. Couldn't get her up on her feet. I told the fellows that was shipping her, I said, "We can put her on if you want me to put her on." I said, "We'll just put the capstan to her, drag her on." He said, "All right, drag her on." Just ran it out and put it around her head, and put it around her horns, and started the capstan, and she began to crawl up the stage plank on her side. There happened to be a nail up, up there, the head up a little. One of them in her side just split her hide about three foot long. But the old cow went on the boat.

Q: Guess the owner had a fit when he saw that?

A: No, he didn't care, he didn't care. I had to get his permission to do that. There was some very wild times on the boat trip. All them musselers, they would go up on Saturday, between here and Madison, they would go up on the boat Saturday. There would be 25 or 30 of them maybe. And back there would be half of them drunk. They would want to fight and everything else, you see. There wasn't nobody but me, rest of them didn't take any responsibility for it at all. I had to take care of it. I had to carry my gun. I got a permit to carry a gun to protect myself. At two different times a fellow cornered me with a knife, and he was within two steps of me. I couldn't get away. The guards were blocked with freight, and I was against the stanchion on the outside. He had that knife up there where my lips were and I had my gun in my pocket with my hand on it. I says, "If you come another step it will be the last step you will ever make." He took my word for it or I'd of had to shoot him if he didn't.

Another time there was one fellow, he got drunk on there, and it was a stormy night there. We didn't get out on time up there at Madison, had to stay till after dark and the river was so rough. We had a cabin full of women. The wind let up a little and we started out. He went in the engine room; the cabin of the boat was on deck. The door opened from the cabin into the engine room. He went in there and pulled the electric wires off the engine. Stopped the engine right out in that rough water. It wasn't out very far. The wind was kind of blowing a little bit onshore. I was out on the head looking after the boat, the women all come running out and said, this fellow was named Wayne Stewart, said he throwed a spittoon at a woman in there. I was pretty well worked up about him pulling the wires off the engine. I was running, and met him coming up to the cabin about half way, and I hit him just as I was running. I think I knocked him about 20 feet. I picked him up by one arm and a leg and butted his damn head again the wall. He was plum out. I drug him out on the guards

John Knoepfle

and left him and went back to get the boat tied up. When I got the engine started and went out to look for him, and he was gone. So he got off of there and left.

What I was going to tell you, this other time, probably a month or two after that why a fellow fell down there, he was drinking a little. He was dressed like a cowboy, he was about a six footer and he had a red handkerchief around his neck and a big cowboy hat on. I saw Wayne and him talking confidentially down in the guards and I suspicioned something. So there was a side door on the cabin and one in front. So Wayne Stewart come in the front door and this other fellow come in the side door and they was meeting there in the center of the cabin, but they hadn't got together yet. They come right up to our office, office was in front. I was in the office. They both had their knives out, cussing one another, they were going to fight right there in the cabin. Well, Wayne knowed I was coming after him first, so I just slid the gun up my sleeve, I had on a coat, and just slide the gun up the sleeve and held it in my hand. I walked up to him and I said, "Wayne, what in the world do you mean here?" He drawed that knife out stab fashion and hit me, wasn't over an arm's length from him and I just let the gun slip down my hand, stuck it right in his nose. I said, "You drop that knife and you drop it quick." Boy, he dropped it. I'd have shot the son of a bitch if he didn't. All them things on boats, have to fight them, and them all wonder I hadn't been killed.

Q: Was Wayne a local fellow?

A: Yes, he lived up here.

Q: He wasn't a musseler then?

A: No, he wasn't a musseler.

Q: I suppose the musselers must have been white laborers. They weren't colored?

A: Oh no, they were white people. But they would get drunk and there was always a percent of them that wanted to fight. If they would go on and tend to their business, I wouldn't bother them, you know, but they would get after me. It was like they would always get after me. I'd knock the son of a bitches in the head and everything else. I never did get hurt but it's a wonder I hadn't. There was a fellow one time on there shooting in the back of midship; it was on a steamboat. Shooting through the midship and it was pretty cold and all the passengers were in the cabin. I heard him shooting out there and I went out and talked to him. I said, "Buddy, you ought not to be shooting out here. You might shoot somebody." When he saw me coming he stuck the gun in his pocket. I walked right in front of him. You know they say when you get close to a mule he can't kick you so hard. I walked right up in front of him and was talking to him. After I'd told him he shouldn't be shooting there he tried to pull that gun out of his pocket, you know. I reached over with the left hand and catched his wrist and hit that son of a gun with everything I had. He couldn't fall down because I was holding him up. I pulled his hand out of his pocket a little bit and wrenched the gun out of his hand and stuck it up to his belly. I said, "I don't know whether your damned old gun will shoot or not, but I might try it on you if you try anything else." All these things . . .

Q: Made for a pretty interesting life I guess.

A: Well another instance I had, I was up at Turner's Landing, that is on the Indiana side. There was some people lived over across the river called Lewellen, called Lewella's boys. They pulled over there in a John boat and pulled right behind our wheel just about the time the pilot couldn't see him back there in the bulkhead. He pulled right behind there and the pilot was ringing the bells to back out. Well he saw the wheel was going to catch his boat and he run to the shore end of the boat and jumped out in the river. He was about ten or 12 years old and the boat went under the wheel. We had the boat swing away, our boat swung away from him, had the rudders out before starting down river. The boat swung way out there and he couldn't swim. He was just kind of treading water. He was just in the water there with just his mouth sticking above water. I was in the office, I heard the thing bump the wheel and the engine stopped and all. The passengers ran out on the guard. I went out to see what was the matter. As soon as I got out I saw that boy out there treading water. Well the crew on there, our boys had gone on the top of the boat. We had wooden life floats up there. They'd tried to throw a wooden life float to him, but he was too far away. I saw if something wasn't done the boy was going to drown. Wasn't any time to get a boat over or anything like that. I grabbed a life preserver, we had life preservers over the guard, we had a string of them on the boat. I grabbed it and run, never took my watch off, had my money and everything, my clothes on, just jumped in the river. Swam to that boy, picked up one of those life floats between me and the boy. They say you catch a fellow drowning in the river he drowns you if he grabs you. One of those life floats was right in my line, I just took it put the end out to him and he caught it and I towed him back to the boat. Another minute he'd have been drowned. There was I expect 40 passengers standing along there watching, looking at him. Nobody made a move to help him. They'd just stand there, let him drown. I don't know, I guess I was a kind of peculiar being, I don't know. Lots of people lose their head, you know, in case of a fire, or any danger or anything, they lose their heads. It never worked that way with me. The more danger there was the cooler I was.

We come in here one time from a Madison trip and we had more than we could carry. It was in wheat time, lots of wheat shipped here, to Madison Mills. We had a barge load and we thought after we come in, we thought we'd tow that wheat on, we thought we'd tow it up the river about ten mile and tie it up so we could keep from dragging it aground the next day landing with it. It was troublesome to land with a barge ahead of you and take on passengers. So we started up with it just about dark and the engineer figured we didn't have enough gasoline in the tanks. So he had a barrel of gasoline on there they pushed it up on the block with a faucet in it and up at the head of the cabin, that was where the tank was down in the hull, put the funnel in the tank and held that

John Knoepfle

barrel up and run gasoline in. Had a lantern, they set the lantern down below them, the head of the boat was up you know. When it was not loaded, the head of the boat's up, and the back was lower. So they set the lantern back of them on the lower part, a little ways from it, and they spilled gasoline and the gasoline run down on the lantern and took fire. Instead of shutting that faucet off on the hole in the barrel, he could have shut the faucet off and save the whole thing. He just jumped and let the barrel run over, just fed that gasoline down the guard and the boat burned up in 20 minutes, fed with a barrel of gasoline. We had that barge on there and there was two men on there that undone the barge and went off on the barge. That left the pilot, the engineer, and me on the boat. Well, I got the fire extinguisher and it would just cut a little black hole through the blaze. I couldn't do anything. I saw it was time to get off of there so I went up over the opposite side from where the fire was up on the roof, put a skiff overboard. I just threw it down, it went in the river end way, and filled it about half full of water cause when it come up, it come back to the boat. So I took the oars and went down and got in it. Didn't know where the rest of them were. Found the engineer standing on the back guard, just back of the wheel as far as he could get on the fantail. A row of life preservers right over his head, he never had a life preserver on, and he couldn't swim. I took him in. I didn't know where the pilot was; going around the wheel, damn if there was the pilot in the river holding the wheel without a life preserver on. The pilot had two life preservers right over his head in the cabin or in his pilot house. That just gives you a little example of how people acted. Them two that took the barge away, they never thought a thing about us, all they was thinking about was themselves. They took the barge away and let us go to the devil. They never thought about anything. I don't know what would have become of them if I hadn't of got the boat down and picked them up and took them to shore.

Q: According to that article about you, you are about 85 now. How are you spending your retirement, just puttering around up here?

A: Well, just a short time ago I passed the examination for a driver's license. I drive my own car. I have got a Chrysler with an automatic shift, fluid drive, and I go anyplace I want to go. But that's not very many places because I don't want to go very many places. I have my garden here, and have my chickens. I got my cats.

Q: Some of your chickens have gotten on the tape.

A: (chuckles) I have a whole lot of things to wear my time away. I work when I feel like it, and when I don't, I don't do it. I have plenty of money to take care of me the rest of my life. I have an income. I am a notary public, I do notary public work. I can do that, and I sell eggs. I take subscriptions for any magazine in the United States, any paper. All of them things pass the time away, try to keep busy. In addition to that, see those piles of books over there? And I read.

Q: Oh, you are a detective story fiend!

A: I read anything that can be read. I got the United States world news, in that magazine there. Those are all magazines.

Q: Oh yes, I see in here. Oh yes, the "U. S. News and World Report."

A: That's a wonderful book, it gives news from all over the world. Got everything, it's very educational to read that. I don't know what I'm storing them up for. My wife died about four years ago. That's her picture up there. We were both married at the same age when we were 20 years old and lived up to four years ago together, and raised five children. One of my daughters lives with me. Her husband died and she owned a farm out here on the . . . a 105, 106 acres. But she is selling it now. She is keeping house for me, she's here a part of the time.

Q: Well you made a nice tape I think, and I thank you for taking the time.

A: I have good health and there ain't a thing the matter with me in the world and I just ain't got no steam behind. I get out and work maybe for a half-hour or something and if it is anything strenuous at all, I, why I'm in, I'm all in. My heart gets to beating too fast, but I putter around and do this and that and the other, anything I want to do. It keeps me busy, you know. You just can't sit down and wear out. When you get old, you can't sit down or you will die a little bit. I'm always busy at something. I putter around in my flowers. I decorate the walks out there, and I did all that painting out there on the front, and built those little settees and one and another. I do all kinds of work. I did carpenter work in my earlier days, and I always thought if I hadn't of taken up the river business I would have been a cabinet maker. I always liked to do fine work. So last week, I have a grandson, just a little fellow about five years old, and he wanted a wheelbarrow. Wanted his daddy to make it and he said that he would make it, "When I get time." So I made a wheelbarrow, and I painted it all up dark mahogany and painted the bed pink, fixed it all up, and put a grin on the front of it, and put his name on both sides, and boy he was tickled to death. It was a real cute thing after I got it made and painted up. So I always figured I could make anything. I have done everything in the world. Right after we was married I bought a lot around here on the other side of town and I built me a house. I didn't have no money. I went out and cleared rock for the foundation and hauled them in and built the foundation. Went to the woods hewed out the sills with a broad axe. Hauled them down, they were 30 feet long. I built the house and made the frames, made my door and window frames, and built the house and plastered it with the old fashioned hair and mortar plaster. There was only one day, I hired two men to help set the frame up after I got it together. There wasn't a nail drove in the house, but what I drove it. I never did see anything that I couldn't do that anybody else could to.

Q: Well, we are just about finished on this tape.

A: Well I got so much stuff on there you won't know what to do with it.

Q: Yes I will.

Question: We are at the Greene Line Wharf. Would you begin by telling us something about yourselves?

Bee: This is Bee Hines, I put most of my time on steamboats. My age, 61 years old. Born 1895, in the state of Kentucky, Rochester, Kentucky, a small town. Not a railroad in the whole county. I left there on a steamboat, mostly on account there was nothing else there to do in the wintertime. I put most of my time on the farm in the summertime, wintertime mostly on the boats. I signed up Cincinnati, left near Beaver to do steamboat work. I fired and roustabout, then deckhand so far. Then the other things, I helped the man around engine room, cleaned up the engine and things like that. That's all.

Leslie: My name is Leslie Souther, I was born on the 29th day of March, in 1885, 72 years old. A greater portion of my life, in my early life I farmed. When I got to be a man, able to do most any kind of work, I taken up steamboating. Frankly, I've done more steamboating than anything else the rest of my life. I worked on boats, years ago when all the work was mostly done by hand and by men, no trucks, no dollies, no conveyances. Drays, wagons, and conveyances like that, haul to and from wharfs and boats where the landings were. All freight was handled by hand. We carried freight on shoulders, we carried freight in hands, we rolled barrels, we carried boxes, things like that. There was no trucks and it was very hard work. But we did that at that time with a perfect will in mind because we knew nothing of the time that would change to the day.

Q: Supposing we talk first about how the heavy loads were carried into the boats. Can you do that?

L: How the loads were carried into the boats. Sometimes we would have two men, sometimes three men and four carrying a heavy box and things like that. There would be a man on each corner, two men in front to turn the back, catch on each corner with the hands, two men on the back corner would catch it with their hands and face towards them, two men walking in front going towards the boat or off the boat with a load, with two men behind walking behind them. They'd carry freight like that. When the barrels were heavy, one man on each side at each end of the barrel would roll, we would roll at a very good speed if it's very heavy; and a small barrel, there would just be one man in the middle would roll that. When they had such things as sacks, that didn't weigh over 125 or 100 pounds, carried that on our shoulders. Boxes, likewise, smaller boxes we'd carry one under each arm. Bags we'd carry on our shoulders. If we had something like bundles, things like that we'd carry on our shoulders. If it was heavy likewise we'd carry it under each arm, one under each arm.

Q: That must have been exhausting work.

B: Yes, it sure was.

L: Sleeping and things like that we wouldn't want to talk about I guess?

Q: Sure talk about anything you can remember.

L: Well at that time you had no beds. We'd sleep on freight piles, such as that. Slept underneath the boilers in cold weather, on the guards of the boat and the head of the boat in the hot weather, but we had no beds to sleep in. Mostly slept on top of freight, the best that we could, the best we could make out, make a conveyance for ourselves. And any time that the boat landed they called all hands, day or night, and we went to work; as long as the freight lasted, why we worked. We have worked as high as ten or 12 hours at one landing, and sometimes longer. We'd only have time to stop and eat and no rest periods, eat, and then we would be back busy working again until the cargo was loaded off or on the boat.

Q: When you said you slept on the freight, I suppose after you loaded hay, it was a little easier sleeping. (laughter)

L: Bags beat hay. Hay was in bales you know, and such things as bags of wheat, corn and things like that.

B: Fertilize.

L: Fertilize, sleep better on that than you could on a bale of straw or hay. Could sleep on the bags because they would give to your weight and make a better bed for you.

Q: Did either of you ever load hay on the boats?

B: Sure.

L: Yes sir, we have done all the way from 50 to 1,000 bales of hay on board. Tobacco, we did 50 to 100, from 50 to 100 hogsheads of tobacco. That's a cask of tobacco, you know, that's you call a hogshead. Weighed anywhere from a 800 to a 1,000 or 1,200. You rolled them on the boat, rolled them off, roll them on the boat at the loading point, roll them off at the destination where they went.

Q: Did you load the hay Bee, and could you describe that?

B: Sure, they'd put hay on our shoulder.

Q: Other men put it on your shoulder.

B: And they would take it off.

Q: You didn't lift though or put it down?

B: No two men would lift it up on your shoulder. All you had to do is take it to the boat and two fellows would take it off and set it down.

Q: How heavy was a bale of hay?

B: Oh, sometimes in late years 1925-1926, some of the bales, the hay they was making then was awful heavy and most all alfalfa. But the other hay was kind of light, about 110 pounds, 120. This alfalfa hay weighed about 140 to 150.

Q: I see, and a day of that would just about break your back.

B: You see, I weighed more than that. (chuckles) I supposed to carry as much as I weighed. I weighed 165 pounds and I carried about 165 pounds. (laughter)

Q: Leslie, someone told me that the *City of Louisville* loaded sunflower seeds, down below Madison. Do you remember anything like that, either of you?

B: No, I don't.

John Knoepfle

L: Sunflower seeds let's see. Not only just in bags, we had sunflower seed in bags just like you would load corn and any other grain. The sunflower was not as large as bags. But the sunflower seed would be in a smaller bag, say 25 or 50 pounds. Other grain would be probably a couple of bushels, 50 or 60 sixty pounds, corn and wheat. But sunflower bags wasn't in as large a bag as other grain that we had on. Sunflower seed would be in small bags because they'd go to so many different places. Wouldn't be like corn going on at one landing going off at another, sunflower seed would go to different points up and down the river. Some to one place, some to another. Corn and wheat, generally those went off in larger amounts but anything like sunflower seed, and stuff like that, that was supposed to be a more valuable kind of grain you see, it would be just be probably a small sack going to one place, then maybe one to another.

Q: I wonder if you could talk about, I know up north now that was all cut nails and stoves and wire, could either of you talk about that?

L: Sure, I lifted Pittsburgh Street freight here to Pittsburgh. We used to come by landings. There was Rochester, and now Rochester's in Pennsylvania. In Pennsylvania we used to get a lot of heavy stuff there, such as plumbing stuff, water sinks, basins, things like that, toilets. We'd get a lot of heavy stuff like that, you know. Then we'd get iron. We'd get iron in Ironton, Ohio, such things as nails. And also at Point of View, at Point Pleasant, West Virginia, at Point Pleasant there was a wharfboat. Point Pleasant, West Virginia, we'd load kegs and spikes, nails, shovels, picks and things like that, we'd bring down the river then. We'd load that on at that place. That came directly to Cincinnati. In Ironton, Ohio, we got nails, cold iron, chains and such as that. We'd load it on there and that came directly to Cincinnati.

Q: Was that the wire?

L: Wire, we got wire at Ironton, Ohio, we got a lot of wire, and also stoves. We loaded a great many stoves. That was almost each trip. That was two trips a week. Sometimes we would get as high as 100 and sometimes 150 stoves at one time, which was very heavy cargo. And if we was loading, unhandy of wheels loading them, why we'd have to carry them. We couldn't roll them, had no way to truck them, had to carry them on our shoulders.

Q: Was that a stove?

L: Yes, stove and sometimes heavy stove, why we would do one in front and one behind to carry a stove.

B: Had large and small, two-capped stove and four, the four-capped was more stable.

L: Some loaded upright stoves and some of those large . . .

Q: Put two men on a four-capped stove?

B: Sometimes three.

L: One on each corner and one in front.

Q: I remember when I first talked to you Leslie, you said sometimes the men would be so exhausted that they would fall asleep in the lines.

L: I've seen them do that.

Q: Could you talk about that?

L: In places like Grandview, Indiana at the Cadick Milling Company that was when we was working in the trade from Louisville to Evansville. They would stop at Grandview, Indiana. There was a large mill there that they called Cadick Milling Company. We'd pick up wheat from most any way landings and unload it at Grandview. I've seen men walk in line at Grandview, shipping out flour, going to different places. We'd load flour, sometimes 500 barrels, and 1,000's of sacks, and also 1,000's sacks of feed. I've seen men work in line one behind another, if you stopped them from anything, fix your dunnage so he could take it down and store it away correctly like it should be. When you got ready to take it down off a man some of them would be asleep standing in line. Yes, I've seen that. They'd have to be waked up before they could walk up to you, so you could take the load off his shoulder.

Q: Did the loads ever carry them over into the river or anything?

L: No. (laughter) Always stop them on the head of the boat.

Q: I think you mentioned some of the men died from that work.

L: Oh yes, a man fell dead at South Carrollton, Kentucky in line working. He had a heart attack, fell with a load on his shoulders. I taken care of him, he died. Worked out! He suppose had heart failure, they didn't call it that at that time. He was overworked, fell out. On the boats running from Paducah to Florence, Alabama we used to load up Tennessee River. We'd be down the river, most always coming from Florence to Paducah with a load of lumber. We'd stop at landings, at Rich Landing, Mouse Tail, Rat Tail. They had a chute built on a hill and it extended from the hill to the front part of the boat, what we call on the head of boat was on the front part. Come down the chute and we'd catch it at the end of the chute and raise it on a man's shoulder, carry it into the boat and they would store it back of the boat. Before they started stowing on the deck of the boat they would open up what called the hatch, back in the midship and also on the head. Two men would take it off the man's shoulder back at the hatch and lower it down in the hatch, shove it down, and there would be men down in the hull of the boat would catch it down there, and load it down in the hull of the boat. Took care of it down there, and after we got it loaded as much as we could stand to load in the hull of the boat, we would start to storing it on deck. Close the hatches, we'd start storing on deck. And we've carried lumber for a night and a day, on boats carrying solid lumber, nothing but lumber.

Q: All railroad ties up in there I guess.

B: And we loaded some of them too, up in there.

L: That was on towboats. Carried on a towboat. We'd go up and make a tow, take a boat and leave away from Paducah with 25 or 30 men, seven eight nine, six, ten barges at a time, going up the river and they would go up the river as far as Florence, Alabama and load coming back down. We'd load the barge, leave some at one landing, some at another: Pittsburg Landing, Rich Landing,

John Knoepfle

Goose Pond, Saltillo, Cerro Gordo, other landings, Waterloo, Riverton, places like that. We'd stop and unload a barge, sometimes two barges at one landing. Then we would tie up the barges and we'd move down to another landing and we load like that until we'd load as much as from six to ten barges of cross ties. After we would get them all loaded, why then we would tie them together. A boat would hook up to them and we'd be headed for Paducah then.

Q: How much did you get paid for that labor?

L: Two and a half cents a tie.

Q: Was that what that was?

B: A lot of those southern boats paid that way, a penny a bag or two and a half cents a tie.

L: That's right. We carried corn for penny a bag up the Wabash River. We'd carry that on towboats. Take a large barge and go the river, 15 or 20 men, why they paid a penny a bag for carrying it from on the bank in on the barge. Men raised it on the bank, and then take it down and store it on the barge until you would get the barge loaded. Then you would have another barge, you'd load that. You'd load sometimes as high as four barges. Shell corn in sacks, they paid a penny a bag bringing it on. And then when we landed at Henderson, Kentucky the other men had a wharfboat there, that's where we would carry it. And when they tied it up there, why they had other men that worked there, that lived there who'd take it off the barges at the same price. They'd take it off and stow it in cars so they could take it in to the railroad.

Q: I guess you could make more a penny a bag than you could paid by the day.

L: Oh you could make more at a penny a bag, at that time they didn't pay very much; about $1 a day or $1.50 a day was about all you could get working on different boats. In later years they started paying $2, $3, that was the best price. Rush season, apples, wheat, corn, things like that, sometimes they'd get a raise to about $4.50 a day. They always called it by the month $3, was $90, $135, $120 or $2, $3 a day. While the $4.50 got $135 and all day in town. Sometimes they'd strike on the boat and want more money and they asked them say, "Well we want so much and so much, and all day in town." All day in town, that's when we'd catch the boat that evening leaving port. You'd get paid for that day when you'd leave that afternoon. Probably won't go to work until the next morning, but you get paid for that day when you're leaving town. That was what they called, "All day in town." (chuckles) We wanted $135 and all day in town. That means you'd have a day coming when you shipped out on a boat.

Q: I wonder now if we could distinguish between the functions of the various men who worked in deck gangs, there are deckhands, stevedores and linemen.

L: Lineman, their job was when the boat landed was to catch the lines. If they landed at a bank landing they'd go to a tree and make the lines fast around a tree that would hold a boat into the landing. When the boat swing into the landing they got a line fastened to the tree that would hold the boat so that the boat wouldn't drift away. They'd stop the engine and stop the wheel and the boat would lay dead still almost until you had made your landing and got what you was getting. The lineman would make the lines fast, and then they would either raise up the freight that you was going to pick up or they would take the freight down that you was bringing off the boat. The lineman, that was their job, take down the freight that comes off, raise up and put the freight on your shoulders that goes in. That was what they called a lineman. The deckhand, he stands at the head of the boat tells you, which way to go with a load so you won't get too much on one side, "Cross over. Go down one side. Cross over to the other side." The stevedores was inside men that stored the cargo that you brought in from the banks or wharfboat where you was going. That's the stevedores that takes it down and puts it away properly like it should be placed.

Q: Now who carried it?

L: Roustabouts was the one that carried it.

Q: I guess it was the linemen who got wet when the boat pulled out, they were the ones who got dragged by the lines.

B: Oh no, no. Sometimes he would miss the stage and jump in the water, maybe he was only drunk. (chuckles) He had to catch the stage, size it up see. We got to jump on it. Well, the stage would be down in the water, boat backing out, wind blowing, see. That's why he'd get wet maybe. Make a landing. Sometimes the winds off the shore, winds blowing the smoke clean out the river and he have to jump in the water. He don't get out there, with his line have to get out there with the line, make it around a tree, and get a capstan there would pull in it. The furthest man juggled the line, I never juggled the line up. I've jumped in water and waded up to my knees.

Q: You were always fast enough to get on.

B: Let go of the line, sometimes you had to chop it with an axe. Why I would have the axe out there and go to throw the axe on the stage, jump on the stage, the wind was blowing out off shore. That's the only thing you could do. Couldn't wait out there until they come back and get you. May not come back not this week, maybe next week.

L: Sometimes at landing, and storm, the wind would be high, you couldn't get the boat in properly sometimes to the bank like it should be for a man to get off the stage. Then it would be necessary for them when they got close enough that they'd jump in water with their line, they'd take the line and jump in the water knee deep, or less than that, and run till he could get to a tree you see, and make the line fast, so the boat could slide back then, and hold the boat in to the shore. Sometimes they'd have to jump in water because the boat couldn't get close enough for you to let the stage down beyond the water. Therefore you'd have to jump in the shallow water with the line, and run out on shore and tie your line on a tree. Got to swing in and lower the stage down over above the water.

Q: We discussed too, using the lead lines.

B: That's on account of shallow water. If you are going down on a heavy loaded boat, like down here below Fernbank, a place down there you come to one in

John Knoepfle

to a bar, can't none go past that and that water so shallow you've got to have something to tell the pilot how deep the water was. You drop that lead line down, tell you how deep it is. About five foot there. Years ago they could get over the sandbar down there, and again they couldn't. At Rising Sun we were going down and didn't have nothing on the boat but people, got stuck on that sand there. Sometimes you miss the channel. If the channel comes this way, comes right this way and cuts and moves back out again, you're liable to miss it. You're left hard aground. Soon as you get hard aground, you got first to dam up here 36 or 37, in order to let the water down to pull it off, just come on back off, and then come forward. The sands ain't no gravel there they'd stick, the water run so fast through there, water.

L: Tell something about how to handle the lead-lines see, the man who's running that job kind of a line.

B: Oh the lead line see, a man stood on the head of the boat. He'd drop that, take that line and throw it down. He knew how far it was to get the rope down to the boat and how far the boat was above the water. He'd have to guess, he'd have to tell the man how deep that is. If the line goes down ten foot, he'd have five foot of water beneath there. Sometimes the head of the boat would stand about five foot above the water, sometimes three foot, six foot, seven foot. You have good water, you come ahead. If it hits down there, not hit no bottom, you had good water again. Until you hit that, most of the line in your hand, you're high above it, the boat shallow water there. You have to stop from coming ahead, again we stopped from coming ahead, went hard aground anyhow. We was going down some place like that, you'd always cut them down, try to drift through, some people just all good water down there, come ahead, come ahead half head, stick a boat there for four or five hours. We was going on the *Cincinnati* one time, down here below Vevay. We was down there like six hours. Nothing on the boat but people. Had something to eat on there, and was nothing to do. Just had to wait for the water come back. We had a good time. We had to go, and go to sleep there. It was the only thing you could do.

Q: I understand they sang out the marks?

L: If they got to shallow water, the man who dropped the lead lines, he'd holler, pass the word back to the man standing on the roof to pass the word back to the pilot. He'd holler, "Three feet!" He'd pass the word to the pilot, "Three feet! Four feet!" He'd pass the word, "Four feet!" But if it drops down, say, to six foot, he'd say, "Mark Twain!" He'd say, "Mark Twain! Twain and a half! Twain and a half! Twain and a half! No bottom! All right, come ahead and take your lines up!" You'd wind your line up. As long as, up to six foot, you would call the number of feet that the water is "Three feet! Four feet! Five feet! Six feet!" He'd have to slow down, but when you sounded down and she's over that it's around eight or ten feet you holler, "No bottom!" Then he'd reel up the line, and then the man come ahead and to run the boat because the water was deep enough for him to come on over.

Q: Well the roustabouts, it was his job to entertain the passengers wasn't it?

L: Well they did that on the boats when they'd have a lots of passengers, they'd do that. The passengers would want to see the boys dance and hear them sing like that. Well we had some pretty good singers on board, and get out on the head of the boat. People throw down money. They got a big kick out of seeing the roustabouts dance and scramble over the money, dance and sing, then they'd throw money down and everybody would be trying to get it. This fellow would be on top of the others. They'd be scrambling, that's what you call a scramble. They'd get a kick out of seeing that done, sing and entertain the passengers on the boat, then you'd have a money scramble.

B: They'd get a kick out of something else, take a dishpan, put about that much water in it. If you got good enough to put your mouth down there and not get any water in your eyes, you got a quarter or a half dollar in there. You'd get it.

Q: You ducked for the money in the dishpan!

B: You don't have to . . .

L: Watermelon eating. Slice up the watermelon on the head of the boat.

B: See who eat it the quickest.

L: The one that eat the quickest, why he's the one that got the prize. They had enjoyment, entertainment like that.

Q: Get a stomach ache too, I suppose.

L: We had some men on a boat that could eat a slice of watermelon just zip, do that as though it was nothing. (laughter) Yes, we had all that fun, enjoyment. They'd get a kick out of it, passengers would get a kick out of a great many things.

Q: I understand gambling was almost a sacred pastime.

L: Whenever they would get through working, sometimes they'd not go to sleep, they'd just start a game and have gambling going on. Some few would be sleeping the rest of them be gambling. Most all the time there would be some kind of a game going on.

Q: One man told me that on one trip the passengers backed various of the rousters who were gambling, all the way up the river.

L: Oh, they'd do that a great many times. They did that on excursion boats. Give you money to gamble or gamble in a game with you. Passengers would get in the game, a game on deck of the boat. Passengers come down and gambled in the game and if you got broke, why they'd give you money. They'd furnish the fellows money to gamble with just to see them gamble to them shoot craps, and shoot craps with them. Passengers would get in the games with them. They all had a joyous time shooting craps together. Well there was some good times on a boat, but mostly it was tough.

B: At that time it was.

L: Very tough. Summer seasons when they had pretty weather like it is now had a lot of fun on the boat. When it hit that freight pile, that's where bad luck come in. (laughter) Landed, you'd have to get probably, why we landed down

John Knoepfle

at Islands Landing below Louisville with Allen, Captain Bo Allen that used to work here. We landed down at Islands Landing, and a man hollered, waving his lantern, says, "What have you got? We've got few apples." Captain says, "How many you got?" Says, "We got 1,700 sacks, and 500 barrels." (laughter) That was a few, he got a few apples.

B: On the *Tell City* going to Nashville. "Hey, Cap, you got any corn with you?" "About how many bags?" He said, "Help yourself." (laughter)

L: Land in there and load till we got it all in.

B: He said, "Help yourself."

L: He says, "Help yourself, Captain."

Q: Before you go on to something else, I know because a number of men have told me that certain of the mates were cruel. That they carried these ox whips and leaded chains. Would you care to talk about that at all?

B: It would look a little embarrassing to his people.

Q: You don't have to mention the names.

B: Mention the names. Was mates on the boats that carried sticks. Every landing when he came on watch he had a stick. A man got slow in line and tired, he would punch him up with that stick, and if he didn't do no better than that he would strike him sometimes. Strike him on the ribs, ribs with the stick. Punch him up with that stick, got to keep up, keep step, keep up with the gang. If a man would kind of get mad or something because he do that, he couldn't keep up, a man sometime would be so tired he couldn't keep up, give out, why they would strike them with a stick. I've seen that done. I've seen men, fellows get unruly. I've seen the mate take sticks and whip them for that. Had no chance to strike back because deckhands, you would have the mate and the deckhands too to fight, couldn't win. Beat up fellows a lot of times. That was done years ago, and there was lots of men got beat up on the boats. Severe whipping, for being unruly, something like that. Yes. I've seen them. Most anything, going on in the crap games. Sometimes they'd have fights in crap games. Sometimes there was feeding time, what you call grub piles, when they'd feed they'd call that grub pile. They bring down food in pails like dishpans and cartons and things like that. When they'd start to dishing up the same amount to each and every one, sometimes the men would get to fight with the grub pile. Someone would say he didn't have as much on his pan as the other one. Get into an argument that would cause a fight.

Q: I've heard sometimes the captains of the watch were meaner than the mates.

L: That has happened sometimes a captain of the watch when he would go to wake you up, after working maybe eight or ten hours, steady work, hard work, lay down and go to sleep and at the next landing, the men would be sleeping, hard to wake up. They would get sticks and wake you up with a stick. They done that. Deckhands and the captain of the watch would do that. When he called you, some of them would only call you once and if you didn't move he'd hit you. Wake you up rough. But in late years they broke that all up, you know.

Before we quit steamboating they broke that custom. Men would ride boats that had any fighting on them ride them, they had to put him off on account of that. When I was riding boat from, all away from the time we left town almost till we got back there'd be somebody that would have a fight. The mates would be whipping somebody, or deckhands or somebody like that, tough on boats at that time. It was say, 45 or 50 years ago there was some awful tough men.

B: Sure was.

L: Mates, deckhands and captain of watches and some of the roustabouts just as bad. Linemen were bad. Come out and the linemen would be raising the load on you. If you didn't get up just exactly so that they could lay it on you like they wanted too, they would fight you. Didn't get off where they could take the load off just like they wanted to they would fight. Had all of that back in them years. As times grew more and better condition why they slowed down that. Some of the people got in trouble about things like that. Man would get lost on the boat, why that caused the company a lot of trouble. There was one man you see on the river now today. He's on the *Delta Queen* wouldn't ship a drunk man. If a man was drunk he wouldn't ship him.

B: Sure wouldn't.

L: Tell you too, you get on this boat and you fall overboard, tie the boat up, lawsuits and things like that will happen. Leave you in town, that won't happen. Can't get on when you're drunk. Wouldn't ship a man out of town drunk. That was Captain Doc Carr, he's on the *Delta Queen*. Wouldn't ship you drunk. If you got drunk he wouldn't ship you. Leave you in town.

B: Pick you up next trip.

L: Pick you up next trip. He wouldn't take a chance on letting you get drowned. Some of the others didn't care, they'd tell a man that was a good hard worker, everything like that, some of the mates would give you a break. Go ahead on aft and go to sleep. When they say go aft, that means, go to the back part of the boat, go lay down and go to sleep. When you wake up you'd be sober, and then you can go ahead and work. Some of them would take that kind of chance. Well, they didn't so often much as lose a man from being drunk because the men would go back and go to sleep. The men that didn't do that, sometimes a man would get lost.

Q: I understand. Captain Jesse Hughes told me this that when the boats would land and they needed men, the mate or the clerk will come out with tickets and they hired by tickets, is that right?

B: Yes, that's right.

L: Now if you need extra help, like you're leaving from here, if you're going to say, going to Pittsburgh. We'd get up here in Ironton, there's lots of men around there that want to work and you're short of help, well you hand out tickets, at a certain time you see. Punch your ticket at a certain hour, start to work, well whatever they're paying, 50 cent an hour, $1 an hour whatever they're paying. And they got the cargo all on, then they'd punch the ticket and

John Knoepfle

send you up the office to the clerk or else go up with you to the office, go up to the clerk, would pay you whatever you had coming. They used labor that way. The boat come in port. The roustabouts was working, go up the hill, and crew off the boat would be paid off coming into town or get paid off as soon as the boat lands. They put on what you called laborers. Men in town that used to work right here all the time on all the boats didn't depend on anything, but the labor on the boats when they come in port. The men on the boats when they get paid off they'd go on up the hill until the boat gets loaded and gets ready to leave. Then they put on laborers, they give them, all men, labor tickets. Line up and a man would hand out tickets down the line until he got as many he wanted, and then they would start to work. They had men to take care of the freight just like the men on the boat, but the deckhands and captain of the watch, they stayed with the boat to tell you where the freight was and where to put the freight, on the head of the boat. They had stevedores, they had had stevedores here on a wharf boat in Louisville, Kentucky, at Pittsburgh, Evansville and other places, unloading and loading the boat just like the men did, the crewmen did that was on the boat. Laborers that take charge of the boat knew all about it, just as much the men who rode the boat about how to take the freight.

B: Oh yes.

L: Some of them knew better some of them was old retired.

Q: I understand that a rouster could, if he had a mind to, he could find ways of we call it goofing off, hide in the toilet or someplace like that.

B: Oh yes, that's just how that would be.

L: Up on the roof and get in the yawl. The yawls on the boat are covered. Raise that covering on the yawl, get inside the yawl, go to sleep. Some of them would have different places. Some of them would go down in the hold, go back in the excelsior pile, got excelsior on the boat to cork the boat in case it springs a leak, pull that out and get in behind there. I goofed on board once and didn't intend to. Had a cargo of coffins on the boat. I got in a coffin, got in the empty coffin, laid down and went to sleep and when I woke up I had slept so long they thought I had got off the boat at the other landing. When I woke up and raised up, the roustabouts all were scared of me. Man, why it took a long time, we was, something like about 45 minutes getting them reconciled. (chuckles)

Q: Did they think you were a haunt?

L: They run, and I say, "Why? What are you running from me for, don't you know who I am?" They say, "Les?" "Yes, this is me, I was asleep in that coffin." They say, "Ahh!" (laughter) Well the mate he come down. I said to the mate, "What is the matter with these fellows?" He says, "Huh." He come excited. "Huh?" I said, "You know who I am. I just got in the coffin and went to sleep and overslept." "Well they told me you got off on the landing." I said, "No, this is me." And he looked, "Yes." He was kind of scared himself. He went up on the head of the boat. He said, "Boys, that's Les. What are you all running, what are you ascared of him for? He just went to sleep in that coffin." Some of them,

"Huh?" I said, "Yes." They said, "Aw, man." Yes, I goofed off on that time. I never did do that no more. I was slumbering on board.

B: I did on the *Indiana* one time, I was on up on the roof, the smoke stack, they looked for from about one o'clock that night until half past six the next morning, I lay sound asleep on the smoke stack. They had a place underneath the pilot house where they kept the ropes and things like that, some old pieces of life preservers and things like that. They'd discard them and threw them underneath the pilot house. I went under there. They didn't know I was under there. Nobody knew I was there. I slept, well they had made several landings. I woke up and come down. They'd say, "Where have you been?" "I was asleep." They looked for me and didn't find me. I was right on there with the gang working. No docking you, and nothing like that. Oh sometimes a man would get unruly on board, they'd put you off at a landing.

Q: You getting out of a coffin reminded me, I read that some of the boats were thought to be haunted, like I think the *Speed* had a bad reputation, the rousters didn't like to work on her. Could you comment on that?

L: Yes, I think they got that reputation, I think from Haunted Hollow they called it. You've read about Haunted Hollow?

Q: No I didn't.

L: Oh below Louisville.

B: That Evansville.

L: Evansville that's right. A landing, they called that the Haunted Hollow.

B: That's what it was. Somebody said a man . . .

L: On the *John K. Speed*

B: Waved lantern landing out there, so the boat went into the bank. I don't know. I wasn't there. I don't think I was on the boat that trip. Said the man had a white horse and rode up on the stage and on back, on back to the deck room. Said a man goes back there to tie the horse up. The man got off and back there ain't no horse. That kind of upset him a little bit.

L: I've been hearing that for the last 45 years.

B: I wasn't on the boat.

L: I wasn't either.

B: Spect I'd got off.

Q: A man came on and disappeared!

L: A man came on, on a horse.

B: The horse got in on the stage back in the back of the boat, you go back there tying the horse up see what man went there don't find no man, neither, no horse.

Q: A man came on and disappeared. And that started them on the *Speed*.

L: That started saying it was haunted, that was the haunted . . .

B: Haunted Hollow down there, which I know there was boats that stopped there a lot of times, we didn't nothing. And I hear the captain up there and he was hollering, "Where you at?" Nobody answers.

L: Or you see a light sometimes.

John Knoepfle

B: A light come on, seems to glow for a landing whistle. And you go in there, see what the man had. Don't see nobody or hear nobody. Back it on out.

L: Nobody there. Boat just back out, go ahead. They call it Haunted Hollow. They give it that name Haunted Hollow.

B: Tough one, too.

Q: A hard landing to make in there.

B: No, ain't so hard landing to make, but you go into a place like Newport. Somebody in this house over yonder. You go in there. You see somebody's head over there and can't find nobody, you get moving you self.

Q: I imagine I would, dark night.

L: You remember seeing this before you got there, but then when you got there you don't see nobody.

Q: I heard on the *Speed* that they were so frightened that a small boy got ahold of a rooster's tail feathers, he was waving it around and they thought that was bad sign and when the boat landed, I don't know whether it was near Louisville or not, but he grabbed this tail feather and he chased all the roustabouts off the boat and it took them about a week and a half to get another crew. (laughter)

L: I never rode on the *John K. Speed*.

B: Me neither.

L: Well, I could have rode on it but at that time I was on other boats, you know. *John K. Speed*, I think she runs from here all the way down. And at that time I was running on boats up Green River, and places like that. I was at Nashville, Tennessee River, Cumberland River, and Green River.

Q: What did they pull out of the Green River, Leslie?

L: All kinds of stuff, almost anything a man could imagine. Now they carried, after you would leave Evansville, the boat would load a cargo at Evansville of groceries, feed, and machinery and such equipment for farmers, like barbwire and fencing equipment. Carry a load out, unload that going up, coming back down they'd get cedar posts, they'd get cross-ties, they'd get lumber, hickory wood that was cut for timber, short wood that was cut for automobile spokes. And they would get corn, they'd get wheat, they'd get tobacco on wagons and roll the wagon aboard the boat, they'd get hogs. They'd have what you would call a stock trip. The first trip you carried cargo up and back you loaded up with materials such as wood, lumber, anything that you get that the man would have on the landing. The next trip was stock trip, principally for stock. Now they'd drive stock in on the boat, they'd put up a gate in front. Down the guard, they'd put up a gate in front of them. They'd put cross pieces across from another deck, up on top, over the hogs. They'd put up the gangplank and they run sheep up over top of them. They'd take them down and run another drive in with a gate in front of them, then they would put up a platform again, run them up over the top of them. Cattle, hogs, sheep and all that kind of stuff. Doubledeck.

B: What trip was that they had that, the Evansville, Green River, upstairs up on the boiler deck?

L: Oh we had chickens, eggs, calves, such as that we had up on boiler deck. That's the boiler deck where the passengers and people, they would have them tied all up and down the guard. And chickens, had them stacked all along the roof, up around where the pilot house was, all like that. Coops of chickens. And near Thanksgiving and Christmastime, they would carry turkeys all night long, stacking them on the roof. Then when you get in, then get your money before we got to town. Paid off 20 miles from town there. Paid the crew off, and got to town, tie the boat up, and then the laborers would take it. The laborers sometime would be way in the afternoon before they'd get the boat unloaded. Then they would start to loading up again with a cargo to go back up the river. Then the summer season we going up the Green River, they'd make one trip to Bowling Green with freight, and the next trip we'd go to Mammoth Cave. Then they would carry excursion, see to the Mammoth Cave. They'd go to Mammoth Cave one trip, Bowling Green one trip, the next trip to the Mammoth Cave.

Q: Those were those little packets out of Madison, weren't they?

L: No, packets out of Evansville.

Q: Evansville.

L: Evansville to Bowling Green.

Q: Do you remember the names of those boats?

B: Yes. One was named the *Evansville* and the other was named the *Bowling Green*. Then they had another boat named the *Hazel Rice*, and they had a boat that run out of Bowling Green to the Mammoth Cave, that was the *Chaperon*, same name as on this boat out here. The *Chaperon*, that was a packetboat, an old sternwheel boat *Chaperon*.

Q: Did they ever run the little boat the *Hanover* down there that you know of?

B: Oh, the *Hanover* run on the Kentucky River down there. Usually out of Louisville, up in the Kentucky River.

L: *Hanover*, hauled from Louisville up to Hanover landing. There's a landing down there they call Hanover, between here and Louisville, Hanover landing.

Q: Oh yes, by down in near Bethlehem, Indiana.

B: That's right, just about.

L: Hanover landing, yes we knew that, and then we had a boat run on Kentucky River then called *Corker*. Oh they had a bunch of them small boats.

B: That was a pretty good sized little boat.

L: It would be a steam boat, gasoline boat, she come to Louisville one Monday morning around about 8:30 or 9:00 o'clock, 600 some odd bales of hay on her. She'd didn't have but three men on it. The engineer was the pilot, and the pilot was the engineer. And two more fellows, one cook. Come with that much hay on her I says, "You've been loading all week, ain't you?"

B: We used to land down in the Louisville trade, the biggest landing we had for hay was Buckeye, that's down river here 20 years ago. Buckeye landing, we'd stop there and get that 1,000 bales sometimes, hay all across the head, hay in the deckroom, hay in the midship, nothing but bales of hay.

Q: Boy, that would have made a fire, wouldn't it?

B: Oh gee I should say it would. If it would have caught on fire there wouldn't have been no way to save the boat. That was before they built the sprinkler on the boats, you know. Late years they had pipe running all over the boat, you know, front and aft part, clear up to the front and all the way to the back, and they'd turn that water on and it just spray all over. Course it would be hard to burn up a boat now like they have them fixed with those sprays. Back in those days there was no such thing as that. Nobody never had a problem with those things. If a boat caught on fire, it was just a fire, you had to put it out with buckets. They had hose, as far as that goes, probably hose on there, but you couldn't, load of hay would have just been a fire.

Q: You mentioned loading sheep before and I've read that a lot of these boats had a goat, a ram on board.

B: You'd have to be there. The rams, catch a ram sheep in the wool and pull them him along behind you. The rest of them would follow you and that sheep. (laughter) You get your hand in his wool, and go pull and they'll follow on. You turn him loose, you have to catch another one.

L: You could load sheep on a boat, if there was 1,000 of them they'd be over on the bank, like a landing over on that bank, they'd have them in a big pen. You would go out there after you put the stage down and put the gates on. You catch one sheep and start it on the stage and let it go into the boat, they'd all follow that one. Here they come just as fast as they could come, one right behind go down on the guard. You'd have no trouble at all they'd go right on by.

B: Easy.

Q: How about hogs?

L: A hog is the hatefulest thing that ever was. (laughter)

B: We'd have to carry him in that thing.

L: We'd carry them in yes, a hog is well sometimes we didn't take time to try to drive them. If they was small lots of like 25, 15 or 20, ten or something like that the lineman would catch the hog by its ears and throw him down by his feet. One would catch by his feet and the other by his ears, throw him down, turn him over on his back. Well, a man would walk up to him, to the linemen, they'd raise him up while you walked under him. They had his legs up in the air. You catch him in each flank right in here up on top of his shoulder you catch him in each flank, put him down on the shoulder. His head swings down behind you. Well, you can just light out and run with him, going in on the boat. Or they'd raise them and bring them in on the boat, they'd have him in on the boat in less time than you could take a seine out to the pen to get them, they'd have them aboard on the boat. Then when you would go to let him down, you'd have his butt, the hind part you have in front of you, you got to stoop over this way and hold him in your arms and just let him slide down through your arms. Put him down perfectly easy.

Q: Did you ever carry hogs in chain bars?

B: Oh yes, them bad ones.

L: (laughter) Yes, sir.

B: Did you ever see one with tushes that long?

Q: Tusk?

B: Tush, tush.

L: That's what you call the tusk.

Q: That must have been an old boar!

B: Could have been.

L: Throw him down, put him in the chain bar.

Q: I heard up in Catlettsburg that there was an old blue boar up there that threw six roustabouts in the river.

B: I wouldn't doubt it.

L: Catlettsburg! We had some of them on Green River that was just as bad as there ever were. Had some awful bad hogs and cattle, too.

B: We had one of them old steers, an old bull rather, about this tall and about this broad. Right between my, there . . . when they got him, I think I'd haul him by the legs. I put a rope on his legs, pulled up on his legs and pulled up underneath up to hold enough so we got a rope on his head. After we got the rope on his head, opened the gates and let him out. Well, he come out and started to charge the boat. I went around a tree in order to check from hitting those guys down in front of him, why he fell. We rolled him over.

L: Yes, I've seen cattle so bad . . . that rope on top.

B: If he'd have hit that fellow in front liable to kill him.

L: Start punching him around in there and just when his head went to drop around his neck rolled up on it. Then somebody come on in the gates and put it on and then you turn that loose and open the gate and get out of there. We have them fight and do everything else when we got outside.

B: Some we got up there from, we went down. Me and a boy called Thomas Jefferson. He was a small fellow. Well small, littler than I was. We went out to get a calf, the calf was just about this tall.

Q: Now wait a minute. He is about what, about four feet tall?

B: Oh, the calf, I'm talking about the calf.

L: About three feet.

B: Yes, that calf, you see, he wasn't no young calf, he was an old calf. We goes out, out there to get him. I say, "How many men do you need?" Say, "Just you-all two to get him." I go out there and one was standing, one was standing, steps up there, old man standing behind the steps. I say, "How is this calf if you-all got him tied here?" He says, "Well, just thought would tie his feet like that." I say, "He ain't no bad calf, is he?" He says, "No sir, he ain't hurt nobody. Not yet. Not on this farm." Tried to untie the rope, couldn't untie the rope. One of us always kept a knife, cut the rope and that calf come running up. Raised up on him, I slapped him on the head. I say, "I know what to do." I took the rope

John Knoepfle

and doubled it up and hit him, knocked him down, knocked him. He just hollered and squalled.

Q: He was a mean one.

L: He was mean. I knew there was something wrong. They had him tied.

B: We've got bulls on the boats. They'd shine a light over the pen, what it was, they'd come, "Humph, humph," pawing the dirt. You was, you know you'd go, I mean, you put loop in the line, you know, and get up on top of a fence, and slide it around his neck and when that catch on, you'd pull it, you see. That noose would grow tighter and tighter till we'd choke him down. Go around his head and get ahold of his tail. When we moved cattle, you know when they was contrary stubborn, you'd get enough men on the line to pull him, and he was holding back, why you just get behind him and twist his tail. That's the way we'd get cattle coming on bad. When we get behind him and twist his tail, he can't stand it. He's got to go when they twisted his tail. They'd lead him with a line, pull him with a line, and twist his tail you get him aboard the boat. Oh we had some awful times.

Up Green River the people had some cattle in the woods and pastures, and things like that, hadn't seen anybody. And when they'd get them up you know, they'd let them into an old barn or something up there. Put one out there and they'd follow him in then, and they'd shut the door. Well, when the boat come, why it's our roustabouts, it's our turn to get him. Now there's a barnful, maybe ten or 15 wild cattle that ain't used to being handled, no kind of way in the world, don't see nobody. Sometimes you got to take them out one by one. Can't drive them out of there, no kind of way. Couldn't seine them, you know. They have a cloth with sticks fastened on it, called a seine. It was long enough to go from here out to the end of that other room. You'd put that seine around them. You go around and put this seine up, after you drive them in that seine all of them, being in that seine. Well somebody on the side near the boat, just start to backing up with the seine, well you just make them keep on. It's just like a fence around them. Well, some of them would just jump up and over that seine. He'd go and knock the seine down. Get another running. Why, he'd have them right back there again the next trip. We'd have them right that thing too before we'd fool with it again. And sometimes we wouldn't get them all, the entire bunch of them sometimes for two or three weeks, but we would eventually get them all before we got through with them. Whenever we got one far as the bank landing there, we would have to we was going to get him. If we kept bringing him there, we was going to bring him away from there. That's all there was to it.

Q: Now Bee, you were mentioning a bank on the boats you knew earlier. Could you elaborate on that?

L: Said he wants to talk about this bank you knew.

B: As I was saying a while ago the bank we used on the boat. That boat was heavy loaded, most of it from Pittsburgh meeting the Rochester, Vanceburg,

Kentucky down to landing, mine. Ask if we could take them, so we did, and sent them upstairs, put them upstairs. They don't know how they're going to get up there. Only walk up the steps. We'd be behind them that's all.

Q: Would you talk a little more about those chain bars? I know you carried barrels in them too? Can you discuss that?

L: The chain bars, two sticks of wood about four feet long and the chains was about two and a half or three feet long. They put chains on each end and a couple of chains in the middle. Now when we got something heavy that a man can't carry by hand or on his shoulder, lay it on that chain bar between them two sticks on them chains and two men can carry it. One would pick up on the front and the other one pick up on the back and they could carry it. One man was back to the other one, and the other one and following carry the chain bars like that. If it was too heavy for two men to carry it, four men, one on each corner, pick it up, and put it on their shoulders. Two men in front and two men behind, and whatever it is you've got in the chain bar, you carry that like that. That's a heavy load. Didn't use the chain bar except for too heavy to carry by hand or on your shoulders. You'd get barrels and such things as boxes of meat, ice, heavy wood. There were some other things that I can't remember we would carry in the chain bars. But principally we carried things in chain bars that we couldn't well carry on our shoulders and in our hands. There were large boxes you couldn't carry in your hands, could be carried on our shoulders. Put four men around that load the chain bar, and then a man on each corner pick that up and put on his shoulder, and four men could carry it like that. And a smaller box that was too heavy to carry for one man, why you'd let a man turn his back to it in front and he'd catch on it with his hands and a man on each corner behind. Well the man in front he'd start forward and the other two men would follow. That's what they called the three-time around. If it was heavier than that they would have a four-time around, two men in front, two men behind carrying the box. If it was too heavy for that they would put a man on each corner, and one in the middle. They would tumble the box, roll the box over and over. That's what you call a tumbleweed. They tumbled that box. Tumbleweed that box. Too heavy to carry, why the mate would holler, "Tumbleweed that," and they would get around it and start to roll it, and roll it on the boat.

Q: I would like to question you. I know the bank was steep and I know they had various ways of getting a lot of that freight to the top of bank, and Bob McCann told me that he had seen the remains of little train railways in various parts of the rivers they used. Did you ever load stuff onto those cars?

L: A small rail, it was very little railroad rail, only they were much lighter and some shorter. Well they had them in bars. If they were light enough, two or three in a bar. But if not, they have them single. Well, you'd put a man on each end and a man in the middle. Three men could carry one of those small train tractors. If not they would put more men on. They put four, five, enough to carry it all the way up that hill and they would have the linemen take it off the

John Knoepfle

man's shoulder in front, lift it up off them, then the other men could turn around let it down without it falling off and hurting anybody.

Q: Wonder if I could stir up your recollections about the Silver Moon and the pleasures up at the top of the levees? (laughter)

L: At the top of the levee at Cincinnati there was a saloon, dance hall, gambling place, they called the Silver Moon where the roustabouts principally would go to that place and drink and gamble. Well, we had some of the men that was made up of all the boats from different parts of the river, some come up the river, some come down the river, but a great many times the roustabouts off the boats, off of one boat and off the other boat, they'd get there. Some of them would call them the cheap roustabouts because the boat he was riding didn't carry as much money as the one he was riding. They'd get into arguments and that would start a brawl. Sometimes they would have some pretty nasty fights. Cutting and throwing beer glasses and things like that. But seldom anybody got hurt bad enough for them to have to go to the hospital or get killed. There were some few got killed but not very many, only a couple in my recollection got hurt bad enough to go to the hospital, and one got killed. One fellow he had a knife and the other one, he was real bad. He went upstairs and got a gun and come down. That fellow jumped behind a post, but that didn't do him any good. Shot him just the same. Killed him. But more or less they got along fine when we all was drinking, but once in a while up the river roustabouts and down the river roustabouts would get together, why they'd have trouble. If it wouldn't be over drinking or sometimes it would be over women or something like that. One call themselves a little better, and then they had boats fellows run on excursions like that. They thought they were superior to the ones that run on the packetboats, thought they was better than they was. They didn't want to associate with them. Sometimes that bunch would get in trouble and have a brawl. That's the way that went.

Q: There was some hard feel about the Lee Line rousters.

L: Oh yes, the Lee Line boats, they was down river boats, you know. They called that the down river boat and the boats that run in these upper rivers, that runned up the Ohio River carried the freight up that river. And some were going down river from Louisville; some from Evansville had the freight, had to come up to Louisville. They'd hire that kind anywhere the boats went. The Lee Line boats they'd come in here from Memphis. They had their roustabouts. They were down road men. They got pretty good money. A lot of fellows up this way didn't get anything much, a dollar a day, or something like that. Well, they'd take to cracking about one was on a cheap boat and another was on a good boat. Well, they would crack, "You fellows don't get enough to eat on that boat." Sometimes that would start an argument around the crap game or around the bar where they'd be drinking. They'd get to fighting. Well the most usual thing they'd fight with their hands, you know. Somebody would separate them, and pull them out, have them make up, and then come back again and drink, you know. The boys would make up. It would be all right again.

Q: Was there a downstairs place in the Silver Moon?

L: Yes that was on the corner of Sycamore and Front.

Q: Was that the Silver Moon?

L: No, the Silver Moon was further up the block. The number was 324, that was the Silver Moon. On the corner, I don't remember the number, it was on the corner of Front and Sycamore Street. It had a saloon upstairs and had an underground there downstairs underneath, a gambling house. Well now you could get the drinks upstairs and go downstairs to gamble. At that time, that was a tough place, that was a tough place! Guys would get to drinking up there, get down there and get to gambling. Guys would get to fighting around there. Well, they allowed women to mingle with them, that was one thing sometimes start fights, about women. Sometimes it was over stakes in the game.

Q: Do you know the name of this other place?

L: I can't think now just exactly.

Q: Do you know Bee?

B: No, no I was thinking what it was, I can't think what the name is.

L: Tom Evans had the place at that time, but they had a name for it. I can't think of what they did call it. Anyhow it wasn't Hole in the Wall, but like that. Hole in the Ground, Hole in the Wall, something like that. (laughter)

Q: That's an odd thing because everybody knows about the Silver Moon, but if you say this other place was . . .

L: That was an older place than Evan's place was. The Silver Moon, oh the Silver Moon, it was running in the 20s.

B: It wasn't Snyder, was it?

L: No, Snyder Tavern was across the street right where the . . .

Q: I remember the rousters had nicknames for a lot of the towns up and down the river, do you know those names? They called Cincinnati Rag Town.

L: That's right Cincinnati was Rag Town. They called Memphis Jim Conan.

Q: What was that?

L: Jim Conan, that was a man who had a big business place there, the roustabouts and a great many other people that wasn't roustabouts in Memphis, that was the big place where the people went to have a good time. What you call a honky tonk because it was run by a man by the name of Jim Conan, they talked about Jim Conan. St. Louis they had the Bucket of Blood and Booster's Place. The Bucket of Blood no, Nashville had the Bucket of Blood. St. Louis had Booster's Place there. Nashville, Tennessee they called that the Bucket of Blood, and Louisville, they called that. Now Paducah they called Gold Tooth Annie. Evansville they call that The Loving Light City, and what the devil did they call, named Louisville. Grayson and Green, that was Louisville. Those were two noted streets at that time. Green Street now is Liberty Street. And

Grayson Street now is Cedar Street. They changed the names. Grayson and Green, that was the red light district.

Q: Which place was String Town?

B: String Town?

L: That sounds familiar but I just can't place that now. String Town. They called this place Rag Town. This place must have been a rag town for years. The roustabouts, they called this place, they get the raggediest roustabouts out of Cincinnati than any of the other ports down the river. Call it Rag Town on account of that. Nashville, they called that the Bucket of Blood because they had more fights down there than they did any place else. Cutting, bad guys with knives, you know, cutting around there.

Q: How about some of the upriver towns?

L: The upriver towns didn't have very much trouble. Charleston, Huntington, take Bowling Green, there's names for those, too. Can't recollect the names of what they did call them.

B: What did they call Pittsburgh? That may have been . . .

L: Smoky City.

B: Smoky City, Smoky City, hard to think what they called Huntington now.

L: Me neither.

B: Gives up real soon.

Q: It sure does, doesn't it?

L: That's right I used to call the names of all the, the names of those little places. They even had a name of Madison. I can't think of Madison now, Shawneetown.

B: Yes, Shawneetown, below Evansville.

L: Can't think what they did call . . .

Q: I know Leslie, he says can't carry a tune. But I know the rousters had a whole bag full of songs they used to sing. Do you remember any Bee offhand?

B: I'll tell you about the only one I remember at the same time. But see, some of these songs was pretty bad, you know. Can't put it in there.

L: I meant by telling him I couldn't remember enough of it, you see to lead a verse of it so it could be sung. If I start to singing two or three words of it, if you can't recollect the rest of it, why you ain't singing at all.

Q: Or even a stab at something, I know there was keg rolling songs, as they rolled nails in at Wheeling. Does that ring a bell?

B: I couldn't hardly, I remember one that I used to sing all the time.

Q: How did that go?

B: Oh, that's a tough song.

L: I don't think we can hardly accommodate you with a song cause I ain't much of a singer. And my recollection ain't no good. I couldn't sing very well or with somebody. I would lead off with a, I forget the song.

Q: Most of the times the deck songs . . .

L: We'd sing some songs on board, somebody would lead you know and we'd all join in, sing like we always did, come in on the chorus, something like that.

Q: Do you remember any of the choruses?

B: I can't remember now.

Q: How about telling me about some of the other roustabouts who were rather well known, I know there was one named Chief. Did you know Chief or Pride?

L: Sure I knew Pride.

Q: Those men?

L: Yes, that was John Moore. John Moore was one Pride. We had two or three Prides. John Moore was one of them. What it looked like.

B: John Moore . . .

L: We had one called Doll Eyes. He was out of Nashville. His name was Evans, called him Doll Eyes. Another one we had, another one out of Nashville to call Black Mouth. Well, they had a nickname for me when I was on the river my name they called me Hog.

Q: What?

L: Hog, the old original Hoghead they used to call me. More people knew me by the name of Hog than they did to the name of Leslie. There were people who never knew my name. They thought my name was Hog. Everybody called me Hog.

Q: Did you have a name too?

B: Oh yes Been Everywhere. Every time they looked for me, I'd be somewhere else. They called me Been Everywhere. They . . .

L: Yes, we had some others, let's see. Ah, Red Shirt Boy. I don't remember either one of them's names. Had one they called Bees. His name was Albert Davis. As, Shorty, we had several of them. There was one fellow's name . . .

B: What about B.S., not B.S., B., ah, B. Walker? What was his last name?

L: I don't know either's last name.

B: They called him Bee Walker I think. He's around.

L: And Slew.

B: Yes, old Slew. He was a heavy-set fellow.

L: Oh, we had some awful names for them, Bad Eye.

B: Woo Hoop. He was a great big fellow.

L: Called him Woo. His name was Hoop. Devil, his name was Dan Parker.

B: What was the other name?

L: Ralph David. Had two devils, Big Devil and Little Devil. Big Devil's name was Ralph David, Little Devil's name was Dan Parker.

B: His only . . .

Q: How did they get the name Devil? (laughter)

L: Bad name. Always fighting. Then we had, Quick.

B: He was another bad one. He'd fight all about.

L: Can't think of Quick's name. Now what is Quick's name?

B: I don't know Quick's name. One called Ralph, called big Ralph.

L: His name was George Little.

B: George Little!

L: Then we had Little Chicken.

B: What was his name?

L: Ed Grimes was his last name. I can't remember what his last name?

B: I can't either.

L: Oh, wait a minute. I'll tell you just in a second. His first name was Herbert.

B: How about Kirk?

L: White, something like that.

B: Howard.

L: Howard White. Tex, his name. And one we called Connecticut.

B: George Cain.

Q: Wonder where all those men are now?

L: Dead most of them.

B: Most of them fellows we called names is dead. George Penn ain't. And a couple of others, calling names, they ain't dead either.

L: Oh, that guy what used to work for, I seen him this morning, called him Kidney. His name's Davis. I don't recollect his first name.

B: Alexander.

Q: I am curious about a point. I think it was heard from Stogie White told me the captain and the mate got a cut out of the rouster's wage for allowing them to gamble on the boat.

B: No, that was saying something like this, if you wanted to gamble on a boat you didn't have any money, you'd go borrow that from him. You have to pay him a quarter or something extra when you won it back. That was the way he'd get his cut out of that.

Q: Oh, you paid him interest on the money from him.

B: That's right.

L: Well, they charged as high as 40 cents for $1, get ten cents on each quarter.

Q: Well rousters didn't end up with very much money at this rate, did they?

L: No, they'd borrow to get money to drink with and borrow money to gamble with. Then in later years, long toward the last of it, why they got a cut out of the game, even. They'd loan out the money, 20 cents on the $1. But the man that run the game see, they got a cut out of that, 50/50 cut out of the game, out of the take off as they call it now. The man who run the game he had to give them half. They got that kind of stuff going on there, the last go round. If you were a deckhand on the boat or stevedore, or coal man, if you wanted to run the game they'd loan the man the money, but he had to give them half of the take. He'd cut the game just like they do in town or any place else. Why they kept the money in a box and when the game was over, they opened up the box. He had to have half of the take. They did that, and they stood for it. I borrowed many a dollar and drank with it. You know, a dollar'd buy four half pints of whiskey with it, two half pints, and then a gallon of whiskey. Whiskey was watered down it was 25 cents a half pint. In the Louisville trade, the Louisville and Evansville trade Tom Cordie was a first class seller of whiskey. A big fat man there for years. They called him Uncle Joe. When they would get to singing a song, on the boat, "I'm going to stop by Uncle Joe," that meant that they were going to stop at Tom Cordie and get that brandy. He sold brandy 25 cents a half pint. That was Tom Cordie, "Stop at Uncle Joe's." You would hear guys singing sometimes, "Oh I'm going by Uncle Joe's." "Help me get to Uncle Joe."

B: "Take me down to Uncle Joe."

L: That's about all the information I guess we could give him.

Q: Before I quit I would like to ask you a few other points though. Just speaking of the gambling, did you know Joe Bates?

L: Yes sir.

B: Why, Holy Jesus Christ, that . . .

L: Gambler that ever lived.

Q: Well he must have been a prophet of gamblers from what I understand. Did he end up a rich man?

L: Nope he had a problem, it was whiskey.

Q: The people I talked to were always saying that he won all the money.

L: He used to he was lucky.

B: Well, you see in the way of people telling you he win all the money. If he was gambling, he'd gamble, only when he would gamble, he would make seven out of his nine, eight, and he was winning.

L: He was running the game when he was one man that operated the game, he gambled in the game himself. Well by him having more money than the other people he would freeze you out. That's the reason why he was so profitable in gambling. He would gamble himself. When he would open up with a game, why he would gamble himself. He would be right in there gambling. Why, he'll have stakes to gamble with. More so than the other people. Yes, that was why he had to quit steamboating, got sick and wasn't long before he passed away. He made plenty of money while he was on the boats running the game, and deckhand too, and then he was what you called a general purpose man on the boat. He could act mate if you didn't have no mate. Why he knew how to handle a boat just like a mate did. Lowering and hoisting the stage and how to come ahead, how to have your lines, a general purpose man on a boat just the same as a mate. Some of the captains on the boat didn't have no mate, why they had him working. He'd be on the same watch that the captain was on. He'd be the deckhand, or he used him as a mate.

Q: Now just a question, I guess 500 pounds is kind of a round number for about the heaviest weight the rouster carried, is that right?

L: 200.

B: You know what I say a while ago, I weighed 165 pounds, couldn't carry much more than my weight. At 165 pounds, I may carry ten pounds or 20 pounds more that's about all.

L: They used to compare, they used to compare, no more, the men not that strong anymore.

B: No sir.

L: 200 pound, man now can't carry 200 pounds. I could carry 250 pounds when I was at my fittest. Now I can't just carry 200 pounds. I can carry 150 pounds all right, but you get anything over that, why I wouldn't be so lucky carrying it.

Q: I can't even take a deep breath myself without . . .

L: That don't compare no more. Years ago they'd look at a man if he was a roustabout they'd say he ought to weigh about a 150 pounds. Put anything on him weighing 150 pounds, he could carry it. There were some fellows that didn't weigh over 125 that could carry 200. Strong men. One of the strongest men that ever I experienced being with, their natural strength was in being a roustabout or a railroad man. You find some small men that had more strength than many large men. The small men were powerful men. That boy Little Devil we was talking about, why he could carry a barrel of salt. A lot of men weighing 200 pounds couldn't carry it. He was a man who weighed about 140.

B: What town was that? I think it was Calhoun. It was on the head of the boat, put it right down there, salt. Drop in the bucket, old clerk, barrel of salt.

L: I carried a barrel of salt. I carried it. There were four barrels of salt, or four barrels of flour, and a barrel of salt sitting together. Well, they had to climb up on top of them. They had some other freight stowed on top of them. When they was taking that off of there they raised the barrel of flour and actually they had no business starting it. Well, they just jumped around it and raised it up. Well, when they laid it down on me I knew it wasn't no barrel of flour. Well, I just carried it all through the freight house. I was a good man at that time, and when I got up there, the lineman went to take off me, it went through the floor. (laughter) Floor! A barrel of salt weighs about 280, 280 pounds.

Q: I'll be darn.

L: Broke . . .

B: A barrel of flour . . .

L: I used to carry a box of picks. A box of picks weighed 200 pounds. Put them off at coal mines, miners, you know. Mines the same way. You get, have a lot of pick and shovels, and things like that, box of picks weighs 200 pounds. But I carried them. You know I carried a box of spikes, carried ten inch spikes, carried some bolts. They all weighted around 200 pounds. Some of the men couldn't carry it. They'd have to load . . .

B: Put them in a chain bar.

L: One by one chain bar because there was no trucks. The first flat truck, the truck that I seen used, flat truck. Go in the wharfboat and pick out the freight. The people coming from first one small town and another, come in after the freight that they had shipped there from someplace else. The clerk would pick that freight out and put it flat trucks and push it out to the edge of the wharfboat to load on wagons or whatever was there. And trucks I forgot now they didn't have them, just drays and wagons, that was all no trucks at all. I first come to Cincinnati in 1913, you could stay here two days and would never see an automobile, now trucks big trucks. I recollect in Evansville the first truck that they had in that town, the first truck they had there, the Evansville Brewing Company bought that, they was electric. And I recollect the first two men on an automobile in Louisville. Wasn't two automobiles in Louisville when I first come down there. That was Jeff Donavan, old man Bier, Frank Bier, and Jeff Donavan. They both had a car. You could stay in Louisville a week and you wouldn't see nobody riding in a car. A car from someplace else.

Q: Well, I wonder if just at the end now you could tell me a little bit about the boats. I know that rousters had different opinions about different boats, or else they would never have called the *General Wood* the *Work House*. (laughter)

B: Well, about the *General Wood*, I'll tell you she was a great deal that boat. It was hard and too much. And make 100 or 200 landings from here to maybe Pittsburgh. She was a *Work House*.

L: Yes, she was a *Work House* for this reason . . .

B: To go out of, way too much work for anybody. Which means *Work House* that's all it was too.

L: Pick up, on that side, and pick up that landing. They'd hoist you see, there and lower the stage, slip the dish. Well you know what they meant. They meant hoist the stage up and put it down on the other side because they was going right across on the other side. They'd hoist the stage up, put it on around instead of putting it in the middle of the boat, just carried the way around.

B: The other side.

L: The other side course, she's slacking off, she's going on apples, chickens, problem is they take on that boat, the *General Wood* called, bales of paper, rags, iron, nails; grocery, stoves, picks, oil drums, iron, the oil . . .

B: Oil yes.

L: Oil, if she was coming down the river we'd bring lots of oil, you know from up the river. We'd haul crude oil on barrels going all across the river. The boat be down the head of the boat blocked off with oil, drums of oil. We'd roll that oil on there. We'd go on the river, we'd go on to Little Creek ran down at the mouth of that river where we used to pick that up. The name of that town can't think of the name of the landing. We get sometimes six barrels of oil in one place, roll it on the head of the boat, and get the head of the boat blocked off and roll it down the guards. Roll it right out to the very area so when we come to that carrier freight so that we could pass by the ends of it go on back to the deckroom. We'd have freight loaded back to the deckroom hauling in for A & P, they had a lot of chickens, and then this crop, corn and cabbages. They had an awful lot of perishable stuff on there, A & P, Great Atlantic and Pacific.

B: Atlantic and Pacific.

L: Ship all that grocery and stuff out. Load up with that, then you'd have to unload at this Way Landing, so much of this, so much the other. Be working all

John Knoepfle

the way down from here, all the way down from Pittsburgh down here to New Orleans. That was the boat, they called it the *Work House*. It was.

B: Yes, the *Work House*.

Q: How about some of the other boats?

L: Well, there was Green River boats. They were *Work Houses*.

Q: They were.

L: They were *Work Houses*.

Q: The Green River. Up here.

L: I'm talking about the *Gordon Greene*, the *Evansville*.

B: *High Crown City*.

L: I've seen them boats when they'd back out from port, at Bowling Green, I've seen them back out from there several miles down to Clark's Landing. That would be the first place to turn around. We'd land over at Plump Ridge at Johnson's and get cedar posts and down over to another landing to get that stuff and right back over here, they'd just back down. Didn't turn around just backed down all the way to Clark's Landing, and when they got to Clark's Landing they'd turn around and head out for Woodbury, go on down to Woodbury, and then all the way down the river, then turn around. It was the landing down below Woodbury that you'd just back out from one, would swing the stage, go right across the river. They'd haul: hickory, hickory wood, cross ties, lumber, cedar posts, hoop poles. You don't see them anymore at all. Hickory withes, you know, cut in two to make hoops for barrels.

Q: Oh yes.

L: They called hoop wood.

Q: Barrel making was a big industry in the valley wasn't it?

L: It was.

B: Yes.

L: Staves, staves.

B: The Skilesville Landing's up in my home town. Skilesville Landing, Rochester.

L: In Rochester.

B: I'd get off of the boat at the lock and go in and cross the river left side of old Rochester. There's Bowling Green, there's Rochester, there's Wilson, there's Hettenger.

L: Wallace Brown.

B: Wallace Brown. I'm back here, I'm back here, I'm back here now.

Q: Felt good when you got home.

B: Oh, sometimes I'd go there, sometimes I wouldn't, I would stay on the boat. Then sometimes I'd land up there be about three miles landing back in up there going up.

L: Going to up there.

B: At Bellevue, Bellevue, Kentucky.

L: It's what you call a swap trade. There's two boats, the *John S. Hopkins* and the *Joe Fowler*. There was a landing at Lee Rock, that's what they called it. Coming up the river it was called Pull Tight. Going up the bank there was a railway cut out, it was from here there to the wall and the bank was as high as this wharfboat is from down the deck up to the top. Well, that narrow chute where you go through when you load, was the four men around the load it would squeeze just barely can go up through it. They called it a Pull Tight. Then there's another one where you go up this way, you turn at this corner and go that way, you can't go straight all the way up the hill, you go up this way and you turn and go that way, then you turn and come back this way, and it's the top of the hill. They call that Tooloo.

Q: Tooloo!

L: Tooloo.

Q: You have to zigzag up that hill.

B: That's right.

L: It was so steep you had to zigzag to get up to the top, and I've seen many a man who would get up to the top. He would almost be ready to fall, be out of breath. Take the load off of him and he'd lie up there. And we'd work right there for as many as three or four hours at a time.

Q: Well, Leslie you're pretty much in retirement, I know. What are you doing now, Bee?

B: Sitting here. (laughter)

Q: Maybe I shouldn't have asked the question.

B: I'm ready to retire too, getting older.

L: Yes, I don't do much work now.

B: I worked enough I think, plowed, milked cows, had to go get the cows, feed the hogs, that was about as good a job as any other I worked. I had seven head of cattle to feed, six head of sheep, four hogs to feed. And, two cows to milk and I told the woman, well she could milk the cows, I'd go get them.

Q: Then you went out and steamboated for the rest of your life.

B: Found something else to do.

Q: Well, it was good of you people to come down and make the tape.

L: Well, yes.

Q: I'll switch her off then.

John Knoepfle

Question: This is Johnny Lawhead, he operates the ferry between Coney Island and Brent, Kentucky. Carries passengers back and forth on a ferryboat. We are going to talk to him now. Just wonder how long have you been on the river?
Answer: Been on the river since 1933, this makes the 23rd season operating.
Q: Have you always operated boats back and forth between Kentucky and here?
A: That's right, I started the original ferry service. There wasn't any ferry service when I started here in 1933.
Q: How many boats have you had?
A: This makes the fourth boat.
Q: How long is it?
A: The boat is 36 foot. It's a Navy surplus from World War II.
Q: Do you carry as many passengers as when you first started, or just how many passengers do you carry on your boat?
A: The capacity of the boat is 38. Of course, my business increases each year. I haul more passengers each year. Each year it increases.
Q: Tell us a little bit about your first boat. What was it like?
A: The first boat was just an 18 foot motor boat and hauled six passengers in it, called it the *Whoopee Girl.*
Q: Personally, I remember you had one called the *Ferry Queen.* I think you had a model A engine in it didn't you?
A: Yes, that's right. That was actually the 3rd boat, the *Ferry Queen.* I built that boat in 1940 with a little 30 foot cabin scow.
Q: That was about your second boat was it?
A: The 3rd boat, the 2nd boat was the *John D.* She was a 30 foot cabin scow I bought.
Q: All those boats were used for passenger service!
A: Strictly passenger service, I never hauled freight or automobiles or anything. Nothing any bigger than a baby buggy.
Q: Did you ever have rough water to contend with?
A: It gets a little rough here, mostly from waves when the big boats are passing. During storms I mean we see one of these electrical storms building up, I don't ordinarily run across the river. I won't haul passengers across the river in a storm. I'll stay tied up to which either bank, the storm is going to run itself out.
Q: I understand this past Saturday evening it was you had a lot of trouble with fog.
A: Yes, that was the first time I ever actually got fog bound. I couldn't make my trips. Of course I won't say it was the worst fog that has ever been on the river, usually the fogs occur later on in the mornings and I don't get caught in them. This one happened to close in at 12:30 at night and I made the 12:30 trip,

it took me 20 minutes from the time I left Coney Island to reach the Kentucky shore. Ordinarily it's a five minute run.

Q: What are some of the most exciting experiences you have had on the river as far as boats are concerned or having to contend with big boats? Have any trouble or run into any big trouble with them?

A: Actually no big trouble. A little government tugboat almost took the tail end off of my boat one afternoon about the middle of the afternoon about three, well actually it was about four o'clock in the afternoon, a bright and sunny day. He coasted down the river and he shut down right off the end of the dike and I thought he was just clearing a channel to let other towboats pass so I blew the whistle and passed astern of him. He didn't answer my signal so it was about 100 feet between his paddlewheel and the end of the Coney Island dike at the stone wall. So I blew my signal and went between the end of the dike and his paddlewheel on his boat. Well he has a diesel electric operated boat. He sits up there and operates, the pilot operates his boat like I operate this boat. He has got fingertip control. The minute I nosed the ferry in that opening, I had about 50 feet to my left, the paddlewheel of the towboat's about 50 feet to the right to the end of the stone wall and the minute I stuck my nose in that opening he started backing on his paddlewheel. Well I couldn't turn out of that situation. I either had to try to back out or run out. I knew if I tried to back out I would lose too much time and he would probably hit me so I had to open the throttle wide open and run through there and he just missed me about five feet back there and threw water all over the rear deck. One couple sitting back they had to run inside the boat to keep from getting drowned in the water he threw on there.

Q: A narrow escape.

A: I almost fainted up here at the controls of the boat, I thought he was going to tear the whole tail end off the ferry.

Q: Well I see we are about here at Kentucky now so thank you very much for your all information.

A: Yours truly, appreciate it.

Q: This is the 30th day of June a blue morning aboard the steamer *Avalon*. We are here making a tape recording of the trip out from the public landing of Cincinnati to Coney Island. At present you can hear the music of the calliope, which is one of the last two on the river. By coincidence both calliopes are within seeing distance of each other. Since the other calliope is aboard the *Atta Boy* on Captain Reynolds Hiram College Showboat. This particular calliope is a bit out of tune. Calliope playing: "The Bells of St. Mary," and "DuDu Liegst Mir Im Herzen," are being played by Ray Mensh who is the Campbell County Juvenile Officer, who is just up here this morning for the lark. The first pieces that you heard were by a young boy named Doc Hawley from Charleston, West Virginia who came aboard solely to play the calliope. We are now out on the starboard bow, port bow of the boat and we are going to attempt to record the

John Knoepfle

commands of Captain Wagner as he goes up on the bridge, which is a little structure here and gets the boat underway.

Captain Wagner: Get up here someone and get your picture taken, get in the paper here. Get up here and be a waving at him. Give him a chance to warm her up a little bit, back her on a straight rudder, Destrow. (whistle blowing) All right stop her a minute. I've got a line out there yet. All right, let's go. Hold it Jimmy hold it. All right let's go.

Q: Now we are down on what would have been known as the bull rail section of the boat and we are merely listening to the boilers. We are now at the stern of the steamer and if you listen closely you can hear the two powerful driving arms that turn the sternwheel of the steamer. These work alternately. I suppose in order to keep from shaking the boat to pieces. What is the technical name for the part of the boat we are on?

A: The fantail.

Q: Fantail, and we are back here at the very stern of the boat and this huge pile driving sound is the sound of the sternwheel beating the river. How many planks are there on the wheel do you know mate?

A: I couldn't tell you actually.

Q: What are these driving arms called?

A: That's wheel arms.

Q: Wheel arms.

A: This one right here.

Q: Yes.

A: That's what they call the pitman it turns the Wheel.

Q: Fine thank you very much. Now we have come up into the pilot house, topside of the steamer and we are here with Captain Emory Edgington and Captain Wagner. Captain Edgington can you tell us how long you have been on the river.

A: About seventy-four years.

Q: Fine, maybe captain Wagner will talk to Captain Edgington? Just ask him to tell a few stories.

W: Captain Edgington how many years?

A: About 74 years since I started to steamboat and I have done everything on a steamboat except chambermaid. That includes deckhand, cook started in as a cook, and clerk, captain, mate, engineer and pilot. As I said a while ago everything but a chambermaid.

W: When you started out boats were a little different than they are today weren't they?

A: Oh yes, my father owned a little boat called the *Katie Prather*. She was what you call a sandy gyper. She had a steel shaft clear across the boat with a wheel on each end of it and the machinery was a threshing machine boiler with the engine fastened up on the boiler and run to a drum and around that shaft and that operated the boat coming ahead or backing. She was a packetboat and run the local packet trade up around Manchester, Ohio, and Vanceburg and Maysville.

W: Well, tell us some of the experiences you have had since you have been steamboating. What would you say was the most interesting thing that happened to you in these 74 years you have been here on the river?

A: The most interesting thing to me in my earlier steamboating days was the low water and getting boats over a sandbar. I have spent as high as 24 to 26 hours on a sandbar trying to get the boat over. One instance here in Cincinnati when I working for the White Collar Line I worked for about 18 hours getting a up over the Seven Mile Bar up here, and when I got her up over I got orders to come on back to Cincinnati after all that hard work. I've had fog and all those things to contend with. As a matter of fact I operated the Chilo and Cincinnati packet, oh a number of years ago, seven days and six nights in fog that never raised. I did that with a little pocket compass and got in Cincinnati about an hour late, and then back up to Chilo about two hours late over my regular time. That was a sort of an innovative experience to do that successfully, which I did. Then I have towboated. I quit packetboating about 25 years ago, 30 years ago, I can't recall that exactly. I have been towboating up until about three years ago. Towing coal over from Kanawha River points to Cincinnati, Louisville and Huntington. Mostly out of Huntington. I worked for Island Creek Coal on two shifts. The first time for about eight years and the second time about seven. I worked for the Ohio River Company out of Huntington and there I worked two shifts, the first time about four years and the second shift about seven years. And I worked on other towboats. I worked for T. J. Hall towboating the first time, towed coal out of Kanawha River. I have been on this boat through the summer here between Louisville and Pittsburgh.

Q: The captain is busy now. He is going to pass a coal tow, which is coming downriver. That is a sternwheel tow coming down isn't it? It's the *Omar,* the great sternwheel tow.

W: Want me to call him and see what he wants to do? WS6270. Steamer *Avalon* calling to *Omar.* Come in Cap.

Omar: I'll . . . Cap if it's all right with you.

W: That will be fine then, that will be fine. Thank you for coming in. If you have nothing else? WS6270, the *Avalon* all clear of the *Omar.*

Omar: WB7754, the *Omar* clear of the *Avalon.* (whistle sounds)

W: Pedal operated. This makes an amber light, two different pedals. You manage to push the pedal down far enough that it makes this go down so you have an idea that at night or the day too, you can see that amber light on top of the pilot house.

Q: I'm not recording now until I get by that boat.

W: Maybe you can tell us some of your experiences on the river as captain here or any other place.

John Knoepfle

A: Well most all of my steamboating has been on this type of vessel, passenger boat. I started out on the *Island Maid* right here at Cincinnati in 1927 and then I got away from the river I only worked one season. I stayed away until 1933, and then I came back and went on the *Island Queen*. I worked on the *Island Queen* then a couple of years and got my mates license and I worked seven more years, and then I was gone a while. I stayed away from the river seven years. When I came back out of the service why I don't know the water was in my blood and I had to come back.

Q: Were you aboard the *Island Queen* when it . . .

A: Yes I was aboard the *Island Queen* when it burned up at Pittsburgh. But I don't like to remember it. This is steam steering gear, the more modern steering rigging is what you call a hydraulic. That's an oil fed into these cylinders, which is the same as the steam one.

Q: This boat hasn't always been run by oil has it? Although it is running by oil today.

A: By run you mean firing? No, this oil furnace was put on her last year at Owensboro and put new boilers on her then, and they put an oil furnace on her and now she is fired by oil instead of coal. It is not any more economical but cleaner and you don't lose as much time getting fuel. We don't have to stop every coal pile to get fuel.

Q: How old is the *Avalon*, Captain?

A: They tell me she is 40 years old. I don't know just exactly, I think that is right. She was originally built as a ferry boat for Memphis, Tennessee. She was called the *Idlewild* at that time. She was rebuilt this last spring at Point Pleasant, West Virginia with a practically new hull under her. They put pontoons on each side, three foot and a half on each side, that makes her six foot wider than she was before. Now she's 46 foot wide. I should say 47 foot wide.

Q: How much of a draft does the boat have?

A: About four and a half feet. It depends upon the number of people they have on her and when we have capacity it might put her down four inches deeper than normal when she hasn't got any passengers on her.

Q: Captain Arthur Schletker tells me that you've hauled probably more coal into Cincinnati than any other man alive.

A: I believe he's exaggerating a little bit on that. I have piloted a whole lot of it down the river all right on these Ohio River boats and the Island Creek boats. The Ohio River boats have been towing on an overage, well the largest tows, regular tows is 20 barges of coal, which is about 19,000 ton. The Island Creek, the tonnage wasn't quite as heavy. They had smaller capacity boats, smaller horsepower. But they would tow ten to well, from six to 12 barges of coal.

Q: Did you tow coal in your earlier days on the river?

A: No, I didn't commence towing coal until 1908. I worked for T. J. Hall on the steamer *Douglas Hall*, a towboat out of Kanawha River. They were all good pilots, Captain Jim Rowley, as I said before, different ones. I am really the only one of the boys in the family that done any towboating to amount to anything. I had one brother that towboated a little bit on one boat. But he didn't tow coal. Not for very long. None of them liked towing coal. Oh in 1899 or 1900 up to 1900 we used two boats the *Bellevue* and the *M. P. Wells* as towboats. We towed brick from Blairville up here and sand and gravel from Manchester Island down here to the foundries and freestone, the paving stone, from the mills at Buena Vista, Ohio where they saw the stone out of the hills there and made paving stone. Now that's all done away with anymore. They don't do that, and they don't haul that sand and gravel anymore from Manchester Island or anyplace else unless they ship it by rail to Pittsburgh. That they might do, I don't know. There is just one thing about the whole thing I spent my life at it. As I said a while ago I've been on this boat I think this is the 5th year and I call this a vacation, not work lots of times. My son and daughter-in-law have a farm out above right up against Blanchester, Ohio and we just bought that farm a couple of years ago, and I had a farm a mile below Moscow, Ohio 47 years. As a matter of fact, all steamboat people, and especially pilots, look out see these farms going along the river and they make up their minds that they are going to buy a farm, quit steamboating, go out there and spend their days out there. But I haven't accomplished that yet.

Q: I see. Well you still have plenty of time.

A: I hope. I hope I have.

Q: Did you ever come close to losing a boat on the river, Captain?

A: Never had an accident at all. The only thing that has happened was sinking a barge running under up at New Martinsville. It was the *Omar* and there was a hole in the bulkhead, of the barge on the head, nobody knew it and it filled up and it was after night. I'd had the search light out on it 20 minutes before that across the head of the tow and everything appeared to be all right. The next thing I knew I heard a lashing snap. I had my search light on at that looking down at dam 15 and threw the light down on it and here the barge was going under. I pulled the boat hard down away from it so when it came back I saw there was no chance of evading, of course I stopped the boat. No chance of saving the barge though, but I didn't want it to hit the side of the boat and sink her, so I pulled hard away from it. That's the nearest I have had to any accident. I've always consistently tried to be careful and I have been careful. That's been one of my principles, always not to be in too big a hurry to avoid safely.

Q: I wonder if you remember the ice gorge that wiped out so many of the boats?

A: Yes, I was with the government then on the engineer corps and was Captain of one of the boats and we had the fleet laying under the ice piers at Maysville, Kentucky in 1917 and 1918. I saw any number of wrecks going down the river when the river broke up. The only thing we lost out of that fleet was one of the scows on one of the dredges. They eventually found that down about five miles from the Ohio River down above Henderson, Kentucky opposite Evansville, Indiana. They finally got it. I don't know how they got it though, that country is all flat down there. That's the only thing we lost in that ice, that is for the government, in the fleet we had. But it sunk the *City of Cincinnati*, the *City of Louisville* and banked the *Bonanza* and did a lot of damage at Cincinnati and sank the *Princess* down the Kentucky River, and did a lot of damage up the river too. There were some boats went down the river that I had boated on from upriver, just went on down the river and one or two of them didn't sink at all. They went down with the ice and didn't hit any big piers, and one little boat I was told, I didn't see it, called the *Helen E.*, she was froze up in a big flow of ice and she hit the bridge pier at Cincinnati. And that flow of ice sheared off, it sheared that ice flow off, and didn't hit the boat at all, she went on down they caught her way down around Louisville someplace, eventually.

Q: Were you in Cincinnati during the great steamboat fire?

A: No, I wasn't there I was upriver on a boat.

Q: Maybe you were lucky to have been up the river then?

A: Well I don't recall what boat was on, I was on several at that time. But the *Tacoma* and several boats and the *City of Cincinnati*, the *City of Louisville*, I've been on them. I run Captain of those boats, on the *Tacoma* and the *Courier* in the Maysville to Cincinnati trade. I was learning the river at Louisville on the *City of Louisville*, and the *City of Cincinnati*. I have had a varied experience on the river and I think most steamboat people have, and I as I said a while ago this is vacation for me. Because I think I would rather pilot a steamboat than eat. You know what I mean.

Q: You are a lucky man.

A: Well I've pretty good health and I have always taken care of myself. Never drunk in my life. I don't, hope I won't be, in fact I know I won't be. I won't drink that much, in fact I don't drink anyway.

Q: Did you handle any of the wartime shippings?

A: Not any on the wartime vessels. I was on a towboat towing coal at that time. Captain Schletker was though. He was on several of them.

Peggy Knoepfle: I would like to know one question. What actually is the chain of command on a boat like this? Who is actually in charge? Are you in charge?

A: No, I'm not Captain Wagner is in charge and he's in charge of me and so far as navigation goes, except he can't tell me what to do in the way of where to navigate or anything like that, but he can order me to land, or to back out, or run slow or something like that. I think it's all right. I can refuse to do that if I think in my judgement that it's not safe to do it. That's the law as far as that's concerned. We hardly ever exercise that because we all work hand in hand, of course there has been crews that have been at loggerheads. I never was in very many of those crews. I've run captain for several steamboats, towboats and packetboats in my time, I don't want any more captain's jobs.

Q: Too much trouble?

A: Too much to worry about. Captain Wagner and I were talking last night. He was talking about the worries he had, and I said, "Well, I wouldn't have your job on a silver platter at all." Not that I couldn't do it, but I wouldn't have the worry of it. It is a worry.

Q: Can you tell us something about the other boats that you were on?

A: I don't know, they were all good boats and it made a good business and when business got bad they laid them up. What happened to our boats of my family. We got into competition with the White Collar Line and the C & O Railroad combined, and they broke us up, and we didn't break the C &, O but we broke the White Collar line up. Both of us lost.

Q: There was a river war on at the time.

A: Just between the White Collar Line and our local boats. They wanted the local business too and they cut rates and so did we. We hauled stuff for less than it cost and eventually we broke up, several of them done that though several companies.

Q: That would have been in the twenties I guess?

A: It was back in 1901-1902 and 1903 in that neighborhood.

Q: I guess things were beginning to get rough for commercial haulers back then.

A: No packet business anymore at all outside of this excursion business like this boat is doing. The Streckfus people have a boat at St. Louis they run and do the same kind of business that we do except they stay right there at St. Louis and they have the old *Cincinnati*, which is called the *Admiral* now. Wait a minute now I'm not sure I've got that right. No, she is called the *President* and the *Admiral* is the one at St. Louis. They are big fine sidewheels, the *President* is a duplicate of the *Island Queen*. They were both built the same time, the same size, machinery and everything. I haven't seen her since the Streckfus people got it because I haven't been to St. Louis or New Orleans really. I have never seen the *Admiral* either, but I have seen pictures of her.

P: Wonder if you have a favorite spot or on the river or a favorite town?

A: I was born and raised in Manchester, Ohio that's my favorite. It's my birthplace. I had the calliope player play "Long Long Ago," yesterday when we passed there. That was one of my father's favorite songs and I heard him sing it many times, and he would lay his head back and enjoy it. It is pretty too. He's laid away there at Manchester. All my immediate family is. I lost my wife three years ago, it will be in October. She is buried up there at Neville, Ohio that's about two miles above the farm I owned for 47 years. We stayed on the farm until she passed away. None of us care to stay there now. My grandchildren all live out around Dayton and Hamilton and I have a granddaughter at Oxford and a grandson at Middleton and one works in Dayton and he lives in Williamsville. They've all got children, so I'm a great grandfather.

Q: When did the Edgington's first come on the river?

A: I think it was my father and I think it was 1874 or 1875. The first boat I remember him being on was a little boat called *John Kyle* and little sternwheel boat, a packetboat.

Q: Where was that Captain?

A: That's was up around Manchester. She run from Manchester to Portsmouth.

Q: Had a produce trade, a huckster trade.

A: A local packet trade we called it. We carried everything passengers and we carried all sorts of freight. Coops of chickens, barrels of flour, sacks of wheat, bales of hay.

A: I have a chew of tobacco once in a while, not very much, to keep from smoking too much. Dropped in many a load of coal in there. That's Coal Haven. Tied up in there and delivered from there.

Q: Did the railroad pick it up from this point on the river?

A: No, we would take it down to what they call Fifth Street just above Mississippi Valley plant down there. It was their landing and we would unload it there and it was put in cars down there. The Queen City Coal Company that's where they got their coal at too. In fact the Island Creek owned was also the Queen City Coal Company.

Q: Did you ever build any boats yourself?

A: No I never did. My father did though. Well I know of four. My first trip to Wichita, Kansas I went by B & O train and we crossed the Wabash River at Vincennes as it just got daylight enough I could see a few things. I looked down out of the window and saw a little boat called the *Racket*, he built that boat. She was way up the Wabash River, she was a little sternwheel boat. He built her. That was funny to see a boat he built way up there at Vincennes, Indiana.

Q: We were talking to Captain Reynolds recently on the *Atta Boy*. He has the Hiram College Showboat crew now. Did you ever do any showboating?

A: No, I never did. That was one branch of it I never was in. I knew a lot of the old ones. Price, and I can't think of the other one now.

Q: Bryant.

A: Bryant, Price and French, and I piloted a boat called the *Wabash*. Cincinnati to Parkersburg for this man. I was trying to think of his name, I can't think of it now. He had a showboat up there at Parkersburg, ran that quite a while and he went bankrupt and that ended that. The people that built his show boat, they had to take over the unpaid balance, so I don't know what has become of it. That *Wabash* she finally wound up in a fire up here opposite Higginsport, Ohio. Burned there. They made a towboat out of her. She was originally what they called a corn boat out of Wabash River. That was the principle freight, corn. (wind) Big wind here out of that holler.

Q: Yes, the wind is picking up now.

A: Well it's coming downstream now.

Q: The wind makes it difficult to pilot.

A: Well, you have, you have to know that wind blow, side wind, it will blow you side . . . .

Steamer Avalon 2, July 2, 1957, Cincinnati, Ohio

Question: We are aboard the steamer *Avalon* on the second of July. Captain Schletker has gone up into the pilothouse and pretty soon he's going to ring the set of steamboat bells, which Mr. Courtney Ellis, the engineer, will interpret.

Courtney Ellis: The sound of this is the come-ahead bell "strong." That is the gong, which we use for reversing the engines. Then this one sound is the backing bell, that is the back half-head and that is the back-slow again. That's the come-ahead slow bell. That's the stopping bell. That's the stopping bell. That's the gong to reverse the engines. From the time I was ten years old it was my ambition to become a steamboat engineer. My grandfather was a captain and a pilot. When I finished school at the age of 17 I went on the rivers as a striker engineer, which is known as an apprentice engineer. In those days it required an apprentice to serve until he became 21 years of age before securing a government license. I followed that procedure and at age 22 secured my first assistant papers. Operating under those for some 18 months, then I secured the chief engineers papers.

Q: Can you tell us what boats you were operating on?

CE: At that time I was operating out of Evansville, Indiana on some small boats, packet boats, one of them known as the *Bowling Green*, the other as the *Evansville*. Then from *Evansville* I went to St. Louis, Missouri, and there I operated on the big sidewheel packetboats, the *Quincy*, the *Saint Paul*, which operated from St. Louis to St. Paul. Also, on the excursion boat, *Belle of the Bends*, and on the transfer boat, transferred railroads across the river. Then I later became a chief engineer on Missouri River boats, towboats and on two occasions was shipwrecked, once on the Missouri and once on the Mississippi. The Missouri River incident was a small boat and we were caught in a severe windstorm late one March afternoon and the boat capsized. All hands went overboard on the shore side but it was necessary for me to go overboard on the offshore side because the boat turned turtle. As I came up out of the cold waters I was looking at the bottom of the boat and swam ashore. On another occasion I was on a car transfer boat, this was a railway car transfer boat, and we were filling coal from Illinois to Missouri, and a railroad ballast, which is known as chat, crushed stone from Missouri to Illinois. Early in February 1918 after the ice had run out of the Mississippi River we were well loaded one night, February 28 to be exact, and in entering the incline in some manner the stem of the boat, which was known as the *St. Genevieve*, belonged to the Missouri & Illinois Railroad Company, was struck against the incline in trying to pick up the cradle. The cradle is a platform so to speak, which is used to run the cars into and off of the boat by the switch engines. Repeated efforts and constant diligence was carried on during that evening to try and save the boat. But all

John Knoepfle

were in vain because finally she went down with four carloads of coal on one side and four carloads of chat on the other side. The crew members stayed with her until the water was up to their waist and I personally waded out in water up to my chest and climbed up over the roof and got into the lifeboat and as we entered the lifeboat the captain and the other engineer and some of the deck crew, someone failed to put the bung in the bottom of the lifeboat and there we had a stream of water two inches in diameter running into the boat. But that we managed to overcome because we held our hands and our feet over it until we could row ashore. This happened at two o'clock in the morning and it was very cold, but we made it and no lives were lost. After the sinking and destruction of this transfer boat the railway company put in another boat known as the *Kellogg*. Then World War I came on and it was necessary for me to leave the river and seek other fields. After World War I, I was engaged in the U.S. Engineer Department on towboats and dredge boats around St. Louis for a number of years. Then became associated with a large multiple line insurance company as their boiler inspector and consulting engineer. At which time I spent 35 years on this job and after reaching retirement age and training some men to take over my position I was retired by my good company, and then after some years of rest, two years of rest, I decided to come back on the rivers to my first love, the steamboats. And I am now enjoying very pleasant days and hours with some of my old friends and associates from back during the real old paddlewheel, sternwheel, sidewheel steamboat days.

Q: Thank you. Now this is Johnny Dobbs who has been a pilot on the old Tennessee River.

Johnny Dobbs: Yeah and I'm sitting right here looking at you. (chuckles) Well I was born on the island called the Jolley's Island at the mouth of the Hiwassee River, and the Tennessee was running by too. I was plowing Old Buck down on the island, the steamboats would be a passing along and I kept a watching them, losing about a half day of plowing watching them go by. Finally got interested in them, got me a job as night watchman on one of them, the old *Joe Wheeler*. I stayed on that boat for about 20 years. I clerked boat four years, and then Captain Robinson got me to go in the pilothouse. He learned me the pilot business, and I steered that boat in that packet trade there. I remember long enough there was a lady that wanted off at Jones Landing and I carried her baby up and set it down on the ground. That girl baby grew up and I carried her baby up there and put it down in the same place.

Q: Is that so?

JD: Then finally I got my first pilot license in 1908. I worked on the river from 1903 until 1953 before I quit. I was laid off for a while, I'm still on the river right smart. I remember one time we had to go through the mountains down there, it's what's called first part in Tumbling Shoals, and then you hit Suck Creek, and then you go on down and hit the Pot, the Pan, and then the Skillet. Then you run out of the mountain again. There is about nine miles there and

I've counted 38 stills was making whiskey in that nine miles from Suck Creek Road to Kelly's Ferry Road. They made good corn whiskey because I've been around all of them stills. Another time I was going up the river one evening about sundown and we had a lot of chickens on top of the boat. I let the boat swing in under a tree about sundown and all these chickens flew up in that tree. So I went on to Kingston and left Kingston the next morning and come back down about time for them to fly down and I let the boat go in under there and they all flew back down and stayed with us. So after that I was on, well I have been on several boats. I was on the old *N. B. Forrest* it ran between Chattanooga and Kankakee. The *Joe Wheeler*, the *Chattanooga*, the *John Ross*, the *James N. Trigg*, the *John A. Patten*.

Going down river on the *Patten* one time and the *Parker*, a towboat laid around there until we got ready to leave about ten o'clock to have a race with us. So we got down the river about eight or ten miles the *Parker* pulled away from us to go around the short side of the island, thought she was going to beat us. She got away about 100 yards and blew up, I seen her boilers go 100 feet in the air and set down in the island over there. Just got away from the *Patten*, and she had two or 300 passengers on there. It might have killed a lot of them if it had happened about five minutes sooner. One of the boilers is still sitting on the island sitting in the mud. That was 1910 I think when that happened. Blew the pilot out of the pilothouse into the river and the engineer into the river. The fireman, never seen or heard tell of him anymore. The pilot was standing in the pilot window he had a man steering for him. It killed that man that was steering for him. So that was a pretty bad thing to happen. I never had very much trouble on the river.

Q: Well that must have been an awfully difficult river to pilot.

JD: Well, it was crooked and a lot of shoals and dams and everything. Then we had Hiwassee River to run to Charleston and all that, you know. Had a lot of good excursions out of Chattanooga and I stayed on from 1903 to 1953 and got off a while and now I'm on the excursion *Avalon*, way up here around, I been to Pittsburgh on her, first time I was ever up in there. It's a pretty river up there.

Q: It is indeed.

JD: Yes it's pretty all up in there.

Q: Were you ever up on the French Broad?

JD: Yes, I've been up in the lower end of French Broad, but not up on it much. I've been right at the mouth of it, French Broad and Holston. I've been right around up in there in the lower end of but not very far up on it. I've been up to Ocoee, and above Ocoee at Savannah Landing about 30 miles above Charleston, Tennessee, the Ocoee River, on the Hiwassee River, and that's where the Ocoee comes in up there. Of course they've got a big dam on the Ocoee River now from Charleston up there. We used to carry excursions out of Charleston once a year called the May boat ride. We would go to Charleston and pick up a crowd and bring them out to the mouth of the Hiwassee River and Tennessee

John Knoepfle

River, and turn around and take them back. That took about all day and generally we had all we could carry and plenty of good chicken and stuff to eat. The people would bring it on the boat.

Q: What kind of a boat were you on then?

JD: I was on the *Joe Wheeler*, a packetboat and freight boat.

Q: Can you describe that boat?

JD: Yes I was on that boat about 18 years. I got on, I worked for the Dixie Sand and Gravel Company 14 years on the *W. H. Klein* towing sand and gravel from below Hales Bar. I went through Hales Bar in that 14 years in a little over 9,000 times with three barges. The lockmaster said I didn't knock enough concrete off of in that length of time to fill a half gallon bucket. So I done pretty well.

Q: Could you tell me offhand about some of the produce you were shipping?

JD: Well we shipped chickens, eggs, cows, hogs, horses and everything practically on the river, corn, hay and wheat and all that. We would load down cotton, fertilizer and all that kind of stuff. I've boated enough fertilizer out of Decatur and Bridgeport, Alabama to raise Sand Mountain six inches. (chuckles) A lot of fertilizer. In five weeks we would handle anywhere from 500 to 600,000 sacks of fertilizer. It had to be carried on and off by man. Had good men in them days, they could work. They wouldn't carry two sacks off now. I had two on there got to bragging, which could carry the most and so they got to carrying. I put five on one of them and both of them carried five up the bank, that's 500 pounds. The other boy come in and I put six on him and he went up with it, and the other one had shot himself about a year before and broke his leg and I was afraid to put six on him, afraid I would break it again. (chuckles)

Q: Were those roustabouts?

JD: Yes, roustabouts. Carried 600 pounds of fertilizer up that bank. He was a man and they was good workers in them days. I miss all of them. They are all gone, practically all of them. At one time I was the youngest pilot on the Tennessee River and now I'm the oldest. So time passes right on. I'm going back home, I've been away from home now four months, the longest in my 50 odd years steamboating. When I get to Paducah I'm going home again.

Q: Well good. There must be whole towns that were there when you started that aren't there now.

JD: They didn't move any towns over there when they built them dams. They are all still there. You leave Chattanooga, you run into Hales Bar, then you run into Bridgeport, then you go a little to Hobbs Island and down there at Decatur, and then Florence. Then on down through Perryville and down on in there right on into Paducah. I went down there the 19th of February this year and got on the *Avalon* and piloted it to Knoxville and back to Paducah. The captain run out of a mate, so I just used my masters license and acted mate for him up here.

Q: They hauled a lot of railroad ties out of Florence.

JD: There was a lot of railroad ties down there, I've hauled many. I've loaded many a barges of cross ties up on the Tennessee River on the boat and carried them into Chattanooga. Put it off there. Back in the old raft days, I talked to raftsmen 70 miles above Chattanooga and asked one of them where so and so was that I knew, and he come back and told me he was landing at South Chickamauga Creek, that was 70 miles they had talked to one another. They was running that close together. You know rafts of logs going down the river. I run a store boat about two years during that time, sold goods up and down the river. I knew from Decatur, Alabama and Six Miles River practically to Kingston, Tennessee. That's about 350 miles. I got off the boat one morning at Pinhook before breakfast and started out the road, and smelling that good country ham and I got hungry. I said, "The next house I pass cooking that ham I'm going in and get me a sandwich." So I went to the backdoor and knocked on the door and took my hat off and stretched out my arm and a woman came to the door and says, "Come on in, Mr. Dobbs, we are just serving breakfast now." People I knew, you know. And that's just the way it run.

Q: Can you tell me something about that rafting?

JD: That raft logs? Well you see you take all up Clinch River and French Broad and Emory and all them rivers, all the year these old raftmen would build up a dam and when the rains would come in the fall of the year late, why they'd come out. I've known them to run by me when I was on my store boat, they would come by me. I got acquainted with 100s of them. I'd sell them stuff on credit and they'd pay me when they would come back up the river on a boat the next Sunday. They would run for sometimes four days and nights talking to me another from me raft to another. I've seen them stacked there at Chattanooga seven miles to the Cincinnati New Orleans Bridge. I've seen them landed there and they would be five and six wide out in the river. When the sawmill would get ready for them, they would just drop the raft into the sawmill and they would pull it up and saw it up. That's the way they done it, them old logs. You take Poplar Creek on the Clinch River. I've seen Poplar logs come out there be, a floating four feet high. The prettiest things you ever seen in your life.

Q: I bet they are. About how long ago was that?

JD: That was back in 1902 and 1903 and 1904 and along in there when they run them thick. I've come in on a steamboat and got behind them at Soddy. It's about three or four miles through that island, through them shoals. Have to back up and float behind them until I could get out. Couldn't get past them at all, had to back up and floated with a raft of logs through so we could get out, until we got down where it was wide enough to get around them.

Q: Must have been big rafts.

JD: Oh they was, some of them would be a thousand feet long and maybe 50, 60, 80 and 90 feet wide. Loomis and Howard bought most of it there. A big sawmill there on the bank at Chattanooga. I've watched them pull them out of the river and saw them up and make lumber out of them. The old raftmen would get their money, and then go get drunk. Some get on the *Joe Wheeler*. Got 100 night one night on there and the cook cooked a thousand biscuits and they ate

John Knoepfle

every one of them. We tied up our barges and loaded all the freight on and made a hard run to Kingston and put them off before breakfast and they sure did cuss us out. (chuckles) They was mad because they got off before breakfast. You are getting the whole history of the Tennessee River.

Q: That's right, I'll get as much as you can give me.

JD: One night, I clerked the boat four years, and one night a man named Ralston, Mr. Ralston and his wife and two babies were on the boat. One of the babies was about three years old and the other one was in her arms. I carried the little one, three year old, it was a pretty steep bank and set him down on top of the bank. Wasn't thinking about anything and when I got back to the boat and got the baby out of Mrs. Ralston's arms and looked around and he was rolling towards the river and he was going to go on the barge. I didn't have time to give Mrs. Ralston back the baby, I jumped in the river ahead of the little fellow rolling down the river, with her baby in my arm. She fainted on the boat. Said that man jumped in the river with my baby. I had to jump in there to catch little one coming down the deckhands came around and got us all out. I got out and she got all right. After that I met the man and his boy on the Market Street Bridge 15 years after that. He said, "Here is the man that saved your life." I looked at him and he says, "What do you think about it now Mr. Dobbs? Do you think you could save him?" I said, "No." He weighed 365 pounds. If he rolled me again now he'd knock me plum across the river. I'm going to tell you about when I quit farming that was the best job I ever had in my life, plowing Old Buck. I got to arguing with my daddy and we was talking, it was 1903 in July. I got to talking to him, I was 17 years old and I told him, "If ever I do get 21 years old I will never plow anymore." I says, "I'm tired of it, especially for the other fellow. If ever I plow again it will be on my own land." We plowed on, we was making our last round and he stopped about halfway in the field and made me stop to talk to him. He said, 'Now when you get out son, you don't never have to plow another round if you don't want to." When I had gotten to about ten feet of the end of the row and took that old double shoveled plow and I commenced riding and when I got it up the beam the mule stalled it. He drove up and said, "What are you doing son?" I said, "I'm setting my plow down and I'll never take ahold of another as long as I live." I'm still living and I ain't had ahold of one since. (chuckles)

Q: Well tell me about that country twix the rivers they were just talking about.

JD: Where was that?

Arthur Schletker: Up at Grand Rivers you know, up at Kentucky Dam. It takes the train one minute to go across.

JD: It doesn't take long.

AS: Up there around Kuttawa and Grand Rivers.

JD: I worked on the Kentucky Dam. I was there working for the government, had a little boat called *H. P. Powell* and all I had to do was to stay there. They was filling the lake and if anybody got caught on the islands and couldn't get home I had to go get them off. But never did nobody got caught, so I laid there in Blood River for about three months and didn't even move. I had a good time, going the country there and a man was smoking his tobacco and I thought his house was on fire. I run to the house and told him his barn had burned up and he said, "That's all right. I'm just smoking my tobacco." So I didn't know anything about smokehouses.

AS: Do you know about how down there around, what's the name of that town where that preacher wouldn't go in? I started up the river with him. I said, "Now, brother, I want to tell you something. This is bad country." He said, "Well, I'm a bad man. When I'm with the Lord, I'm with the Lord regardless. I'm used to Paducah." And this little town was called. Oh, there's Panther Creek, you know back of Panther Creek.

JD: I know Where Panther creek is. I went up in Panther Creek one time with this little boat and waves were up and had to lay there all night. Fellow had a little old store up on the bank. I went up there and set around there until it got dark and went back to the boat and covered up in blankets to keep the mosquitos from eating you up. Got up the next morning and went up there and him and his wife was eating breakfast and they had some of the best looking coffee I had ever seen. I said, "I'd give a dollar for a cup of coffee, but I ain't ever got no cup of coffee yet." The boys come over, we moved on down to Blood River and got down there old man Miller, the boss I was going to work under, he was cooking breakfast and had a good pot of coffee everything, I sure did eat.

CE: You don't mean Golden Pond do you?

AS: Golden Pond, yes!

CE: Where the owls and the chickens fought every night?

JD: I told him about the chickens flying on and off the boat.

AS: I don't know if you did or not.

Q: Yes, he told me about that.

JD: Well I'll tell you another one about going up the river in low water. We went up river one time in low water and told everybody it was the last trip for that year. Coming back down right above a big shoal we run into 1,000 coops of turkeys. Got them on the boat and got down there and got hung up on them shoals and an old mate, he got to walking around, nobody paying much attention to him, and he went and filled his pockets full of tacks and opened them coops of turkeys up and nailed their feets to the floor. Pulled out his pistol and shot it and they flopped their wings and raised the boat up and we went on.

Q: You can't fool me on that. That was the *Katie Prather*.

JD: Was it?

Q: Yes, that happened up here at Brush Creek.

AS: Well I'll tell you just something like that I heard. A goose, they nailed him down. Do you know how Golden Pond got its name? Well I know the story very well.

CE: The town in itself was down in a little valley.

AS: I named a light after Earl Jacobs, right down from it.

CE: And up on the westside of the hill. The town in itself was in a little valley and upon the side of the hill there was a big sawmill there and they had a pond that was used to feed water to the boiler. In the late afternoon when the sun would go down and sink behind the hills there, it would cast a reflection or a shadow on this pond and make the water look like it was a golden color. That is the origin of the name of the town of Golden Pond. But today there is no town there but the pond is still there. I've stopped many times to look at it.

Q: A saw town went out with the lumber going!

CE: Yes and then the town was moved about a mile down the hill. Yes, there is still a Golden Pond Post Office midway between the Cumberland River and the Tennessee River and it's called Twixt the River. People in there have a reputation of being pretty rugged.

AS: That's where the route of the new canal, the proposed canal from Tennessee to Cumberland River after the Barkley Dam is built is the route of this. Right across there above Eureka. You know Eureka Bridge. That's a bad bridge to hit now let me tell you.

CE: I have ferried across the Cumberland River at Canton. There is a little town called Canton at the Cumberland before they built the bridge, and then over on the Tennessee River, I've ferried across there, and that was called Egner's Ferry. Where the bridge is now over the Kentucky Lake.

AS: Wasn't that the sandy River? No, that was Centerville. Sandy River was Centerville. I named a light after Earl Jacobs right up in there someplace. Do you remember when the *Blue Spot* laid out in that Ingram Bar there for many years? There was a whole boat laying out there. It was sunk, in a sunken condition. Just like we have one up here in the Ohio River that way. It's surprising, you take these towns along the Ohio River and places, it's just like at Shawneetown. They went to move Shawneetown back on the hill, I was surprised, I went out there one day, saw a whole grain elevator going out the road. A little bit later, here was the city water tower on a truck going on out the roads to a new town they established on the hill back of Shawneetown.

CE: Well that's what they are going to do with the town of Kuttawa. A lot of people cannot correctly pronounce that name. K-U-T-T-A-W-A is pronounced Kutoy and it's is only about a mile from Eddyville where the Kentucky State Penitentiary is located and Lock F is there too. Now to get back up there to Canton and the Cumberland River, right below Lock E is what is known as Devil's Elbow. A pilot has to maneuver around there.

AS: Devil's Elbow?

JD: In the river there in 1934.

CE: A pilot has to maneuver around there?

JD: Yes, I found the end of it down there.

AS: Money Cliff and those places like there where . . .

Q: Tell me about me about that finding the end of the river.

JD: Well, we were working for the Dixie Sand and Gravel Company and they had three new barges built at Nashville. So they sent a little diesel boat they had over there after it and sent me with it. Had a pilot go with me to Nashville, but when I got to Nashville they called him to work for the government and he left me there and I had Mr. Paget, my boss. I says, "How are you going to get back out here?" And he said, "You're going to take it back out." I said, "Well supposing I sink it?" "If it does, it belongs to the company and there won't be nothing said to you about it." So I brought that and I got down to Devil's Elbow down there, I thought I had found end of the Cumberland River. I stopped and backed up and fiddled around there a while and finally I got around it. I got the barges all back to Chattanooga all right. He said, "I told you, you could do it." (chuckles) I said, "Yes, but I wouldn't do it again for $100."

AS: Is that below Eureka?

JD: I don't know where that is. Devil's Elbow is down below Eddyville somewhere.

CE: No, it's just above Canton where the bridge crosses there and just below Lock E.

AS: Lock E, yes. I know that I went up there. I went up on this boat the *Avalon* one time and just because those fellows weren't used to this kind of boat, I was going to make the locks for them. They had several fellows, one of them is Buchanan. I don't know if you know him or not.

JD: Buchanan yeah I heard of him.

AS: He knew the river all right, but he was afraid of the boat. Well anyhow Lock F was down and there was nine inches of a drop. Well a man waved at me to go on the outside way. First, I came in and got in shape to go in the locks. I saw the ripple over the dam and I started up with this boat. Believe me Mr., I gave her all she had and it looked like climbing a mountain. All of a sudden she got to the top and she made it. Bo was up there with me and he said, "You had better stop her." Of course, I stopped her in that bed down below. I upset this boat three times trying to get her straightened up there, it was so swift Finally we wiggled in among those pilings and got into the lock. Nine inches was a little too much for this boat, but of course with a towboat it would have been all right. It would have had something to steady her. Of course, if I would of had something on the head of this boat it would have been all right too. But it didn't have anything and she just kept on climbing.

CE: You know right below Devil's Elbow and the bridge at Canton the packet boat *B. S. Rhea* went aground there one time. The water was falling so fast and before they could get her backed out she was hard aground. They simply left her there all summer long. She stayed there for six or eight months. I have a picture of her on the ground there. It's a good picture. They went out and shored up under her cylinder timbers and round her guards to keep her from breaking off, a wheel off. She stayed there for several months and there was a big flat rock that sticks out there and there still is. That was the *B. S. Rhea*.

John Knoepfle

AS: That wasn't at Money Cliff was it?

CE: No, that was right there at Canton.

JD: That place I went around there was a bluff come way out towards the river. Just a big flat rock came out in the river there.

AS: They tried to steer that several times with that *Yocona*. She sank twice up there.

JD: Now I'm going to tell you about going through the mountains right below Chattanooga from Suck Creek Road to Kelly's Ferry it is about seven or eight miles and all of them stills around there. Boy, there's some gals down there that sure can sing too. A revenue man by the name of Jim Jones tore them up all the time. He called me one time, I was raised with Jim and he called me and says, "I want to make a trip with you down river tomorrow." I said, "There ain't but one way you can go down there with me, Jim." And he says, "What's that?" I says, "Come in the pilothouse and sit down and take your hat off." I said, "You can't get off of the boat nowhere between here and down there and back." I said, "Now if you want to go with me that away, you can go. I have to go through them mountains every day and they have all kinds of rifles down there. If they found out I was carrying a revenue man down through there they would shoot me out of the pilothouse." So he says, "I will go with you John, I don't care." We got down there and he offered me $10 to land and put him off. I said, "No, I told you, you would go back to Chattanooga." I took him back to Chattanooga. He went down there the next morning and got about 12 or 15 of them. They never did know that I done it though. I've got holes in the pilothouse and on the stacks and over the kitchen back there. It just like to killed the cook, he had just stepped away when a bullet went through there. They shot at me, but they didn't shoot at me an account of that whiskey business, on account of the waves turned a boy's boat over and made him mad and he just cut down at me with a target, you know. Then his daddy came to me in Chattanooga and begged me not to do anything with him. He said, "I won't let him have the gun anymore, I'll take it away from him." I knew the man and I told him I wouldn't bother about it and just let the boy go. "But tell him to be careful about shooting, he might kill somebody." And he did.

AS: The first trip down the river that I ever made below Cincinnati right below the Suspension Bridge here at the high speed boat called *Florence Marmet*, we took part of her stuff off her. We had the Fall City Dock there, we had a lot of parts of different boats that we put together and made the *John Barret* out of, *One Armed John*. We went up here below Ripley, there was a place out in the river with a red buoy on it, called Dover, Kentucky. It was a place where the trucks would drive out in low water and put stuff on the packetboats. We landed again that way and put about five heifers and a bull on there and to take to Barrett's Quarry down at Rappolees Landing. You know that's in the Cumberland River where they had that big landing. Now it's a limestone plant. They crush rock, there's crushed rock, mountains of it down there.

JD: Barrett's Quarry.

AS: Anyhow I go down there and I tried to milk this cow and I couldn't milk. I was a city boy. I couldn't milk this cow, and a colored fellow he did, pretty good. So we drank milk all the way down the river. We got that thing off before the ice started up in this part of the country. We was down there, Harry Dawson was the pilot, Clem Carter was the Captain of her, I was the second engineer on there. Hiram Howe was the chief. We left here with the first tow of automobiles that ever left this part of the country. Loaded them on these big pair of long barges that could only run in daylight. That was before there was any dams in the Ohio River outside of 37 down here and they were building 48. No other dams in here. Gee whiz, small boats were all aground down lower river and this *John Barret* was so light that we passed a lot of them just by more luck than sense. Just by drifting slowly by them. We would get by with no power.

JD: My wife was born and raised in England. One time she went back to England. I got her to come back and so we got married.

AS: Where did you meet her at John?

JD: Met her at a little town called Grayville up at the mouth of the Hiwassee River.

AS: And she come from England over to a place like Grayville?

JD: So she never asks me about when I'll be back or when I'm going. I don't ask her anything. We just go off and come back. We have been married 43 years and we haven't had any short words yet. My boy has been in the Navy nine years, he just got back from Malta. I went with them to Bath, Maine last year about this time. We was on the road up there in his car. We got to Bath, Maine, stayed there through the last 4th of July, and then he got transferred from Bath, Maine about a month ago to Jacksonville, Florida. But they sent him to Malta and he spent 15 days over there. And they sent him back. Now him and his wife and two babies are home and here I am stuck off up here. I'd give anything to be there, but I'll be home some of these days to see them kids. They call me Mule, you know, I ride them they call me Mule all the time. We have a time, them kids. I talked to them Sunday and the little one, one is four and the other is just going on two so the one four year old says, "Mule, when are you coming home?" I says, "I'll be home some of these days."

Q: I understand that the Tennessee is so narrow that the branches of the trees scrape the pilothouse sometimes.

JD: Well that is just in places. It's not that way now because we have got some places 15 miles wide now. These lakes have made wide rivers out of them, made oceans out of nearly all of them. It used to be you would get up Hiwassee River to Charleston, 18 miles you could come out of there easy in a hour you know, you'd be scraping trees on both sides. Same way with Clinch River in above Kingston, all them little rivers, used to be riding both banks coming up.

Q: Imagine those boats you were on didn't draw much.

John Knoepfle

JD: Well, loaded they would draw about five and a half or six feet, light they would draw about 28 inches.

AS: . . . One of them over in the *John Ross*, he was telling me about fellow named . . .

JD: That's one, I watched on the *John Ross* coming on over from Dayton to Knox, that's where the first pilot wheel I ever had ahold of was on that towboat.

AS: She was the funniest tramp boat I ever saw in my life, and she was a packet-boat. She had a scow bow you know, and cabins, and everything on them, looked kind of funny.

JD: I stayed on her with Captain Joe Thompson.

CE: Captain Dobbs were you ever on the Chattanooga?

JD: Yes, I have been on the Chattanooga.

CE: She was the Gospel boat called the *Meggido*.

JD: Yes, she come out of the old *Meggido* when she come to Chattanooga, what they . . .

AS: She was built here, wasn't she?

JD: I don't know where she was built at. We carried excursions two or three years with her out of Chattanooga.

AS: She was converted years ago into a . . .

JD: I guess that's about played out, ain't it?

Q: Oh, no.

CE: This *Meggido* boat was built somewhere in the upper Mississippi River, probably around Wabasha or Winona. Some fellow was somewhat of a religious fanatic and he built the boat to carry the gospel to the various sections of the country. In other words, he had his crew on there, his preachers, his choirs, leaders and directors. He operated several years as the gospel boat and the word Meggido is a Biblical term. Finally he was played out and the funny thing about her captain, her Texas was the same width as her cabin. Ordinarily a Texas on a boat is narrow. But on this boat the Texas was the same width as her cabin, I have some pictures of her.

AS: Did they have a runway around then?

CE: No.

AS: How did people get in and out of there?

CE: Well they did had some short steps up, short steps up like you . . .

AS: Oh yes, I see.

JD: Well, I'll tell you some more about the *Joe Wheeler*.

CE: After they converted her to the Chattanooga they removed that Texas and her pilothouse sat right on hurricane roof.

JD: Back to the *Joe Wheeler* again. That's the boat that run between Chattanooga and Kingston, the whistle on there run through that for 80 years. There was never another whistle in the world like it. I never heard another one sound anything like it. It was the prettiest whistle ever was. It was so clear you could hear it 21 miles, I have. We'd get to Cottonport every Sunday morning about ten o'clock just about the time for church and everybody in Cottonport would come to the river. Leave the preacher by himself. Didn't make any difference about him, he got to where he came with them. Sometimes he would preach to them right there on the bank close to the boat. It was a fact that way, we got many a letter wanting us to stop blowing the whistle there at Cottonport but we got ten times more from the people telling us not to stop blowing.

AS: No doubt you fellows know Henry Carroll.

JD: Yes, I heard of him.

AS: He was down there, he was on this *Greenbrier*, see. We hired pilots to go in different places. Well Henry Carroll was our Tennessee River pilot one time.

JD: I have seen him at Florence many a time.

AS: We stopped at Perryville one time and everything was going good. Perryville was known as rough tough customers. This old preacher come in, and doggone we didn't have nothing else to do, and we went to church that night. This was a knocked out church right up on the riverbank. And by golly come there with a mule and doggone, he reached in one pocket and laid the Bible down and the other one, doggone, he laid a pistol down. He said, "I use this to preach the word of God." He said, "And I use this to protect myself again ruffians." And they were all scared to death of him. "Brother Carroll, lead us in prayer." And Henry Carroll prayed there for an hour it seemed like.

JD: We went to Knoxville on the *General Joe Wheeler*. The boat was named after General Joe Wheeler. We went to Knoxville when she was new built and brought him downriver. Brought him down the river on his boat that was named after him. The *Joe Wheeler* was a pretty boat in my opinion.

AS: Stay and eat supper with us.

Q: Oh, I better go back, I think.

JD: Well, you might near got it all, so we'll call it a day, what do you think?

AS: But you can stay here and eat dinner with us.

Q: All right.

JD: Yes, stay and eat dinner with us. It won't hurt you.

AS: Tell him that again.

JD: Paul Perryman, Mississippi River pilot, he was on the Chattanooga and he's coming out of Suck Creek, awful swift water, and she got away from him and run over and hit this rock and we changed the name from Suck Creek Rock to Perryman's Rock. It's got that name yet.

AS: Well, Paul Perryman was a funny kind of a guy. You know Bruinski? You know little Will Bruinski? He said one time that Bruinski, after they shut down C & I Business down in Joppa, he was going to get a new job, draft work up in some bank in Chicago. Was going to raise the window so the people would have plenty of air.

JD: Well you couldn't get through the mountains back in low water times because no boat wasn't stout enough to push through the mountains, you had to put outlines and wind them through there.

Q: Capstan and a line.

JD: Yes, we had to put the lines through there. These old mountaineers would come down and lay lines for you on those swift waters. They'd carry them up, three or four of them would carry them up and we'd wind through with the line, you know. I never was on a boat that had power enough to push through them.

Q: Captain Hornbrook was on a boat called the *Bessie Smith* up through there. Bought it at Smithsonia.

AS: The *Bessie Smith* was running out of, *S. H. Clarke* now not the *Samuel Clarke*, she was a big boat, but anyhow the *Bessie Smith* was built at Point Pleasant. She went up in the upper Allegheny River. She was owned by somebody up in there, and this old Captain Smith run her for a long while. You remember, there was a bunch of them Smiths were all Tennessee River pilots. One of them called Yellow Dan, you know.

JD: There was Roy Smith, Roy's still living, he lives at Paducah.

AS: His brother was Roy, and oh his brother, what was his name? He was on the boats quite a long while.

JD: Well, there was Billy Smith, Roy, and . . .

CE: Captain Dobbs, who was it owned that boat that ran on the Duck River called the *Lula E. Warren*?

JD: *Lula E. Warren*. Well, now the Dayton Coal and Iron Company down in there and she towed coal, towed iron ore from Dayton to Knox on the Tennessee River the last time.

CE: She was built up in there on the Duck River.

JD: I don't know where she was built, but anyhow the Dayton Coal and Iron Company bought her and she towed iron ore from Knox to Dayton.

Q: Every time I turn that off you start up with something. He, Schletker did that to me over at his house a whole afternoon.

JD: Did he? (laughter)

AS: You get to thinking and all that stuff kind of comes to you. You know Duck River Sucks was always the place the pilots all hated to go down there. What is that name in the bends down there? I put a day mark up there.

JD: Big Bend Shoals or what?

AS: No, down through Duck River Sucks. Right before the Sucks.

JD: Oh that's the . . .

AS: Crossing there.

JD: That's the Pan when you get down there, the Skillet.

AS: No, I mean this is way down in lower, the Duck River Sucks. The Big Four Landing you know, and all this. This dam there takes care of that a whole lot now. This Kentucky Dam takes care, it's in the Kentucky Dam area. That's the Duck River I'm talking about. Then of course, we used to land at Leadbetter, you know they had iron, they used to get iron out of there. John Rowland and his brother. What was the other Rowland's brother's name? Two Rowland brothers. They had the *Enterprise* up there for a while. The *Enterprise* she was a light boat. Charlie Merges built her. He built her in Brownsville, Pennsylvania. I think Charlie Merges was in the Combine office there for a long while.

CE: Well, there was a fellow down there at . . . trying to think of the name of that town. They built the *Lula E. Warren* and he named it for his daughter, and on Duck River, he had a big general country store and cotton.

AS: Well, wasn't she one of . . . Kentucky boats?

JD: She sunk up there around Big Creek. The *Lula E. Warren* did.

AS: What was she named, one of these Kentucky River boats, what was the name of that? Ellen, Helen, you know Grainger was captain of her. And Cy Korm was engineer for a long way.

JD: That company up there bought the *J. J. White*. I guess you have seen it or heard of it? It came up there, it was a pretty good little boat, and Captain Thompson and I had worked with him two years or three, and Cap was pretty bad then. Before I was coming into the creek there, the general manager of the Dayton Coal and Iron Company was out on the bank. He thought Cap was cussing him and he was just cussing the boat you know. And he fired him. They put a ad in the paper for a pilot. I was always pilot on the *Joe Wheeler*. So I just got on a train and went to Dayton to see about it. I went in the office there and was talking to a manager there and he said, "Well, you want to go down to the river?" I said, "No, I know what kind of boats you got down there. I just want to know what is the matter with you and Captain Thompson?" So he said, "That's my business," and I said, "Yes, and it's mine too." I said, "You've got a pilot down there, and if he can't give you satisfaction there ain't a man in the world can. If he can't do that work there is not another pilot that I know of that can do it as good as he can. He has been in that trade for 20 years that I know of." I said, "You've got the best pilot on the Tennessee River for that job, and I'd advise to keep him cause I ain't going down there and I don't want his job," and I says, "I'm going." He says, "Well, he's leaving here." I says, "You'd better stop him if you want a pilot because you ain't going to get none."

So I went downtown and I met Captain Thompson, he was coming in town, fellow bringing him in in a dray and had his trunk in there. Put it off at the station and I went walking around and he looked at me kind of mad. He thought I had come up there to get his job. I said, "Come here a minute, Captain I want to talk to you." He says, "What about?" I says, "I want to know what the trouble is down there." Well he says, "You know I cuss a whole lot and he thought I was cussing him, and I wasn't, and he fired me." I says, "Well now before this train leaves he is going to be down here to see you." He says, "How do you know?" I says, "I have been down there and talked to him and I told him he had better keep you if you could." And so before the train left he came running. I said, "Now if put a $10 raise on. Don't go back if he don't give you $10 more." So he came down and I seen them meet on the corner of the depot there. I was standing on the street watching. He stood firm and the man gave

John Knoepfle

him a $10 raise and he went back and stayed there as long as the *J. J. White* stayed there. Never had any more trouble. I couldn't stand to see him do anything to Captain Thompson. I told him, "I wouldn't have the job as long as Cap Thompson was living. You've got the best man I know of worked under him two years. I know what he can do and that's the reason I'm telling you. If you take my advice you'll get down there as quick as you can, don't let him catch that train, and send him back to that boat." He went down there, and he went back and he got a $10 raise. They paid off in gold there all the time. Got him a $10 gold piece. Next time I saw him he said, "Johnny, I got that $10 raise." I said, "I know you did." He said, "Much obliged." I asked, "Captain, did you think I come up there to get your job?" He says, "I didn't know."

AS: This is Captain Lawrence Allen, just got up here and he's got a cup of coffee in his hand and he says he can't talk very much, but he has a legend of experience in the lower Ohio River, especially between Louisville and Evansville, Indiana, were he run for many years on the steamers *Tarascon* and *Evansville* and several others. Then in later years he would have spent 14 years on the *Chris Greene*, running between Cincinnati, Louisville and West Virginia. Now from there, go on, Bo, tell him something.

Lawrence Allen: I was on the *Gordon Greene* about 14 summer seasons between Cincinnati and New Orleans, St. Paul, Minnesota. I was on the Greene Line. Stayed with them till they went out of business with the freight business, then I went with the government, worked four years, I've been on the steamer *Avalon* six years. Nice boat to be on. I've been on about 98 boats all together.

JD: Go ahead and talk. We ain't bothering you. Go ahead and talk.

LA: I can't think of nothing, just getting out of bed.

AS: I know, but that ought to make it still better.

LA: Yes, it ought to be better, oughtn't it?

AS: I'll tell you, the experience, you had more Ohio River on those Greene Line boats, the *Gordon* and the large one. The *Delta Queen*, you was on her for quite a while and also on the *Chris*.

LA: On the *Delta Queen* two years.

AS: Tell him some stories about either one of those boats.

LA: I'll tell him the one about the wild goose down at Grandview.

AS: That's right.

LA: Well, I was working for Doctor Mayo on his boats, I believe it was. They had a gun on there. What was the Doctor Mayo boat? The *Glenmore*, and I saw a big bunch of wild geese, bunch of wild geese across the river. I was coming up the Kentucky shore and the mate got his gun and he shot the bunch. He killed two. And he said he got the one he shot at. It was darn near a mile from the bunch of geese. Saying that he got the one he shot at, you know. (laughter) But he didn't get them.

AS: He didn't get them.

LA: No, the river was too low.

AS: That was the Doctor Mayo, on their boat.

LA: Yes, on Doctor Mayo's boat. Those were the surgeons, you know, from Rochester, Minnesota. The Mayo brothers, the Doctor's Mayo.

AS: Captain Allen was pilot on their boat at one time. And of course, he's been lots of time in the lower Ohio River. And boy, I want to tell you if there's ever a man knows the bottom of the doggone river, he showed me several places, and I found my way up through, so I have especially down French Island country.

LA: I like to stand watch with him. He started telling these tales. (laughter)

Q: Did you know an Ordie Devers down in that section of the country Captain?

LA: Devers? I've heard of him.

Q: Had the *Grace Devers*, the *C. C. Bowyer*.

LA: Oh yes, *Grace Devers*.

AS: I knew the *C. C. Bowyer*, very well. She's from Mount Vernon, Ohio. She's named after a banker up here at Point Pleasant. I knew him personally very well. The boat was called the *C. C. Bowyer*, and then of course I think the *Grace Devers*.

LA: Yes, *Grace Devers*.

AS: I don't know if he's had the experience of a lot of these others we have around here.

LA: *Grace Devers*. I'll tell you one of the fastest boat was ever around that part of the country, that *Speed*, you remember the *Speed*, don't you?

AS: Yes, I do.

LA: She'd go from Evansville to Spottsville in just one hour, 18 miles.

AS: Evansville to Spottsville. She had a long stroke.

LA: Yes, long stroke on her.

AS: They had her around here for a while. The Marmet Coal Company owned her.

LA: You remember?

AS: Tony Perry owned her.

CE: I'll tell you two other fast boats they had around there too Cap was the *Grand* and the *Rapid*.

LA: *Rapid*, yes.

AS: I remember the *Rapid*. When she sank I saw her, I saw her sink at Paducah.

LA: Paducah.

AS: Yes, you remember the cut down, in the ice? Funny thing she laid again the wharfboat, a big float of ice came right over foot of the island and run right in the side of her and sank her right at the Paducah wharfboat, and I was laying on Owens Island on the *John Barret*. Seen it happen. Seen her going down.

LA: Sunk her there?

AS: Right there, yes.

CE: You know, those two boats were built to run between Grand Rapids, Michigan and Grand Haven, Michigan, on the Grand River. After the trade

John Knoepfle

played out, they sold them, and they brought them, got them across Lake Michigan some way and brought them up into the Wisconsin River, through the Wisconsin River into the St. Croix River and down in the Mississippi and that's how they got . . .

AS: St. Croix. Yes. That's in Stillwater.

CE: I'm not sure they came down the Wisconsin River into the Mississippi River.

AS: On high water they could do that. Same as boats that were built in Wabash River around Terra Haute, and then have come down this Wabash River. You know, there's been boats going up there. Now the *I. N. Flesher*, you know, Frank Norwood and those fellows, you know, they towed corn for years out of Wabash River bottoms.

LA: Yes, used to be packetboats run up there, too.

AS: They did? Well, packet boats before my time.

LA: Well, I know of a fellow had a freight bill dated way back then, I guess 60, 70 years ago. That freight bill on some place up the Wabash River.

Q: How did they load that corn on? How did they get it on?

CE: By hand.

LA: By hand. And they had a chute that goes down, too. Put it in a chute, you know. Goes down on board.

AS: Same way that they load ties on the Tennessee River. They'd put a buffer down at the end. They'd slide these ties, some big hefty grab one of them on their shoulders and go on with it.

LA: Yes.

CE: Put it in the chute and down she goes.

LA: Get a cent a tie, loading them.

CE: They'd wet the chute every once in a while to make it slick. One time I was on the little towboat up the Green River called the *Samuel* had all these roustabouts there on there you know, and was loading ties. They always had a captain of the watch, you know.

LA: Oh, yes, the head one.

CE: He would store the ties in the barge as they come down the hill.

LA: Yes, he was just like a deckhand.

CE: Well, all the roustabouts up on the hill were carrying the ties from the tie piles to the chute and they got into an argument. I was standing out on the head of the boat and they were just arguing, and there wasn't these ties coming down. The old, old roustabout down in the barge storing them away said, "Hell with that argument up there, lower away the wood." (laughter)

AS: Lower away the wood! They'd get in the middle of them and stack them up. And that's what they used to do on the *Paducah*. In the last days out she'd take two or three carloads of that. And I was up there when Irvin Cobb, you knew of course I told him all about Irvin Cobb up in the upper river, and Lon

Shell was there and was mate on there and that old captain, not Dick Willis, just died here not too long ago, had a big mustache.

LA: Where'd he live, Evansville?

AS: No, Paducah.

LA: Oh yes.

JD: Oh I'll tell you who you're thinking about, Captain Peter I. Wilson.

AS: Pete Wilson, Pete Wilson's right. And he says, Gill come crying. He says, "Cap, I got that fellow Cobb on here and he's giving these roustabouts money," and he says, "I can't get this boat out." The captain says, "See what I can do with him. I don't know." He said, "Maybe Red Schletker can do something with him." So he turned them on and I eased on up to him and said, "Hi, Mr. Cobb, how are you?" I said, "Would you like to take a walk up to the store here?" Cuba Landing you know. So, gets on up to the store there and he says, "You don't think there'd be half a chance of getting a little liquor around here?" It was during Prohibition days, you know. I said, "I don't know, but it could be." So I called up this old colored fellow as we walked along. I said, "Uncle Henry, could you give us a little liquor?" He said, "I don't know." He said, "How much you want?" I said, "About a quart." He looked around. He said, "I don't know." And then he called me back after I got away. He said, "I ain't got it in quarts, but I got it in barrels, in charred barrels." I said, "Uncle Henry, how much is this barrel? Wait a minute, come here." I said, "How much is this barrel?" He said, "$5," I said, "$5 for a barrel?" And they were the cutest little barrels and they were charred, you know. And he, Cobb said, "Well, can we taste it?" "Yes, sir." He takes a doggone nail and drives it in there and doggone, Cobb gives him $10 for it, and he pulls through a reed straw you know, sipping it. Right through the straw. "How's that taste?" And after we got down to the river, time that the boat left, I says, "Now Pete, you tap the gong." I says, "And I'll get him on down here." He said, "Well, what are we going to do with the whiskey? How are we going to get this whiskey down there." I said, "I don't know." But I said, "Uncle Henry, do you think you can get this?" He said, "No, sir." I said, "$5?" "Yes, sir." So he got another $5, and doggone, he takes it out and puts it in a gunny sack and takes it to the fantail. We get to Paducah the next day says, "Where's them roustabouts get that whiskey you had there?" I said, "Whiskey? I don't know of any whiskey." He said, "Well, anyhow, I don't know. They never emptied this boat as quick as they did in their life." They got hooked for it you know, they left at six o'clock, left Paducah. Zelzie Riley I was telling you about was clerk on there, I picked him up, he's chief engineer at Christ Hospital out here now. I picked him up off the bank right there at Paducah. He was with you for a while on the *Gordon Greene*, wasn't he?

LA: Yes.

AS: He was getting a license on her anyhow.

Q: Captain Allen, what were some of the earlier boats you were on?

LA: The first boats, I started on a boat named the steamer *Tell City*. She was a packetboat, freight and passengers. And there was the *Morning Star*, *Tarascon*, there was a boat running on in my youth named *Alton*, and one named *Glenmore*, and I spent the last days of my river life, about ten or 15 years, I was working on other boats, like towboats.

AS: How long was you with the Evansville and Packet Company, you know?

LA: I'll tell you, it was about 15 years.

AS: About 15 years on the packetboats, the *Tell City* and *Tarascon* and the boats that they had there during low water periods.

LA: I was on one boat named *Nashville*, was one of the boats. I was on there ten years and six months, and never lost a day.

AS: Let's go on up there. Show me how to shut that thing off. Shut her off now anyhow for a while.

LA: I went down one morning, put the nickel in there. Felt in that box, was just running over with money. Somebody put money in there, walked away, thought it wasn't going to hit. I couldn't find out of course, who it belonged to. Yes, about $2 worth of nickels.

JD: I put a nickel in there.

AS: Well sir, that light below Evansville, that flashing green light, I was waiting for the power company to come there and put the light in. The power company, and they were going to connect the electric light on to it. And I saw this small half ton truck or something going along there. They're just stuck in the mud. A couple big bruisers got out of it, and tried to push, they couldn't do it. Well, I got a whole gang of men. I says, "Boys, let's go down and give them a push." We didn't know what it was. And that thing was filled full of nail kegs, five nail kegs filled full of money. And doggone, these boys give them a push, and these, "Here boys come on." He'd throw them, reach in a whole hand full out of there and hand them money, like that out of these kegs there, those nail kegs was full of money they got out of those slot machines at the Trockadaro. The big bruisers had guns on under their arms.

Q: Where was that, Captain?

AS: In Evansville, right below the Evansville waterworks. They was stuck in the bank, and I never saw anything like that in my life before.

LA: Giving it to them by the handful?

AS: Yeah, they give them to the boys. You know how much after that. And they were just reaching in all denominations. They were just as free with half dollars and dollars as they were with dimes. Bands of, "Here, boys." Each one of them got $4 or $5 out of it. At Three River Island, the Grace Park Race Track. Now they call it Ellen's Race Track.

LA: Ellen. Named for Jim Ellen.

AS: All in Kentucky, an old slough down through there.

LA: You know Joe Opman, didn't you, Captain?

AS: Yes.

LA: Why, he said he's been up through that place. Before it closed up. All a big island there. Still belongs to Kentucky. Had a big race track on it.

AS: Well, somebody told me, you take . . .

JD: The island where I was raised at the Cherokee Indians lived on there, the first governor of Tennessee lived with them on it. A long time ago. Known as Jolly's Island. They built a big mound on there. They built a race track. Old man Colonel Bray had a lot of race horses, he built a half mile race track around it. I've seen people in there from Chicago, everywhere getting on them races.

AS: Well, by jingo the Tennessee River's full of shell mounds.

JD: I'll tell you, if I had all of the pots, arrowheads, and tomahawks, and everything like that that I broke up and throwed away, I could be worth a million dollars now.

LA: What, throwed them in the river?

JD: You'd just go along on the ground, just take your hand that away, you'd stick yourself a handful, I'd take a spool of thread, we'd take a spool of thread and string them, just all on that spool of thread, you know, and then get to swinging and watch them run and watch them leave you know, and scatter them everywhere in the world. I think I've found pretty pots you know, and everything like that. Why I got an uncle, and you have heads, heads on them, he was plowing and he hit something, and he stopped and dug it up. Old man and old woman and five children made out of stone. They were sitting with their hands up this way, you know. And he dug them out and took them home and left them setting around in the chimney corners and around. Some fellow come through one time and gave him $10 for them. The last I heard of they sold for $300,000 in St. Louis.

AS: You still hear about that family killed right back of Paducah, you know, the whole family of them, even the dog. Carved out a monument, you know. They've got a fence around it. They have an idea it's about as far as from here to that there bulkhead and about from here to there wide. All right, Joe. We ain't mad at you now, Joe. Think we're mad at you, cause we ain't.

Q: You were talking before putting a harbor boat crosswise to get them through that canal in Louisville. Can you tell me something about that?

LA: Yes in high water you know, we had not quite enough water to go over the falls, they'd come down Grassy Shoals by Jeffersonville. We had boats there that were pretty good boats that transferred.

AS: He knows more about them falls than anybody around here.

LA: Put this towboat right on the head. You want to shove her into the bank, you blow two whistles, and you want to bring the head away from the bank a little bit you blow one whistle. And one to stop and shove them right on down into canal almost at, go right down from Fourth Street down the first, the falls. They'd have these towboats to hold them in there.

Q: Did you ever navigate over the falls yourself?

LA: Sure did. I was running them falls for years.

John Knoepfle

Q: Could you describe getting down there? I don't think there's anybody around anymore that's piloted over low water.

LA: No, nobody but I went over there 21 feet through the locks once.

AS: 21 feet.

LA: See run them, all the locks on the fall. And there's a fall when the river's down, the falls, you go down to six feet right now. Just like it was forever.

Q: Do you steer by certain eddies, and lights, and marks?

LA: Yes, we had marks to go by. A place they call the big eddy. Go over the falls there. That's the biggest fall right below Jeffersonville. Running the big C & I Bridge on into New Albany. Yes, I run them falls, all kinds of weather, smoking lights, torch lights.

CE: Now you take when they complete that Barkley Dam, Cap. There will only be two locks between the mouth of the Cumberland River and Nashville. That will be Barkley and Cheatham.

JD: And then Cheatham will back the water up to Old Hickory.

AS: They're going to put, they're going to put locks in then at Barkley Dam, are they?

CE: That's my understanding.

LA: Oh, that would be faster at Paducah, then you get . . .

CE: You go up the Tennessee, then come through the canal.

LA: And they'll be lots of business up the Cumberland River then.

JD: Oh yes.

AS: Wouldn't that be quicker?

CE: I don't believe so.

AS: Coming all the way around Paducah and on up in there.

CE: It's 13 miles from Paducah up to Smithland.

AS: And 30 odd miles up the river to Eureka.

CE: Well, I believe you call it 20 miles up to Kentucky Dam Gilbertsville.

LA: That will make a big cut off won't it?

JD: Yes, it will make a cut off all right.

CE: It's going to take a long time before they get that canal cut through.

LA: Yes, it will be a long time.

AS: I wondered about the boiler codes and everything else. (laughter)

JD: You mean he's still got that thing running here? (laughter)

Q: This is real authentic stuff. The only one who will want to listen to it is another inland steamboat man.

LA: Before the dam was built, you used to carry lots of ducks and geese and stuff like that, Cap?

AS: Oh, it's just like when they built Gallipolis, or when they built the other ones. The people kicked and kicked. When they put the lock in Gallipolis, then they wanted 11, 10 and 9 in the Kanawha, and 26, 25 and 24 in the Ohio River. And the people kicked to beat the band. They didn't know what they were kicking about. Now they wouldn't have it the other way.

LA: I've seen these boats boat going down one time largely loaded with geese in the creek ran aground.

JD: Where was that?

AS: Loaded with what?

LA: loaded with geese.

JD: Geese!

AS: All right.

LA: And she was hard aground. So they decided, the mate said, "I'll just take geese out of the coop and put them in the hull." Well they put all these geese in the hull and he got down there he hollered, "Shoo!" And every one of them jumped up and the boat jumped and moved. forward. (laughter)

AS: All right that's three versions of it you've got now.

Q: Yes I'll write an article on this: ducks, geese, turkeys and chickens.

CE: All right, I'll tell you one about the geese. In the fall of the year you're going up the river you know, and you run into a flock of geese, and the geese is going south. And you get, the headlights blind them, they just fly at you.

AS: I've seen that.

JD: I'll tell you what I've done one time. I was on a little boat called the *Pilot*. We was up the Hiwassee River. Millions of wild geese flew into the search lights, and I grabbed one of them, and I had to turn the son of a bitch loose. He'd of flew in the river with me. I had him by the legs, too.

Q: Big geese down there!

AS: Did you ever knew George Trapp? Well, George Trapp and I for fun, we got into a restaurant down there at Osceola. He says, "What do you want?" He says, "I got wild goose." He was going to give us something wild.

LA: I did a true story. I was going down one night down at Sugar Creek Bend. I heard an old walloon hollering. It a dark night and raining. So I throwed a headlight out to see what he was doing. Throwed the headlight out and, my God, 1,000 ducks I guess in a bunch. They got started towards that headlight and we got 14 ducks for dinner next day. There was a racehorse up that day named Walloon. I bet him, he win. That's sure enough a true story.

AS: By jingo, I was coming up from Cairo and right above the Cairo Bridge a fog shut down on us. And Chandler was on there with me and I said, "Chandler, what are we doing to do?" He said, "What do you want to do?" I said, "I don't know. If we keep this away, we hit a bridge pier, we just hit it. We'll try and keep close. Maybe we can shove her ahead or back." Well, finally we landed. We hit a sandbar, and none of us knew where we was at, and nothing else, and the ducks were flying right through our search light by golly, and some of the boys got a couple of them down below, but I never got any. But I got something to eat out of it anyhow. And as soon as the daylight come up by golly, hey looking right up above, like we was looking at the Suspension Bridge here, we were looking right up at that Illinois Central, that I C Bridge.

LA: Right on to it, wasn't you?

AS: Right on to it. We knew where we were before we shut down. Well, that's the way it goes. When you get in those fogs.

JD: That old fog on the Tennessee River When we was running chickens and corn.

AS: Yes.

JD: They fly off the wrong port, they got lost. (laughter)

LA: You knew Mike Caplinger, didn't you, Cap?

AS: What?

LA: Mike Caplinger run on the Green River. Well, Mike's coming down the river, claims he's the best pilot on the Green River, he's coming down one night. Of course they had a dog on the head of the boat in a box. He's a coasting along working slow, and he heard a dog bark. He said, "That's Brown's dog. I know where I'm at now." He went on down a little further, and another dog barked. He thought he heard another. He said, "That's Smith's, I know that's Smith, right on out here on the bank." Come to find that dog's on the head of the boat, in that box. (laughter)

CE: Did you ever hear the story about Knight Bolls? Did you ever know Knight Bolls, the Green River pilot? He ran over the saw log raft up there at Lock 3. This is a true story, too. I'm writing a story about it.

AS: Green River, that's right.

CE: This saw log raft was anchored; it was tied up on the Ohio County side right above Lock 3. That's a little town called Rochester. Come out of the lock there, foggy as the dickens, the raft had a shanty on it, you know was a tent. This tent was mildewed. And there was eight men in that tent, separated four white men and four colored. They had a little boat, the *Samuel.* I fired her for two and a half years. She just drove right up on to that raft, pushed that tent right down in the river and drowned all four of those white men; those colored's took out on the raft you know all of them got off. Well they sued Captain Bolls and they sued the Erin Log Tie Company, and I've been doing some research over there at Hartford, Kentucky on that. That happened on January 4, 1909.

AS: That so!

CE: No 1906 is when the accident happened, the trial came up in 1909.

AS: Well, you know Gene Ross, don't you?

CE: Oh sure.

AS: You know, Gene can play that mockingbird whistle any kind of tune.

CE: Can play a tune on it.

AS: Can play about like a calliope.

CE: Yes he could.

LA: Yes he could play that thing couldn't he?

CE: Yes he was known all up and down that river.

AS: Oh gee whiz, I'll tell you one time we was laying in the mouth of the Green River, Captain Hill and I, I hollered, "Oh, Gene!" He blowed the whistle, dark, some fellow come up and held her, he just played "My Old Kentucky Home."

CE: Yes he played that and . . .

AS: On his mockingbird whistle just as good as anybody can play it on the calliope.

CE: "Old Black Joe."

LA: Yes.

CE: "In the Sweet By and By," "Dixie."

AS: You know what a mockingbird whistle is don't you?

Q: No.

AS: It's a steam whistle built with a plunger in the side. They can raise up and down, same as you have a slide trombone. And you can change the tune of the whistle by shutting off part of it.

CE: Like blowing in a bottle with water in it. Gene was good. Everybody knew him. When Gene died they brought him back up there at Morgan town, that was his hometown. There's a cemetery there called River Valley River Cemetery. Gene was buried there, and Charley Thomas was an engineer on those boats.

LA: Yes, I've stood a many a watch with him.

CE: Yes, and Abe Johnson, and when Abe Johnson died, five miles down the river, a little place called Aberdeen, the water was up all over the country, so they had to bring him up there in a yawl, had to bring his body up in a yawl. And I guess that was his last trip on the Monogahela.

AS: Well, we took Fred Bower's daddy 22 miles up the Kanawha River on the *Greenbrier* when he died at Point Pleasant. That's that engineer you know, and then we never knew that he was ever going with me or anything. That was in one of them floods, I don't know what year it was. Anyhow we had the whole cortege on the *Greenbrier*. The whole funeral outfit.

LA: Yes.

AS: And we done you know that's the doggone, of course we was hauling milk back and forth in those different places in the high water. Doggone loads up, I was wondering if have lucky enough to get back into the Ohio because there was no place, you could hardly see where it was. I know about how it was according to the light in the rig. But I just didn't know if we could get out or not. We did before the water fell. Always had the idea about the old *Virginia*, she was caught you know, and we didn't want to get caught in there. Just like, know the story about this, had the *Tom Greene* whistle safe on. She had cut across up here. And there was a little old harelipped fellow, captain of a little ferry boat called the *Whisper*, and he come on up there with us. He said, "I'll tell you boys, by God that whistle is up there, couldn't get her off." (laughter)

LA: Which towboat?

CE: You were talking about being above Cairo Bridge, Illinois Central, Cairo Bridge there. I was in a little boat up in Missouri River called the *Fairmont*.

AS: Yes, I know the boat.

CE: We'd made a trip up to just below Omaha, Nebraska coming back down, had barges of willows you know, for rip-rapping, we went aground right above the St. Joe, Missouri Bridge. And he backed, and he backed, and he backed, and he couldn't do a god dang. Well, one of those Hecht, John Hecht, that boat was named after, the one that had the double wheel, the *John Hecht*, he came down to me and he said, "Chief, we'll have to stay here tonight."

JD: I knew him a bit.

CE: And she was just anchored out there, and so I said, "Above this bridge, Captain?" He said, "Oh, she'll be all right. I got a anchor out." All during the night you could feel her work out take a little lunge like that.

LA: Yes.

CE: Next morning that boat was rounded to and just floating there just as pretty, so we just backed her out and went on down the river. You know that sand just cut right out from under.

JD: Yes, you can do it.

LA: We used to get over Blue River that way.

AS: Did you?

LA: You're aground just pull out you get a strain on the anchor and the sand will all cut out.

CE: That's right, cut her right out.

LA: Be afloat the next morning.

CE: Yes.

JD: I was going to tell you about rafting the logs passed Chattanooga and they couldn't stop it, they had to go through the mountains. Right below Suck Creek they had what they called Dead Man's Eddy there. A great big place that the river goes around and around. They were having a square dance up there in this man's house, and this raft would go down there, and would come back up by it, you know. Next day a fireman, he got out of it sometime, he told somebody down the river. He said, "Every house in them mountains had a square dance last night. Every house I passed, they was playing it." He was just going around and around there at Dead Man's Eddy there. (laughter)

AS: Well, that was like this radar done to me up here. This radar, this boat was coming passed by golly. Above the Lock 31 here, coming down. Mister I was just lucky to get in again the bank there above that.

LA: Yes.

AS: Foot mark, I didn't know where I was at.

LA: That radar won't show nothing coming down streams like that.

AS: Doc's got more business here. He brought some milk to drink.

CE: Good old cow's milk.

Q: Well I'm going to shut her down.

AS: All right.

Q: I'm going to check all your stories with Mark Twain's.

LA: Mark Twain! (laughter)

James P. Stutzman, June 26, 1957

Question: I have come down past Sayler Park to Lock 37 to talk to Mr. James P. Stutzman about his river experiences.

Answer: This cold winter started December 8th.

Q: This is the ice gorge.

A: Yes, this is the ice gorge, December 8th, this dam was still up yet, and they had this heavy snow, and then it snowed all that night and by the next morning the river was froze over. Now the government had a fleet right above here and the only boat that was in there at that time was the *E. A. Woodruff* and I was on the *E. A. Woodruff* at the time, and we ran out of coal and luck had it that a coal barge had broken loose. Well, I'm a little ahead of my story, first the ice broke a little bit and broke a barge loose up around Campbell's Creek Coal Company. Well this barge came down as far as Taylorsport and we got the barge in alongside of the *Woodruff*, and if it hadn't of been for that the boat, wouldn't have had any coal all winter. So, then the river just froze over completely from one end to the other and I think it was in February, sometime in February. I don't know the exact date, why we started getting warm weather and the river broke. It moved for about, I would say for about eight or nine hours until it gorged down around Sugar Creek. The river rose up to a stage to approximately about 62, 63 feet here on this gauge at 37. That gorge held until the river got to that stage and in the meantime, why we had pulled the *Woodruff* in close up to the top of the bank here, when that let go down there why the river fell ten foot an hour. The river fell so fast you couldn't get the boat out, the *E. A. Woodruff* was caught up on the bank up there. She set there for I expect about two or three months and finally along about I think April or sometime in March we had high water again and it came in and floated her out again.

Q: It was lucky she was caught on the bank.

A: Oh yes, she was a steel hull, she was one of the very few steel hull boats on this river, the *E. A. Woodruff* was. She had a double hull under her, and she was kind of unique built because in olden days that was just about the only thing there was to keep the channel clean and kept the logs out of there. So then in 1919 why she started out and for two years she really had all she could do to clean the river up because there were boats that sank from Pittsburgh to Cairo. It was just an unbelievable number of boats that were sunk. She worked around down there in Paducah down there in the harbor for about three months just getting all those wrecks out of the river. Then in 1920 was her last trip and they brought her in and laid her up and they didn't use her any more until they started. In fact, they used her up here as a shop boat until I don't know the exact dates when they took her up to 36. They used her up there to furnish steam for the cofferdam when they built the bear traps. Then after that job she was

John Knoepfle

brought in and sold. I think she was used for a wharf boat down in Louisville for a long while. That was the first boat I worked on, the *E. A. Woodruff.*

Q: Then where did you go from the *Woodruff?*

A: From the *E. A. Woodruff* I went over on the *Miami.*

Q: What kind of a boat was that?

A: That was a towboat. I worked on the *Miami* for about two months, then I went out on the *Oswego* dredge boat and we went up to Dam 21, they were just building Dam 21 at that time. We stayed there all summer and worked there, filled the cofferdam, one thing and another. Then when we came back in, then I went on the *U. S. Guyandotte*, fireman there with Captain Edgington, Emory Edgington, and I stayed on there for about three months, and then went over to Captain Meldahl. Now that was in 21 and then I stayed there all year, and when I came in I got my first engineers license, second engineers license. Then I left the government and went to work for Island Creek Coal Company. Captain Waters was the chief engineer on the *Robert P. Gillam.* She was a sternwheel towboat, just about the biggest one there was around at that time. I worked for them for about six months towing coal from the Kanawha River to Cincinnati. Then I came back to the government again as engineer on the *Scioto* and I was on the *Scioto*, well first one and then another. They used me just any place on any of those boats, and then I went over as engineer with Schletker, he was chief engineer on the *Ottawa*, and I put one summer in with him. We towed cement from Hannibal, Missouri to Cairo, Illinois. That was in the year 1923 I think it was, they were just building these locks then. Then I went back on the *Scioto* permanently, by that time I had my chief engineer's license and I went back there permanently. I stayed there until 1928, chief engineer on the *Scioto*, and Mr. Soudrett here, he was engineer here at this place and was an elderly man, had quite a lot of background.

Q: How do you spell his name?

A: John S-O-U-D-R-E-T-T. Everybody on the river knows old John. Him and I traded jobs. I came here, engineer on the dam, and he engineered on the *Scioto.* I was engineer here until 1937 until the flood, until Mr. Oliver retired. Andrew Oliver, he was lockmaster here, and he retired and I was appointed lockmaster here and I've been lockmaster ever since.

Q: You are still holding back all this water!

A: Yes, still hold back all this water. But in 1937 we held back too much. In 1937 there was just a little bit too much water for us and I hope I get away from here before it comes again that strong.

Q: You talked a little about the earlier boats. You were with the government service and I guess you were working with lights and day marks.

A: No, my job was pulling the dredge boats. We pulled the *Marietta* dredge, and she loaded these scows, and we towed them away. These dumped out on shallow water. One year we also towed the *C. B. Harris*, a big suction dredge they had. The most interesting trip I made was in 1927 when they had the big flood down on the Mississippi River, although I was chief engineer on the *Scioto* I went down there as second engineer with a man named Bill Barrett on the *U. S. Iroquois*. We went up every side river between here and Baton Rouge, we thought we would never forget all those people and that tremendous amount of water of course, now they have this thing all pretty well leveed out and I don't think they have ever had anything like it back in there.

Q: What actually were they doing up on these side rivers?

A: Up at first we was taking people out. The headquarters were at Natchez, you would go up those side rivers, the Red, Black Rivers, all those rivers. We went up as far as Monroe, Louisiana. I tell you there are places up in there that they had never heard of a steamboat. That river was just all over everywhere, you just can't imagine how that river was. Then after that we went back, was sure that all the people was out, why we went back and brought out cattle, because every place there was a piece of ground was full of cattle and anything that could get on it.

Q: Must have had a deal of trouble getting . . .

A: They did! It was really interesting, and that's one thing that I always did praise the Red Cross for, the Red Cross did a wonderful piece of work down in there. Nobody knows just what hardships those poor people did go through.

Q: That was on the *Iroquois*.

A: That was on the *Iroquois* that's right. Then when that trip was over I went back to the *Scioto* again and stayed on the *Scioto* permanently.

Q: Can you describe the *Scioto* for us?

A: The *Scioto* was a sternwheel boat. I guess she was about 800 horsepower boat and Captain Chandler was Captain on her. She was a good, clean boat and I enjoyed her very much.

Q: Now what was the operation on the *Scioto*?

A: You mean what she did? She was the one that towed the dredge boats. She towed the dredge boats, and she was the last boat the government kept. At one time the government had, well there were three boats like her. There was herself, the *Scioto*, the *Guyandotte* and the *Miami*, were all the same size. Then they had the *Cayuga* and the *Ottawa*, was the same size and the *Iroquois* was a smaller boat. They kept the *Scioto* to the last, she was the last one they kept. Now, they don't have any more sternwheel boats at all. Everything's gone to diesel now, there's no steamboats, only these here large ones, but I have a hobby now, I have a movie camera, and I really dwell on that. I expect in the last two years I have shot I'd say 3,000 foot of film. Just sternwheel boats mostly, I dwell on sternwheel boats because I think I will always have diesels. But that and old steam railroad engines, I've got quite a bunch of them. Because they are just about out, too. Yes, everything is going at once, but I'm a great lover of steam, but can I see that the other is the most economical.

Q: Tell me something about you were with Captain Edgington for a while.

John Knoepfle

A: My actual experiences with Captain Edgington, in his younger days he was very precise and everything. I can remember him when I first started to work for him. He had us out scrubbing the smokestacks when the boat was going up the river. He was really a character in his younger days. I tell you, he was sitting here in the office not long ago, he came in here. But Captain Edgington was one of the good pilots. It used to be before these locks and dams were in and we were dredging, maybe you'd see those coal boats, the *Joseph B. Williams* and the *Moran* and all those boats come down out of Pittsburgh. The only time they came down outside of in the winter was when there would be like now, see they'd get some rain up around Pittsburgh, then they would all lay-up up there and have their tows all ready and the more a raise would come, here they'd come. Then the river would be full about a day or so until they would get those by. They would have all wooden boats. Of course, these boats here now carry a whole lot more coal than those wooden barges did, and then another thing they did before the dams were done, they used to get them all ready, and then they would throw what they would call a splash. They'd get these boats ready at Point Pleasant, and then the last one got through 29 why then they would throw the bear traps and throw a bunch of water behind them and float them on through. There were a very few times that some of them didn't lose some barges somewhere along the line because in them days you had to be a pilot. You just had to be a pilot, you had to know where these rocks were and you didn't have to be like these boys now when the government has it all buoyed out for them. I didn't know until the other day some of these boys don't even have to have license now. Yes, I was talking to a boy out here the other day. A boy went up here with three barges, he told me he didn't have no license.

Q: I'll get a job!

A: I'm not kidding you. You don't have to have a license on these diesel boats. But I understand that Ashland, Mississippi Valley and all these here other out-fits do make them take a pilot's test they request, but I don't think it's the law. I don't think it's strictly the law that they have to have a license.

Q: But you have to have a license for steam!

A: You have to have a license for steam, that's right but you do not have to have a license for them. I think that's wrong. Some of these boats are bigger than some of those steamboats. I don't think that's right. They have really been fortunate they haven't had more accidents. These boats are really pretty big. I'll tell you something else I saw, I don't know the exact date, I'm poor on dates. I saw the big fire at Cincinnati, when the *Island Queen*, the *Morning Star*, the *Fred Hall*, the *Chris Greene* and some other Greene boat, there was about six of those boats burned.

Q: Where were you when this happened?

A: I was right on the levee, I was uptown and heard them hollering about the big fire down on the levee and I went down there. That was about the biggest thing that I have ever seen. If that wasn't a pitiful sight. See all those boats and the *Fred Hall*, I think she came up there to help someone. She came up there to help pull them out and when she pulled, I know the *Chris Greene* was out in the middle of the river burning up when I got there, and then she took fire from that out there. That was really a terrific fire, to see all those big boats being burned up. I think that was in January, let's see, he was elected in 1920. Well anyway, I think, it was in 1921 that they were having the centennial of Grant Memorial at Point Pleasant, West Virginia. President Harding came here.

Q: Ohio.

A: Yes, Point Pleasant, Ohio, and the government furnished all the boats for the officials to ride on. There was senators and a lot of congressmen and that, but there were other boats there. They had a parade up there. They took the *Cayuga* up there a couple of days ahead of the rest of the boats on account of the security, and there were all kinds of secret service men around there, and we all got a kick out of it. The crew that was on the *Cayuga*, why they weren't allowed to go or come while she laid there at Cincinnati. They had to be for about a day or two ahead of that on account of the security. She laid up on the upper end of the wharfboat, the Cincinnati-Louisville wharfboat at that time. She laid there by herself and the rest of them had to lay down in below there because of the secret service men all around there for a day and a night. Captain Tony Meldahl was the Captain of the *Cayuga* that made this trip. I never will forget Captain Meldahl told us afterwards, said President Harding came up in there in the pilothouse, and he stood up there with him while he was piloting his boat up the river. Captain Meldahl said President Harding asked him, "Captain, just how much do you get for piloting this boat?" I never will forget Captain Meldahl. He spoke of that many times. He told him, "I get the magnificent sum of $157 dollars a month." And he said President Harding laughed, "You mean to tell me that that's all this pays?" So it wasn't very long afterwards that they all got a pretty good raise after he was here. Of course, Harding only lived, I think he died the next year. He was very much interested, and made that trip to Point Pleasant and came back. Of course, I wasn't on the boat when they dedicated these locks and dams when Hoover was here. I think Hoover was on the boat Schletker was on, wasn't he?

Q: Yes, he was.

A: He give you all that. But I know we have a model here and President Hoover got off here and they demonstrated that model here.

Q: Was that a working model?

A: No, it was an actual one. It was an actual wicket and everything that had the same size. It wasn't a working model like this one we had in the office. But he had the actual wicket down there.

Q: I heard that there is a model of one of these dams that sit in a hotel lobby, has water in it and all and drunks come in at night and put goldfish in it.

A: Well, I don't doubt that. They had that last time I seen it, they had it up at the Netherland Plaza about two years ago, yes they do have. It's a pretty good size model.

Q: We're going to talk about Captain Meldahl again.

A: One of my memories with him was we was turning the wheel one cold morning and I had on mittens because in the olden days mittens used to be more practical than gloves because they really kept your hands warm. Back on the wheel one day, had a mallet in my hand driving up wedges in the wheel. It was cold, this mallet slipped off and just missed Captain Meldahl's head. He hollered at me, "Take those boxing gloves off before you kill somebody." He was really a fine man. He was very kind. I think Mrs. Meldahl is still living. I think she is. I was talking to somebody here the other day. I think if you get to talk to Emory Edgington, Captain Edgington, he was up, because they all live up in that country, up there around Augusta, up in there someplace.

Q: You actually fired the boat!

A: Yes, I was firing. You see you had to have three years firing, or two firing and one year before you could make application to license. Then you got the first assistant license and if you was just on a small boat, why then you only got a tonnage license. Say you was on a boat that was only a hundred tons. Well then that's all the bigger license, they would put tonnage on your license. If you had fired and been on a larger boat than that, why then they would give you all gross ton, that entitled you to be on any boat. My licenses were all gross ton.

Q: What exactly did a fireman do?

A: When you are with a company on one of these coal boats, the boat runs continuously. You are on six hours and you're off six hours. You don't do anything but fire. You don't have any time, only to fire.

Q: You shovel coal.

A: That's right, there wasn't no stokers, you shoveled that coal. The only help you got was maybe the deckhand would pull the ashes for you. If you dropped out, you cleaned the fire, why then maybe you could get them to help you clean and pull the ashes out. But of course, they always thought they were over worked because they had to continuously keep wheeling coal, because they wheeled, some boats had what they called coal passers on them, boys that didn't do nothing. Maybe they would be two assigned to a boat to a watch, that would just do nothing but pass coal, they called it, wheel coal continuously.

Q: Coal monkeys.

A: Now in olden days when I first started on the *E. A. Woodruff* the only way you could get coal on her, you had to carry it on there. You carried it on there in a box. Each box held three bushels. She had colored people on there and there would be one man in the front of the box and one behind it. There were handles on each side of the box and that's the way that coal was carried in there.

Q: You didn't have a special name for that box, did you?

A: No, there wasn't a special name for that box. Just coal box. They carried that coal out of the barges. Just have to carry that up there. You could hear them singing coming up out of there, that box a swinging.

Q: Sang!

A: I tell you, you had to be on your job because the man in front would throw the man behind over into the coal box when he emptied up there because they never stopped. It was just one continuous trip. I have seen, down at Paducah at West Kentucky Coal Company, I have seen them put as high as 1,200 bushel of coal on that boat in eight hours. They would have that many men.

Q: Eight-hour watches.

A: That coal company, you know, you'd go in there and buy so much coal. They'd go up on the levee and hire these people, the coal monkeys. They'd come down there and box it up in there. But there wasn't no wheelbarrows or anything like that. Just one string carrying that coal in there. So then, what I was going to say, fireman never had no time to do anything else but fire. But now on the government boats at the time when I fired for them, they only run 12 hours a day. Then you would have to fire one of the watches, and then your night watch, you would be night watchman, or you had to clean the engines.

Q: Twelve on and twelve off.

A: No, six on and six off. What I mean, that was 30 days a month or 31 if they was in a month. It wasn't like these boys got now. I get a kick out of them now. They get off here at Cincinnati. They tell me they're going home on their time off. I think now they work 30 days and get 27 off. (tape off for a while)

A: Three dollars and something a month and my board.

Q: What boat was that?

A: That was on the *E. A. Woodruff*. Then on the *Scioto* I think it got up to about 48 dollars. Then it just came up, came creeping on up and I don't know just what they do get now.

Q: You made almost as much as we teachers make.

A: Yes, that's right, of course right now they are getting too much. We work by the hour, we don't work by the month anymore.

Q: Can you give me a few more details on firing?

A: Well I do know one thing, if an engineer wanted you back there, he could really kill you. Yes sir, he could really kill you. I never will forget I had a boy working for me one time and he tried to tell me that you couldn't burn him out. I got a kick out of him, he was watching me continuously. But on this boat, she had a two-inch stream of steam going into her water intake, and that was to keep ice from forming on the side, you know. This was on the *Scioto*, and this boy he bet me that I couldn't get him. So we was on a straight stretch there one day, had plenty of time, and boy he was coasting along there. So I just walked over, he didn't know anything about this, where you could turn this live steam value. I opened that thing up, that steam started going down, and I seen him jump off his chair out there. He was firing his boat, and the more he fired, and

John Knoepfle

the first thing you usually do when you fire, that's the worst thing you can do is to go loading up the boat up with a lot of green coal, see what I mean. Because then the first thing you know nothing is burning. I tell you I let him go, the boat was carrying about 225 and I let him go to where she got down to around 275 and I saw how hot and how worried he was. I went back and shut it off and he never did know anything about it. The steam just came right back up and I never did tell the boy to this day what happened. But he never did tell nobody he couldn't be beat.

Q: What kind of a fire then would have been ideal?

A: When he puts the coal in because if you just put the coal in there, just enough to keep a good bright fire going, and a good fireman can tell just about when it needs coal, just about like they do on these stokers on railroads or any place else. They watch that and if you load up, putting coal in, you've outdone the fire in your furnace. The least coal you use, the better off you are. They used to, in back up as far as 1923 and 1924, all up and before that, apples used to be in season brought down the Mississippi River by the Eagle Packet Company, and then they were put on the levee there.

Q: At St. Louis?

A: At St. Louis on the levee. This afternoon in one July or August afternoon a couple of boats would come in there and they had all these apples, all different ricks of them, all around these barrels up there. We came in there with the *Scioto*. We was going to wash boilers and lay up for the evening. Then they would run these lines up between . . .

Q: Wait a minute, you were on the *Ottawa*!

A: Yes, on the *Ottawa*. They run these lines all up through and around in between those barges and ordinarily it would of been all right but Stretch and I were both in a hurry to get off that boat and a little bit careless. The *Ottawa* had, when you pulled her levers down, they called it levers, that was the thing that held the valves up. Well in place of me taking a chain on there where you could chain levers down, in place of that, well I didn't pull the chain but did set the steam off on the jack and that let the levers fall. In the meantime, the fireman came along and wanted to coal the boat down, he opened the throttle valve and thought the boat was going to blow through, right through the valves. In place of that the boat took out. She just started up the river there and these lines all around these apple barrels, you never saw such a commotion and throwing apple barrels and rolling them in the river. And Captain Emerson Moore was Captain on her then, and he could get kind of loud anyway at times and I tell you he came down there. If he didn't get on me and Red.

Q: As I understand it that *Ottawa* had these piles underneath and it could sit in the bottom of the water. Is that right?

A: No, the barrels, now you see, now like this would be the levee. Why these barrels, there would be a bunch of them here and a bunch of them there. We just run our lines up through in between these barrels. When the boat started up, why she just ripped our lines out underneath of them, you see what I mean, throwed apples everywhere. That was really some sight over there at St. Louis, in the fall to see all those apples come in. It was really a catastrophe, when the Eagle Packet Company, when they all went out of business over there.

Q: I understand when they were parked out there at Paducah they didn't have insurance on these boats.

A: Well I doubt it myself because the last one, the one the Greene Line bought was, I think she was the *Golden Eagle*, wasn't she?

Q: The *Cape Girardeau.*

A: I think she originally was the *Golden Eagle*, and then they named her *Cape Girardeau*, after that they named her the *Gordon Greene*. I made a trip for the Greene Line. The only packet boat I ever worked on in my life. I made a trip for a boy who was on there named Nelson, Nelson Howe, an engineer. He called me one time, and I wasn't working at that time, it was in the winter time, and he was on vacation, and he wanted to know if I wanted to make a trip to Charleston on the old *Andes*. Did you ever hear of it?

Q: The *Andes*!

A: Yes, the *Andes* and I made that trip to Charleston for him. I think it took about three or four days to make that round trip. When I came back, why we came in, they paid me a magnificent sum of $10 for that round trip. I said to Nels Howe, "Do you mean to tell me Nels, that is all you make on this boat? Don't you ever call me to make any more trips for you." I said, "I would rather fire for anybody than engineer on a boat for $10 for a trip to Charleston." But they never did pay very much on those packet boats. That's the reason they were always having trouble getting men on them.

Q: I guess it was before your time. Dent Stanford was Captain on there.

A: On the *Andes*, yes it must have been before, he wasn't on there, Chris Greene was on her that time. Captain Chris Greene, he was really a fine man. I tell you I always liked him. I expect I talked to him just about two or three days before he had his heart attack. He was a very fine man.

Q: Well now tell me you talked about apples over in St. Louis, what about the produce up along this valley? I know they hauled apples out of the northern part of the state here too, didn't they?

A: I tell you the apple business and business up in here was never like it was over in there. That's a great county for that over there. Calhoun County and come down out of that Illinois River, oh up even far as Keokuk, Iowa, up that far was all apples up in through there. At that time that was the only mode of transportation there was up in there.

Q: Captain Wisherd.

A: Yes, he came from up there. That's just like down in the lower river. I was telling these boys when I went first down in the lower river, that was the only boat that traveled down on this lower river from Louisville down. I was talking to one of these boys here the other day, from Rockport to Owensboro, and he didn't believe me, so I had to go prove it. There used to be two little boats running between Rockport and Owensboro. One of them was the *Messenger* and one was the *Inquirer*. They were boats about 40 feet long, well I think they made a trip about every two hours. That was the only mode of travel there was. There was another one that used to run from Evansville to Shawneetown.

Q: Do you remember the name of that boat?

A: The *Bay Queen*, they run down in there. But about the boats, another one that I remembered where I met my wife on. There used to be a little boat, *McCandless Brothers*.

Q: How do you spell that?

A: There was Fred and Les McCandless, they lived at Golconda, Illinois and they always had a boat that always run from Golconda, Illinois to Paducah, made a round trip a day.

Q: How do you spell this Illinois name?

A: G-O-L-C-O-N-D-A. Golconda, Illinois. Their first boat was the *Dorothy*. Now this *Dorothy* was a beautiful boat and she would make that round trip. In fact that *Dorothy* was just about the fastest thing in that lower river. It was a good size boat, it was a boat as big as the *Andes* or any of these boats up in. But they lost her, I don't know how they did lose her, but they did lose her. Then they bought this small boat. They had a little boat called the *Pearl City* and they run her from Golconda to Paducah. I was engineer on the *Scioto* and the reason I'm telling you this, that's how I met my wife. So the river was so low that the *Scioto* couldn't run and we were laid up to conserve coal and the dredge boat was banking a cut down by Pryor Island.

Q: Now what do you mean by banking?

A: Just throwing it out on the bank. We were just going down, just throwing it out on the bank. We didn't have enough coal in the scow to take it away from her so she would just bank it out. She would come back and bank another one. Just banked it to make a cut for the boats to get through, the river was that low. Well Captain Chandler this morning ask me if I would like to go to Paducah with him. The *Pearl City* only drawed about a foot and a half or two feet of water. I said, "Well I really want to go to Paducah to get me some clothes." He said, "Get ready," and he blowed that boat to come in. The *Pearl City* came in and came in there and picked us up and we got over on there. I went back to the engine room and there was a little kind of a waiting room for passengers.

Q: You mean a lady's room.

A: Yes, that's right, went back in there and there sat this lady and this girl. Well I didn't pay any attention to them and I went on back in this room. By the time I came out, when I come up in the pilothouse, why here is this lady and this girl was up in the pilothouse. This lady was a relative of the owner of the boat, and this girl was going to Paducah with her. They introduced me to them and I never thought much about them. We sat up in the pilothouse and talked and I never thought anymore about it. I got off the boat. In the meantime, I told the

Chandler, "Why, I don't think I'll go back tonight. I think I will stay in Paducah tonight." I said, "I'll come up on a boat tomorrow." I stayed down there that night. The next evening when the boat came out, why I went down there, and lo and behold who was the first one I run into but this lady and this girl again. So her and I we got to talking and I asked her for a date. She said, "Yes, I can come up the next night." So I was up the next night. Met her in November and married her in February, that's pretty fast.

Q: You sound like you were the victim of a conspiracy.

A: We have been happily married ever since.

Q: Wonderful. Tell me, down in that lower country did you know of a man named Gordon Devers?

A: No, I didn't.

Q: Had a boat called the *Grace Devers* and the *C. C. Devers*.

A: Oh yes, I remember those boats, but I don't remember the name.

Q: Do you remember what runs they made?

A: I think they went up the Tennessee and the Cumberland Rivers. I think they mostly towed. You see there used to be another company in there, Airlord Tie Company. There were an awful lot of railroad ties towed out of Tennessee and Cumberland Rivers.

Q: What is the name of that company again?

A: Airlord Tie Company. A-I-R-L-O-R-D. Those ties were towed to Joppa, Illinois. Then I think the Illinois Central Railroad came in there. That was a great business in that lower river, those railroad ties because that was the only way there was to get them out of that Tennessee River. I have seen barge after barge of ties in there being unloaded, most always they were unloaded by hand too. Carried out of there by colored stevedores, carried out of these barges, there wasn't any such things as derricks in those days. Carried out on barges.

Q: Don't remember what they sang do you?

A: No, but they was always happy go lucky down in there. That lower river down in there, when you go down in there it don't seem like the same place anymore. At Cave In Rock, Illinois, I went to see that picture, the one Walt Disney had. Those pirates and that down in there. See, my wife, she came along. It's only about oh I guess about 30 miles from Golconda. The last trip we went down I went to see those old markings. If you are ever in that country you should go see that. In that cave, there's a lot of those old writings and things in there in that cave. That was really an interesting place in there.

Q: One other point, I have been attempting to trace this, if I were taking a hypothetical trip on of those tows, such as the wooden boats down there, I wonder if you can remember any details about towing down that lower river coal boats?

A: Well I'll tell you, they had more coal lost down in there, because even with the lock and dam system, they have to dredge continuously down in there. In them days, it's just like I was telling you here. If you got caught in between,

John Knoepfle

there was a bar at Shawneetown, the Shawneetown Bar it was called. I'd venture to say that the river would get down to where there would be only a foot of water through there. Down there where we was, down there at Pryor Island, why there were just times the river was spread out all over thing and the river was so wide you could almost get out and walk across. I have seen the time down there where we would take the steamboat and just wash out the sand with the wheels to get anywhere. They just had the one suction dredge at that time, the *Indiana*, I don't expect anybody, I guess a lot of fellows don't remember her, the *Indiana* suction dredge.

Q: Some of them down there did.

A: Did they? She was only a 15 inch dredge, and then they got the *C. B. Harris*, I think she was 22 inch.

Q: L. C. Riley, I think was on that.

A: Was he? I have a brother that was an engineer on her for a long while.

Q: What was his name?

A: George Stutzman. He engineered for Carnegie Ohio Barge Line. He's engineer on the *Pittsburgh*. You take in olden days down there you went down in you used to say, "Never let them big gates close on them again there at Louisville." They always called them the big gates at Louisville. I've heard it many a times, "If I never get up by here again, I'll never let them big gates close on me again down there." I'd say from August until the first of January there just was no water in that lower river and it used to take a pretty good raise to soak those sandbars up that stand out dry for all summer.

Q: So getting those coal boats through at that time was a hazardous affair.

A: I'll tell you there were just lots of them that just never made it. They just never made it. Somebody told me one time not too long ago about the *Sprague*. I think she started out up here with 50 some and got to Memphis I think with about 15. Just strung them things out everywhere. Have you ever seen her?

Q: No, just pictures.

A: Sometimes if you are ever in Vicksburg, she's at Vicksburg there. I drove 100 miles out of the way here not long ago just to take a look at her. I think they charge you. I didn't go down on her we didn't have time. I understand you can go on her for a quarter. They keep her up. I don't think anybody would begrudge giving a half a dollar or $1 to go on her.

Q: If I get to Vicksburg . . .

A: Me too. She was really a wonderful boat, or she was, and that *Joseph B. Williams* that was another big fine boat.

Q: Were you ever on her?

A: No, I was never on her, I just saw her. I just saw her go down the river. Down that lower river. She was a magnificent boat. Now West Kentucky Coal Company built one right off the pattern for her and they named it *Charles F. Richards*.

Q: Paddle!

A: No, I meant the pattern. She was the same size and everything of the *Joseph B. Williams*. I expect in her time the *Joseph B. Williams* was a prettier boat than the *Sprague*. She wasn't near as big as the *Sprague* but she was really a beautiful boat. The *W. K. Field* that was another big sternwheel boat. I think Island Creek finally ended up owning her. Going back to all those old boats makes you feel bad about them being gone.

Q: Well, I've never seen boats like that.

A: But I understand, Mr. Long told me the other day that I guess the *Omar*, you have seen the *Omar*.

Q: Yes, I have.

A: I think she's going to be running for about five years. They have got five year plates on her again the other day.

Q: Still up in this river.

A: Yes, she goes right through here.

Q: I locked through on her in fifty-five up above Coney Island.

A: Did you? He told me they put her on the ways the other day and her hull is in wonderful shape think she got papers for five years again. You know those boats are not laid up as much as these.

Q: That's what Captain Brasher said.

A: Yes, they are not laid up as much as these diesels are. Because Mr. Long told me the other days they got five years on her again. Is this it?

Q: Well, I thank you for talking to me.

A: I really appreciate it. You come down anytime.

Q: You are a man the river has been good to.

A: Oh yes, I've got 39 years. I mean with the government, of course I have done other things. I remember talking the other day, "What are you going to do when this new dam's done?" I'll be ready to quit. I'm not that old but at the same time there is no use starting anything else.

Q: Well all right, we will cut it off now.

John Knoepfle

Ed Taylor, July 29, 1957

Question: We are at Millersport, Ohio with Ed Taylor. Can you say something about that sunflower deal?

Answer: About this sunflower deal you see they raised these in vast quantities, and then they have a receiving day along in the fall and they bring these in from all around. So it starts about seven o'clock in the morning clear on receiving until nine that night. They would have a string of wagons a half mile long. Then the boat come out in that evening and pick them up. I saw the *Louisville* lay there for I believe about two hours and two minutes with 31 roustabouts carrying. Well they had such a large pile that they had to make the second landing made the, too far to carry them, and dropped it back out in the river, and then dropped the gangplank down where they would be closer by. It would be two out on the bank hoisting and they would set them up on their shoulders, and they would carry without ever putting their hand on them, they'd just catch them on the point of the shoulder, and then see like that and they'd have their hands in their pockets going up singing up the gangplank.

Q: They carried those seed in sacks then!

A: In sacks. Oh you see sunflower seed is not too heavy and they could get around 140 or 50 pounds but it would be a sizeable sack maybe four foot long. They would just set them around on the shoulder like that and stick them up and over and never spill a one out of all that lick of seed.

Q: Wish I knew what they were singing.

A: Well I could tell you something one said as he went up the gangplank. He said, "If you want a hoecake baked good and done stick it on a roustabout's heel and turn it to the sun."

Q: Is that so?

A: Yes that's so. Some a singing one thing and some another. Anything to break the monotony.

Q: In other words, raising sunflowers must have been a big thing down there.

A: That was at that time, that was in a sunflower district about all of them raised sunflowers and it seemed as though that crop and market for it. Now Kansas raised a lot of sunflower seed at that time but it seems like that's kind of gone out and soybeans has taken the place of sunflower seeds. Now dad he bought sunflowers there for two or three years. I believe they went to McCullough's at Cincinnati. Maybe you recall the McCullough Seed Company, then at Wood, Stubbs & Company at Louisville they bought a lot of them. But I'd say in recent years I haven't heard of any market for sunflower seed. I don't I know I reckon the soybean took the place of the sunflower seed.

Q: I think you said earlier that you shipped hogs by boat too.

A: Yes, I can tell you a little incident about the hog situation. That was back in 1917 and 1918, the winter was so cold and the river blocked. There was a neighbor down there, dad was buying hogs and shipping out. A neighbor down there, I guess he'd noticed what had happened during the night. See he had some about ready to go and he called dad up and asked him about the hogs. He said, "Yes," after he'd made the deal, he said, "bring them up." He said, "Did you look toward the river this morning." Dad looked up and she looked like a big field. She had blocked during the night and there wasn't a boat a moving.

Q: Precisely where did you live down there, Mr. Taylor?

A: We lived about 15 miles below Madison in what is called London Bottom.

Q: London Bottom!

A: Yes that would be the, I think it's the second bottom below Madison. You see, every time the river turns, or rather the hill turns, you would have the channel on first on one side the other. One way the river turns or the hill turns, you'll run the channel towards the hill all the time. That throws your bottoms maybe over on the Indiana side, then the river turns and run again that hill, that throws the bottoms all on it, and that's the way it meanders around down following the valley.

Q: You were in a rich bottom there.

A: We were in a pretty good bottom down 15 miles below Madison.

Q: I guess you had a landing too.

A: Yes, we had a landing. I'll tell you a little story about that now, that I think, if I come in up here and miss the landing, of course we have got just about 100 foot to come in on and if you are over that you are on somebody else's territory. But there along the river you know they can bump the bank most anywhere along. My father was coming up from Louisville on the *Corker* that one morning and it was along in March, the river was high and the wind, the upstream wind was blowing, and the river was so rough. I saw that *Corker* try to make the landing three times, and then put him off about quarter of a mile down along the cornfield or rather where the corn was the year before.

Q: They did!

A: Yes every time they would start to the bank, of course they would have to shut down some. The wind would take them and just turn that three deck steamer, and that was a sizeable boat, probably a 150 or 160 foot long, and then they wonder about this little boat of mine. You just come in and put it on a dime. You just don't know. It's just not all roses with steamboating.

Q: Light draft and a high freeboard.

A: That's right, all riverboats, what you term, would be light draft, you know. They started out with shallow, I guess there's been some carried a sizable lot of freight, wouldn't draw over 16 or 18 inches of water. I've read about in the *Waterways Journal*, different boats, you know. Several have asked me about this boat, said you ought to have this up on the Lakes. I said it wouldn't stay on the Lakes more than one big storm. They wondered why, steel hull and all. "Well," I said, "it doesn't draw enough water." I says, "You have to get down six or seven foot anyhow into the water."

John Knoepfle

Q: What do you draw on that boat?

A: I draw about 19 inches, it's 22 at the aft and 16 in the bow, light loaded. It'll average about 19, 20 inches I guess.

Q: Well let me take you back now to your experience of shipping on that earlier river. How about things like . . .

A: Like the time I got the hogs in the river down there, waiting for the mail boat? Well there is a landing just below us there about two miles, which was what they called Mail Boat Landing. These big sidewheels wouldn't land only, outside the wharfboats, only in deep water. You couldn't land it just anywhere. So they had what they called the Mail Boat Landing down there and they shipped from there. They shipped hogs, fruits, cattle, anything. They had stock pens there. And one night they got these new pens and opened up for the gang-plank, and some way they let these hogs get out and they had the roustabouts, but some of them got into the river and they had them out with what they call chain-bars. Have you seen them?

Q: Yes, I have heard of them.

A: Well a chain-bar, two fellows can carry a pretty good size hog with them. It's two poles I'd say six foot long, strong say two and a half inches in diameter, with chains across them. They would lay that right down across, with two chains across, lay it down across the hog's back and throw him over, and then the hog is on his back and they'd just pick it up, up like you would pick up a wheelbarrow, a man at each end. They'd carry 226 pound hog and he couldn't get out of there. Just carry him right on and turn him right out again. They was out there that night, some of them got in the river, and I don't know whether they got all of them or not. They got part of them on the boat, but the ones that got away, they had the roustabouts out there, trying to catch hogs, and they got the gate broke down some way. They'd aimed to drag them right up, and then they had gates on the gangplank, and they would take them right around from one pen to another.

Q: Must have been a hard lot for those rousters!

A: It seems like that would be a pretty hard life, but I guess steamboating, and then the cotton fields, were kind of the second nature. Well all river life, like other life was more or less rugged in them days than what it is now. Even farm life then you did it with more main strength and awkwardness then than what you do now. So it's all kind of done mechanically, you know.

Q: If the machinery is good. Well tell me about you must have raised a lot of corn too.

A: Yes, they did, now this county that I moved from over here, now you ought to get this, raised the most hogs per square mile of any in the United States.

Q: What county was that?

A: That's Rush County, Indiana. They raised corn and hogs there, if you've got 50 acres you put half of it in corn and feed it all up to hogs, and if you have got 500 acres you will probably put half of it in corn. Corn in about half of it. It's strong ground and they raise and feed, they get a lot of corn out of Illinois. They feed up all they raise there because they do raise so many hogs. That's their main goal there, corn and hogs.

Q: Guess they just supplied most of the market up at Cincinnati and maybe Louisville too.

A: Yes and they ship a lot of it into Indianapolis. Indianapolis I just noticed in the quotations on the hogs was running heavier receipts than Chicago.

Q: Is that so?

A: But it's right in an awful hog producing district. I can tell you a little joke on a fellow out home there. He told his boy he says, "You see that stump out there. Go drive it out, it's probably a hog." Because they do raise so many hogs you know.

Q: Well did you ever ship corn by river?

A: We did when we moved away from the river. That's the only time. We fed most of our corn down there.

Q: What other stuff did you raise down there?

A: Just clover is a three year rotation like corn, wheat and clover. Some oats, and then now they're getting to raise quite a lot of soybeans.

Q: This is an offbeat question, but did you fellows plant by the light of the moon down there?

A: Not too much. But there is something in that. If you plant corn in the light moon and it will grow a lot heavier foliage, taller stalks, your corn will grow taller than it will in the dark moon. Then any root crop you are supposed to plant like potatoes, or anything like that in the dark of the moon, they'll root deeper. Whether, anyhow in the potato set up, it will keep them from sun burning. You plant them in the light moon and they will grow right on top of the ground. A lot of them will sunburn. They set on right up close to the top of the ground and in the dark moon they will root down deeper. Here's another story, they say if you build a rail fence, you know we used to have lots of rail fences, build it in the light moon and it will stay on top of the ground and if you build it in the dark moon the second rail will go out of sight, just go out of sight keep a sinking.

Q: Somebody else told us all about that you set the worm of the rail in the light of the moon.

A: And it will stay on the top of the ground and I have heard old timers say that, that the second rail will eventually go out of sight, just keep sinking. Freezing and thawing, it will just keep sinking.

Q: I wonder where those farmers down in that part of the country came in from! Were they over from North Carolina, that part of the country.

A: Well, that I don't know, a lot of them, these people I was telling about right below us I don't know just exactly, I think they came from New Orleans. The older generation is very wealthy, they said when old man Herold came there he had a barrel of gold. Anyhow he started, his boy run through with a hat factory

John Knoepfle

somewhere, don't know where it was, then he run through with a fine steamboat on the river. They were very wealthy and they were from New Orleans.

Q: Do you know the name of the boat he had?

A: No, that was before my day, the younger generation was living here at this farm where they were shipping these hogs from I was telling about getting in the river. It seems like that this fellow was kind of a playboy and he just run the older folks crazy, started with first one thing, and then another and I know the steamboat entered into it along in his life there and he run through everything.

Q: Well you said that you knew a number of rivermen down in that section of the country. I wonder if you could, tell us something about those men.

A: Some and maybe not too much. Now this Sanford Smith, he ran on the river there for years. I think he owned a share in this Hanover Packet and he was captain of the *Hanover*. This Jesse Singer, he was on the same boat but whether he had a share in it or not, but he was a licensed engineer and a pilot on it. His brother was the regular engineer. It used to be in case of storm, in fact I think Sandy Smith was the only one that was authorized pilot and captain. Jesse Singer was the regular pilot, Sandy Smith was clerk on there. If they had a severe storm, they said that Sandy would go to the wheel, Jesse would go to the engine room, and John that was Jesse's brother. He would take up some other office. In other words they would just step down to each one's capacity.

Q: The *Hanover* I guess was a small sternwheeler.

A: It was a small sternwheel packet. It ran from Bethlehem to Madison six days a week. Now you talk about them Turners was quite riverboat guys. There was four or five of them brothers, and they owned a fleet of boats. They owned the *Kathryn*, the *Revonah*, the *White Dove*. Then they expanded out and bought the *Ohio*. That was a three deck steamboat, run from Madison to Louisville against the *Corker*. That's where they made a fatal mistake because it was hitting the White Collar Line then that could run a big steamboat for nothing in competition. I could tell you a little story about on the 4th of July all of them steamers would run excursions somewhere. So the *Corker* and *Ohio* started down the river from Madison taking an excursion on the 4th to Louisville and they was about neck and neck. A couple of girls over on the bank hailed, so both of them both answered the hail and started in. Well the *Corker* beat the *Ohio* in and the clerk run off and the girls commenced moving back, said, "We wanted the other boat." The clerk just grabbed one of them and said, "You are going today with us for nothing." Said, "We won't charge you anything," and then the *Ohio* went on in and picked up the other one and the girls got together when they got to Louisville. There used to be quite some rough times in competition on the river. This Turner outfit used to scrap the *Hanover* right smart. You talk about the way times were back then, they cut the fare that you could go from our landing 15 miles to Madison and back for 15 cents. Well that would ordinarily be a quarter, but in competitive business. Then the *Hanover* went into another trade for a while and then your fare went 40 cents. But that competition in rivermen it works that way.

Q: One of those photographs that we looked at the other day was the *Hanover*. It was so small I thought it might be somebody's private boat.

A: We have a picture taken out of the *Waterways Journal*, it was at Louisville with the *Hanover*, I think the *Revonah*, there was about ten, including several big steamboats, at the levee at Louisville in 19, it could of been in the teens, I don't just remember whether it was in the teens or 1920s, but it was back in the heyday of the river.

Q: You've built a number of boats yourself, maybe you would like to tell us about those.

A: The first one was a small boat. It would carry about 20 passengers, but it was a sternwheeler, then this next one it was about in Indiana in 1936. The next one I built was this one I built in 1950 and sold in 1953, had a capacity of 125.

Q: Were you running those boats on the river down there?

A: This was on what they called the Muscatatuck River or Big Otter Creek. It was about like a river sometimes, but it would be a small river.

Q: I guess you were running little excursions through there.

A: We had a kind of a little park built up there in our farm. Had a place for picnics and like of that. I built this little sternwheel boat to operate there.

Q: What was the name of the boat?

A: I called that for the boy, the *B. C. Taylor*.

Q: I see.

A: Then the next one was the *A. M. Taylor* for the wife. Then in the meantime the boy gets married and got a couple of little girls there, Judelle and Becky, and of course I had to name the next ones for my granddaughters so that cut me clear out, I never named one for myself. This one has a capacity for 300.

Q: This one on the lake now!

A: This new one I have.

Q: Would you describe the building of that boat?

A: The first one here, we built from the keel up. We laid the keel, we built it right here beside the house and the timbers, we brought a Dodge truck over here from Indiana. The timbers for this boat I built here, the first one, come from down around Greensburg, Indiana. We had it loaded down with the overloads, all it would carry, the timbers. Then we took the same truck and went to Cleveland and I believe we got 2,300 foot of red cypress for planking. About 300 pounds of brass screws to put that planking on with. No nails whatever was used in it. Was all put together, we even plated our bolts, we couldn't buy bolts of the size we needed, we fluxed and plated our own bolts. We put the planking all on with brass screws on account of the corrosion. We don't have any of that.

Q: How did you ever figure out how to construct that wheel?

A: I guess it was just from watching the construction of them on the river, just about the balancing of them, and about how they were put together.

John Knoepfle

Q: Did you ever get up into the shipyard in Madison, things like that?

A: Not too much because the shipyards at Madison were pretty well going out at the time. This one down at Marietta, I about lived down there all during the time I was building this, see they built this steel hull for me, for this boat.

Q: Oh, I see.

A: The Marietta Manufacturing Company, and then I brought it up here. Took six semis to haul the seven pieces up here. It was built in sections, and then brought up here and put in the drydock and welded together. Had 96 man hours of welding on it. The welding was parched together watertight. It's got four watertight compartments bulkheaded and it's built out of quarter inch plate steel, the hull weighing 23 tons. Then we launched it and I started putting the superstructure on. I constructed all that myself, outside of hiring some day-labor on it.

Q: That little boat was kind of an expensive proposition wasn't it?

A: You mean this last one?

Q: Yes.

A: I got just about as much in the hull of this last one as I had in the entire boat of the other one I built, music and all.

Q: Well I tell you if you continue at this rate you will soon be building huge steamboats.

A: The next one will be a sizeable boat if in ratio with the last. But the wife says there won't be any next one. I don't know, maybe she knows.

Q: She's wanting to put the clamps on you.

A: Well we've worked pretty hard for this one. Long hours to get it in. We christened on the 16th day of June. We christened the other one on the 16th day of July in 1950, this one christened on the 16th day of June in 1957.

Q: Did you have quite a little party when you christened this boat?

A: Yes when we christened we had guests from the Marietta Manufacturing Company. In fact the master of ceremonies was the Vice President of the Marietta Manufacturing Company. Then we had the engineer with us that had done all the calculation of the hull and gave me a lot of aid in securing such things as my chains. There was a part that he and I discussed quite a bit, he said it would take two and a half inch pitch lower double strand or two single strand to transmit the power of a 150 horse diesel to the wheel, the size of wheel I was planning, which cost me better than $31 a foot and took 37 foot of it. I tried to talk him into two inch pitch and when I checked the figures on it there was 70,000 pounds difference in the strength so him being a MIT graduate I moved out of the picture. But the other chain would have cost me about half as much since from bicycle chain up to two inch pitch is standard chain. The other is industrial chain moves into . . . .

Q: It's more expensive then!

A: Yes, special built.

Q: Did any of the old rivermen come over to the . . . .

A: I just forget, there were several up from down at the Marietta Manufacturing Company, but you don't know Captain Stone I reckon at Point Pleasant?

Q: No, I don't know him.

A: He runs the Stone Towing Company. He has two towboats down there. He gives me a lot of lake tips on some of his experience. I can tell you a little instance there that we conversed over the phone about, of course this was a wedged wheel, the others I had always put on were keyed on. So this was a hex shaft and you wedged it on. It took 96 steel wedges, with a slight taper so they drawed well, but what got me was that you set this all up with wood first around there. Said to use soft pine. Well it seemed I couldn't get my wedges just right so I thought well maybe the wood would soon mash out anyhow, because you sledged those wedges under it. So I come over to the phone and called Captain Stone and asked him, I says, "What is the prime factor of that wood being in there? Does it need to be in there other than to see your wedges so we could line the wheel up right and fasten it to the shaft?" Well he says, "Not in particular." He says, "Just so," says, "that wood you will mash out anyhow." He says, "We have tore up old steamboat wheels that had some of that wood in them yet, that was pressed so tight that it made it waterproof, you know just like steel pretty near, and had been in the river for years and was still solid." Well I went over and I took out the wood and tried my way. By the time I got one bunch of wedges in, you wedge from both sides, the other side was a falling out. Pretty soon I had a basket full of wedges and no wheel wedged yet. So I finally come back to his to what had been tried out for a 100 years probably and she is running today without any trouble at all.

Q: With all wooden wedges in there.

A: Well with the steel wedges in, but we drove them. You take your wood wedges around to line your shiv or your wheel flange up, then you start driving your wedges from both sides and you sledge them, you just squeeze that wood completely out of there until it's not thicker than a pancake. Just squeeze it clear out. Because you know the whole turn of that wheel twists on that wrist you know, and I painted that of course, and it's never broke the paint yet. So the wedges are, well you take an eight pound sledge hammer with both hands and some fellow holding the driving pin and sledge for all your worth, you know you are driving them awfully tight. I says, "How tight do you drive them?" He says, "Drive them till they ring and you can't drive them any further, your hammer just bounces, and you don't drive any further." (end of tape)

A: On an eight inch stroke, so you know that is a very light taper see, it has an awful drawing effect, and that would just draw until, well with all that power that I'm putting on that, it has never even put the shaft in the wheel in it. So, I still come to his way, and the way it's been tried out. But I thought I had a new way of putting in wedges, but it didn't work out. So they say experience is still a good teacher. Now this pilot wheel is built out of white oak and the black walnut finished in natural wood with brass screws, and it seemed like that was

535   John Knoepfle

something you couldn't buy, there was lots of them along the river different places. Why, some member of the family in the steamboat line, had a place for them, and the only thing for me to do was to build my own wheel.

Q: So now you are enjoying the fruits of your labor out there on the lake.

A: I guess you might put it that way. Them wheels, as I say you can't buy them, so about all of them have gone either air or hydraulic steering. The boy wanted me to put that on this boat, but I wanted the old effect of the of that wheel. I know this fellow was up here from Marietta as the master of ceremonies, he was up in the pilot house and he said, "Why Ed, this wheel will kill you. Why don't you put air steering on something like that?" "Well," I says, "people on the bank, they wouldn't see me roll the wheel then."

Q: Those old pilots with the big sidewheels used to climb up the wheel spokes.

A: Yes and roll the wheel, change it over from one side to the other. Whenever you can get an advantage of changing over like when I am backing out up there I'll ring down and stop the wheel, and then let that choke it a second, then I can turn my wheel because the action of the water has ceased to pulling against my rudders and it will be about one-third as hard to turn. I'll roll it over to the other way, and then ring up my wheel and we are off. You can change that rudder much easier when you don't have the water action from the wheel against it.

Well really I think what knocked the packets out was good trucks and better roads. Now when we lived on the river, why that was the only means practically of transportation. The Ohio River outlet was the main way of transportation. If we bought a piece of machinery, it was shipped down the river on the boat and picked up at our landing, and that was just about it. When I was say, along about 13 years old, they would have what they would call a coal barge rise up around Pittsburgh maybe along in June and you would see coal fleets coming down and empties going up, anytime of the day you wanted to look there would be some going one way and some another. The river was full of coal going out. Now they've got a lot of . . . and them was all big sternwheelers.

Q: Let me keep you on that for a little because I have been trying to follow the picture down. Those were leaky coal boats weren't they?

A: Those were the old wooden barges. That was before there was any steel barges made. They was made out of pine fir about five inches thick and nailed together with square wrought iron nails about 10 or 12 inches long. They would get that coal barge rise, and then they would have them all loaded, and then they would bring them down the river, of course there would be . . . maybe you remember the *Sprague*?

Q: Yes, the great *Sprague*.

A: That towed I believe six or seven acres of barges at one time; it is at Vicksburg, Mississippi now as a museum. It costs probably a quarter to go through it. I was over when they brought the old *Snyder* down and give it, I was down seeing it come through lock 16, and was down there at the celebration when they landed in at Marietta, and that I believe was next to now the *Monongahela*, she has been on the river since. Some of them said that was the last of the sternwheel towboats. But the *Monongahela* has been running some since. But it was pictured and offered in the "Waterways Journal," in some of the later issues, I don't know just what ones now.

Q: Well there are sternwheel tows still on the river because I saw one yesterday.

A: Cap stone has one, this man I was telling you about it down here.

Q: Well up there is a smaller one, it's the big tows. I think the *Orco* and the *Omar* are still on. The *Omar* is going to be good another four years I have heard.

A: They tried to sell the idea that the *Snyder* was the last one, but there was same others on there. In fact, when I made up my mind I was going to build a boat here, I was a checking on boats and there was one down around New Orleans, just what I needed, and the price was about right. The transportation of it here, then getting it from Zanesville, and it had to be all cut up and rebuilt. I found I could build brand new cheaper than for what I could get that one for.

Q: I wonder if you could come back a little bit to those coal boats. Did you ever see any of them of them going down up around your part of the country? Because I know they sank all over the river.

A: No but I can tell you about one of the windiest fellows we had down there. They said there was a coal boat went down not too far from their place and they hired him to dive down and he did it until he brought all that coal up and loaded up. Would dive down and load up a bucket and come up. He was just the windiest fellow there was around.

Q: That would be about 2,500 bushels to bring up.

A: That would be quite a lot. But if you knew the character why it belonged to him. (chuckles)

Q: I know that a lot of river people used to go out in low water after the sunken coal.

A: There is coal barges sunk and they are buried half in the mud all the way from Pittsburg to New Orleans right now.

Q: Yes I've heard that.

A: I rather hated to see, well maybe I'm a little old fashioned I don't know, I just hated to see all of them sternwheelers and sidewheelers go out.

Q: Well they must have been beauties.

A: Oh yes. It used to be that a packet would start out in the spring of the year, and that is the season would open up good for shipping, why they would always aim to have it trimmed out and a new coat of paint. The prettiest thing in the way of a boat I believe I ever saw. Maybe it's just because the setting of it and the nature of the trip was so fitting. We was leaving Madison there one December raw evening on the little *Hanover* and just as we backed out, there was a big Mississippi boat laying in there brand new, called the *Alabama*. It was a big steamer, awful pretty, so we came on down the river around to Hanover Bend, and there wasn't a boat in sight, so when we landed in at Lees

Landing there is where I was telling you about all these sunflower seeds being picked up, that big steamer passed us and it was just about such an evening that you would have liked to jumped over on it and followed it on down to New Orleans. Just threatening snow about every minute.

Q: Did she have red stacks by any chance?

A: I don't remember about red stacks, but I know it was snow white, trimmed in green and had a green sternwheel. It was as bright as you ever saw. It just looked like sunshine.

Peggy Knoepfle: Can you tell us anything about any of the old excursion boats on the river?

A: Well the old *Homer Smith*, I know they used to want to paddle me for going out and riding the waves. That was back in 1916. The *Homer Smith* that was a big five deck excursion boat. It was running out of Louisville then, and I had a boy, friend over in Kentucky, just across the river from me, and about five o'clock here would come the *Homer Smith* around the Hanover Bend up there. Why we would get in them old leaky john boats and we'd light out for the middle of the river you know to catch the second wheel wave, which was about as high as a house. It just looked like it would pick the river up, of course I reckon I didn't realize about the danger of the suction of the boat if we'd get too close, something like that would suck us in and the wheel would catch us.

Q: That sounds like it could be a disaster. They say you could hear those big boats too! Captain Paul Kelley who is pilot on the Delta Queen now was telling me you could hear them way down river.

A: You can hear, maybe you have reference to the music or calliope.

Q: No, not only that, but the sound of the scapes and all.

A: Yes, now these sidewheelers, the old *Louisville* and the *Cincinnati*, sister boats, one was up one night and one the next during the week, then on Sunday they had what you called meet the boat trip, now that was quite an excursion trip. One would leave Louisville, I believe 110 miles between Louisville and Cincinnati. One would leave Cincinnati at the same time and you could get this trip, and then around Lawrenceburg, Indiana they would land and the passengers down would get on the other boat and go back to the hometown, and that's what they called meet the boat trip. In fact, I believe I have that right here clipped out of the "Waterways Journal," and telling you now about, cost you two bits I think, to make that trip and for an extra two bits you could get an all-round chicken dinner.

Q: Wow.

Dick and Marie Twedell, March 16, 1957

Question: Now here's your chance to be recorded for posterity, Dick.

Dick Twedell: Yes, that's the trouble with it. Well Marie you can talk about when you were a little girl on the river too? You were raised much closer to it than I was. What was the name, the number of the dam? Was that 4? I thought it was four, it might have well been lock 4. There was at one time a very established beach below there, Jefferson Beach.

Q: Where was it?

D: Below lock 4, which is about twenty miles upstream on the Monongahela, from Pittsburgh. That was, I guess in its heyday, quite a gay place, little dance place there. Was also a roller rink there. This was a sand beach and they had to restore the sand all the time because of the wash away. Above the dam about 400 yards was, above the beach rather was the dam, which was a lock. They had the big cheek wall, which extended downstream about 100 yards past the dam. We used to swim up there all the time. You could walk across the top of the dam, you could always walk across when the river was normal. The water going over the top of the dam would be about five or six inches deep. If you planted your feet firmly, you could walk across to the concrete construction in the middle. We used to except in floods. When there was a flood you couldn't walk across it, be knee-deep as soon as it got knee deep it would knock you right over. Nobody would dare venture on it then because the water below the dam was in pretty much spate all the time.

     The trick we used to do was one year we went up there, it was spring and the water was coming over, real brown, dirty and a lot of debris in it, as usual in a flood in high water. We went down below the cheek wall of the dam downstream, and got a long limb. We stuck it out over the water about 18 inches or two feet above the water. Then we would go back up, right below the dam where the jetty stuck out, retained the dam, concrete structure in the water. Guess in normal times it would be about two feet underwater. We'd dive in or jump in. We always jumped in because we always figured nobody ever got concussion of the foot (chuckles) because of the debris in the water. And then when we came out of the water, the wall would just whistle by almost go whish, whish, whish right by you. You would just be going down at such a speed. Then we'd reach down and grab ahold of the limb we had sticking out, a big sturdy thing. Then we would get back hand over hand into the shore because if we didn't, below the dams, below these cheek walls, they usually piled up great big rubble, piles of stone to retain the river wall, the riverbank. If you kept on going, you might get knocked into these things. Thus the river was going at a pretty terrific pace with a very narrow channel up there at the Monongahela as compared to the Ohio. That was our fun, it was of course, that was early in the spring and our parents never suspected we were swimming.

John Knoepfle

Q: You were just watching!

D: Just watching, just go down, we'd always try to form, we had our own little clique. We always tried to see who would be the first one in the water. The first day of spring, which is only a date on the calendar, we would all get down. I remember one year that we would build a terrific fire, a good one out of all the beach wood we could find, took off our clothes, went in the water for about a minute and a half, dashed out and immediately dried ourselves. This established a record, somebody beat us by two days the next year, within two days before the first of spring. This was done much lower than the beach, actually where you go in. The beach was about, there was some beach at the dam about two miles upstream from where I lived. We always walked, we never hitchhiked, it was considered sort of unsporting to hitchhike, we walked everywhere.

Marie Twedell: John, if you ever get to Elizabeth, the people who live up stream are people who run the bakery called Ulrich, every time the water came up, this was the place their bakery was always flooded. This happened every year that their house was flooded. In the 1936 flood they were just, they just had to leave, they just couldn't stay, most of the time they moved upstairs, every year they cleaned it up, then cleaned up the bakery. The bake shop, which they had right there was a very small thing. This would really be the people to see because they really knew the river. They could tell you every stage, everything that was happening when there was a flood. They knew every boat.

D: You had to know every boat to live on the, to be down there. You knew that the *Donora* made the biggest waves. That was what was important to a kid swimming down there.

Q: Which boat made the biggest waves?

D: The *Donora* supposedly in our day. All the boats, the *Moseby*, the *Clairton*, which was named after the town that I was raised in, and the *Elizabeth*. There were big tows, they were always coal. All the tows were coal, because they would, up in the upper Monongahela, most of the coaling was taking place upstream. One of the boats was the *Clairton*, the *Denora*, the *Elizabeth*. I can't remember now, there were some boats that were, one boat *Hannah* something.

Q: There was *Tom Hannah* or some name like that.

D: It might have been, there was these boats with, most of them had names. There was the *Monongahela*, too. It was one boat, the *Old Mon*, there was the *Duquesne*, the *Homestead*, the *Fairless*, and a few named after the presidents and the vice-presidents of the coal and steel companies. We'd swim out. We'd swim the river, I couldn't do it now, about three and four times a day. It didn't mean a thing. There were drownings all the time. We would swim out and sort of just let the boat breeze by. As soon as it got by we would plunge in the breakers off the stern, and bounce up and down for a while.

M: You used to climb on them, walk along that coal.

D: What we used to do for that was, you could take the bamboo pole that came out of a rug, you had to have something light. We would take a wire loop about two and a half feet in diameter and make a loop on it and tie it or tape it at the end. Then wrap, just sort of step into that loop and dragging a pole behind you, you would swim out into the river. And we'd wait out there about four or five feet from the barges as they went by, sort of treading water. As soon as you saw one of the stanchions or one of the capstans as we called them in those days on the barge, as they go by you hook, you slipped off your pole and you hook, you'd put the loop over the stanchion and you would shinny up the pole and you rode the barge up to maybe, almost up to Elizabeth Bridge, which was down below the dam. You always had to judge how far you could swim back even with the current, and then we'd ride up, and then the river hands didn't chase you off, to accept this fact, on river they would put up with all the termites and trash like that. (laughter) We used to go up and swim back down and start all over again. I remember one time we decided to go up as far as the locks, the locks were about two miles upstream and we thought we would swim back, very courageous, it was a two-mile swim.

We were all pretty sturdy swimmers, better than the average, but not no channel swimmers among us. Then we would get up to the locks and get off and we had arranged it all pretty nicely. We had thrown our poles to one man who retrieved it, or two men and they took them back. We got to the locks and we started swimming downstream. For some reason we didn't, I don't know what the case was, but we never went through the locks on a boat. I think the lockmaster would have chased us off. We started swimming down, and we didn't get quite as far as the bridge, because it was pretty far. So we swam over to shore and we walked down. I was barefooted, that's a long hard walk down a pebbly beach. So, I walked through town. I felt kind of naked in my trunks walking through town and I went back to the beach and I tried through the ash alleys and everywhere else. My feet were just sore and tender. It took me hours to get back, it was two miles. I would stop every once in a while and stick my feet in the water and let them cool, then get back once more on the hot pavement or hot gravel heated by the July sun and once more went back. Now our parents knew we were down here all the time, because there was a magnificent municipal pool. The thing about the pool was you couldn't ride a boat up the river. You couldn't take a bunch of old rusty nails and a hatchet down there and make a raft. You couldn't do all the things that the river allowed you do. You couldn't build a fire, you couldn't stick a potato in your pocket when you went out in the middle of the day, and counting on it being your lunch, along with some spring water. I never ate lunch. I grew to be a gangly youth of 18 before I realized what eating lunch was in the summertime.

I remember one time we had been gathering wood to make a raft and my feet got all wet and muddy. I kept my sneakers on because it was so rough walking, gravel and a great deal of glass in there. I put my sneakers by the fireplace while I went to take a swim and I came back and one of my sneakers was burned. All that was left was this rubber sole smoldering and smelly and I

John Knoepfle

wrapped around my feet with some old pieces of rope and cloth and walked home. I got home and I'll never forget, I'll never understand how I got away with it because all I said was I need a new pair of sneakers. My mother didn't even question the fact that the sneakers that I had burned were two weeks old, and went out and bought me a new pair. This was very unlike my mother especially in those days, in the 1930s.

Another thing we used to do was a tremendous strawberry patch. I guess everybody, somebody had a truck garden. The east side of the river was flanked with railroad yards and our side there was the Union and Pennsylvania Railroad. The other side was the B & O Railroad. Beyond the railroad on the other side was a more of a flatland. Our side of the river, the hills went directly almost into the river. And there was some nice flat bottom land over there, and there was a man with a tremendous strawberry patch. In the spring when the strawberries were in full bloom, we used to go on several of our sort of raiding parties. We would go get a big branch along the river, a tremendous branch it would be. You would put it in the water and part of some other limbs would stick out above the water. We would hang our essential clothing on this, no underwear and no socks. Our shirts, trousers and sneakers. We'd push the thing across the river keeping all our clothing dry.

When we would get to the other side and put on our sneakers, shirt and trousers, and go marauding in this strawberry patch; we would get down and sneak around behind the boxcar and hide, waiting for him and see where he was, try to locate him, then we'd run in and grab a handful and eat like mad up a row, filling our pockets, and our mouths at the same time. Then we would get out and run. If he caught, one time he did, he came out and saw us; he started across the strawberry patch. Now like fools we went down to the bank, over the bank and into the water, stirring up the water. Well it's pretty hard to run in about a foot of water. He was right up the railroad track and we realized we were trapped, so we kept running until we got to a certain point where we stopped, where the woods between us and the railroad track, the willows were pretty thick. And we took off our clothes and buried them. There was some foliage and we walked up the beach and sat there very nonchalantly dipping our feet, in the nude already to swim. He came down and asked us if we had seen any boys. Whew! (laughter) We were still eating strawberries.

M: You were always talking about the river, you were always nude; you didn't say you were little naughty boys.

D: We had our own beach, our own beach to this beach was right around the bend up in the steel mills. The bend was just behind you see where we swam from, where we departed from you see, for all these marauding parties was just around the river from the steel office and was completely isolated beach. There was a row of willows and sycamores between the road and the beach, and then there was the elderberry bushes. E. J. Crossing was the railroad crossing, there was a tower there, we used to drink water. The tower keeper was very kind. If we didn't want to walk way up to this one spring we knew of, which was near the river, the man at E. J. Tower would give us all the water we wanted, just a matter of having some company. You sit in a railroad for eight hours a day you'd want to talk to anybody. A bunch of boys that don't have much to do but get themselves in trouble. Anyhow the man from who we stole the strawberries accepted our story. We saw no boys who would steal strawberries, and he went away. So I don't believe he accepted it, but he was kind of disbelieving and glancing back at us as he left. Also, from this point we were on the other side upstream was a very respectable beach where mixed people bathed, that beach down from Wylie there. There was a gravel area, well it wasn't, I don't know how respectable a beach can get. Well at least people bathed there and they had suits on. We were swimming over in the same area one time, about the same place we would go on our strawberry party and there was a whole packet of blue mud wash, with a sort of a stream washing in there, came through Wylie down Roberts Hollow then.

Q: That was blue mud!

D: The blue mud. It was really bluish mud. We went over there one time and we rubbed it on ourselves to form swimming trunks or just blued ourselves around our midsections and walked sort of out near the beach to spread it around, not too close. There are really blue mud deposits out there, it's really strikingly blue, dark navy blue. This is what we did, this is to be wicked. Then there was sort of a half, operating in the 1930s, a lot of mines up in the area, mines that had been dead for years, opened up for people who wanted to just look through, wanted to provide themselves with fuel coal. They were co-operative things in the neighborhood. The mines had been invented by the regional owners and some coal operators. The local people would in the vicinity of the mine, go in and start digging it again. There was a tremendous old mine with a great huge slag dump upriver, it was dead, and they started operating in the 1930s and had one of the old narrow gauge track going into it and a mule pulling the coal out. We'd go on our marauding parties including going up to the mine, going to the shed there and getting mule shoes, which we would take back out or hang on the branch again. Once more in our basic clothes, we would push the mule shoes across and set up our horseshoe pitching boxes, and use the mule shoes. This is what we did. I never was very good at pitching horse-shoes or mule shoes.

Q: During the 1930s everybody farmed every bit of available bottom land they could. As a little girl on the river you were two or three blocks from it. How close did you live to the river? How close did your mother come to the river?

M: Well about two blocks.

D: You were one block from the railroad track.

M: Yes, we crossed the railroad tracks, which wasn't a block though, it was …

D: It was a half or a quarter of a block due north of Cincinnati, quarter of a square. Then about another quarter of a block, two streets from the river. I remember when I was kid. Guess I was, how old was I in 1937? I was about 20 years younger than I am now. Was about 16 in high school. I remember walking up around it was a treacherous walk because of the mud and water, you couldn't go up the river road walking around the bluffs and back and coming in through hogback down the road and seeing the water lapping up on route 51.

M: The school bus couldn't get through, so we didn't have any school. My brother, he had gotten by three years telling Mr. Bell, who was the principal of Clairton High School, we didn't have a high school in our town, that he had to stay home and help out with the flood victims. (laughter) He'd never been known to do anything like this in his life. But in the 1937 flood we really could not, we couldn't get to school, couldn't do very much of anything and the thing that was most upsetting in my family, our house had never been flooded and my mother went down, opened the basement door and our washing machine was bobbing around like mad. This disturbed my mother to no end. She didn't care who was down there got completely flooded out, she just wanted her washing machine to get stable again and not go bobbing around the basement. Because we were up higher we had all these people staying with us, my aunt and her husband, and their child, and an old man who was related to my grand-mother. I didn't know they, there were other people too. Guess they only stayed with us for one night. I remember this was a very happy time, see I was 15. And having all these people visiting with us because we were up out of the flood district, and people who had never been flooded before were, in 1937.

D: That was a high one wasn't it?

M: Yes and then the volunteer fire department went down with the fire hoses and washed out these houses, the furniture soaked.

D: Oh, that was nice after the flood. You know we went along the riverbank after the flood, after the river got back somewhere close to pool and we picked up all, you know we had, you know kids are always looking around for sort of a clubhouse. There were these chicken coops and outhouses and everything lying up along the bank. You could pick out one of them. If you put it upright and got a foundation for it you had a shelter. I remember one time we came across this. I forget what it was in. There was a wooden box with some Portland papers inside and we pulled them out, real old stock of some bicycle company many years ago, real old picture of an old bicycle. Maybe that company was converted and is now Northrup or something like that. (laughter) Lockheed or something. (laughter) We decided they were worthless because of the condition of the bike.

M: You weren't properly brought up. We knew enough never to touch anything like this because disease was rampant, we weren't to touch anything.

D: There was all kinds of good thing left. I remember I was a kid and I was raised, when I was very young, I was much closer to the river for a while, for about two years. They always had these dredges coming up and dredging where any stream was flushing gravel and soil into the channel. One summer the dredges appeared upstream at New England Hollow. Every stream was called a hollow. So in the upper Monongahela they had nice names. They had names like Starved Gut Hollow and Mutton Town Hollow.

M: That's where you lived, Starved Gut, wasn't it?

D: For a while, and then Calamity Hollow, they're really nice places. A young man and I, he was about eight, seven, the same age as I was, we used to row for water across the dredge. The closest place to get water was across the river and we both, don't know if we could swim very well, maybe could swim the river. We would skiff faithfully over that river for about two weeks and bring back water to the men on the dredge for the terrific salary for 25 cents a day for both men. (laughter) Then they dredged a nice big deep, they kept dredging the stream bed itself right back as far as they can up to the river road or any railroad bed that is there. They gave us a delicious pool to swim in right there away from the river current, the river would back in. Eventually the sides slumped in and filled in and old trees fall across it and makes a nice spot to swim in. As we grew older we would always swim up. I moved later on about five miles upstream. We swam a beach where no females were allowed because of the costumes. This was by the old railroad town. We had a name for it, we used to call it BAB, which in our terms stood for Bare Ass Beach. It was just enough seclusion for us, a good place to lay in the sun and the water was not quite as clean, not quite as safe as a municipal pool, but it had a lot to it.

Q: It had local color.

D: Yes it had local, we had a variety of things we could do in that water.

M: You know Major Bowes had a showboat too that went up and down the river. Do you remember this?

D: No I . . .

M: Because I was only in grade school. Did you ever hear about this?

D: I knew he had a show.

M: But he had a showboat. Remember when he had people win on the radio, and then his winners, this is what they had, instead of stopping at theatres they visited. I don't remember seeing any other thing, seeing them in the theatre, but I do remember seeing them on this showboat and they had these people who tap danced and sang and so on who had won on his, that was there after the Bryant's I think.

Q: That was in Jefferson.

M: West Elizabeth, yes.

D: There was one person I remember down at the old area where they dredged. Some character, was probably as old as I am now, I'm an old character, named Jock Harrigan. He was a very athletic man for his age. He smoked long black cigars and Harrigan was a descendant, I guess he was second generation Glasgow Irish. That's why you count the name Jock and Harrigan together. He was a big, deep-chested man, and everybody respected him on the beach. He

John Knoepfle

would put a cigar in his mouth and swim out and back again. The cigar would never go out. (laughter) This is the thing I think that made him the real athlete.

Q: That was incredible.

D: A tobacco smoking athlete. (laughter)

M: You always remember such happy things about the river. I always remember the children who were drowned.

D: There were a lot of kids drowned.

M: There were these things called step-offs. I don't know what step-offs were.

D: It was a groove in the bottom.

M: Why were they grooved?

D: This meant that rock shelving on the bottom of those ridges, some would resist erosion and some wouldn't.

M: I remember how the whistle would blow and the fire department would go down . . .

D: And drag. They used to shoot guns over the water because they thought the gun would bring up the body. It was typical. You would hear that boom down there. Then there was one particular case, one incident I remember one person ever drowning there in the river. Was nothing to swim out and get in the wake of a boat and bounce up and down in the waves. At eight you learned to swim 50 yards, at ten you could swim 100 yards, at 12 he ought to be able to swim across the river or he had no business down there. We used to get out in the middle and see if you could touch bottom, which meant going down actually with your foot, getting ahold of the mud on the bottom or something like that. You coming up, proving it by holding up a dirty foot or sticking the mud between your toes. Somebody had a canoe on our river, a canoe was sort of like owning a Lincoln Continental today. Had a canoe there on one of those rivers, a rarity. In our hometown, which had a great deal of central or southern Europeans, there was a family named Kareta, who had their only son we knew, who was Benny and he played the violin. Reason I knew him so well was, he was a pretty good friend of my brothers who was also taking lessons on the violin with the same old teacher. There was kind of a sacrifice for a family in those days to put out money for a lesson. My brother went to town there; my brother turned out to be a fiddler. Benny Kareta had he lived would have been a violinist. Benny went out one day in a canoe, and they were going to catch the waves, and the canoe overturned and Benny couldn't swim a stroke. All the time he had been practicing the violin instead of learning how to swim and he drowned. They picked his body up about a quarter of a mile downstream. He came from a family who were very self-sacrificing for him, instead of buying a car they would buy a new violin for Benny. Violin in those days, about a $800 violin, think it was the last one they bought. That was about the price for which you would pay for a normal car. Teach him to give him every opportunity they could. That was a terrific tragedy at the time because everybody realized and respected the effort that the family had put in it. He had been to states in high school competition, champion violin player. A champion violin player that was what he was, and when he went down just, and he went down off Bare Ass Beach, up there where we grew up.

M: He was what, seventeen at the time?

D: Seventeen or eighteen, no I don't think he was through high school.

M: It must have been the year it was graduated, he was graduated with Jack and that was before. He was going to go to Carnegie Tech.

D: Study music, yes. That was just one drowning, and then in our gang, there was a kid named, a fine specimen, Danny Lowes. His whole family was a family of athletes. His sister was a swimmer, swam her way through college in California. Her brothers played assorted football at different universities, and Danny ended up playing for North Carolina State. Danny went down there one day as a very young kid, he was about two years younger than I am, he still is, nothing can change this, and he built a raft. There was a little boy on the corner named Ramus. Can't remember what his first name was, but he couldn't swim, he couldn't swim too well and the raft went over tipped, and the child drowned. Danny managed to get himself ashore safely. Danny went home like little children will. I imagine Danny was about seven at the time.

M: He didn't tell anybody.

D: He didn't tell anybody. He ate a silent dinner and sort of withdrew and Mrs. Ramus started looking for her son. She said, "Danny, have you seen him?" Finally, Danny burst out, told them the last time he had seen the Ramus boy he fell in the water. So, they went down and got the body out. The area was pretty close to shore, so it wasn't too far downstream. It was a pretty typical of accidents you get. I guess the river claimed about an average of two a year. One time after we were married, five kids were drowned in one fell swoop.

M: Five little boys.

D: Five little boys were on vacation from school one day in the fall for some reason. They were playing hunter. Somebody said there were ducks on the water and they put on all their father's hunting clothes, big heavy boots and big heavy coats and got a skiff, a boat on the upper Monongahela was a skiff no matter what shape it takes. They rowed out near the dam 4, and overturned. From then on the problem was getting the kids the bodies out, all five of them. They couldn't make it in their clothes. We still, it is the same area where we used to spend most of the summer when the dam was, when the water was over the dam just at a certain height, about six inches, nice and clear, put your feet on it. I remember I used to, we'd always avoid going over the dam — the downstream side of the dam always had a slope to it so it wouldn't erode — and get caught in that water. The water was over, about 45 degrees. Then there were these abutments below coming in with these buoys in between. We would always be careful for some reason not to get involved, falling over the dam or get in the white water below. So one time somebody was going to come up the dam and he lost his balance and he started toppling over. He rolled down the slip with the water, and of course, all the fun area washes away and it leaves the gravel out and it's kind of rough. He went into the foam, got spattered around a bit, and popped out. He looked happy. So what was left, but we all do this. From then on you couldn't keep us away from the lower end of the dam. We were always in the white water from then on, always off the abutments below, wading around and diving into the foam and coming up. This seemed to have erased the thing that we had avoided so long — and thought dangerous — all of a sudden became just another sport. We indulged in it all of the time.

Q: Well wonderful.

D: Marie, you haven't told about the, who was it lived across, Walker?

M: Howder.

D: Captain Howder lived downstream from lock 4 from on the hill. I'll let Marie tell you about him. He was the ever faithful husband.

M: Yes, he always put his light up on his house. He had this very fine substantial house and he would signal to his wife, you see. Then she flashed the lights in the house and we always knew when Captain Howder was going up the river.

D: I wonder which boat Captain Howder was on? He always had to blow for the lock.

M: I don't know but Mother said the last time I talked to her Mrs. Howder had died.

D: Well Captain Howder is probably long since gone too, isn't he?

M: I don't know.

D: It was the old red brick house up there wasn't it?

M: Buff brick.

D: Was it buff brick?

M: His brother was a doctor.

D: He had to blow for the lock anyhow. How many times do you blow for the lock? Was it three tooter?

M: I don't know. Then he would flash the light up there and she'd flash.

D: She would wake up with the toot anyhow because she lived near the lock.

Q: How did you spell his name?

M: H-O-W-D-E-R.

D: Marie's hometown is a real river town, one of the real old ones.

M: It was a boat building.

D: Boat building town. They used to build the sea going craft there after the Revolution, sail them down the river and rig them in New Orleans and they'd fill up with grain, all the old Monongahela and Western Pennsylvania farmers would load them up and they'd sell grain and boat. The Marine Ways still exist in Elizabeth. That's the principle industry, isn't it?

M: It was.

D: What else is in there now?

M: Well it is just leftover now.

D: It's a dormitory for the steel mills around. People live there because that's the only thing, that's the biggest industry there is rebuilding river craft, restoring it and they're not welding barges very much. I guess the town was formed in about 1790 or 1780.

M: Well no when I was . . .

D: What does it, here about Lewis and Clark building their ships there, their boats there.

M: I don't know. You know Mr. Wiley has written lots of books about this. You know where Wiley's farm is? He was an old, he had a newspaper in Elizabeth when they still had a newspaper. He's written lots of things about this. He's written things that we had to look up when we had history in high school. Let's see, how old would it be, because they had their centennial.

D: Sesquicentennial

M: No, it was their centennial as a town when I was in the 7th grade.

D: It was one hundred and fifty years old then.

M: No.

D: It was Elizabeth's sesquicentennial, the best argument on tape, but it was Marie, that would have only made it 1830. That town existed before 1830. There is a very pretty part of the Monongahela above Elizabeth. There's one part seems to be uninhabited by steel mills. All the flatlands on the Monongahela between Elizabeth and Pittsburgh were taken over by steel mills, or coffers, or glassworks and glassware something like that. Wherever they could put a lot of, a lot of acreage of industrial buildings up. But above there is still some flatland, there is still some nice bends and it's very pretty and it is sort of densely, sparsely populated. There is one terrific bend going up to Monongahela City, which is the next main town after Elizabeth. I guess it's about ten miles upstream. It's called the Cincinnati Bend because it resembles the contours. It's a really pretty spot. On a summer evening it's very pretty up there, willows on the other side, a gradual slope from the flatland up into the hills, a very sheer cut on the southside. Marie was more of a river rat than I am. Her folks live in Monongahela City and some live in Donora.

M: Let's do this, we must do this, you must go to Elizabeth sometime. There are people who could tell you, this is nothing. They know everything about it. Why don't you go there sometime, you'd like it.

D: I will.

Q: Maybe Dick you can tell me about the social status of a captain that you might have remembered?

D: Well there were captains on the Monongahela. I knew two of them. One remotely, that was Captain Howder, and one that lived near us Coleman. They were in those days, course we had a pretty established industrial river actually. They seemed to have the same status as a general foreman or superintendent of a steel mill. They were really separate men. The only difference was you very seldom saw the river captain because he was on the river.

John Knoepfle

M: A very prosperous . . .

D: That was considered to be a fine way to make a living because he was always taken care of and his salary and was always with his family. He had his home, he had his meals provided by whatever coal or steel company he was navigating for. Captain Coleman, I knew his son, grew up with me, I couldn't tell you this day what his father looked like. I have no conception what his dad looked like. His sisters, his older sisters, taught me in high school, Captain Coleman's daughter. This was before, but I don't know to this day what he looked like. Did you ever see Howder or did you know his wife? Did you know Howder?

M: No, I knew his brother.

D: Well you never saw the captain, but you always knew he existed. This was the thing about it, you always knew this man existed, and you knew he was somewhere in the river, but you never saw him.

Q: Kind of a God like creature.

D: Yes, that is right.

M: There was kind of a great drop there from the captain to the, you know.

D: To the river hand, yes, the river hand was . . .

M: Yes, the river hand was an awful low form of . . .

D: He did that because he couldn't get a respectable job. But the captain for some reason he did it because he was a great man, whatever he did. There was a great gap there.

M: The lower ones were shifty sort of people. They were apt to quit this thing and do something else.

D: There were all sorts of people who cooked on there. You would hear of people, somebody was cooking, occasionally I think later on they took, had female cooks. Had women cooks. Originally, they just had men cooks, and we'd see the boats come up, and they'd have wash hanging on the lines.

M: The thing you remembered about rivermen was that they drank. They drank as soon as they hit town and this wasn't a nice thing to do at all; when they drank they got drunk. But not captains, they were different.

D: Captains had families. Your typical rivermen, I guess, was not supposed to have families. Of course I imagine, a pilot or a chief engineer was still respectable. People never bothered to break it down below captain and crew. That was just the way it was. I never knew of a man who would admit he was an engineer or a pilot or anything. He was a captain or a crewman.

M: No, I think there were, I don't think that's true. I think there were graduations in these things. The lower ones were of terribly . . .

D: I used to know about a fellow whose father was superintendent of a maintenance group, a Marine Ways in Floreffe, which is a very minute hamlet above Elizabeth. What company was Bob Coleman?

M: U. S. Steel.

D: It was United States Steel Company, a subsidiary of one of them, he was a superintendent of the repair Marine Ways up at Floreffe, that was a great job.

He was clerk for the whole works and everything else. For a while I guess he was assistant, he moved right up into the company property. You have to realize the coal and iron business in those days and probably still left over now, they make a man a superintendent and in order to assure him a status they provide him with a domicile, which would be equal to his position. Steel for example, my hometown is a steel town. They had a terrific old English mansion up there with a big grill fence around it, which was occupied by the superintendent of the steel mill. That branch of United States Steel, and of course, when he retired or was moved from that branch that house was immediately occupied by the next superintendent. Same way with all the miner subsidiary, including the local plant up at Floreffe. Maintaining the riverboats for United States Steel had this house set up, and Bob occasionally, he used to be the envy of the, because he would get a chance to go down to New Orleans on the riverboat and come back up. I thought this was really great. I used to go up and visit him every chance I got just so I could tell, I wandered around the Marine Ways.

M: Strange thing is this man's son married a second cousin of mine and the son and his wife now live in Detroit. When Richard and I were visiting in Detroit a while ago I went to see her and she said her father-in-law comes to see her occasionally and it is always so good when he comes because he brings this scotch cooler or something like this you see. And it's loaded with steaks and all these lovely cuts of meat and everything because you see these rivermen get all this at very reasonable rates, so he buys all this food.

D: At the commissary for buying provisions for the riverboats.

M: For the riverboats, so he brings all this marvelous food up to Detroit to his daughter-in-law. Seems funny to drag it all the way up there.

D: The most disappointing thing about, the Monongahela where I knew it was you couldn't fish in it. It was dead. It was a dead stream. It was so industrialized.

Q: So many chemicals in there.

D: No, there was some old hands around there including Marie's father who I didn't know, who remember up at Monongahela City when they used to fish for Walleyed Pike in the river and men who used to go duck shooting on the upper reaches of the Monongahela. There were men I have met, man who used to trap for muskrat on Hughes Creek, which now is tunneled under a steel mill. Used to take canoes up there, used to fish for trout in the headwater. Now it's nothing but a typical sulfur bottom, streams that coal residue from coal mines and seepage sulfurized it. All these streams have essentially become industrial sewers, waterways or something like that, but nothing that supports any marine vegetation, nothing that has life in it at all. Once in a while somebody says the bluegills are coming back in. Bluegill is a pretty hardy fish. At the waterworks above the dam there is always catfish on the other side. It's even chancy catching a fish up there unlike they are in the Ohio because the stream is so caustic for a small stream and industry is so heavy around it. The stream has just taken too much.

John Knoepfle

Q: Is it clear there?

D: No, it's not clear.

Q: At Brownsville and places like that?

D: It gets clear up around there. Probably you are getting pretty far above there. Now below Donora, at Donora you are way downstream from Brownsville at Charleroi. You are starting to get industrialized at Elmport. They start dumping there. Then you got all that mine, all coming in from all the hollows between and along all those points between there and Pittsburgh. There are all these hollows pouring all their mud, the creeks coming in there like Peters Creek and Turtle Creek and the Youghiogheny coming in at McKeesport.

Q: What's that that comes in at McKeesport?

D: The Youghiogheny comes in at McKeesport and the Youghiogheny up at the headwaters is very nice. It forms up in Somerset County. I used to go trout fishing up there, become a very beautiful stream, just a slough, not a navigable stream. I think it's navigable about ten miles up from where it comes into the Monongahela, but there is not much up there in the commercial end of it.

M: Twenty years after the St. Patrick's Day flood.

Q: To the day?

M: To the very day.

Q: Amazing.

Question: This is Thomas Wagner and we are in Columbus, Ohio. I understand you began working on the river at a very young age. Can you tell us something about that?

Answer: In McKinley's administration there was pretty hard times and it just started then to get good times, and everybody was working. They would go up in West Virginia and cut poplar timber, walnut and oak, but mostly poplar. There were five sawmills in Ironton and the biggest sawmill in the United States at that time was the Cole Crane Company in Cincinnati. Sometimes they would have, over 70,000 logs a season would get away from them in the Big Sandy and Guyandotte Valley, and come out in the Ohio River. The state legislature had a salvage law, and whoever caught those logs, pulled them ashore, and tied them up, they got 50 cents a log abandoned logs. The logs was abandoned and was free property. It belonged to anybody, but everybody was out trying to catch logs, everybody with a skiff, which they wanted you to do because if a log got below Cincinnati it was just gone that was all. That's how we made our living year after year from 1896 to about 1906. They would catch those logs and pull them into the Ohio side, 50 cents, Kentucky side 25. The legislation changed and the Kentucky side went to 50 cents and Ohio 25. That's how we had to do, whichever state paid the most, we'd land the logs in that state. In those days you went to work when you was 12 years old. You didn't fool around. My mother was a widow, and six kids, and we had to get out and hustle. That's where those logs come in at.

Q: I guess every time you got a nice free log you would have a kind of bonanza then.

A: Oh yes, Wilber Pyle and I, at one time we caught 72 logs one day. They wouldn't give us the money. We had to get Dr. Ellison, he was the coroner, he run the drugstore, he come over and appointed himself our guardian and he collected the money. We were only 15 years old, they weren't going to give us no $36. (chuckles) We lived on the river all the time, us kids. We would make our own boats and everything, of course the men would pitch in and help us. We would tell Pete Newman we wanted lumber for boats. He'd give it to us, take it and dry it and run it through the planer. One board would be as wide and as high as the boat, maybe 24 or 25 inches wide. He would give us that for nothing, of course we always caught his logs. If a log would get away from them, get down, there was no way of getting it back up the river. Nowadays it's pool stage, just like a pond as you come up it, but when that current goes, why they couldn't tow those logs back up the river. But now they can. In those days before they built these dams there was no traffic going towards Pittsburgh on the Ohio River. It would always come out of Pittsburgh.

Q: Now Ironton was the home of the Bay brothers.

John Knoepfle

A: They lived on South Sixth Street in Ironton. They owned quite a few boats. Their small packets ran between Huntington and Portsmouth, daily trips. Let's see, Huntington is 50 miles, 100 miles each day, 50 miles each way. They only charged 50 cents from Huntington to Portsmouth, from Portsmouth to Huntington. They had the *Chevalier*, the *Greyhound*, the *Lizzie Bay*, the *B. T. Enos*, the *Louise*, the *Georgia*. The *Georgia* was the first steel hull boat around the Ohio River, that was a little kind of a yacht. Captain Dess Davis had the *Bob Ballard*, that was a towboat. They towed freight trains across the Ohio River to Ashland, Kentucky. Ore would come into Ironton and it was taken across to the furnace in Ashland. There was another furnace in Ashland. They would transfer about eight cars at a time, they got the freight train across the river that way.

Q: There was no bridge there at that time.

A: There was no bridge there, the Kenova bridge was just finished, but they'd have to send ore clear to West Virginia and bring it down through Kentucky, so they ferried it across the river at Ironton.

Q: Do you have any personal recollections of the Bay brothers?

A: Oh yes, I have. The Sunday morning we was up on the incline, that's where they would put those cars down and Captain Billy Bay got his leg bashed off one Sunday morning up there.

Q: If you would, if you could, talk about that logging a little bit more. You said the logs were branded.

A: When these trees were going to West Virginia they would strip the trees and the ones that were going to be cut, to be on the safe side, they had kind of like a sledge hammer with initials in the end. They'd hit the tree so they couldn't miss having it branded, then after it was cut down they would hit it on the end. That would put the initial and the lumber firm on the log.

Q: What were some of those brands?

A: Yellow poplar was YFC, Nigh was BN, and Newman and Sparta was NS, and Cole Crane Company was CCC, and Cross Ties was CC Clark. You got six cents for a cross tie and 25, 50 cents for a log.

Q: Cross ties were for the railroad I guess.

A: That's right. They were all hand hewn cross ties not sawed ties, they were hand hewn.

Q: I didn't know that. Do you remember any of the flooding of the river?

A: There was never, of course I was just born then, was just a year old in 1883 flood or the 1884 flood. That was the biggest one until the 1913 flood. I had left Ironton at that time. Annually we would have a flood. I got $2.50 a day then ferrying the mail from the end of, as far as the C. H. & D., could go, and then about two miles and a half would be water and I would have to row a boat over with the mail to the other end and transfer the mail across that water. I got $2.50 a day for that.

Q: It must have been quite a strain on a wide river.

A: It wasn't the river, it was the backwater, a creek. The N & W, when it would go down through the water, a guy would have to walk in front of the engine to keep the logs in place. They ran that train as long as the water didn't get to the firebox the trains would run.

Q: Ironton was a big steel center in its day wasn't it? Do you remember much about that industry?

A: I can remember Ironton when the only way they could get the iron in from those furnaces, see there was 49 furnaces within 29 miles of Ironton. They were charcoal furnaces and the only way they could get the iron in was by oxen.

Q: Oxen!

A: They would have from 16 to 32 oxen pulling this iron ore, one ton of iron down those hills. But it paid. I've seen those big packet boats pull into Ironton at eight o'clock in the morning and they wouldn't leave until five that afternoon just loading iron and nails.

Q: Guess they were going south on the river.

A: That's right.

Q: Iron and coal and lumber, that's a lot of industries for a small Ohio town, isn't it?

A: I tell you, Newman & Sparta Lumber Company, when that burned they had 16,000,000 feet of lumber loaded on the cars. They let the insurance stop at noon, and those 16 cars burned up besides 48,000,000 feet of lumber besides that. Started at seven o'clock Tuesday evening and the N & W didn't get a train through there again until Sunday morning. It was stacked 40 to 50 feet high and about three blocks long and about two blocks wide.

Q: I guess that just about wiped them out.

A: It did. Well, it killed old T.

Q: Well you spent a lot of time down on the riverbank I suppose.

A: That's all us kids did.

Q: Do you remember much of the activity that went on when the boats were up along the shore? Could you describe any of that?

A: They had what they called a wharfboat, which was about 40 feet wide, about 112 feet long. The boats would land and tie up to this wharfboat and unload their freight on that. They would never step in Ironton unless it was nails, of course the nails and the pig iron, they would load from the bank. They'd hire men from Ironton to help, of course had their regular crew of roustabouts and it all had to be done carrying it by hand. Carry a keg of nails that weighed 180 pounds. I have seen them load as many as 1,200 kegs at a time.

Q: It must have been awful for labor in those days!

A: We were young guys about 17 or 18 and we'd hire out at Ironton, Ashland, Catlettsburg, we got 75 cents. It cost us 15 cents to get back home.

Q: You worked on this loading and unloading then, so you must have known, I suppose, some of the rousters.

John Knoepfle

A: No, I didn't know anybody. Oh, say one thing this is really important. There was a family named Havely Hasly, they called Captain Havely. Him and his wife they had 15 girls and two boys all raised on shanty boats. They had two big boats, 15 girls and two boys. We would go down there and play. They would take the windows out, the girls would dive out through the windows.

Q: Well that's pretty much a past existence those shanty boats.

A: I don't think there was one girl out of that whole family went bad. Different ones of them were just fine.

Q: Were there many shanty boats up around Ironton?

A: Oh yes see, I don't think they allow them now. But in those days I would say there was 25 along Ironton, nice boats. Even the police, you know, a dirty boat come along there, they wouldn't allow it. They'd just have to move. In those days it didn't matter how high the water rose, if that boat stuck up there that was his then until the next water came and carried it away. Police had to watch that. Oldman Havely would never let his boat do that. He would always keep it in the water. He fished, him and his two boys. Well the girls did too, and he rented boats. In the wintertime why they would all pitch in and make skiffs. Just think those skiffs sold for $15 apiece and he thought he was getting a tremendous price. Now you couldn't buy one for $150.

Q: Well he managed to carve out an existence for himself then off the river.

A: Oh yes.

Q: How did you make out in low water on the rivers? It must have gotten to be the size of a creek bed sometimes.

A: You could never wade the Ohio River at any time around Ironton.

Q: Deep channel there I guess.

A: That's where Bay made his money with those little boats. They weren't little boats, I would say they were 100 feet long, but very little draft. The *Virginia* and the *Queen City*, they very seldom had to lay up on account of low water.

Q: Did you ever go and see any of the showboats?

A: I worked on the stage and that and I got to go to the showboats free.

Q: Could you talk about it?

A: Charley Hunter was a friend of mine from down there, he was the one that coached Edna Ferber on the "Showboat" when she wrote it. He could play any instrument, I don't care what it was, any musical instrument that anybody else could play he could play it better. He was on the *Cotton Blossom* and Edna Ferber got him to help her, you know give her pointers, I think it was the "Showboat," wasn't it that she wrote?

Q: Yes, what other showboats came into there? Do you remember?

A: I don't remember the names. All of them stopped at Ironton. Ironton was a town with the money. Ironton in those days had more money than Huntington and Portsmouth and Ashland put together. They had two or three steel mills and two great big nail mills. I guess they made three or 4,000 kegs of nails a day at one time. I worked for 12 years on the stage in Ironton from the time I was a little kid on up.

Q: They had a legitimate theatre there?

A: Oh yes, Julia Marlowe was born in Ironton.

Q: Is that so?

A: Ben Hayes and I, we still argue about that. He said the book says she was born in England and the fellows that I worked with on the stage when I started there, they claim she was born in Ironton and used to sing on the street corners in Ironton.

Q: Well can you recollect? It would be an interesting departure if you could tell us about the theatre in Ironton.

A: All the legitimate shows, they'd make a stop between Chicago and Cincinnati. They would stop in Charleston, Huntington, Ironton, Portsmouth and Maysville. That's where they would break that week stand. They'd pick up their money there. They had a regular, Elsie Janis and George M. Cohen and all of those shows played there.

Q: Can you remember any particulars about these people?

A: I used to have their pictures and history. Elsie Janis, she was only 17 when she first came to Ironton, of course that Mrs. Bierbower she wanted everybody to see her daughter. They had what you called a repertoire company, they would play six nights and it would be easy to get well acquainted with people, but by gosh you would forget them as soon as they would leave.

Q: In and out. Were you a stagehand?

A: I was a stagehand. I was property man, assistant props, and then property man.

Q: I guess they were rather amiable people coming in and out all the time.

A: Oh yes, they had to be. You see we drank the raw water right out of the Ohio River. You have seen these creeks when they get muddy, well that's the water we would drink. Take that in, of course I was the one that, "Props? Props?" "Yes Ma'am." "Get me a glass of water will you?" I would take that into them about ten times darker than that. "I'm not a going to drink that." I said, "You drink it or else, that's what we drink." They couldn't understand people drinking that. You could take your hand and put it down to hold it like that. Pour it out and your hand would be all muddy.

Q: Well what kind of a theatre going audience was there in Ironton?

A: That theatre seated 800. It was filled nearly all the time every show, of course there wasn't nightly, it would be say, in the wintertime, beside the, of course the ten, 20 and 30 cents shows would be nightly, but the $2 shows would be twice a week, maybe three times a week. They would have musical comedies, just the biggest there were come in there. Only had about a 35 foot proscenium where the Hartman's got about 100 foot, but they'd cut it down. They would have 35 girls on the stage in the chorus besides the men.

Q: This was all in the . . .

A: The "Milk White Flag," The "Texas Steer," all of those shows and the "Isle of Spice." The biggest shows out of New York would come there. John and Ian Campbell, see they were the founders of the town. Those old Welsh nailers back in those days, that was when I was kid ten or 12 years old, that's during Grover Cleveland's administration, whenever that nail mill would work they would make, that was when nails were made by hand, and they got machines though that turned these plates. These were cut nails, not wire nails, long before wire nails. These guys would make $25 to $50 a day. They were nearly all Welsh, Davis's.

Q: That's right, there was a heavy migration of Welsh in the valley here.

A: They were all down through there.

Q: Were the Bays Welsh too? I wonder.

A: Yes they were Welsh.

Q: The Bays came on the river before the Civil War I guess.

A: The old man did. The two boys, the youngest boy of the two boys of Billy Bay, George never married, but Billy married and he had two boys, George and Billy. They left Ironton after and they went to college. They left Ironton.

Captain Volney White

Question: I don't know what your Christian name is Stogie, does anybody?

Answer: Well very few people do, except my mother and a couple cf aunts. It's Volney. V-O-L-N-E-Y. Volney E.

Q: I think the best way to start is to just give us a resume of your on the river experience with the Greenes.

A: To begin with Chris Greene and I were classmates at Woodward High School 1915 through 1919. We got to be pretty good buddies. I used to make trips on weekends on the boats with Captain Greene's dad, Captain Gordon Greene. It kind of got in my blood and the day I graduated from high school Mrs. Mary B. Greene said, "Stogie, we are awful short of help, would you go on the *Tacoma* and help us out?" I graduated high school one night, went on the steamboat the next day, on the *Tacoma* in June 1919. Gradually learned the business, I went on in the office as clerk, mud clerk. Captain Greene built the *Tom Greene*. I went on there as the purser with old Captain Greene himself. Tom Greene was in college. As time progressed I got a pilot's license in 1924. Captain Greene died in 1926. In 1927 I got a master's license. I alternated as relief master on the various boats for Tom and Chris. When Chris decided after his dad's death to come into the office to be general manager he put me Captain of the *Chris Greene*, as regular master. I stayed on there up until they got the *Gordon Greene* in 1934 I think. Tom Greene, Jesse Hughes, myself and several other people went over to St. Louis to get her. Brought her around to Louisville. Chris made a deal, if I would stay on the *Gordon* that summer, instead of going back on my own boat, we'd go to the World Series that fall, and we did. In the winter I went back on the *Chris Greene*. Then 1936 I entered the steamboat inspection service, hull inspection, was in that, started at Louisville and transferred to St. Louis, was over there for five years and transferred to Cincinnati in 1941 and I retired, quit and come to Neare Gibbs in 1946.

Q: Here you've been ever since.

A: Here yes, the only steamboating I've done since I've been here. shortly before Tom died, he made a contract with the *Gordon Greene* to go up the Tennessee and the Cumberland Rivers on some special trips and in the contract he specified he would be on it and he forgot all about it. The boat got over to Nashville and they called up and wanted to know where he was. Well he was in Cincinnati, they said according to contract you had to be here. So he called my boss and myself and wondered if I would go on the *Delta Queen* as Captain and help him out. So I went on there for about three weeks while he made that trip. I got off the first day of July, and in the afternoon of the tenth of July Tom died. Before he died Letha called me from Evansville all worried, that's Tom's wife, shortly later I got a call from my boss to go down to the *Delta* and help them out while Tom was sick. At that time he thought he just had a heart attack.

When I got to Louisville on the train there was a telegram. Tom had died and for me to go on the boat, which I did. I got there at four o'clock in the morning and got on the boat at Terminal Island. I stayed on there practically the rest of that summer until they got organized and appointed a regular captain.

Q: All those deaths were quit a blow to the lines weren't they?

A: Yes, I was pallbearer and at the funerals of the whole Greene family, mother, father and both sons. Pallbearer for all of them.

Q: Now Stogie, will you give us the history of the bell on the *Delta Queen*?

A: I don't know the exact history of the bell other than that it was on the *Queen City* during her life time. When Tom brought the *Delta Queen* around, all they had was the ship's bell, a post, which was a small bell and out of proportion to what we used on the river type boat. So Tom was concerned about where he was going to find a bell that would be suitable for the boat and I saw the *Queen City* bell, which was owned by the Ohio River Company. So I finally finagled around and made a deal with Bill Long of the Ohio River Company to trade him a couple of smaller bells that Tom had on wharf boats for the *Queen City* bell. So he agreed to it and it was on the steamer *John W. Hubbard*, a towboat. So they landed the *Hubbard* into the side of the *Delta Queen* and moved that bell over on there and Bill got the two smaller bells for the towboats.

Q: That's a pretty big bell.

A: Yes, it's a beautiful bell and had a wonderful tone and quite a history coming from the *Queen City*, which had ran her lifetime out and was dismantled up in Pittsburgh in the middle 30s.

Q: Were you ever on the *Queen City*?

A: I made a Mardi Gras trip on the *Queen City* in 1925 to New Orleans. Loaded with bath tubs, passengers.

Q: Must have been a beautiful old boat.

A: It was. It was a sternwheel boat, of course, it had quite a lot of tradition to it. The first boat that I really worked on was the *Tacoma*. She was 190 or a 195 feet long, an old White Collar boat. Ran in the upper trade for years. The Greene Line bought her in the early 1900s. Jesse Hughes was Captain on her, married on there, raised two children up to school age on the *Tacoma*. Ben Pattison was the Captain, Wilbur Chapman later became a crack towboat pilot for the Ohio River Company on the *Omar* after the death of the other pilot.

Q: Do you know how he spelled his name?

A: Chapman? W-I-L-B-U-R C-H-A-P-M-A-N. And Walter Lanham was the mate. I can't think who the engineers were at that time.

Q: That's the one they called the *Tack Hammer*?

A: That's the old *Tack Hammer* and the machinery later was put on the *Chris Greene*, on the new *Chris Greene* when she was built in 1925, the machinery off the *Tacoma*. Captain Greene never had a steel hull boat until 1921. In late 1921 he contracted a Marietta Manufacturing company to build a new 200 foot packetboat with new Frisbie machinery etc., and she was about half done in

November 1922 when they had the big fire down here and the *Tacoma* burned up and the little *Chris Greene*, the first Chris Greene, the *Island Queen*, the *Morning Star*, and damaged the *Coney Island* and the *Greene Line* wharfboats. Then they decided they needed boats so bad that the *Tom Greene* was rushed through completion. She was brought to Cincinnati and the cabin work finished and the machinery installed, the boiler had been put on at Gallipolis, and I did the electric wiring on there. Wired the boat in the winter of 1922 and 1923, the spring of 1923. She started out I think if I remember right in June of 1923 and I stayed on her up until around 1929 or so when I transferred over on the *Chris Greene*. She was bigger than the *Chris*, she had 22 and nine feet and the *Chris* had 18 feet. In 1933 when they switched, I ran in the Huntington trade all those years to Charleston. Then the *Tom Greene* started to run to Louisville about 1930 or 1931, and in 1933 they changed us there where we were opposite boats. Whichever one left Cincinnati at night, which one left Louisville at one o'clock in the morning, they both would be whistling for lock 39 and the lockmaster wouldn't know which way to turn the lock for us. But in the open river the *Tom Greene* was the fastest, she had the more power. But pool water we could about make the same time as she did. There was great rivalry between Tom and I about it to see who could keep the nicest boat and the best bands on there and entertain the passengers best in the summertime. Quite a rivalry.

Q: Do you remember offhand, names of any bands that were on the boats then?
A: We'd pick up, during the depression, you could get any band you wanted from say 1929 on there was a period when music was suffering and these name bands were folding up. We were only allowed three musicians by the boss on the boat, but we would line up with a ten or 12 piece band. These men were hungry and they would go for their meals and bed on the boats. We had some of the best musicians out of big name bands. I remember one year we had a trumpet player out of Kay Kayser's band. At that time he was hot stuff, he ran the band that summer. But there is quite an alumnus around Cincinnati now, the old boys that played in the bands on the boats. One of them, Tommy Thompson, a percussionist with Cincinnati Symphony, he used to play for me on the boat. Jimmy Alton is the chief arranger or something in the music department at WLW. He used to play. Another trombone player is a music director out here in a big Catholic high school on Hackberry Street, Purcell I think it is. Rodney Ellis, he teaches music out there and he was a trombone player on there. I knew quite a lot of them and run into them every once in a while that were on the boat at various times.

Q: I seem to recall when I was down here in 1952 we got into some kind of discussion about racing those boats.
A: Yes, they had several races. The first one was 19 . . . believe it was 1928. It was quite a hectic thing, the *Chris Greene* used to leave down here on Tuesday nights at the same time the *Betsy Ann* did for Pittsburgh. There was quite a rivalry there in those days over when you left each other. So one night the

correspondent up at New Richmond who since had become quite a writer, I won't mention his name but he still writes a column in the paper today, was the local agent for the local news gatherer at New Richmond for the Associated Press. They got on him, he hadn't sent many news items, so he happened to look out and the *Chris Greene* and the *Betsy Ann* were going up by New Richmond neck and neck. He sent a very flowery story into the newspaper. It got out on the wire all over the country, "Guardrails Crashing and Boat's Boilers at Bursting Points." As a result of that the steamboat inspectors had an investigation and they fined both pilots. I think it was Elmer Fancher on the *Betsy Ann* and Vern Stickel on the *Chris Greene* for violation of failing to whistle at one another in passing. As a result of all that publicity Fred Way and Chris got together and challenged one another for a real race. I mean in those days they didn't have television but newsreel cameramen were in abundance and hundreds of newspaper writers from all over the country and they built that thing up until thousands of people witnessed that race from Cincinnati to New Richmond. The *Chris Greene* won the antlers that the *Betsy* had. Then they had another race the next year in 1929 and then in 1930 *Tom* challenged the *Betsy Ann* and that was quite a race. That was the *Chris Greene* and the *Betsy Ann* ran the first race and the last two races were with the *Tom*. The second race was quite disputable. They argued around about which end of the boat was first because they entered lock 35 practically neck and neck and they always claim that the stern of the *Betsy* was over the finish line first due to the *Tom Greene* was a longer boat. The boats continued on up to 1936 when they passed a sprinkler law, which required an automatic sprinkler system, and a lot of expenses and the passenger was a summertime thing in the Louisville trade. So they decided to tear the cabin off, that was shortly after I left them. Shortly after I left they stripped the boats down and made the boiler deck so you could put automobiles up there, tore out the stateroom, and they continued that up until the middle 1940s. Fords one way and Chevrolets the other, along with the general freight. Then at Louisville some union trouble developed and, all I know is hearsay, what Tom told me, that they tried to organize the common help that we used to call laborers. Used to get them pretty cheap but they wanted to organize them into a union and have specified hours and overtime provisions, which made it prohibitive. Revenue was coming in but putting in all that extra labor, if the boat had fog or something, Tom said they'd have to pay those laborers right on until the boat got there and load and unload the boat on an overtime basis. There was a lot of restrictions put on the labor, tell who was to do this and who to do that, so Tom got disgusted and just overnight quit the freight business. Laid the boats up and sold the wharfboats down at Louisville, the boats laid around here for two or three years, shortly after that Tom died, and the boats wound up, the *Chris Greene*, now the hull of the *Chris Greene*, was practically all that is left and part of its superstructure is the Dayton Boat Club up there at Long Shore Harris. And a commercial barge line bought the

Tom Greene and converted her into an auto carrying barge and used her a few years. I haven't seen her the last two or three years, I don't know whether they had did away with her or what happened.

Q: One of these boats is in Florida now I understand.

A: That's the *Gordon Greene*.

Q: The old *Cape* Girardeau.

A: Yes originally the *Cape Girardeau*. After they got the *Delta Queen* they ran the *Gordon* a few years from St. Louis to St. Paul and I guess they made some money with it. They finally laid her up and didn't operate her one year and a group bought her up at Portsmouth, Ohio; they were going to make a floating nightclub and restaurant out of her and everything. They moored to the bank and got in trouble with the state of Ohio about a liquor permit and a lot of publicity ensued and they finally gave it up. Then a group in Owensboro bought the boat and they put quite an elaborate restaurant system on the middle deck of her. About that time Burt Lancaster, of Lancaster Hecht Productions needed a boat for a movie and they made a movie down there, it was a locale of the Green River for the river scene.

Q: "The Kentuckian!"

A: "The Kentuckian," and I was technical adviser in that picture. She didn't have any motive power on, the boilers had been taken off and put on the *Avalon*. So they tied a little towboat on the stern quarter called the *Tell City*, and when the boat's in movement you can't see it in the picture, but the motive power is furnished by the little towboat.

Q: I guess that the sternwheeler was a restaurant down there.

A: That was the *Gordon Greene*. They took her back to Owensboro, then some group down in Florida, Bradenton, Florida bought her and they tell me they have her in behind the dike down there. She is in a lagoon of fresh water and quite a tourist attraction. They're putting on a lot of old relics and I think they have conducted trips over the boat and serving meals on there and what not.

Q: We'll go up to Catlettsburg.

A: What did you want to know about, the log business?

Q: Yes.

A: It was kind of on the decline when I started but it was still pretty active. Catlettsburg, Kentucky was one that looked like a Western town in those days. If I remember right there was 21 saloons on the riverfront. West Virginia was dry and they hit a, like a Los Vegas of the day.

Q: That would have been around 1918.

A: Yes, around 1919 when prohibition came in. The day before prohibition, national prohibition was to start I think we unloaded 3,600 cases of whiskey at Catlettsburg. The log business was still going because I can remember log rafts in the mouth of the Big Sandy down below Ironton, the Hanging Rock, a lot of log rafts along there. The Crane mills were still going up there in the East End and they would back, the towboats would back all the way down with the logs.

John Knoepfle

Q: They would. How's that?

A: Steer them easier, come down stern first so they could swing them.

Q: The logs would be following the tow! I didn't know that, can you talk a little more about that towing logs?

A: Well they used to back all the way from Catlettsburg to Cincinnati, so they could handle those log rafts better.

Q: About how long were they?

A: Oh they were several hundred feet long according to how many sections they had. Then a big raise would come and scatter logs all over the place and they would go out and give two bits for a cross tie. If you had a log or a cross tie that CC that meant the Crane Company or Charley Crane, why they would pay you for holding that log, and then a boat would come along and pick up all those strays.

Q: I knew that, a man named Wagner told us that sometimes as many as 70,000 logs would get out of the Big Sandy.

A: That's true, and then they tell me those old loggers up there, which would come down the Big Sandy, a wild narrow river and see the Ohio and they would just get scared to death and jump right off the raft right in the river and swim into shore. Afraid of all that, afraid to go out on that big water. It was three times as dangerous coming along those rapids in the Big Sandy.

Q: I would like to talk to a Big Sandy pilot sometime. But I guess they are rare birds now.

A: Yes, I think most of them came out on their own power, I don't think they used many boats in the Sandy. I think they rafted them out in their own power with oars. They used to get on those little packetboats with a jug of whiskey in one hand and a grip in the other and go up to bring logs out.

Q: I knew there was, Mr. Wagner mentioned five companies, one was the Newman. Did you ever hear of that company?

A: No, I can remember, one that I remember most was the Yellow Poplar Company up there at Ironton. Here in Cincinnati locally most of the logs I knew of came to Crane. They had several mills along up in the bend at East End, and then in later years they built, the base of it is still there, directly opposite Corey Island dike, it's a concrete pier. That was a whirly crane. A steam operated crane that lifted logs out of the river and loaded them in cars up there.

Q: We were a little curious about Wagner saying there was as many as 70,000 logs that would get away from them, I don't know whether he meant 70,000 were brought down or it is possible that 70,000 logs would get free and they would have to be caught on the river.

A: Well the fellow that I knew best that was in the logging business a long while was the Captain on the *Delta Queen* when he died was Jim Butler. He worked with cranes for years on several of their boats, what they call log boats. Used to lay in the bend at East End there and he brought many a log raft down the river. He died about, well he died since Tom, probably five years ago.

Q: Do you remember the names of any of those little log boats?

A: I was trying to think. The *Crown Hill* was one and I forget the names of the last one. The *Crown Hill* brought down logs for years.

Q: That's an interesting point. Tell us something about the roustabouts.

A: The roustabout was as much a part of the packetboats as the captain. If you didn't have rousters you couldn't do very much and we carried 20 to 25 on deck. That meant two deckhands and they were like junior mates and ran the crap game was their extra dividends at the end of the trip. When you paid them off they got the cut out of the crap game for running the games. But the roustabouts the way the mate would ship them up, he'd look at a rouster and tell whether he was or not. If he had a spoon in his overall pocket that was a pretty good sign that he knew what he was doing because that same type of roustabout followed the circus and the river. When Ringling Brothers were heading back to hit Cincinnati we would have trouble for a few days getting straightened out, they'd take all the rousters that would go with the circus, then they would all drift back.

Q: The spoon was to eat with I guess.

A: Yes, they served in pans and they gave them a tin can. Every colored guy had his tin can and his spoon, that was his equipment, the boat furnished. We used to get them made up at a tin shop, partitioned pans, like cafeteria style. Put the food out in big pans, with big spoons and they would eat all they wanted providing they didn't waste any; if they wanted seconds or thirds, we tried to feed them good because we needed them. The rate of pay was very peculiar $1 a day, that meant a 24 hour day and I've seen the time when up in the upper end of the river in the middle section of the river where we make Ironton, Ashland and Huntington and the coal pile, they would be up 24 hours without a minute's sleep. Working and singing all the time.

Q: A coal pile!

A: A coal pile. We'd go up and take coal. In those days up the Kanawha River we used to coal by hand out of a barge. Shovel it on the boat, and then later they put it on with a crane, but just moved it back to the coal pile.

Q: They did a lot of singing then.

A: Oh yes, sing all the time. The secret of being a good mate, what we would call work the roustabouts would keep them in good humor. They would get to the coon jining, they would unload freight three times as fast as they would without this song that they had. I remember one of them in particular was a song called "Uncle Bud." Some of the verses you couldn't put on a live recording, pretty risqué. One would strike up that, another one was spirituals. They'd set around by their selves and sing spirituals a lot. Some of them were just as good as this Billy Williams quartet you hear on television today.

Q: You don't remember the words to any of the songs off hand.

John Knoepfle

A: No I don't remember the words though they had several of them. "Blood," and one about the "Blood Done Signed My Name," and they used to sing that by the hour. "Uncle Bud" and quite a lot of religious songs.

Q: Ever hear of a keg rolling song from Wheeling?

A: No, I haven't heard that. Might have heard it because they had a rhythm that went like calypso stuff, they would make up their own songs. About every colored guy, one of them would start a verse and make pretty good rhyme with it about one of them in the line, then he would get all tickled up about it.

Q: That's fine.

A: We paid $1 a day was the salary. Once in a while they would want to strike, sit up around the flag pole, we go up to find out what was the trouble, they wanted the cook off of the boat, they wanted this or wanted that or more money. I know when Captain Gordon C. Greene was still alive, we were hauling a lot of passengers, plenty of freight. It was a fertilizer trip, we had the boat loaded down with fertilizer for every bank landing between here and Charleston. The colored guys all went on a strike, so the old man says, "Well let's break it, come on boys," so we left. Two or three loyal old deckhands and firemen and stuff that stayed, and we would go up and entertain the passengers. The boat would blow for a landing. We'd get out and carry fertilizer. The next trip we broke the strike all right, they all came back to work. So they had strikes long before the era of unionism now. Now going back to this roustabout thing, we had a colored fella on the boat, had he been a white man would have made the best mate in the world. Weighed about 350 pounds, a big husky fellow and a great big stomach that was as hard as rock. I have seen fights started among those colored guys and whenever he would see them reaching in their pocket they were going for knives, and he would walk right in between them and bump them with his stomach and knock them about 30 feet. So one afternoon this colored fella that supervised the loading of the freight inside, we noticed there was congestion in there and things weren't going right and I went in the deck room and said, "Where's big Nat?" They said, "Well he's left here. He is sick." I went back in the fantail and he was leaning over the railing. I said, "What's the matter Nat?" He said, "I don't know. I'm awful sick." We took him out to General Hospital. He died that night. He was such a highly respected fellow, everybody liked him. Captain Chris Greene went out to the morgue, I went with him, we identified the body, claimed it. Got a colored undertaker gave Nat a real funeral. Bought him a lot, a headstone in a colored cemetery up between Mt. Washington and California. If you go out there you can see the tombstone today, Nat Stewart. This Al Segal of the "Cincinnati Post," wrote in his column "Cincinnatus," all about what the Greene family thought of that colored fellow, how they saw he had a decent burial, a grave and a headstone.

Q: So it was kind of paternal at times on some boats. I know that there wasn't always. Rather brutal sometimes too.

A: I wasn't around in the brutality days, that day is past. I've heard a lot of stuff, but I think a lot of it is rumor, more so. Grossly exaggerated, a lot that stuff, they tell about putting all the roustabouts in sidewheel boats, and tell them to roll the wheel over drown them all. I don't think that ever happened. I've heard it's the truth, but I doubt it. They used to have a colored mate I can remember, Lou Brown ran on the Memphis boats had one arm, he couldn't roll a cigarette he'd tell the roustabout, "Roll me a cigarette but don't lick it." He was supposed to be a tough character, Lou Brown.

Q: He's rather famous too. Was he colored?

A: No, he was white, he was one of those guys that was supposed to be so tough on the colored fellows.

Q: Horace Lyle told me a story.

A: On one-armed Lou Brown? Back up until a few years ago, Billy Bryant was the last around here except that little *Majestic* owned by Tom Reynolds up at Point Pleasant. He used to tramp all these towns and we'd have a crowd. They knew their schedule pretty well, and one during the trip we'd try to arrange it somewhere where we landed beside the side of the showboat so the passengers could see an old time melodrama and if we were late, many times Bill Bryant, or Bill Menke, or Ralph Gaches, would put on a special show for us after the regular show for our crowd. We'd have maybe 150 passengers.

Q: Who was the last name you mentioned?

A: Ralph Gaches, he just died here a couple of weeks ago.

Q: He did?

A: Yes, Emerson Showboat, he went by Emerson, his right name was Gaches. He died in Chicago about oh, a month or so ago. Must have been a real old guy.

Q: I know his brother-in-law Charlie Alexander.

A: Well they were in an era that went out like the packetboat did, the stage coach and all, the TV and modern transportation and the movie pictures I think is what really killed them, but that used to be quite an event when they landed in a town with the calliope playing in the morning, why they would have a parade and that night everybody in town would be down at the showboat.

Q: I suppose Daddy Price was a little ahead of your time?

A: Well I don't remember much about Price, I think I remember seeing Price's showboat, but the ones that I knew best was Ralph Emerson and a fellow still at St. Louis that's been there 15 years that I know of without leaving the landing over there and still does a wonderful business is Bill Menke. The Menke brothers had several boats. I knew Billy Bryant well. He and I are good friends today. He's out in Hollywood now. He was on a TV show not long ago with Groucho Marx. He's been on several of them and I think he's technical adviser of some movie out there. He wrote a book on showboats. Have you read it?

Q: *Children of Ol' Man River*.

A: *Children of Ol' Man River*, he gives the history of their family. I knew his mother, dad, his wife, all of them, his daughter. I knew her when she was a baby. When I started, the lock and dam program was I'd say 50% completed. Leaving Cincinnati here, the first lock was in operation when I started, was up here at New Richmond. Then there wasn't any until we got to 31 below Portsmouth, 30 was out, 29 was in and 28. There wasn't any 27. We had a trip that normally took five days. I remember the *Tom Greene* was a new boat in September or October. We left here, was 29 days going to Charleston and back. We were stuck 17 days up at a place called Ferguson's Bar below Ironton.

Q: Low water.

A: Low water, everyday a man came down in one of those high wheeled buggies and a horse, crossed the river in front of us. Went across the river and back every morning and night in a buggy in front of the boat. Several times we'd get as far as New Richmond, we'd have to wait on a splash raise. It would manipulate the locks. It made an artificial wave. You would have all the towboats ready with their coal, they would call washing down a splash wave. We'd ride that wave, then get back up the river as far as we could on it, try to keep going. When the water left why a lot of times we would be stuck right where we were.

Q: What is this washing down again?

A: They called it splash raising. The engineers manipulated the locks that they had in existence. He allowed so many feet, so many hours later it would create an artificial wave four or five feet, it wasn't a wave, it was just a rise in the river that would give the towboats a chance to get down with their coal, they would fight their way back with empties where you didn't need the draft. I've seen that happen many a times. A whole gang of towboats in a row riding on that wave. Trying to make it down before the wave run out. They called it an artificial splash into a wave. Funny thing happened in that 17 days I told you we were stuck up there. We were paying all those colored fellows, the law says if you pay them off you have to pay their fare back to where you hired them, which meant Cincinnati. We figured every way in the world to get rid of them; we wouldn't get rid of them legitimately. We had them gathering up wood, scrub the boat, did everything. Finally one night a bunch of lights appeared out on the bank. Was right in Ku Klux area when Ku Kluxers had colored people scared to death, they had seen signs that morning, when all these lights above the boat up there in that field that they thought this was it. They laid there quiet all night, the next morning at daylight everyone asked for his money, no fare or anything and went up and caught a C & O freight train and hiked to Cincinnati.

Q: They saw a sign about it.

A: Saw a sign in the morning, lanterns. We went up the hill to investigate to find out what it was. It was a big tomato field getting frost, they were afraid the tomatoes were going to be spoiled so they hired all the local people to come out with lanterns that night and picked the tomatoes, the colored fellows thought it was the Ku Klux, they all left. It saved us several hundred dollars.

Q: Well, this is a very rich tape, Stogie, and I am happy that you are willing to talk about it all.

Publisher's Note

John Knoepfle was the first poet that I met. He was my first creative writing professor at Sangamon State University in Springfield, Illinois. After graduation we continued through the years to stay in touch with each other. A little over two years ago in November, I was visiting John and Peggy at their home in Springfield, when John asked me if I might be able to publish his collection of interviews, *Men of the Inland Rivers*. John, Peggy and I went out to the university library and met with Tom Woods in the Archives, he gave us an electronic copy of John's files, transcribed from the original tapes made in the 1950s. I gave those electronic records to Anne Kilgore in Ithaca, New York. She converted those copies of originals into word documents for me. She sent me two or three files a month, and I proofed the new files against the original while editing and correcting some typo errors in the original files. During this time I spoke with John and Peggy at least twice a week about the work. John was concerned about two words in the original that he wanted changed, and John, Peggy and I agreed the changes should be made. Concern about the historical accuracy of the book is why I have written this note.

The time period covered in these interviews falls within the JIM CROW period "from the end of the Civil War to the Civil Rights movement" when racial segregation and exploitation was rampant and legal. This is searingly obvious in the division of labor on the riverboats. Black men served as roustabouts they loaded and unloaded riverboat freight on their backs and far outnumbered the white crews, who managed the boats and are mentioned often in the interviews. They were the lowest in the riverboat hierarchy. With few exceptions, the only higher status jobs that a black man could aspire to was cook, or musician. Yet in all the tape recordings John made, there is only one interview where roustabouts tell their own stories. It took John a long time to find the two men he interviewed, he believed that the interview was essential, and greatly valued their willingness to talk to him.

Two disrespectful words in this book were changed, they are: "nigger," and "niggerhead." We changed the first word twenty-five times in twelve chapters. The first word John thought that it should be changed to rouster, or roustabout, for the African-Americans who performed all the difficult loading and unloading of steamboats, and I agree. Following is a list of those chapters with the number of how many times in that chapter it was changed: Anderson (1), Chamberlain (1), Coomer (1), Harrison (2), Lyle (1), Menke (1), O'Hearn (3), Smith (4), Steamer Avalon 2 (6), Taylored (1), Twedell (1), White (3). The second word was changed five times in three chapters: Anderson (1), Coomer (2), Harrison (2). For the second word we found out that it was actually the capstan on the boat. Scholars seeking accuracy may find these original un-changed files in the library archives at the University of Illinois, Springfield.

John Knoepfle

In November one year after I began work to publish *Men of the Inland Rivers,* Professor Emeritus, John Knoepfle passed away at the age of 96. He lived from 1923-2019. He was a wonderful poet, and my friend who shall be missed. I close with these lines from a poem he sent me in a postcard.

> love is like a bowl
> so when you break it
> glue it together
> if it won't hold water
> fill it with apples
>
> john knoepfle

CPSIA information can be obtained
at www.ICGtesting.com
Printed in the USA
BVHW091955050922
646251BV00001B/7